Walls & Frames

Fine Art from the Streets

gestalten

Index

Street art emerged from a generation of artists that proceeded to break down the elitist barriers of "fine art" and redefine the relationship with its environment. This new canvas brought legal and practical challenges and a new language that speaks directly from artaists to viewers, leaving its message uncensored. What began as an anonymous and illegal act of "vandalism" has conquered its discrimination to the point where it has built a respected reputation and moved through the ranks of the art world to some of the most coveted gallery spaces, auction houses, and museums around the world, becoming the most relevant and solid art movement of the last decades.

The street art movement and its principles haven't wavered since they took center stage on the platform of the contemporary art scene. This encouraged a new wave of artists to come into their own, although recognition in this arena did not define the success of their work. These glimpses of artistic, spontaneous expressions—announced vulnerably but unapologetically to the world on its streets—reveal a fearless art movement that is determined to speak up. In a society that is contradictory, often at the surface of controversial issues and volatile situations, street art is an organic commentary, a response from a generation that has learned to question the given. And the possibility of its adaptation into conventional formats, such as canvases and sculptures, allows it to burst and spread in the art circuit.

What the commercial art world once rejected it now seeks out in the vibrant hubs of the world's creative capitals. These are the birthplaces of artists innocently exploring their talent; theirs may be the next statement that grabs the audience by the scruff of the neck and shuffles their preconceptions around until they learn to reassess their immediate reaction toward a new and unconventional form of fine art. More often than not these pieces are a satirical observation; the artists narrate a social commentary that is so clean in its execution of thought that its message is unavoidable. People are more open to viewing work in this way as it is not forced upon them. Outside of a gallery a piece of art does not give the impression it is there just because the viewer is, but more that it exists on the wall in its own right. Its very nature is unobtrusive, merely speaking out on the walls of the world for you to see and consider, should you choose to.

Walls & Frames captures the work of a generation of artists whose talent is born out of curiosity and a stubborn persistence of self-taught expression. The full potential of this expression cannot necessarily be comprehended in those first tentative flecks of paint. More often than not these are also artists with traditional art education backgrounds who have found a new language in street art that focuses on the effectiveness of reaching the viewer through a raw and uncensored self-promotion and freedom of speech.

Many of the artists in this book hail from very different backgrounds, opinions, techniques, and approaches to their art, but they all share the call of public intervention or strong influence of the street. The spirit of this new generation explores many themes of the expected aspects of fine art, sometimes political, sometimes conceptual, yet its delivery becomes an integral part of their process. The "galleries" of the street add another element to the piece and the artists take their inspiration from the streets and the things they observe. Integrating themselves into street culture gives their work a fresh angle, one that traditional fine art might often miss altogether.

It is in this spirit that the street art movement has swept through the rest of the art world, bringing into play a new school of artists with skills that do not just include their abilities with spray cans and paint, but their skills as a self-promoter and a seller of their own creations. These artists have found creative ways to transfer the impact of their street work into the studio. As a result it is an art form that has earned its place "honestly" in the art world.

The curious ambiguity of seeing an artist's work laid out for all to see on a grubby back street on your way home and the same artist's work sold in private galleries and collectors' auctions around the world throws up the question of the true value of art to those who usually dictate it. A new emphasis on the value of art has caused a reshuffle in its worth and process of evaluation. In the true spirit of the street artist, it has thrown up a challenge in the face of its own consumer. What is so interesting about this new expression of art, then, is that it has striven to pursue what it wanted to do and kept its independence, and this is ultimately what attracts the investors later on. Displaying a stubborn dedication to their art, a freedom of expression they refused to have snatched away despite a bad reception, the artists utilized the repercussions of tabooed actions and public disdain as another spark of ingenuity in their work.

Like many areas of the creative industries now, technology is a catalyst, a freedom ticket to your own success through self-publication. The artists have broken down the elitism of art and as a result a new equality has sprung from their choice to show and create their work in a public space. It is honest, an open invitation to its audience to view and critique should they wish, snipping away all of the constricting barriers that usually contort the communication from a piece to its consumer. In this way the traditional obstacles of class and social position that came with access to fine art have been challenged and adjusted. The meaning of fine art now signifies an art that is accessible and engaging to a broad audience, an art literally brought to the gallery of a much wider audience. The image of fine art no longer just means an aristocratic oil painting, but is considered with a more open mind by the general public.

Walls & Frames is intended to be an important reference and inspirational portfolio of a new wave of artists, not only for art galleries, collectors, art investors, and museums but also for general art lovers and enthusiasts.

It is the first attempt to showcase a whole new generation of artists, through selected works of 101 known and emerging artists from around the world bound to the streets in different aspects. The selection was made in order to feature the most innovative and varied styles, techniques, and languages.

Being a relatively new art form with lots of character and increasing popularity, its future is very promising. But as with every fast and over-celebrated success the chances of falling down or losing popularity are big. Reaching this status was a hard task and staying there will be even harder. But as long as the artists have the streets to inspire them and themes to explore there will be more volumes of **Walls & Frames** featuring new challenging talents from around the world.

Maximiliano Ruiz

Aaron Noble

Born in Portland, United States, 1961. Lives in Los Angeles, United States.

I never wrote graffiti. My aim when I started this work in San Francisco in 2000 was to compete with graffiti. I wanted to make something else that was as dazzling, cryptic, and sensual as the brilliant spraycan works that were making my traditional mural painting seem old and slow.

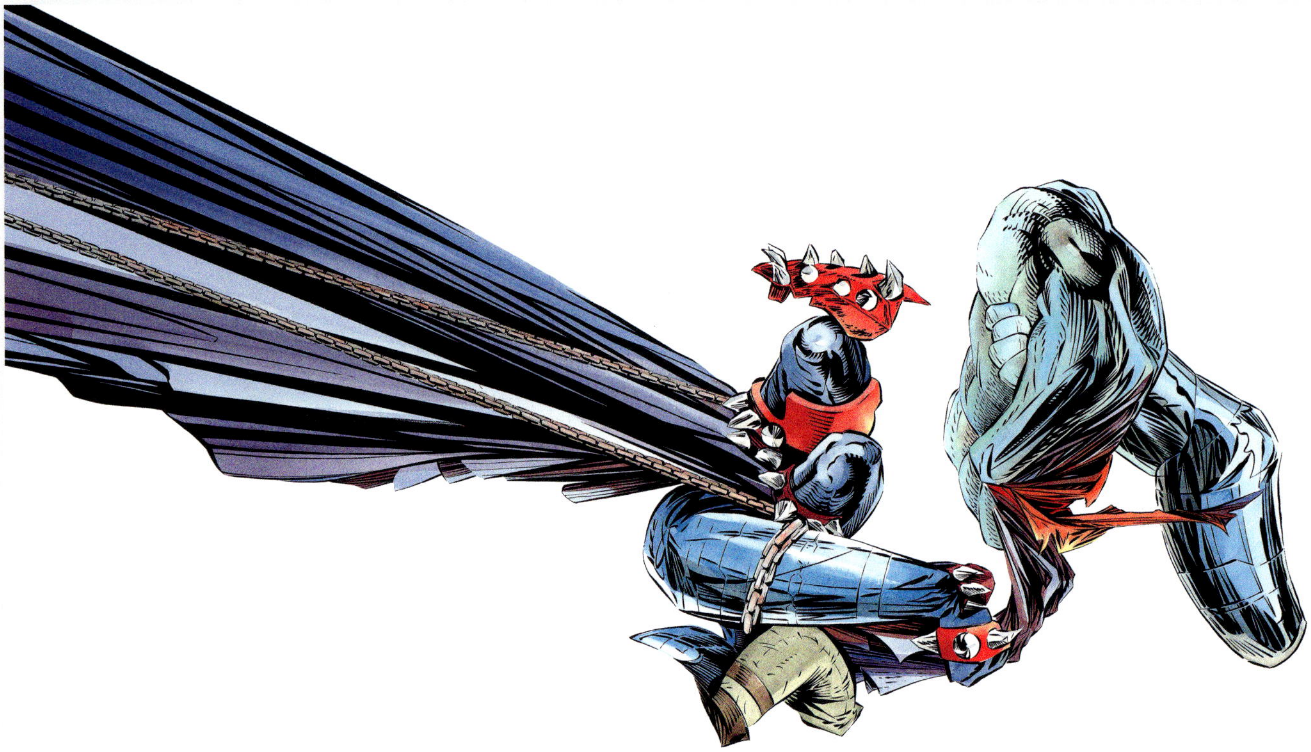

Pawn Checks King / Gouache on paper – 90 x 55 cm – 2008

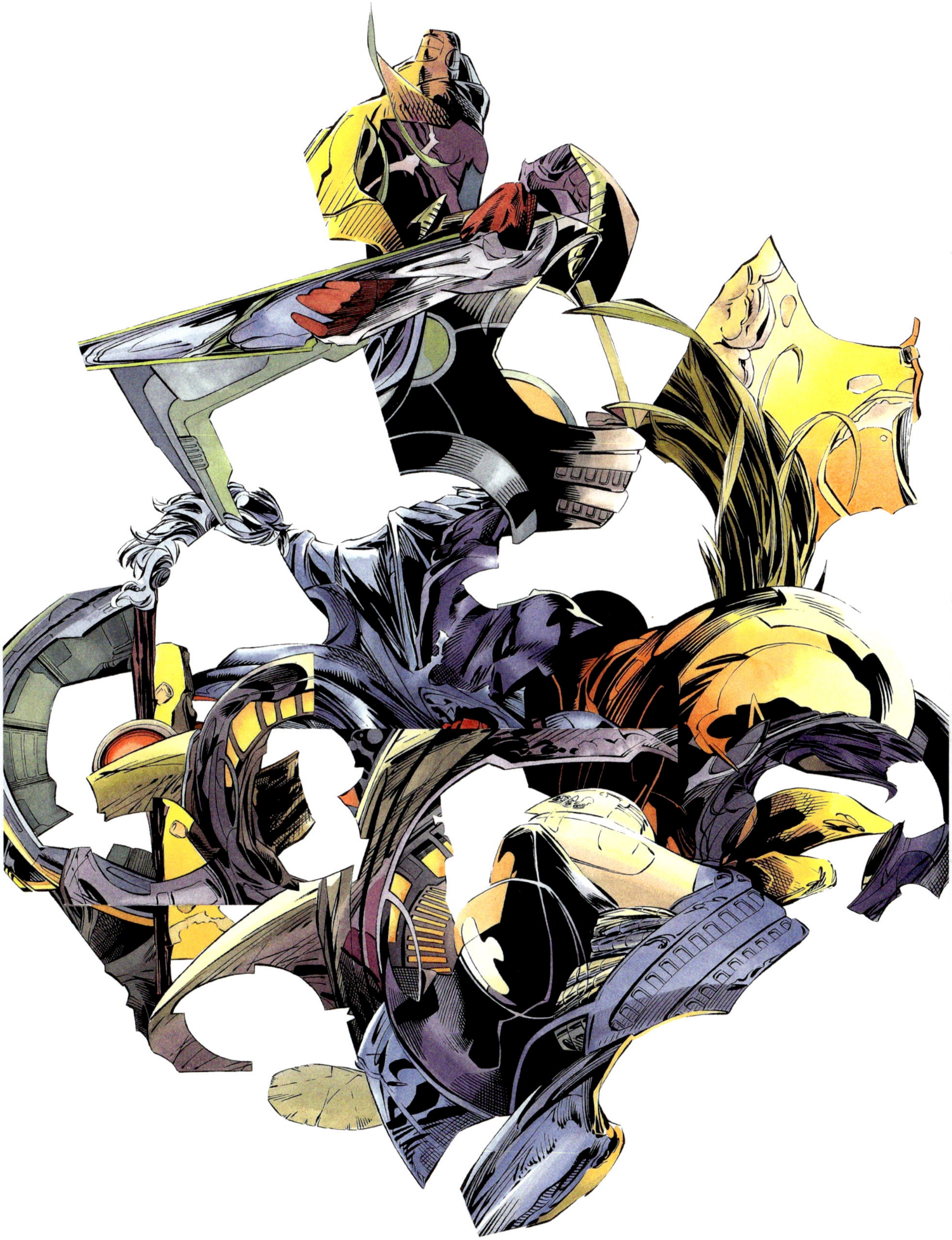

At Work in the Egg Fields / Gouache on paper – 56 x 71 cm – 2010

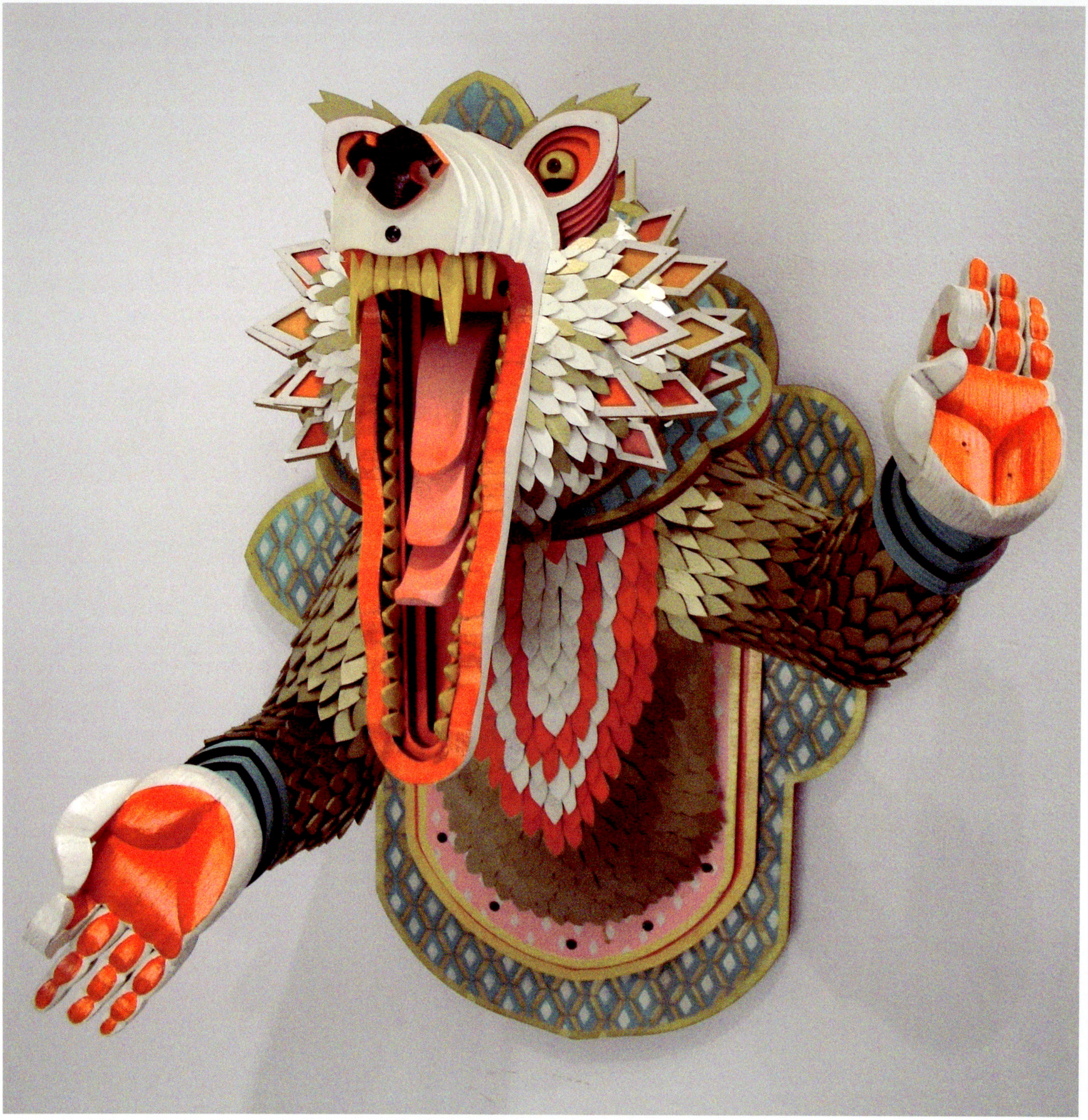

Embracing Stochasticity / Wood, acrylic, and nails – 63 x 71 x 91 cm – 2010

AJ Fosik

Born in Michigan, United States, 1975. Lives in Portland, United States.

I cut my artistic teeth in the city of Detroit. It was here among the rusted bones of American industry that I first encountered the ghosts whose black blood replaced my own. We washed dinner down with a glass of tears from each of the big three and at night we would use the axles of Plymouths and Pontiacs to bar our doors against the wolves and prostitutes.

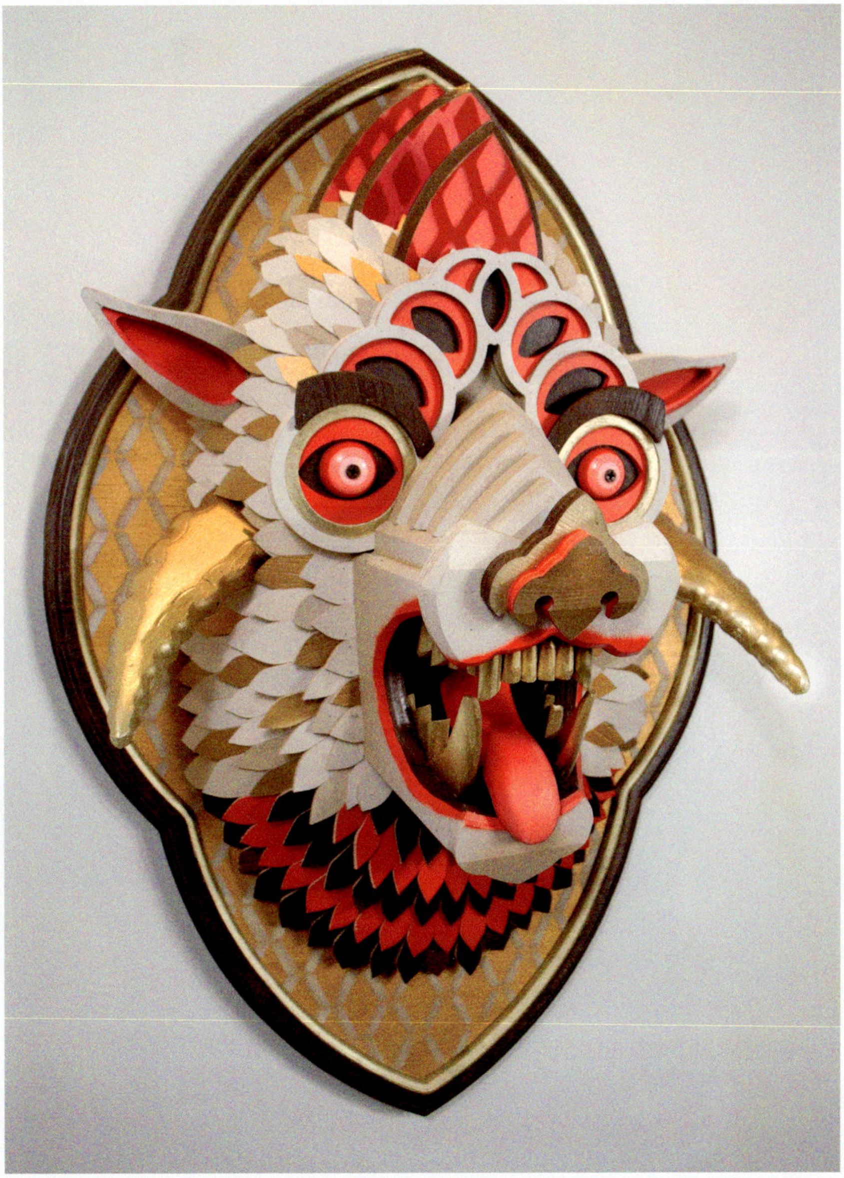

Babylonian Gorgon / Wood, acrylic, and nails – 48 x 66 x 33 cm – 2010

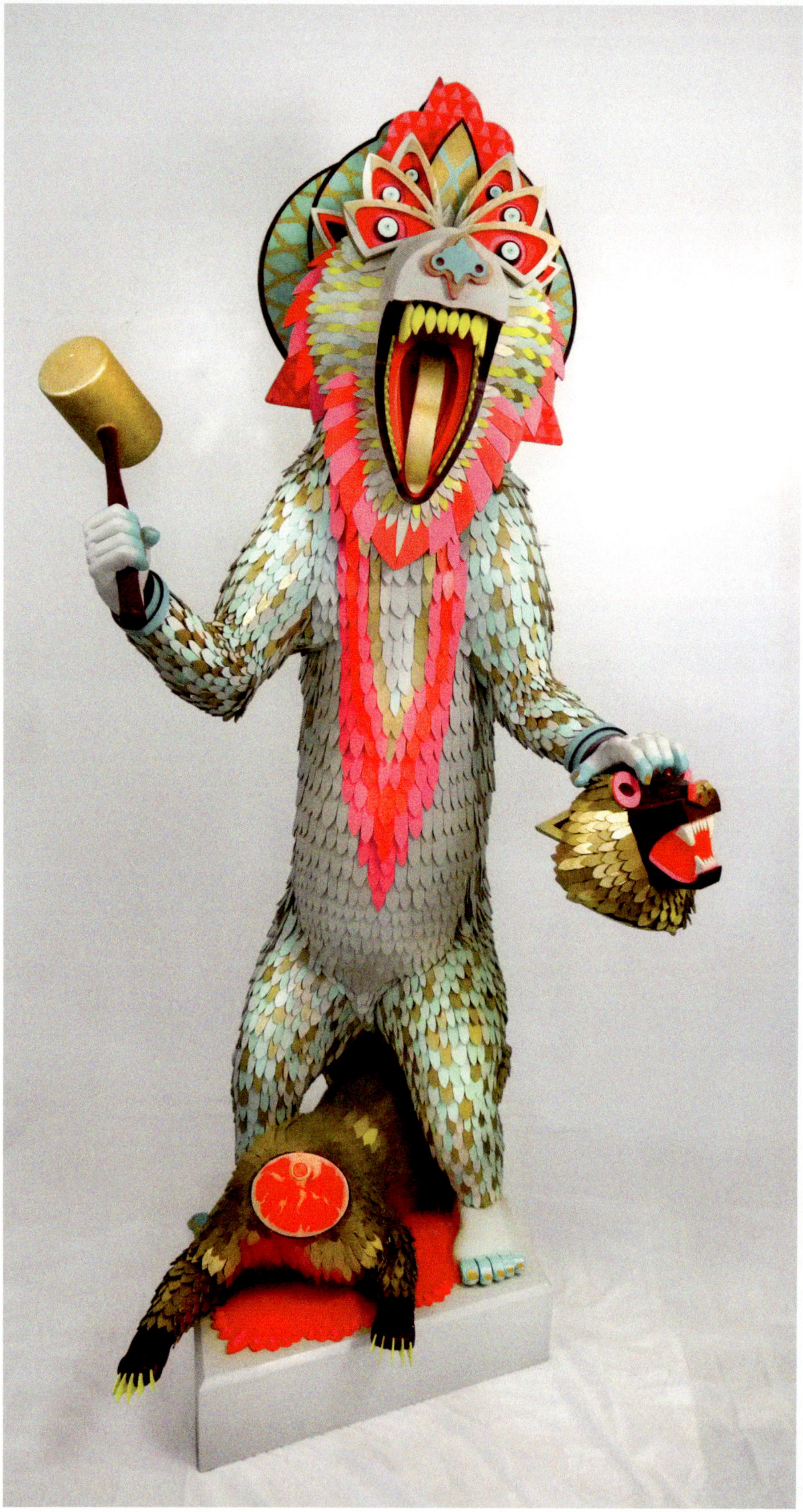

The Third Way Out / Wood, acrylic, and nails – 91 x 213 x 91 cm – 2009

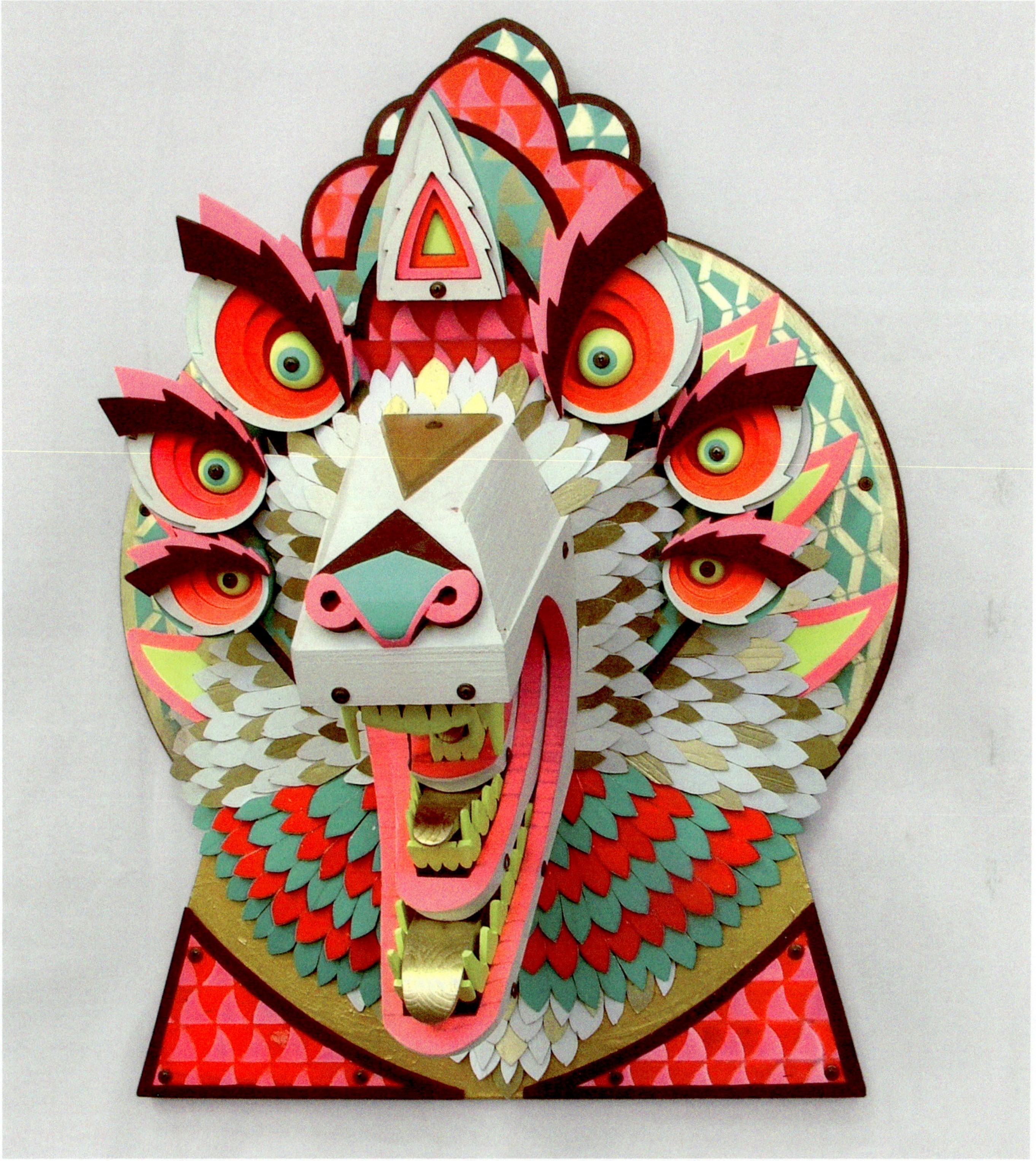

As Good as Any God / Wood, acrylic, and nails – 46 x 63 x 36 cm – 2009

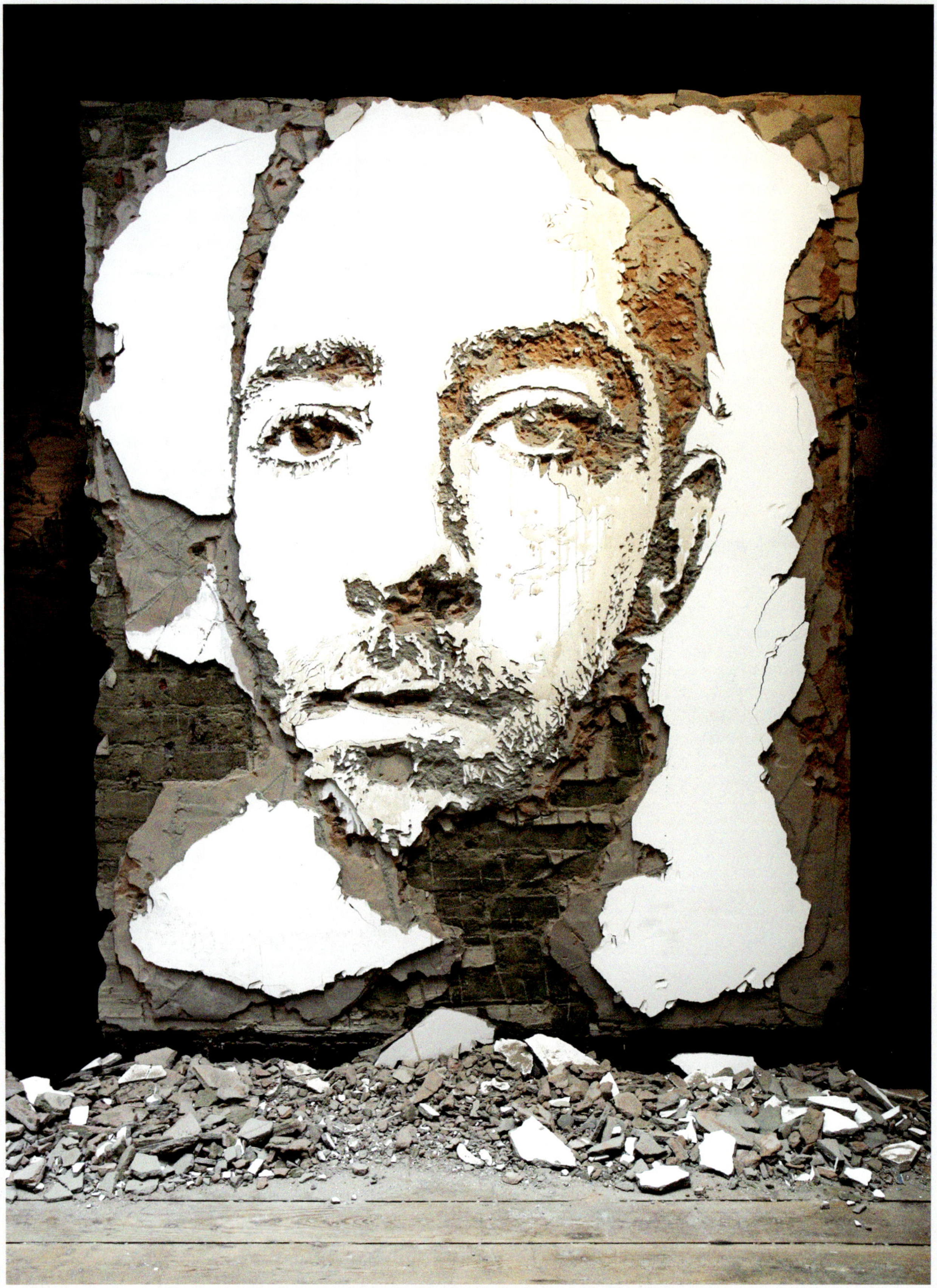

Scratching the Surface Project | Carved concrete – 200 x 300 cm – 2009

Alexandre Farto aka Vhils

Born in Lisbon, Portugal, 1987. Lives in Lisbon, Portugal and London, England.

In this act of excavating, it's the process itself which is expressive, more than the final result. It's a process of trying to reflect upon our own layers. Its aim is not to come up with solutions but to conduct research, to confront systems, materials, processes, elements, to create friction and confront the individual with the process, with the system: an active critical process that stems from the same environment upon which it aims to reflect.

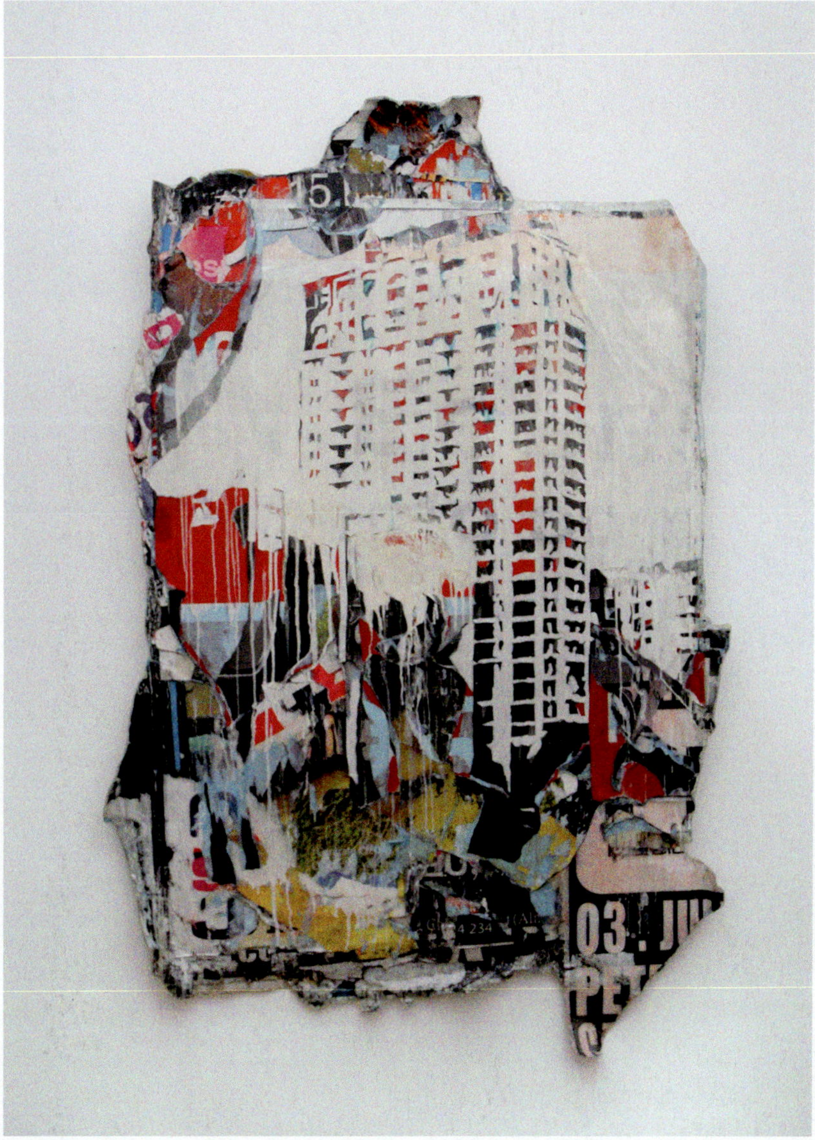

Growth for the Sake of Growth is the Ideology of the Cancer Cell Series / Acrylic and carved street ads – 90 x 150 cm – 2008

Alexandros Vasmoulakis

Born in Athens, Greece, 1980. Lives in Athens, Greece.

My paintings are strongly influenced from my initial street artwork. However, when I exhibit my work in the gallery space, I consider myself a painter rather than a street artist. The street art market can be sweet and cozy for every young street artist, nevertheless it could be a wolf in disguise. Generally, I do not really pay much attention to the location of my work. My first intention is to make something strong and worthy. This can be enough.

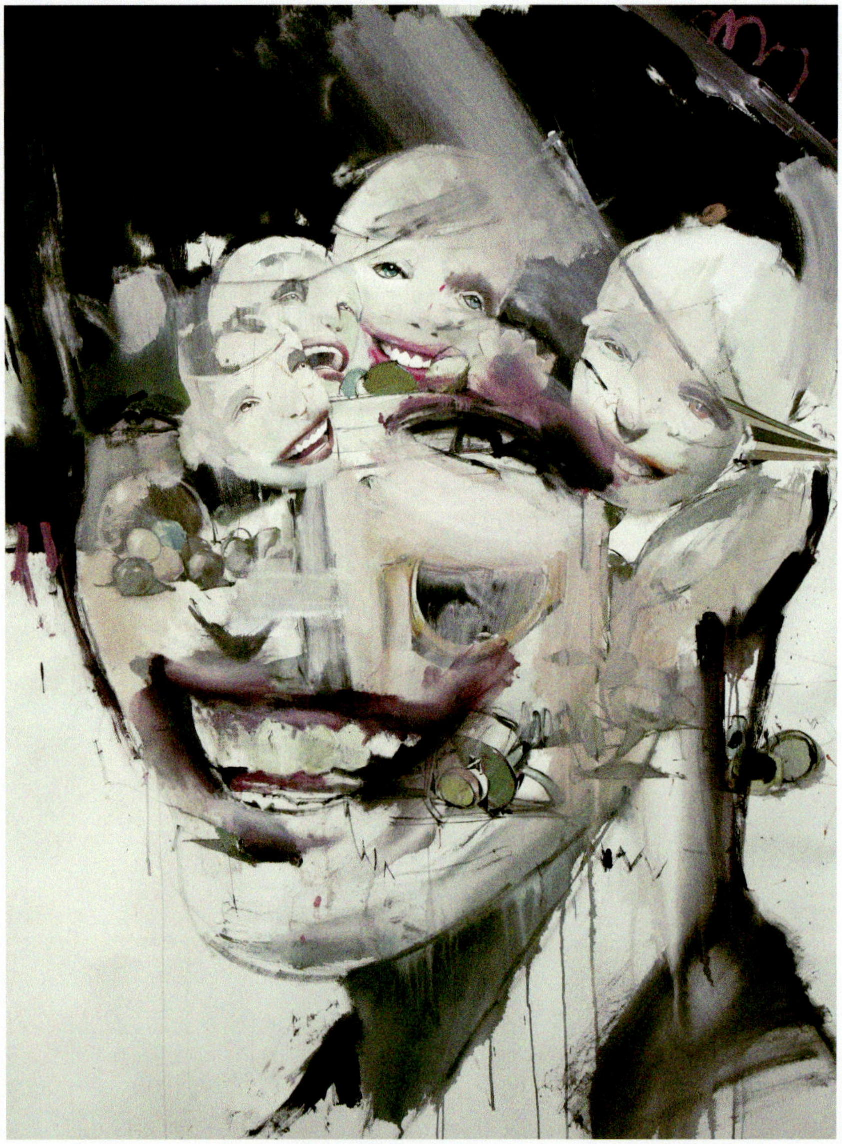

The Wrong Series (Part 2) | Acrylic and ink on canvas – 120 x 140 cm – 2011

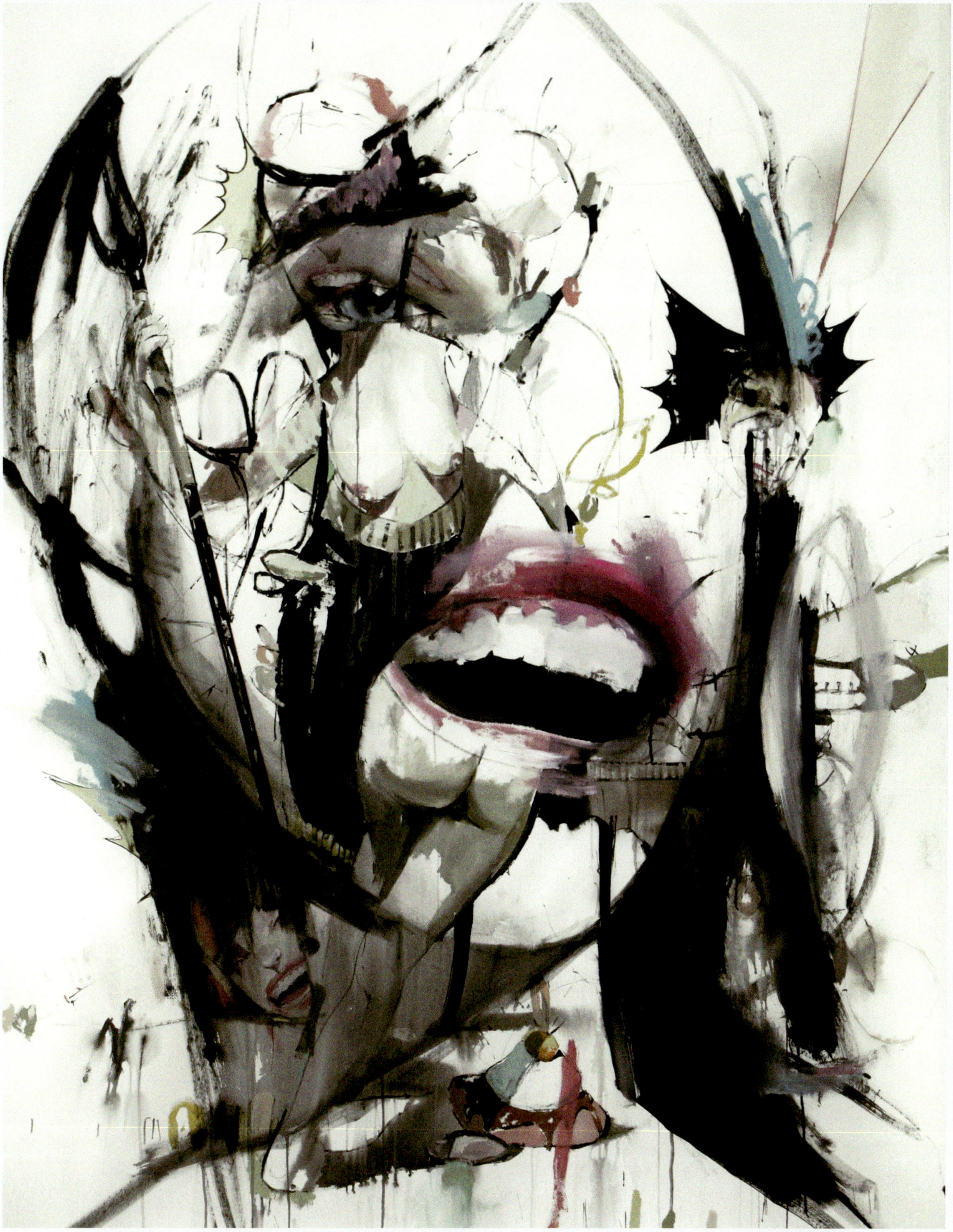

The Wrong Series (Part 1) | Acrylic and ink on canvas – 130 x 170 cm – 2011

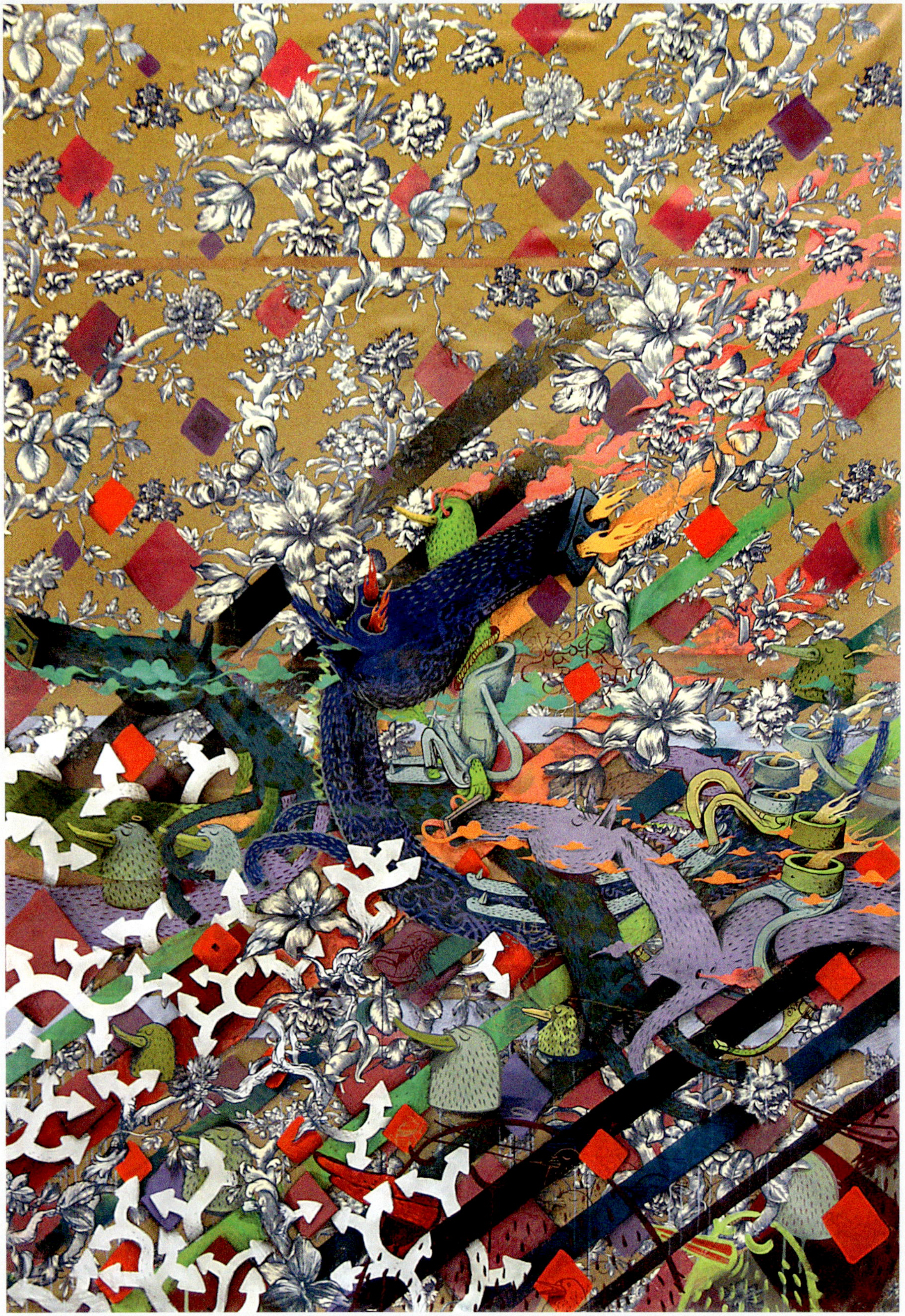

Bleue Lilas / Acrylic and mixed media on fabric – 98 x 149 cm – 2010

Alëxone Dizac

Born in Paris, France, 1976. Lives in Paris, France.

My studio work is basically inspired by the freedom and energy I found in the streets when I started to express myself through my paintings. The street was the only place where I could express myself without any obstacles, while in the studio all of this is differently expressed, although I'm trying to keep spontaneity.

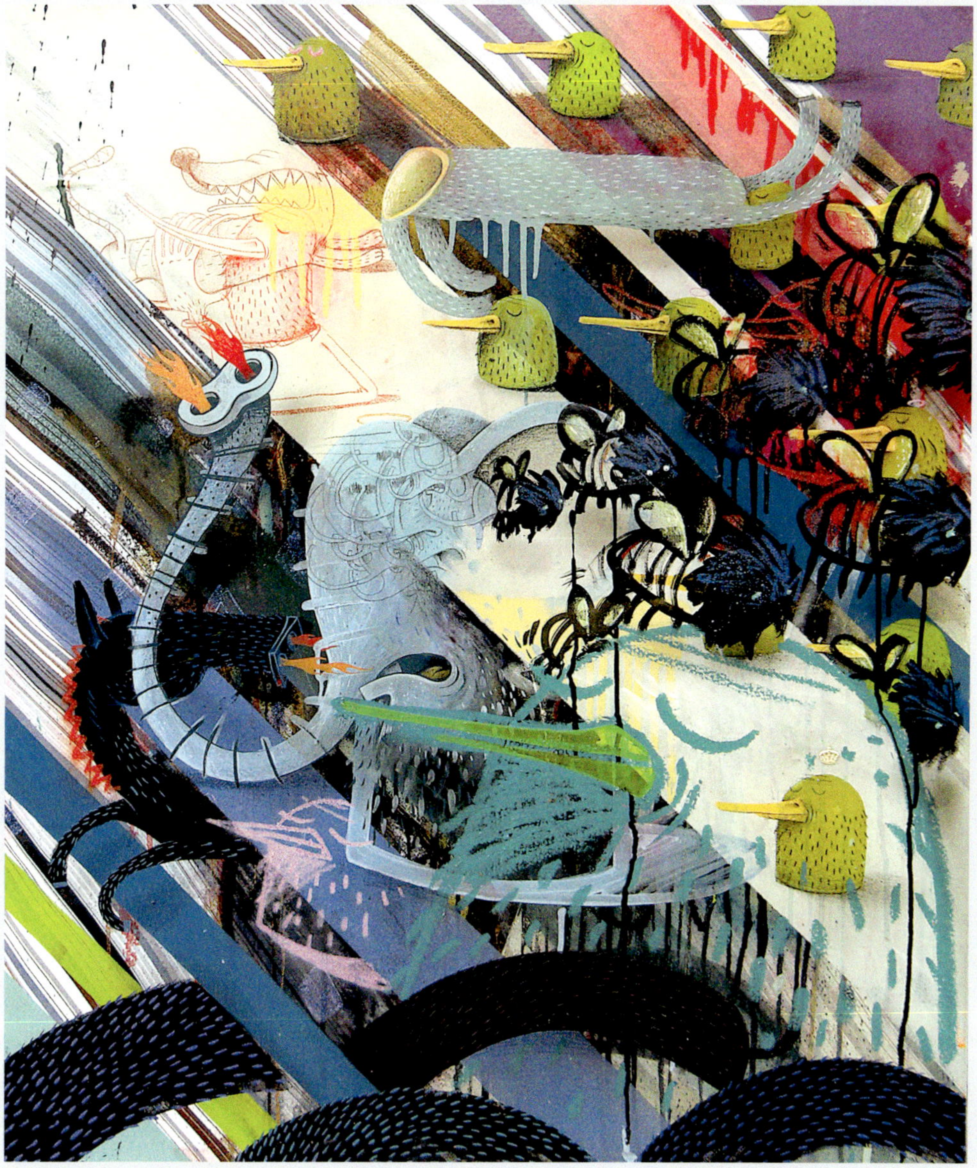

Éléphant Rayée / Acrylic and mixed media on fabric – 73 x 92 cm – 2010

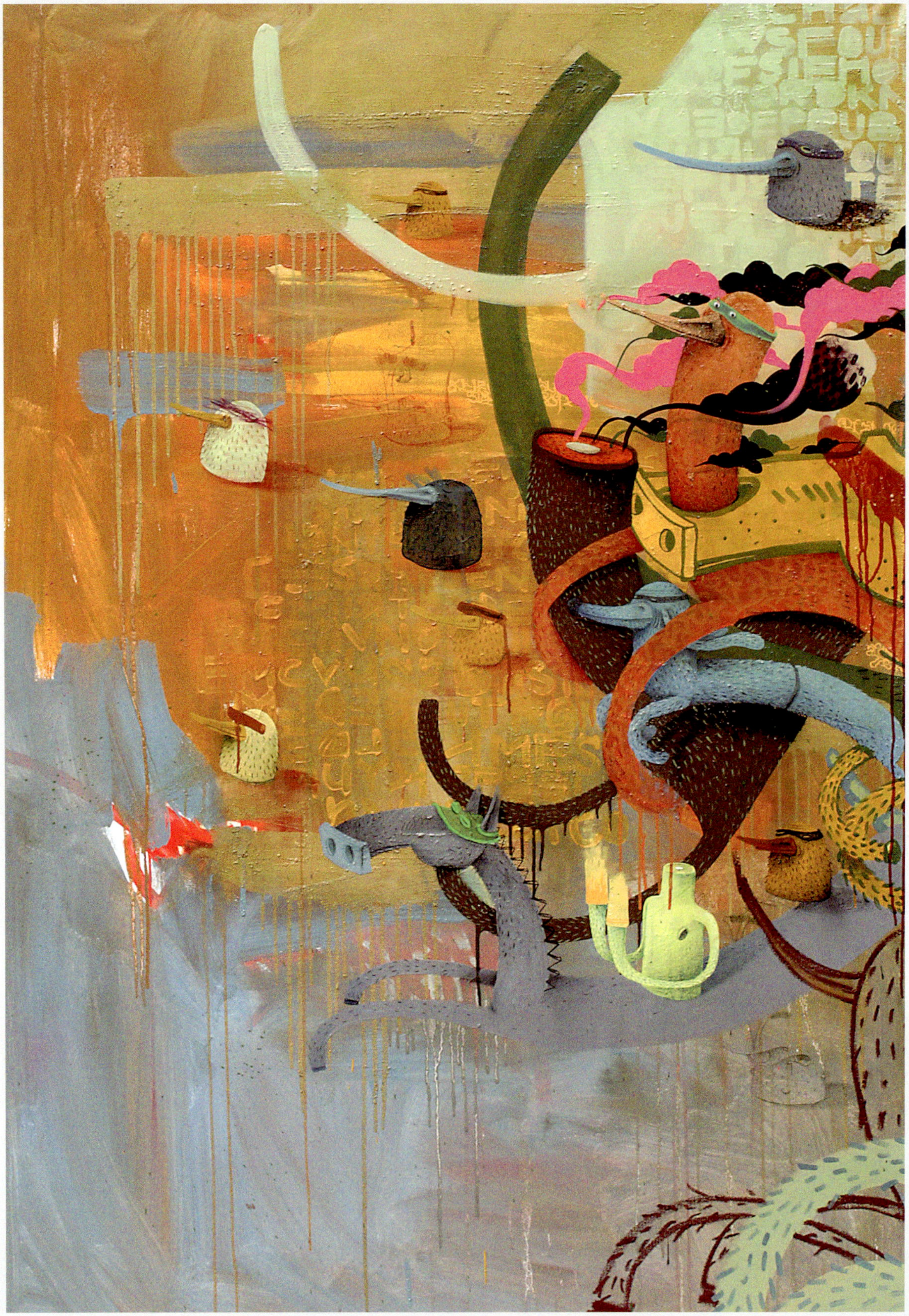

Pinky Cloud **Diptych** / Acrylic on canvas – 114 x 162 cm + 97 x 162 cm – 2008

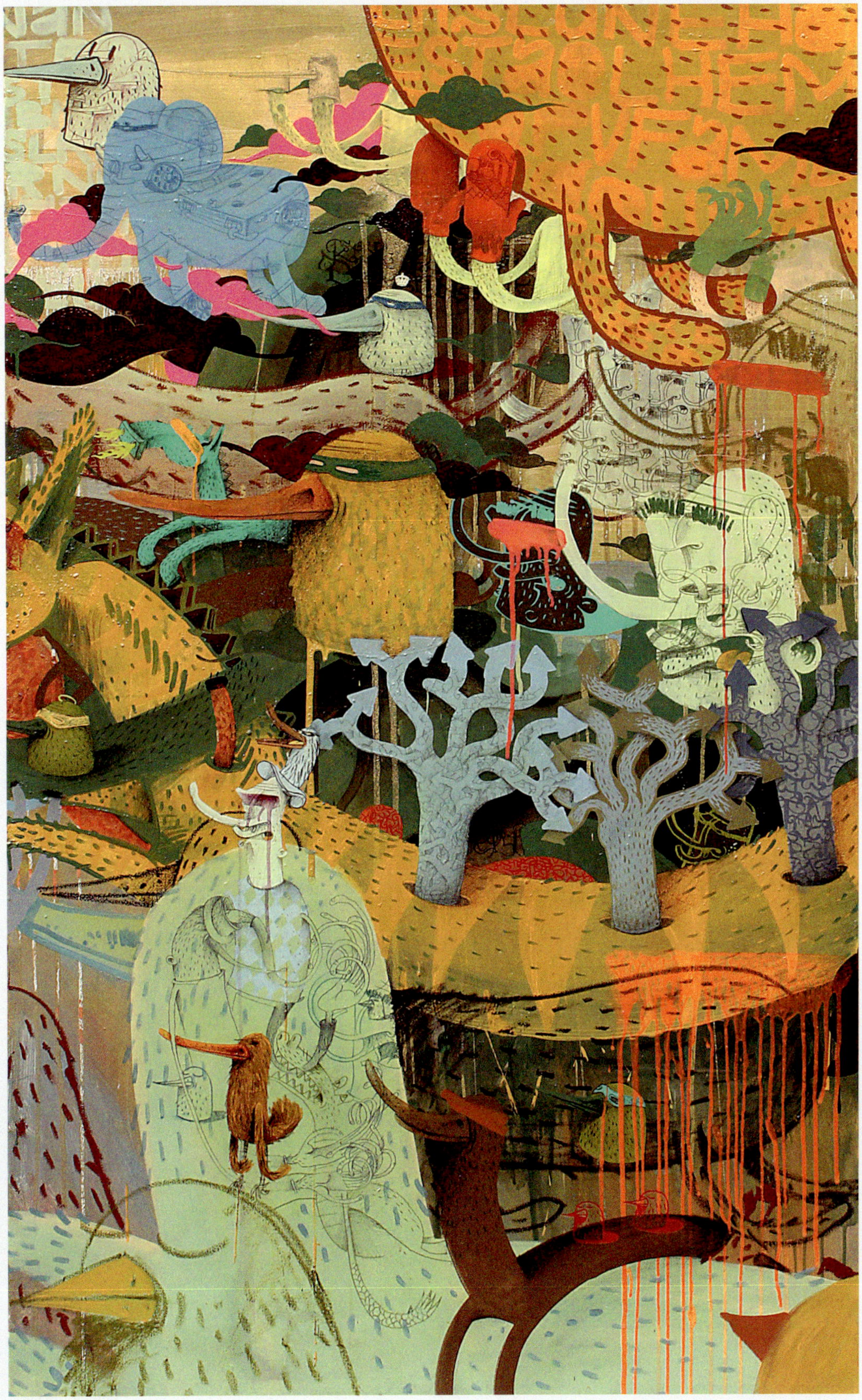

Amose

Born in Croix, France, 1979. Lives in Lille, France.

I've always liked murals made on old walls spoiled by time and weather, where various tints of the wall appear with different textures and different materials. This imperfect and dirty side of the wall convinced me to work my paintings or my drawings on old boards or on some used and yellowed paper, by adding to it a collage of the used papers and pieces of wood found in the street or in abandoned factories.

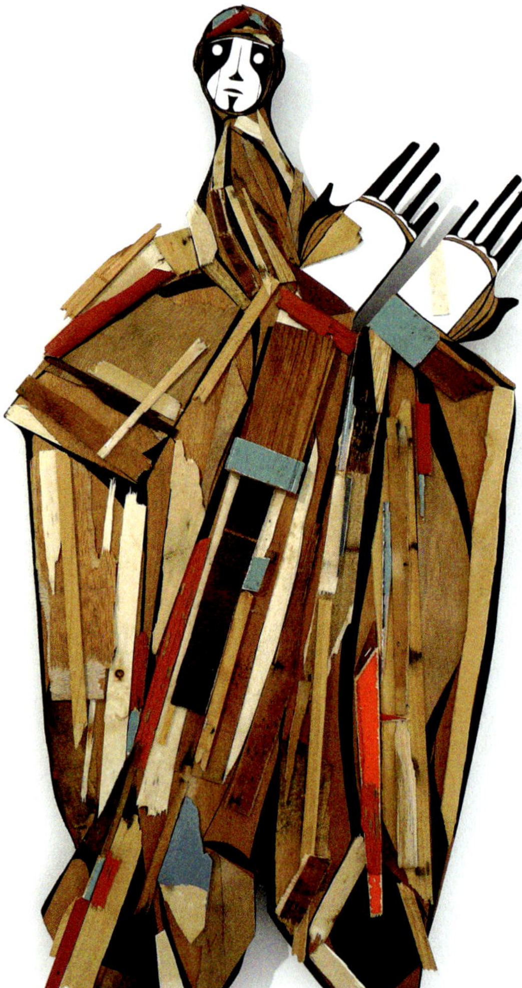

Wooderie / Wooden assembly and acrylic on wood – 55 x 100 cm – 2010

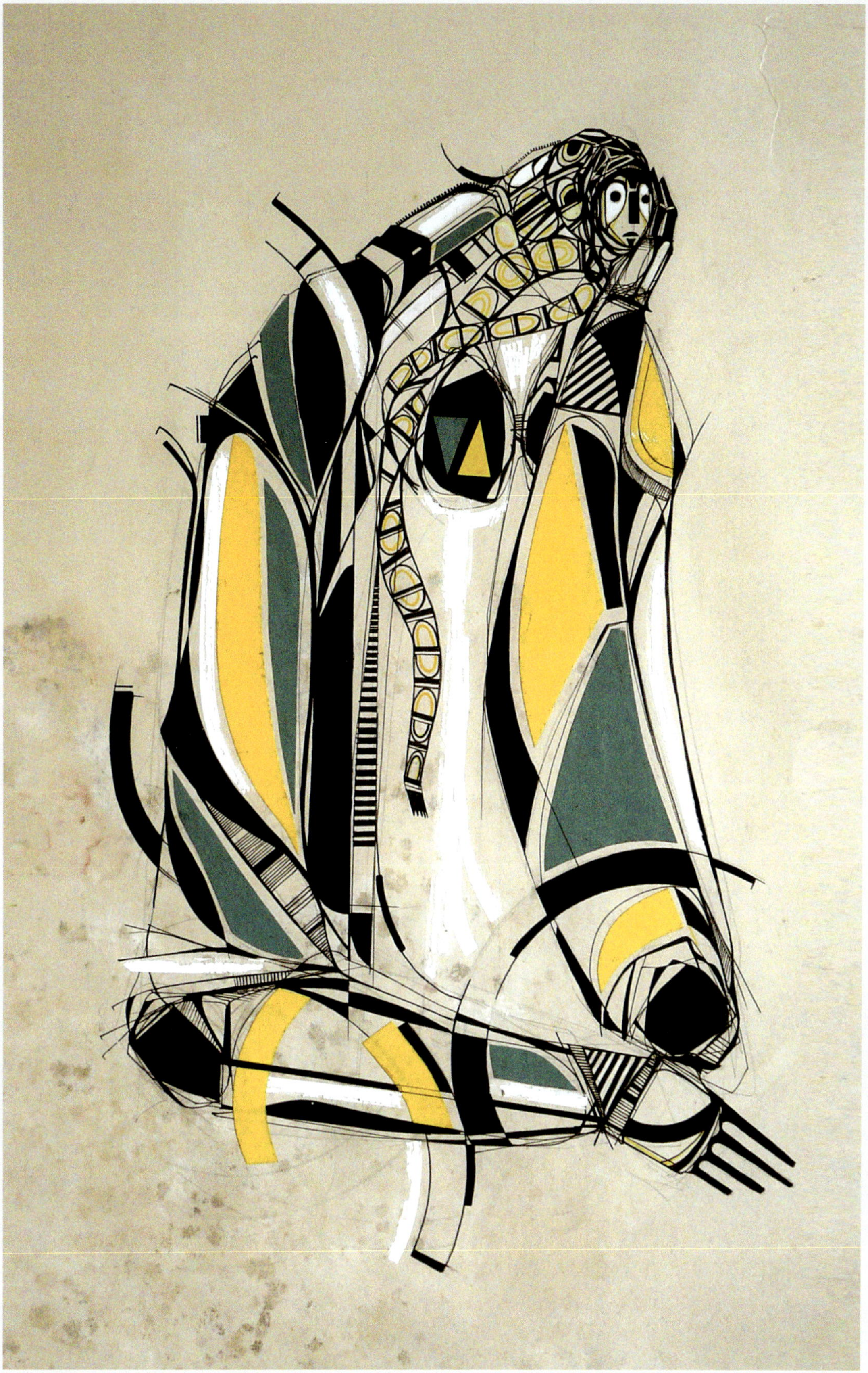

Untitled / Ink and wheat paste on paper – 25 x 43 cm – 2010

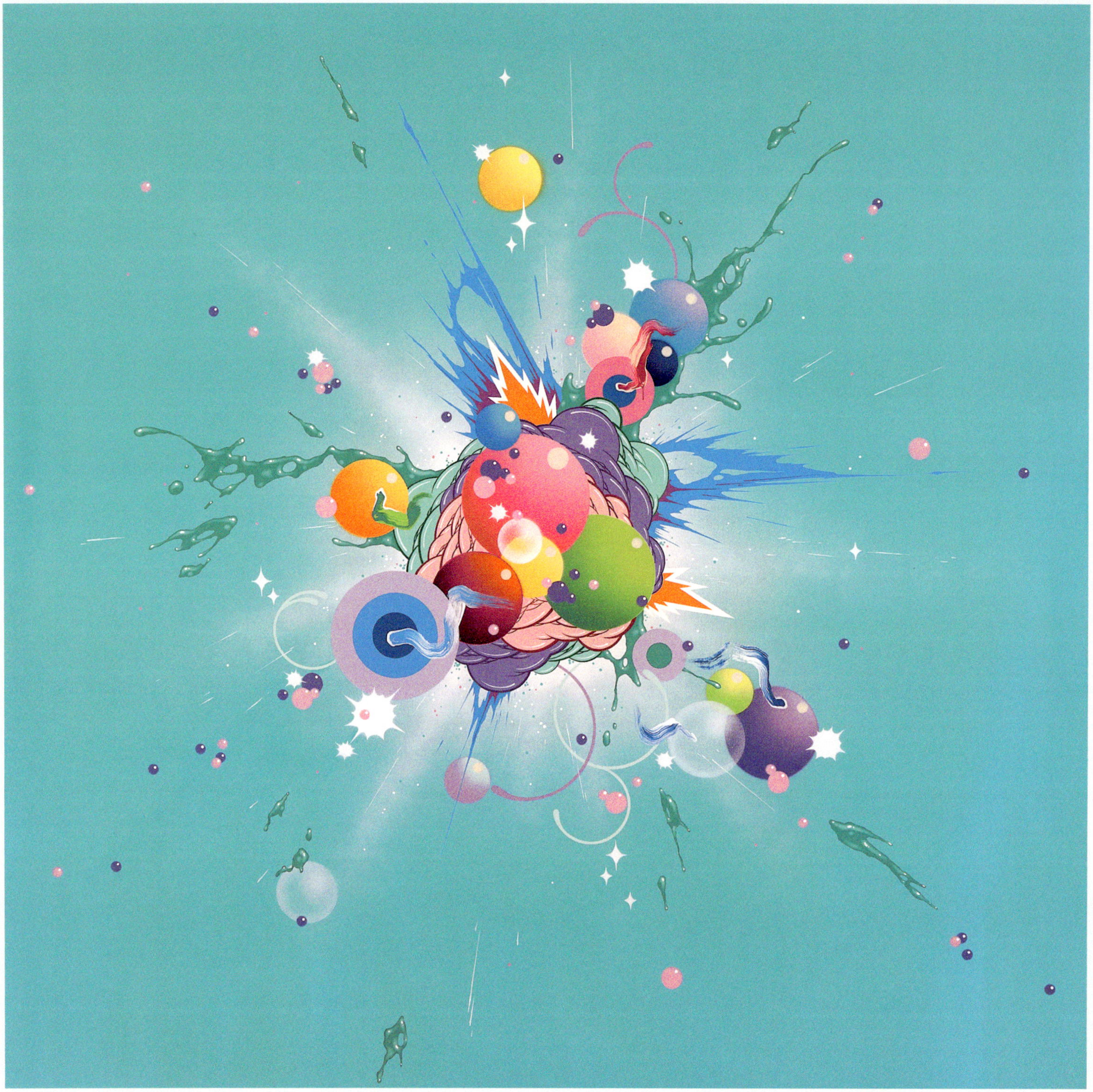

Super Nova / Acrylic and aerosol on canvas – 152 x 152 cm – 2007

Andrew McAttee

Born in London, England, 1972. Lives in London, England.

The roots to my approach can be found in my graffiti past where I painted bright pieces in disused public spaces. Leaving behind a painting that would shine beyond the grey concrete. Therefore beauty is possible anywhere and in this context a form of visual alchemy had taken place. This proved to be significant when confronting a stark blank canvas much with the same intention of making something magical appear seemingly out of nothing.

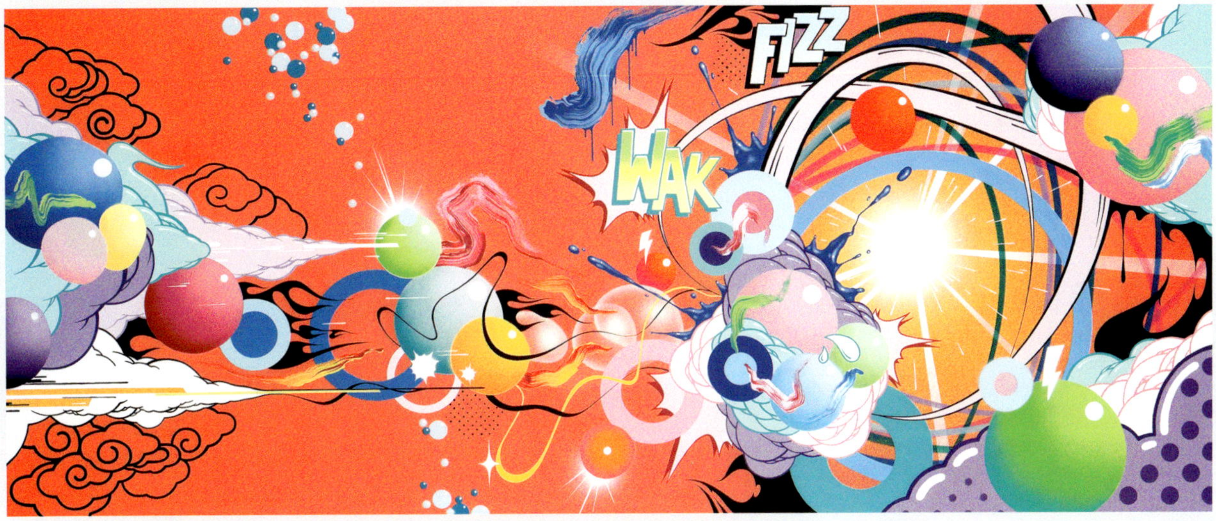

Joy Ride / Acrylic and aerosol on canvas – 203 x 86 cm – 2007

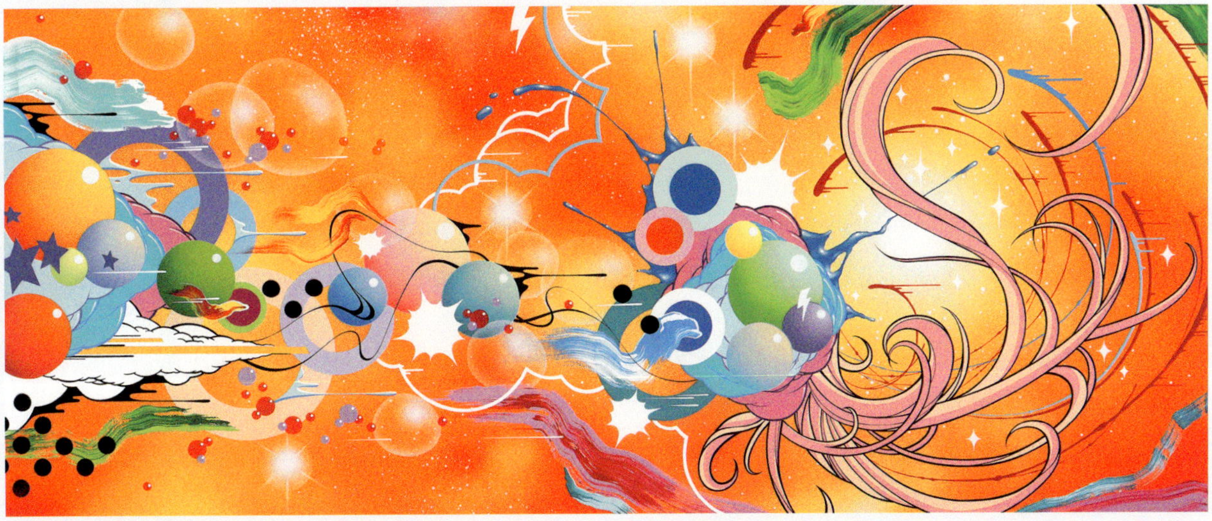

String Theory / Acrylic and aerosol on canvas – 203 x 86 cm – 2007

Anthony Lister

Born in Brisbane, Australia, 1979. Lives in New York, United States.

I am a constructionist from the post-abstract expressionist school of adventure painters. In the studio I am slow and conceptually methodical. On the street I like to act fast and create pieces that are gritty and look rushed around the edges. The street plays a role in my practice by giving me the space to be adventurous with my line. I have found over the years that developing an ability to work on a large scale is quite satisfying and somewhat addictive.

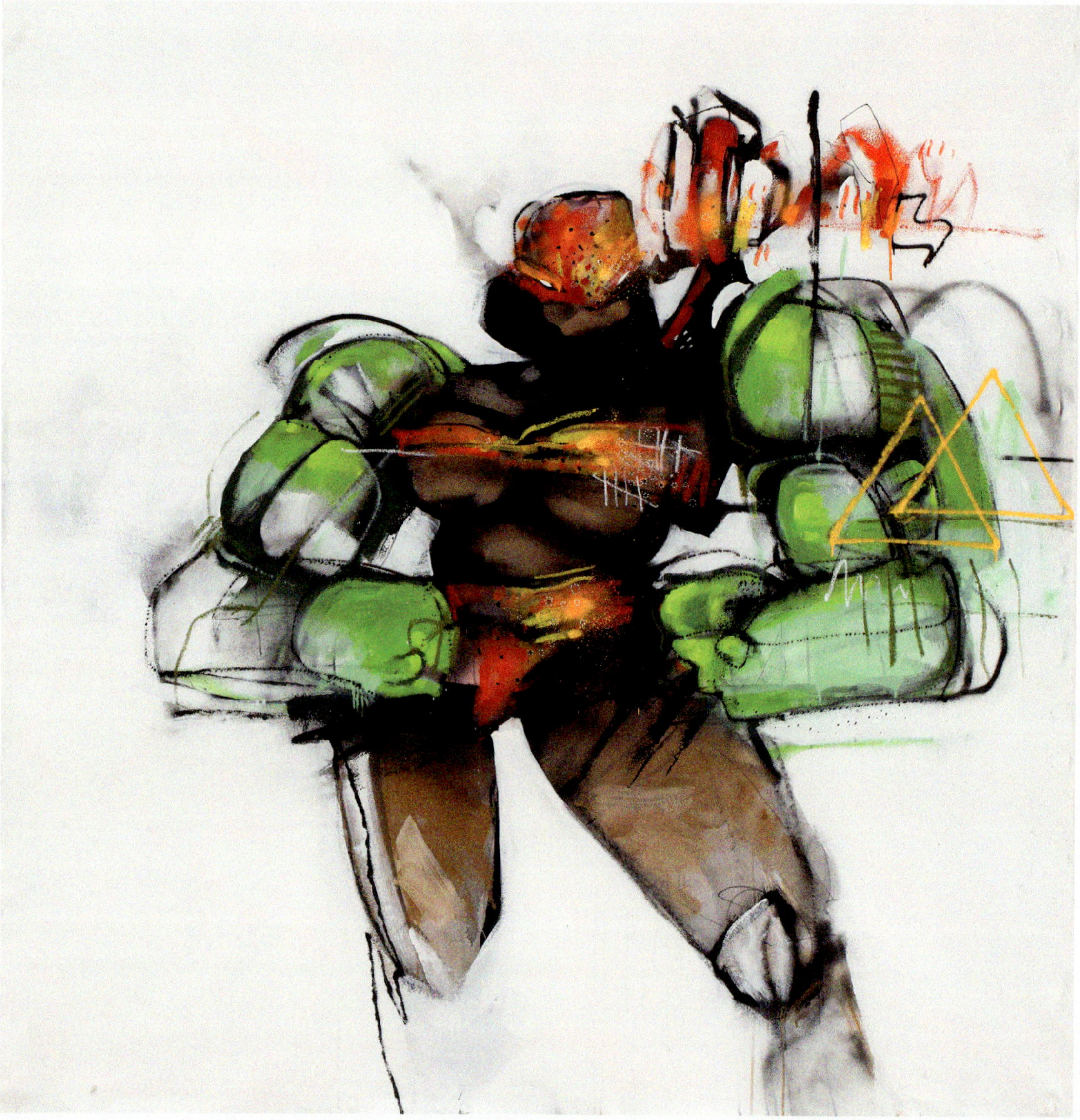

Tribal Hulk Pose / Mixed media on canvas – 180 x 180 cm – 2010

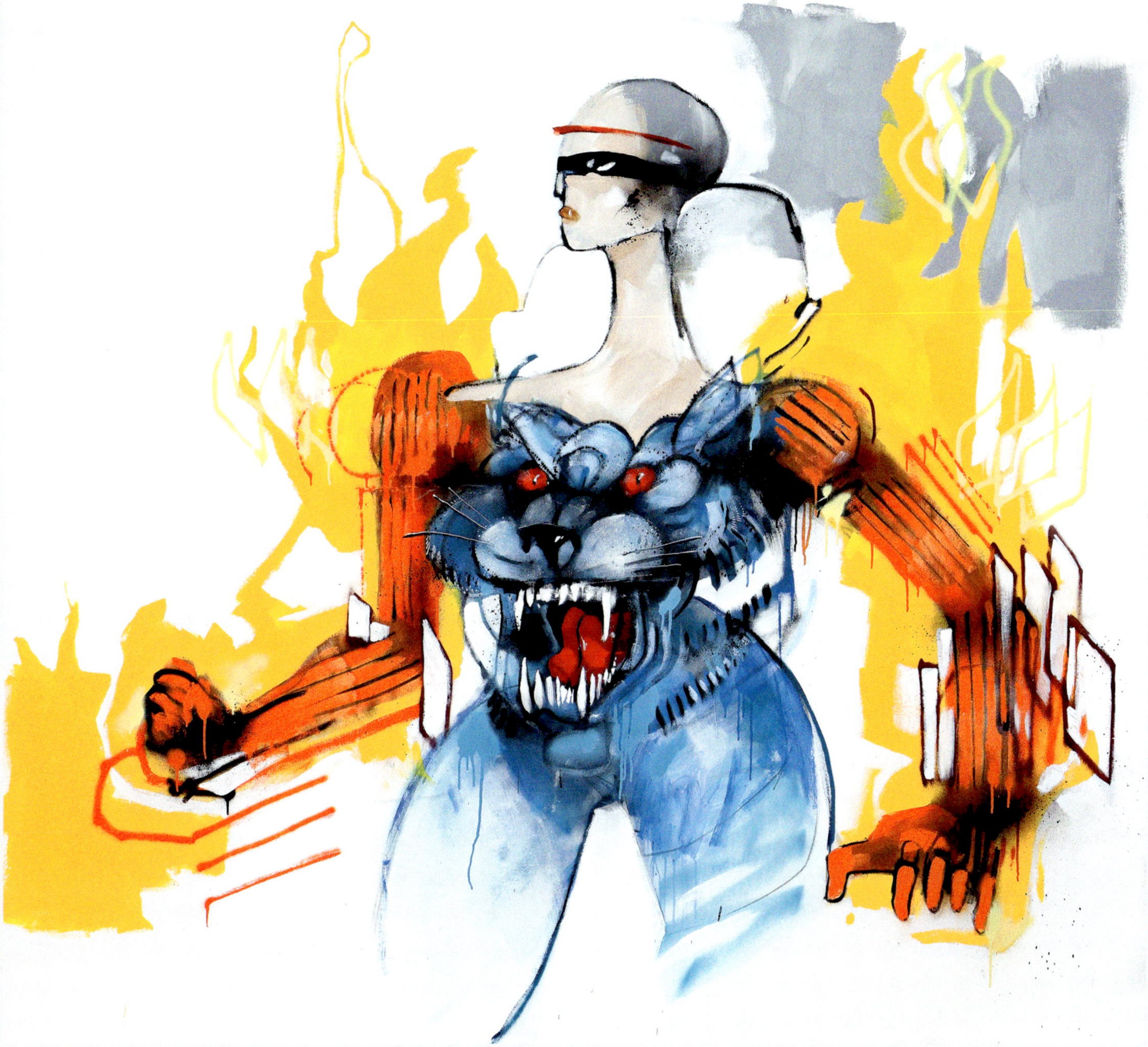

The Way of the Tiger Lady | Mixed media on canvas – 180 x 180 cm – 2010

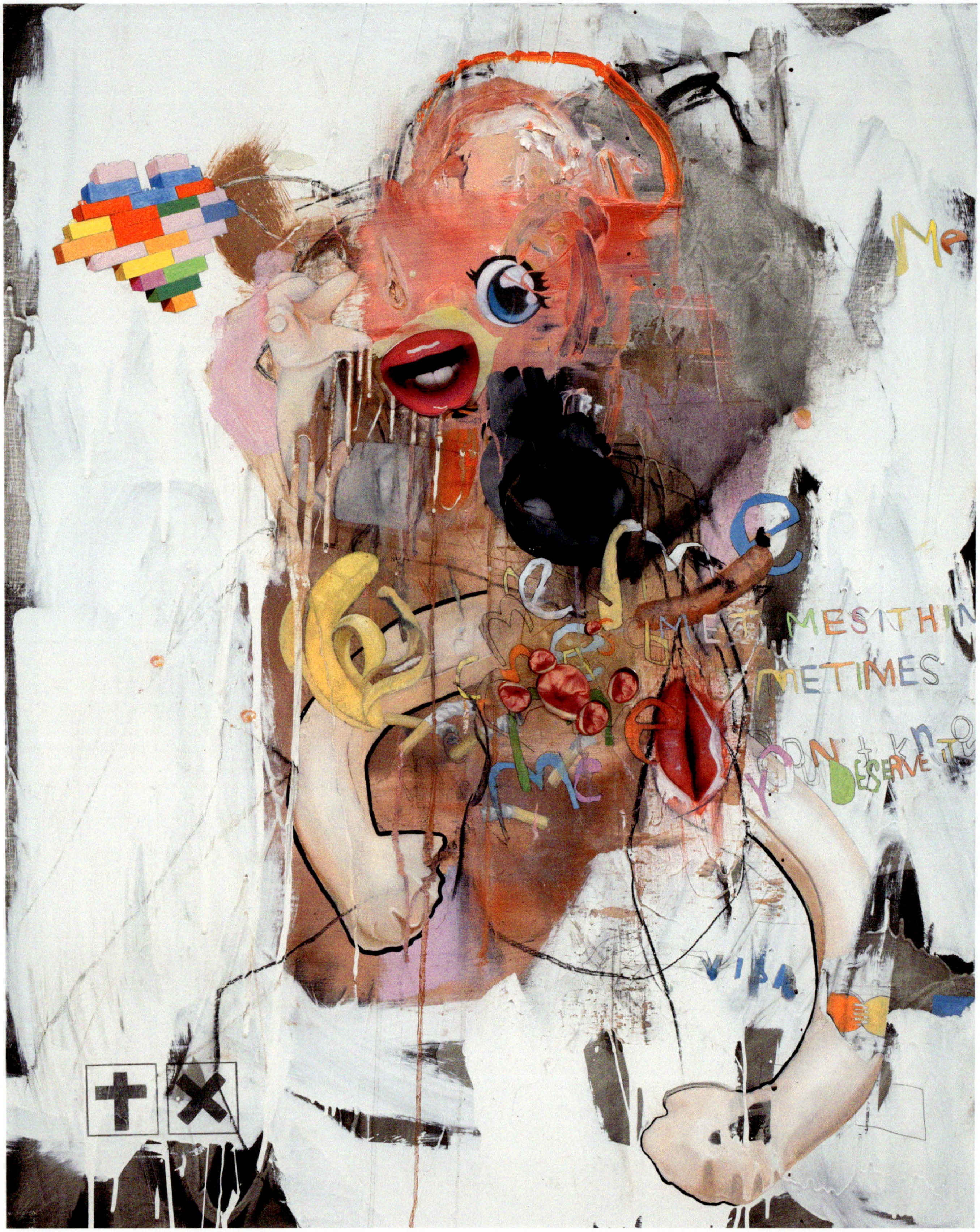

Spasticoid Plasticoid / Oil on linen – 80 x 140 cm – 2010

Antony Micallef

Born in Swindon, England, 1975. Lives in London, England.

For me traveling around and immersing myself in the city environment is very important. I like to watch people and look at behavior. I find the spectrum of rich and poor and how the dynamics function side by side interesting and how this makes a social commentary on a society we have created.

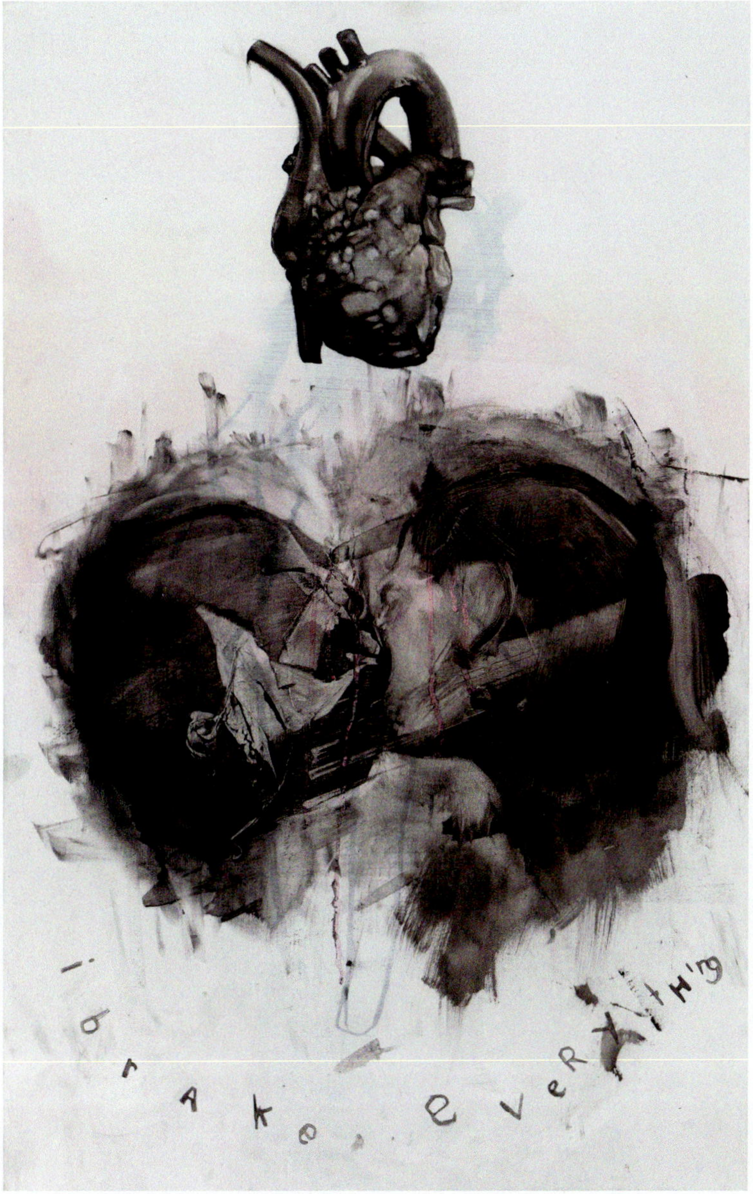

Black Kiss / Oil and acrylic on linen – 80 x 100 cm – 2010

Axel Void

Born in Florida, United States, 1986. Lives in Berlin, Germany.

I don't make a distinction between street and studio work. The difference lies in the context, and therefore the reading of the artwork changes as well. Beyond its physical location, the purpose is the same in each case; the end result is not purely aesthetic, it's at the service of its concept, and nothing more than a tool.

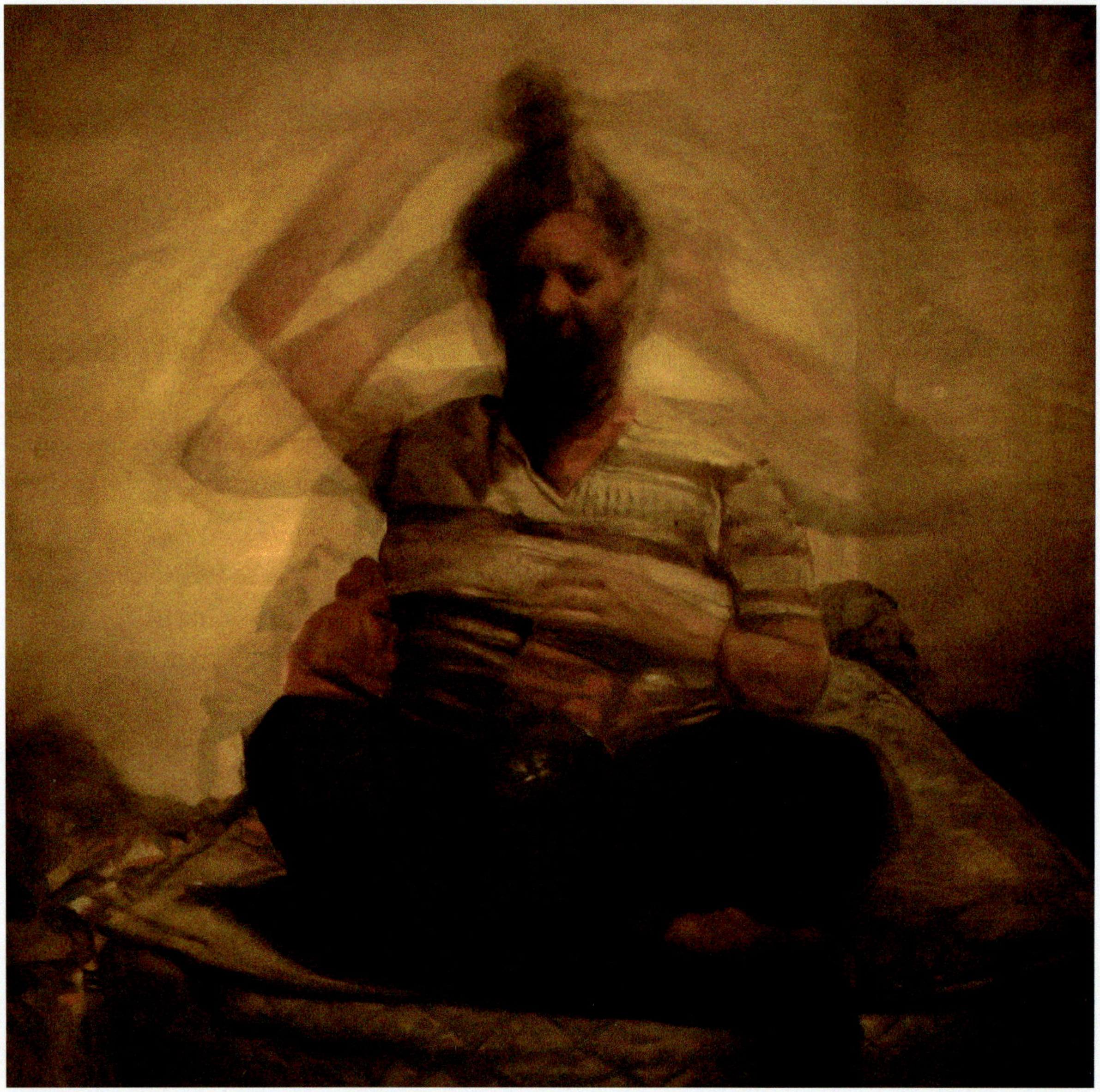

Untitled / Oil on canvas – 100 x 100 cm – 2009

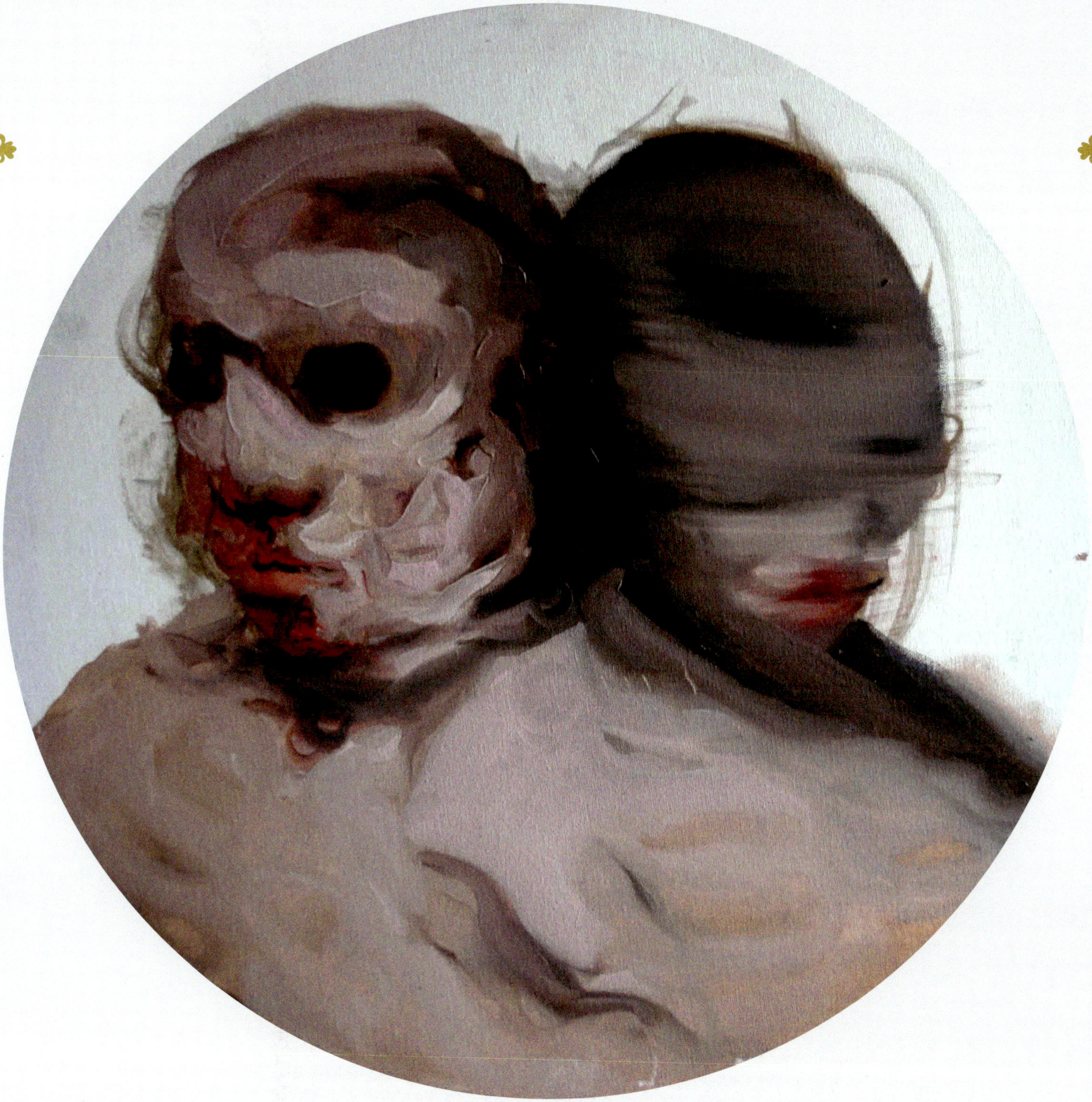

We / Oil on canvas – 50 cm – 2008

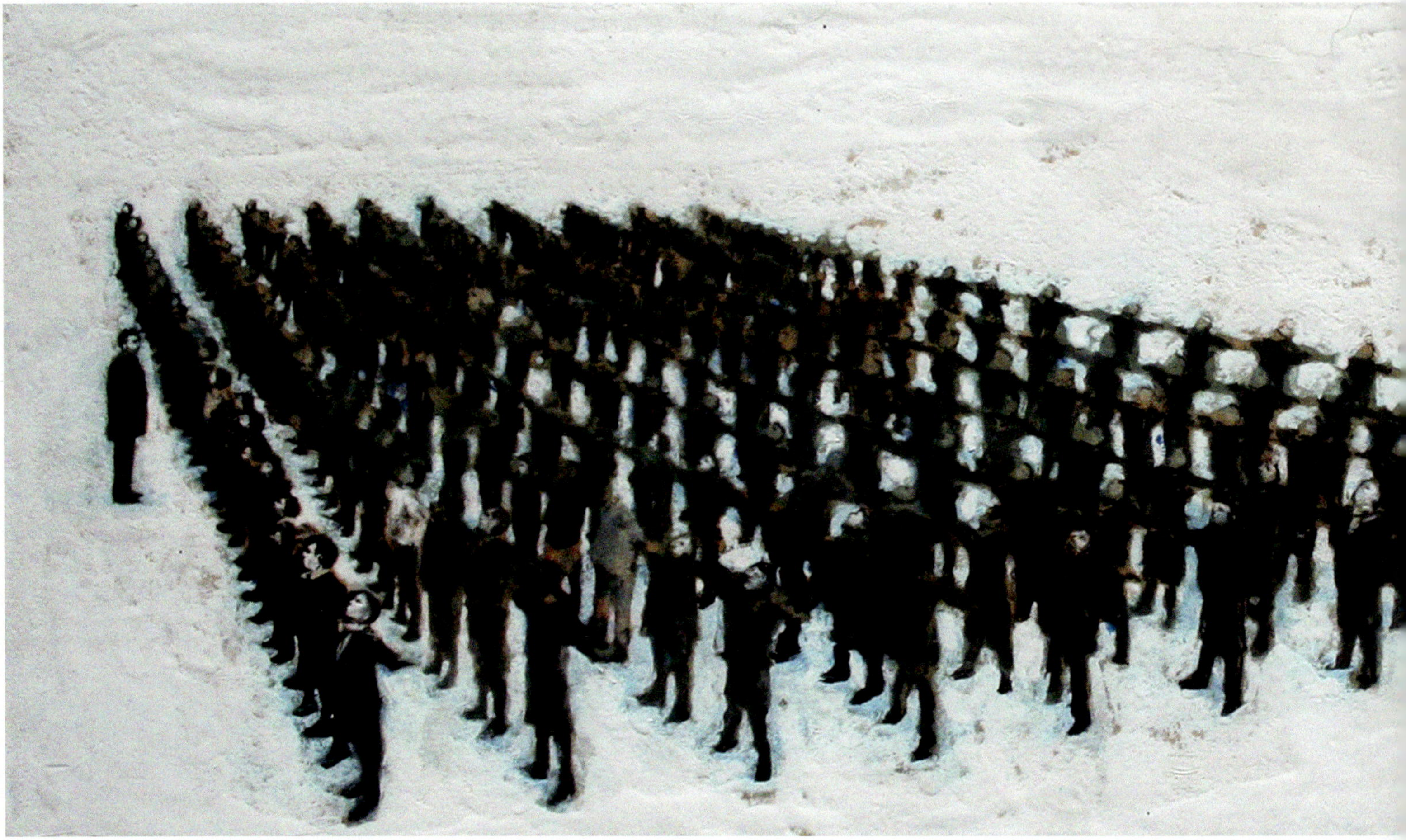

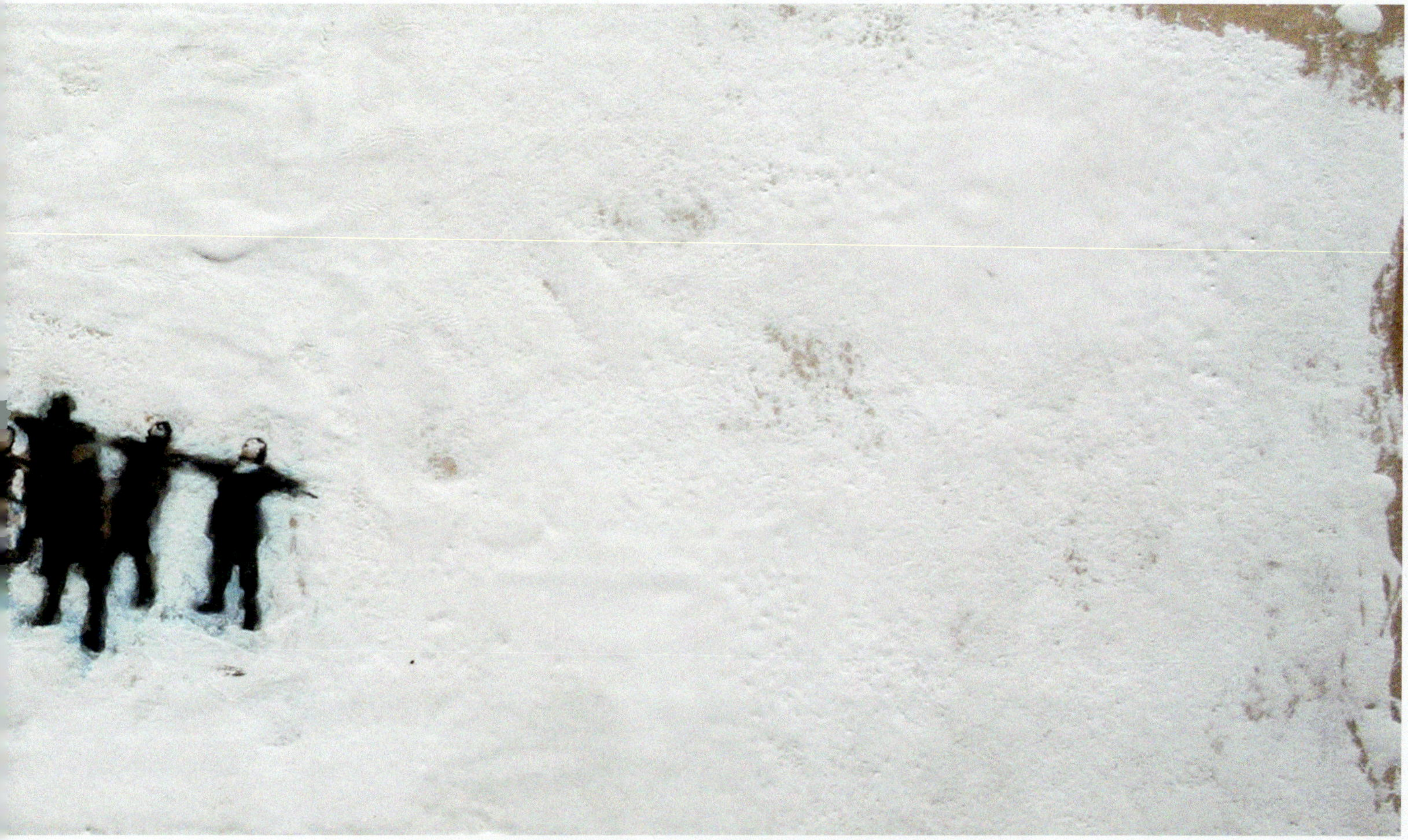

Niños / Oil and enamel on wood – 65 x 20 cm – 2006

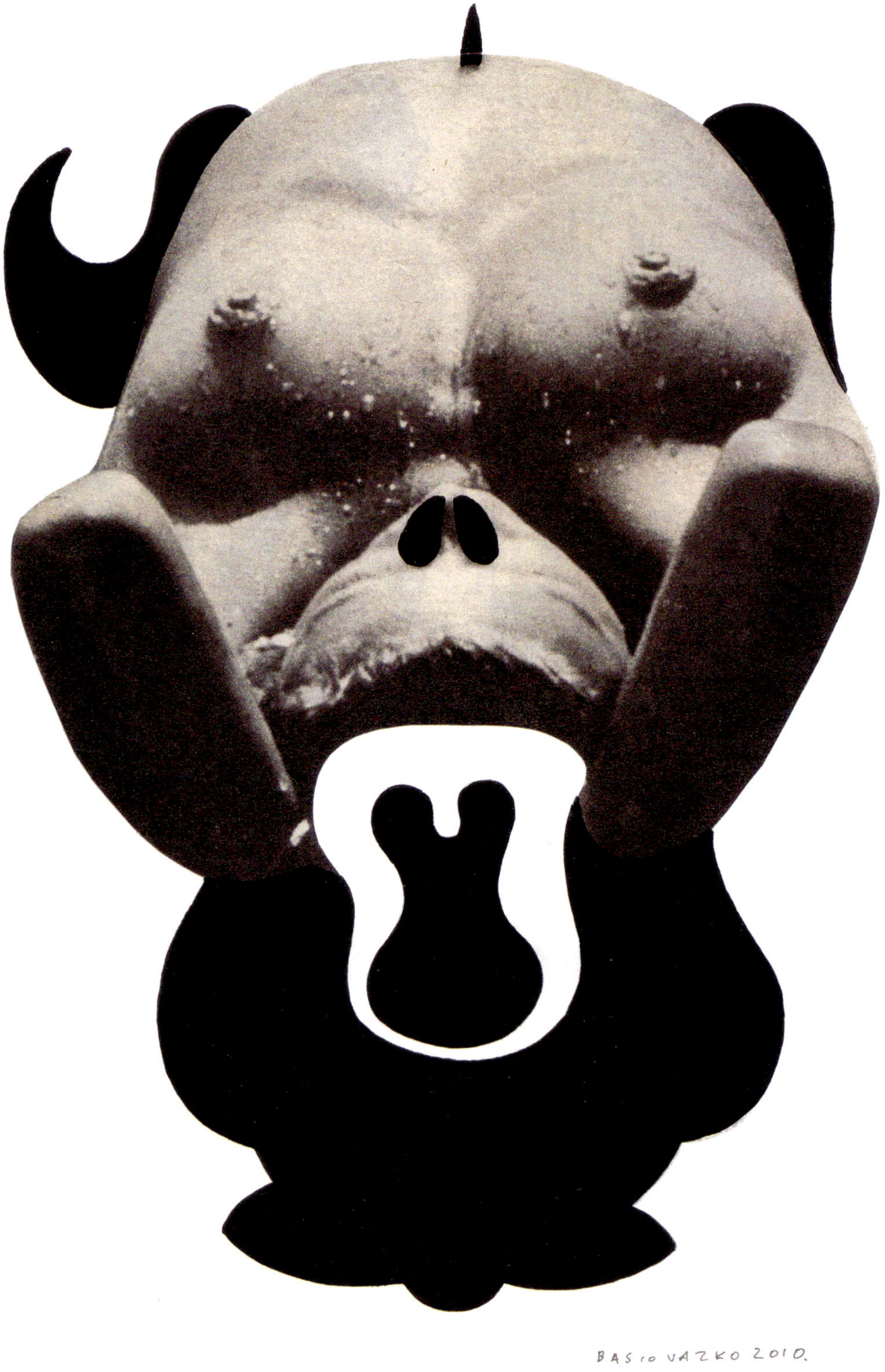

Novedades, Libro de Collages Página #22 / Acrylic and mixed media on paper – 14 x 21 cm – 2010

Basco-Vazko

Born in Santiago, Chile, 1983. Lives in Santiago, Chile.

Painting on the streets is completely different to painting anywhere else I think, mainly for two reasons. First it gives your painting a definitive place in the world and second it gives real meaning to the idea of public space. The only thing I can think of that the street and the studio have in common is that painting stops and marks the time the same way. It doesn't matter if it's a wall or a piece of paper you are painting, it is always the first and last time it would happen.

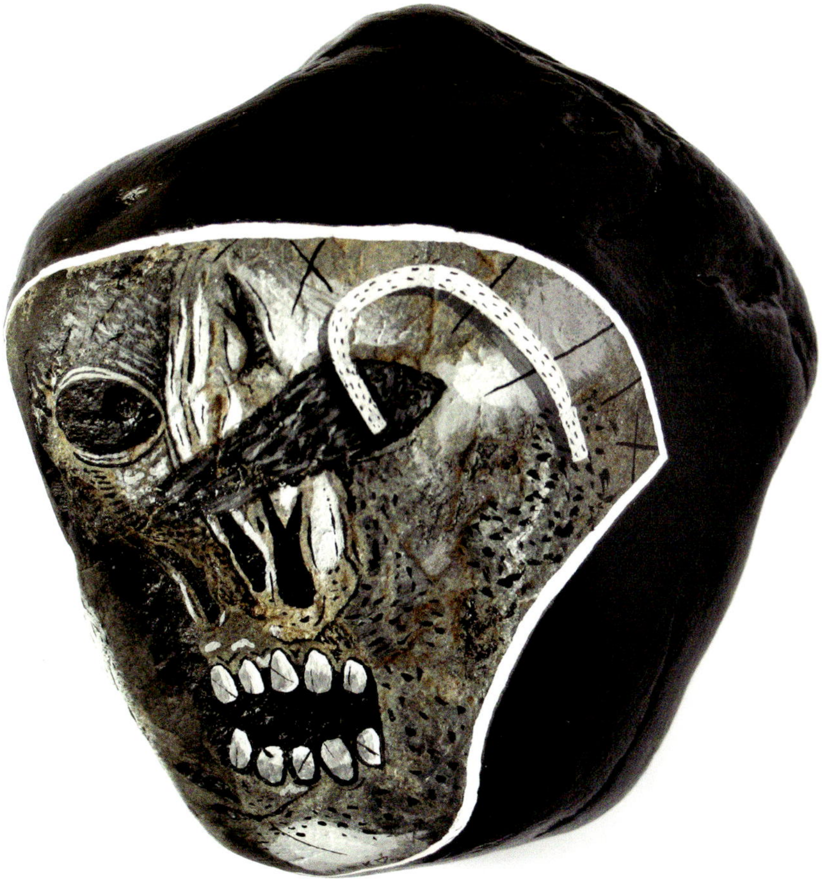

Piedra #5 Sin Título | Acrylic and enamel on stone – 22 x 22 x 25 cm – 2010

Base 23

Born in Kiel, Germany, 1972. Lives in Berlin, Germany.

The ideas of my characters and visions are developed on the streets and originate from 21 years of experience with classic graffiti. My studio work is a direct transfer from walls to canvas with more details on a smaller scale that sometimes lead me to getting lost for days while painting in the Ral Galaxia.

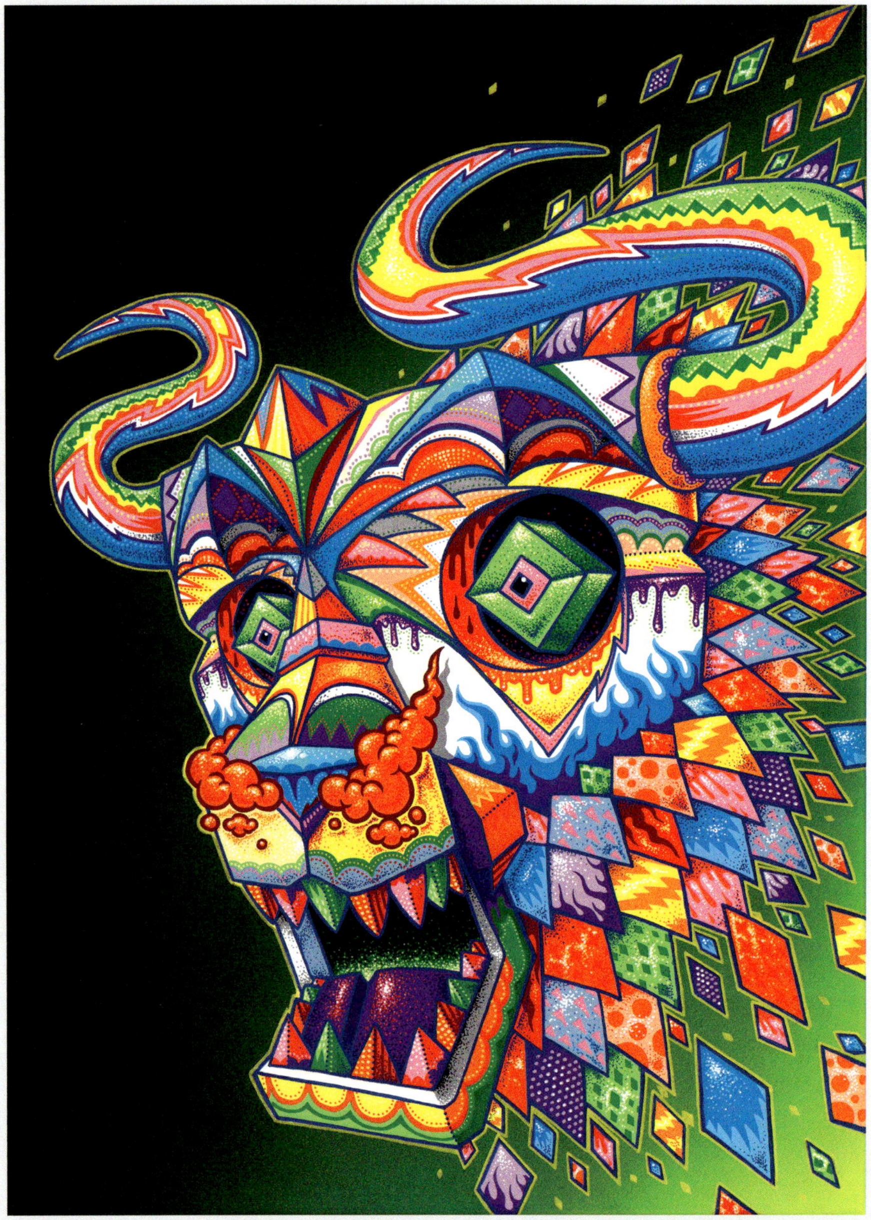

León / Acrylic on canvas – 50 x 70 cm – 2009

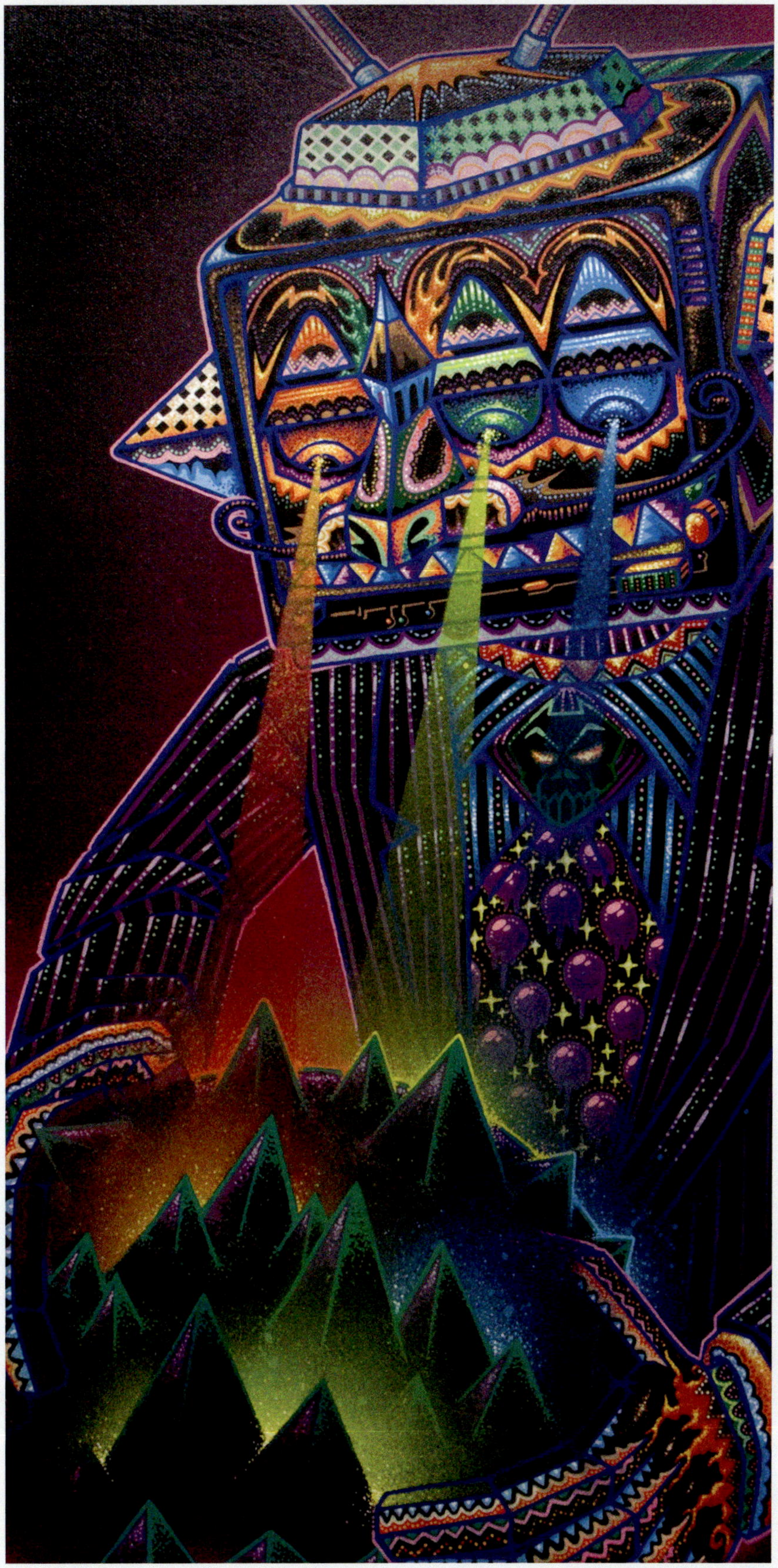

Invasión el Medio de Comunicación | Acrylic on canvas – 25 x 50 cm – 2010

Ben Frost

Born in Brisbane, Australia, 1977. Lives in Sydney, Australia.

I started doing street art in Melbourne in 2001, but now am mostly a gallery artist. I think this transition is because of the amount of time it now takes for me to finish an artwork. I still do a lot of paste-ups, and use stencils and aerosol in my work—I look at a spray can now for what it is: a can with paint in it, rather than it having to be something used on the street and the negative connotations a lot of people unfairly put on it.

Every Man Has His Price | Acrylic and aerosol on board – 120 x 120 cm – 2009

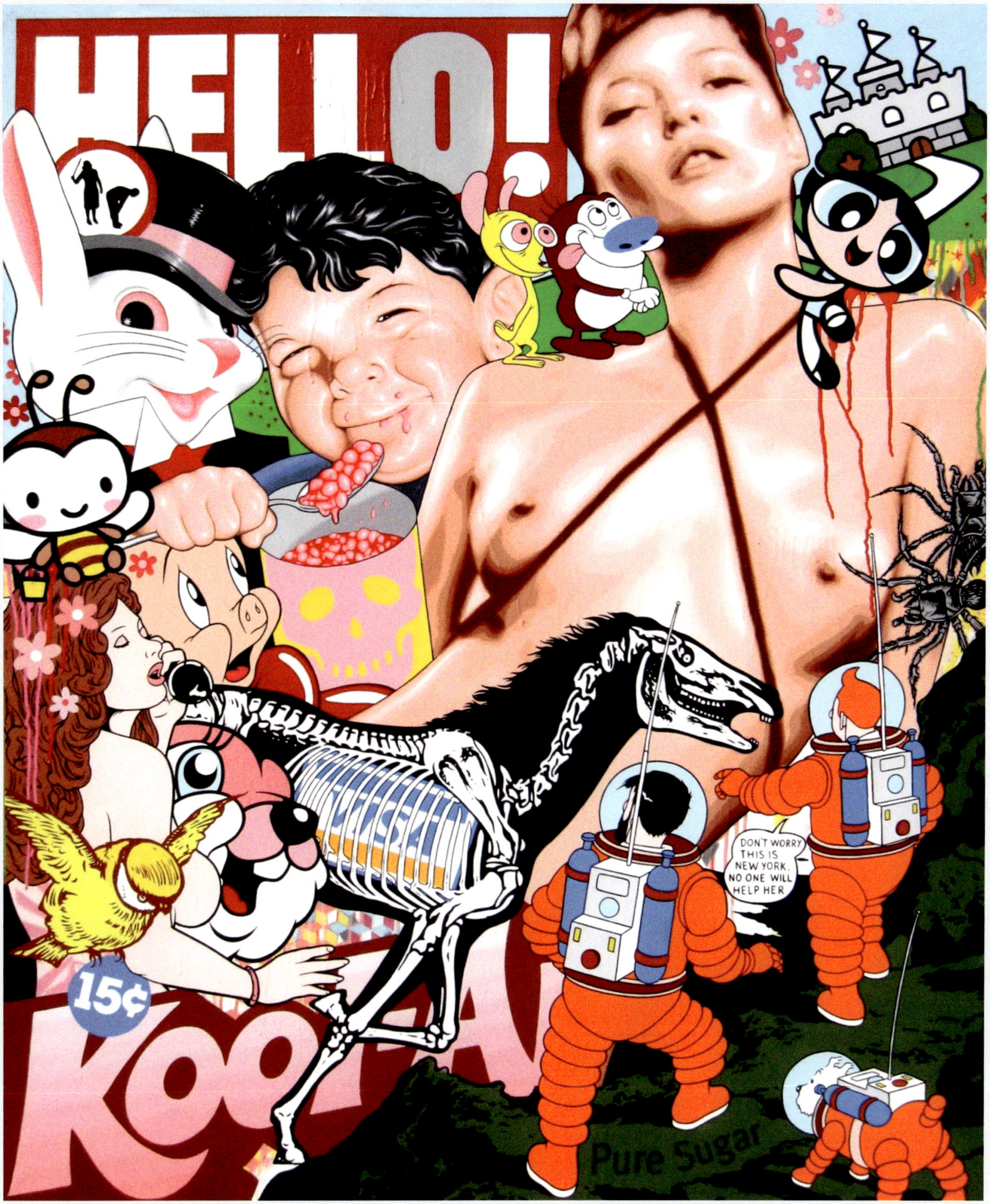

Gathering Moss / Acrylic and aerosol on canvas – 110 x 150 cm – 2010

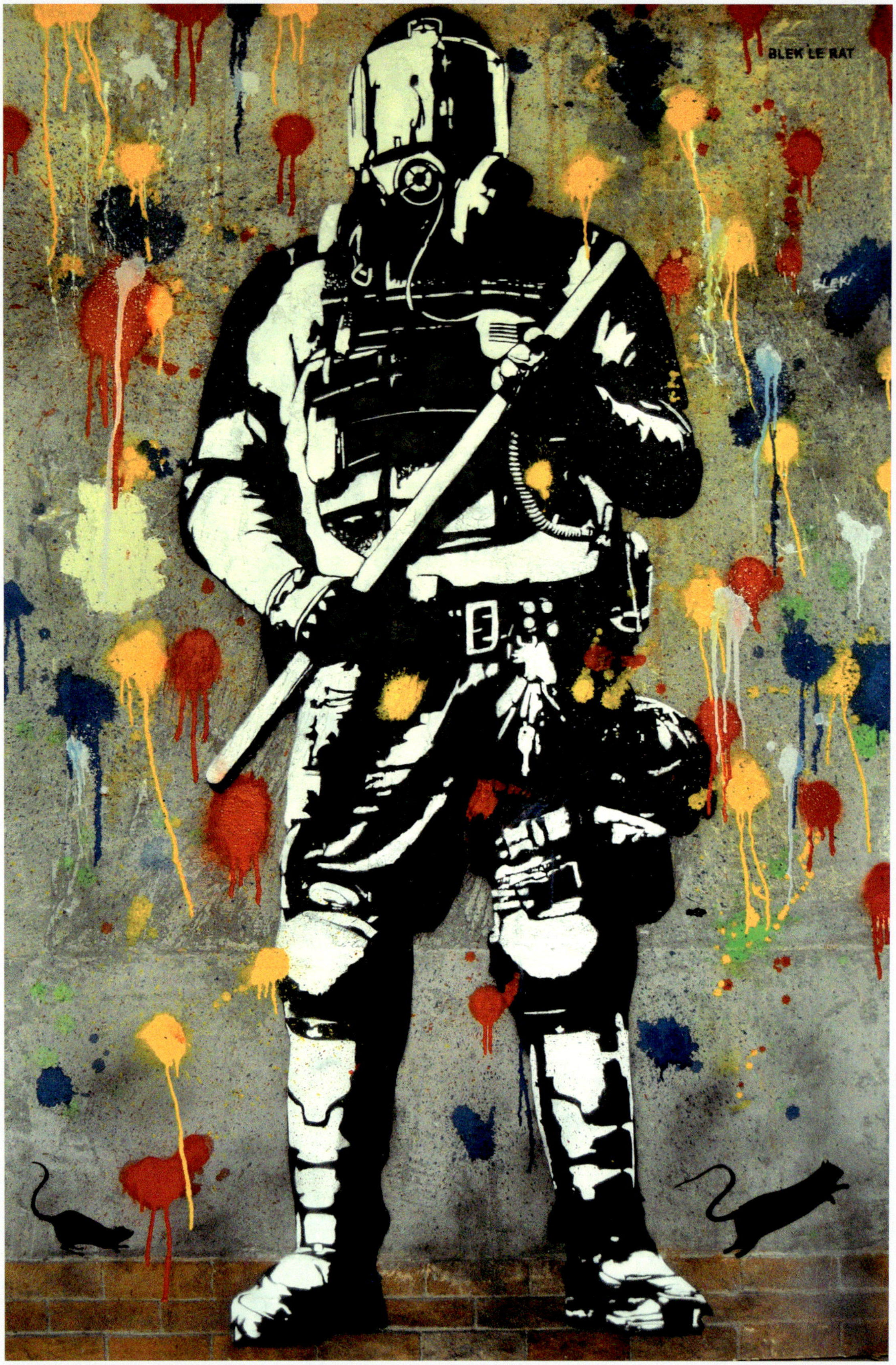

Paintball Cop / Mixed media, aerosol, and stencil on concrete – 130 x 200 cm – 2011

Blek le Rat

Born in Paris, France, 1951. Lives in Paris, France.

Why do the streets and my studio work complement each other? Because urban art is ephemeral; when I leave an image in the streets it only lasts a few hours or days. My work on canvas is a memory of what I did in the urban space before. This memory is necessary for the generations to come, since these painted objects are witnesses of a past they will have never known.

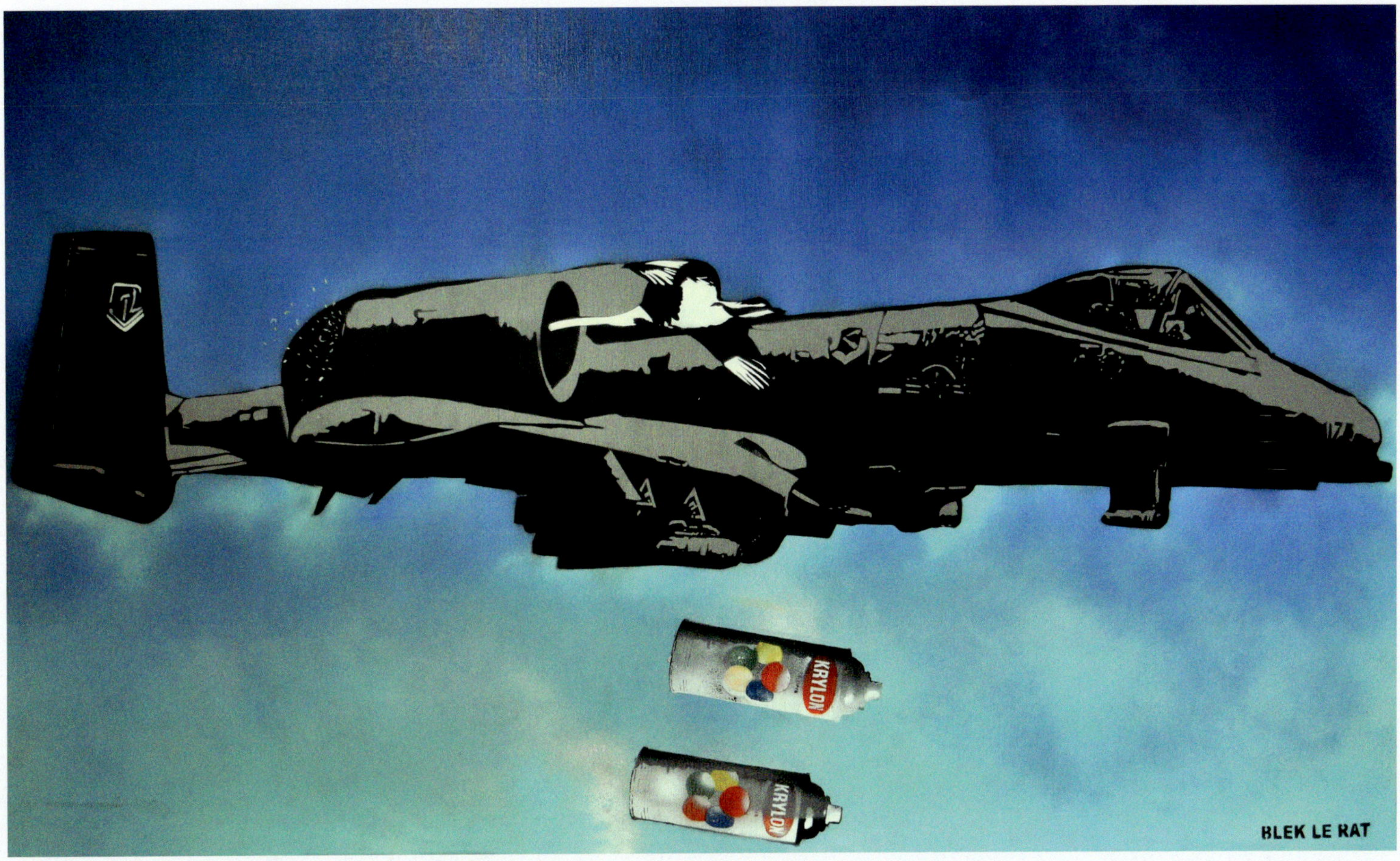

Bomb It / Stencil and aerosol on canvas – 160 x 96 cm – 2011

Bom-K

Born in Paris, France, 1973. Lives in Paris, France.

I love working in the streets or abandoned factories but to me, there's something special about painting on canvas. I feel like I can work on more intimate things in my studio. It offers me the luxury of taking time to think, of erasing things, focusing on technique and so on… More importantly, I don't see how the police will ever come and bug me inside that bubble!

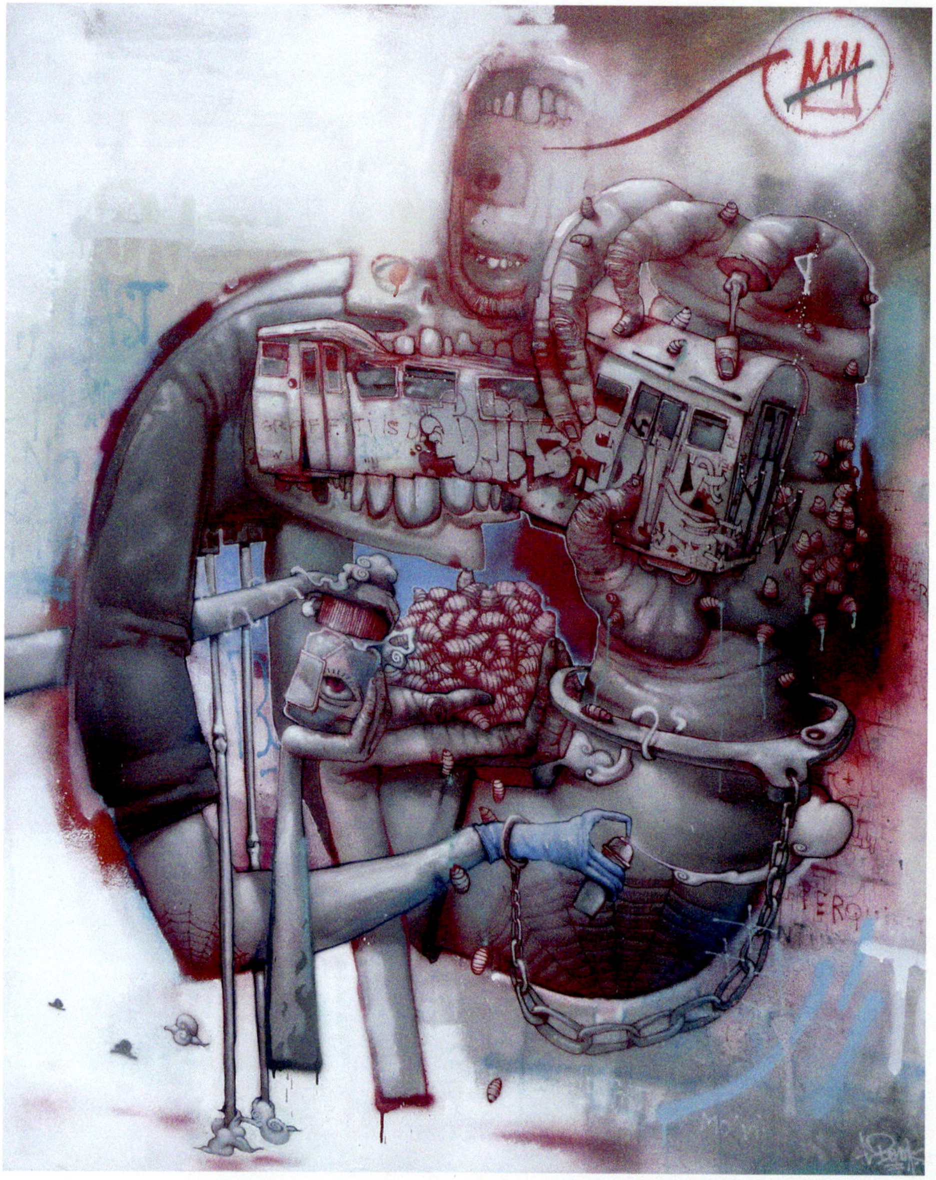

Graffiti is Die / Aerosol on canvas – 130 x 180 cm – 2009

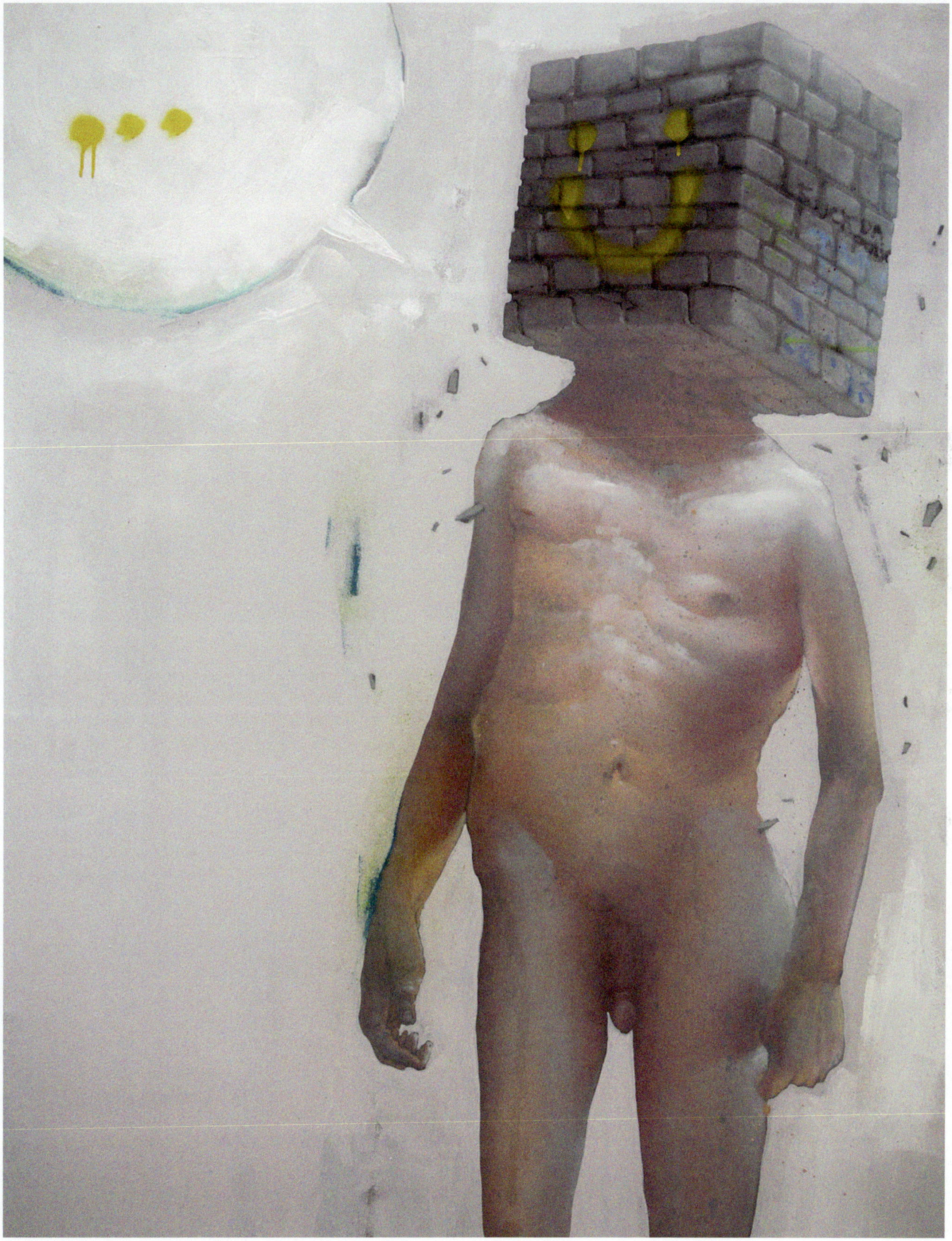

Compulsif Obsessional Disorder #2 | Aerosol on canvas – 130 x 170 cm – 2011

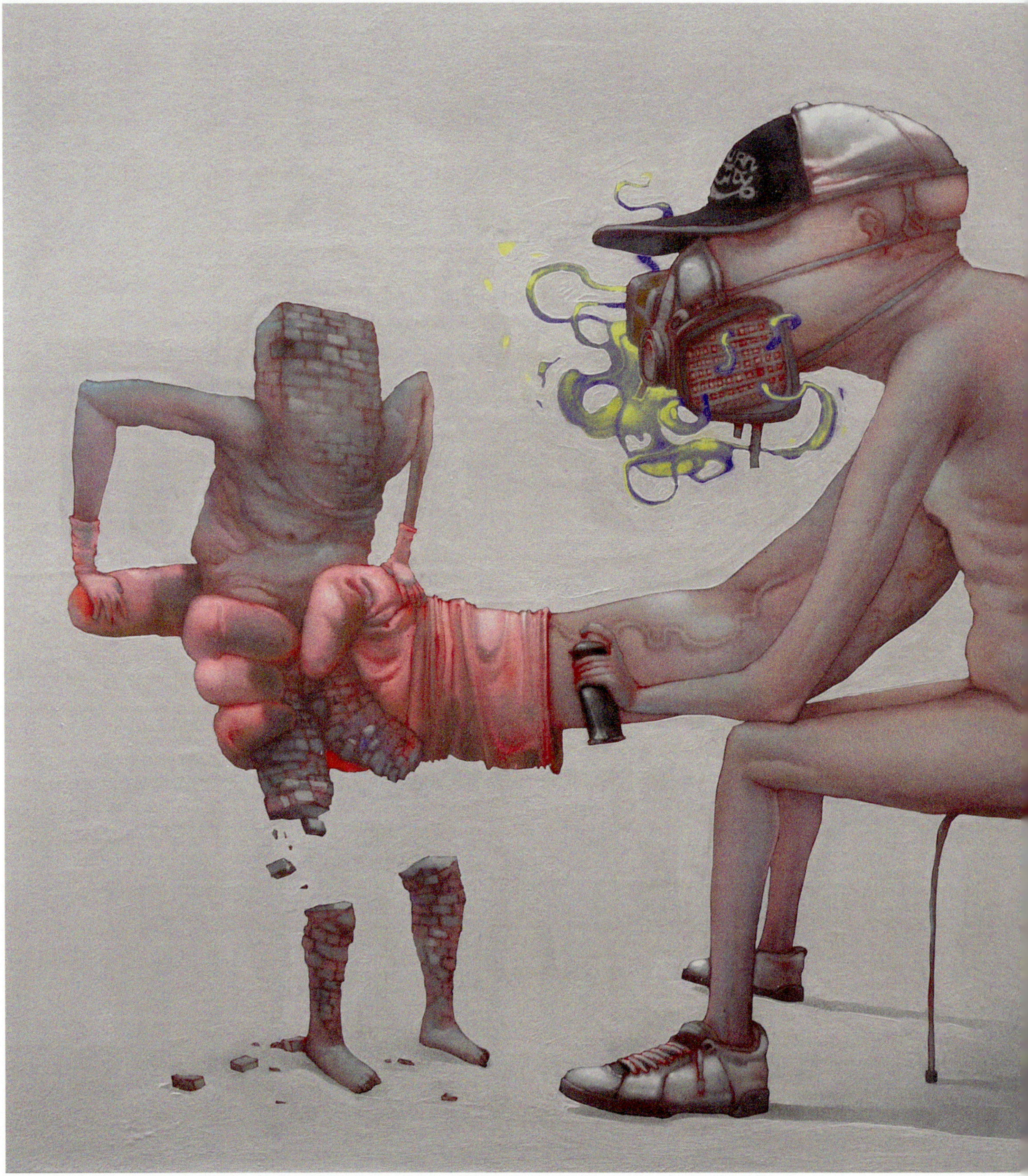

Compulsif Obsessional Disorder #1 | Aerosol on canvas – 165 x 125 cm – 2010

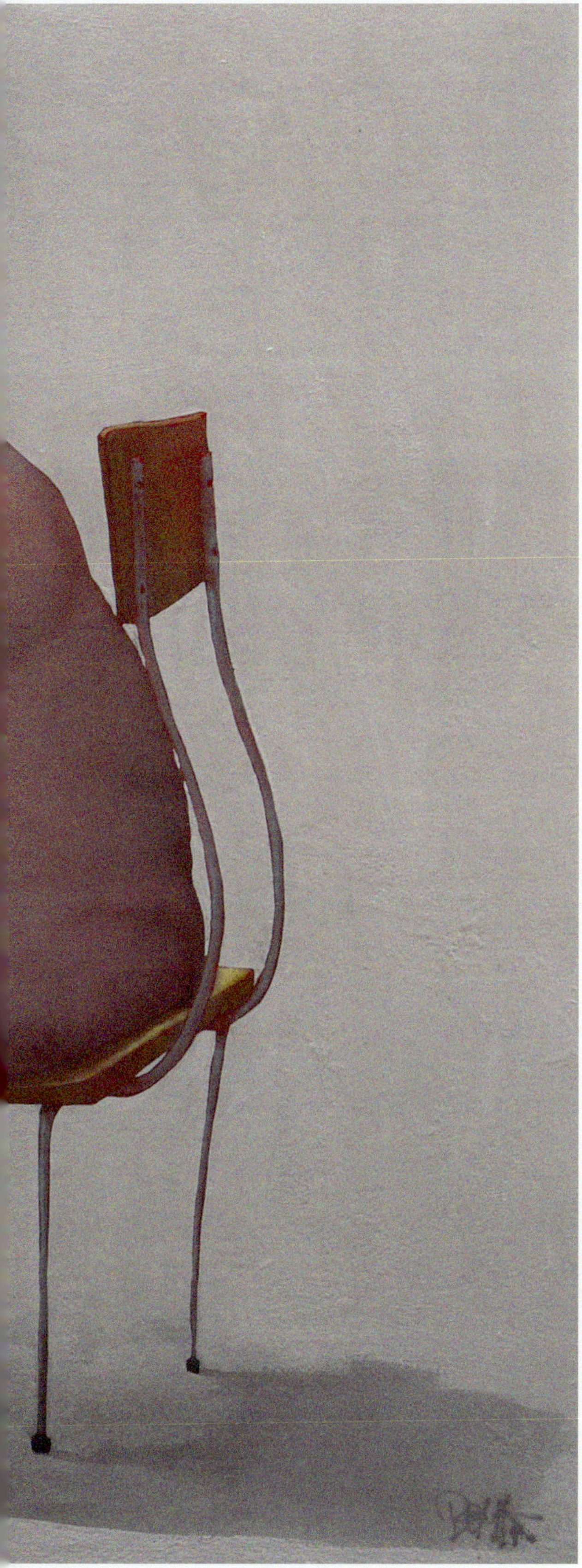

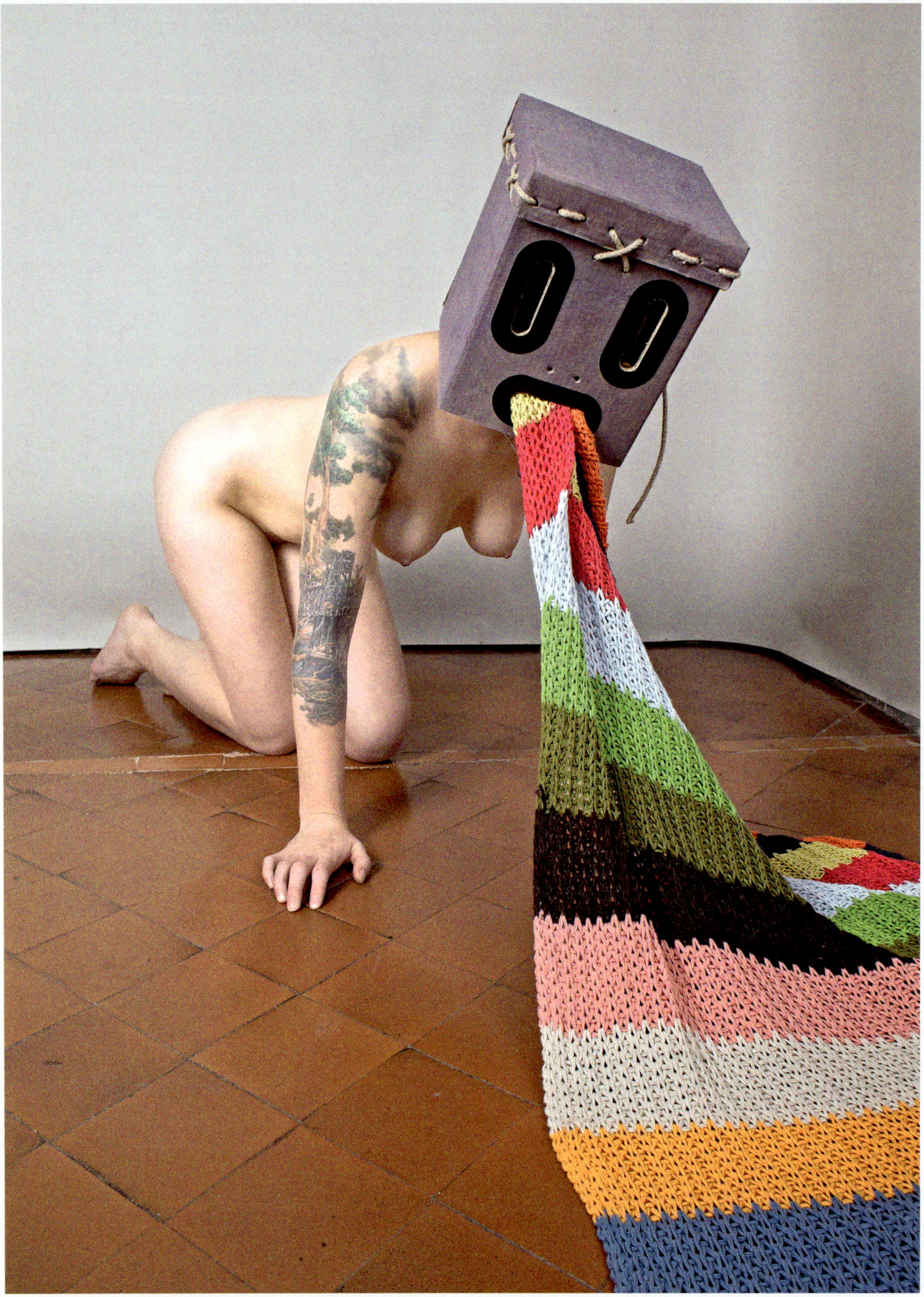

Rainbow Vomit | Photography – 2009

Boris Hoppek

Born in Kreuztal, Germany, 1970. Lives in Barcelona, Spain.

There is no difference for me between studio work and working on the street. Or commercial work and street art. Let's compare art business with street art. Showing in an art gallery or museum is maybe the biggest contrast you can get coming from the street. What's with doing street art for showing it in street art books? Oh man, that's totally uncool, censored in weird ways and destroys the feeling and authenticity of the experience. Better burn books.

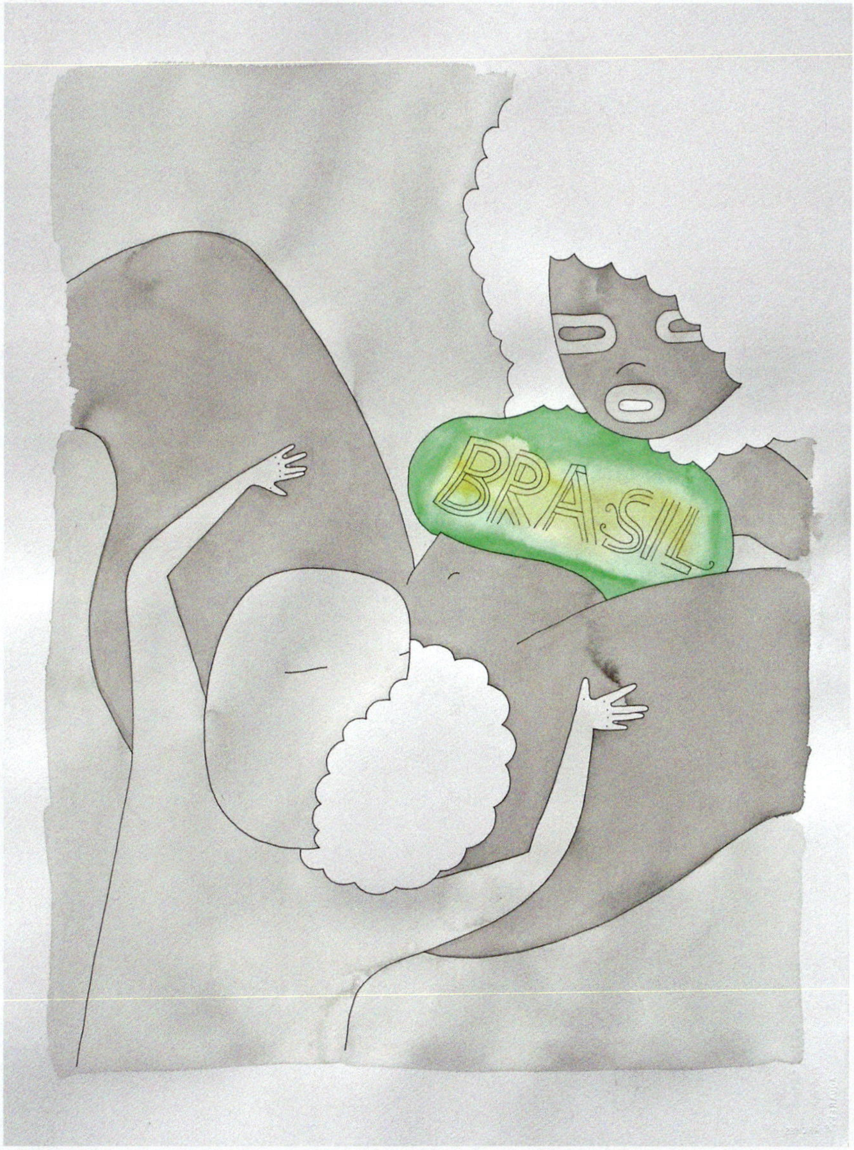

Brazil / Gouache and ink on paper – 56 x 76 cm – 2008

Boxi

Born in London, England, 1974. Lives in Berlin, Germany.

If it wasn't for Berlin, my works probably wouldn't have made the leap to the streets and their walls. Their placement has always been about isolating the figure, so canvas or concrete are just site-specific mediums. Exhibiting them in a "clean" environment, however, clearly shows what they look like without the accelerated exposure of the street.

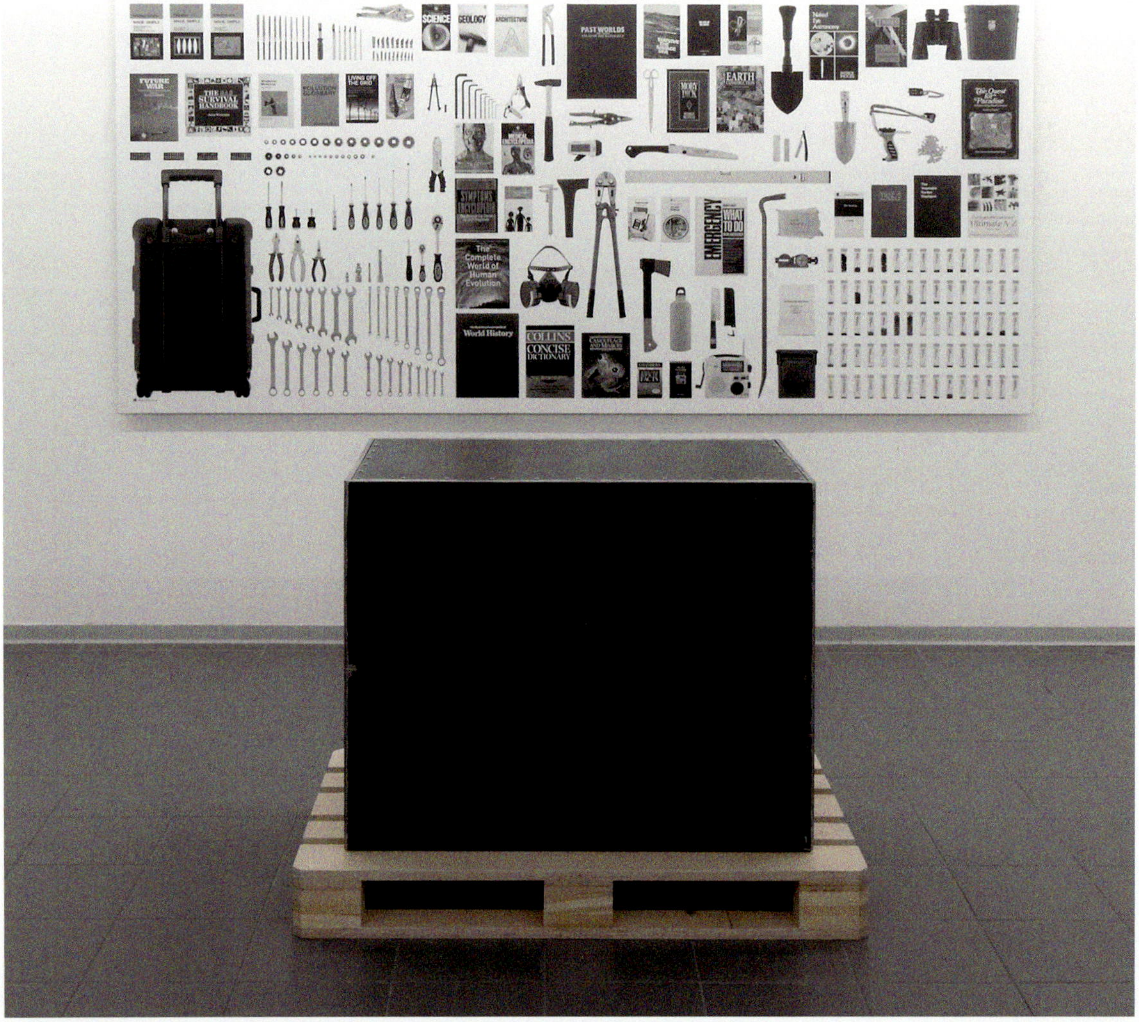

Time Capsule on Euro Pallet and Image With Displayed Contents / Steel, wood, 4c digital print on Dibond, books, tools, and seeds – Capsule 60 x 80 x 100 cm, Dibond 140 x 300 cm – 2010

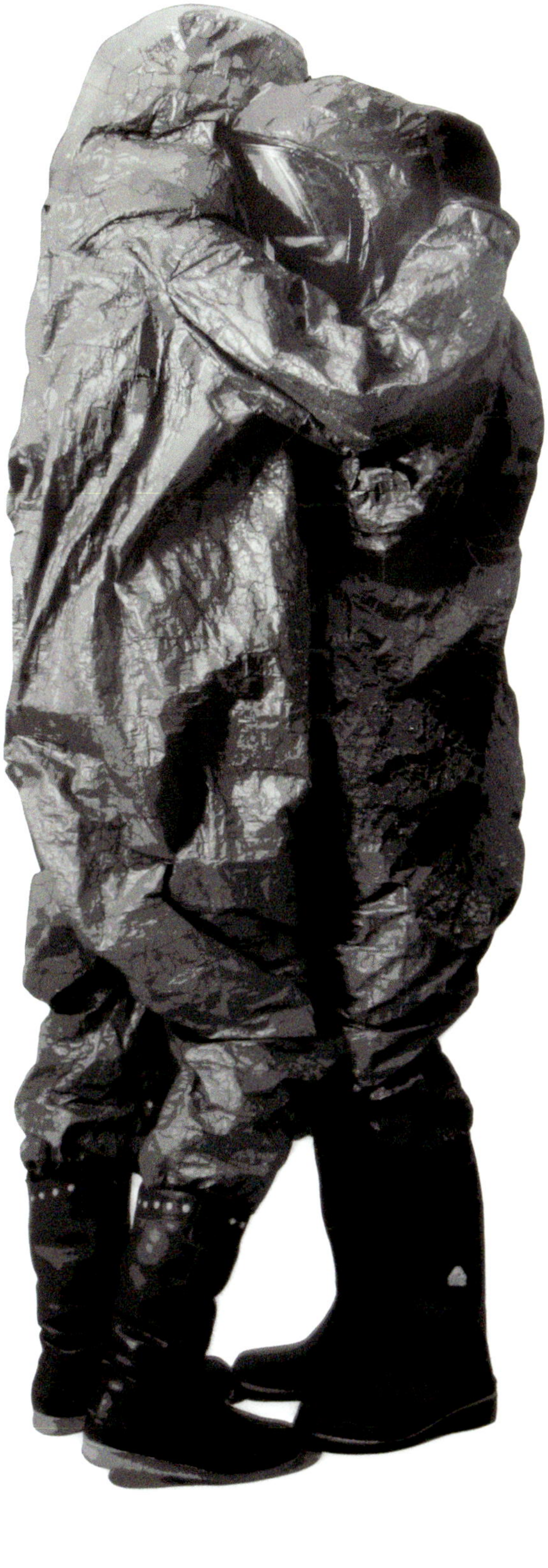

Embrace **ED/8+2AP** / Stencil and aerosol on MDF – 75 x 200 cm – 2009

C215

Born in Paris, France, 1973. Lives in Paris, France.

Working in the studio allows me to explore concepts without any limitations or constraints, while the street imposes upon me each time a context that I need to explore and hijack with a minimum of means.

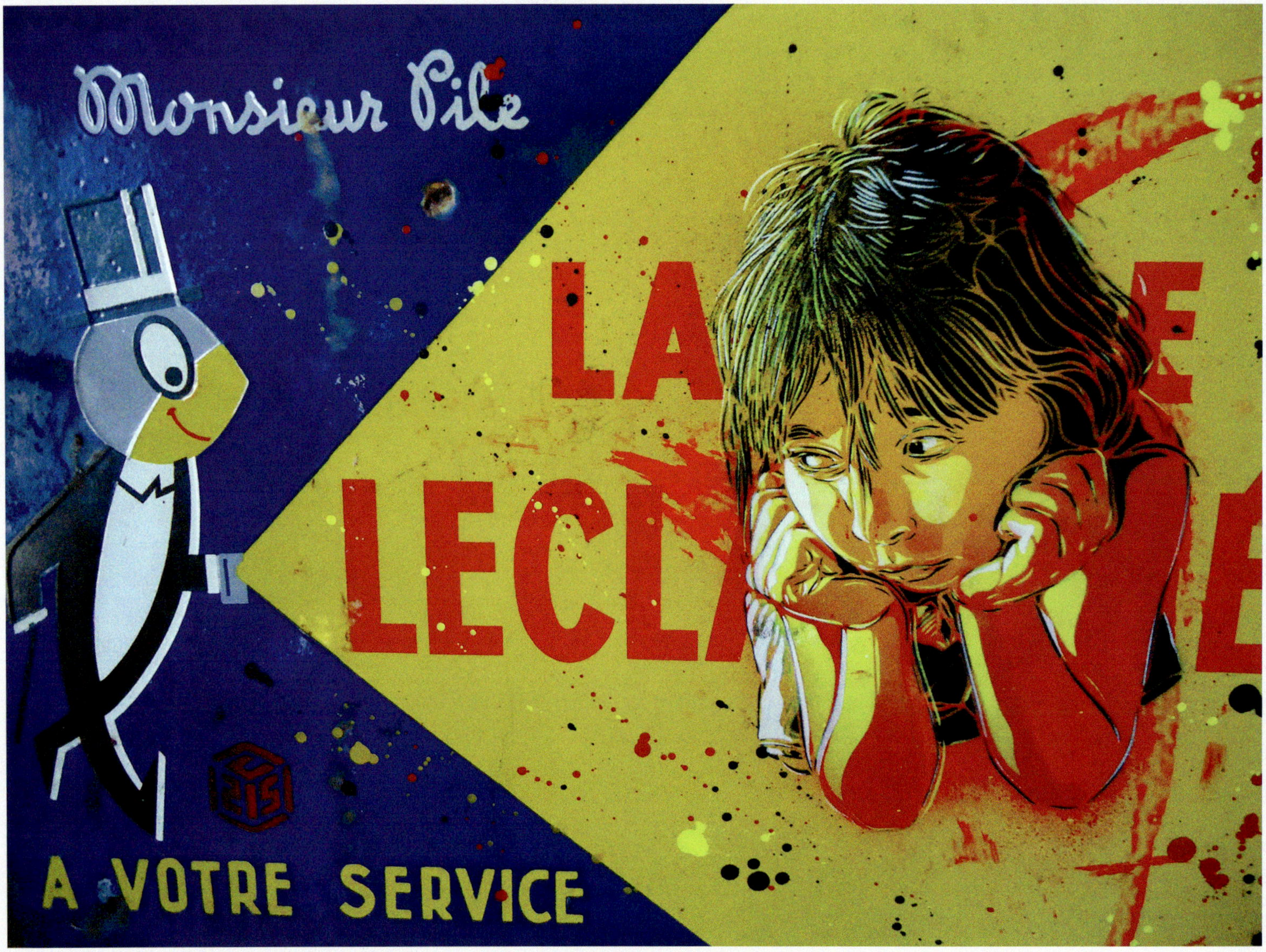

La Pile Leclanche / Aerosol and stencil on found sign – 60 x 45 cm – 2010

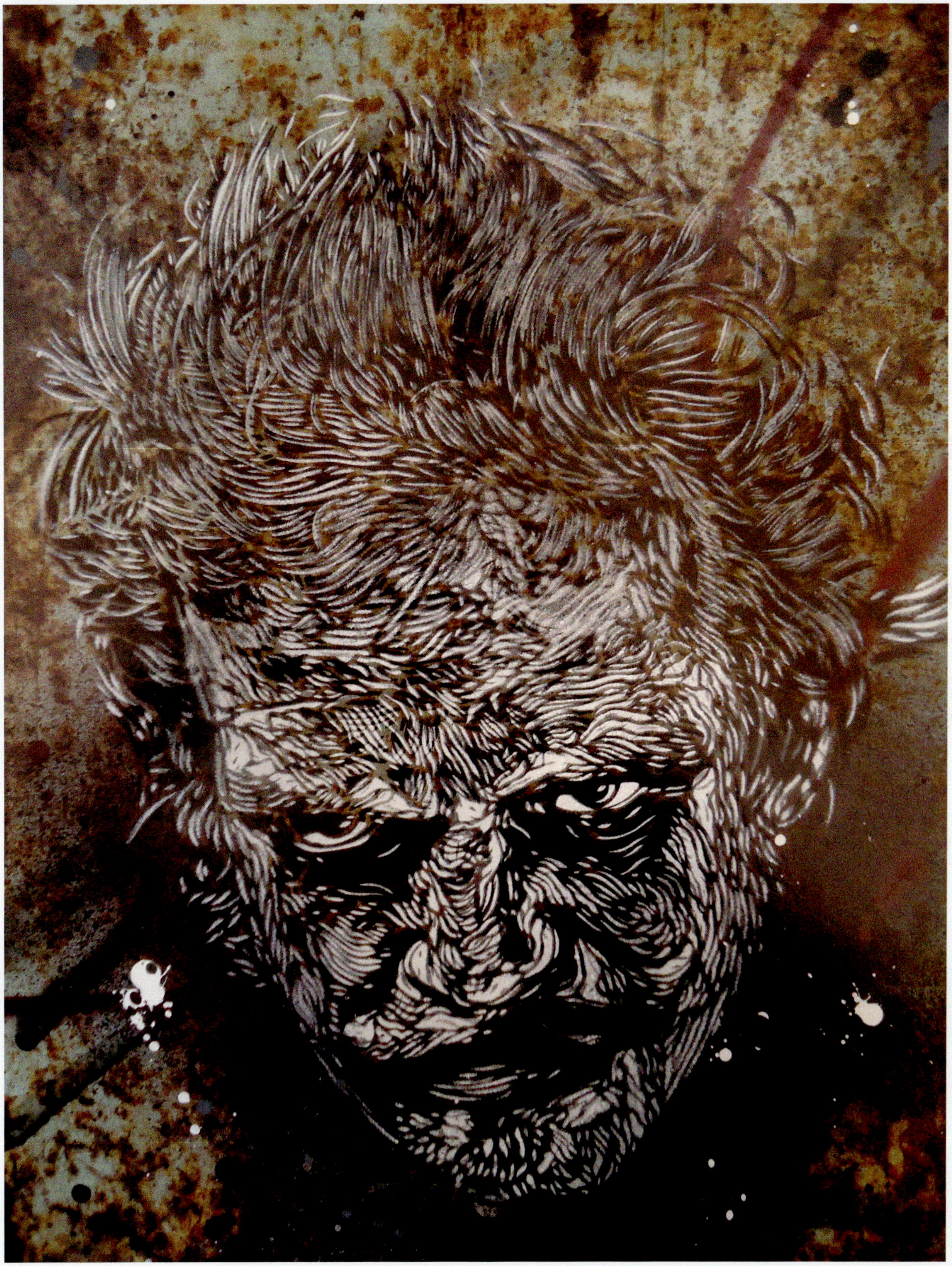

Portrait of Alice Pasquini / Aerosol and stencil on wood – 30 x 40 cm – 2010

Cekis

Born in Santiago, Chile, 1976. Lives in New York, United States.

My studio work is made with the same intentions that led me to paint in the streets early on. It's the simple desire to express my point of view by making portraits that reflect the current society. The purpose being, to feel a part of the city and its inhabitants. Consequently, the subject matter doesn't change from my street work, but I do have a different approach, working the formal elements on my canvases in a more subtle way, aiming to have a less explicit interaction with the audience.

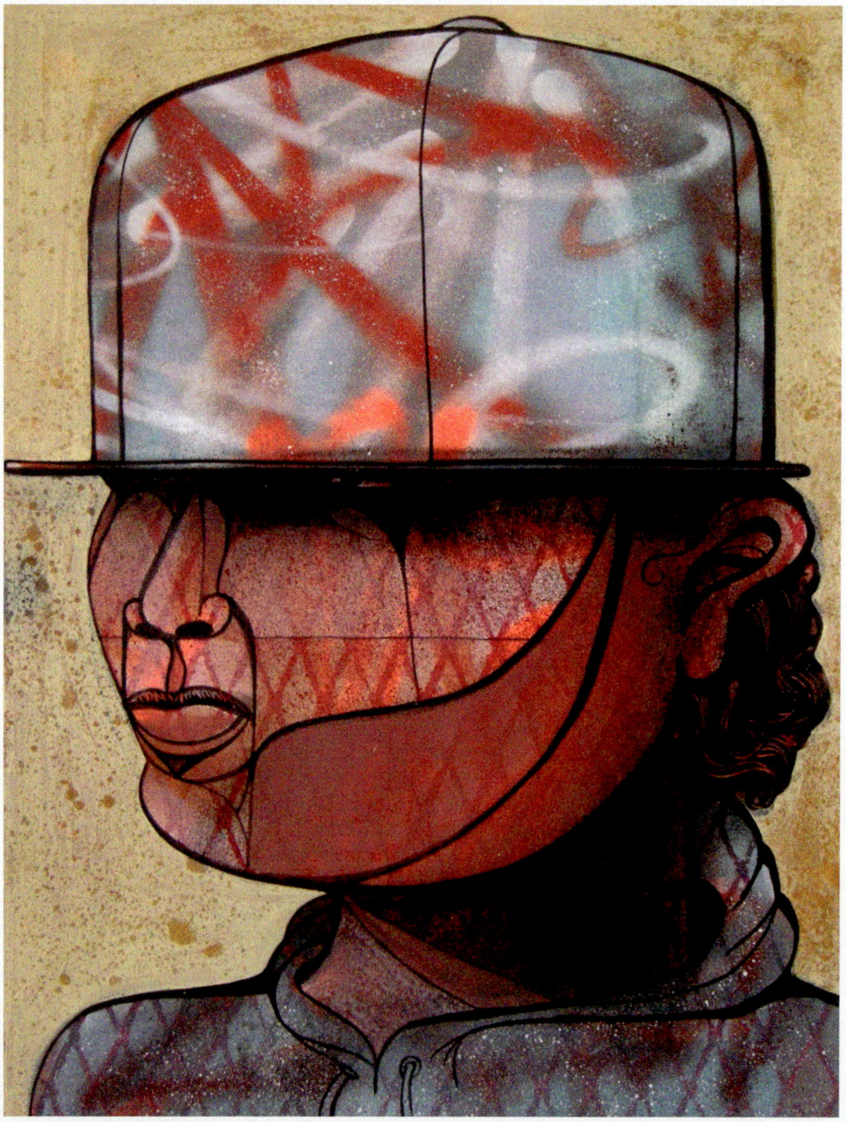

Hiphopized #1 | Acrylic, aerosol, and marker on paper – 56 x 76 cm – 2010

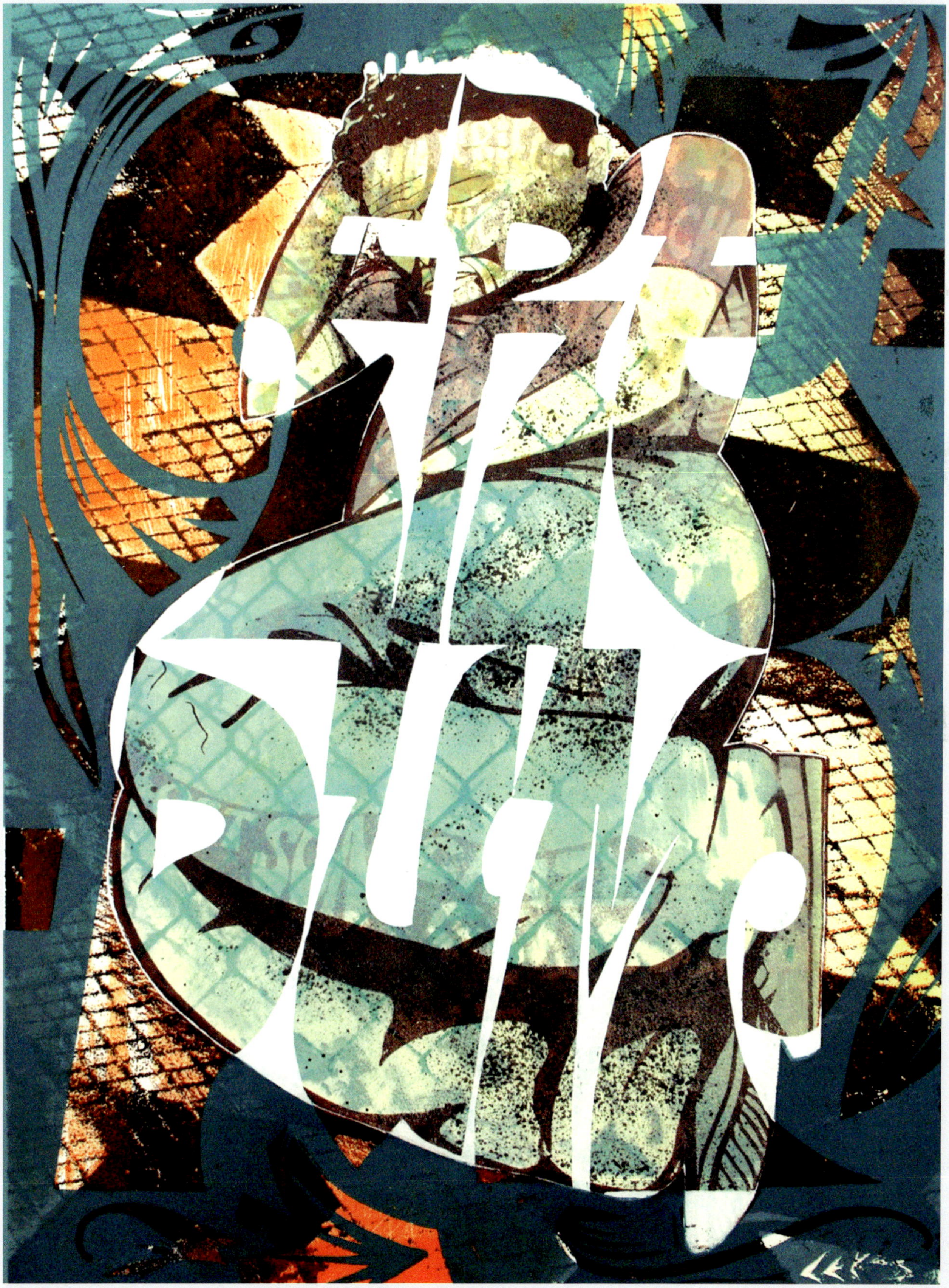

Fre-Dum / Acrylic, 7 colors silkscreen, and aerosol on paper – 54 x 74 cm – 2009

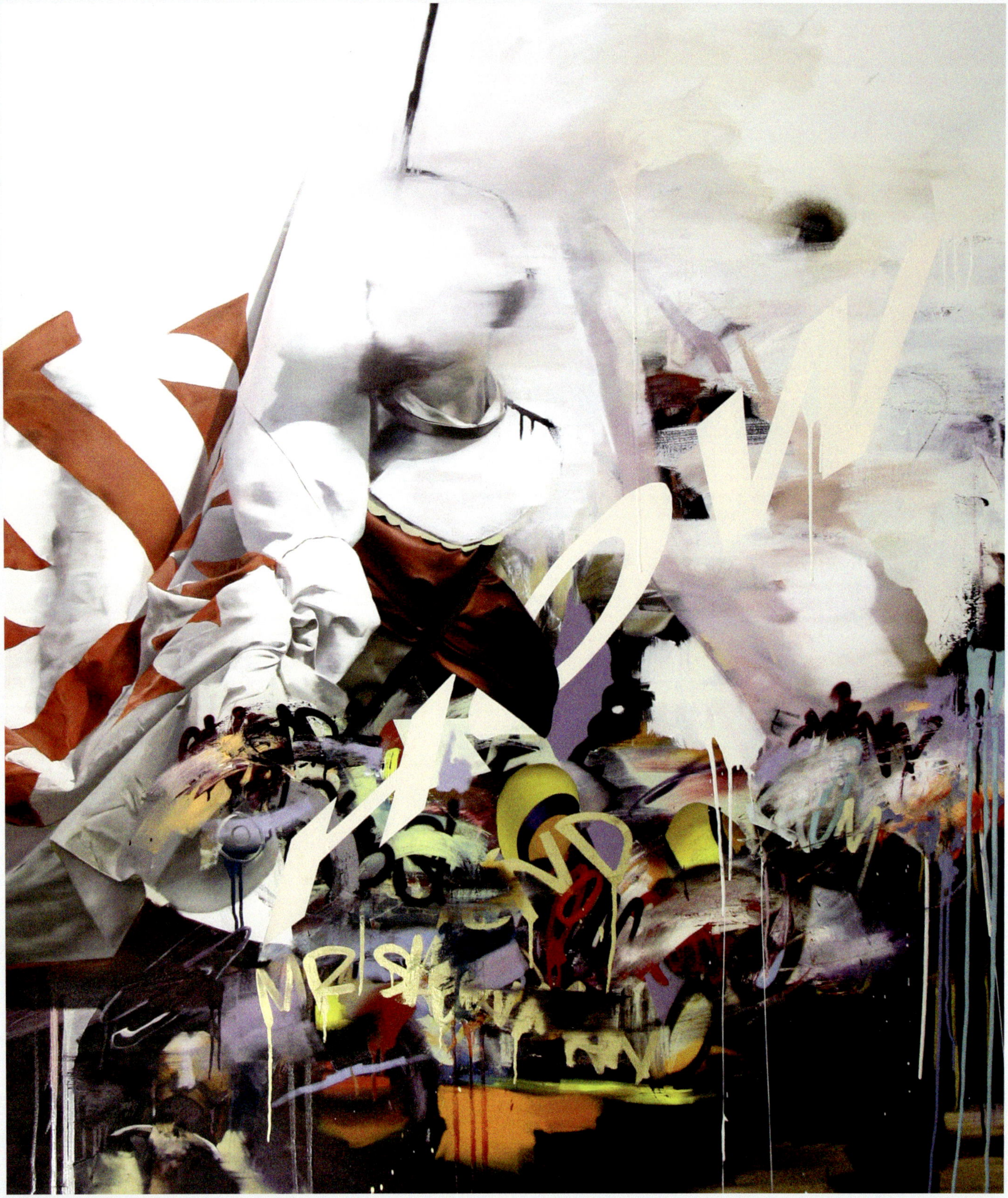

Show Me Yours / Oil and aerosol on canvas – 152 x 183 cm – 2009

Conor Harrington

Born in Cork, Ireland, 1980. Lives in London, England.

In the studio I work on my paintings for weeks and months, slowly building up the layers. I paint the figures with patience and attention to detail, my abstract parts on the other hand are much more immediate and gestural, suggesting the motion and action of painting in the street. I'm a lot less precious outdoors, I don't mind if they get painted over. Sometimes it's nice as I like my walls to be in flux and part of the cycle of the city. On the other hand I don't like to think of my canvases being destroyed. I like to think of them still being around after I'm gone.

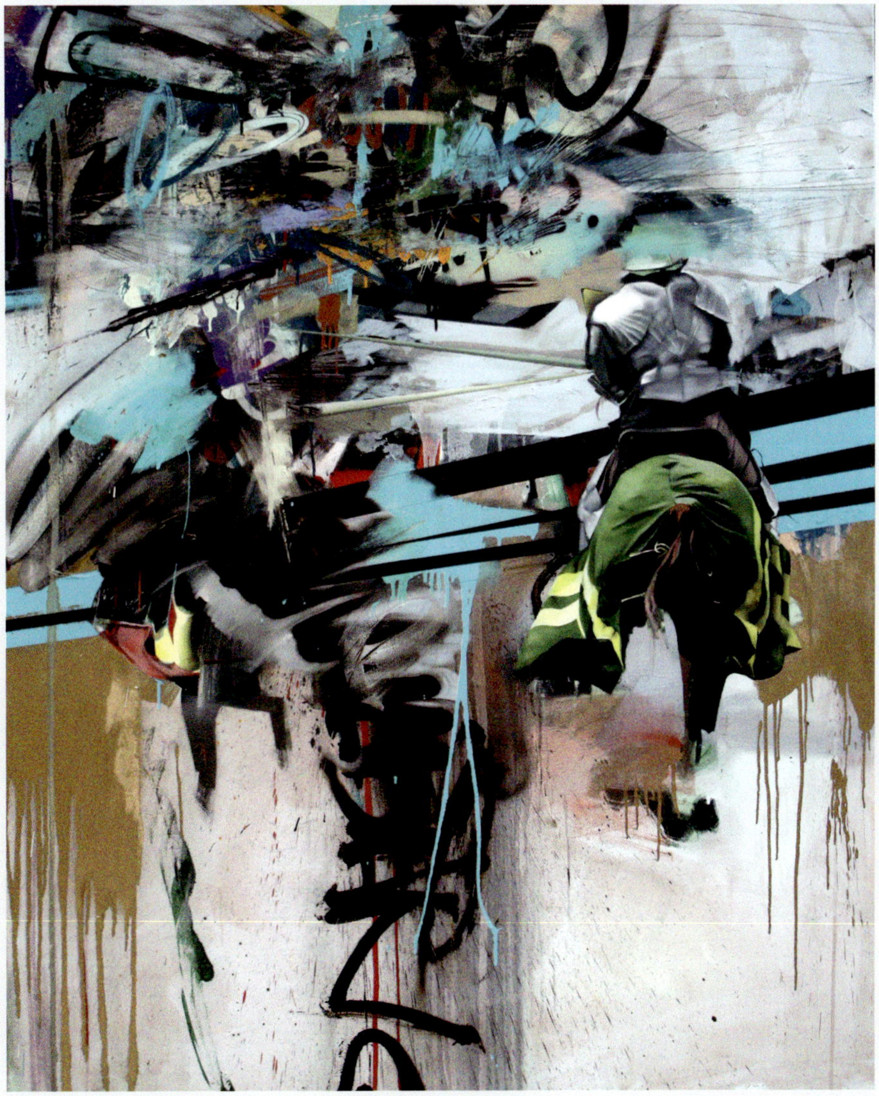

Party Animals / Oil and aerosol on canvas – 120 x 150 cm – 2008

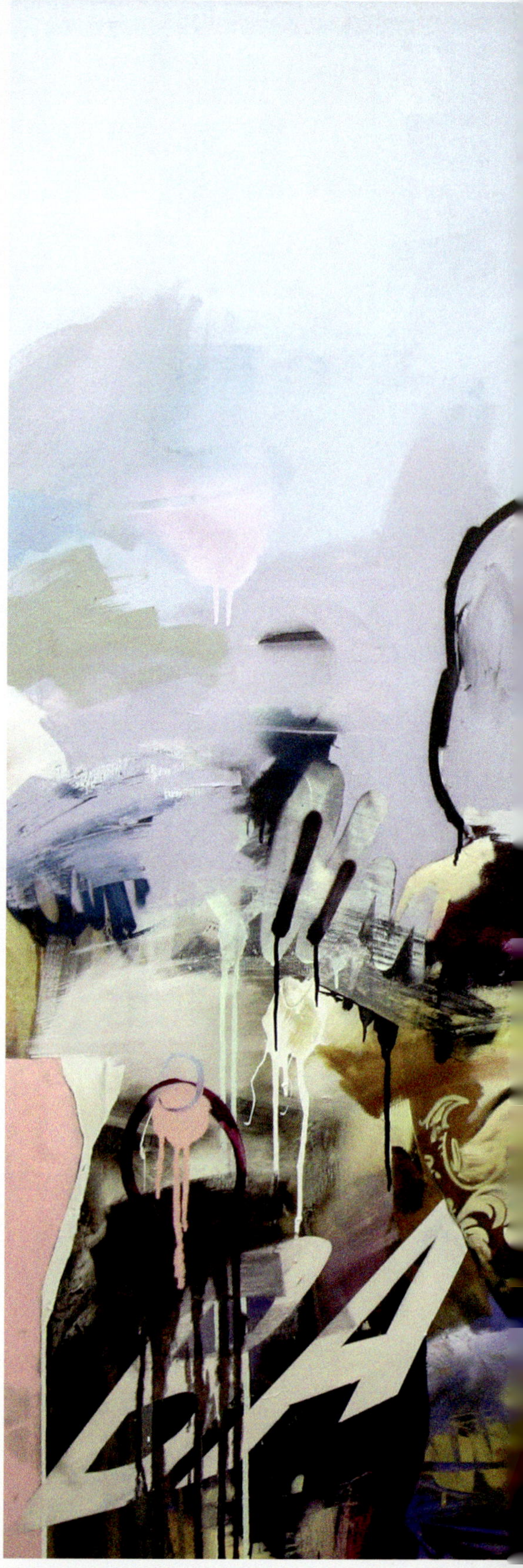

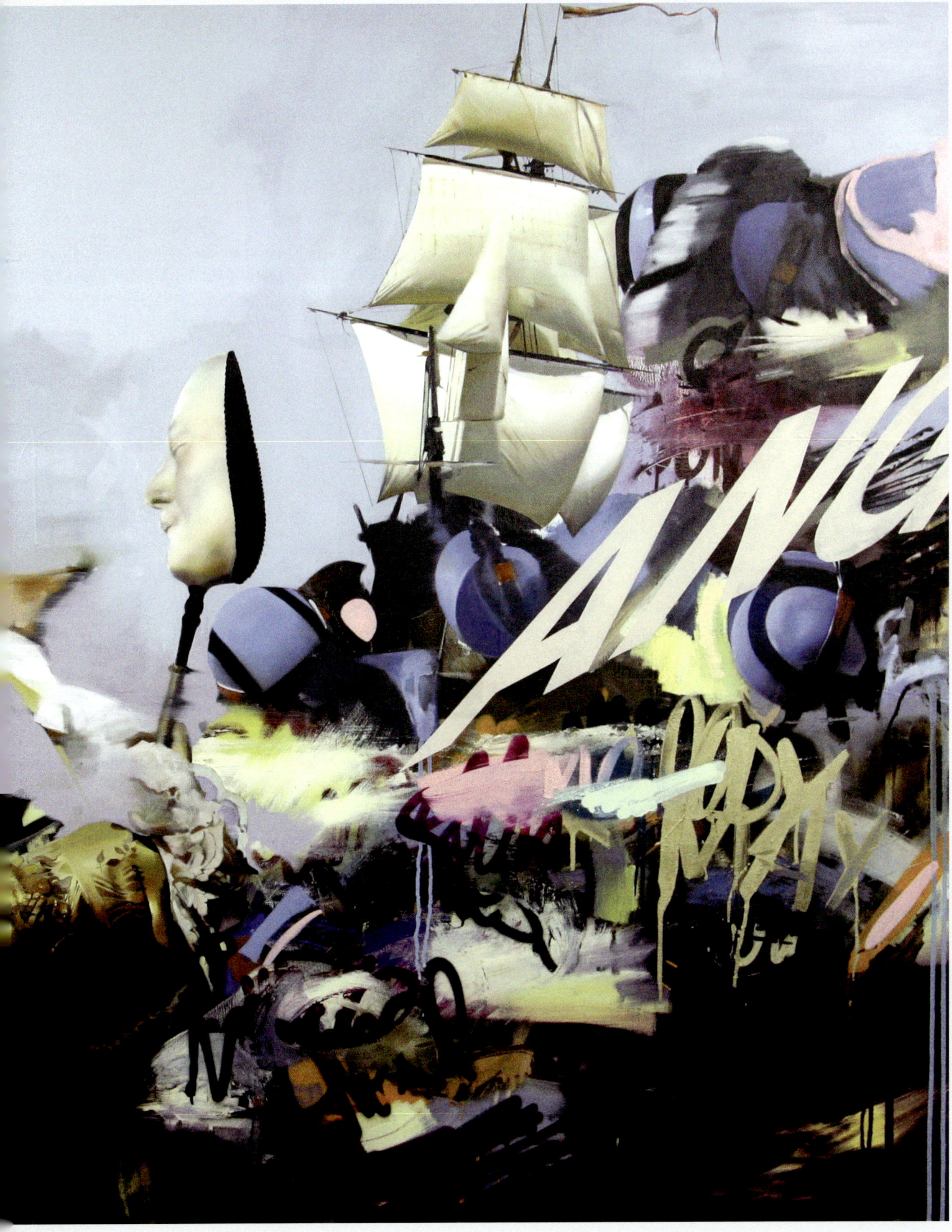

Another Galaxy, Another Triumph | Oil and aerosol on canvas – 183 x 152 cm – 2009

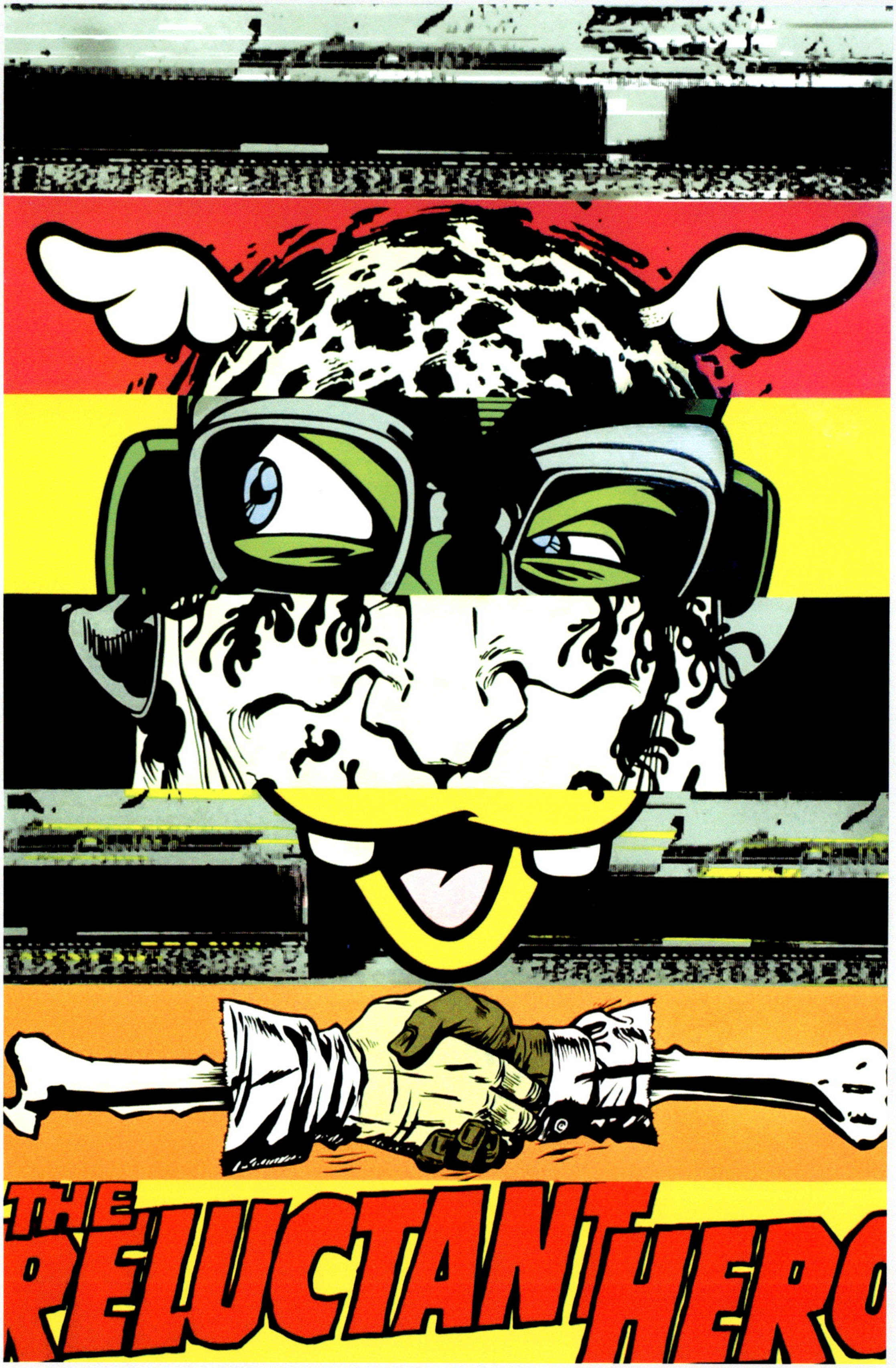

The Reluctant Hero / Enamel and aerosol on wood – 80 x 110 cm – 2009

D*Face

Born in London, England. Lives in London, England.

My work is always conceived in my mind as a street piece, whether it makes it to the street or not. As such impact, concept, and shock are always prevalent. However, placing work within the public domain carries with it immediate juxtaposition, conflict, and social debate; a tag on a wall, a sticker on a lamppost isn't merely a mark made and left by an individual, it questions ownership, this is left to a wide, diverse, unsuspecting audience to discover and digest. Putting work into a gallery environment is nothing short of playing to an audience already well versed. Subsequently I try to make the shock, impact, and physical spectacle of my work in this environment more prevalent.

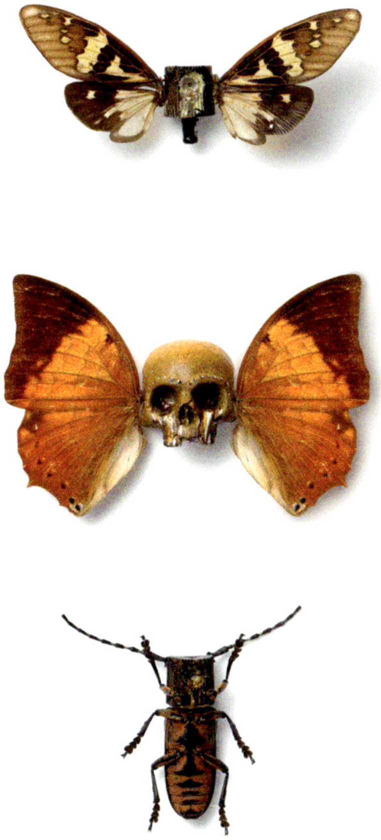

Flutterdies / Taxidermy butterflies and insect reworked with used aerosol caps and pigmy skull – 16 x 23 cm – 2011

Dan Witz

Born in Chicago, United States, 1957. Lives in New York, United States.

Pretty much all the artists I admire were active in other mediums besides painting. Rembrandt and Goya did etchings; Degas did pastels and sculpture; Warhol did films; the list is long. With my street art process I get so obsessively involved with whatever I'm doing that by the end of the summer I'm literally nauseated by it. I long for quiet days in the studio, inching across my canvas, listening to music and wondering what I'm going to have for lunch. But after being home at the easel for a month or so, the difficulty of making paintings begins to wear me down and I get restless and start craving the instant gratification of street art. I'd like to say the two approaches balance me out but that hasn't happened yet.

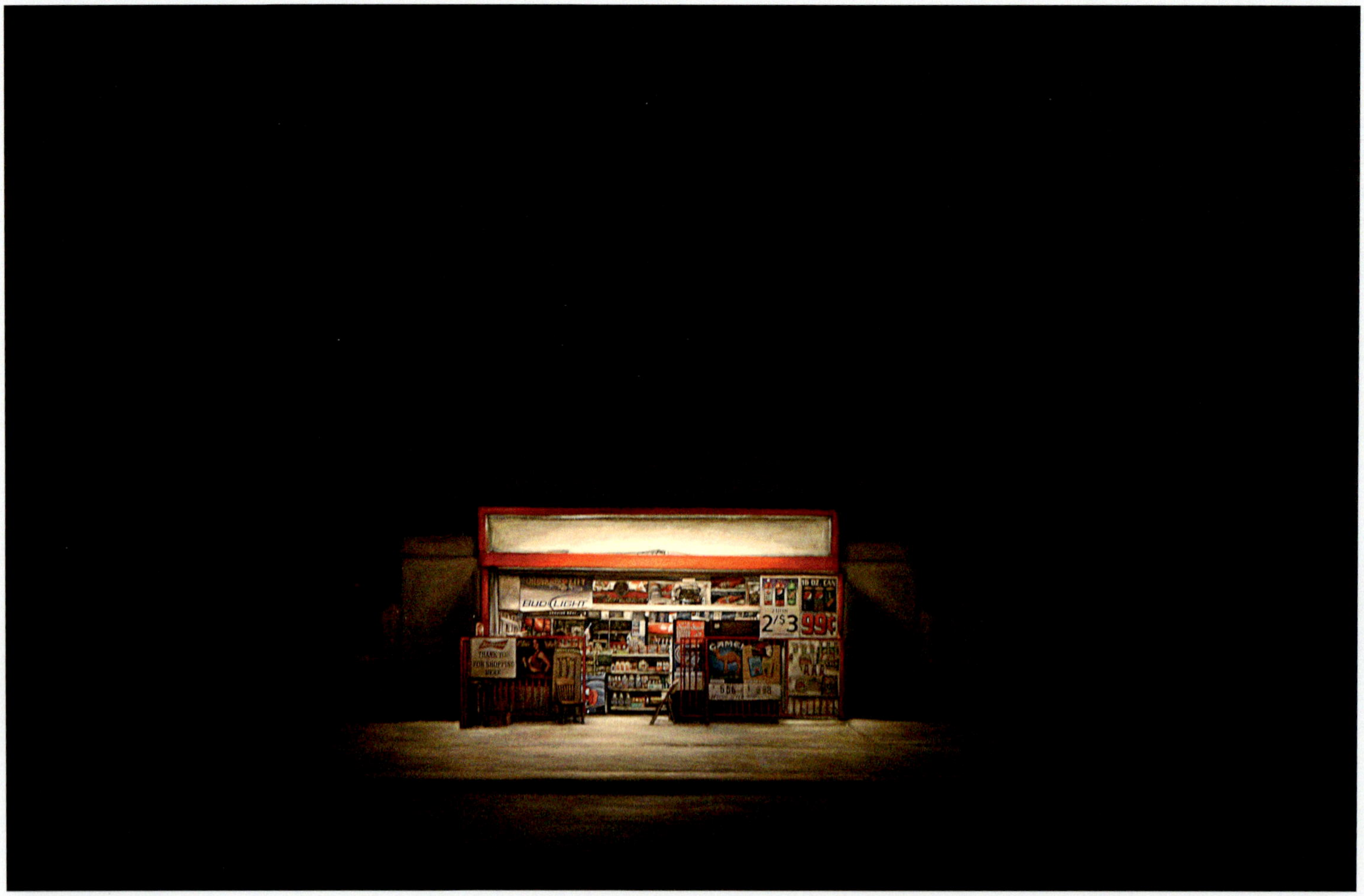

Bodega LA / Oil and digital media on canvas – 183 x 127 cm – 2010

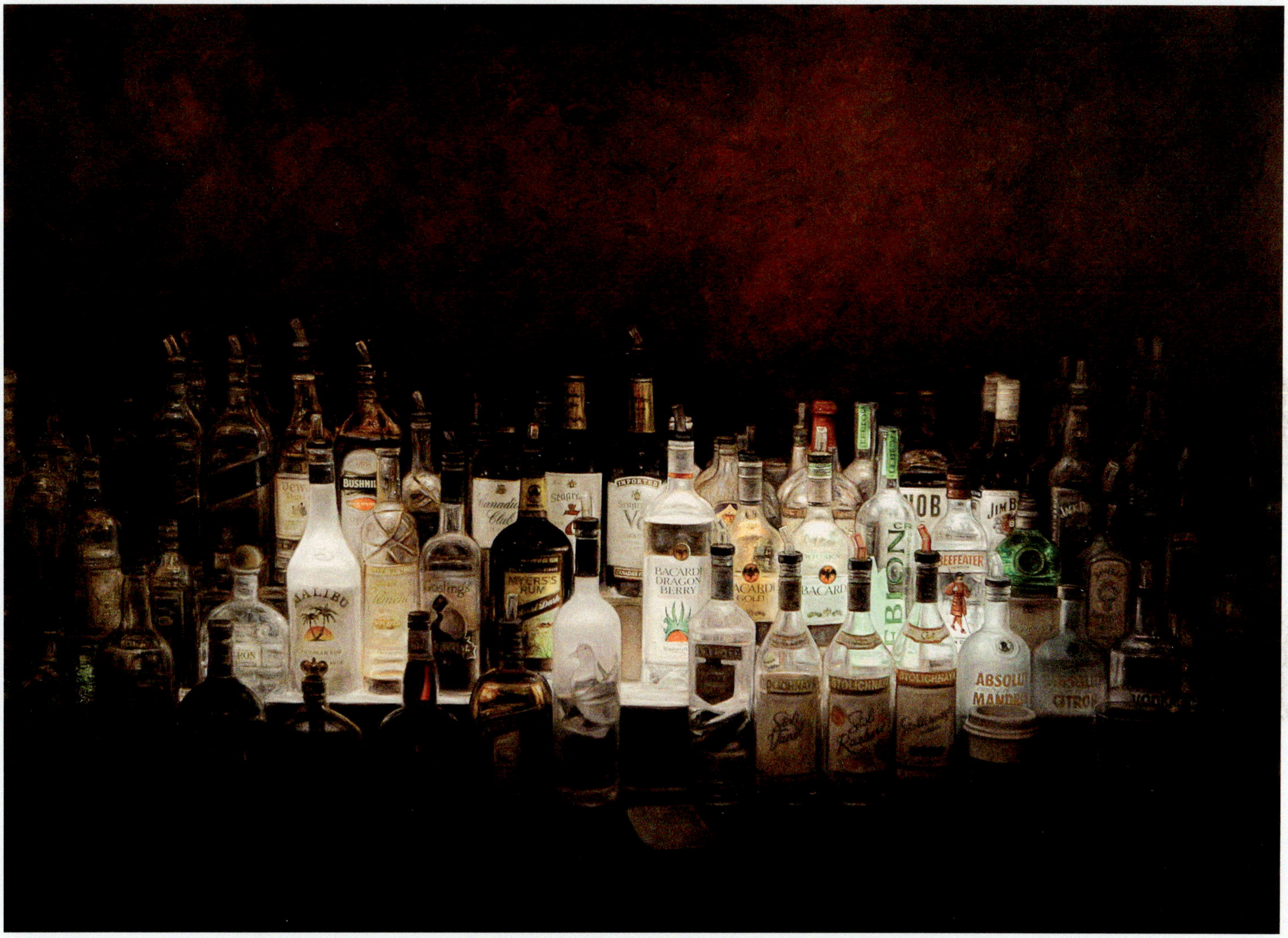

Bar Shrine 3 (M Shanghai) / Oil and digital media on canvas – 137 x 101 cm – 2009

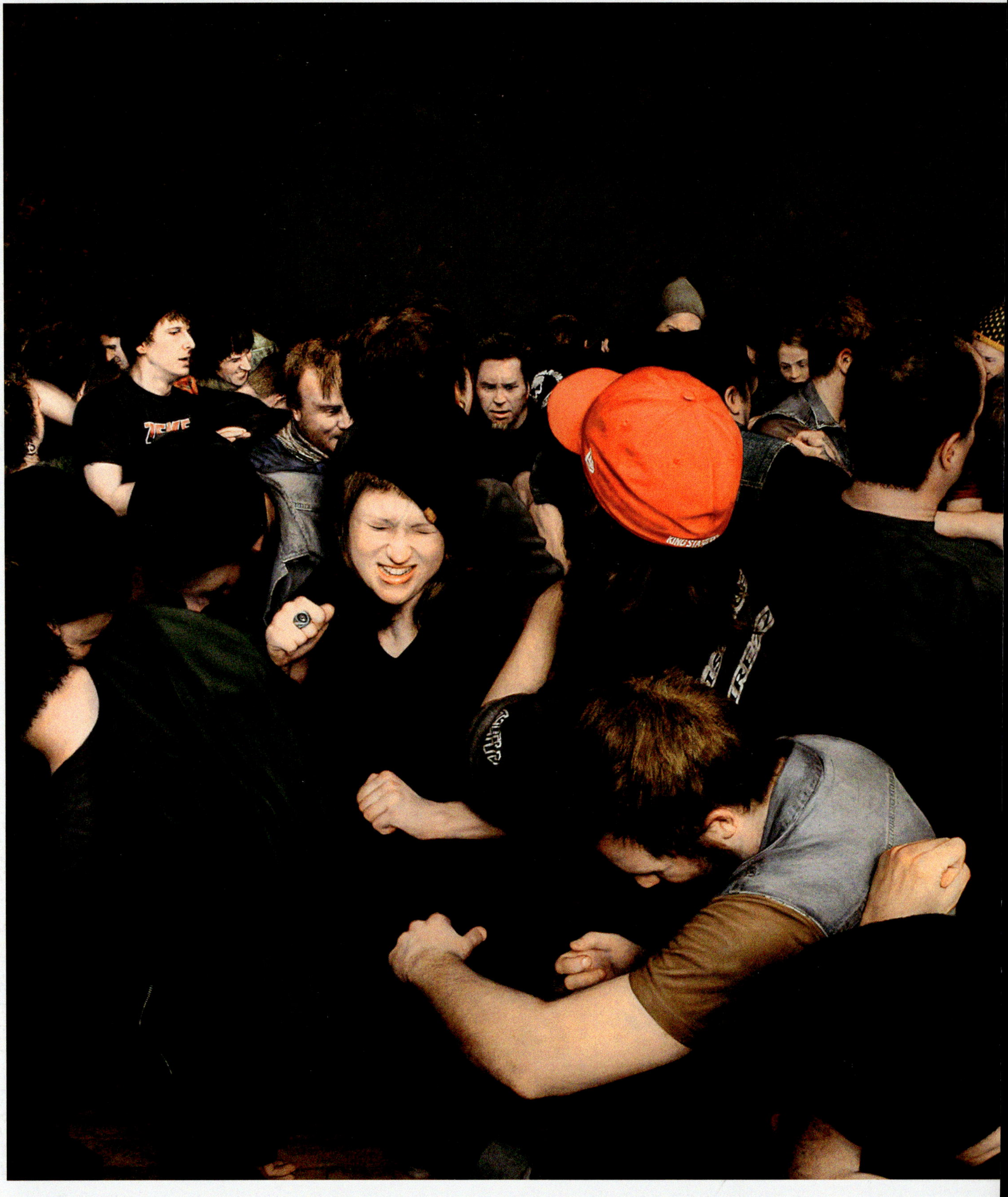

70 *Commercial* / Oil and digital media on canvas – 92 x 86 cm – 2010

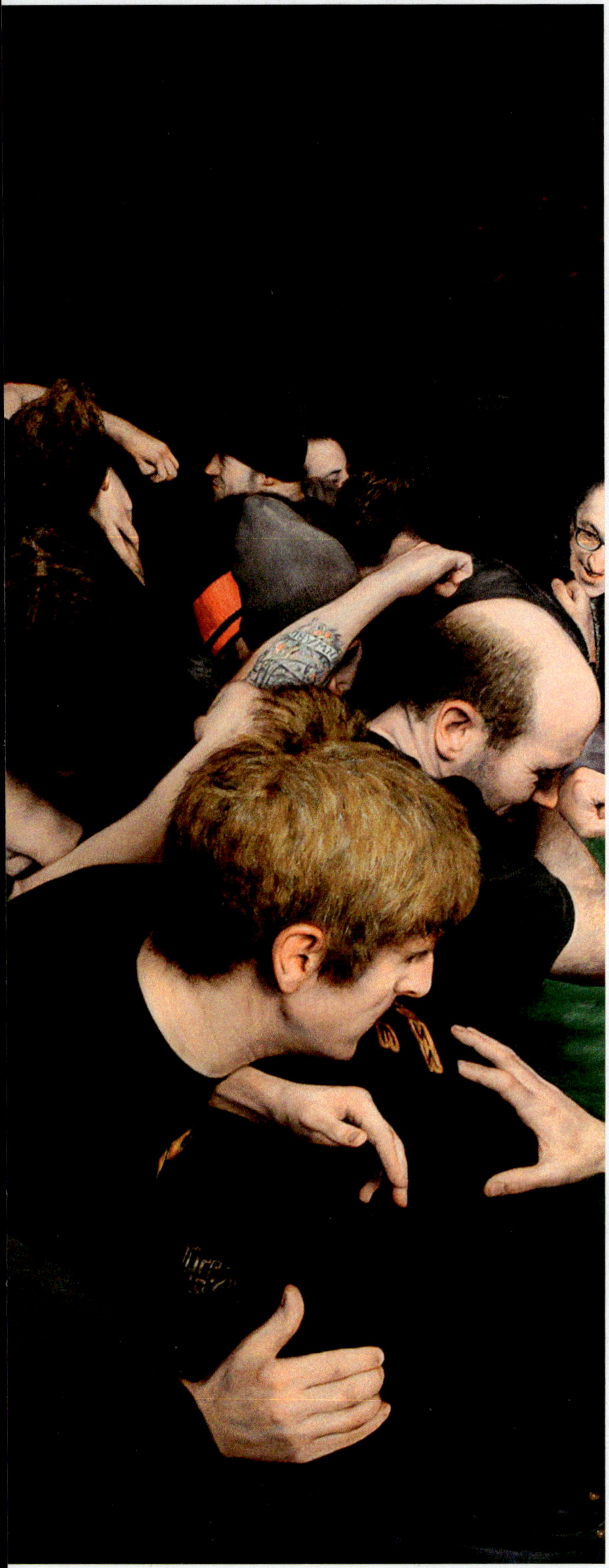

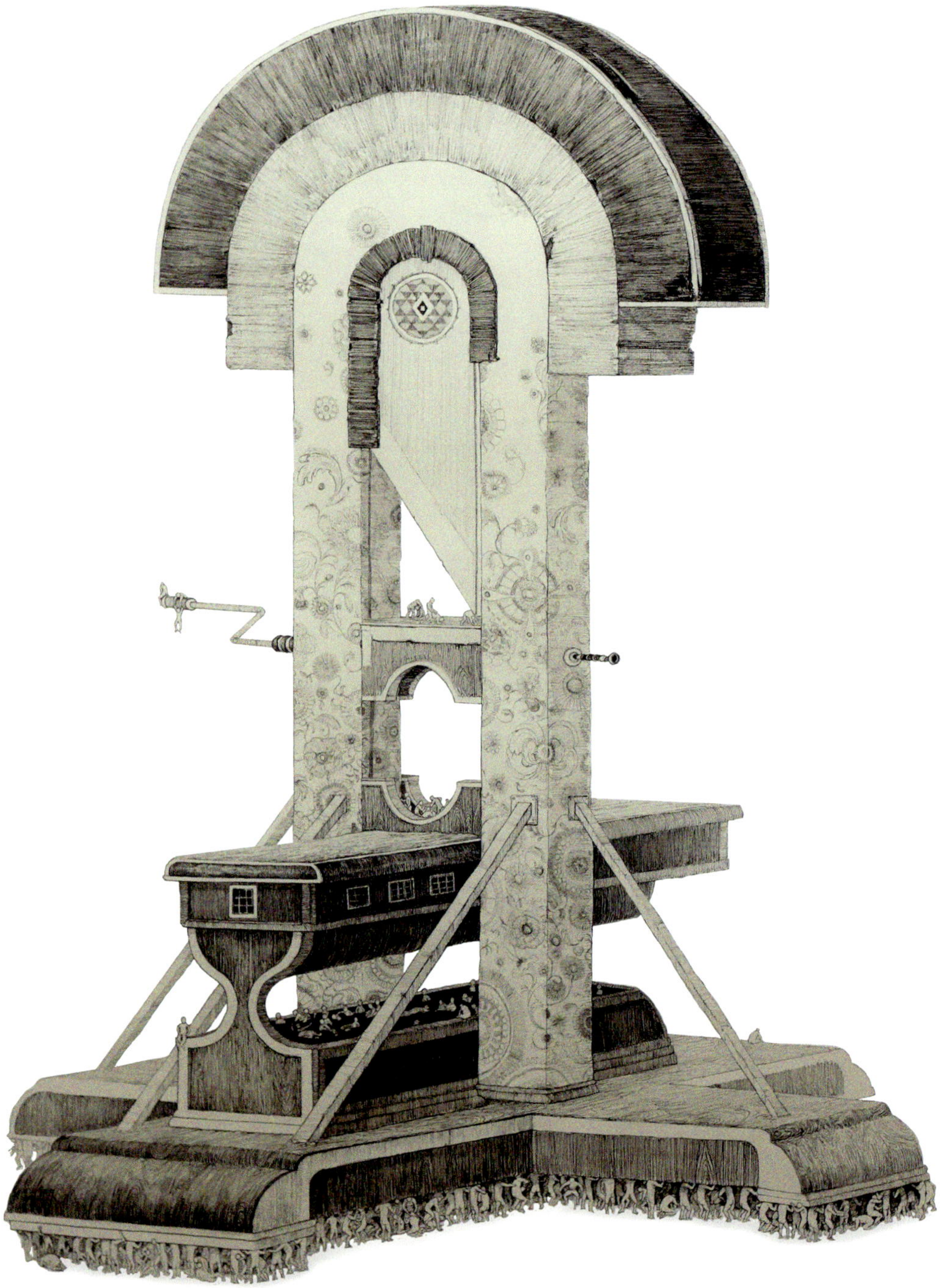

La Fuente / Ink and gouache on paper – 76 x 112 cm – 2010

Daniel Muñoz aka San

Born in Cáceres, Spain, 1980. Lives in Madrid, Spain.

I did not start painting on the streets, but on my street. There are several aspects to this fact that determine my current relationship with it. Relationship somehow exhausted because of the rapid development of this phenomenon dubbed street art in the last five years. This relationship also is affecting my studio work in a critical way. For the first time after more than 15 years as creator and spectator, I think now that the phenomenon is moving ahead of art. In my opinion, there's a lot of garbage being made that passes for art just because it is made in the streets.

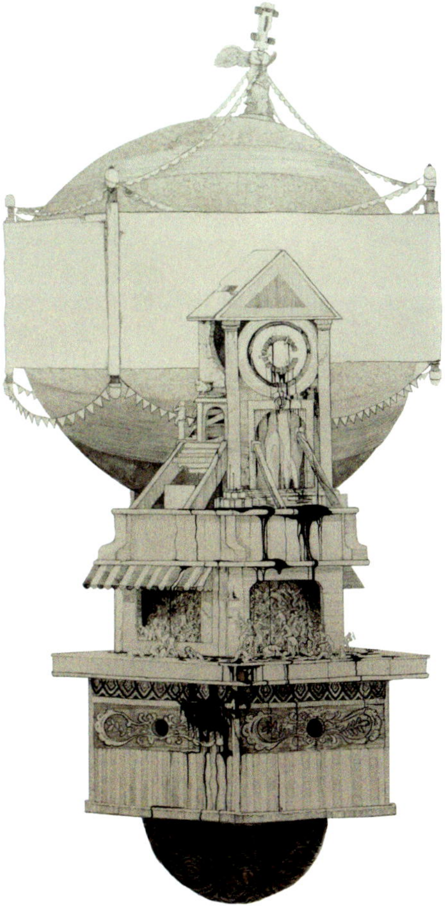

El Club de los Siempre Originales / Ink and gouache on paper – 76 x 112 cm – 2010

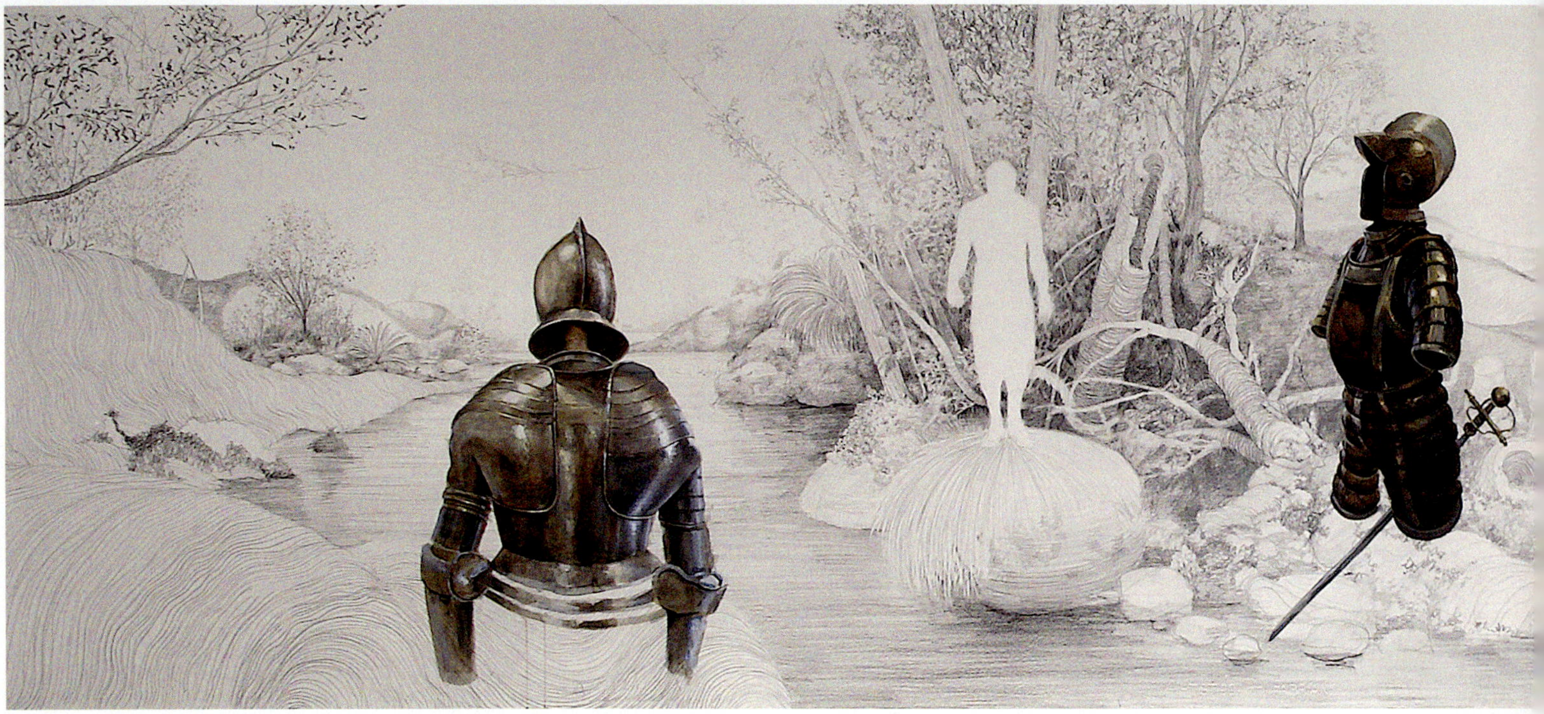

El Traje Reversible / Pencil, ink, watercolor, and gouache on paper – 320 x 70 cm – 2010

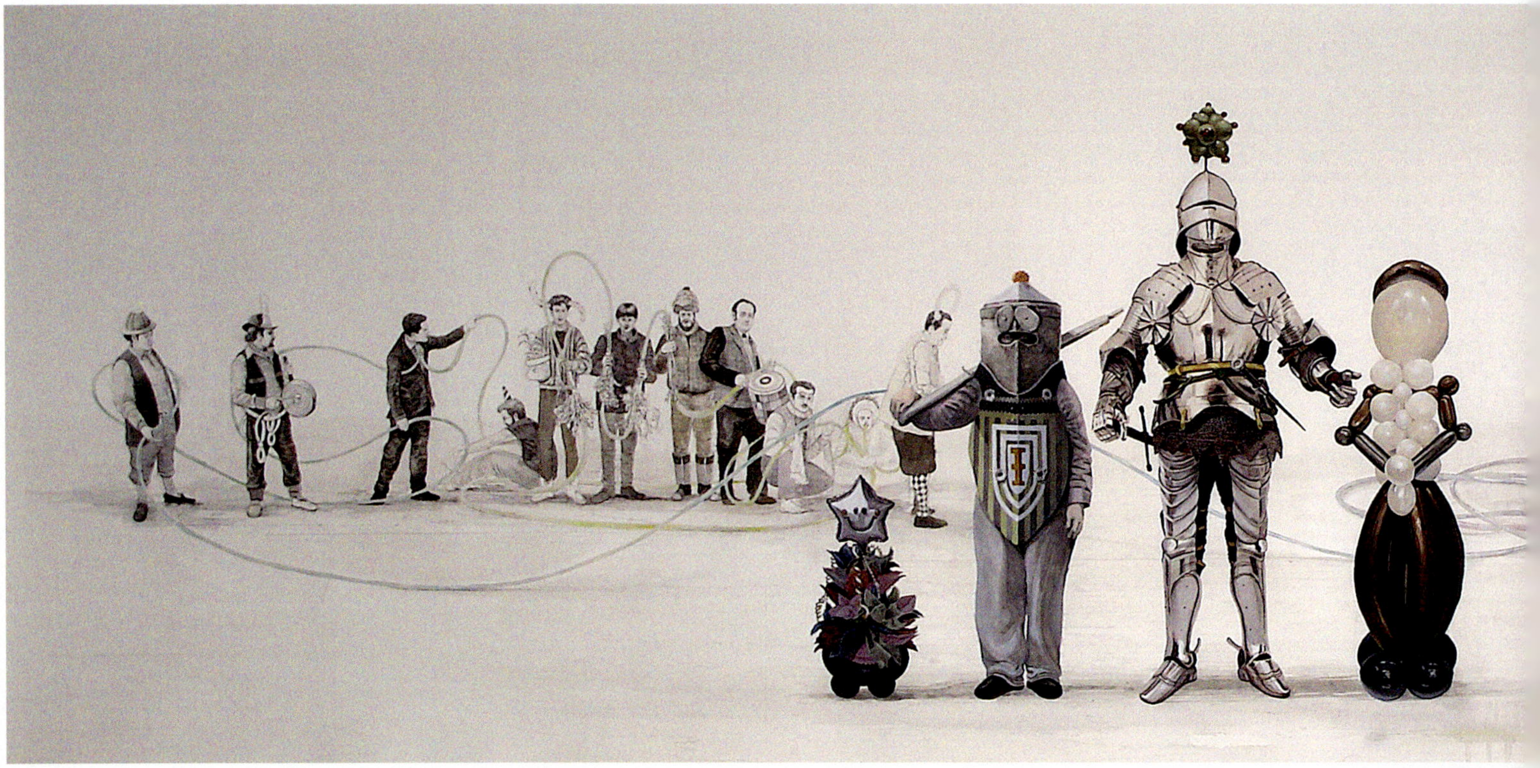

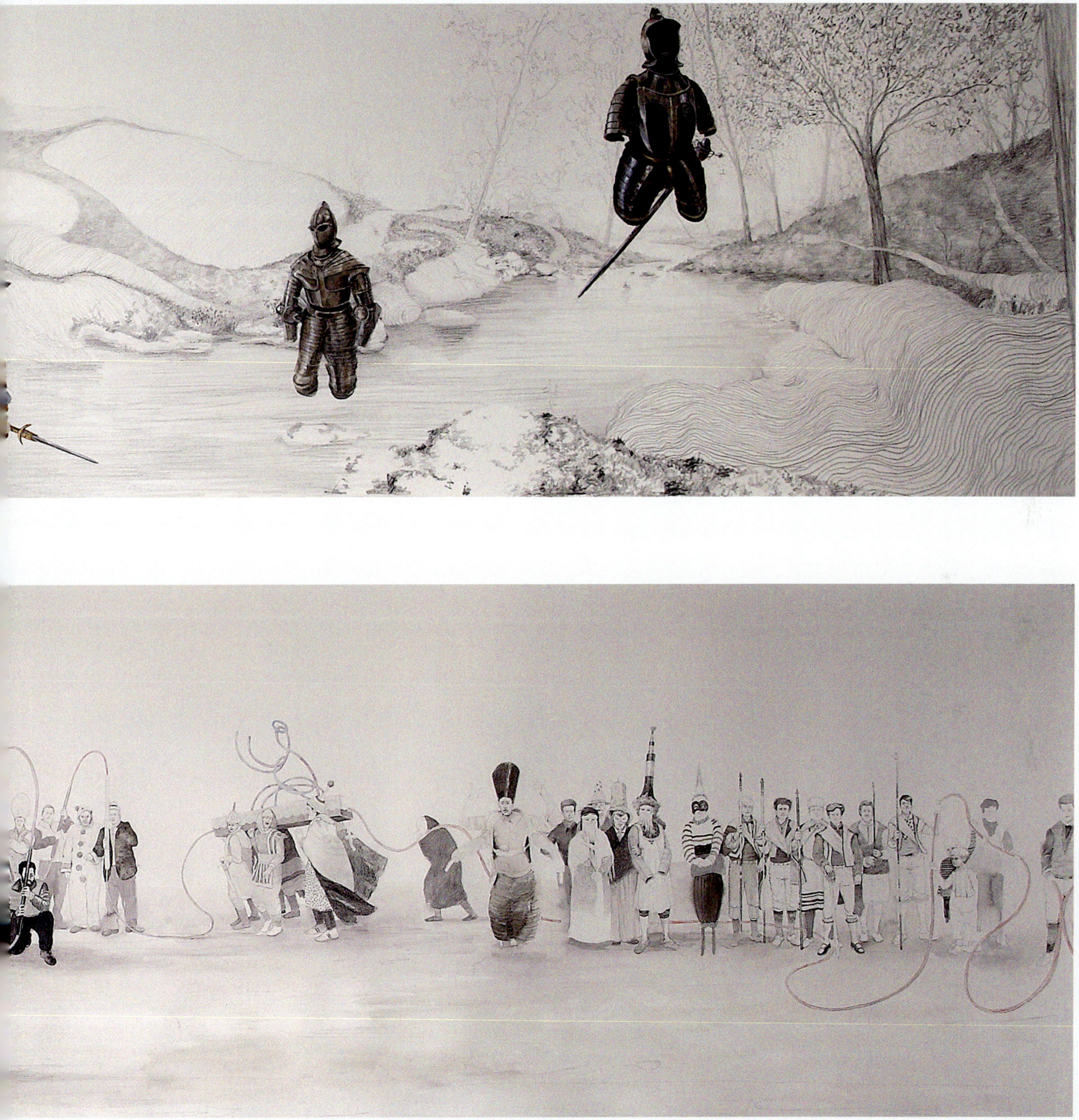

El Frente / Pencil, ink, watercolor, and gouache on paper – 289 x 70 cm – 2010

Dave Kinsey

Born in Pittsburgh, United States, 1971. Lives in Three Rivers, United States.

I am compelled to create due to my passion for expressing thoughts and ideas in a visual manner. Ever since I can remember, I was not only drawn to the arts, but also motivated to create in some form or another as a means of self-expression. In addition to finding the process itself engaging, the ability to utilize a visual dialogue has been an important tool in my attempt to communicate and decipher the complex world we live in by exploring social, political, and even environmental issues.

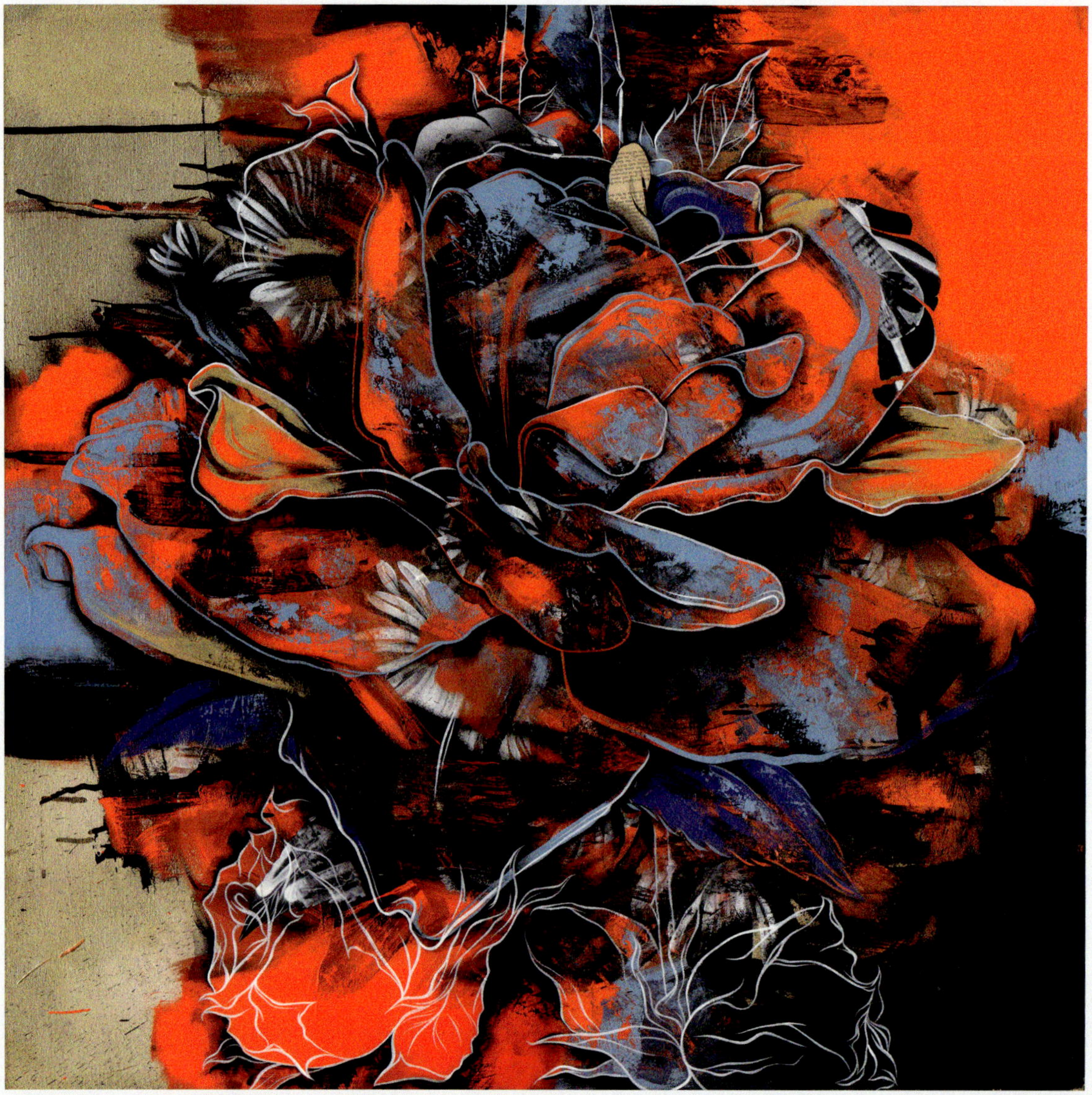

A Rose is a Rose is a Rose / Mixed media on canvas – 101 x 101 cm – 2010

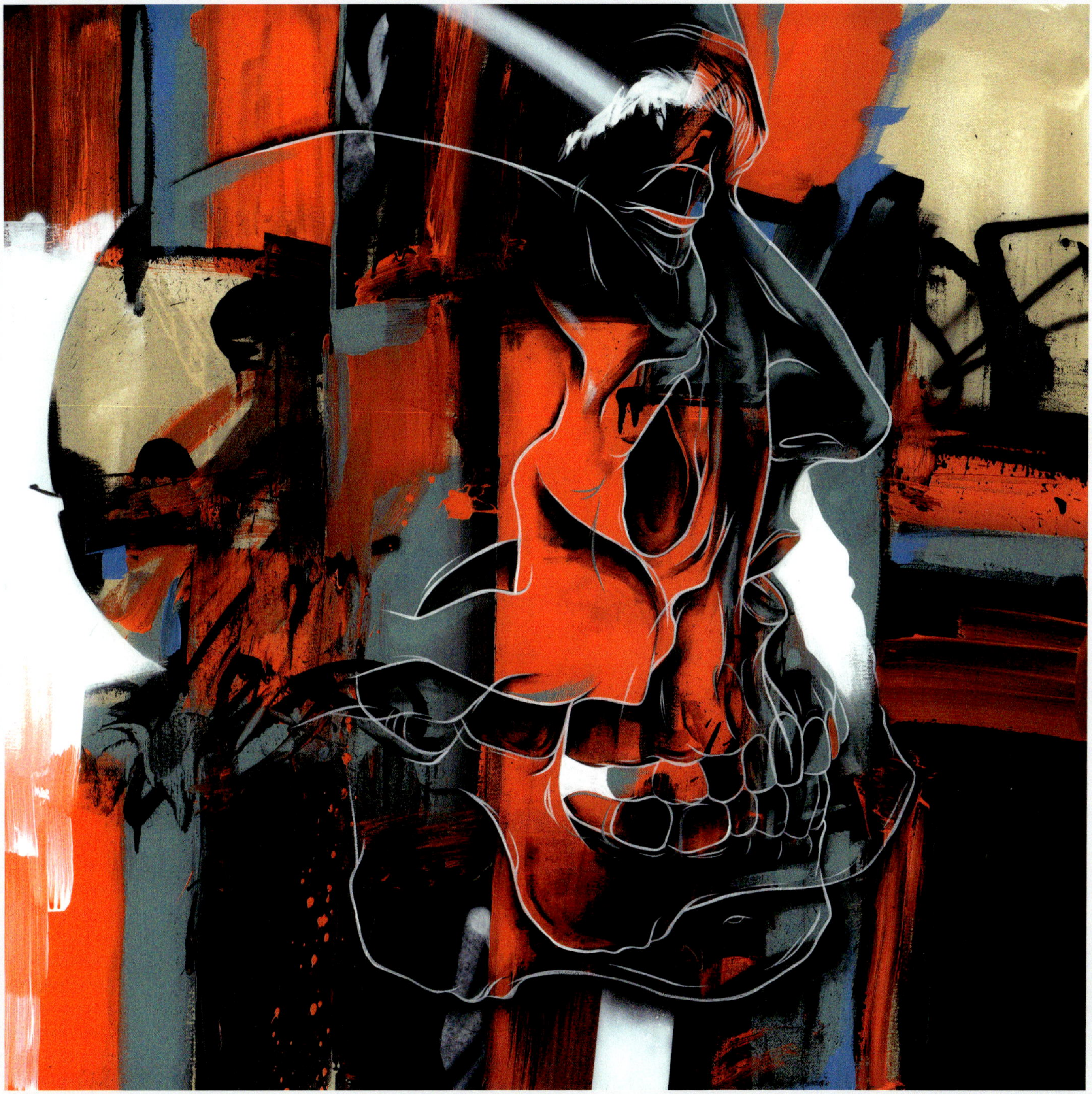

Pendulum / Mixed media on canvas – 81 x 81 cm – 2010

Der

Born in Saintes, France, 1973. Lives in Toulouse, France.

I started graffiti art in 1989 and I did my first 3-D piece in '94. A style which I was going to make my own when I brought my personal touch inspired by the world of mechanics and organics. Meanwhile, I never lost sight of the original calligraffiti influence which remains essential in my quest. This guideline was the main driver of my work with my old crews Truskool and Leclub. My transition to canvas is an obvious follow-up to my work on walls. Using the medium, the means, and the themes, I will represent the past, present, and future of my life.

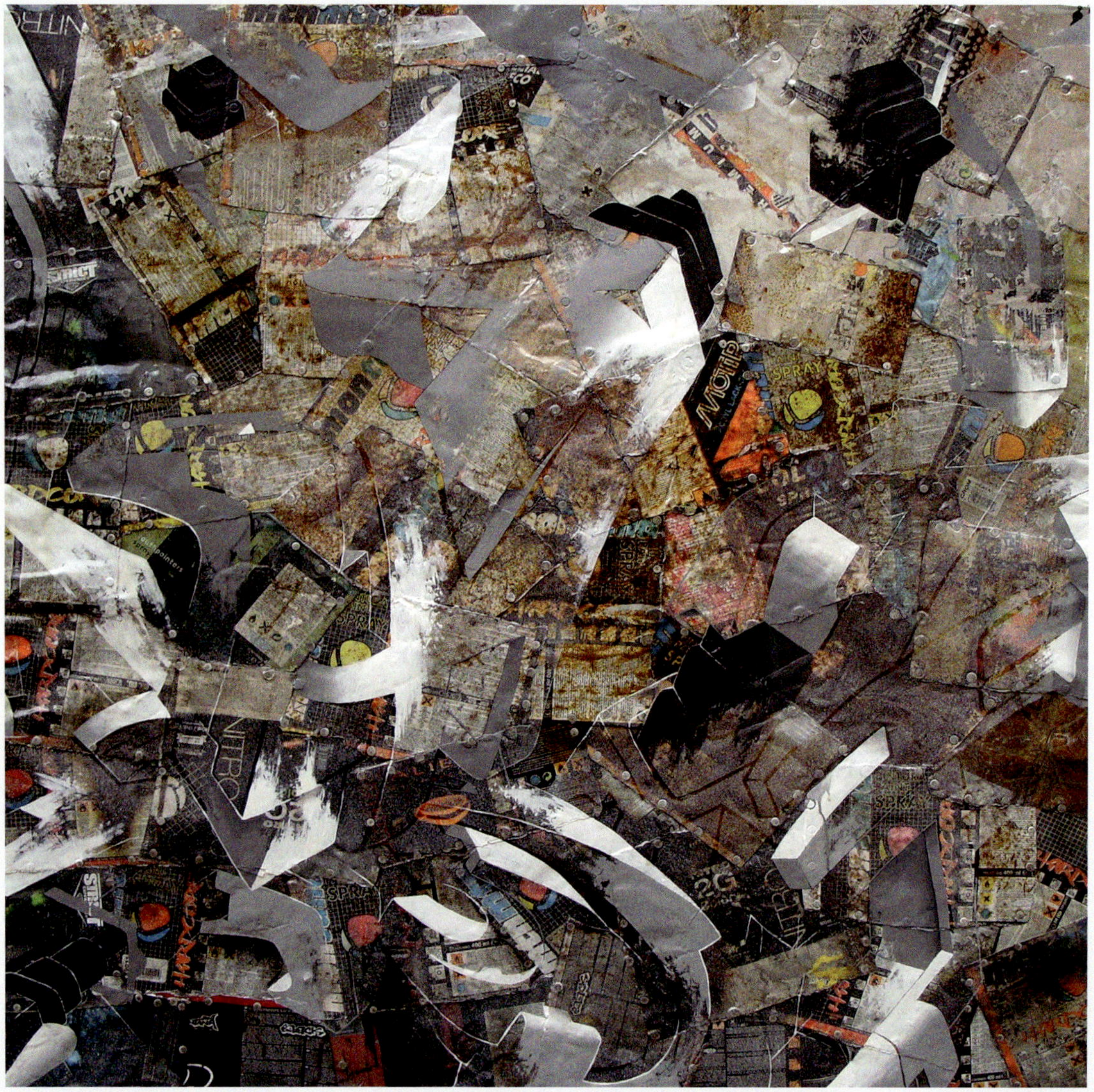

Iron Der / Glycerol and acrylic on aerosol cans – 100 x 100 cm – 2010

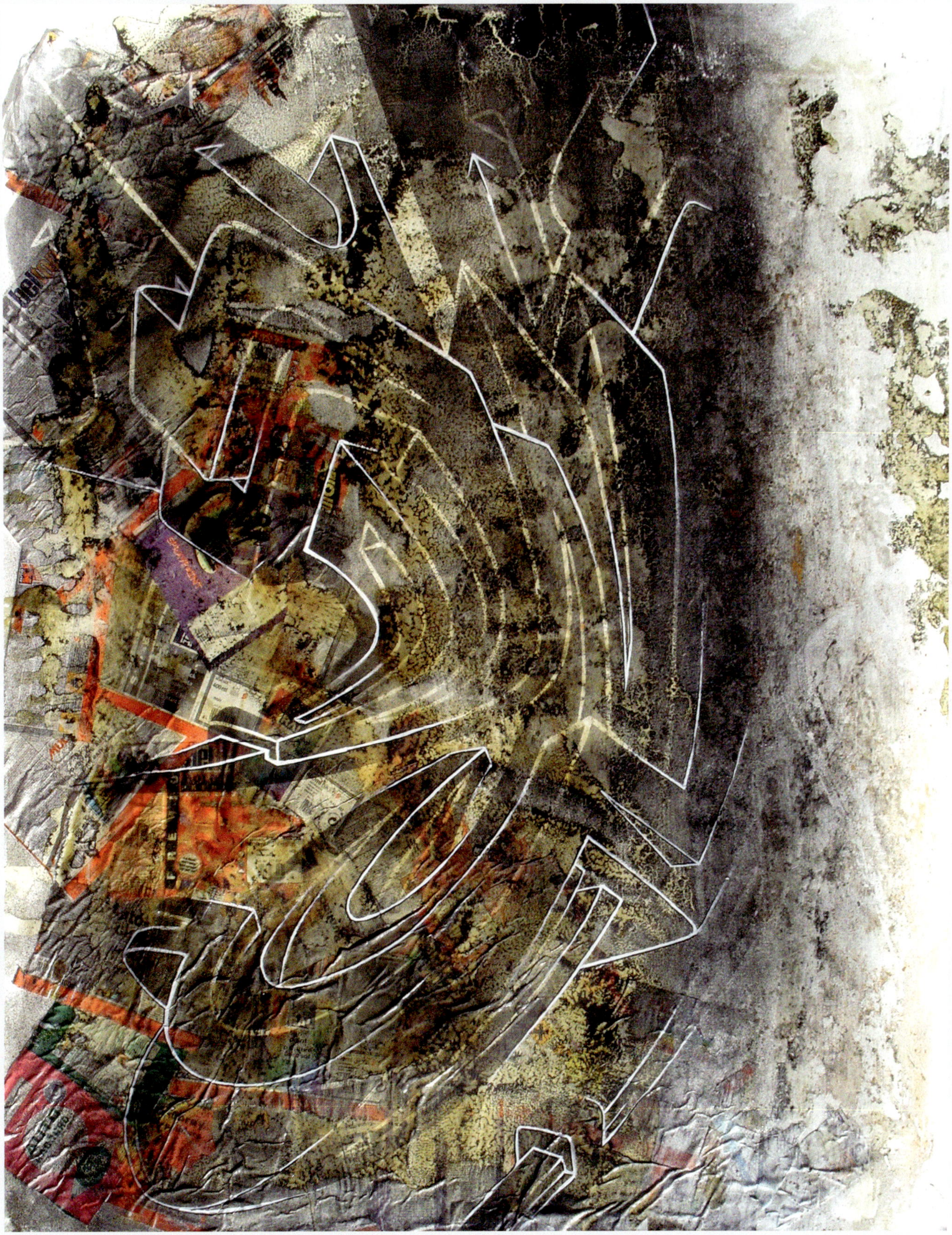

D. Gradation Life / Collage, aerosol, and acrylic on canvas – 70 x 100 cm – 2009

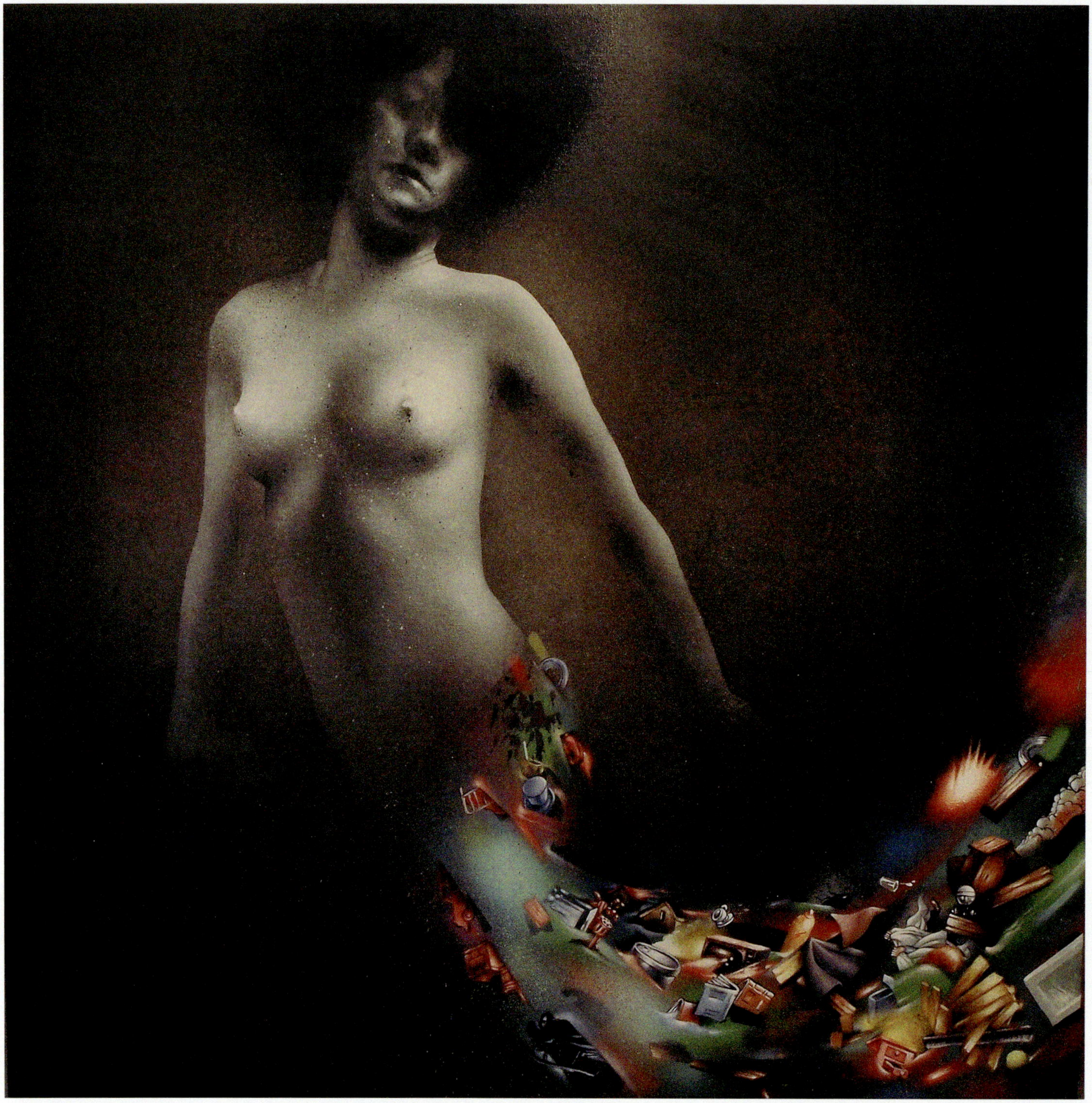

Tempest / Aerosol and enamel on canvas – 100 x 100 cm – 2010

Dixon

Born in Caracas, Venezuela, 1968. Lives in Barcelona, Spain.

My ideas are true to my feelings, and my feelings are true to my art.

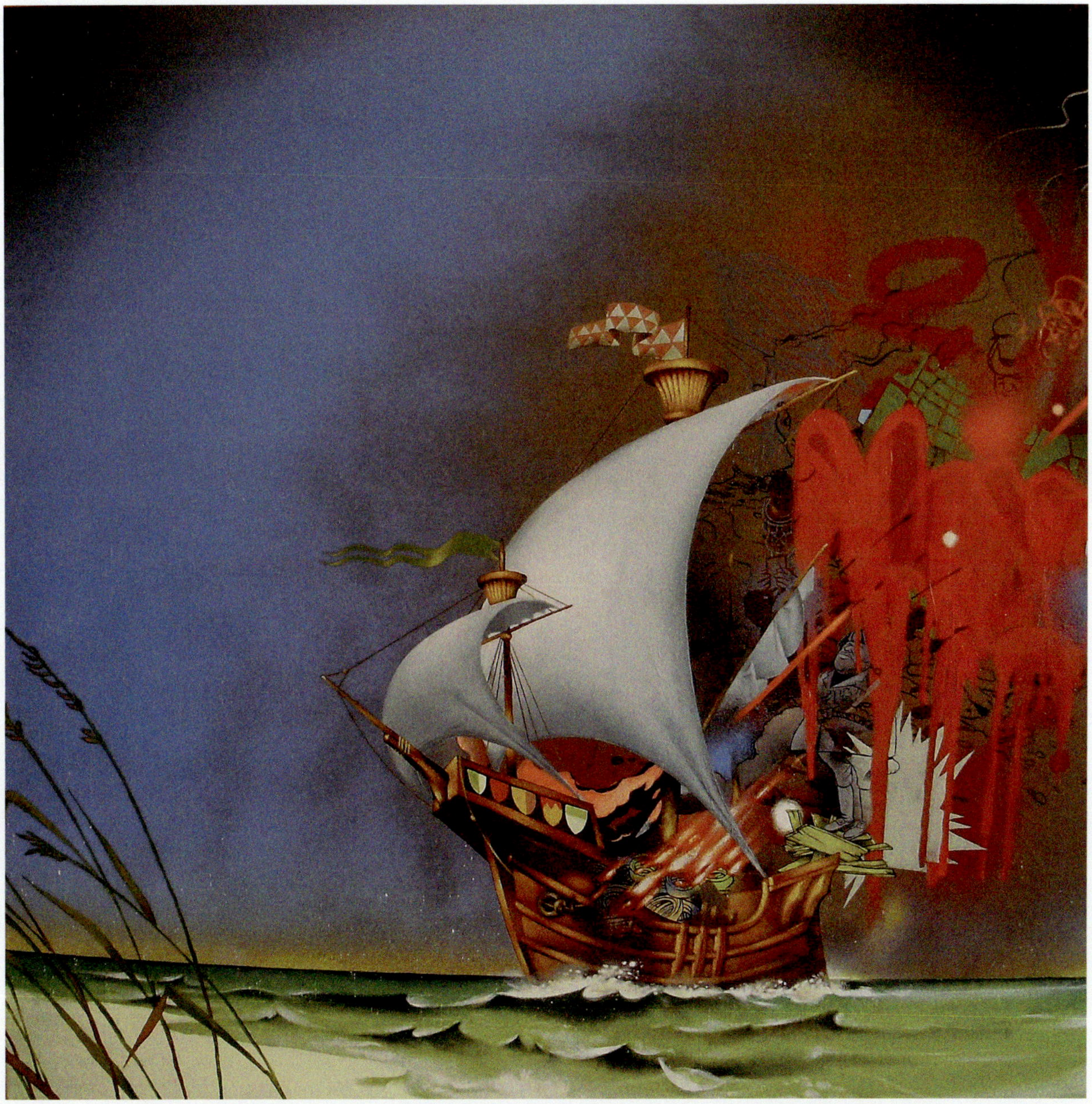

Malice / Aerosol and enamel on canvas – 90 x 90 cm – 2010

Docteur Gecko

Born in La Réunion, France. Lives in Toulouse, France.

I hijack, hack, remessage advertising in bus shelters. The particularity of my works is that my modification can only be seen during the night. However, during daytime the ad modified seems to be untouched. Concerning my few studio works, I keep my concept on advertising: the new message "appears" when someone is in front of the ad.

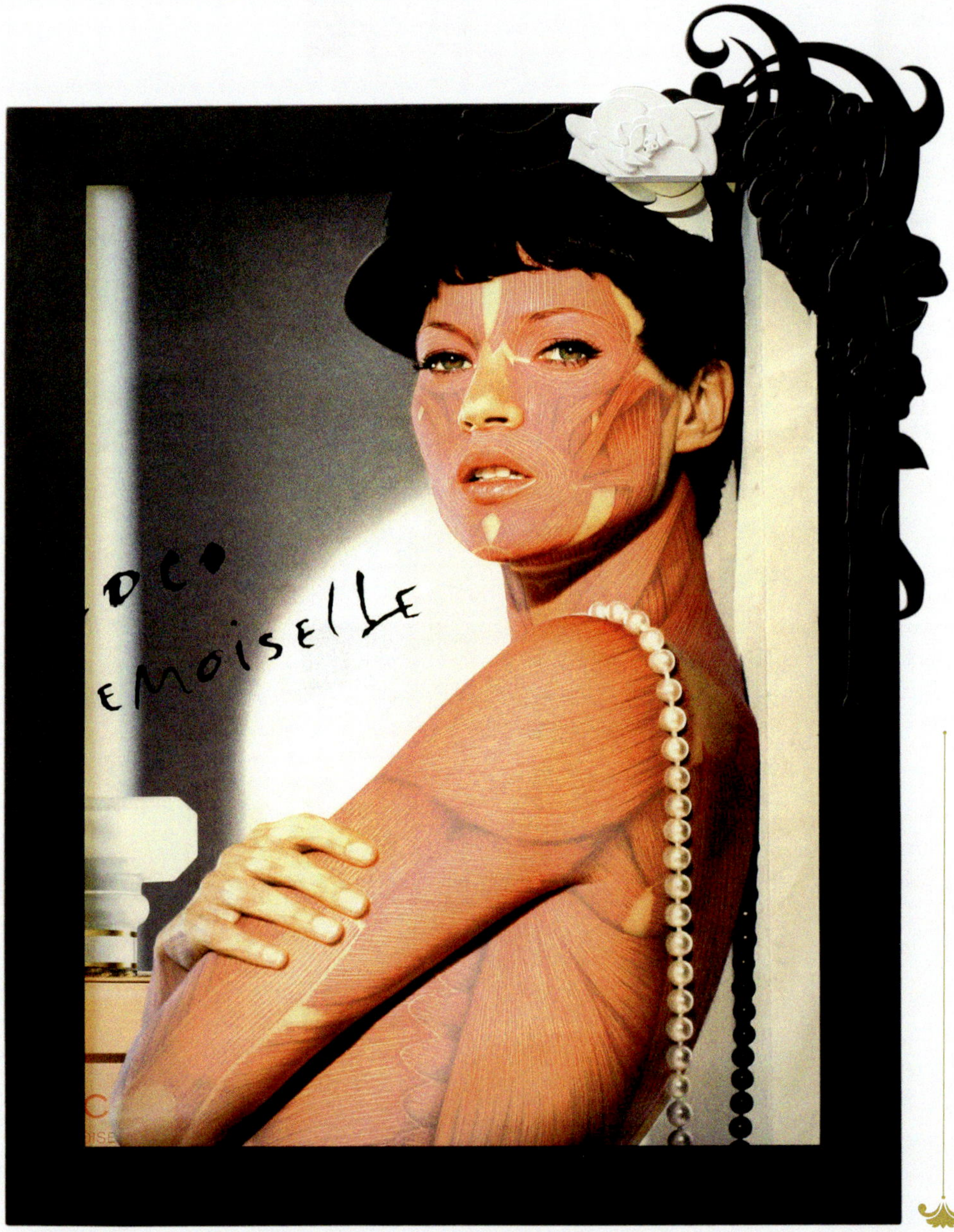

Coco (light) / Ad found in bus shelter, wood, mixed media, and backlight – 110 x 160 x 13 cm – 2010

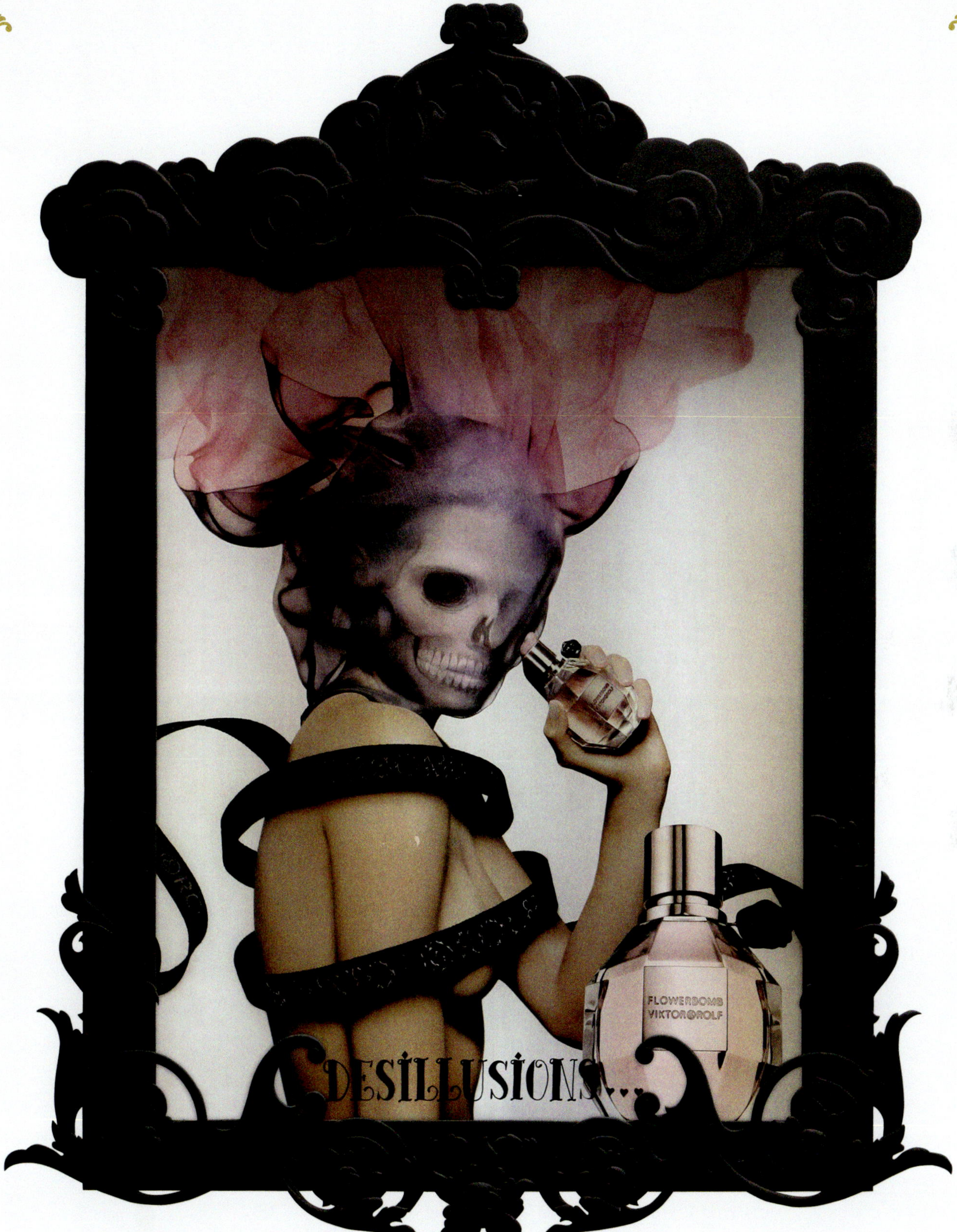

(Des) Illusion(s) (light) / Ad found in bus shelter, wood, mixed media, and backlight – 100 x 130 x 13 cm – 2010

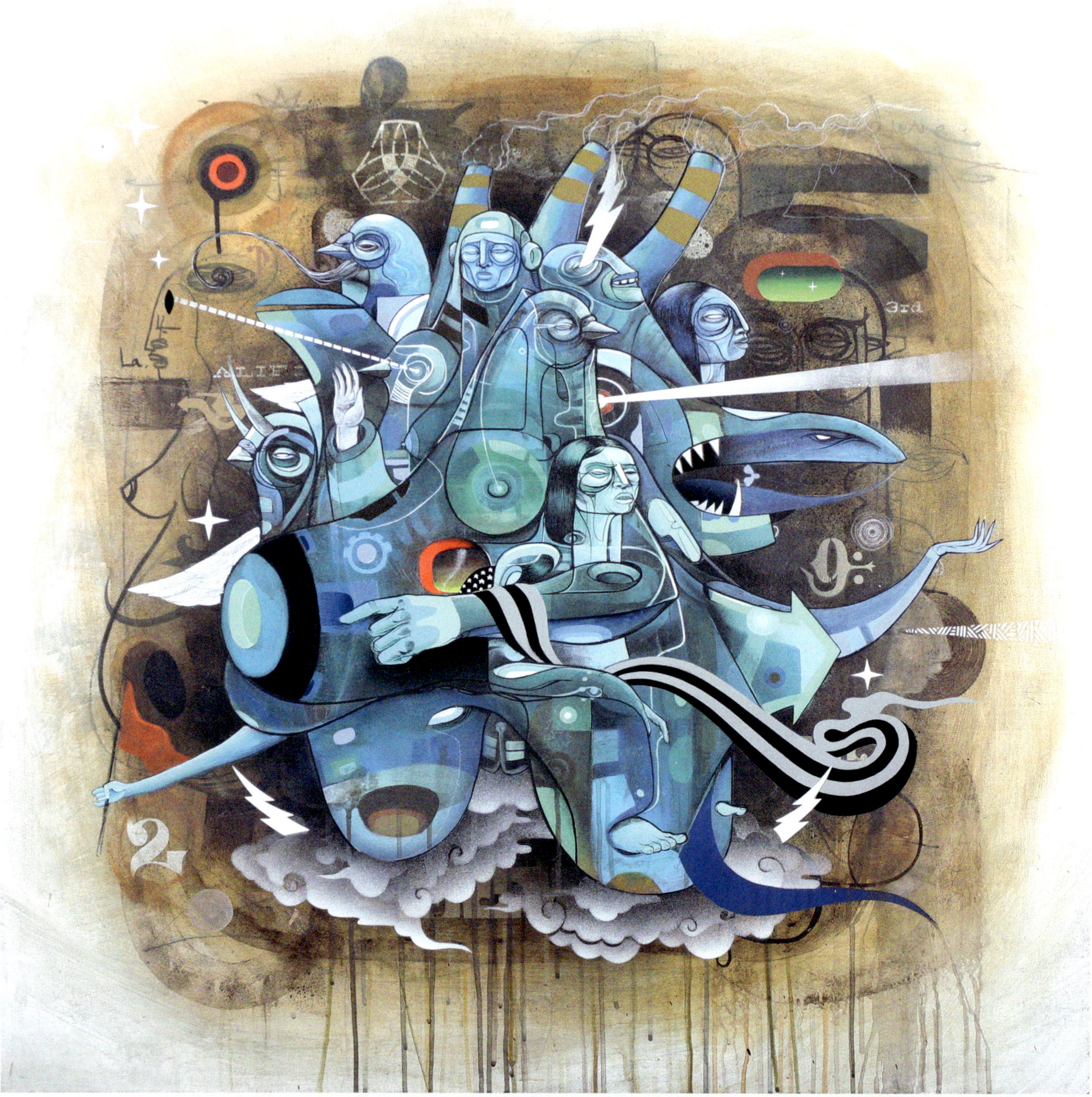

FF Operative Series A3 / Mixed media on wood – 91 x 91 cm – 2009

Doze Green

Born in New York, United States, 1964. Lives in San Francisco, United States.

In the tradition of wildstyle graffiti, the deconstruction of the letter and then the re-juxtaposition of those elements translates into the cycle of "buildestroy." As an artist in the true sense of the word, not a slogan, i.e. graffiti artist, I always retain a sense of my origins but am not wholly reliant on the past. It has taken me from the progression of learning letter forms in their abstraction, to formulating the emerging cohesiveness of letter forms and figurative work. The interconnectedness of all is revealed through layers of color forms and intersecting line work. From the macrocosmic to the unseen.

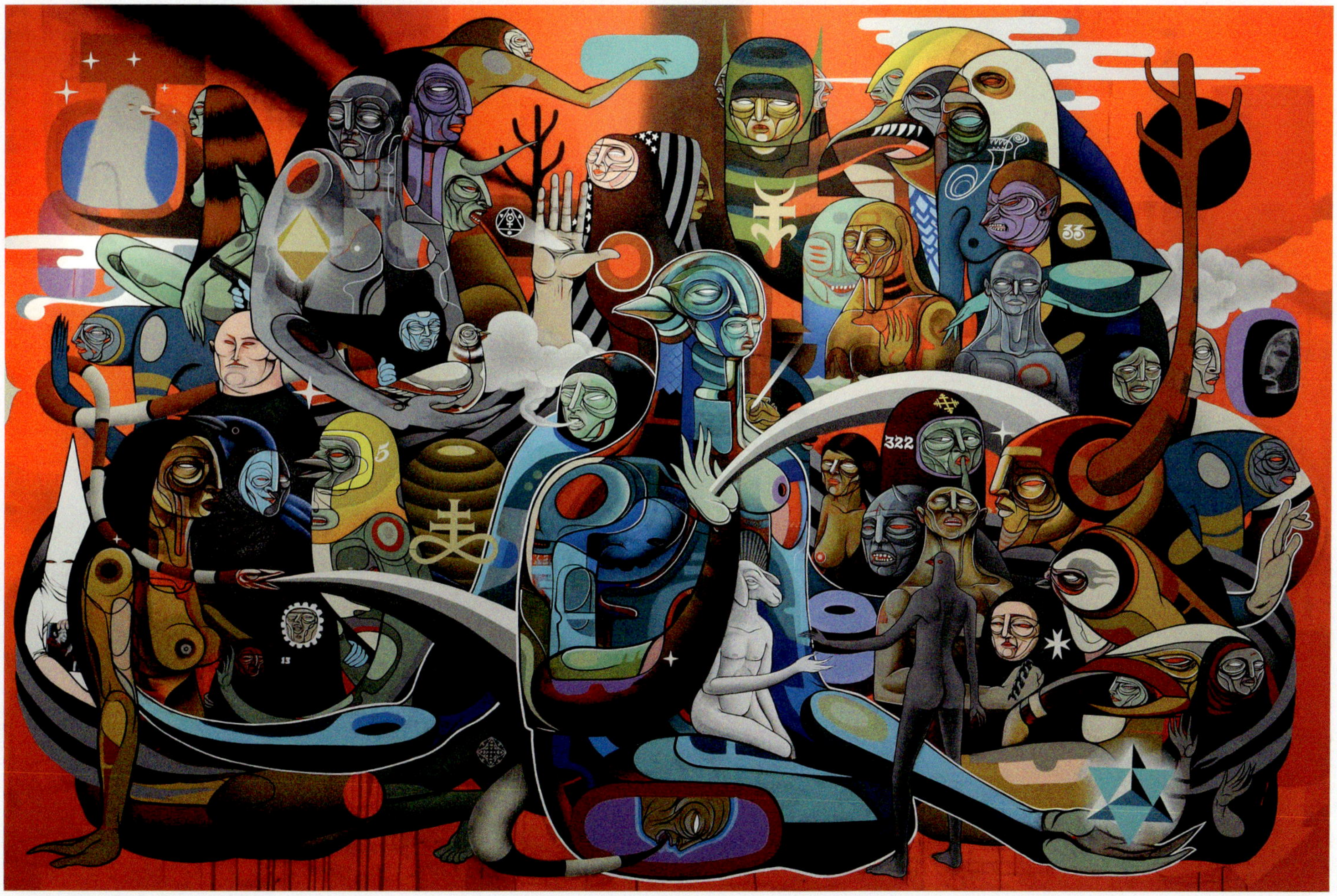

Siddhartha / Mixed media on canvas – 274 x 183 cm – 2009

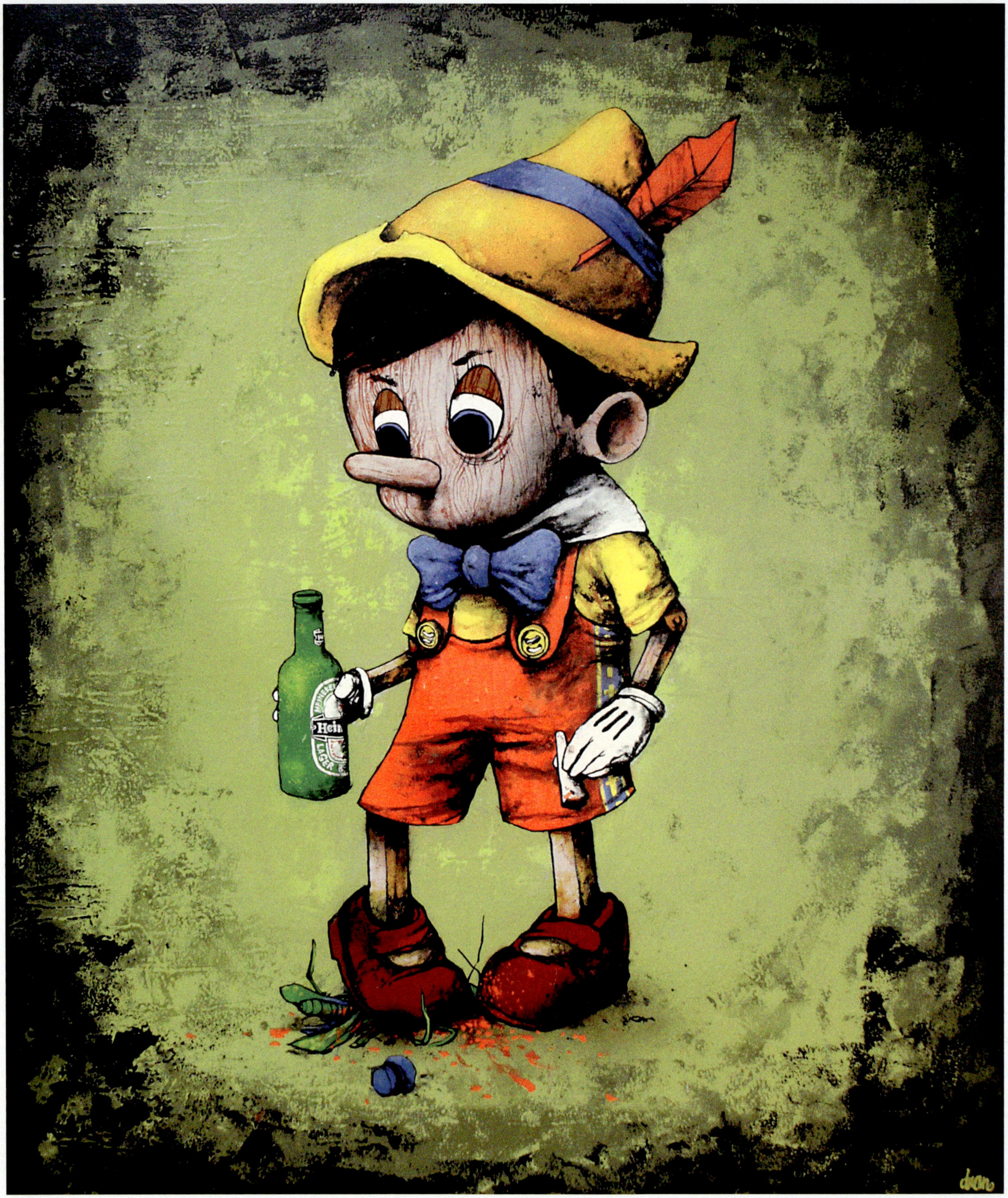

Pinnochio / Aerosol and acrylic on canvas – 100 x 120 cm – 2009

Dran

Born in Toulouse, France, 1979. Lives in Toulouse, France.

The Street unstuck me when I was 14 years old. I owe it my passion and my freedom of expression. I make caricatures about the society of my time. I like to take the clichés that make people look into their selves, and I want to do this with striking images, just like the first graffiti I ever saw.

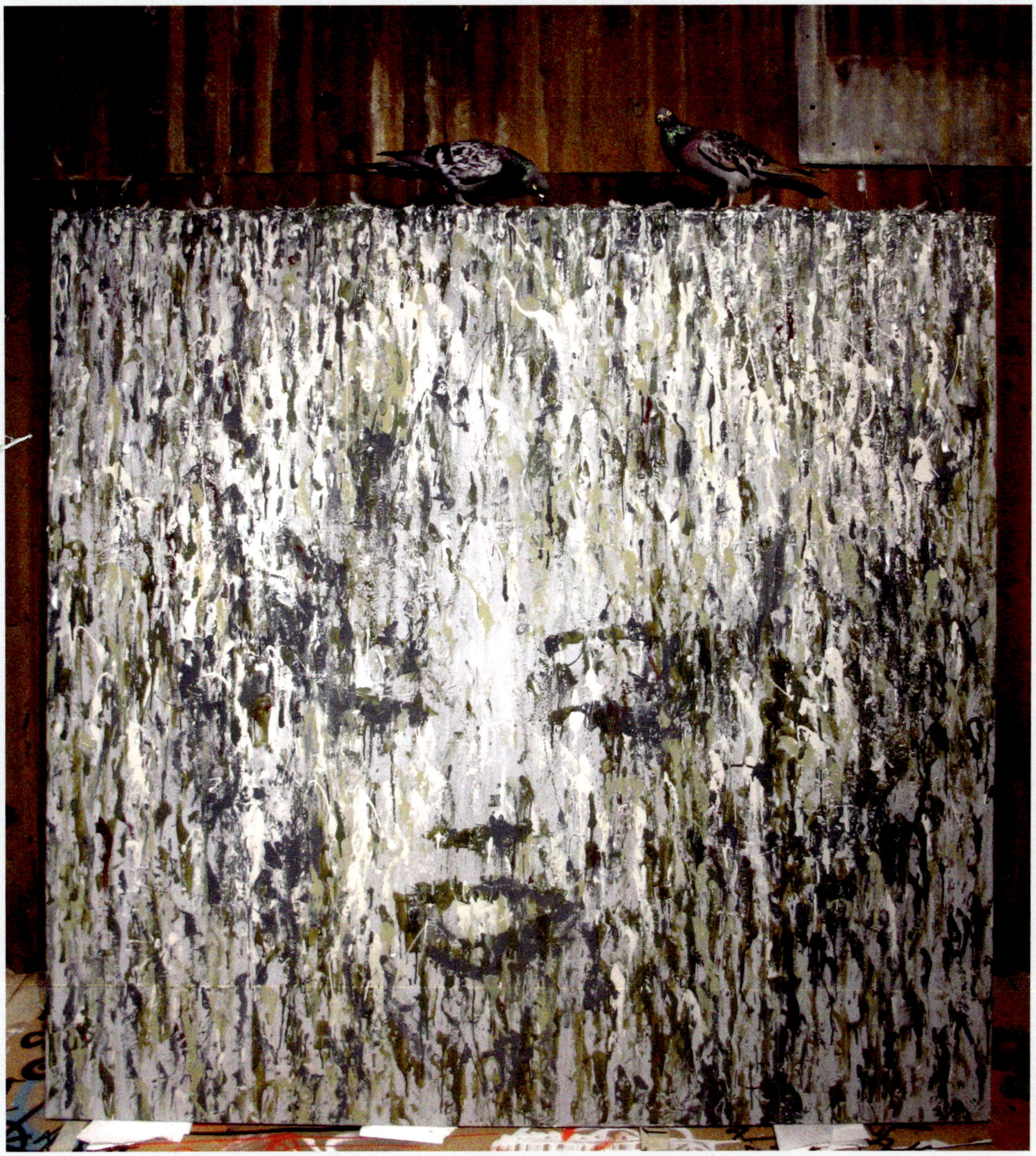

Marylin / Aerosol, pigeons, pigeon feathers, and pigeons spikes on wood – 160 x 150 x 14 cm – 2011

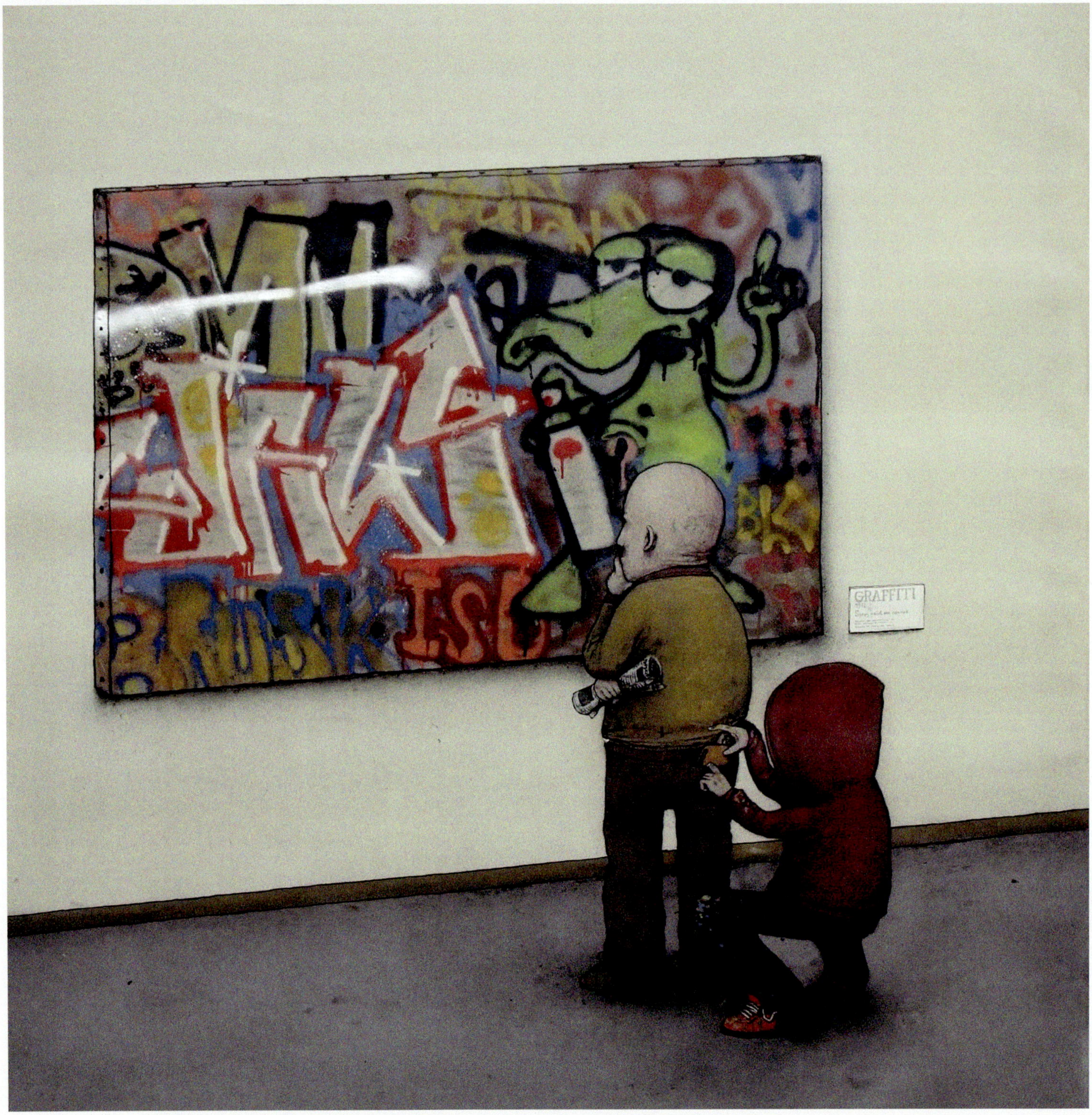

Swindle / Aerosol and acrylic on canvas – 110 x 150 cm – 2010

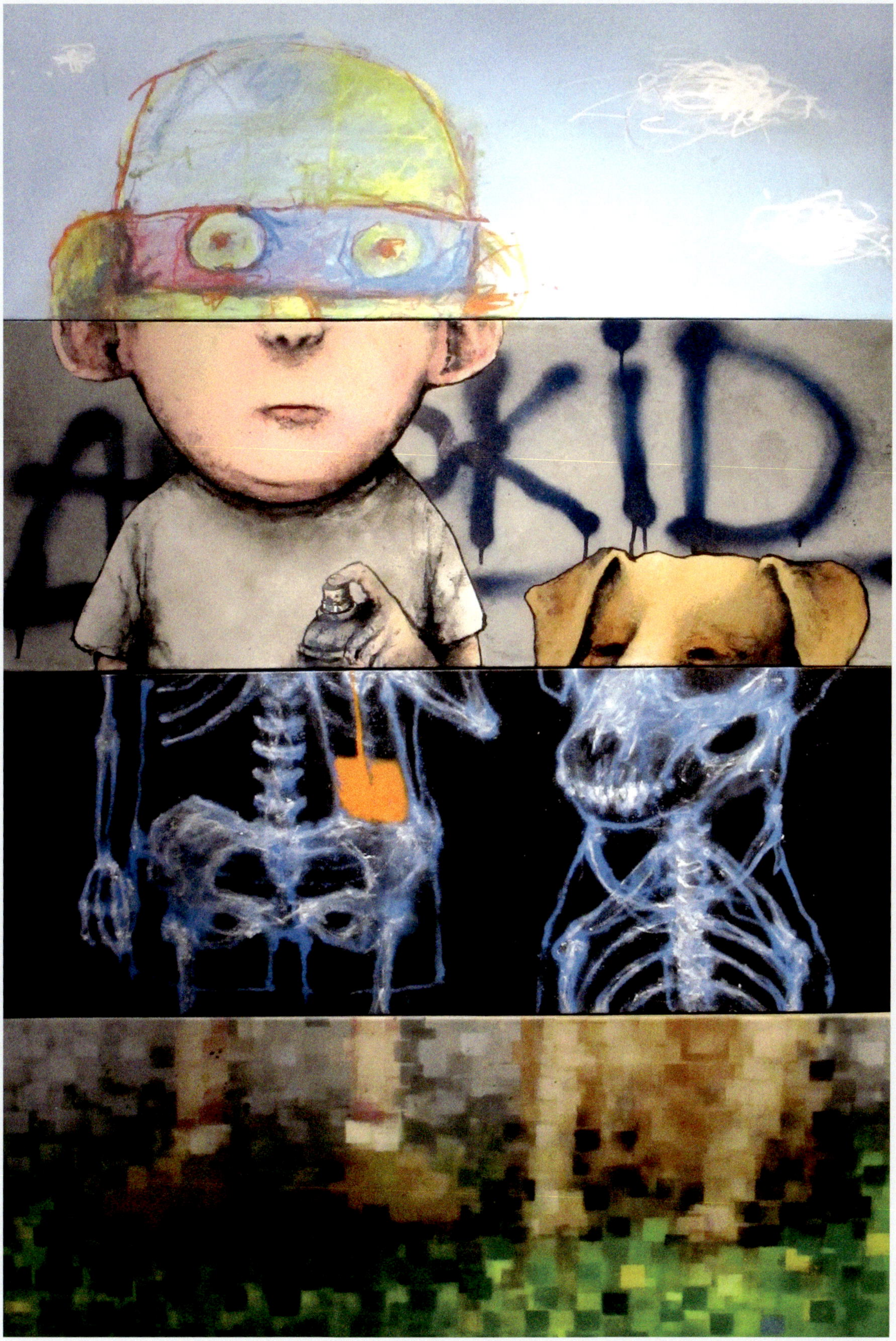

Esquisite Corpse **Quadtych** / Aerosol and acrylic on canvas – 36 x 99 cm – 2010

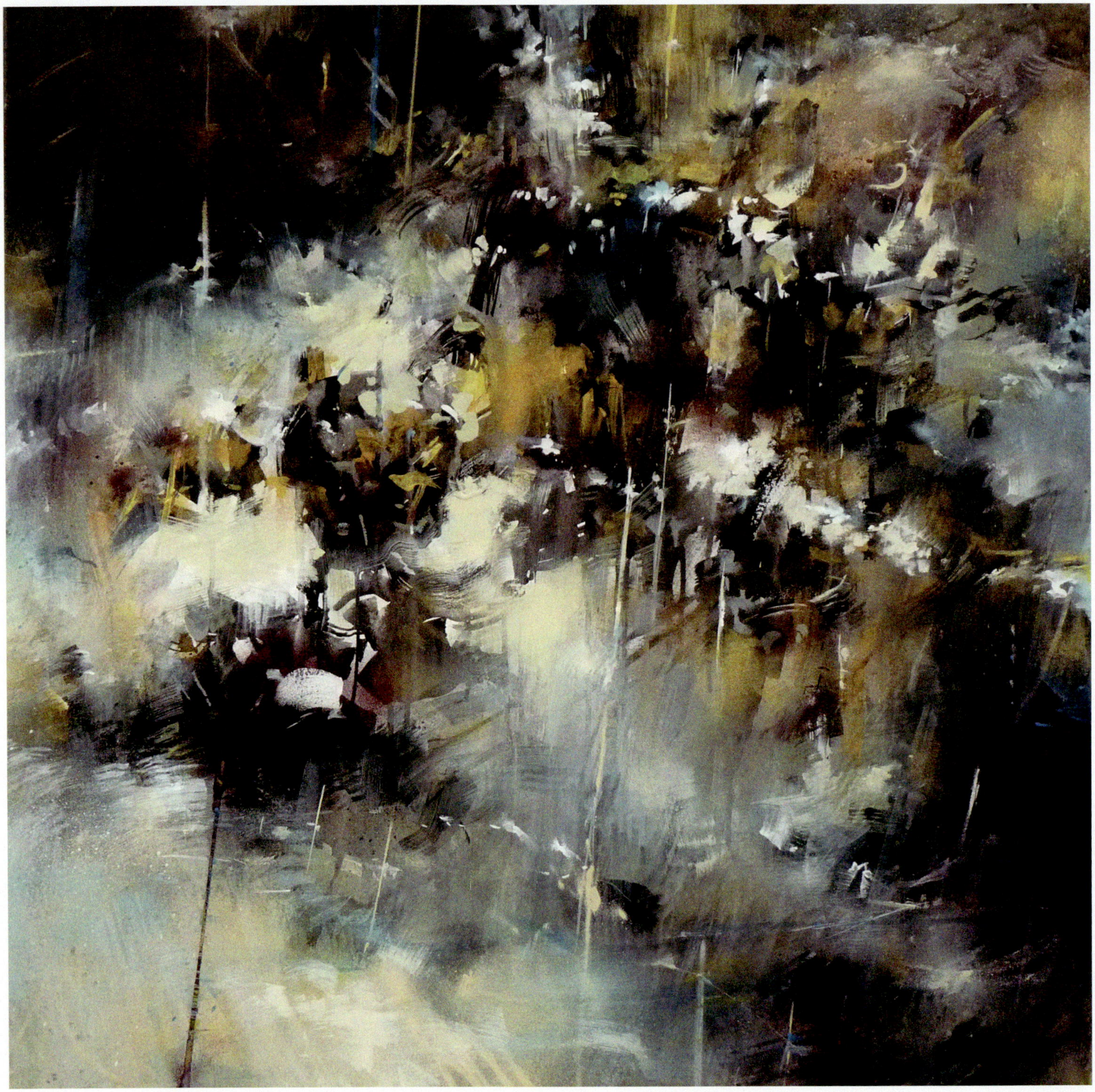

Tides Rising / Aerosol and acrylic on canvas – 76 x 76 cm – 2010

Duncan Jago aka Mr. Jago

Born in Salisbury, England, 1972. Lives in Bristol, England.

To all intents and purposes the street and studio work are one and the same, the main difference being the process; that is when painting outdoors I use my whole body, it is a larger, more physical, and perhaps, therefore, liberating experience. By contrast my studio work is more introspective and reflective.

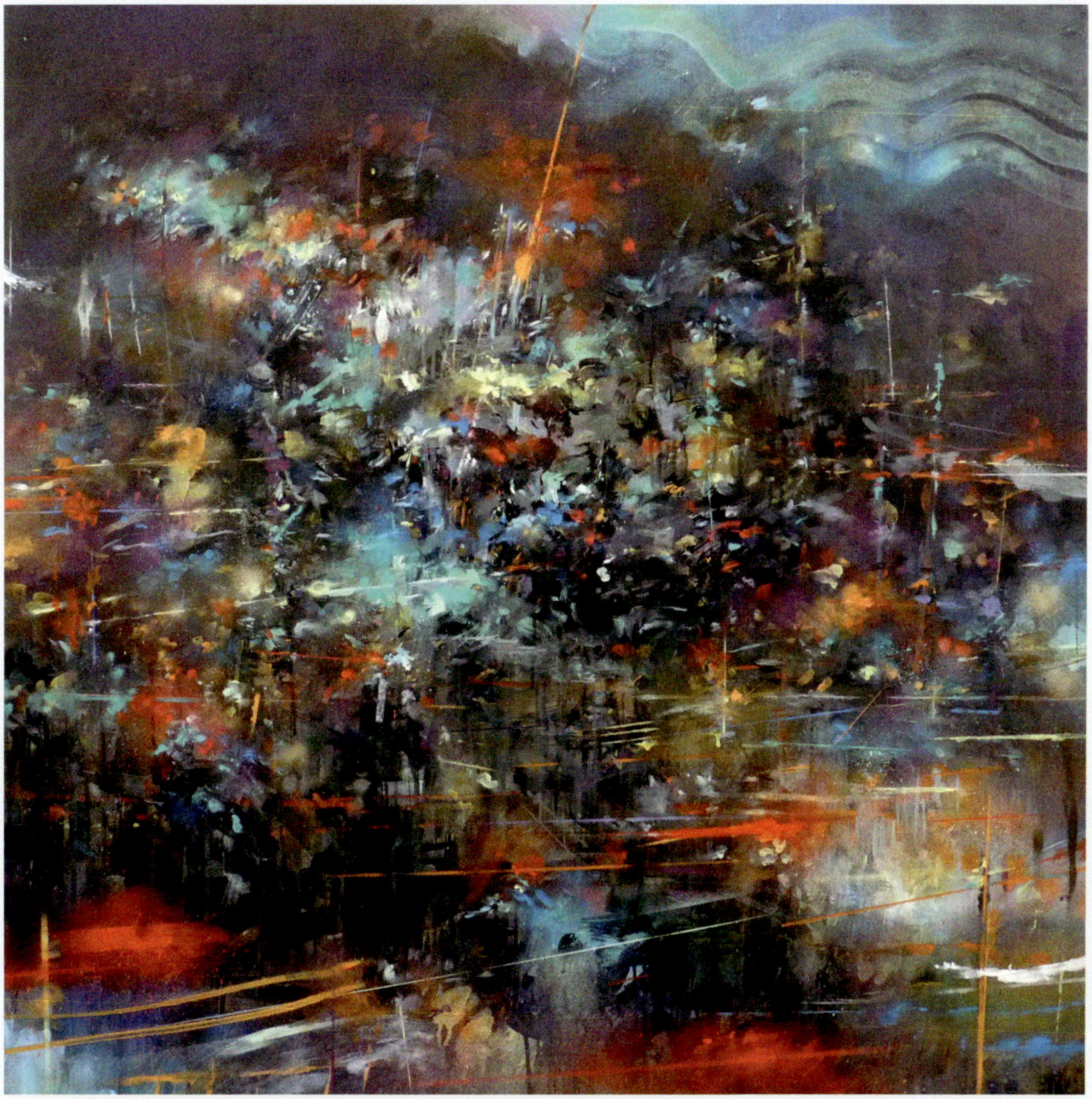

The Hades Shot | Aerosol and acrylic on canvas – 110 x 110 cm – 2010

Eine

Born in London, England, 1970. Lives in Hastings, England.

The work I do in the studio is a reflection of the street. Both environments present you with a different set of challenges. Working in the studio gives me the opportunity to work with materials and techniques that would never work on the street. The studio work represents me as an artist in a different way. For 20 years I painted graffiti with a passion. 99.99% of all that is now gone, once you stop writing graf it gets cleaned and then you're forgotten. My canvases will be all that's left when I'm dead and buried. They will outlive me, that's how I will be remembered.

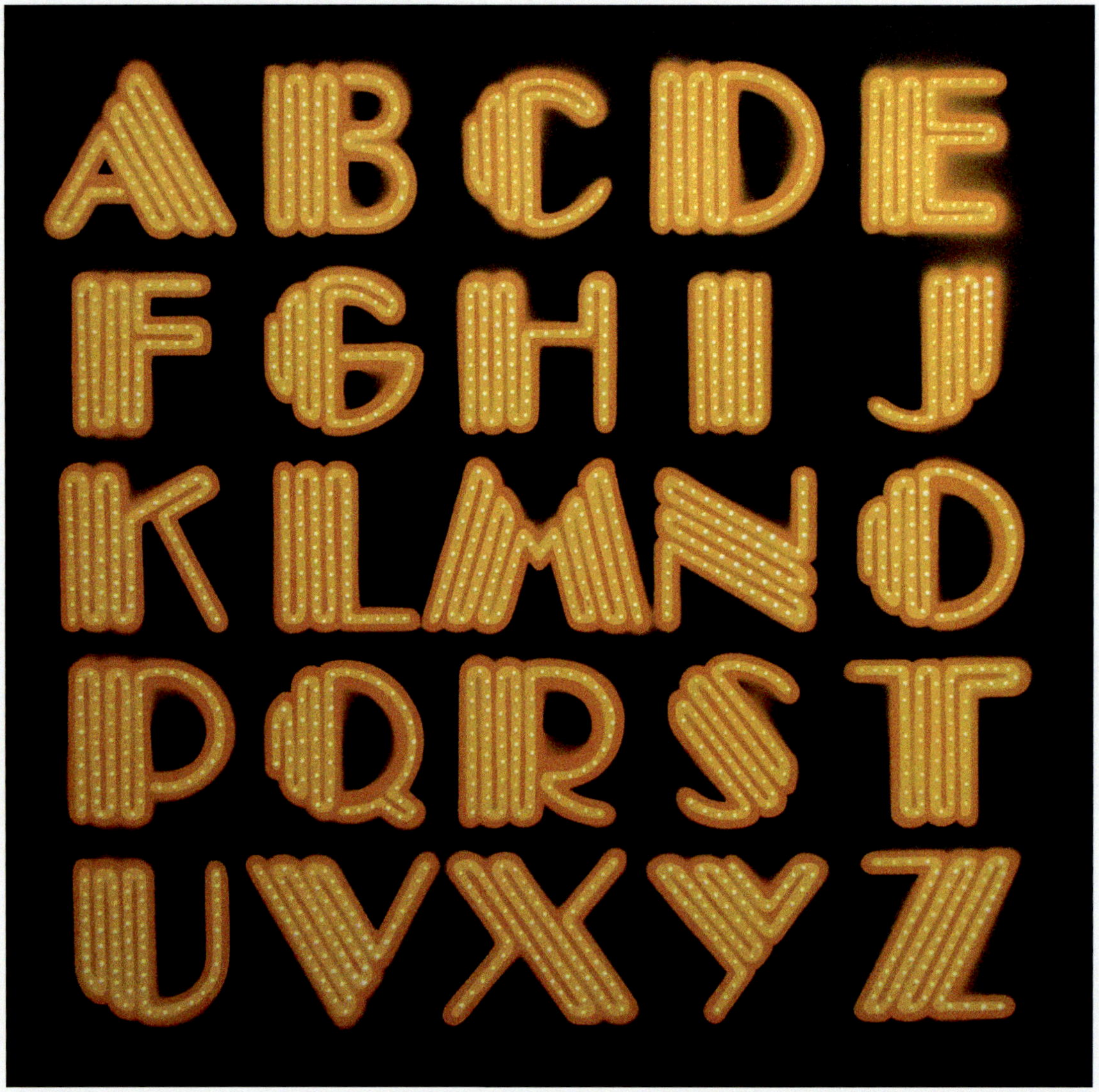

Neon A to Z / Gloss and aerosol on canvas – 76 x 76 cm – 2008

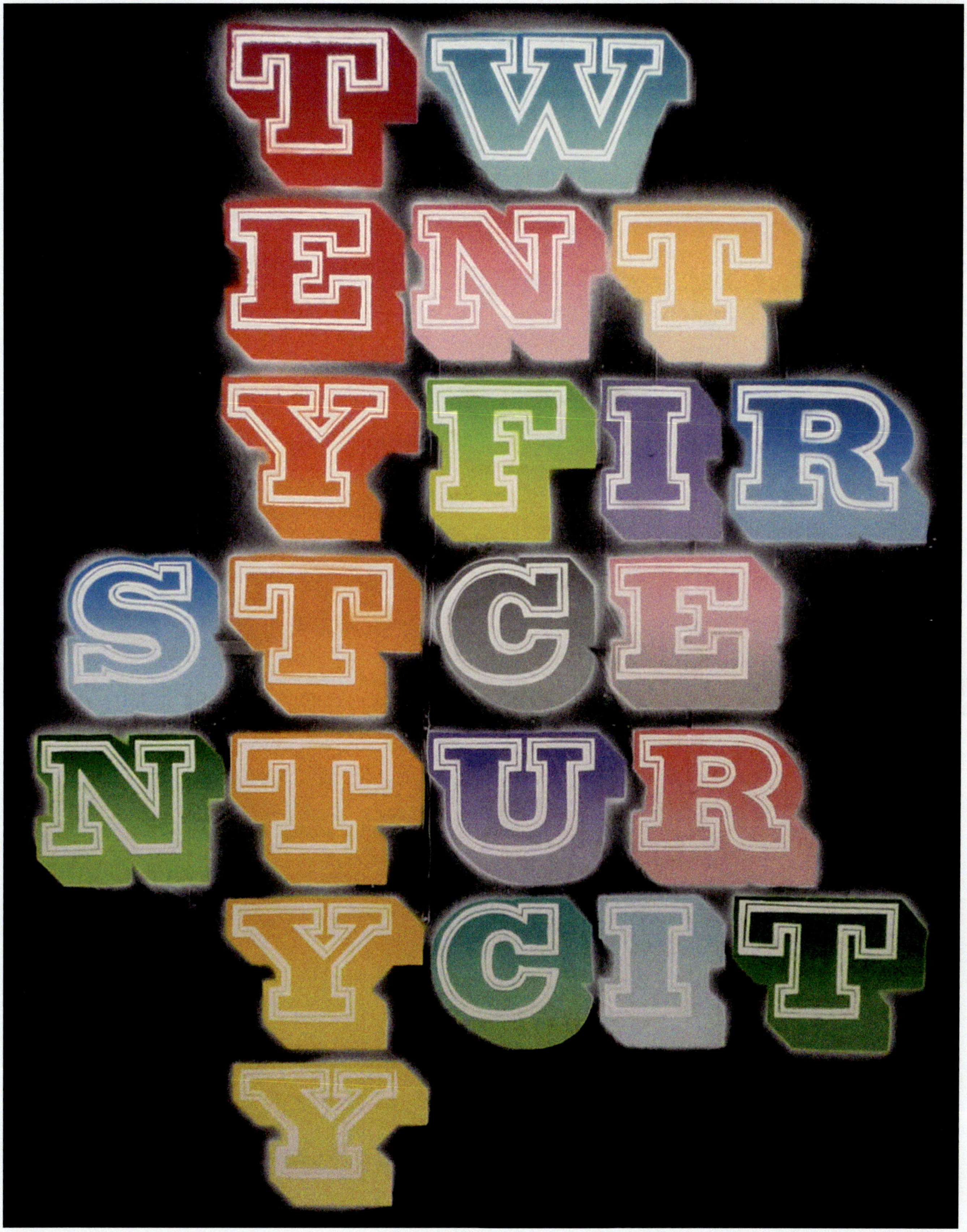

Twenty First Century City / Gloss and aerosol on canvas – 80 x 100 cm – 2010

Ekundayo

Born in Honolulu, Hawaii, 1983. Lives in Honolulu, Hawaii.

Taking a serious risk to create something you believe in is what had the most impact on my studio work. The more time I spent getting caught up and almost getting caught up in all the shit the graffiti game has to offer up made me realize if I was gonna risk all this shit then I better be making something that has some heart. Now I apply that same thinking in everything I do.

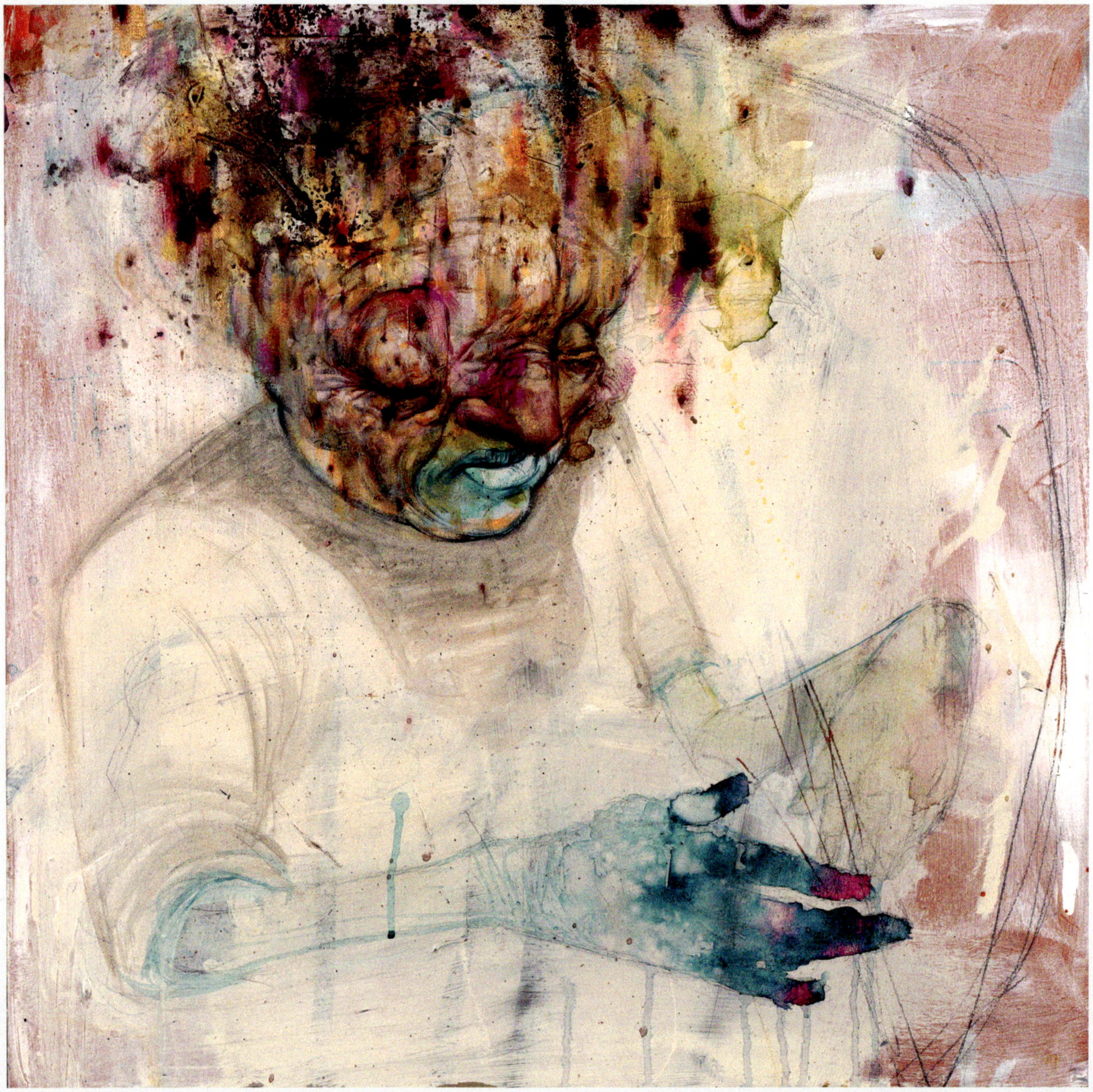

Never Miss it till it's Gone / Acrylic, gouache, ink, and aerosol on canvas – 61 x 61 cm – 2010

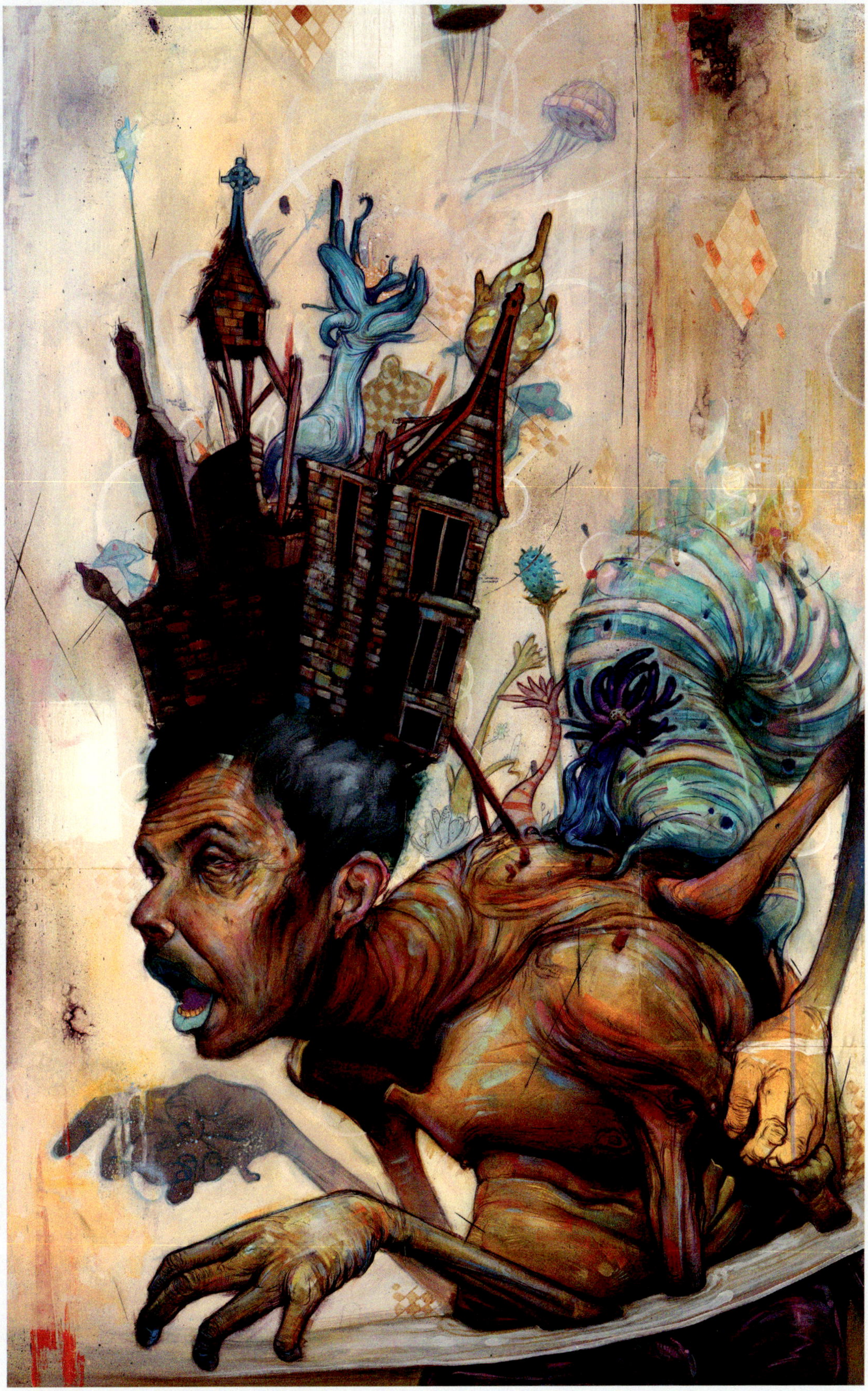

Foreclosure / Acrylic, gouache, ink, and aerosol on paper mounted to wood – 76 x 121 cm – 2010

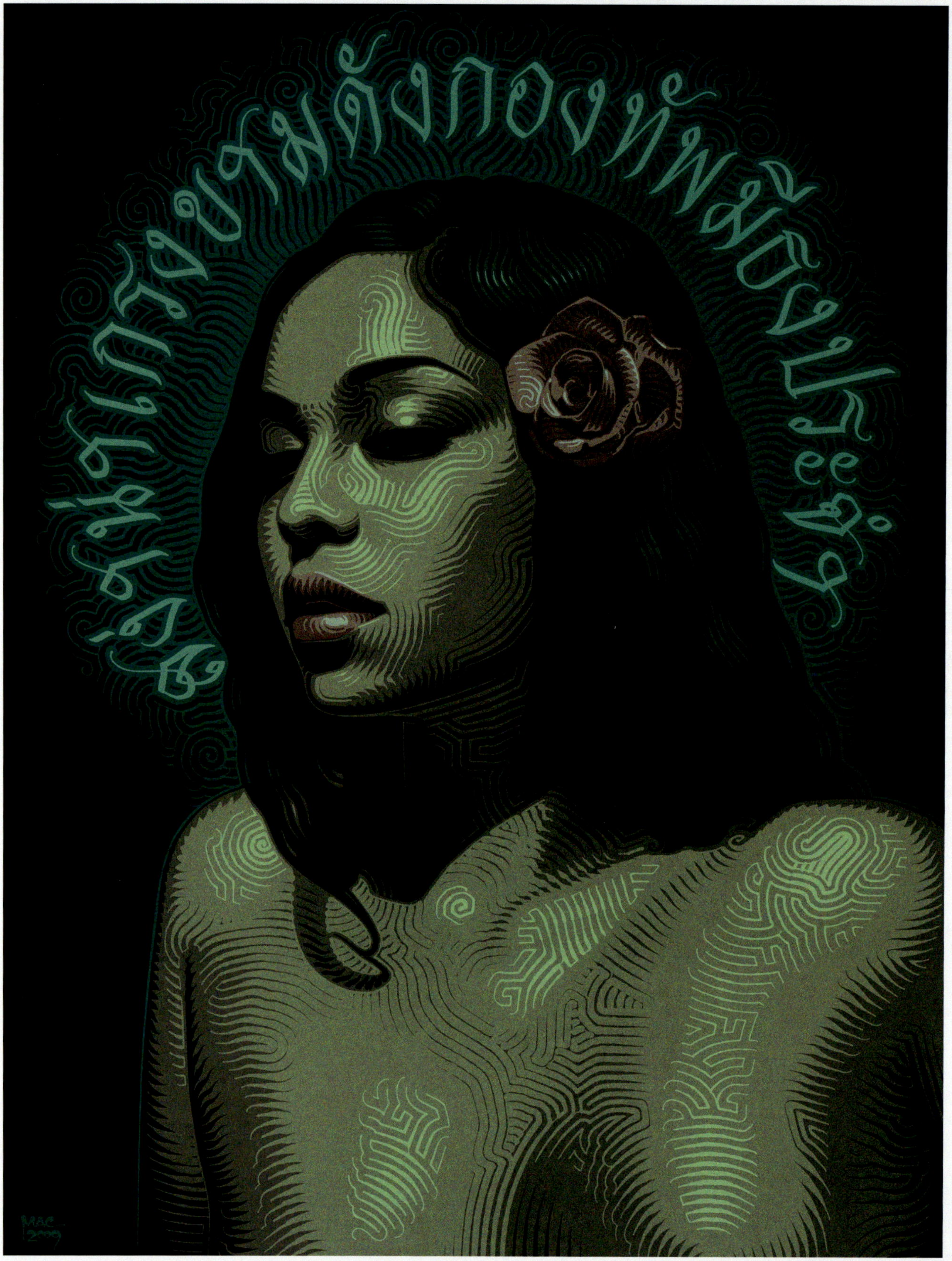

Song of Songs | Acrylic on wood – 92 x 122 cm – 2009

El Mac

Born in Los Angeles, United States, 1980. Lives in Phoenix, United States.

I try to create images of people and scenes, both humble and ethereal, as perfect as I possibly can. This is out of love for beauty and truth and the desire to uplift and inspire. Painting on the streets is the most direct way I know to connect with and impact people, while painting studio work is much more introverted and private. Studio painting allows me to create at my own speed without the urgency of the streets rushing me along.

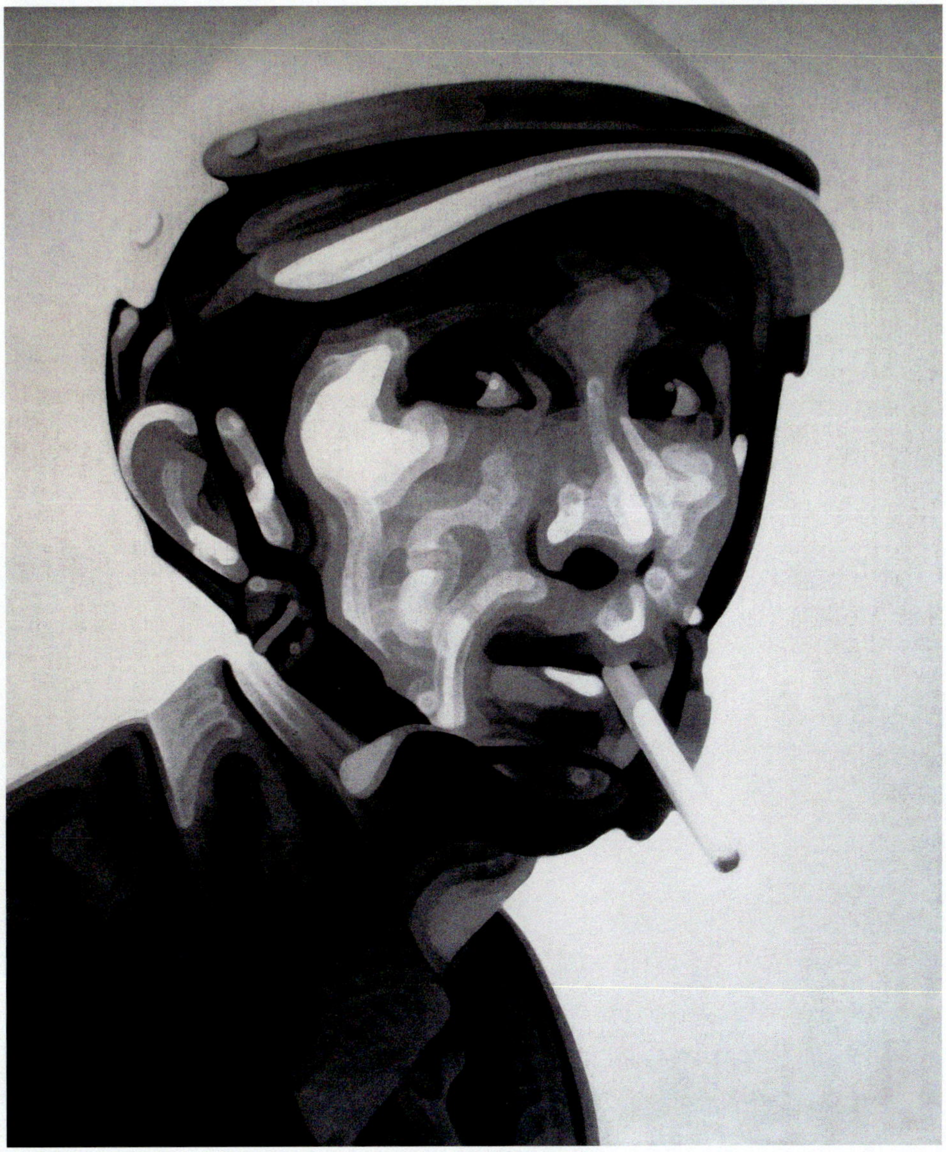

The Motorist | Aerosol on burlap – 152 x 198 cm – 2010

Evan Roth

Born in Okemos, United States, 1978. Lives in Paris, France.

The tag is the primary building block of graffiti. My work deconstructs this form and uses the gallery as a lens that allows others to see the world of gesture, motion, and dance that is written around the city when you learn to look past the paint on the wall. My algorithmically generated prints, videos, and sculptures visualize not the graffiti's ink, but its motion frozen in time.

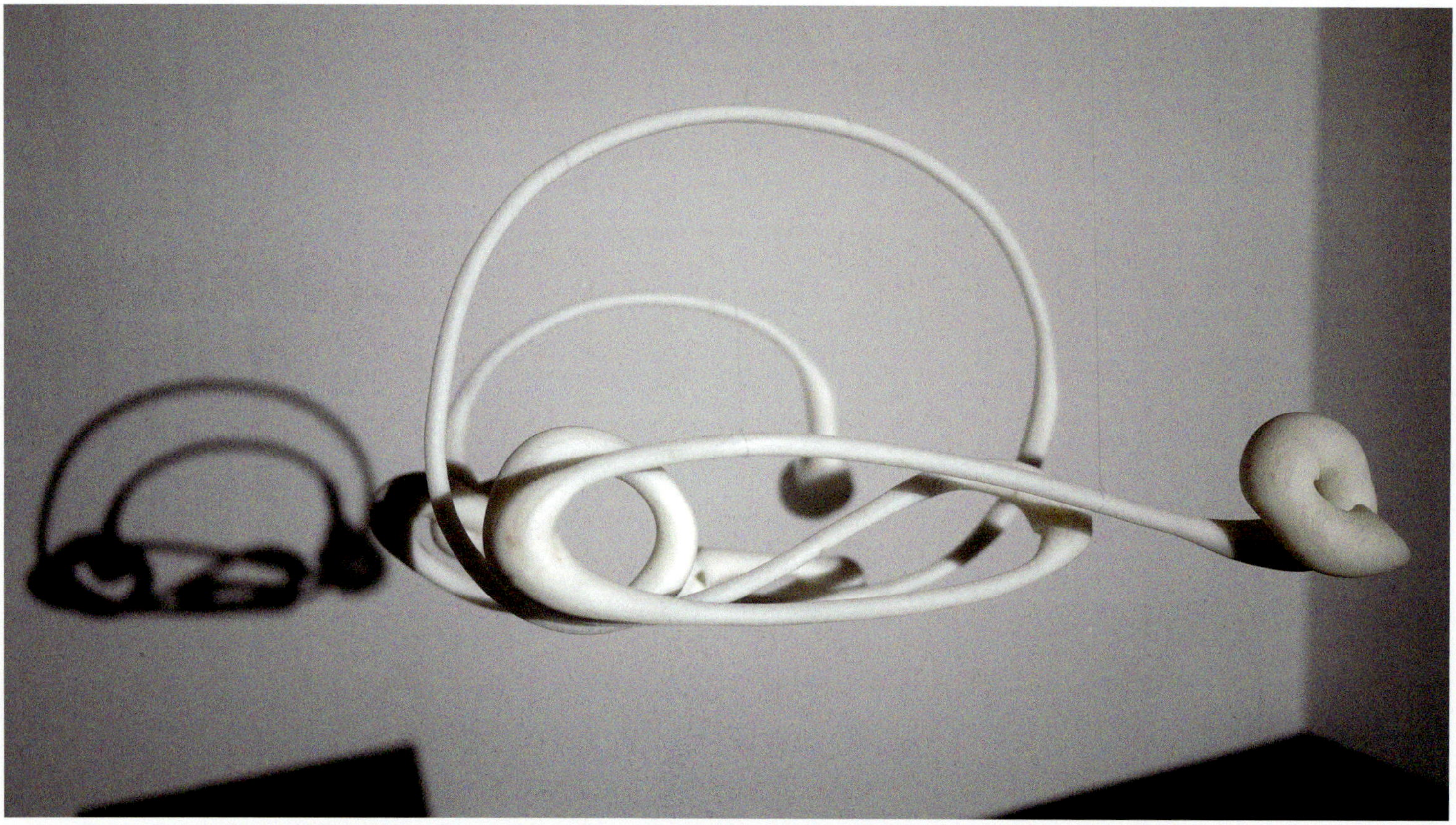

Graffiti Analysis, Anonymous Viennese Graffiti Writer / Motion-tracked graffiti data and ABS thermoplastic – 35 x 46 x 25 cm – 2010-11

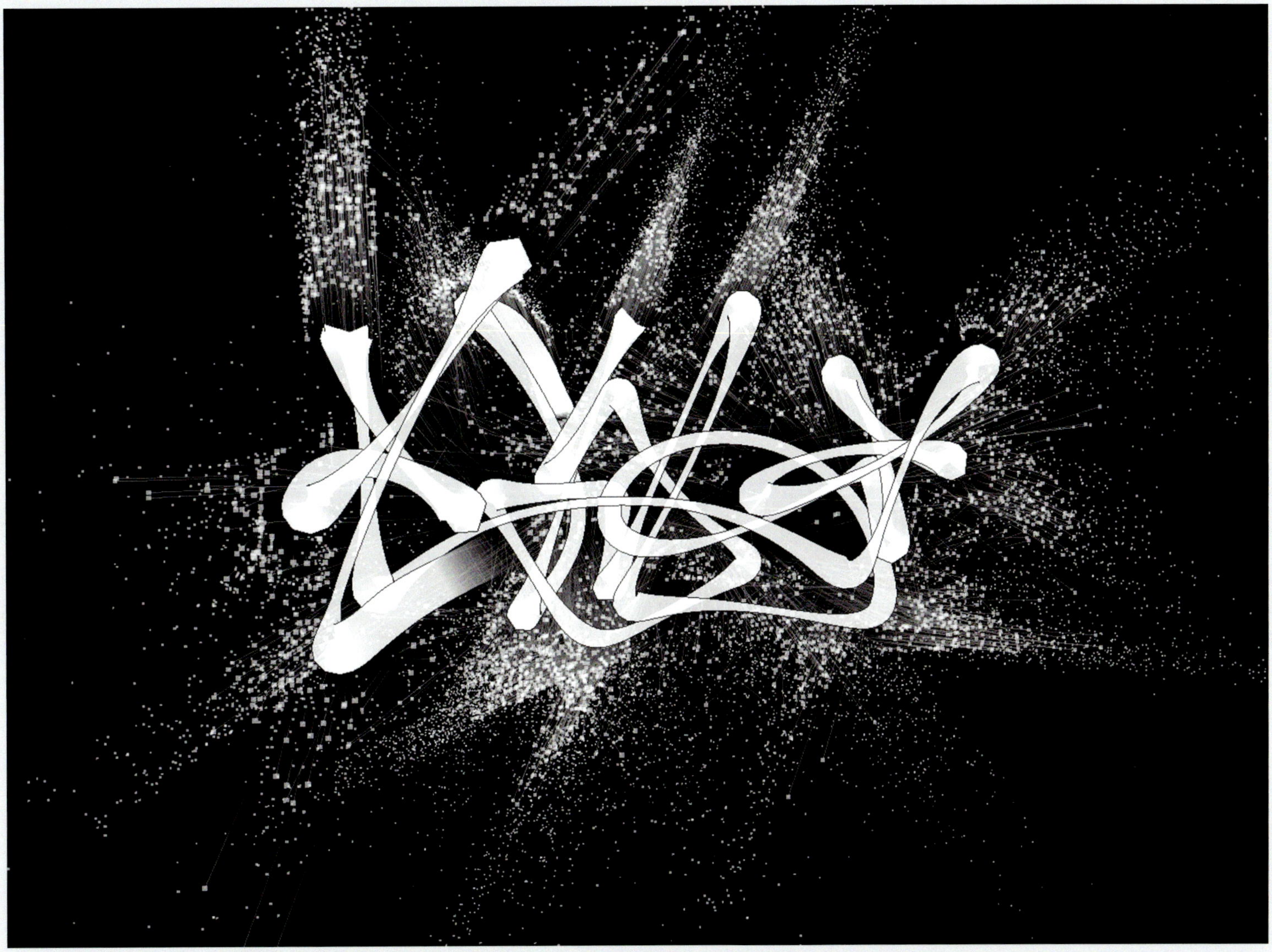

Graffiti Analysis, Paris / Motion-tracked graffiti data and C-print – 60 x 45 cm – 2009

Evol

Born in Heilbronn, Germany, 1972. Lives in Berlin, Germany.

When I do work outside it's always site-specific. I carefully choose the locations I work with, trying to respond to the actual situation and integrate what I find, so that marks (or simple dirt) gains a new perception, and a previously overlooked space or object gets a new meaning. Through rather subtle interventions, I try to create something that's more than the sum of its parts. The same goes for my studio work: the material I work with carries the structures I build on. The only difference in a gallery is that you're free from time constrictions and the audience is already focused.

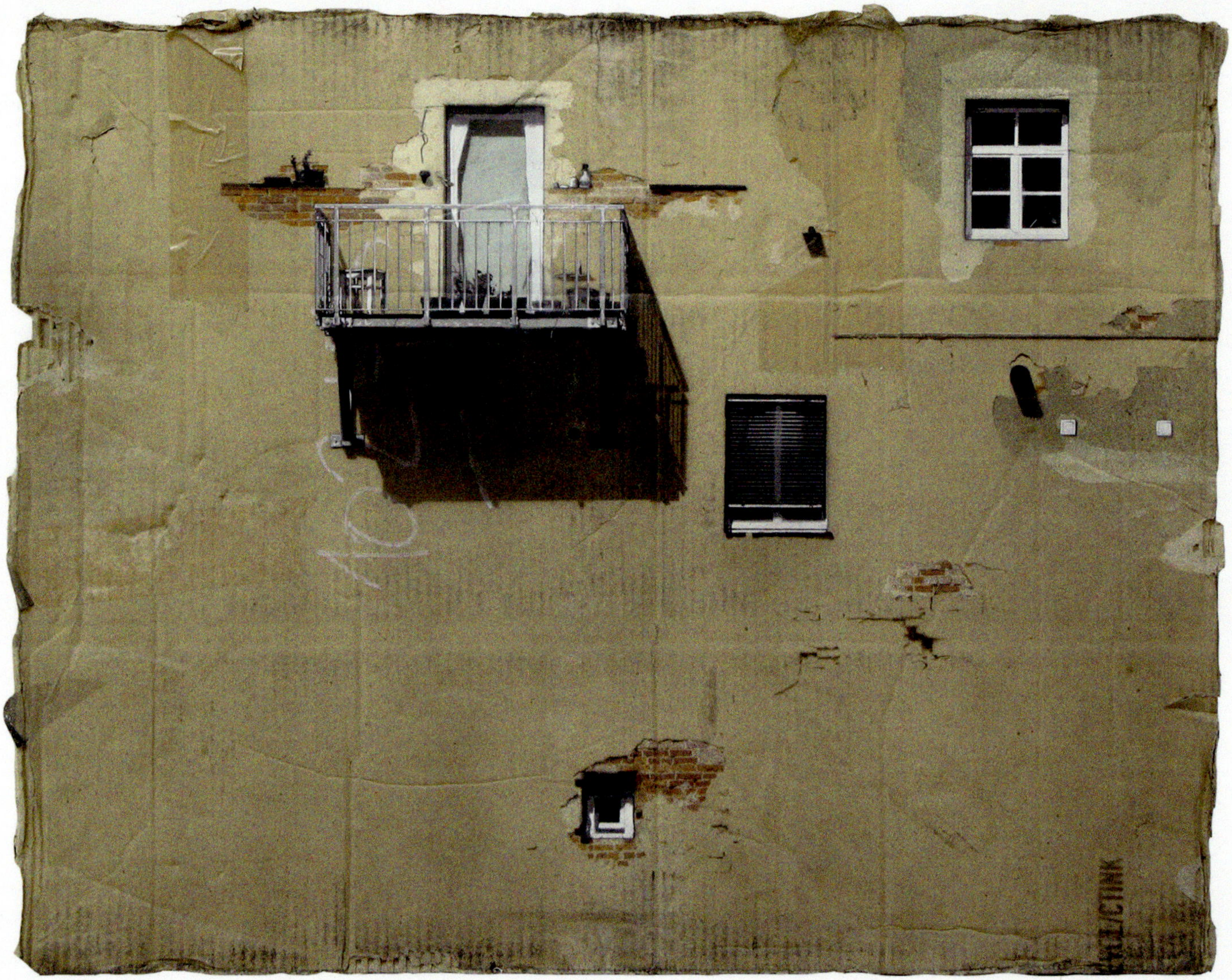

Dresden 09 / Stencil and aerosol on cardboard – 76 x 61 cm – 2010

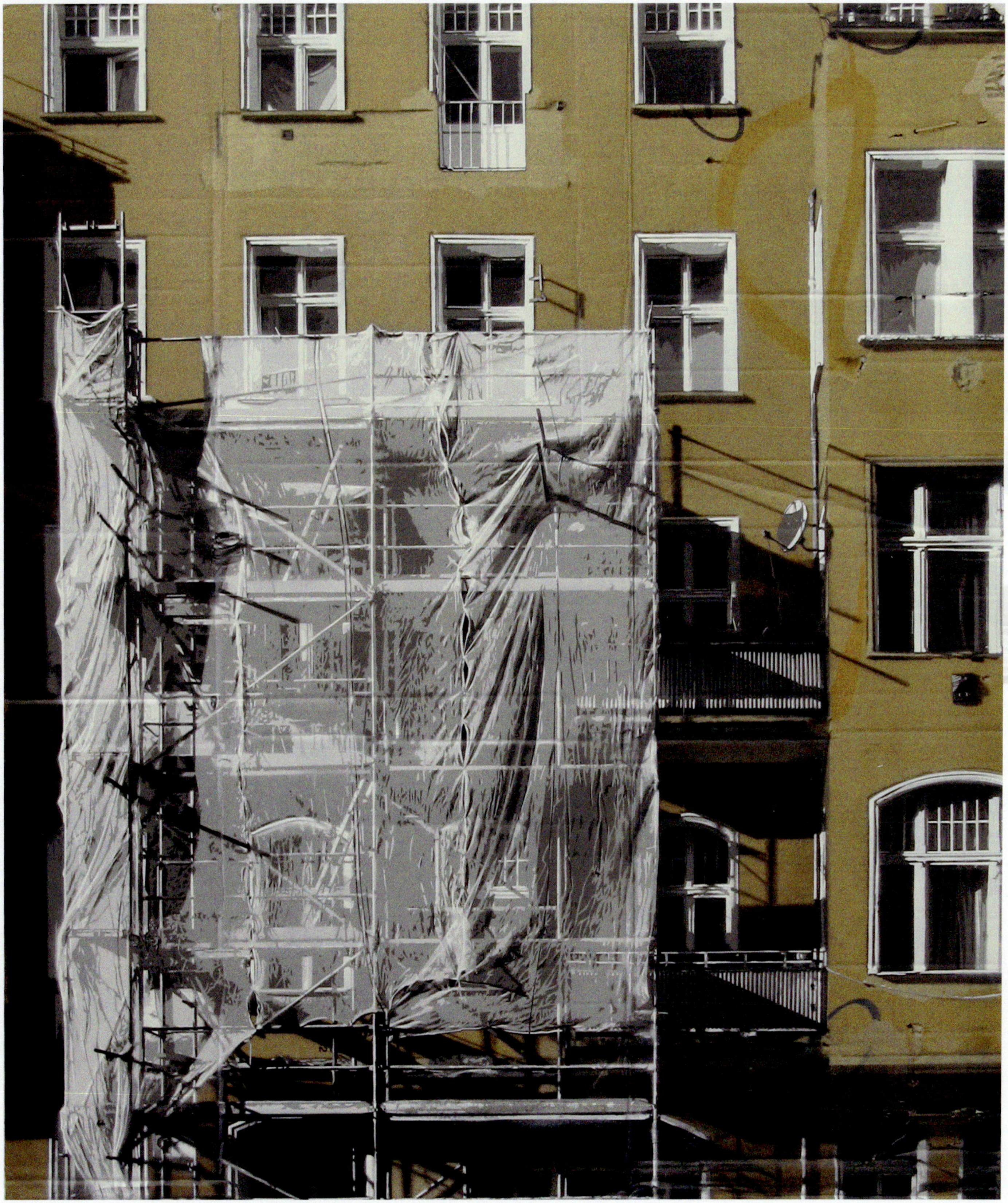

Berlin Shroud / Stencil and aerosol on cardboard – 81 x 98 cm – 2009

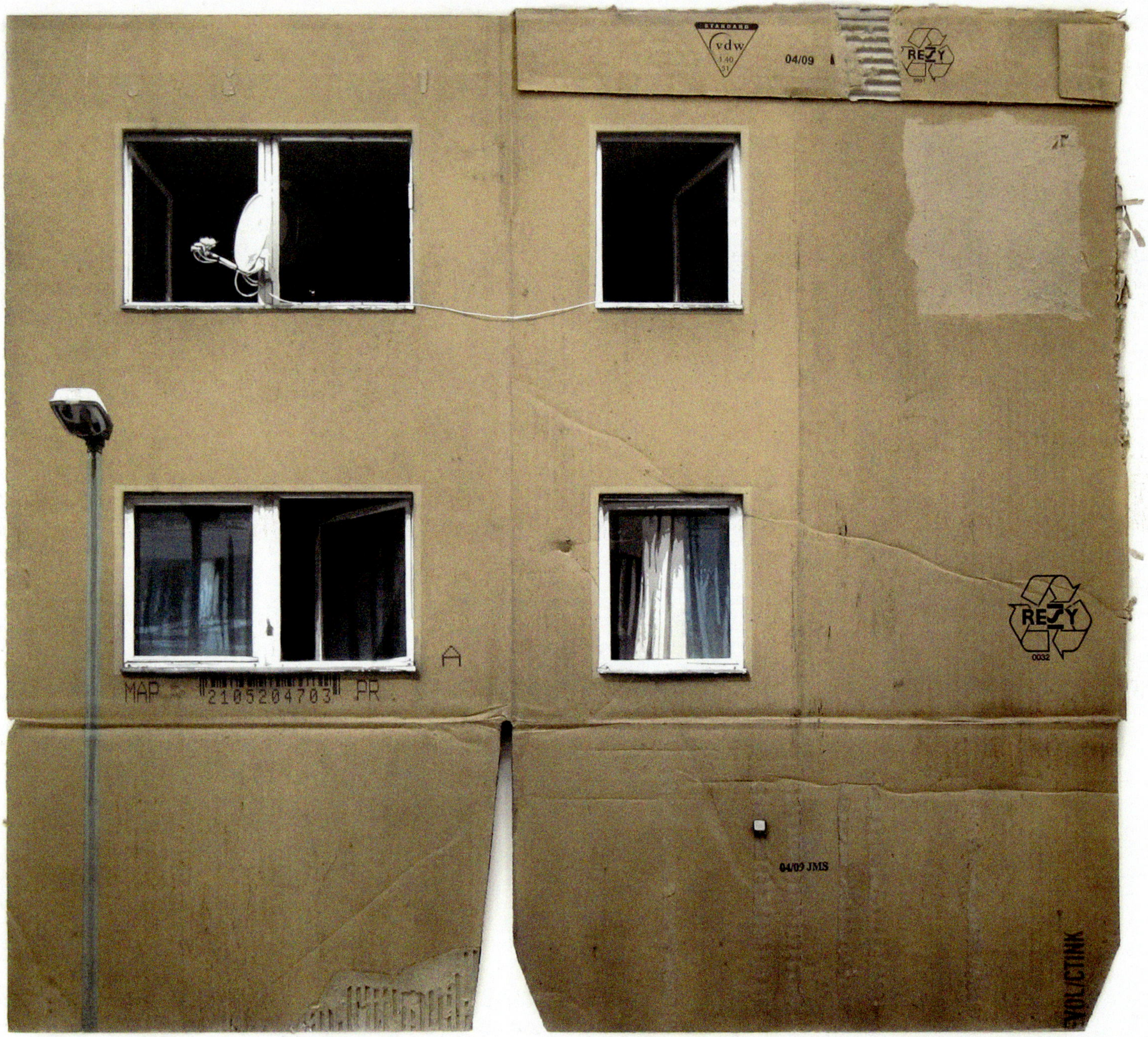

Neighborhood Watch | Stencil and aerosol on cardboard – 80 x 73 cm – 2010

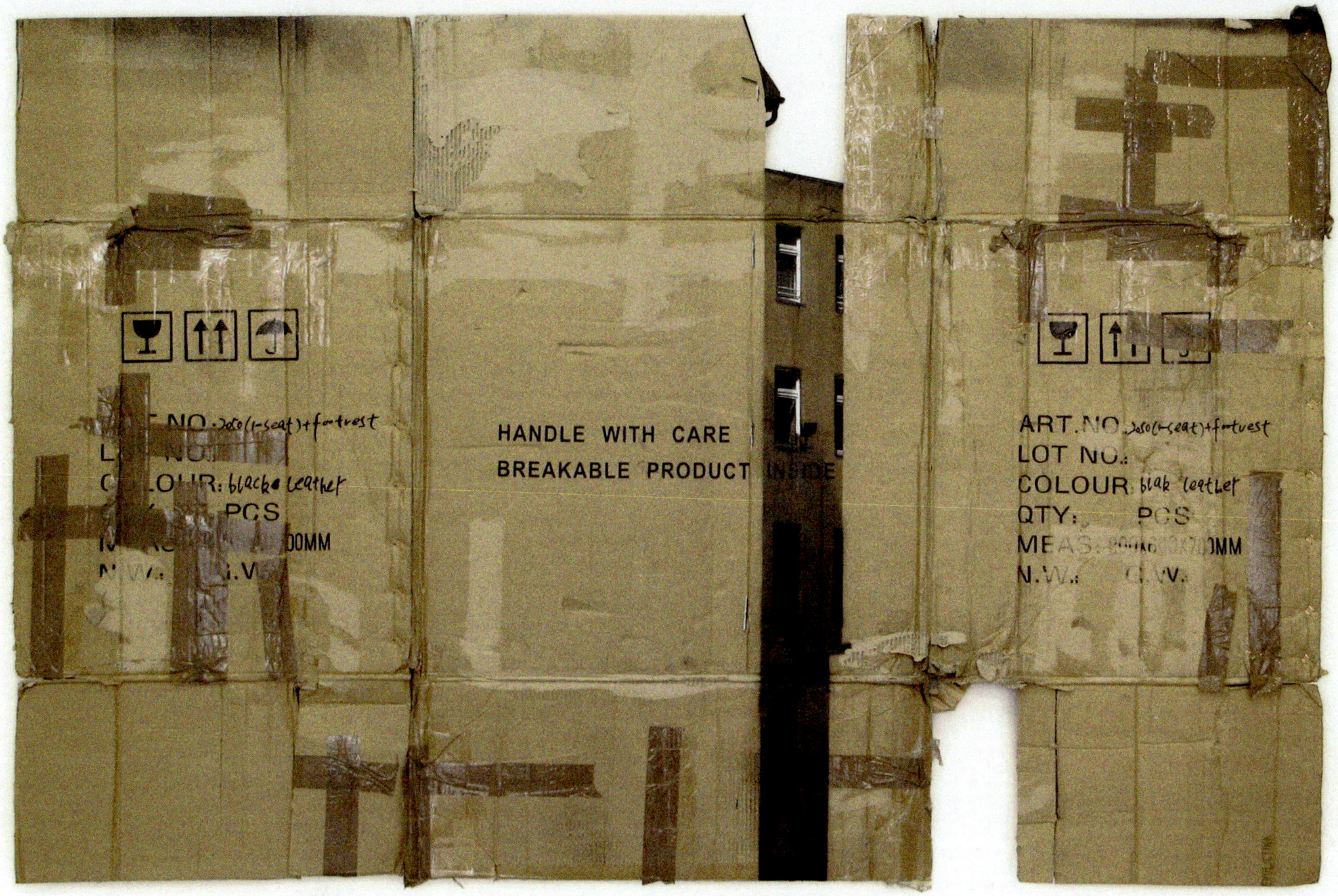

Rauhe Schale (Harter Kern) / Stencil, aerosol, and adhesive tape on cardboard – 208 x 143 cm – 2009

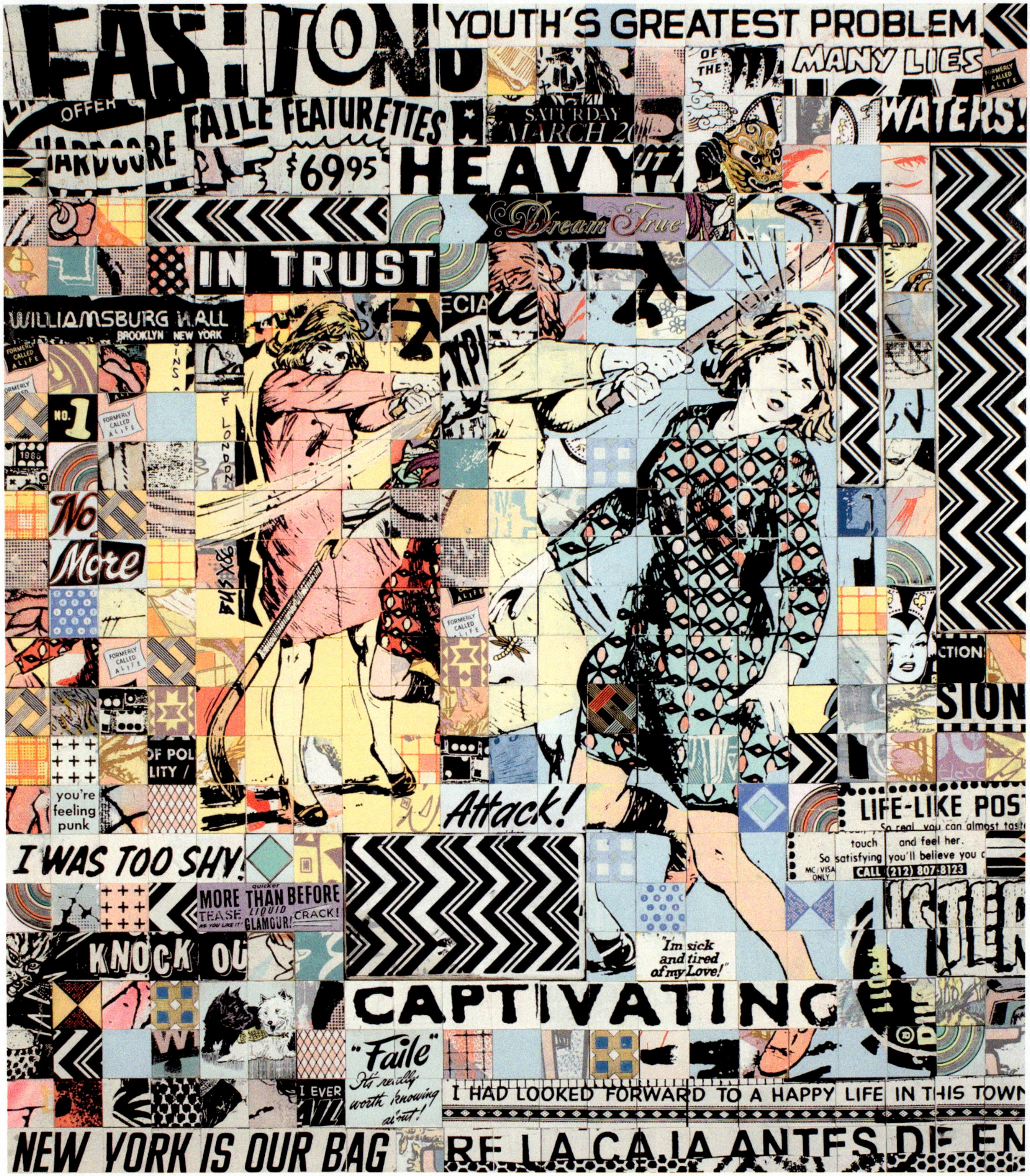

I Was Too Shy / Acrylic and silkscreen on wood in aluminum frame – 108 x 123 x 5 cm – 2010

Faile

Patrick McNeil. Born in Edmonton, United States, 1975. Lives in New York, United States.
Patrick Miller. Born in Minneapolis, United States, 1976. Lives in New York, United States.

Much of our work deals with deconstructing images and the serendipitous layering that occurs through time. It's very akin to the visual tapestry of New York City. There are bits and pieces that you associate with, relate to, and come to know. All these little elements help define Faile. It's something that has a time and a place, it's like a character in a story that is slowly unfolding.

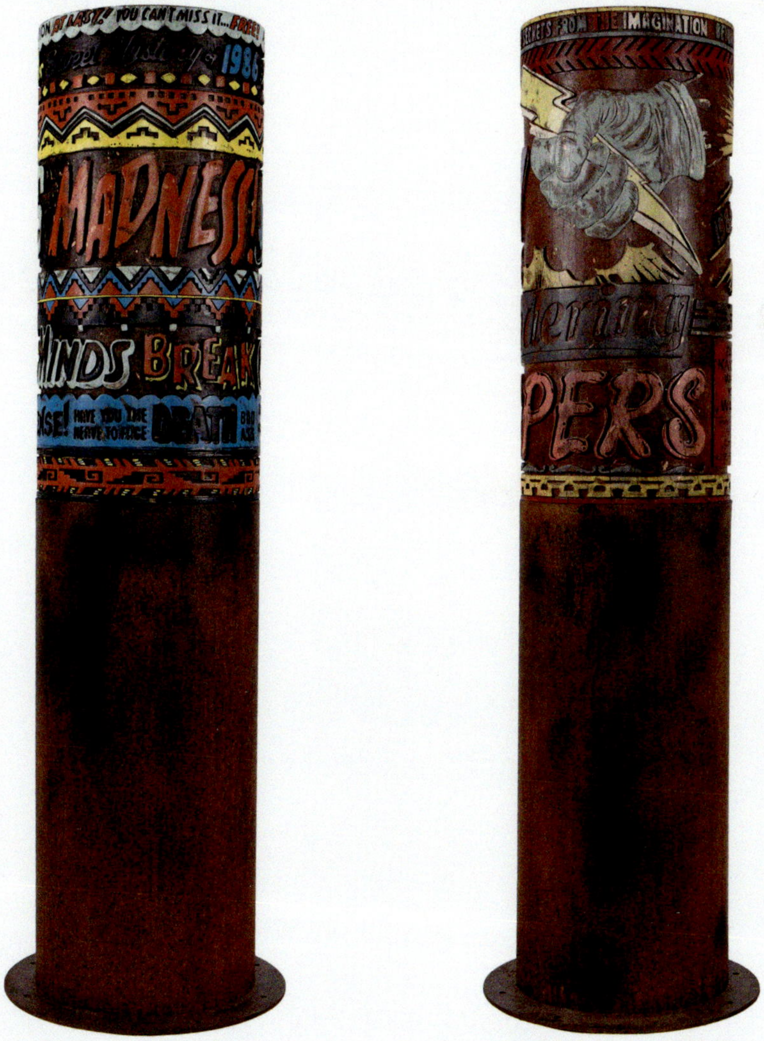

Journey on the Wings of Madness - Walk With Lightning in Hand
Acrylic on hand-carved sandalwood, mounted and rotates on steel base – 35 x 150 cm – 2008

Faith 47

Born in Cape Town, South Africa, 1979. Lives in Cape Town, South Africa.

I empty my being through parables on rusted, lost metal doors. I'm not sure if the inspiration bleeds from my studio nights into my street days, or if the inspiration floods from my street experiences and into my studio cocoon. Which is better... or if it matters. But I know that our minds are complex, our hearts so dark and immense. That the images around us are able to destroy language and borders, overcoming distance and finding stories without words... permeating our ambitions for love.

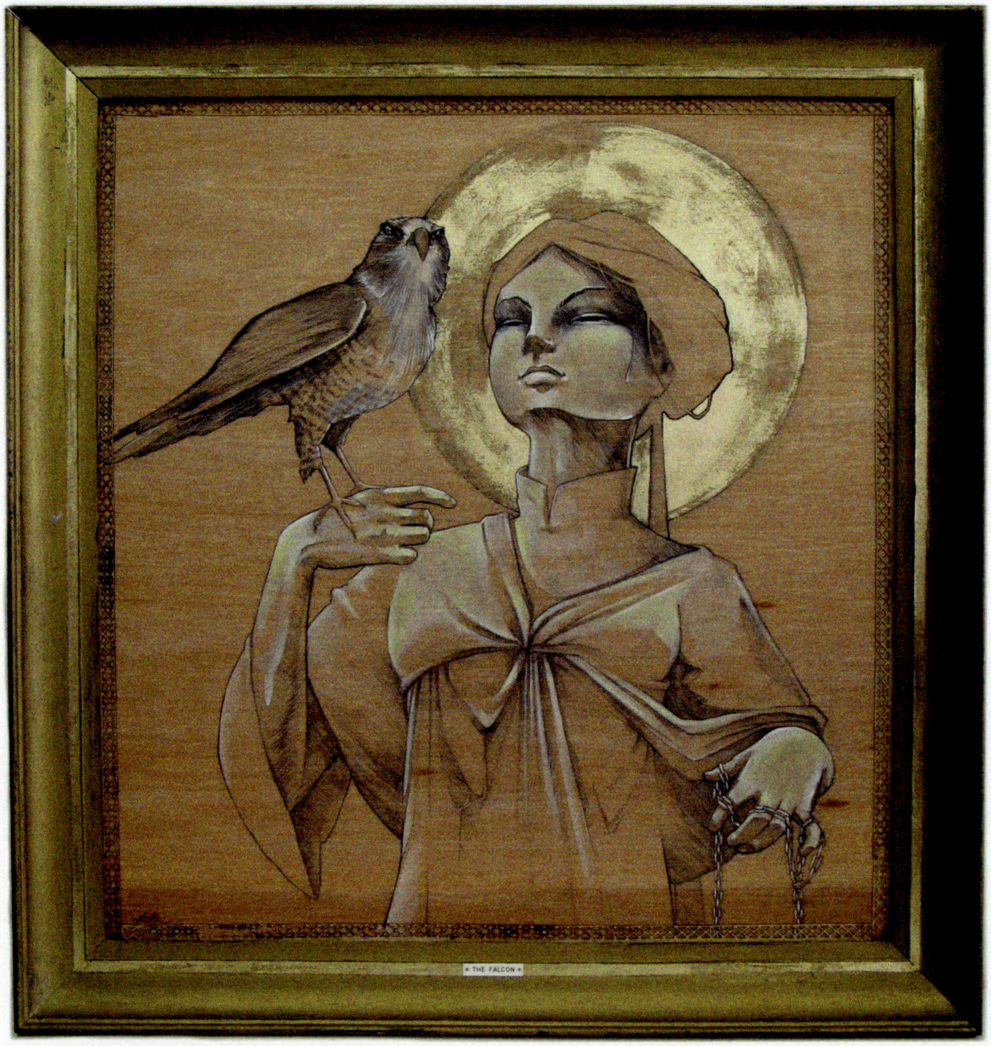

Fortuna / Oil, graphite, and gold leaf on wood with engraved veneer border – 72 x 76 cm – 2010

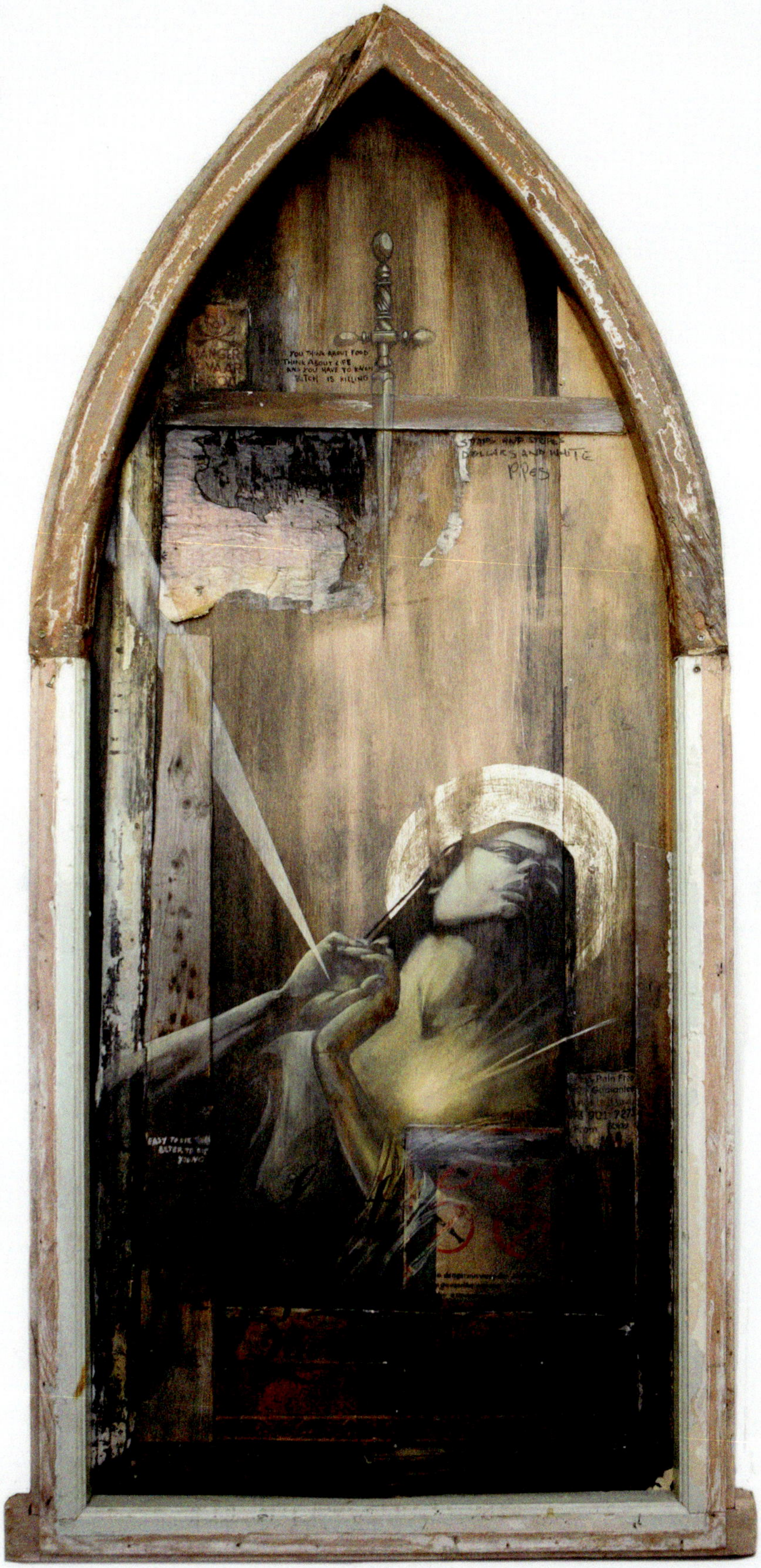

La Mierda que Tenemos que Atravesar Nadando / Oil, graphite, gold leaf, and aerosol on wood – 87 x 200 cm – 2011

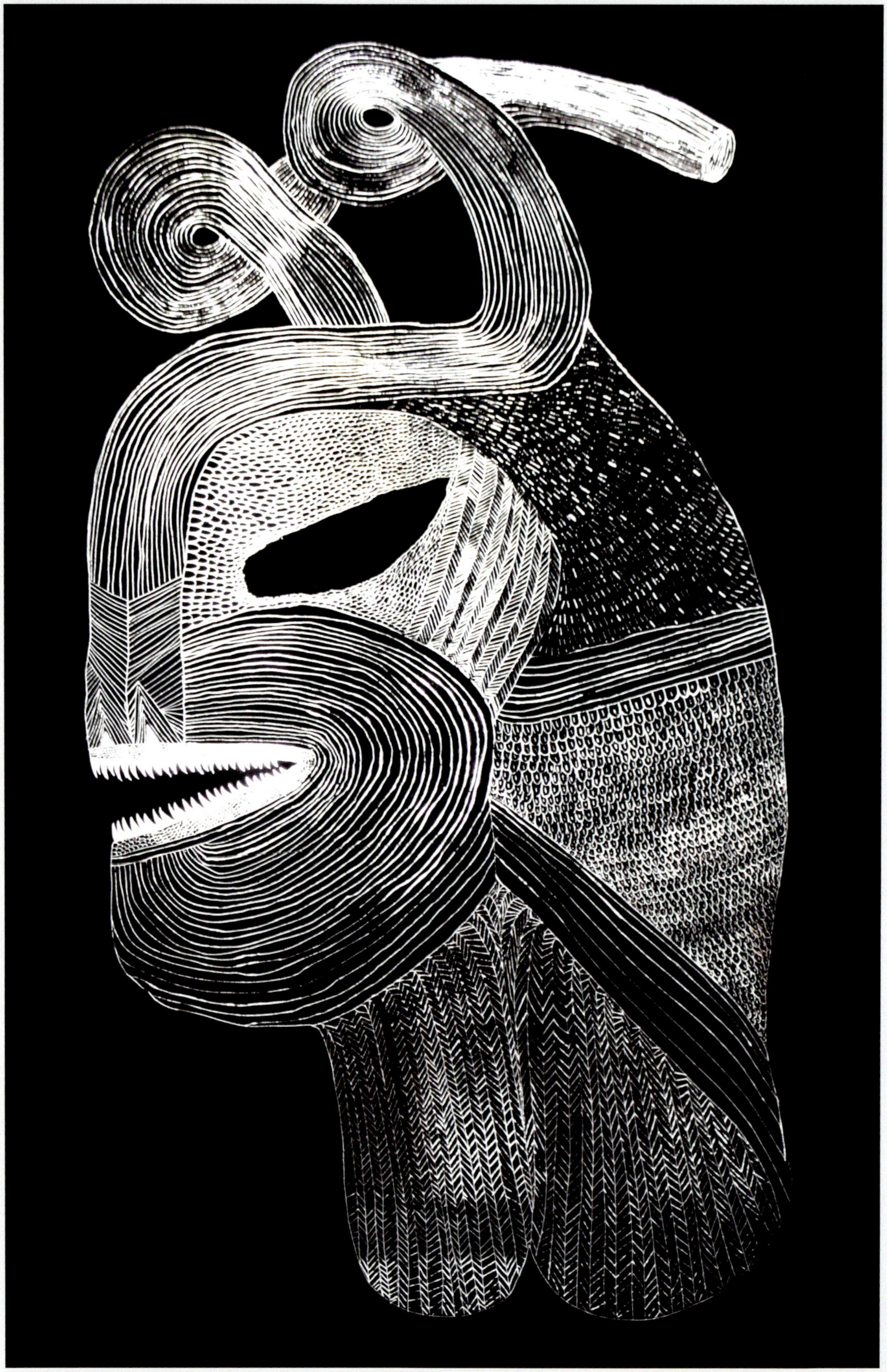

Curves / Scratch on Plexiglas – 120 x 150 cm – 2009

Fefe Talavera

Born in São Paulo, Brazil, 1979. Lives in São Paulo, Brazil.

It is very different to work on the street than in a studio. The street gives you free space, but you are vulnerable for something to happen, it can be with the police or with the same people who go through there. While working in a studio I have more time, less chance of being vulnerable and I take things from the streets to work within the studio. Both spaces are satisfactory, each with its own personality, but I personally take advantage of working in the studio for the pure reason of feeling safer.

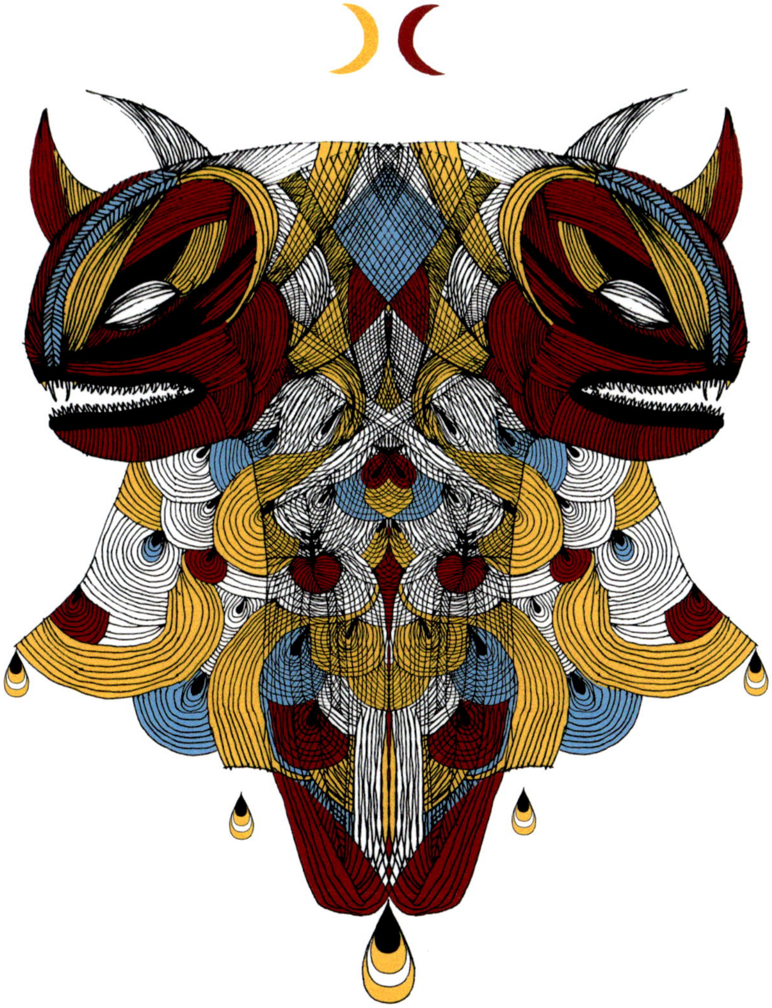

Femme Fatale / Pen on paper – 30 x 45 cm – 2009

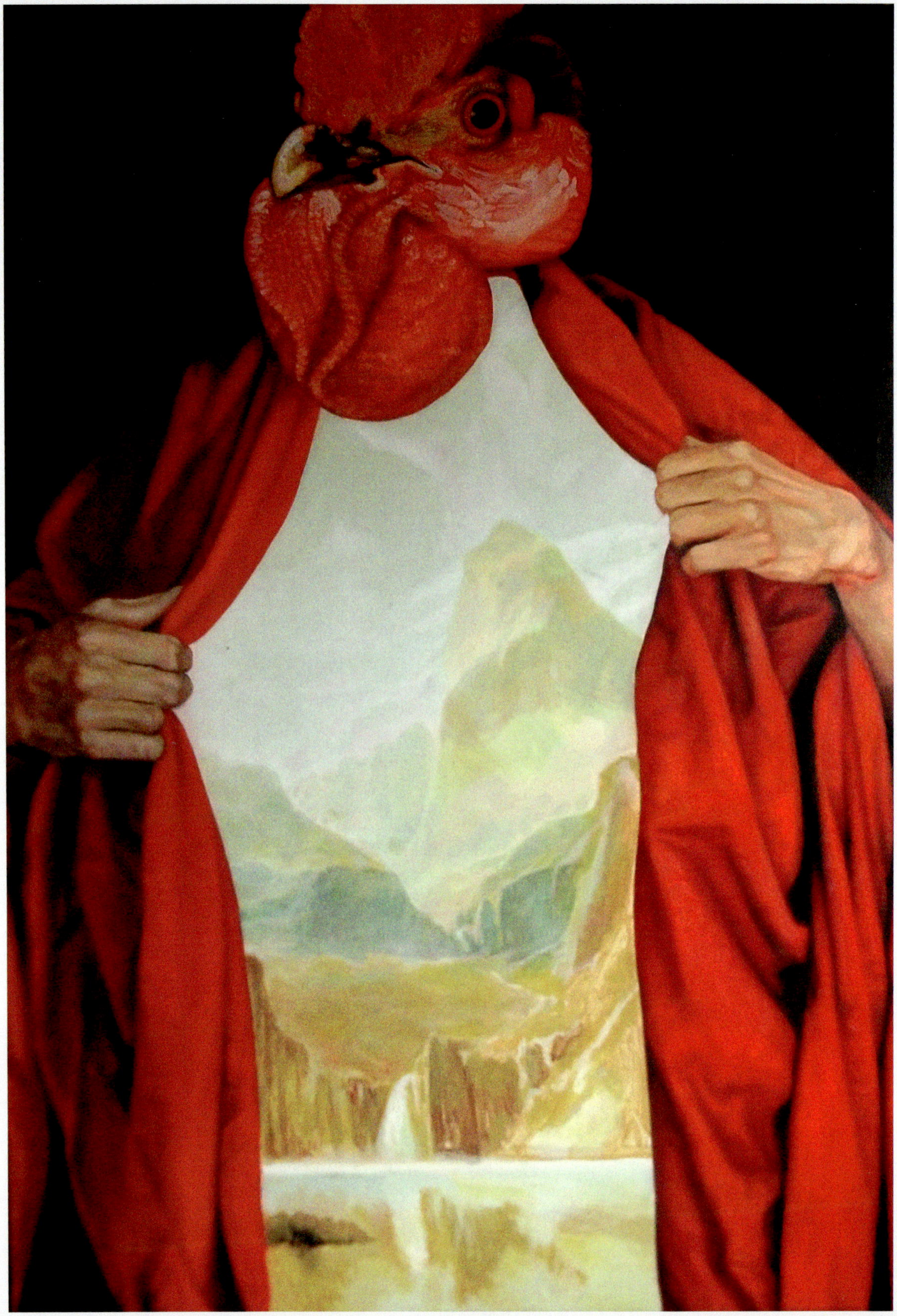

Untitled (Bierstadt) / Oil on canvas – 183 x 244 cm – 2011

Gaia

Born in New York, United States, 1988. Lives in Baltimore, United States.

The streets exist as an extension of the studio and a realm of experimentation that is unhindered by anything but the law. Inside and Outside are not opposed forces, but rather are personally experienced as different media. The work in the public sphere is poetry in the everyday, a strange experience that becomes familiar on the walk home to school every evening. The posterity provided by the institutions of galleries and museums is the opportunity to apply all that is learned from my various adventures and accidents into a clear, unsullied thesis.

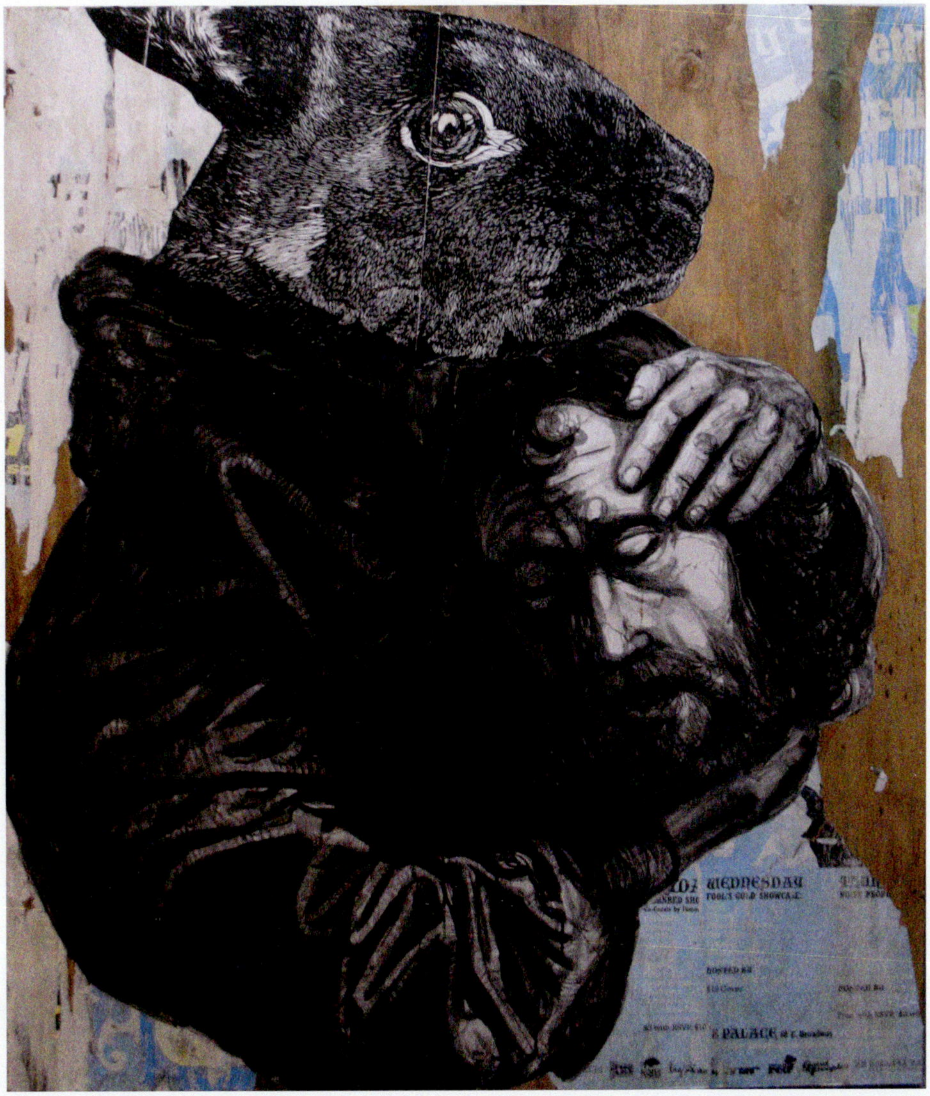

Rabbit Holding the Head of St. John (Caravaggio) | Acrylic and block print on decollaged wood – 107 x 107 cm – 2010

George Morton-Clark

Born in London, England, 1982. Lives in London, England.

Society has evolved a paranoid state of mind because of our ever-tightening freedoms. I see the world as a colliding of consciousness, made violent by its increasing extremes. We are becoming more suffocated in our day-to-day lives by marketing, religious views, and bureaucracy. I use my work to explore the effects of these pressures on each other and ourselves.

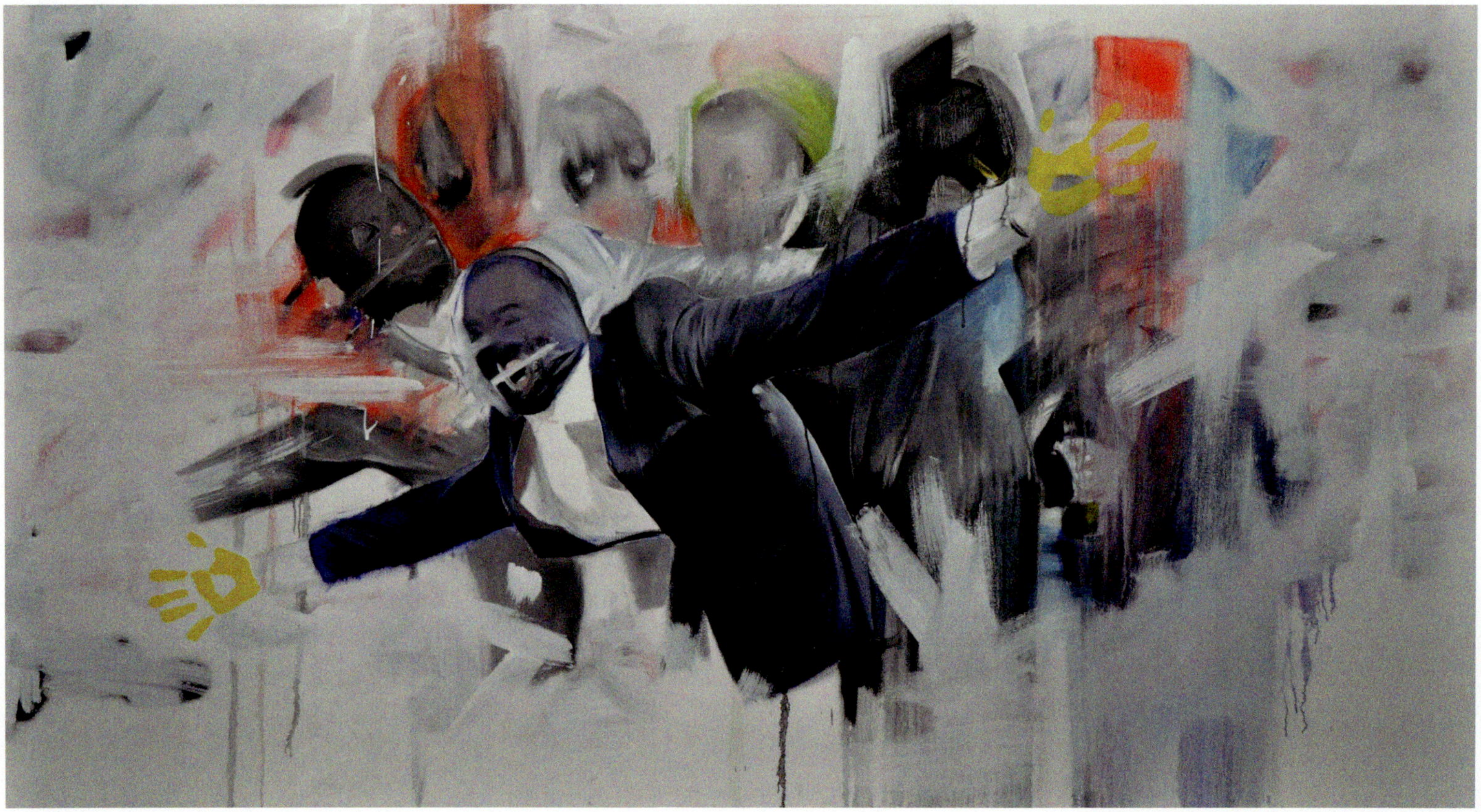

Heroes and Villains / Oil on canvas – 213 cm x 91 cm – 2009

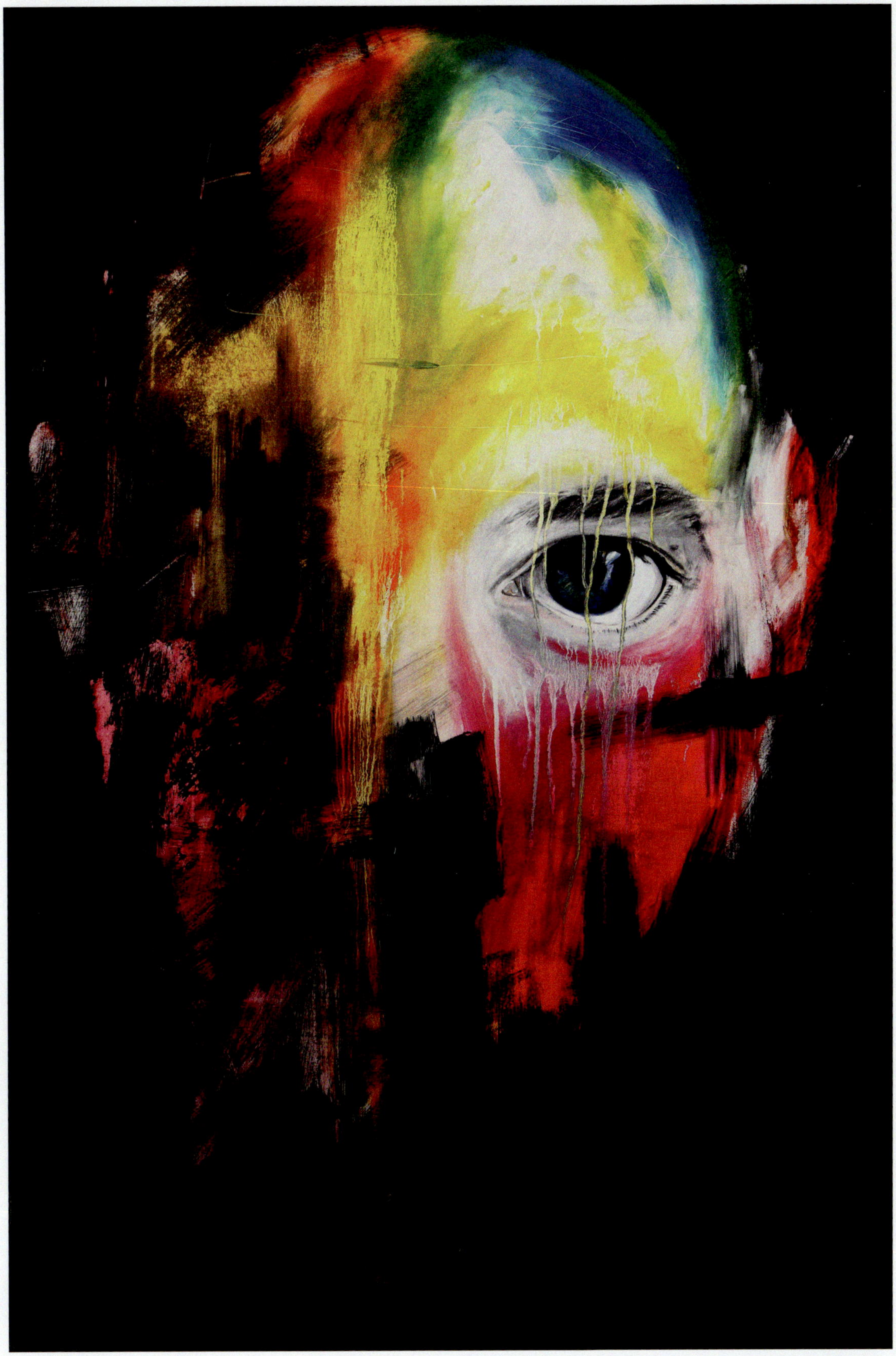

Holi / Oil on wood – 80 x 120 cm – 2010

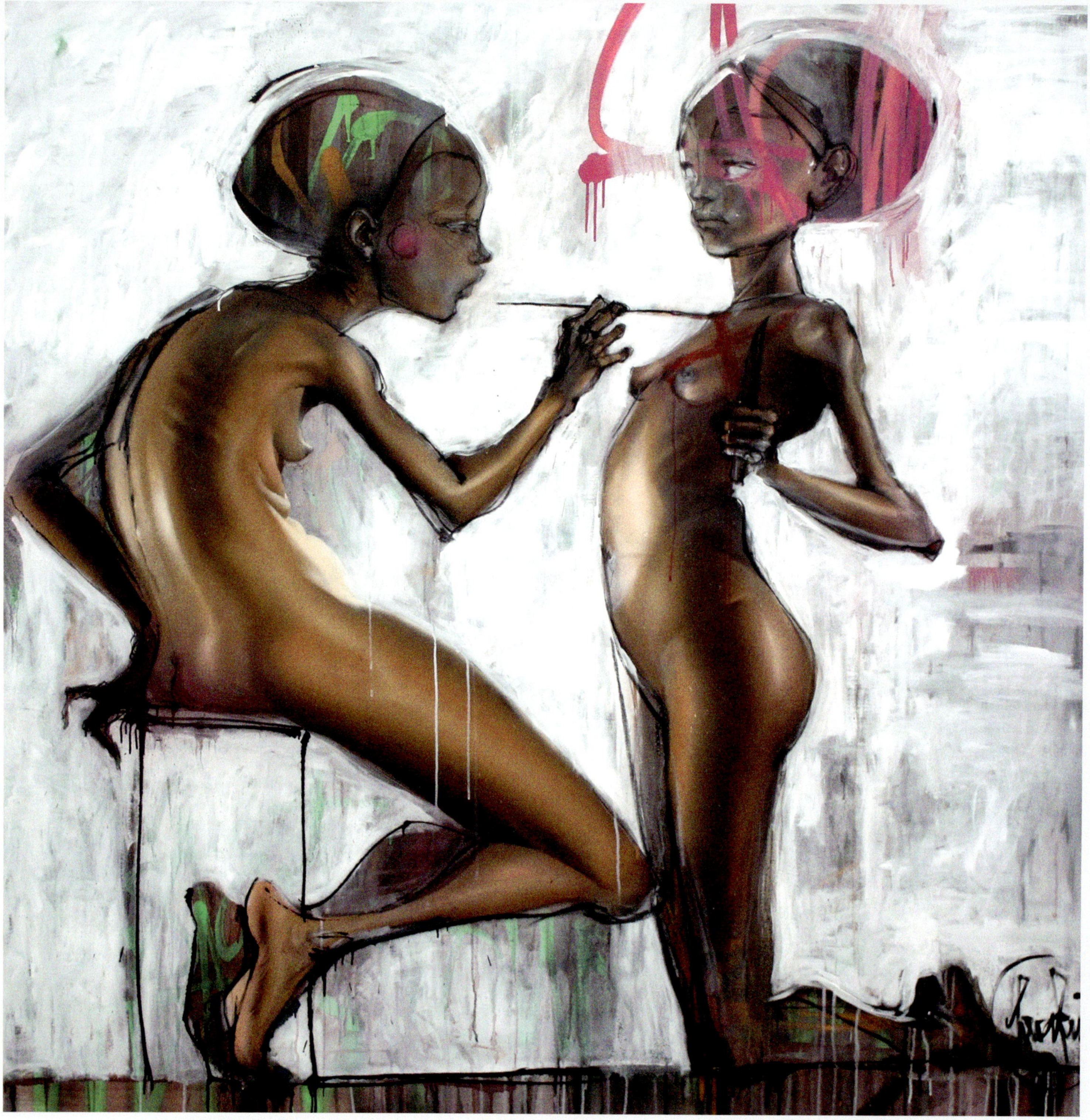

Seek & Destroy | Aerosol, acrylic, and charcoal on canvas – 180 x 180 cm – 2010

Herakut

Hera. Born in Frankfurt, Germany, 1981. Lives in Munich and Heidelberg, Germany.
Akut. Born in Schmalkalden, Germany, 1977. Lives in Munich and Heidelberg, Germany.

Our work is a reflection of our life. A documentation of anything happening in- and outside of our minds. It's a collage without technical boundaries. The only limits to what we do are our own morals. You have responsibility for what you throw at the world. Having somebody's attention for a minute is an honor and a challenge. That's what the streets have taught us.

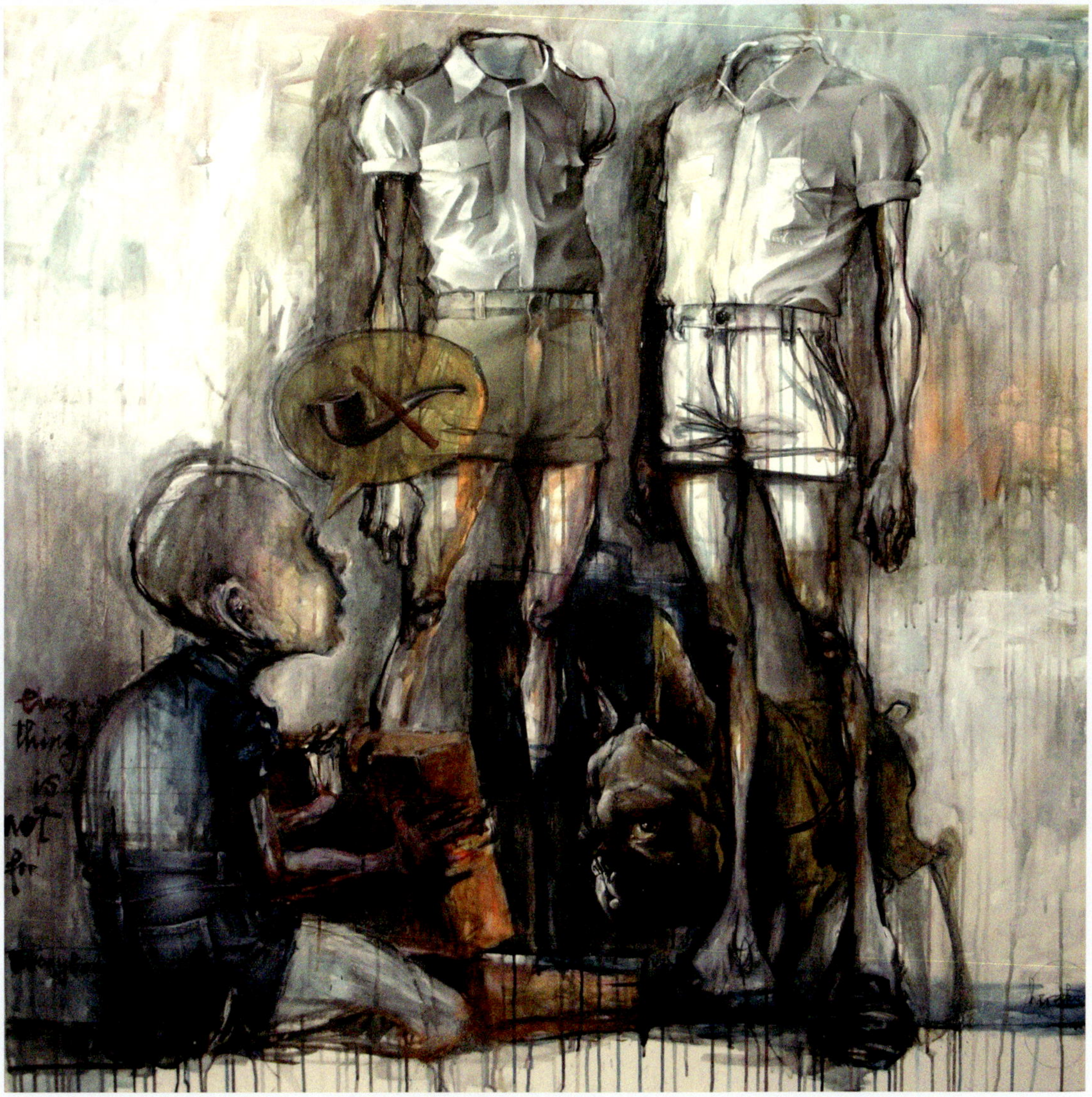

Everything Aint for Everybody / Aerosol, acrylic, and charcoal on canvas – 120 x 120 cm – 2011

Herbert Baglione

Born in São Paulo, Brazil, 1977. Lives in São Paulo, Brazil.

The work I do today is the sum of all my previous experiences, be it punk, Christianity, or the day when I was hospitalized or the dream I had last night, all these are registered inside me and are manifested unconsciously in my work.

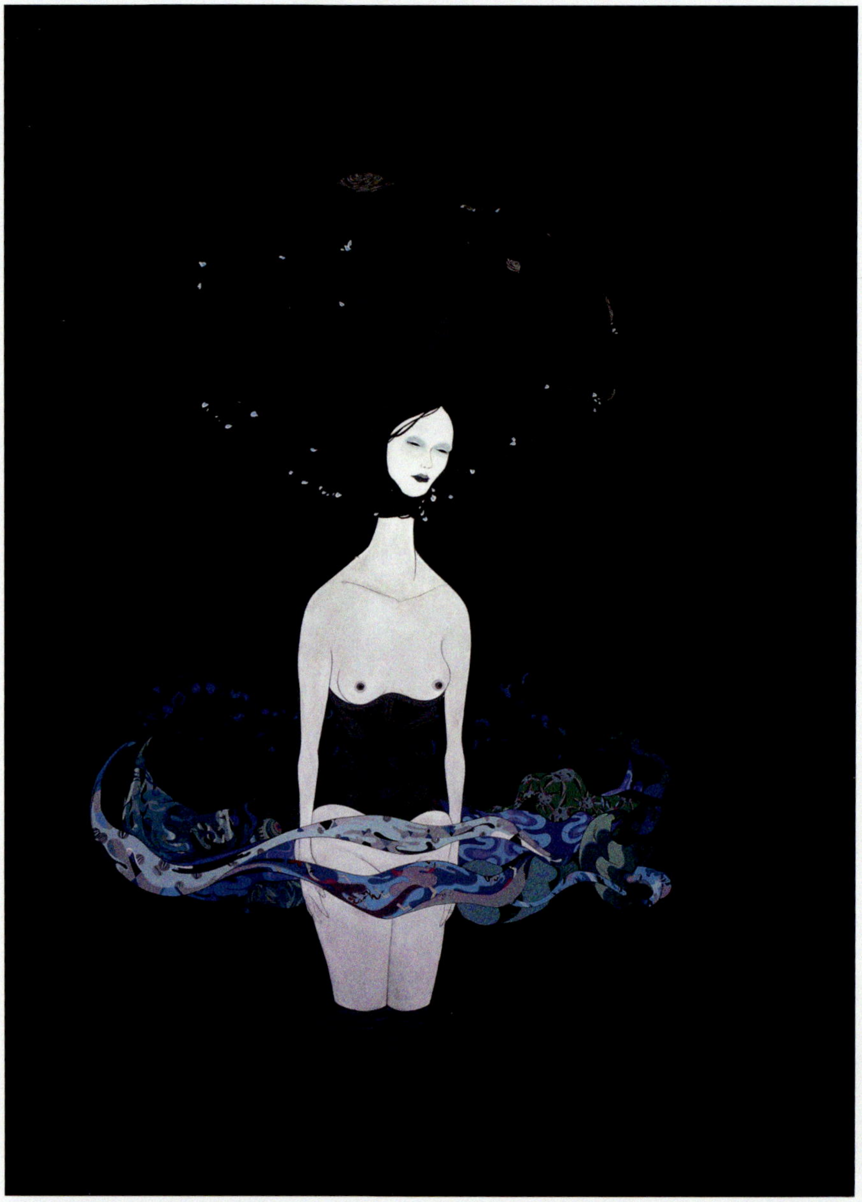

Quando os Barriletes se Vão, a Alma Descansas | Acrylic on canvas – 120 x 200 cm – 2010

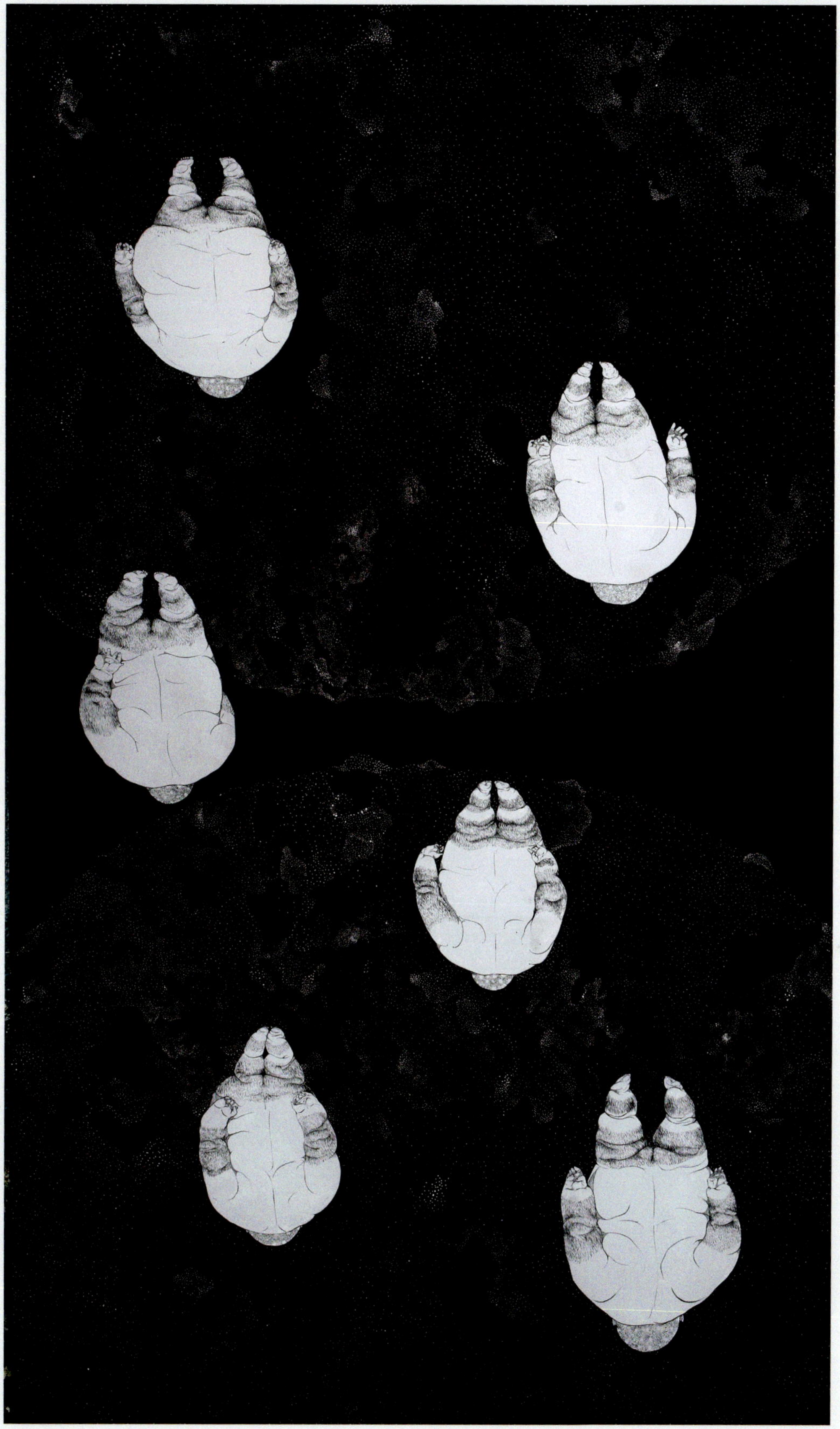

New - Cults / Acrylic on canvas – 120 x 200 cm – 2008

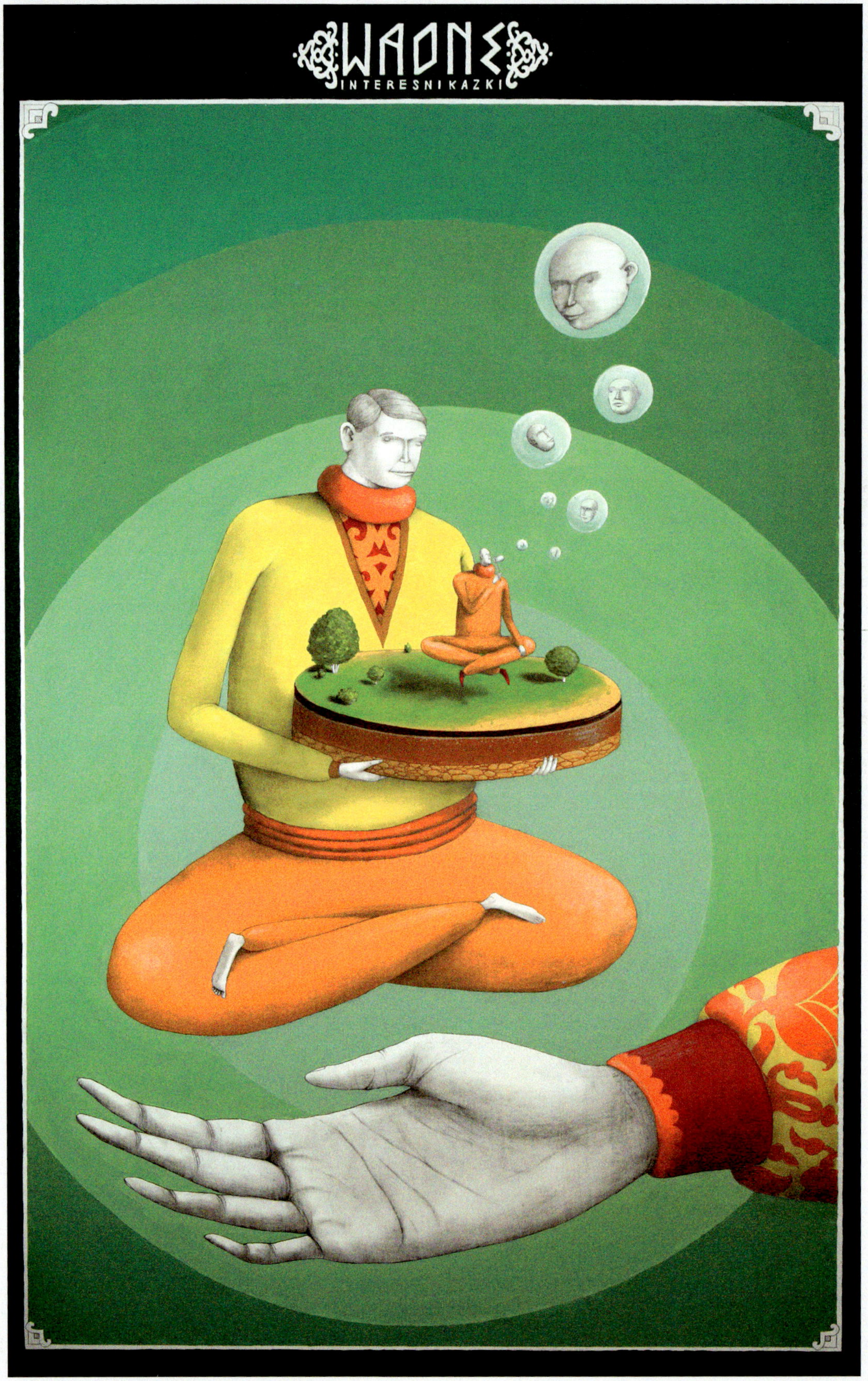

Hierarchy / *Parampara* / Acrylic and pencil on canvas – 62 x 100 cm – 2009

Interesni Kazki

Aleksei Bordusov aka Aec. Born in Kiev, Ukraine, 1980. Lives in Kiev, Ukraine.
VolodymyrManzhos aka Waone. Born in Bogdanovka, Ukraine, 1981. Lives in Kiev, Ukraine.

We found the language of symbols and colors with which we communicate with the audience. At the beginning, we started making canvases only as sketches for the murals. Then this turned into a more serious and profound thing for us. From the beginnig of our art, the connection between our work on the streets and in the studio was direct, a situation that we keep the same. While most of the time we create murals together, we prefer to work on canvases separately.

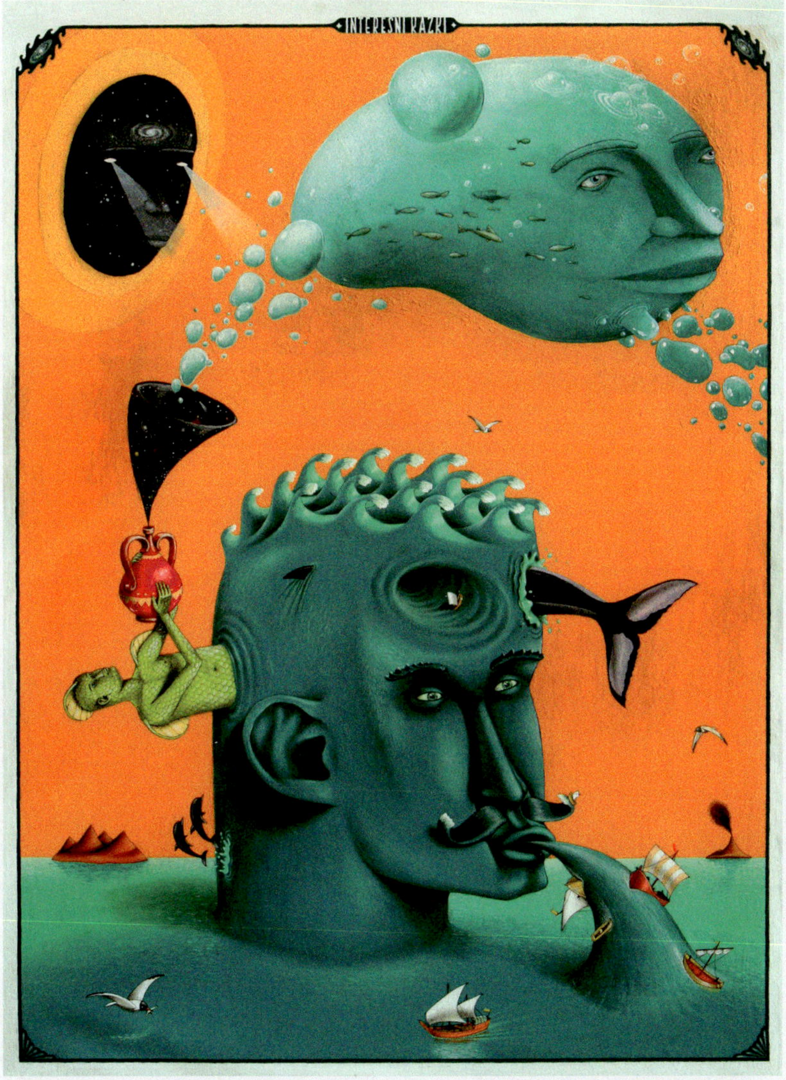

Elemental | Acrylic and pencil on canvas – 50 x 70 cm – 2009

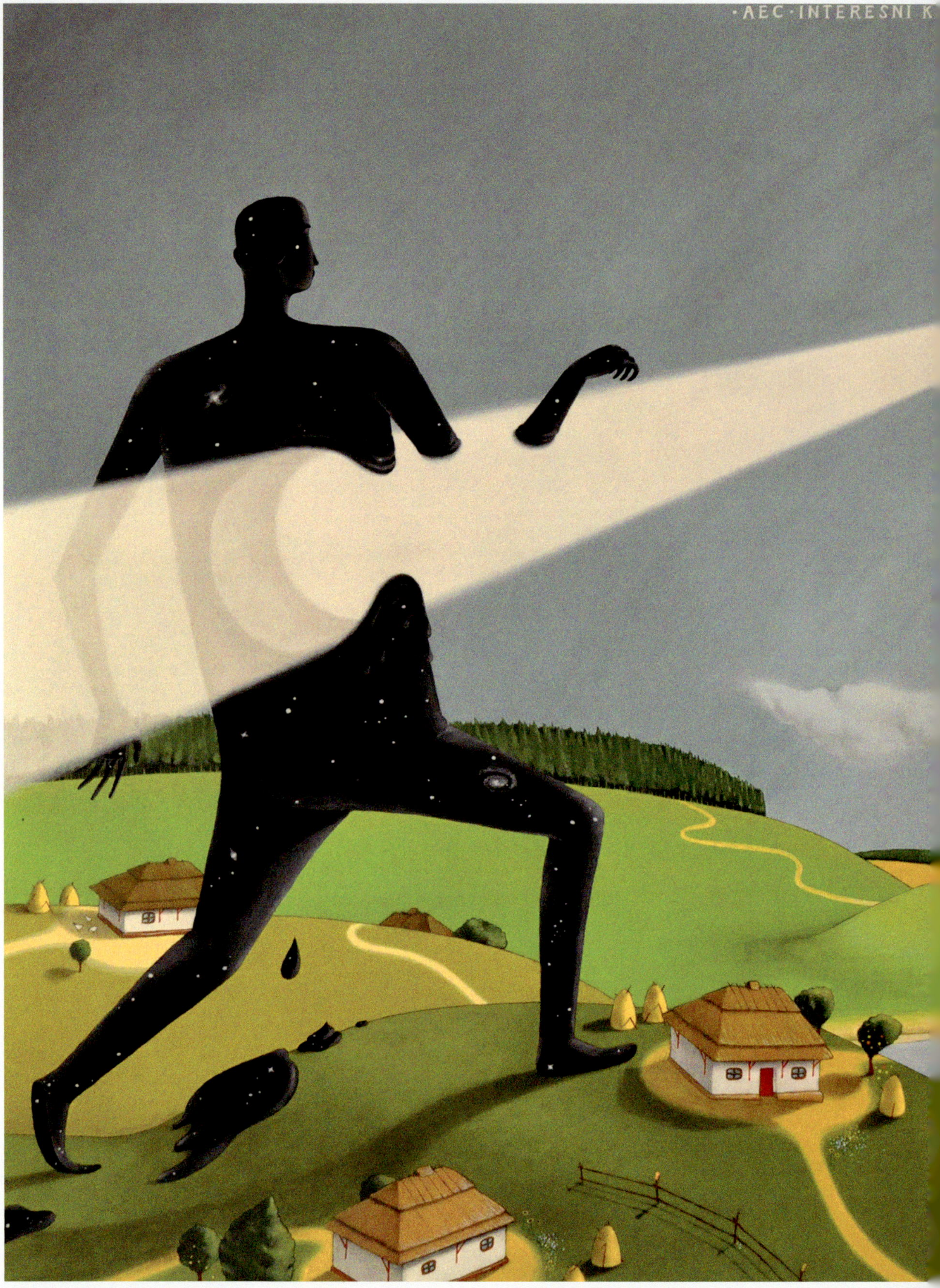

Sunrise / Acrylic and pencil on canvas – 80 x 60 cm – 2011

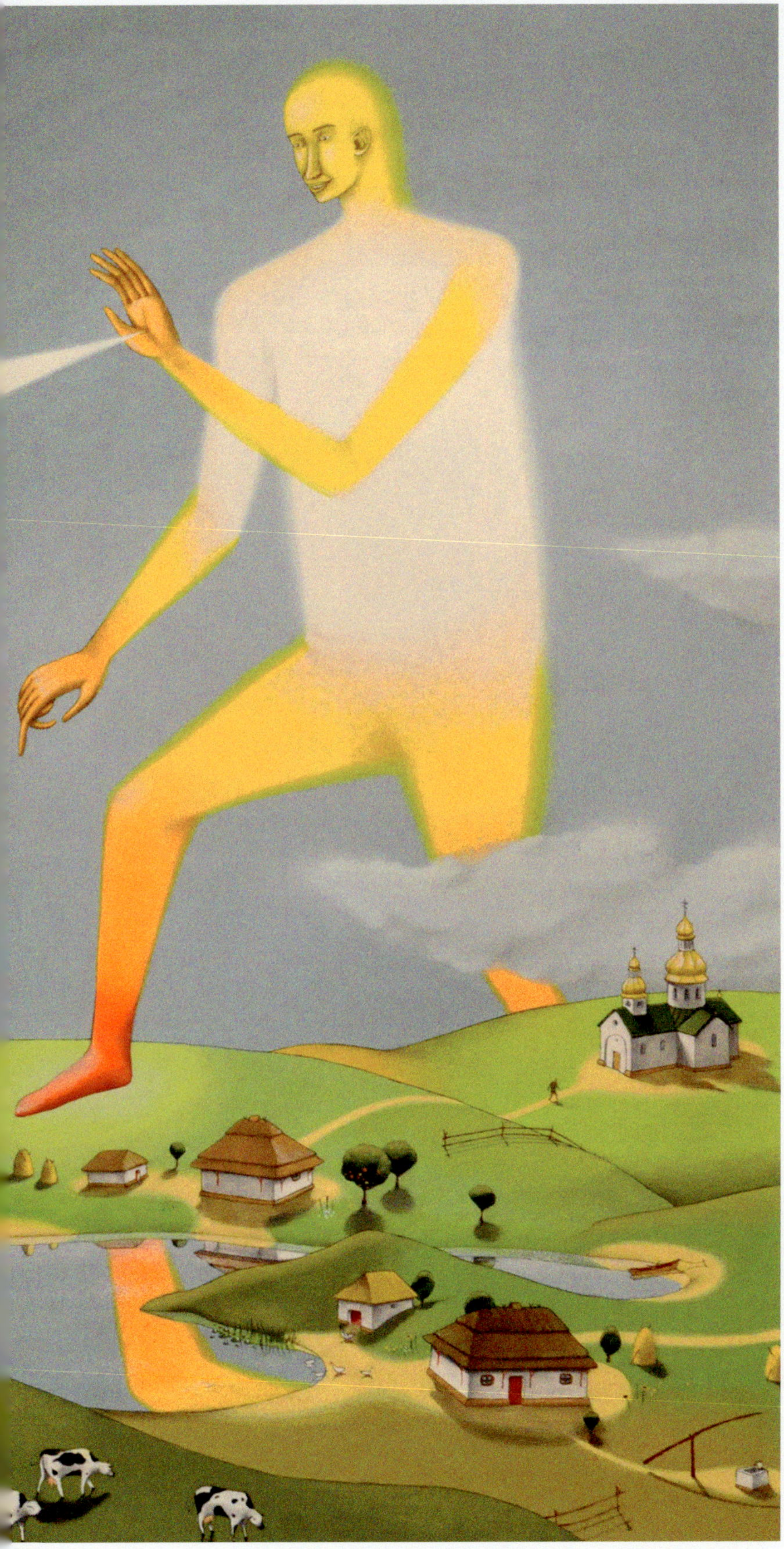

Jaybo

Born in Paris, France, 1963. Lives in Berlin, Germany.

I left home when I was 14. I travel along the street, I had my first kiss in the street, my first fight, my first luck, my first pain and sorrow, I used to make friends in the street and enemies as well. It's in the street that I learned freedom. Now I paint about this freedom which is going to go away more and more as kids are afraid of confrontation and prefer to glue their eyes on their own Playstation brain masturbation. Street made me what I am now, to not be afraid of freedom. Paint is just a hobby. Don't call me an artist, please.

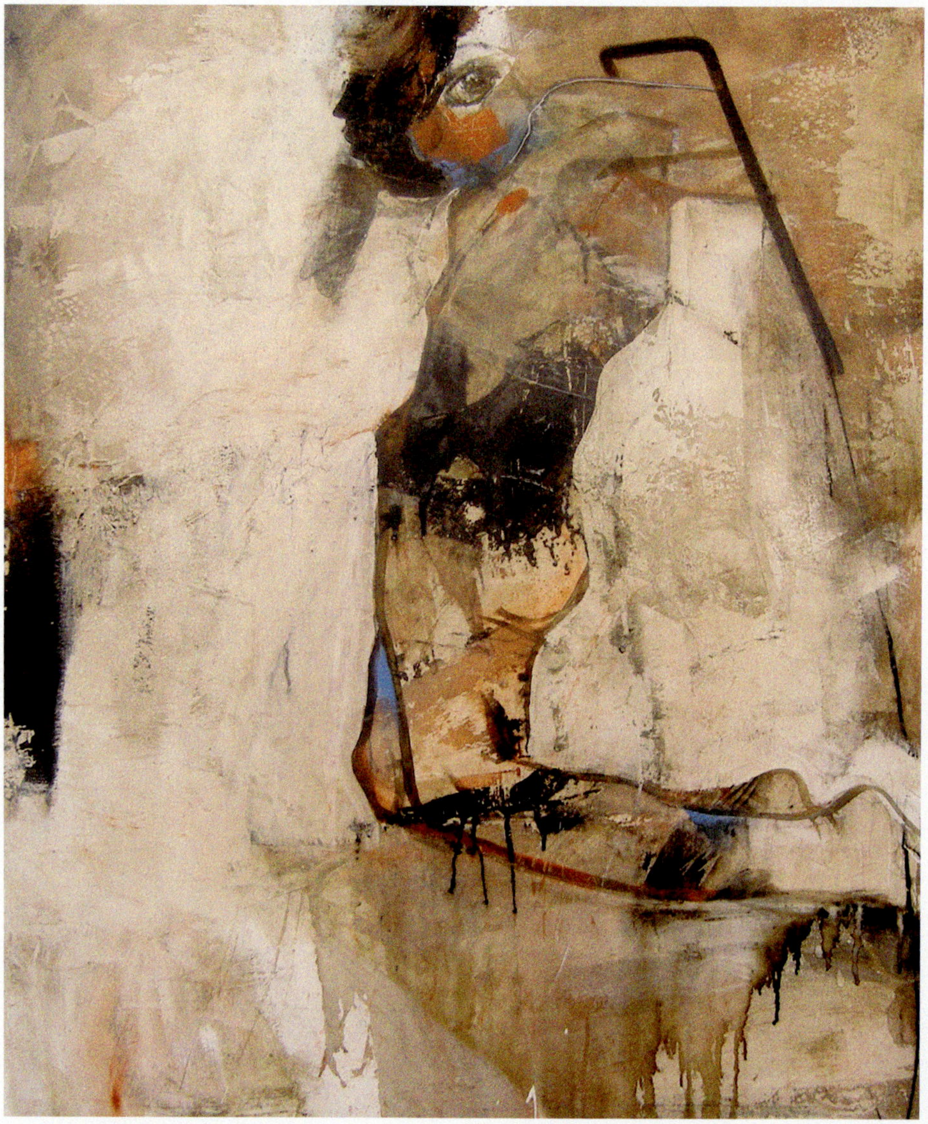

Mr. Nobody is a Painter / Aerosol and bitumen on canvas – 100 x 120 x 4 cm – 2010

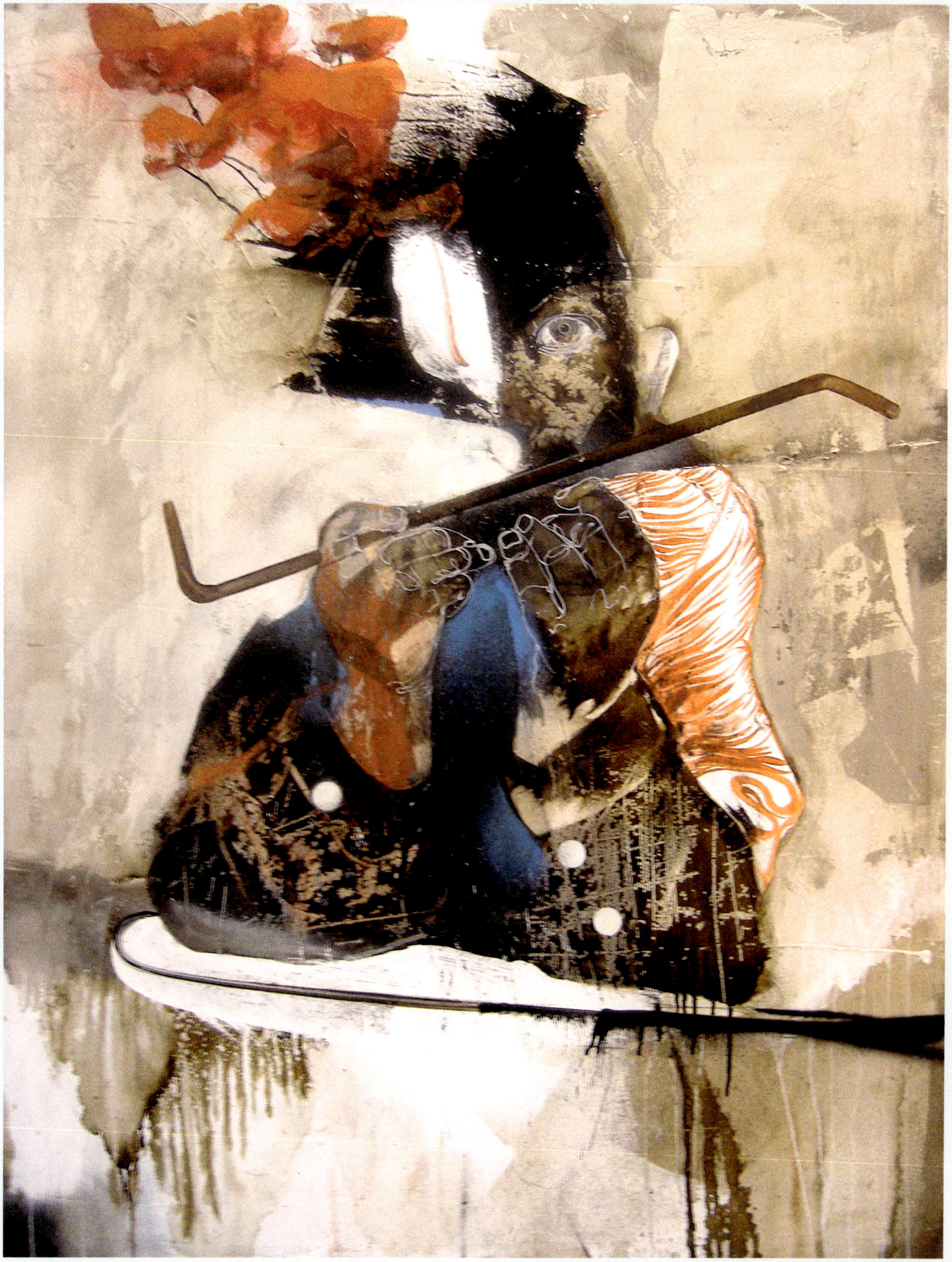

Le Flutiste / Aerosol and bitumen on canvas – 90 x 121 x 5 cm – 2010

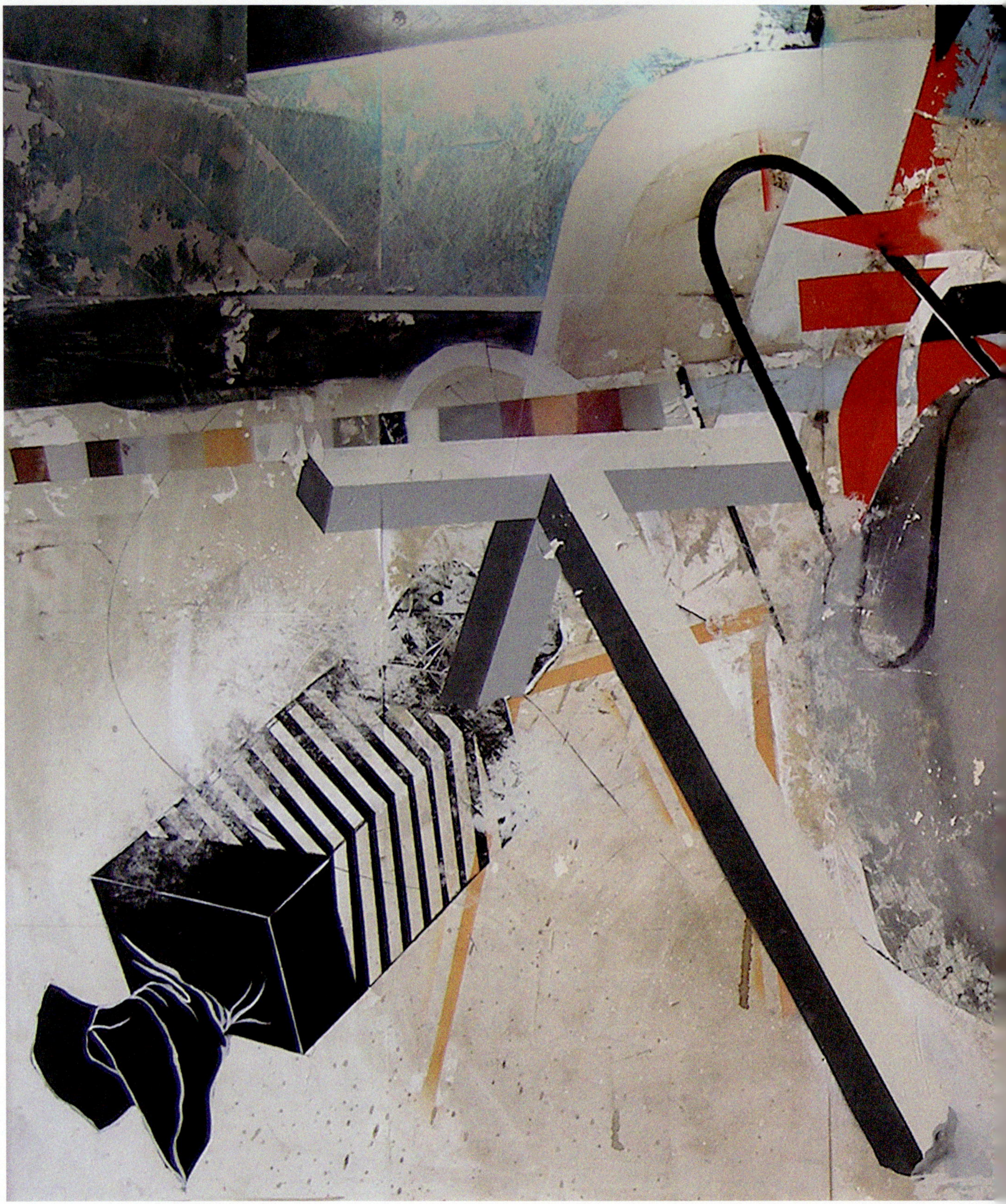

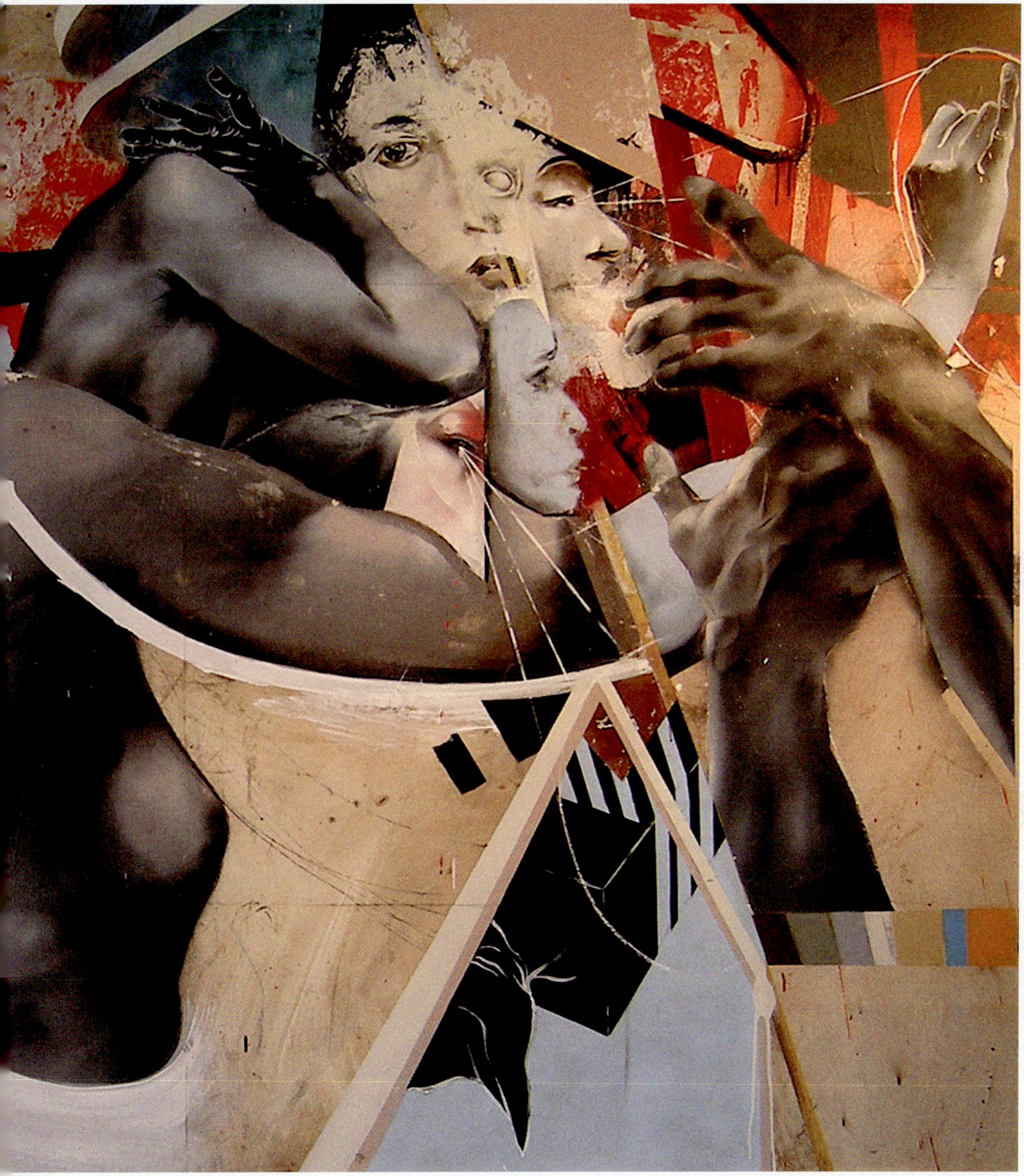

They Buy Things They Don't Need, With Money They Don't Have to Impress Neighbours Who Don't Care
Mixed media, wax light fixture, and varnish on wood – 300 x 170 cm – 2011

Jeff Soto

Born in Fullerton, United States, 1975. Lives in Riverside, United States.

I started painting graffiti in 1989, the same year I started playing with more traditional artists' materials like oil paints. I enjoyed them both, but with aerosol there was the added risk involved and the inevitable adrenaline rush. I rarely partake in illegal work nowadays as a 35-year-old father of two, but I still speak that language and my past reflects always in my current paintings. It is a part of me.

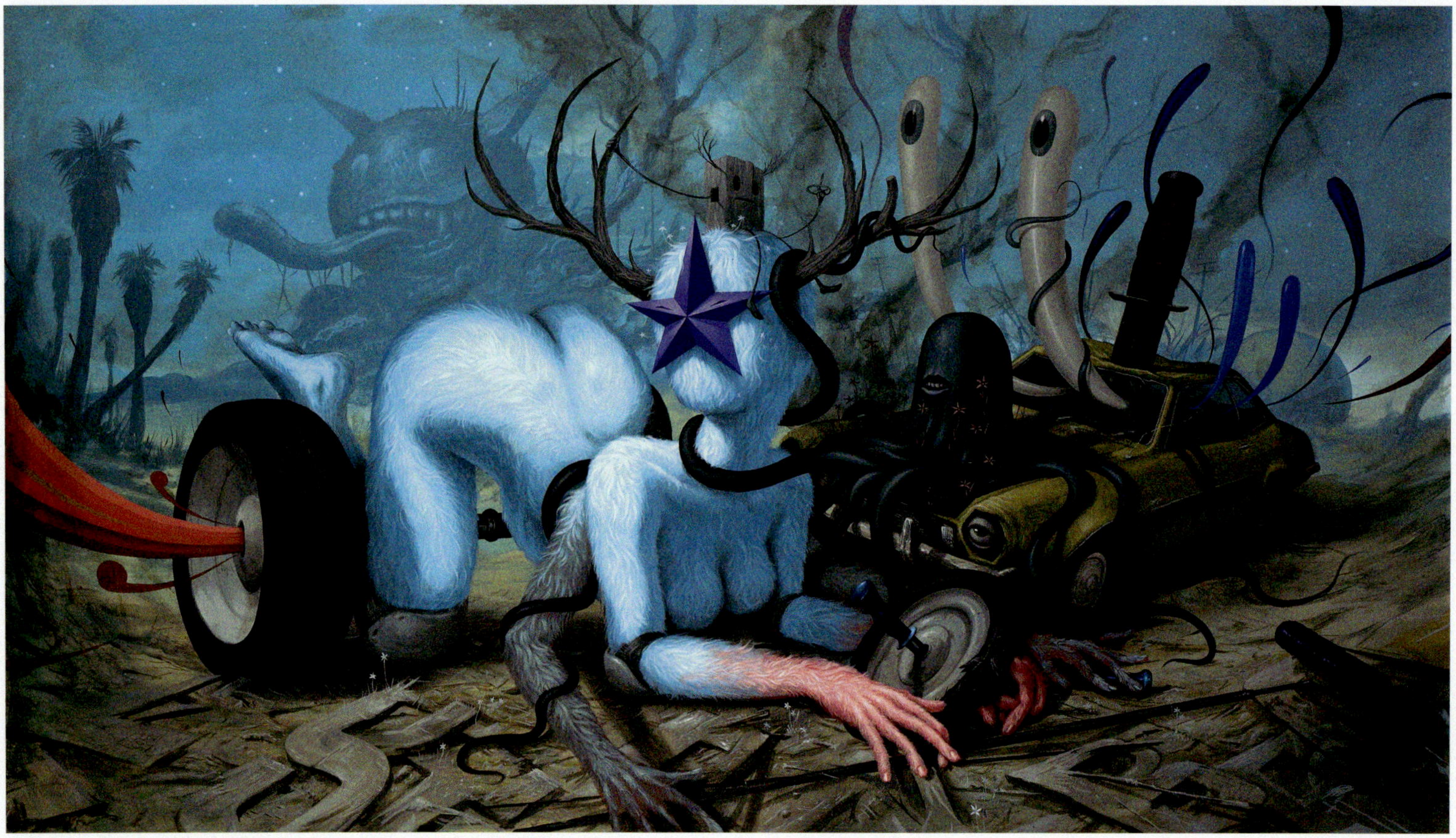

Car Crash / Acrylic on wood panel – 213 x 122 cm – 2010

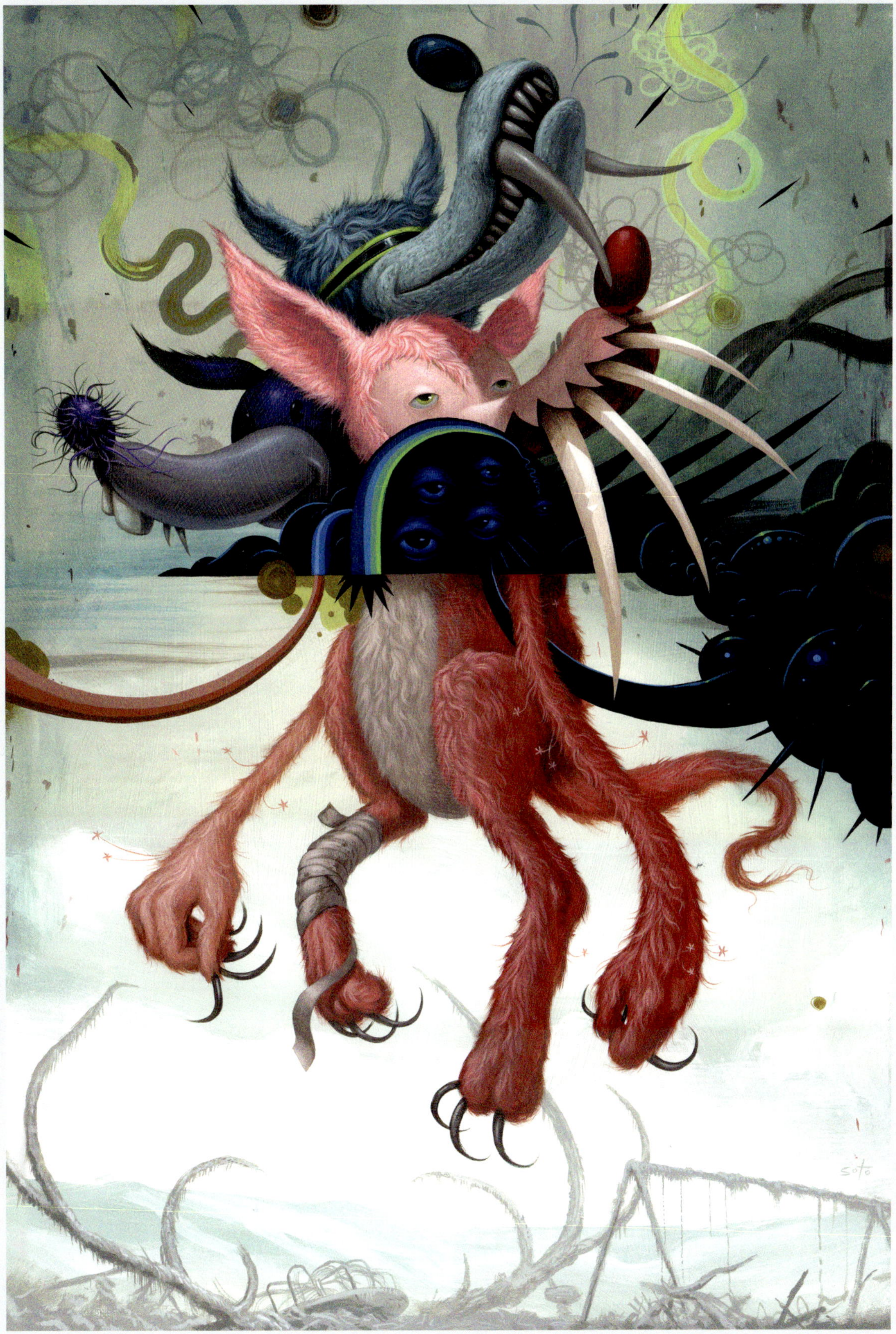

Broken / Acrylic on wood panel – 61 x 91 cm – 2010

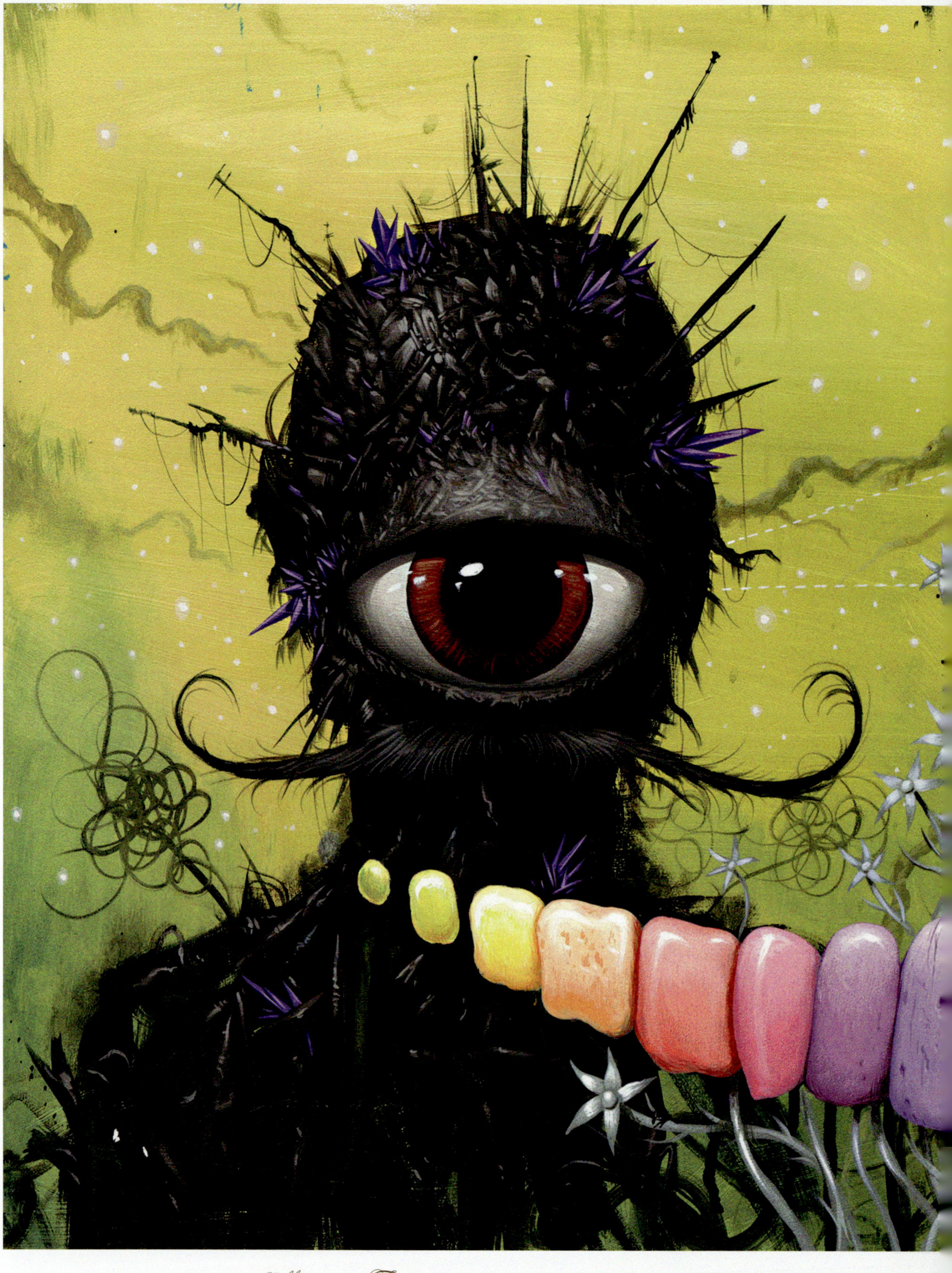

Mother and Father / Acrylic on wood panel – 81 x 51 cm – 2010

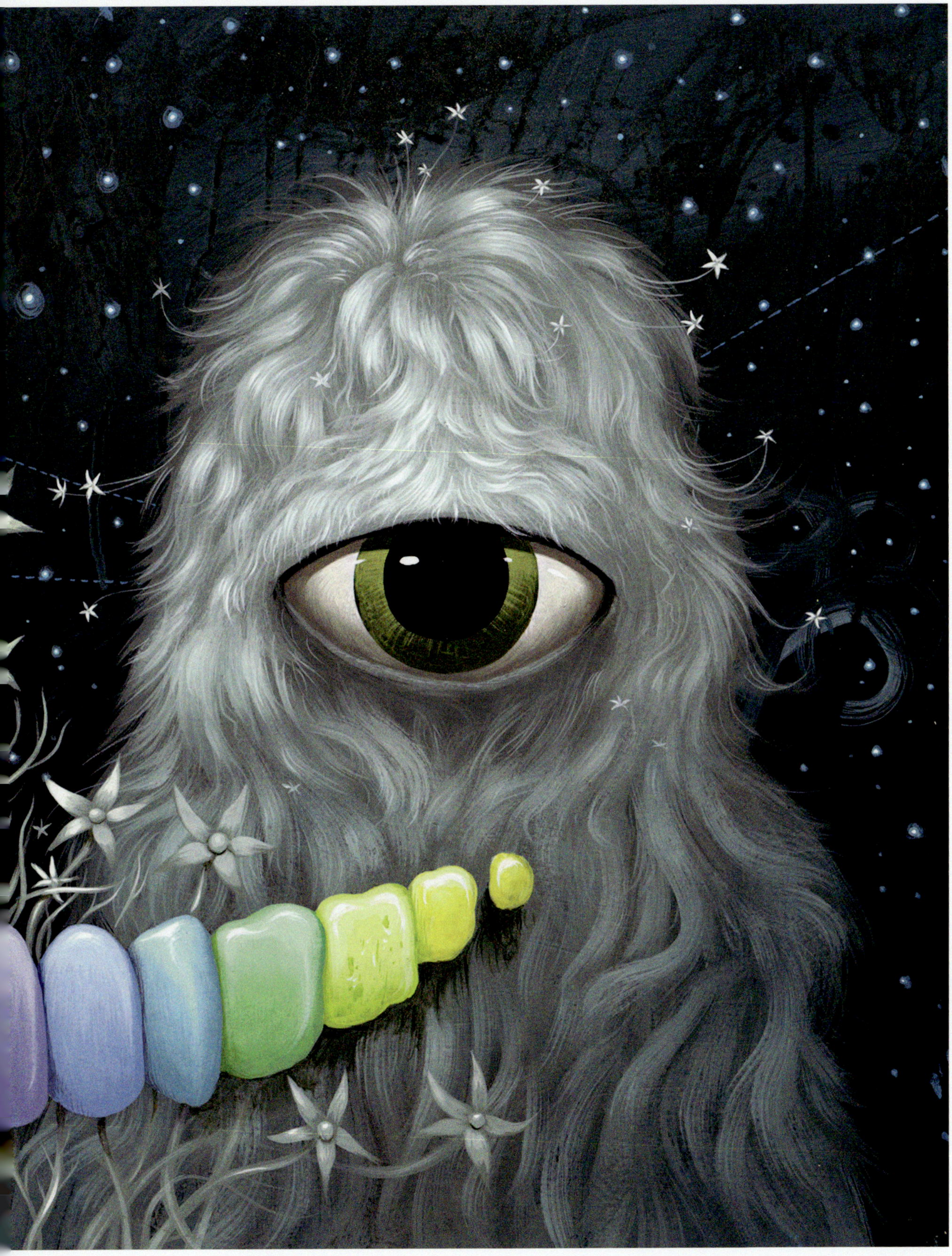

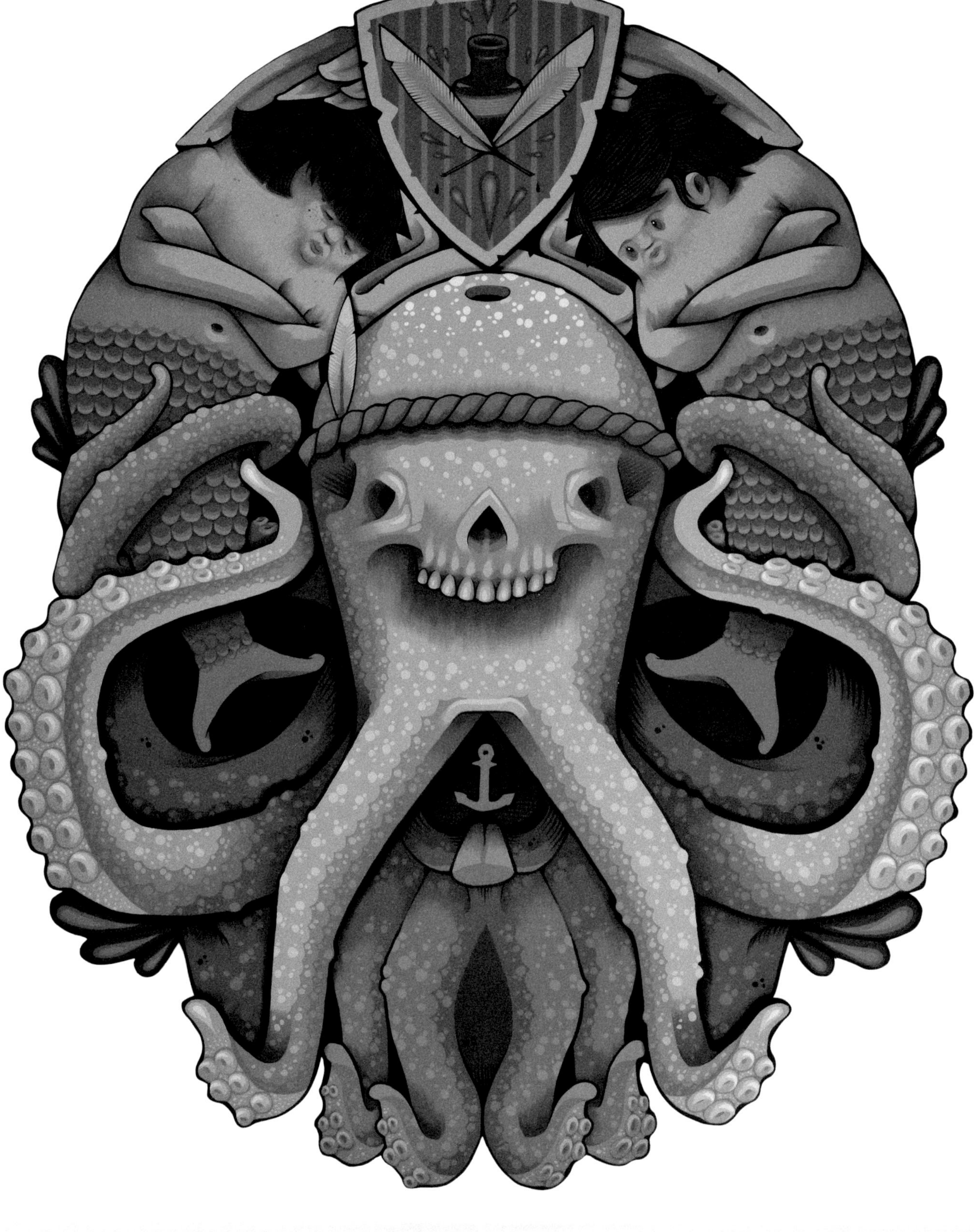

Be Careful Where you Squirt Your Ink | Acrylic on wood – 91 x 122 cm – 2010

Jeremy Fish

Born in Albany, United States, 1975. Lives in San Francisco, United States.

Growing up I spent a lot of time skateboarding and hanging around in the street. now I am older and I sit in my house and make art. Sometimes I go for a walk, or a drive and see someone wearing one of my T-shirt designs walking around in the street. You can also walk down a street into galleries where my artwork is hanging. This is my relationship with the street, and my artwork's relationship with the street. I also live on a street here in San Francisco. To sum up my feelings, I would like to quote the great Grandmaster Flash:

Beat Street
The king of the beat
You see him rocking that beat from across the street
And huh huh!
Beat Street is a lesson too, because you can't let the streets beat you!

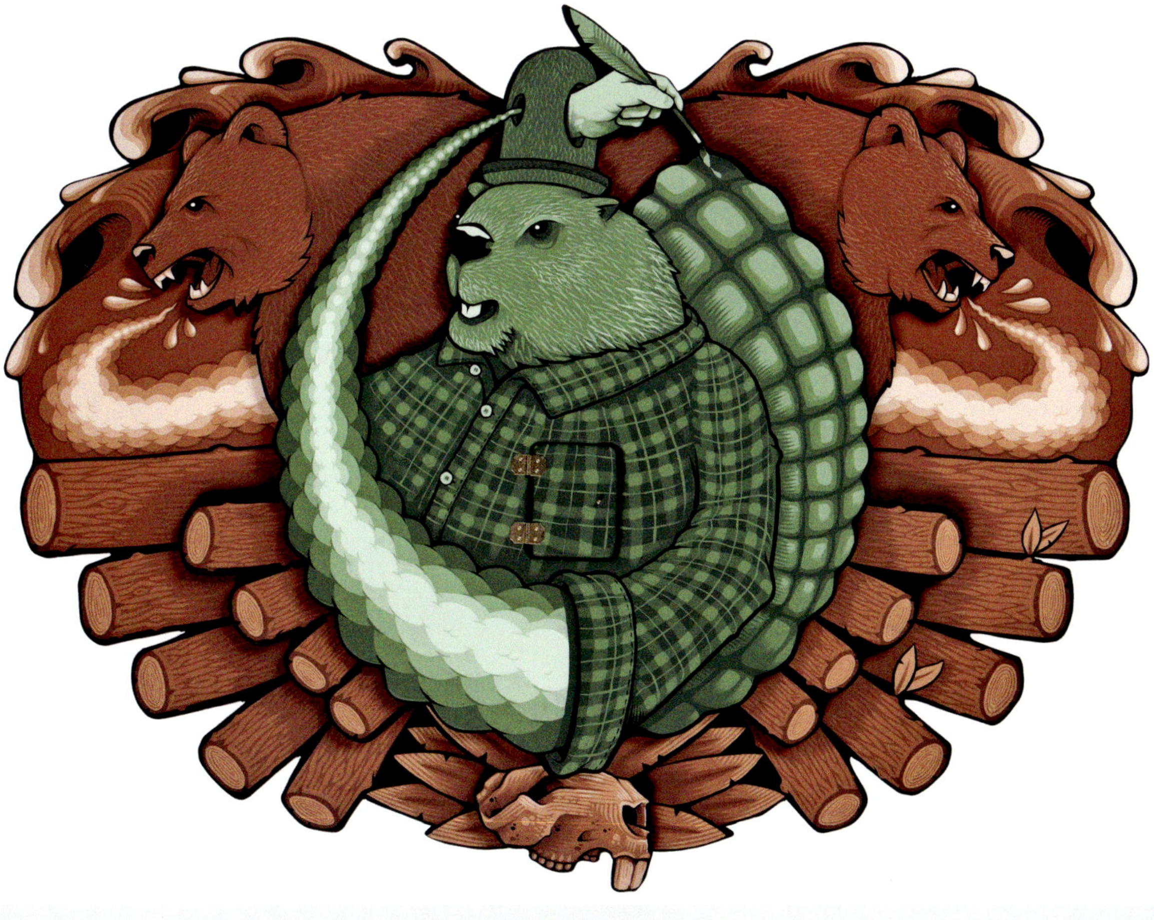

Build a Strong Dam Foundation / Acrylic on wood – 91 x 61 cm – 2010

Jesse Hazelip

Born in Cortez, United States, 1977. Lives in Oakland, United States.

Graffiti has been the driving force of my artistic inspiration since I was introduced to it as a teenager. It has shaped my life and my art in ways I could never access through formal training. My fine art and my street work are contingent upon each other.

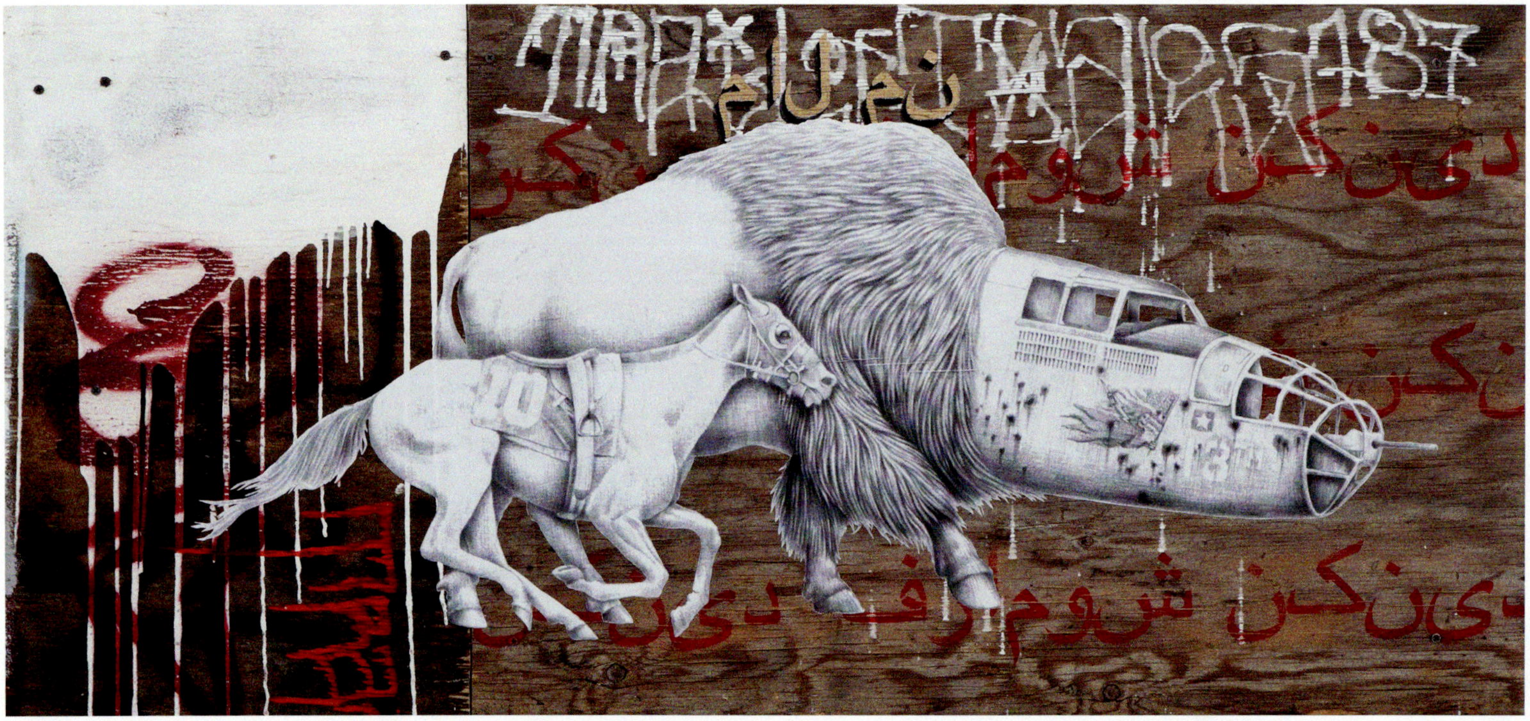

Right Runner / Acrylic, paper, wheat paste, and aerosol on found wood – 157 x 91 cm – 2011

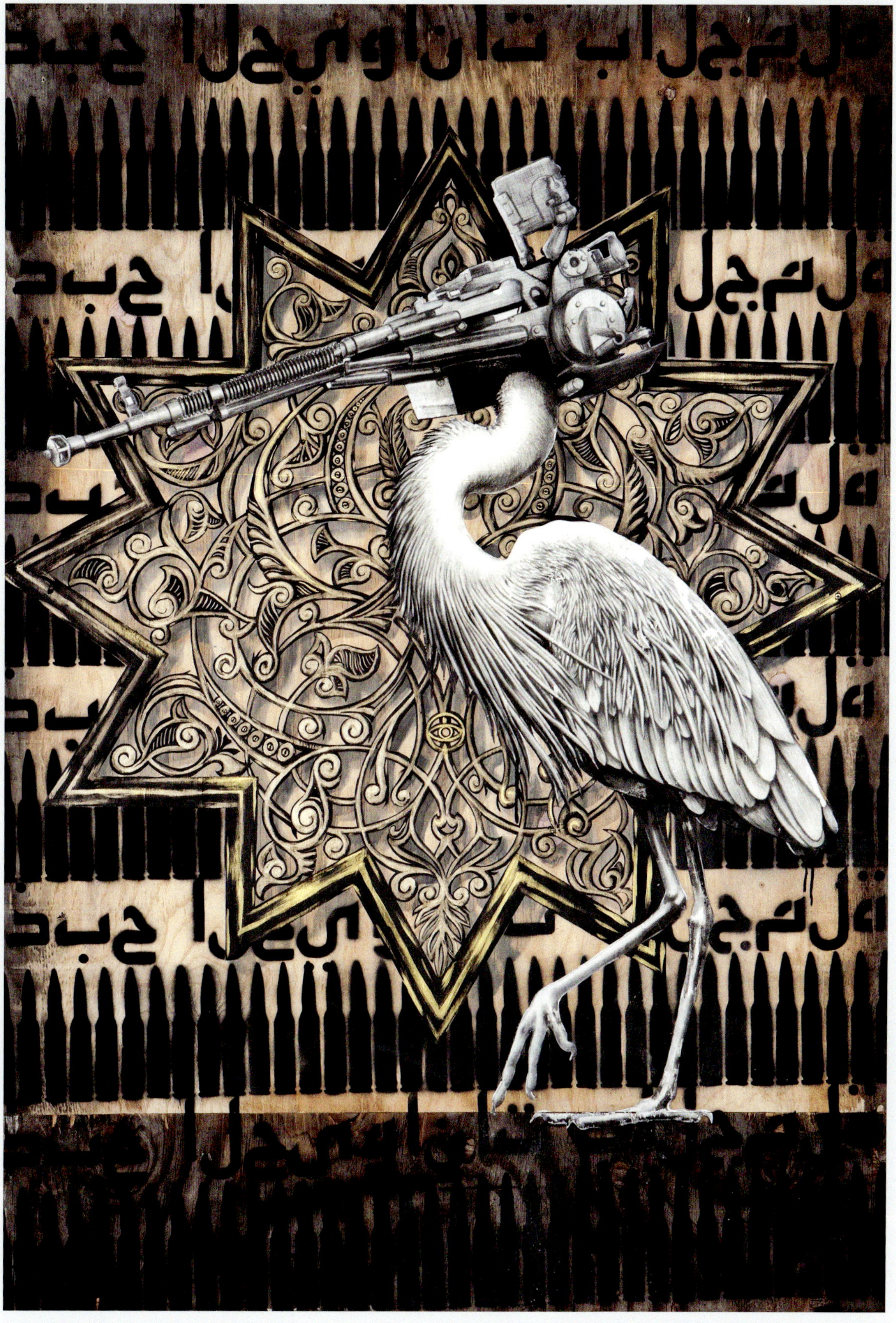

Beautiful Seclusion / Acrylic, ink, gel medium, and aerosol on found wood – 140 x 200 cm – 2011

Johnny "KMNDZ" Rodriguez

Born in Los Angeles, United States, 1974. Lives in Pomona, United States.

I'm amazed how time erodes the things we create. From old roads to old murals on brick walls. I love the layers of paint over mural over old advertisements. While in high school I got into outdoor sign painting and was fortunate to study under an old master. It's a dying art form replaced by digital cutouts of vinyl and laser prints on large rolls of canvas. I think if the sign painters of yesteryear knew what we've become they'd turn over in their graves.

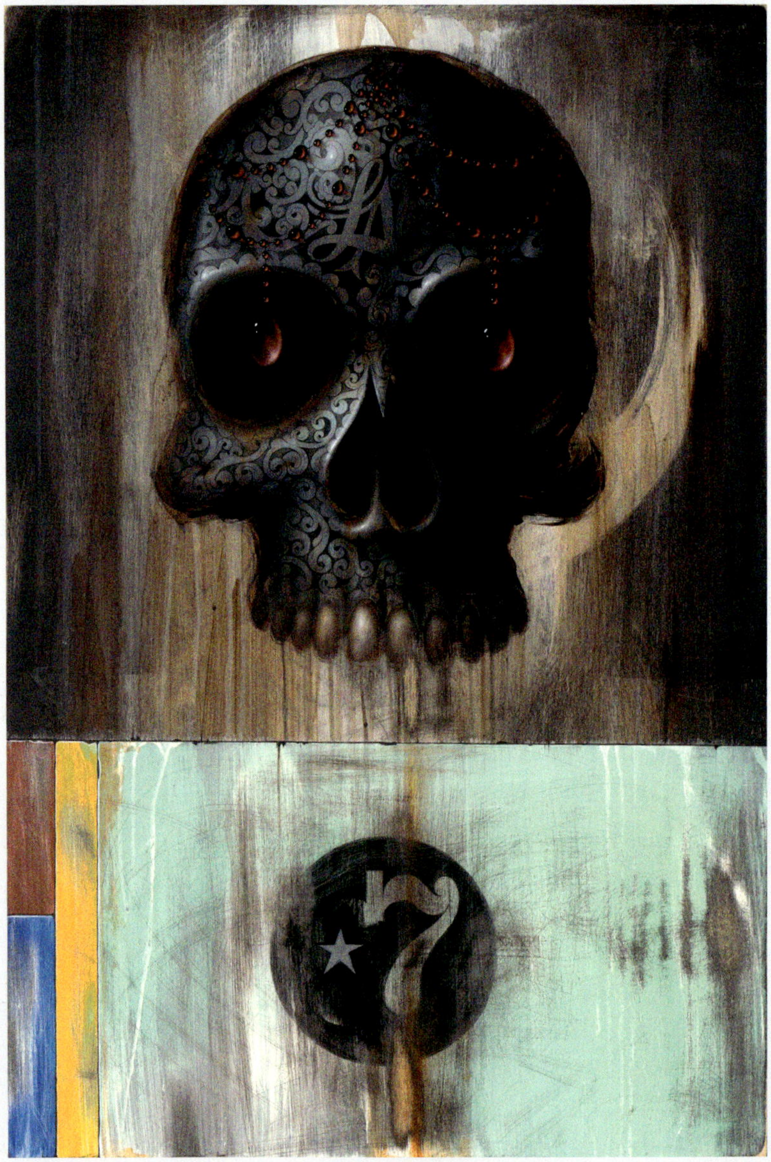

Death Defeater / Acrylic on wood – 61 x 91 cm – 2010

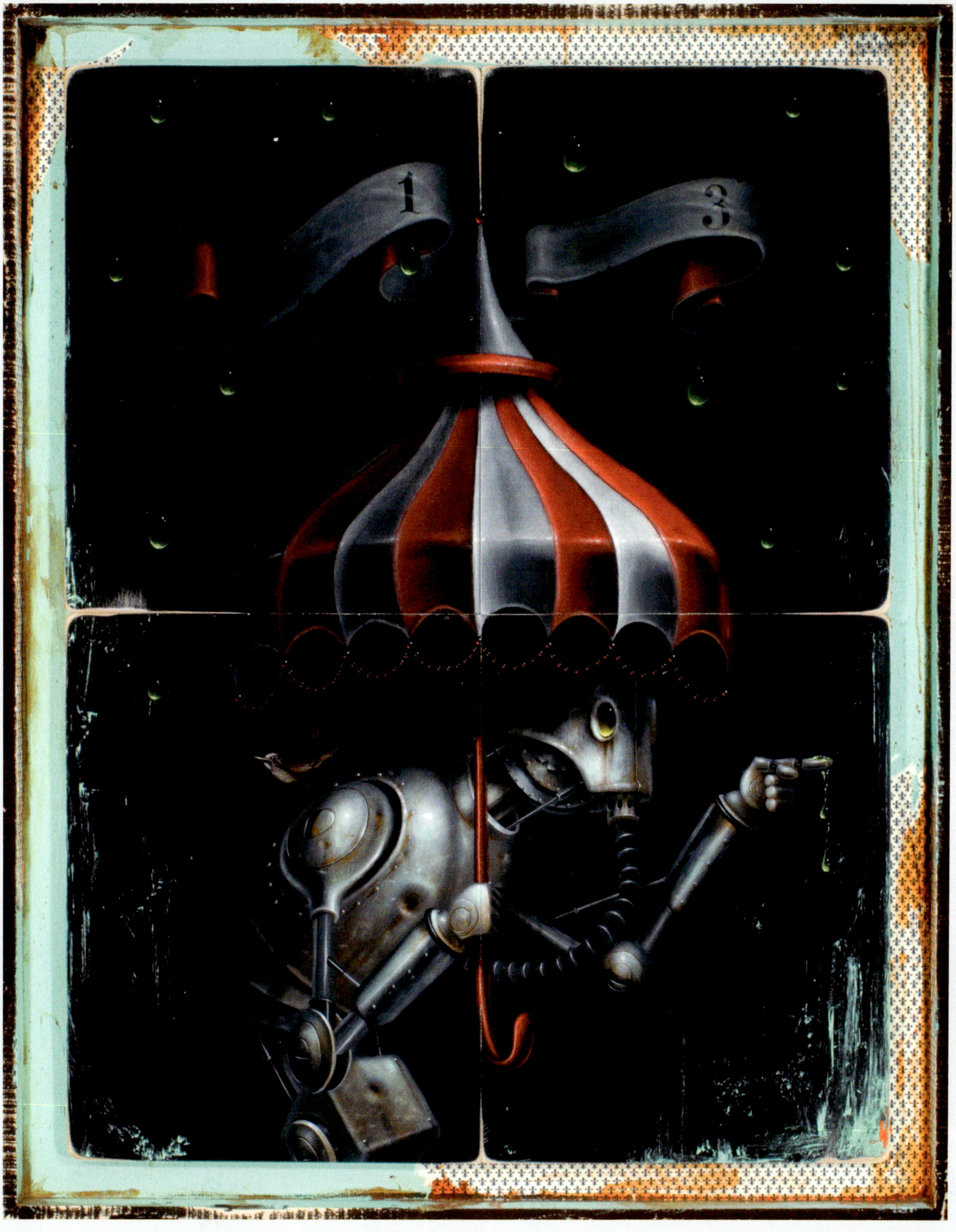

Nothing New Under the Sun / Acrylic on wood – 90 x 121 cm – 2008

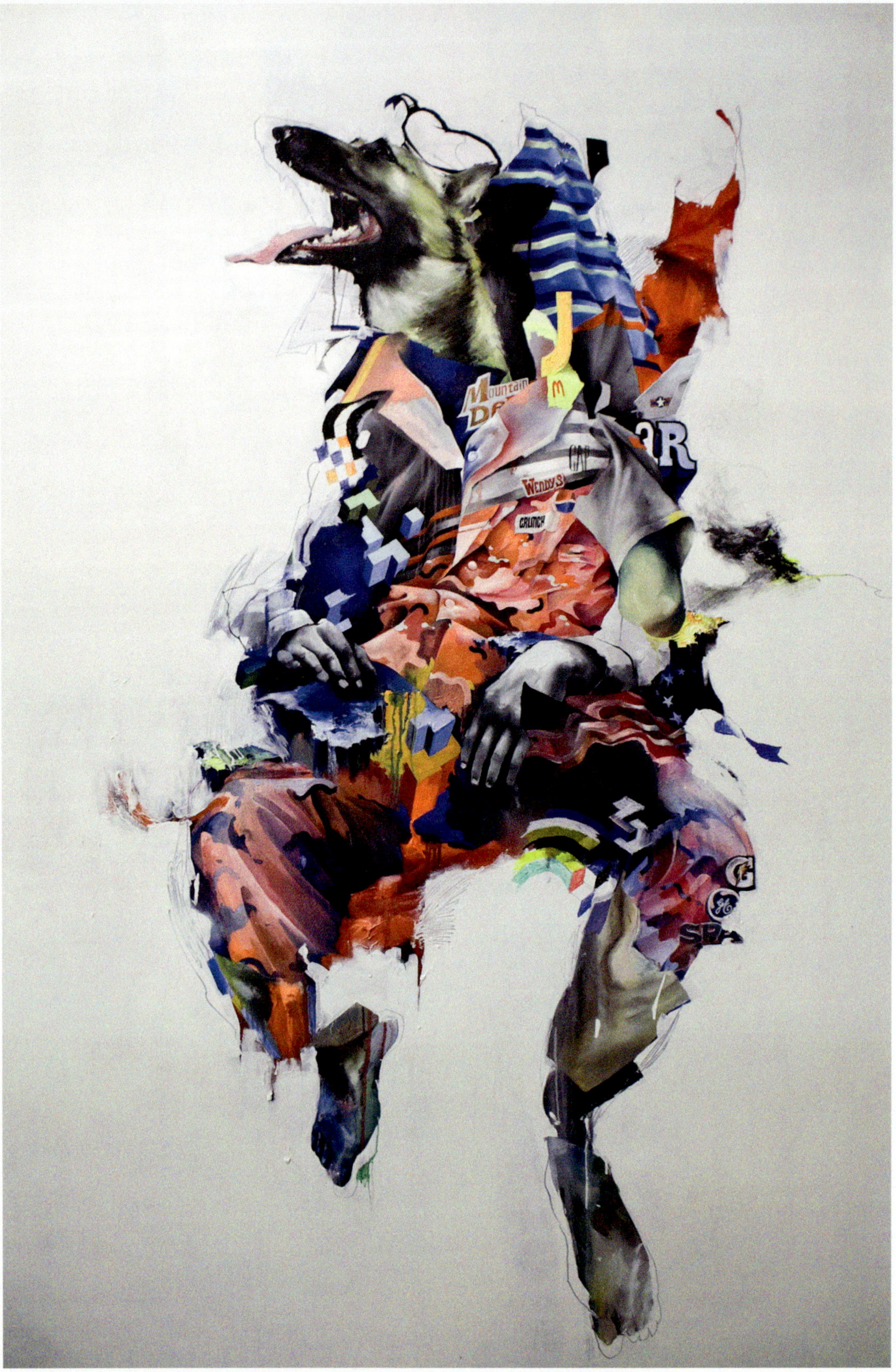

Private David / Oil on canvas – 190 x 270 cm – 2010

Joram Roukes

Born in Lelystad, Netherlands, 1983. Lives in Groningen, Netherlands.

I did graffiti until I found out I was repeating myself and everybody else who was doing it. I just got bored ... and arrested.

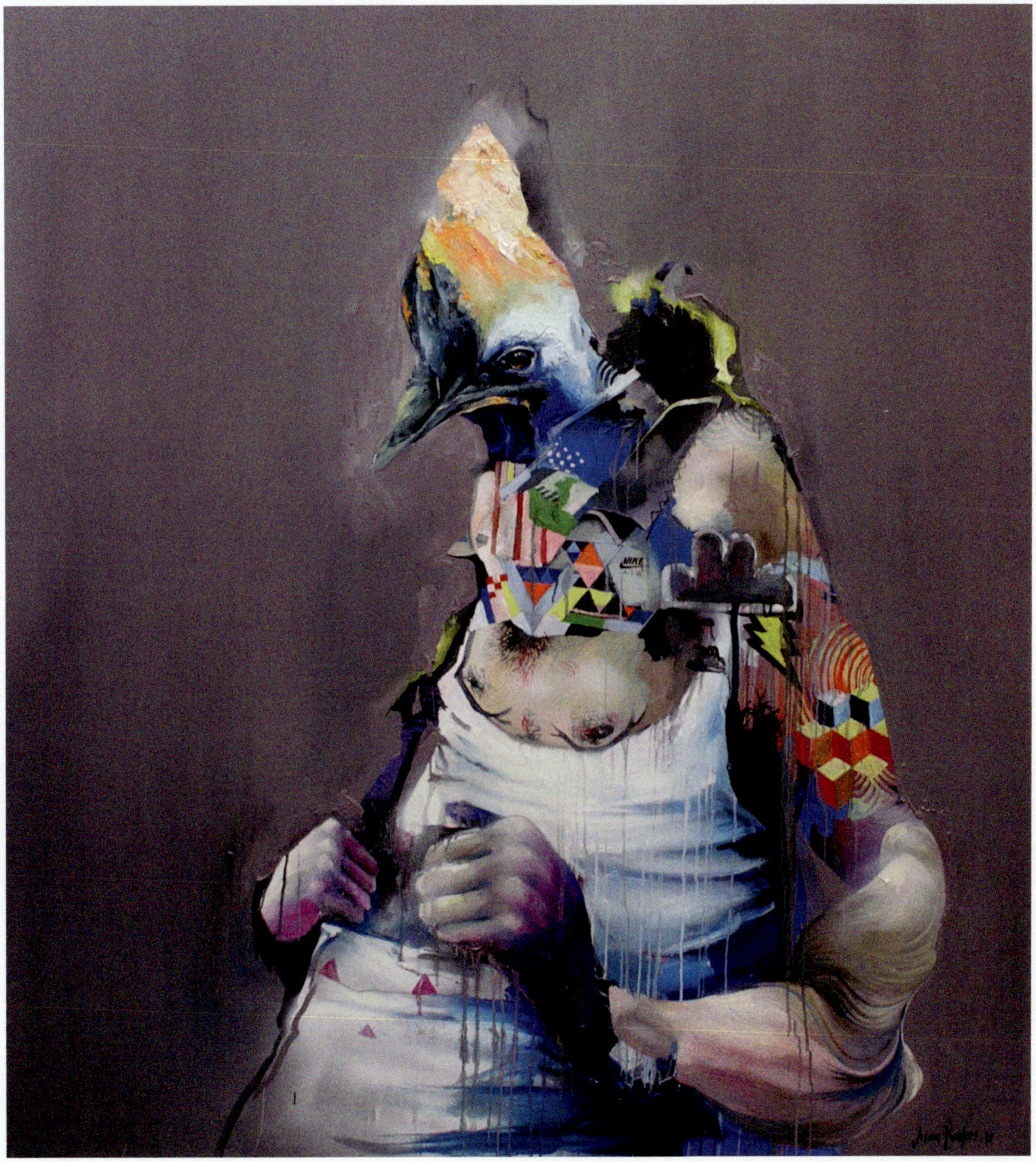

Wifebeater / Oil on canvas – 160 x 180 cm – 2010

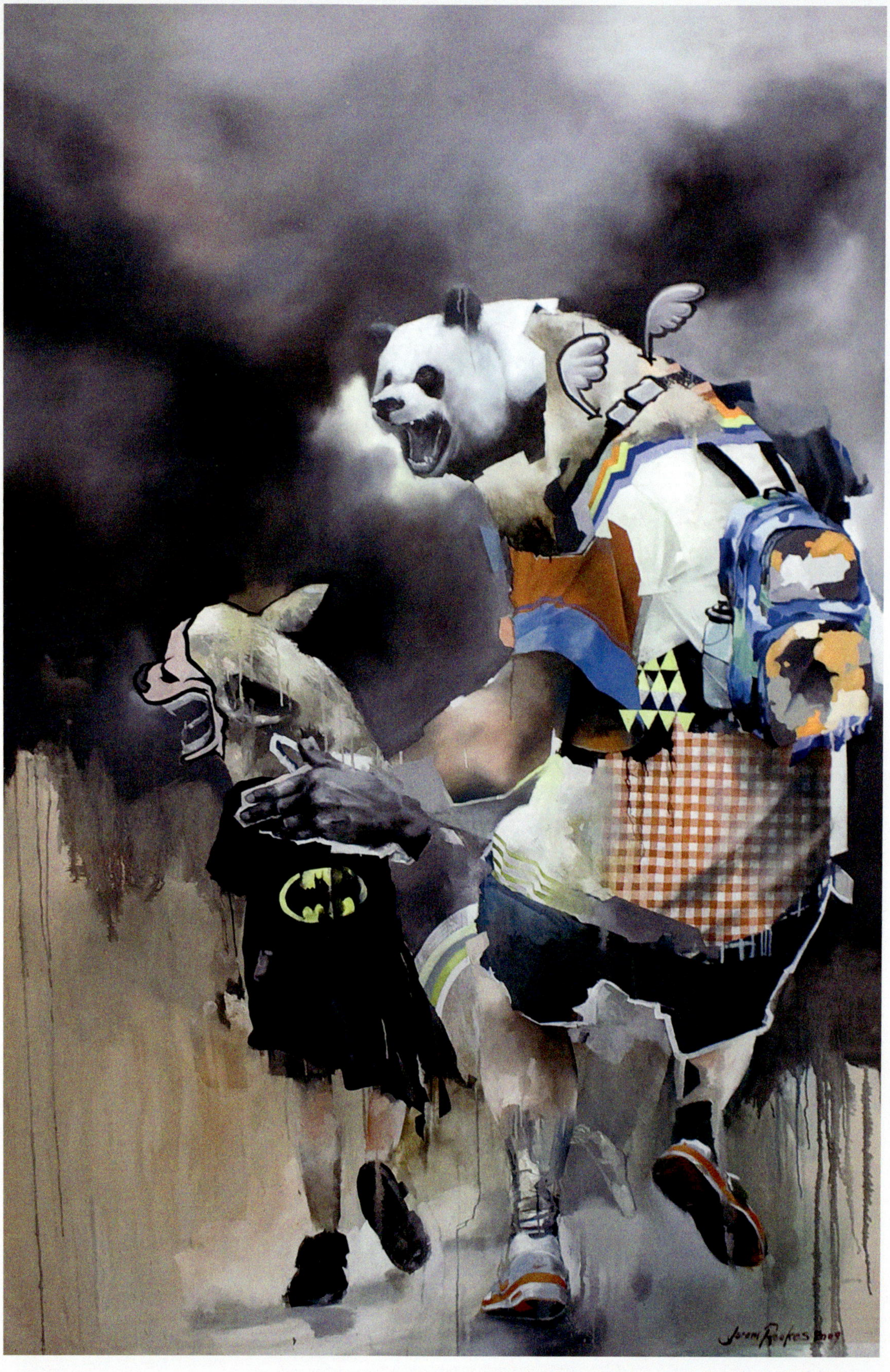

On The Way Out / Oil on canvas – 160 x 250 cm – 2008

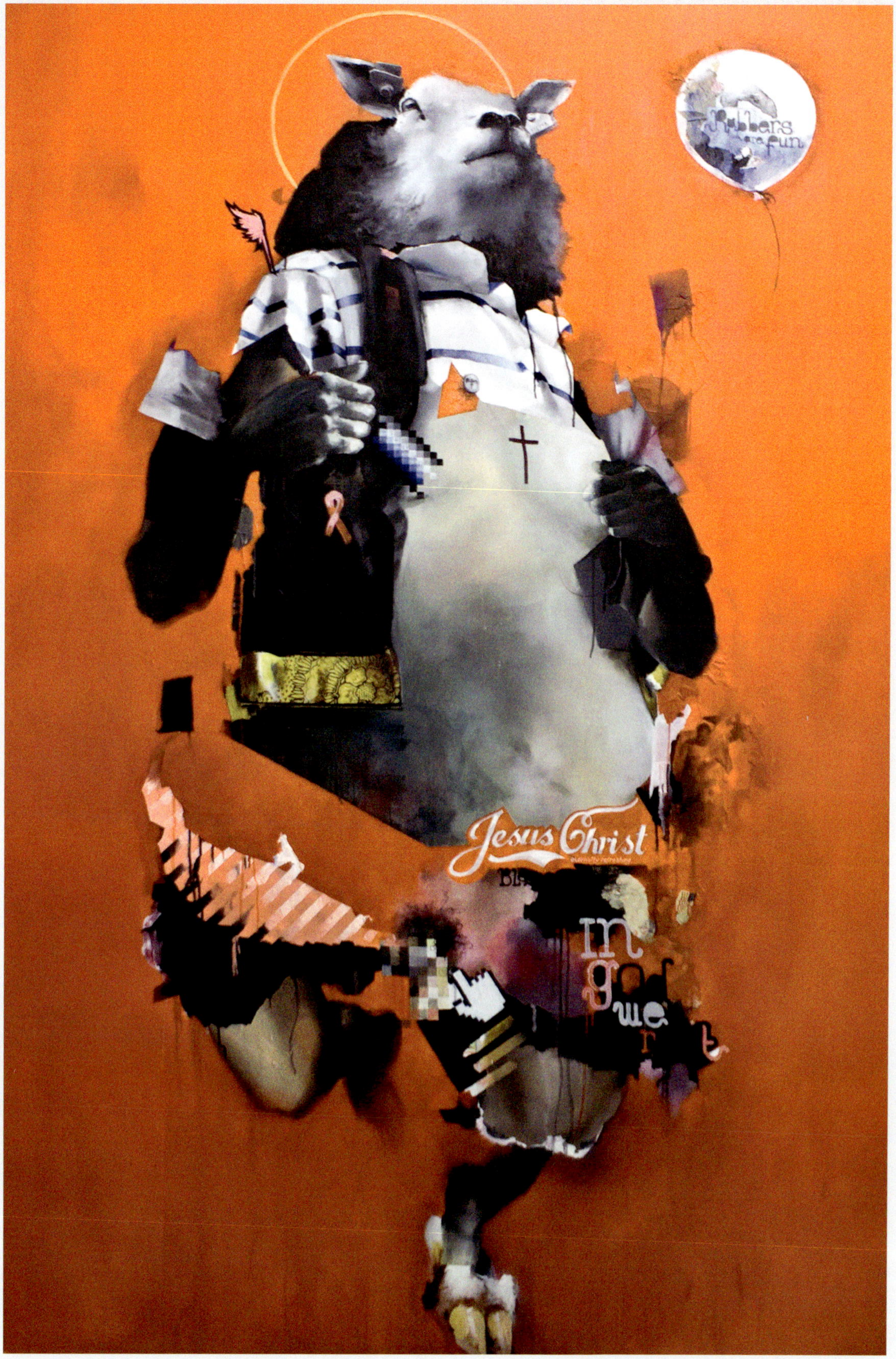

In God We Trust / Oil on canvas – 160 x 240 cm – 2008

Jorge Rodriguez Gerada

Born in Santa Clara, Cuba, 1966. Lives in Barcelona, Spain.

The Urban Analogies series is a parallel direction that is coherent with my street work. I focus on weathered architectural surfaces that show their history and residual memory. While most of the wall surfaces that are being preserved have some kind of historic importance (e.g. frescos, murals, etc.) with these old surfaces I am giving importance to the commonplace for the memory that they possess and the passage of time that they portray.

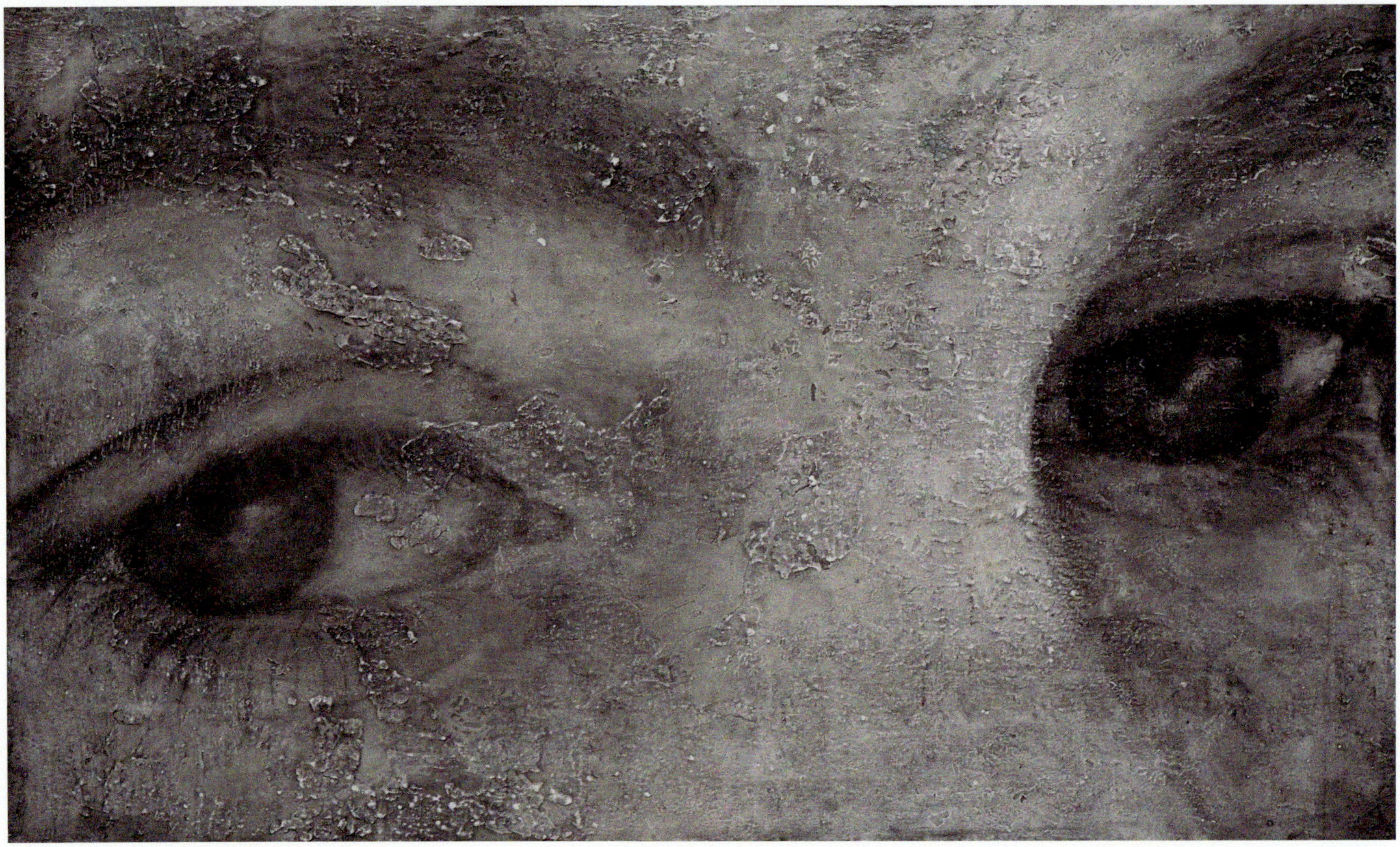

Urban Analogies #16 | Charcoal on 200-year-old wall surface transferred on to wood panel – 150 x 90 cm – 2010

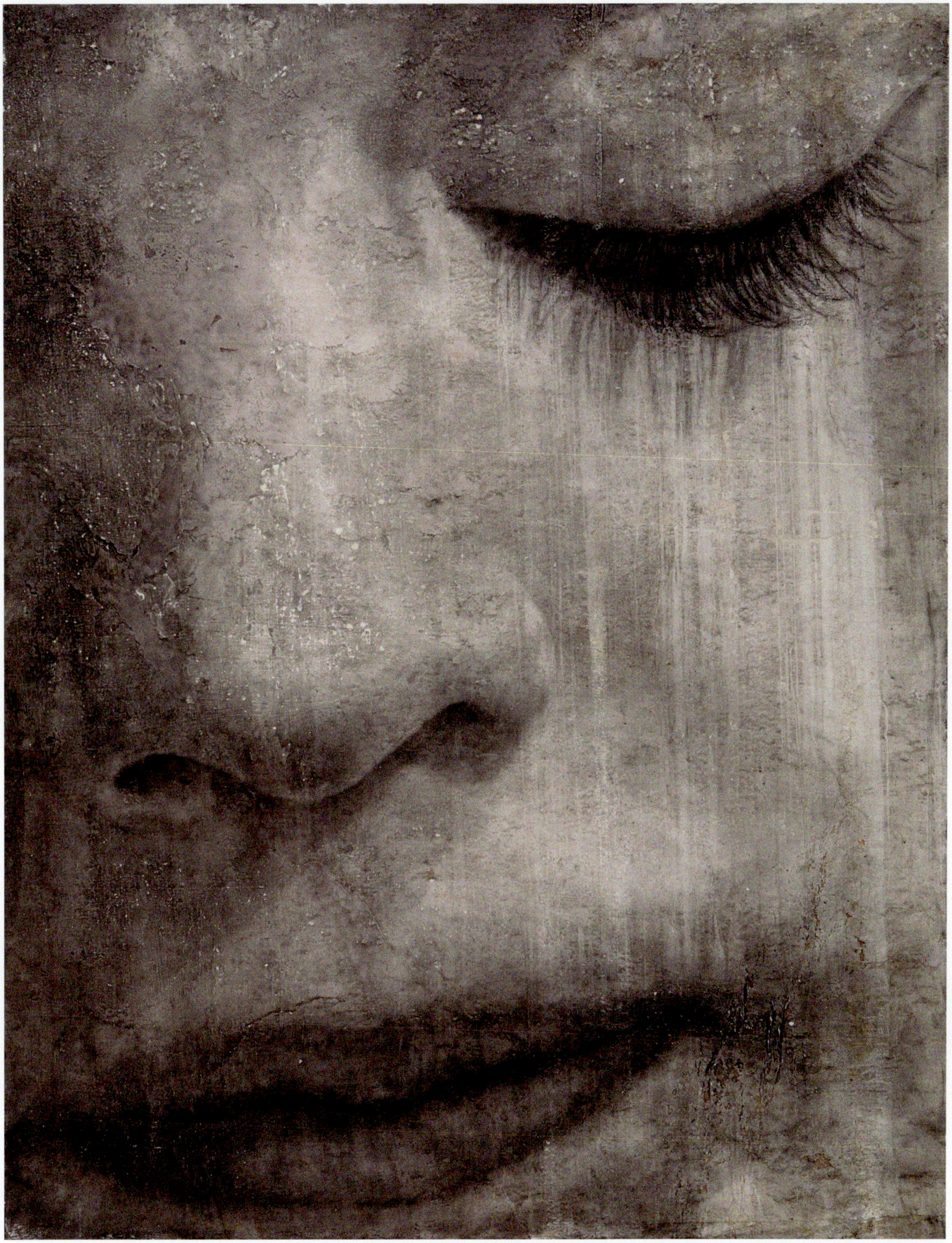

Urban Analogies #11 / Charcoal on 200-year-old wall surface transferred on to wood panel – 90 x 240 cm – 2010

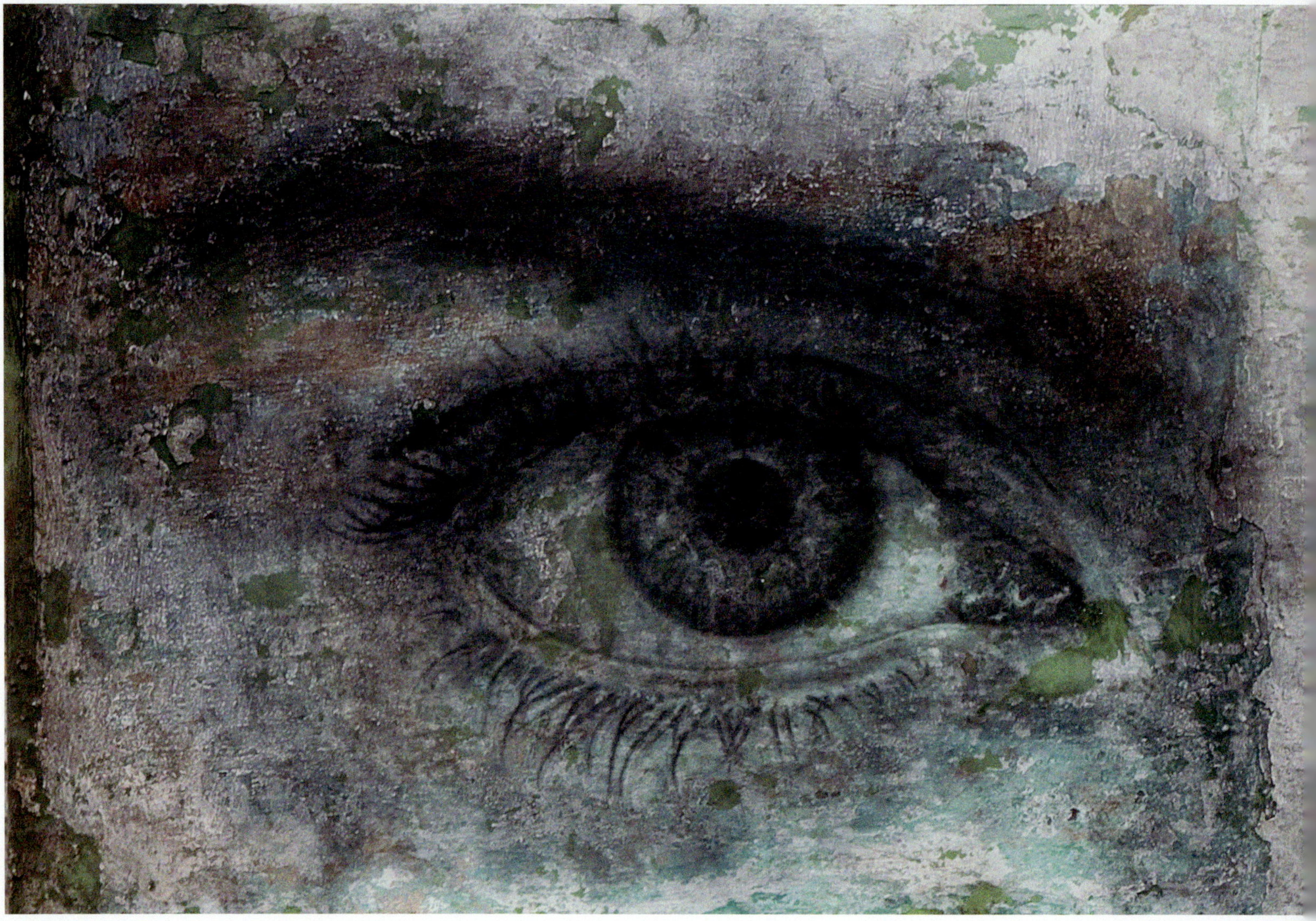

Urban Analogies #19 | Charcoal on 200-year-old wall surface transferred on to wood panel – 300 x 100 cm – 2011

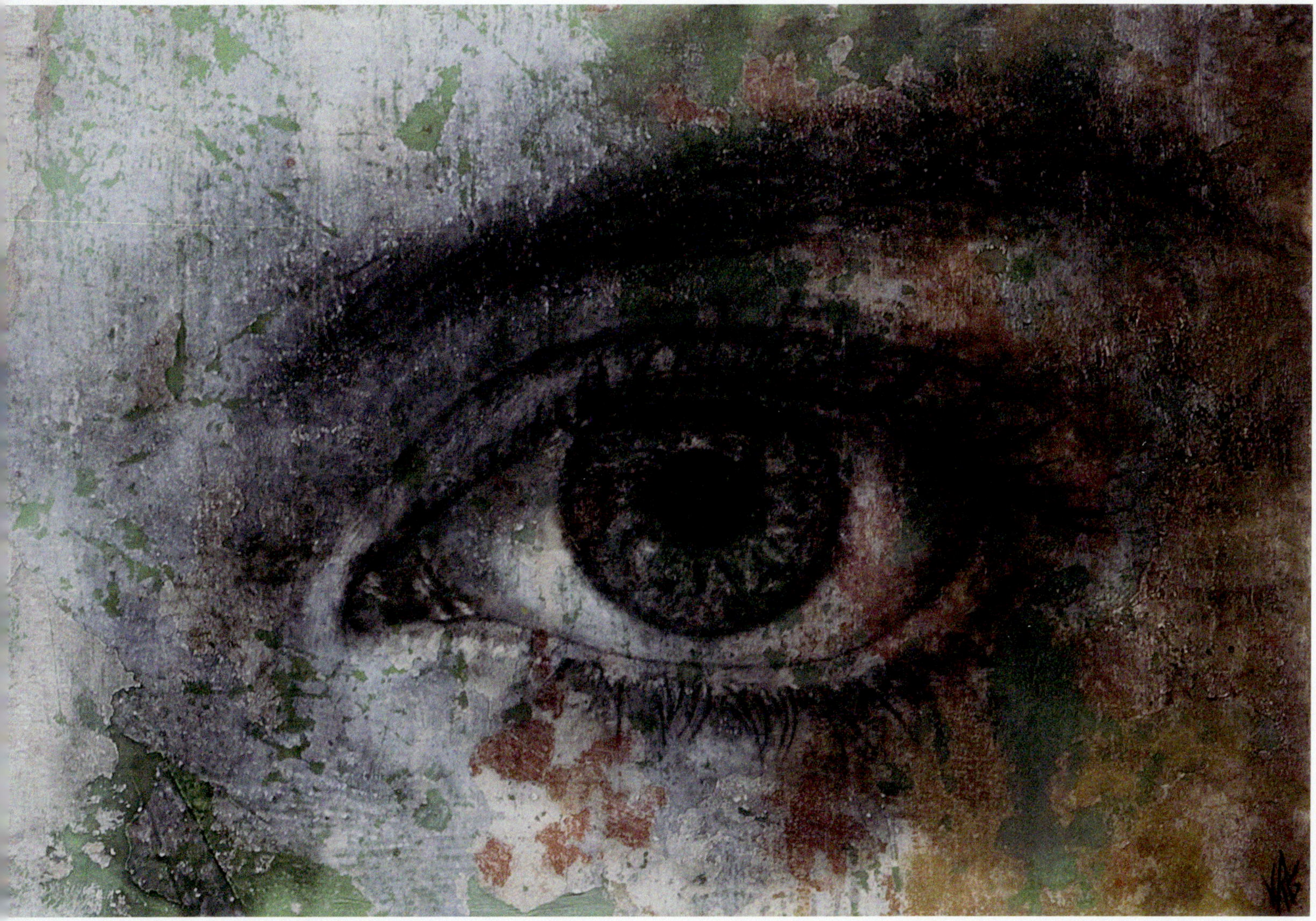

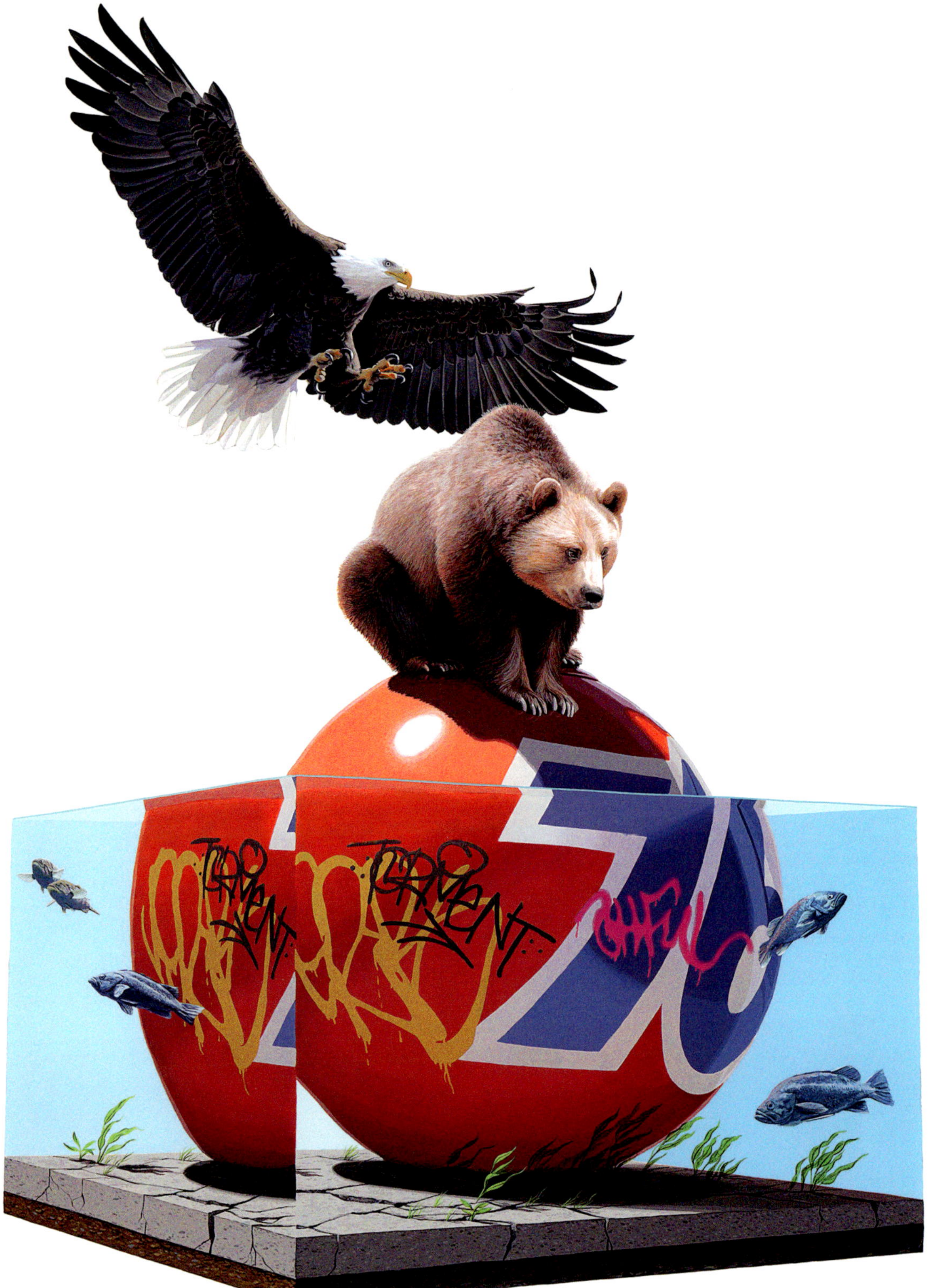

Lifted / Acrylic on wood panel – 76 x 101 cm – 2010

Josh Keyes

Born in Tacoma, United States, 1969. Lives in Oregon, United States.

I think what has changed in the street art movement is the growing emphasis on how creating art in public spaces, even employing the flash mob practice, can serve to generate political action and give a voice to a silenced majority or group. I use graffiti and street art references in my work to convey specific literal messages, and also as a sign or indication of the importance of questioning authority, be it corporate, government, military, or historical in terms of public statues and monuments.

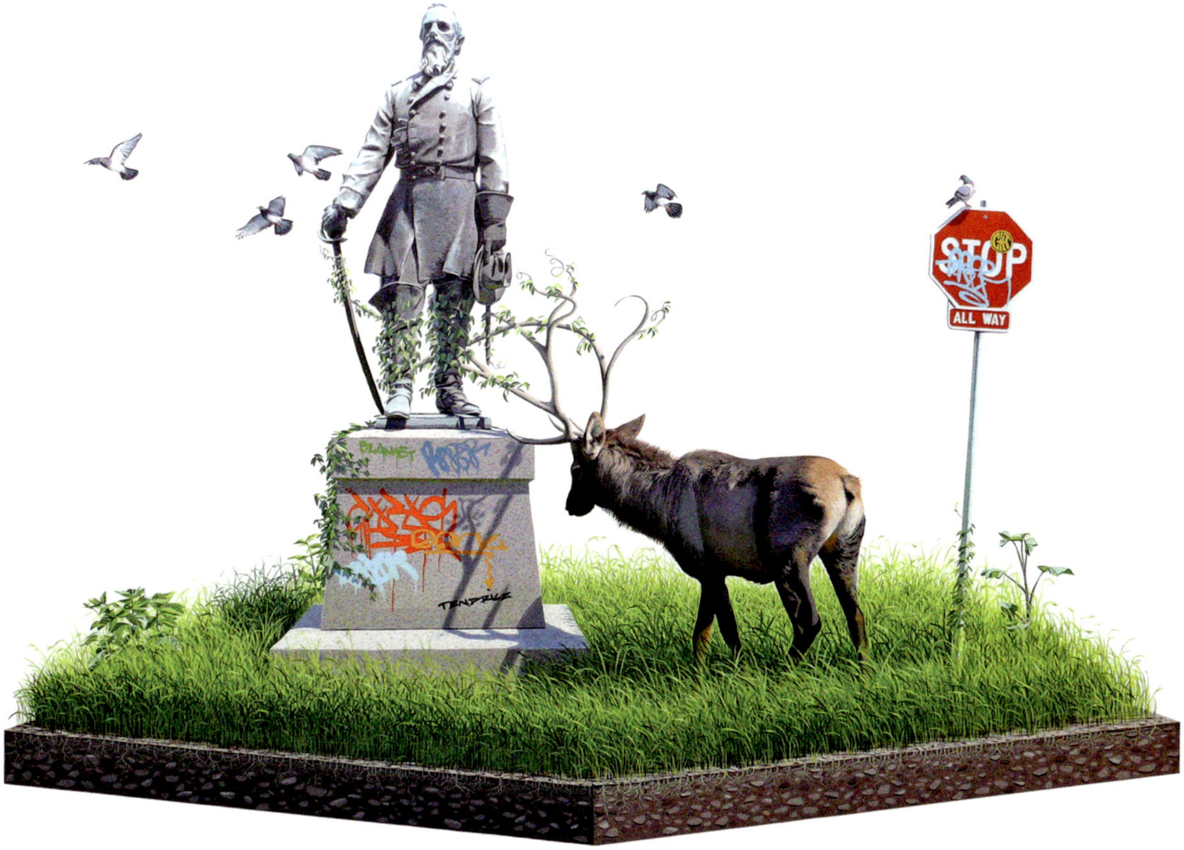

Entangle II / Acrylic on wood panel – 101 x 76 cm – 2009

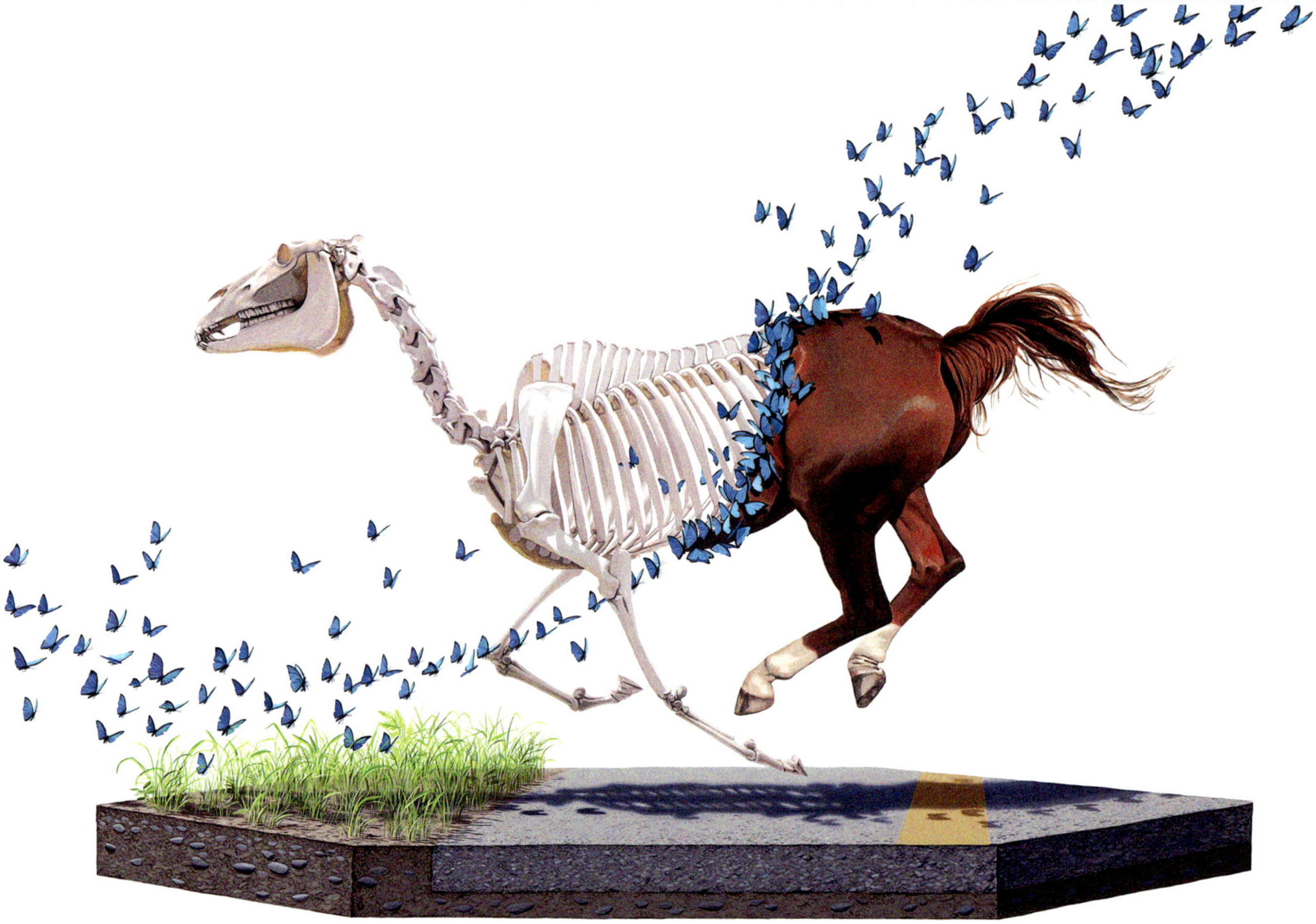

Shedding / Acrylic on wood panel – 102 x 76 cm – 2009

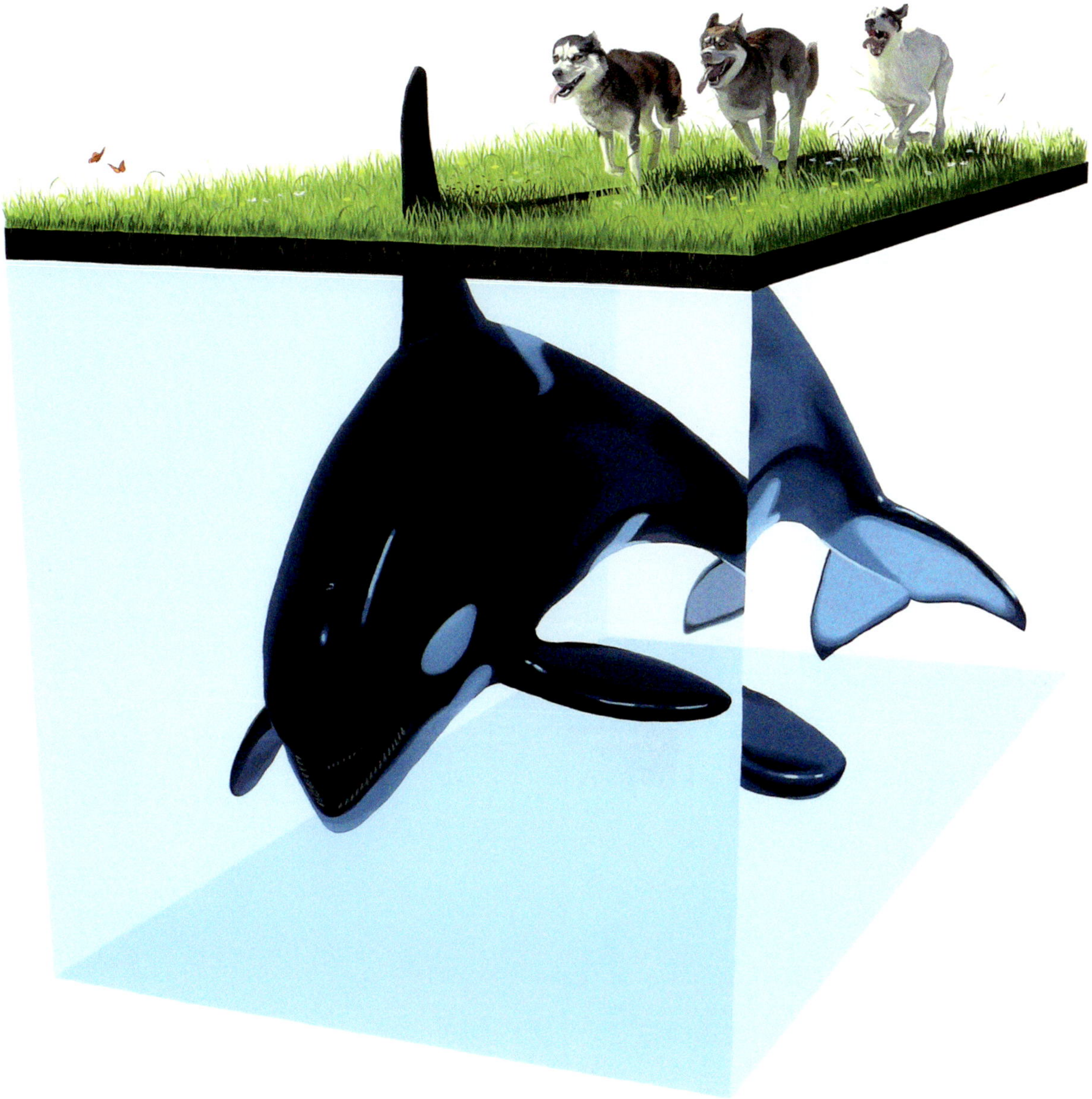

Thunder / Acrylic on wood panel – 76 x 102 cm – 2009

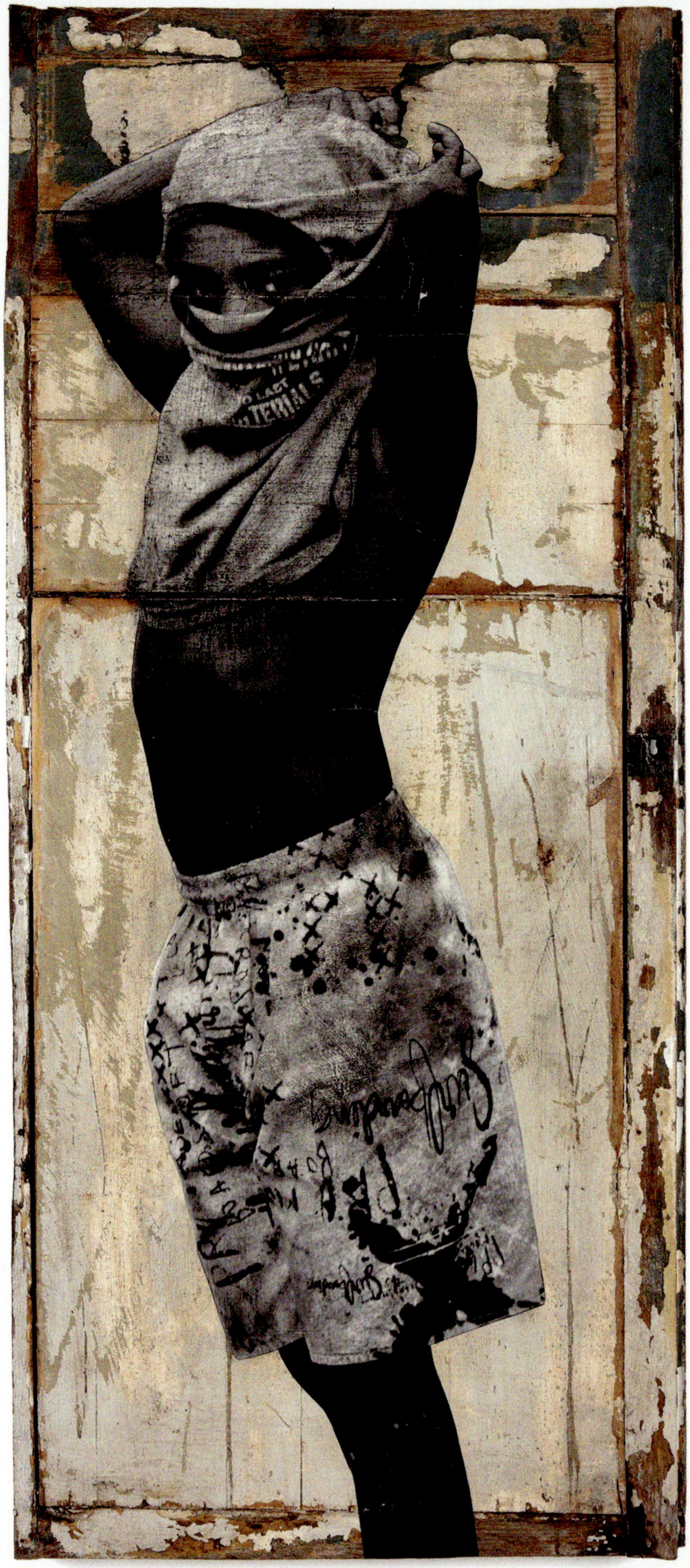

28 Millimètres, Women are Heroes, Street Kid, Favela Morro da Providência, Rio de Janeiro, Brazil

Black and white print on paper pasted on wood – 76 x 179 cm – 2008

JR

Born in Paris, France, 1983. Lives in Paris, France.

For me the indoor work completes the outdoor work. I have never tried to reproduce what I do in the street on the inside, it just couldn't work. Actually, the work that the collector can acquire is the uptake of my work itself. At a precise moment I knew I had to photograph a house when it was falling down into the river in Cambodia. There is something human that touches people and that is above the formal force.

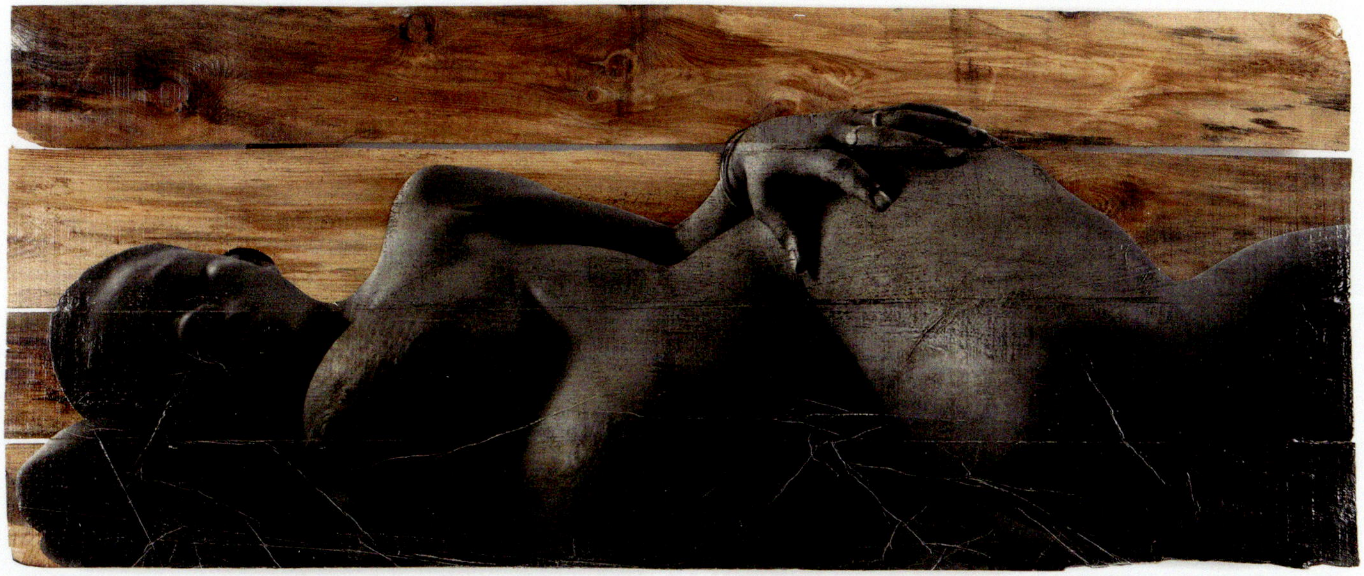

28 Millimètres, Women are Heroes, Femme Allongée / Black and white print on paper pasted on wood – 110 x 43 cm – 2008

Judith Supine

Born in Virginia, United States, 1980. Lives in New York, United States.

When I make art that is outside and illegal it reminds me of my childhood playing in the Dismal Swamp—digging holes, sharpening sticks, eating bark, and building traps for other children. When I work in my studio I am more subdued—drinking tea—more introspective.

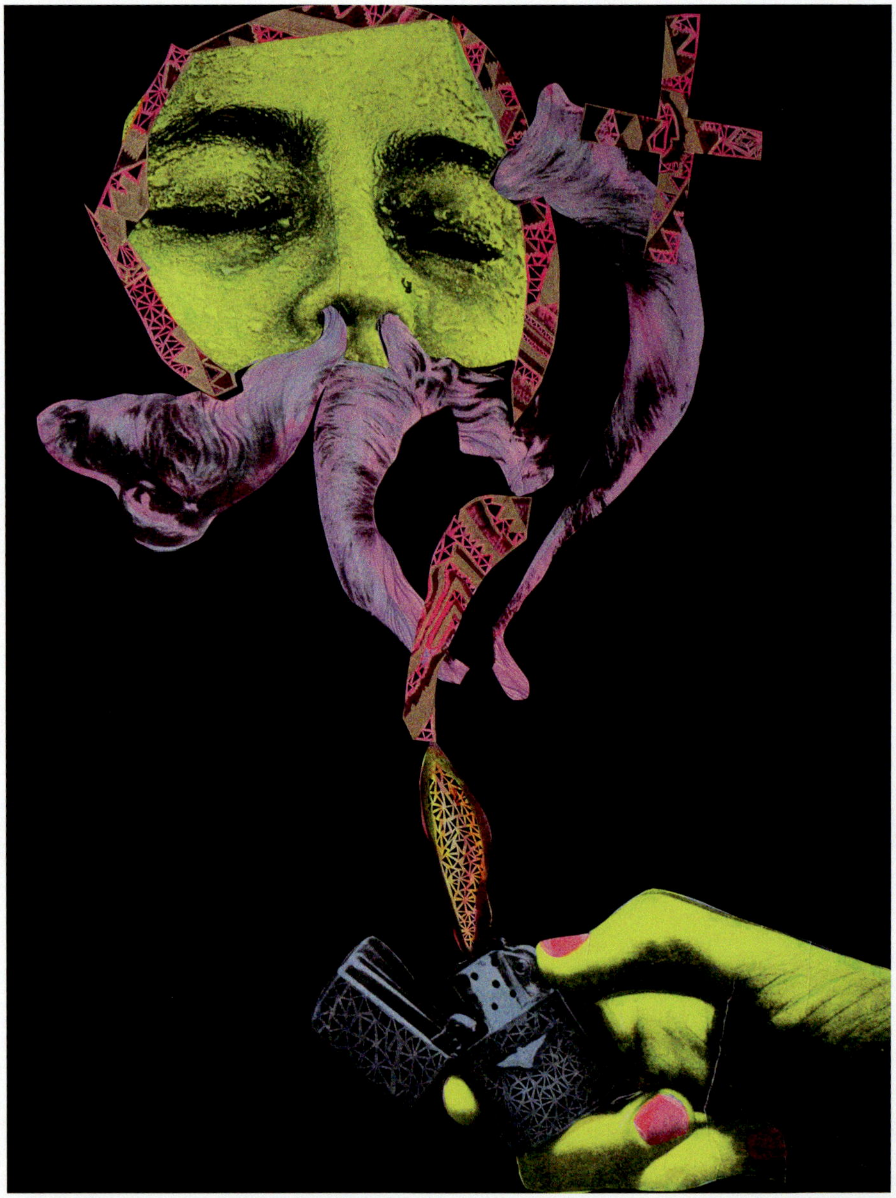

My Father's Wife / Acrylic, paper, and resin on wood panel – 91 x 122 cm – 2011

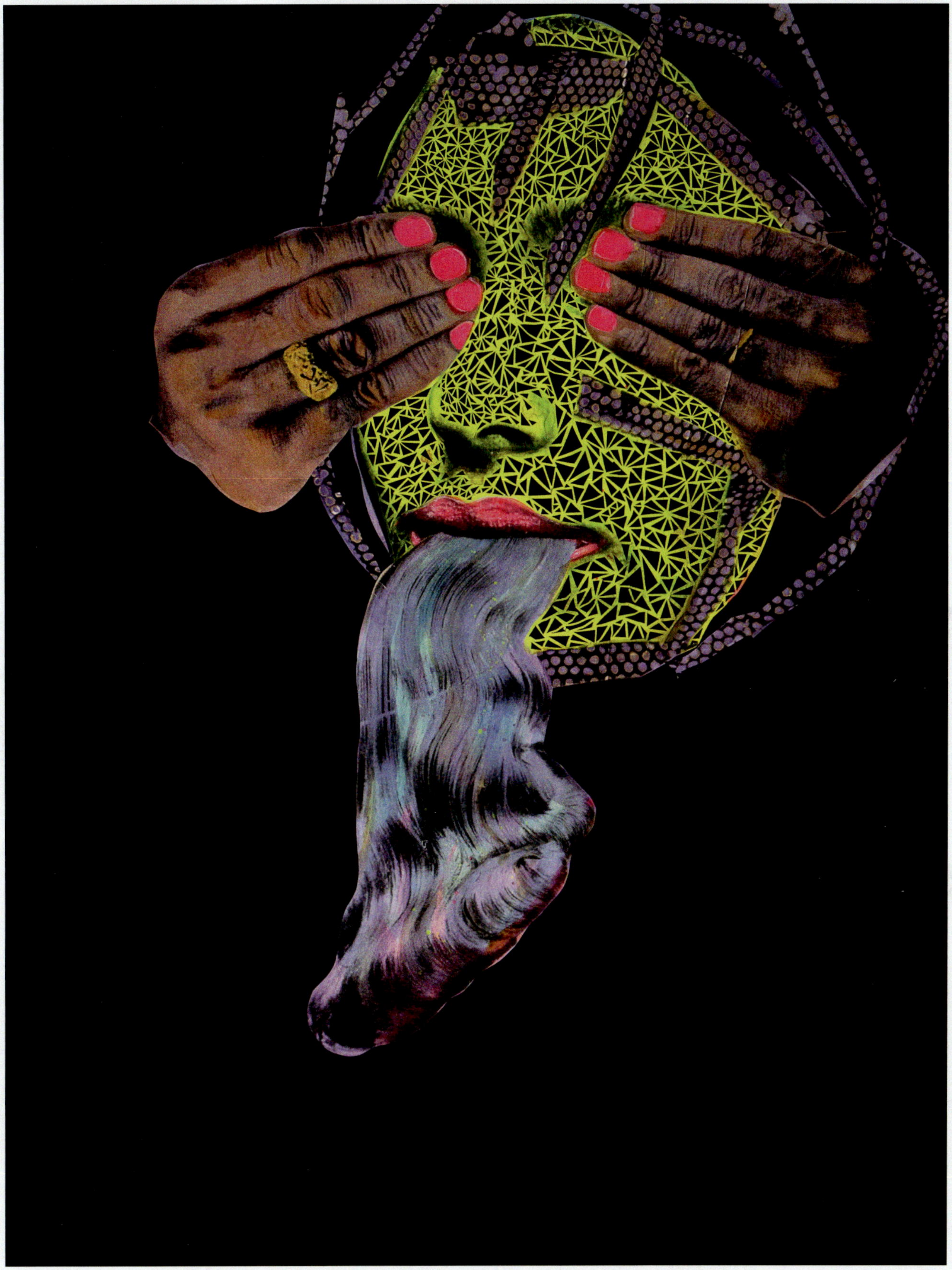

My Mother's Dream / Acrylic, paper, and resin on wood panel – 91 x 122 cm – 2011

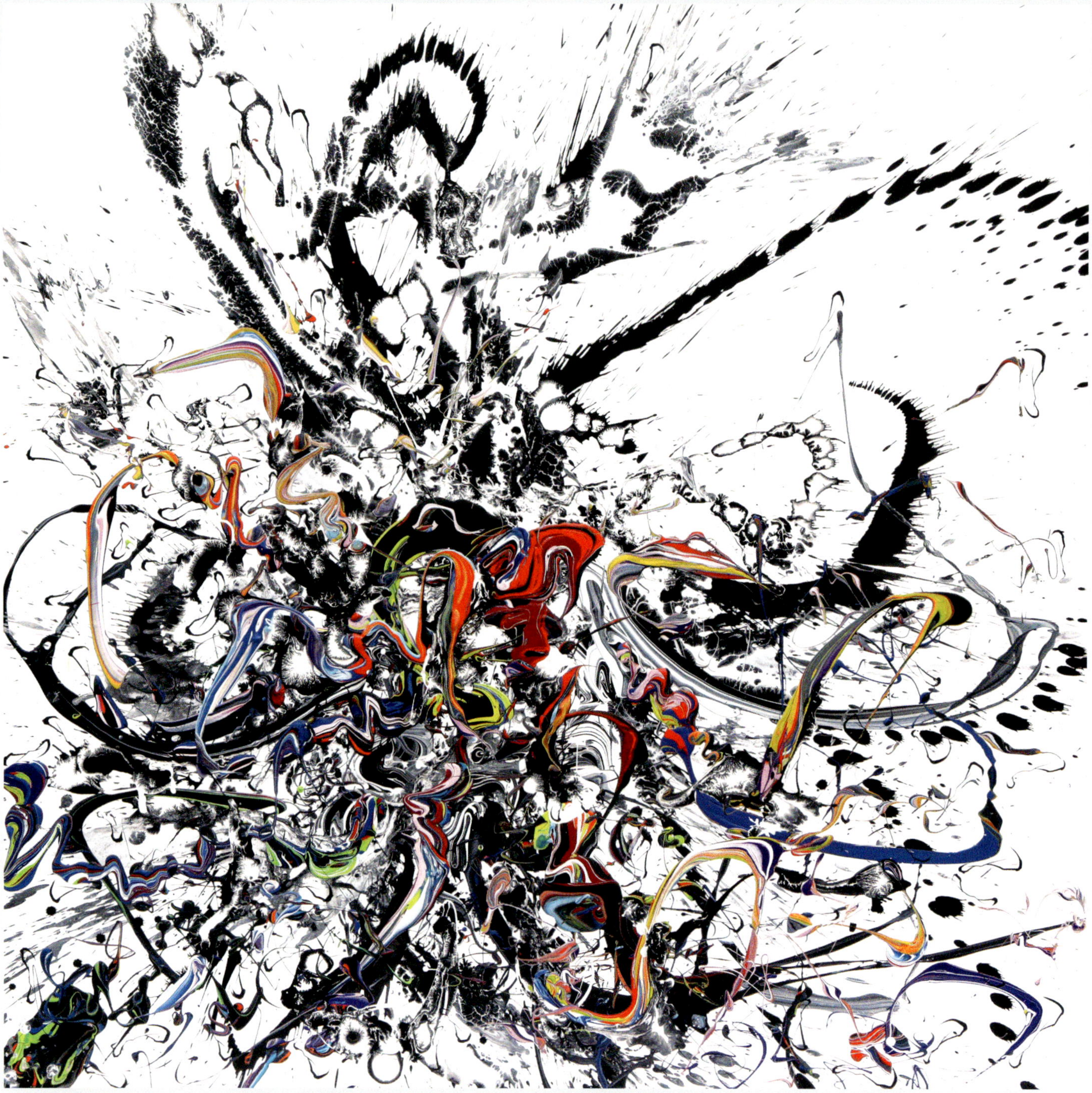

Mother Nature #16 | Acrylic on canvas – 150 x 150 x 10 cm – 2010

Katrin Fridriks

Born in Reykjavik, Iceland, 1974. Lives in Paris, France and Luxembourg.

My passion for architecture inspires me to create conceptual installations, developing new perspectives, various visual writing made up of canvas and paintings. Beyond a modern pictorial expression combining minimalism with abstract expressionism, pop colorimetry, calligraphy, and graffiti, my research focuses on substance, color, and on a thorough technique to bring a new dimension to fine art.

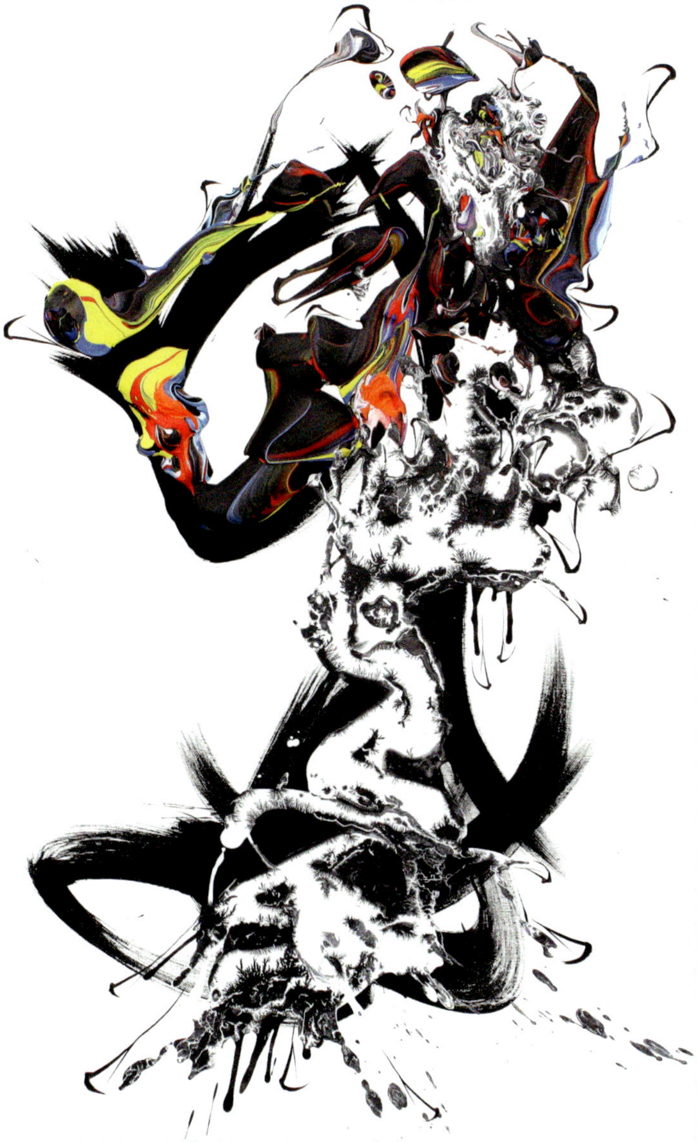

Face, Decoding Us / Acrylic on canvas – 80 x 80 cm – 2007

Kevin Cyr

Born in Edmundston, Canada, 1976. Lives in New York, United States.

Even though I don't physically do work on the street, like graffiti artists, my work is certainly influenced by street art. I like that the vans I've been painting represent working people, and finding vans covered with graffiti adds an interesting aspect to each van, making them into something very unique that is constantly evolving. I often only see vehicles once or twice, and I'm always very excited when I find the perfect combination of an interesting old van and good tags.

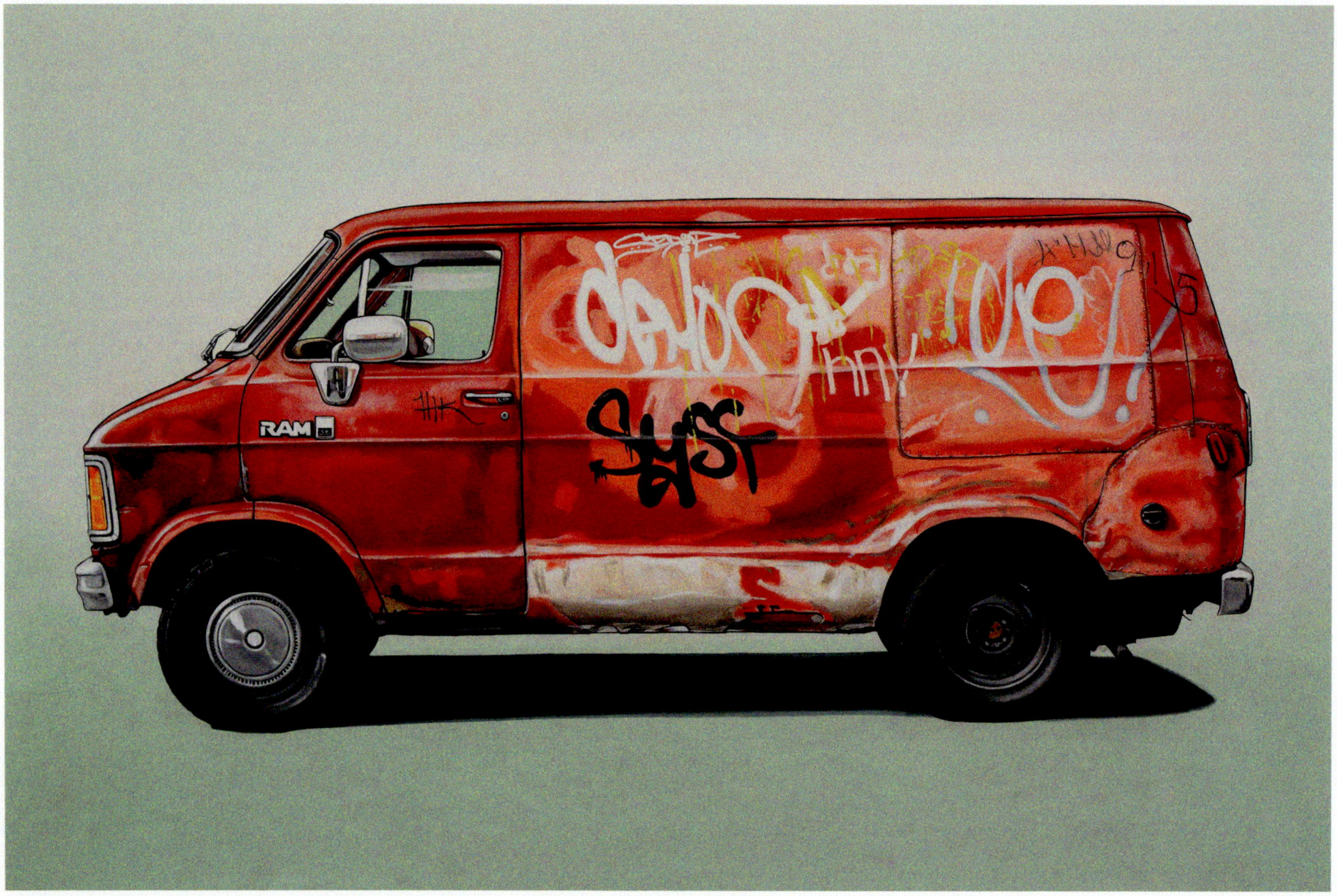

Leonard / Oil on panel – 76 x 51 cm – 2009

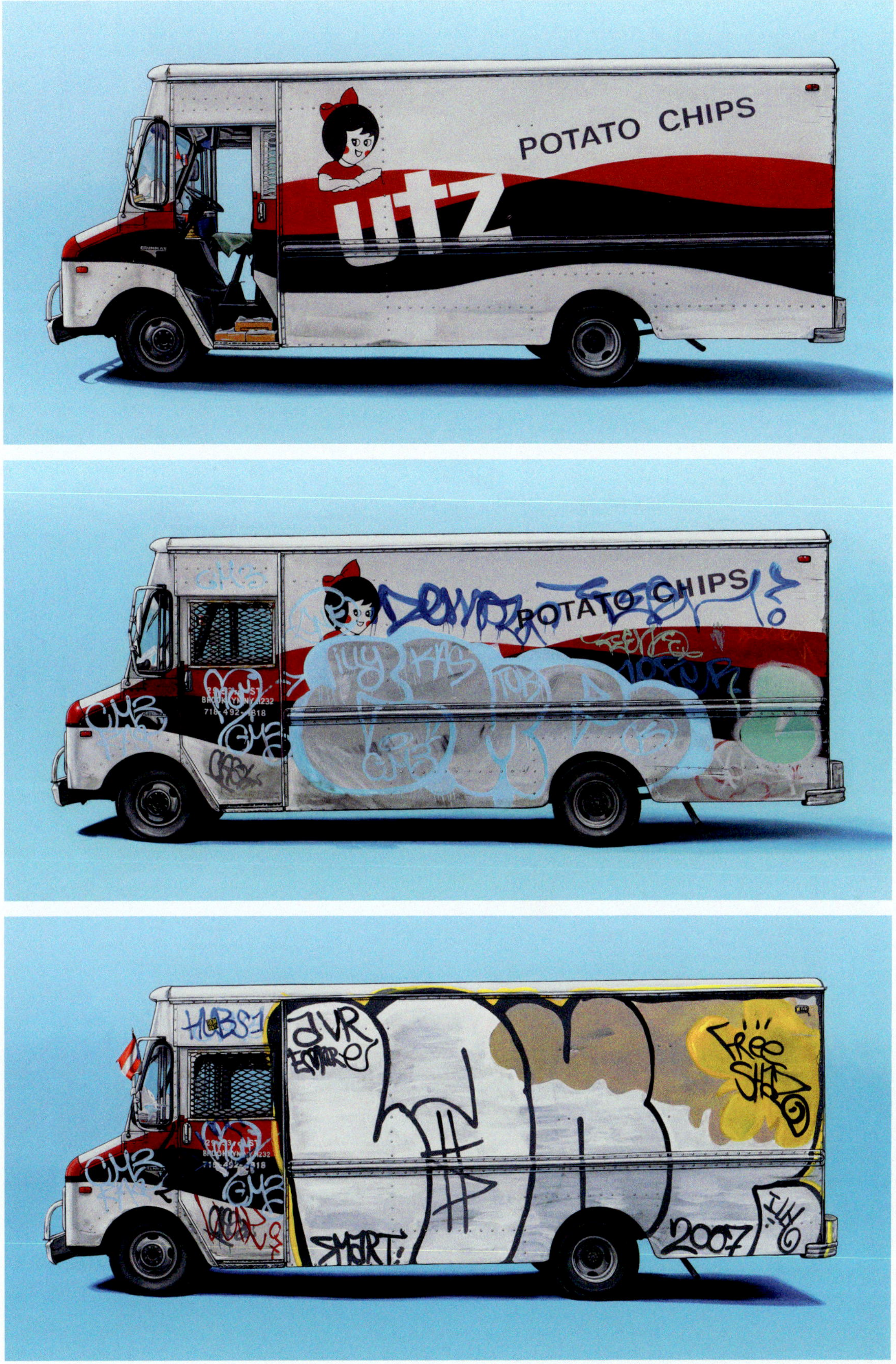

Utz **Triptych** / Oil on panel – 122 x 182 cm – 2010

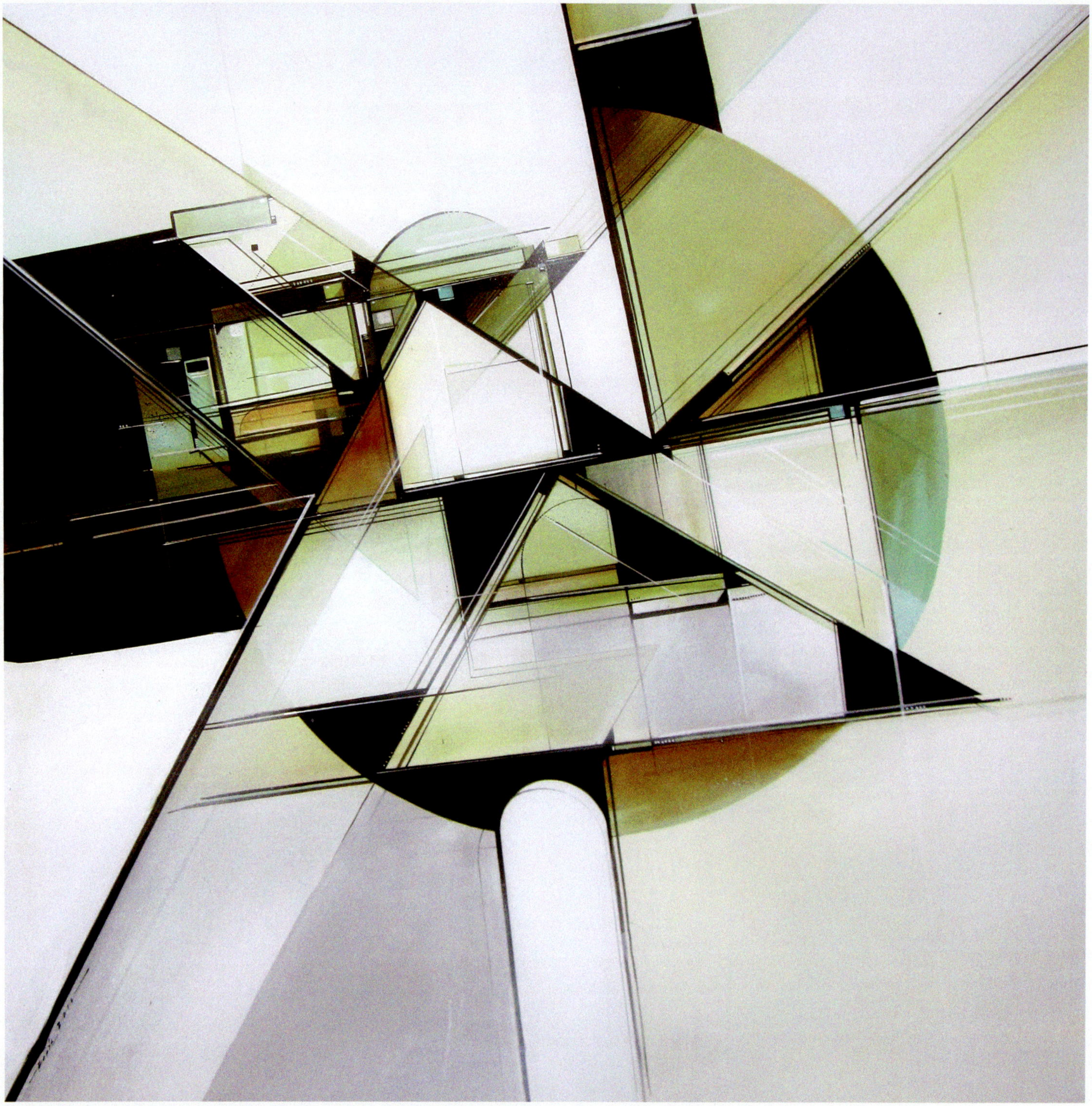

Circulatory System No. 2 | Acrylic and aerosol on primed duck canvas with matte varnish finish – 121 x 121 x 4 cm – 2010

Kofie

Born in Los Angeles, United States, 1973. Lives in Los Angeles, United States.

For me both studio and exterior work are one and the same in terms of technique. There's still a need to balance the studio work with the outdoor explorations with vintage futurist approaches and not care for what an established gallery expects from me. I am still respecting the traditions of my field yet managing to balance techniques and further the art form that gave me these freedoms, recognition, and acknowledgment.

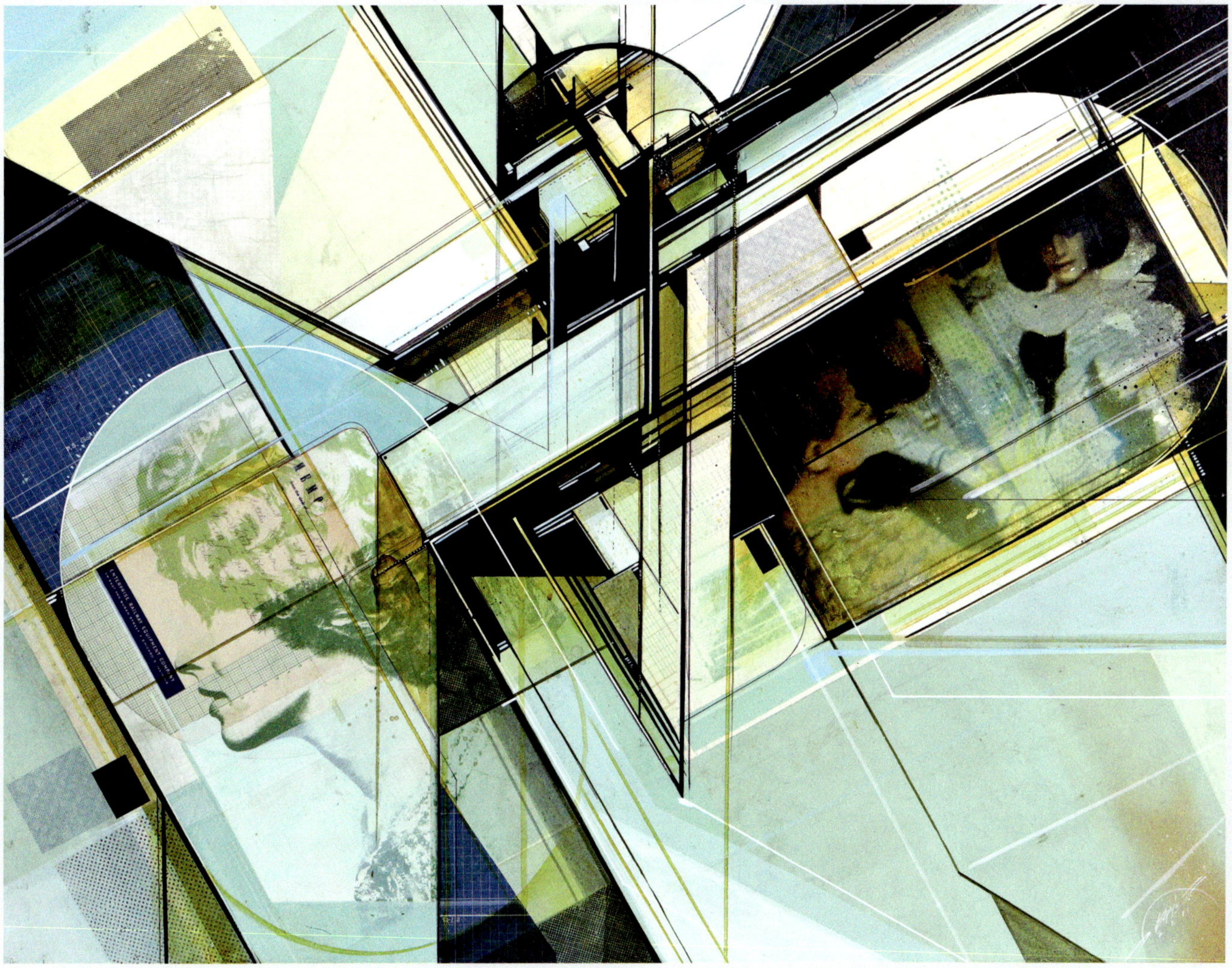

Linear Lovely / Found vintage paper, ballpoint pen, acrylic, white-out, xerographic gel transfer, acrylic, and matte gel on wood panel – 92 x 72 x 5 cm – 2011

L'Atlas

Born in Paris, France, 1978. Lives in Paris, France.

My love for the city came from my fascination for the image. I started to build a personal vision of the city through the lens of my camera. The presence of the writing in the urban space projected me to the other side of the lens, like a calligrapher who would project himself on a paper sheet, to become an actor of this movement we call today street art, or art of rebellion.

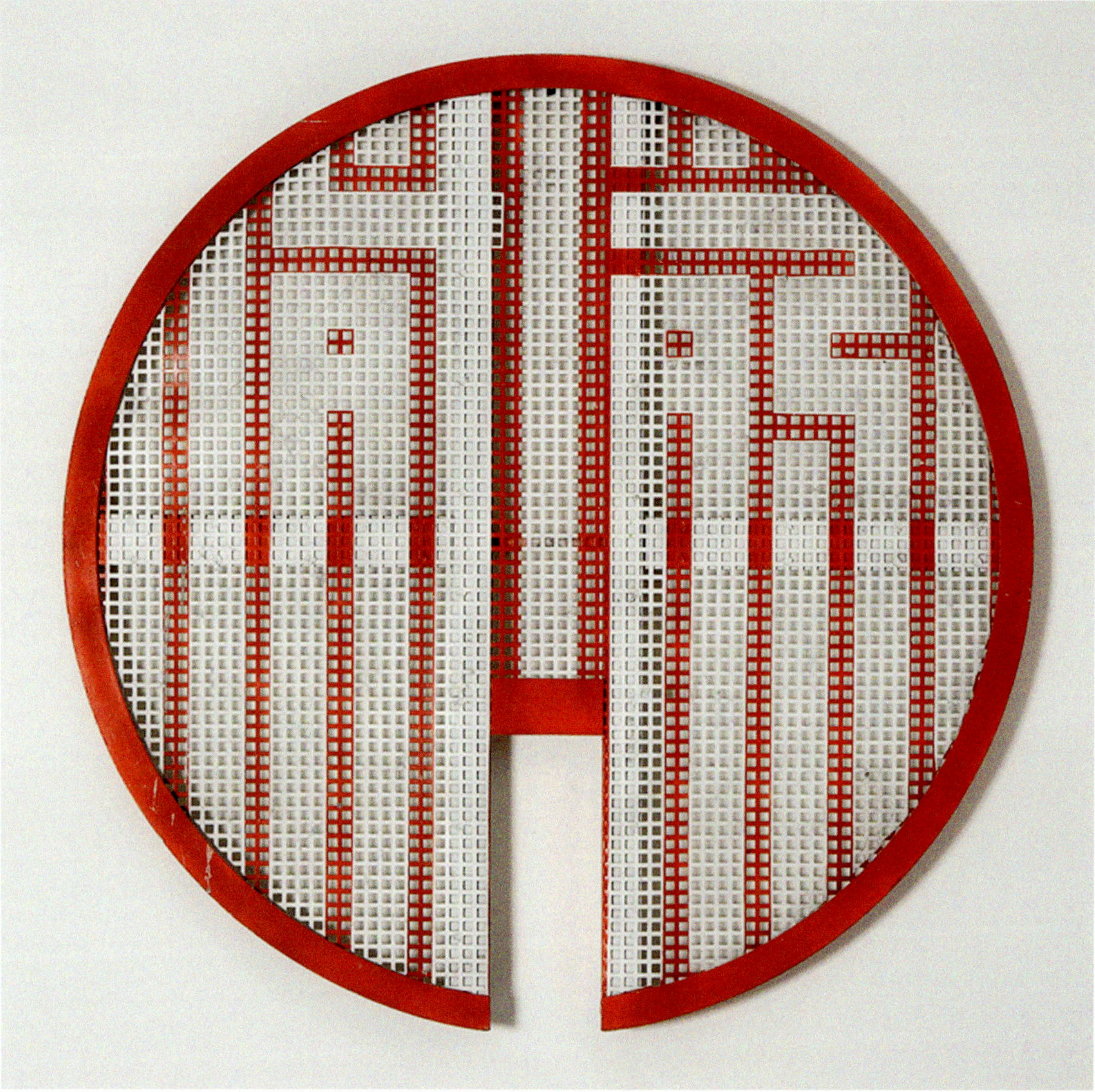

Red Point | Aerosol on metal manhole grill – 80 cm – 2005

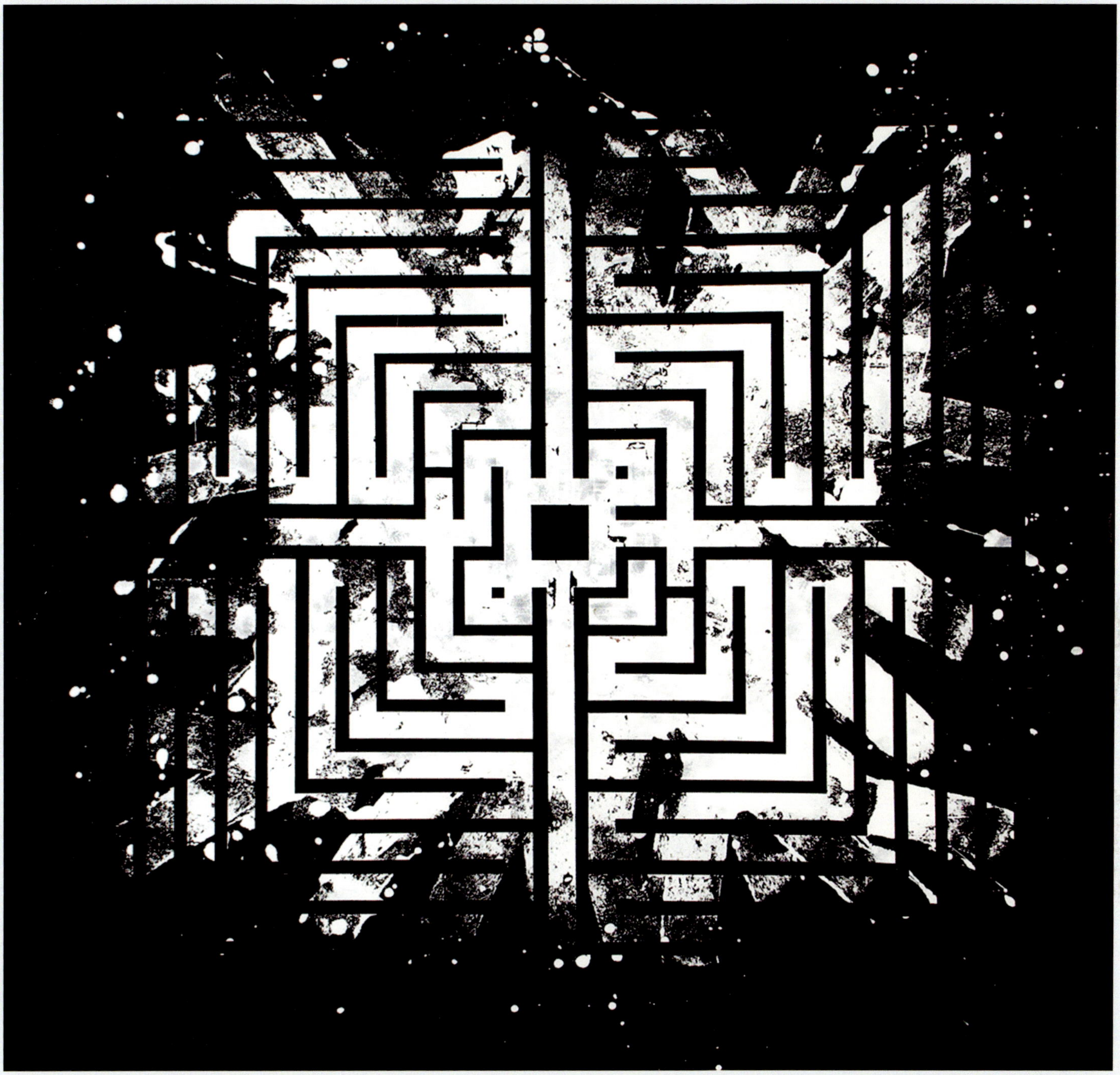

Big Bang / Acrylic and aerosol on canvas – 210 x 200 cm – 2010

Lightgraff

Brusk, Light Writer. Born in Lyon, France, 1976. Lives in Lyon, France.
Guillaume J. Plisson, Photographer. Born in Lyon, France, 1976. Lives in Lyon, France.

More than an art form, Lightgraff is a discipline, an intimate alchemy between our cameras and magical tools: LEDs, neon lights, laser beams, and so on. Like graffiti, it's a science of movement that allows us to ephemerally take possession of the places we go. Lurking, we creep at night, set up our gear and launch in thirty seconds to three minutes choreographies, creating fantasy-like images invisible to the eye...

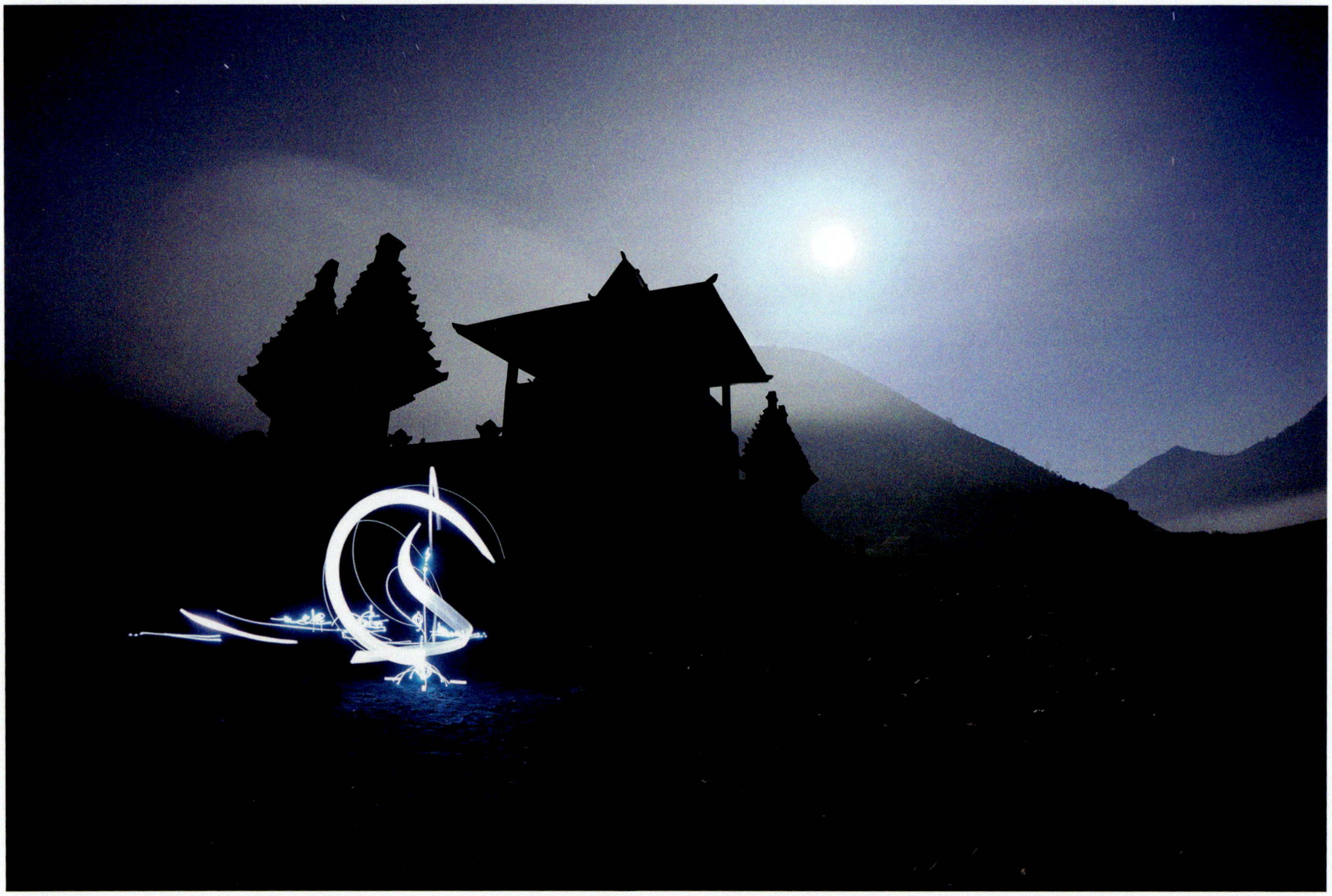

Caldeira of Bromo. Java, Indonesia / Photography, flashlight, neon, and LEDs – 2009

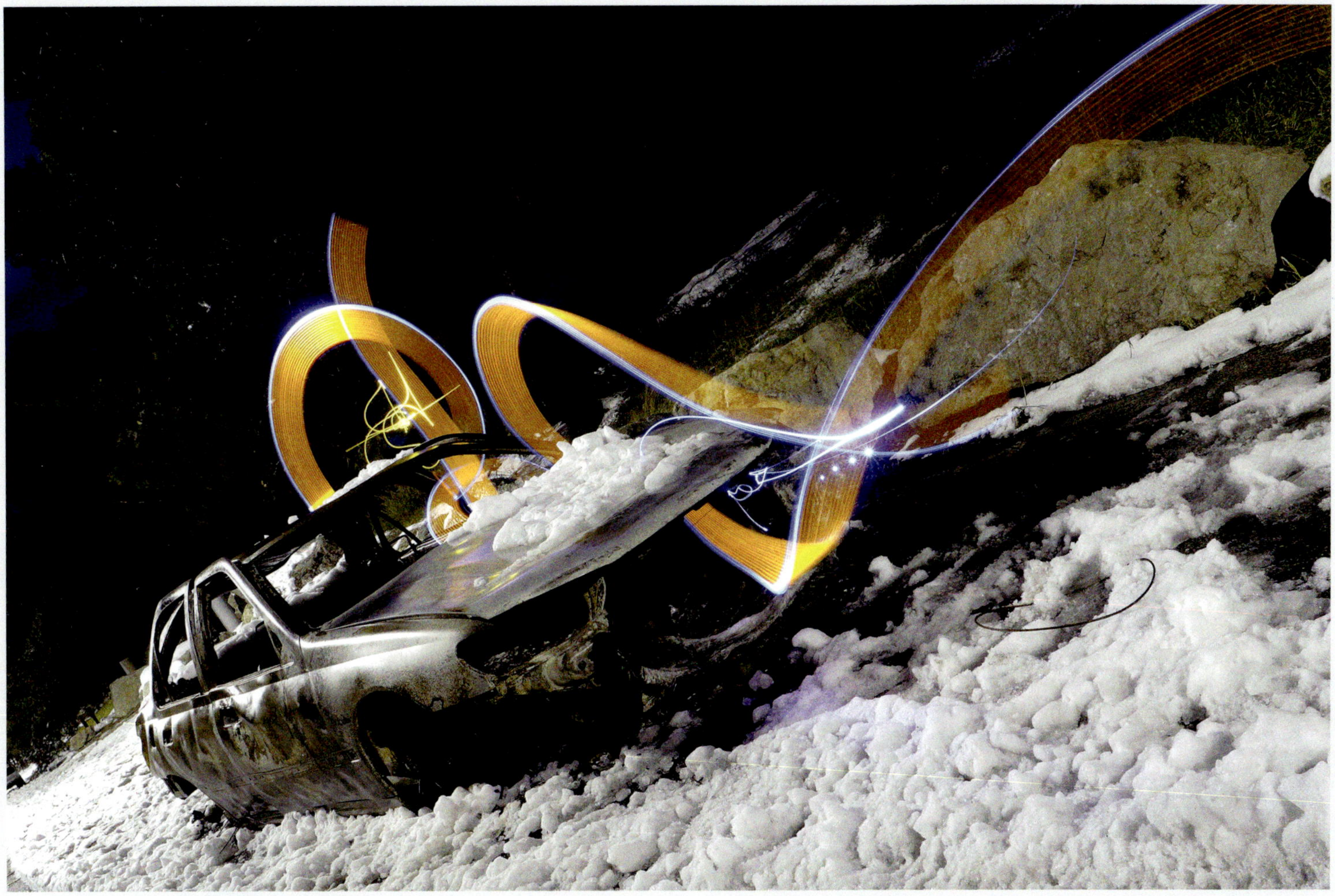

Light Car. Marseille, France / Photography, flashlight, neon, and LEDs – 2009

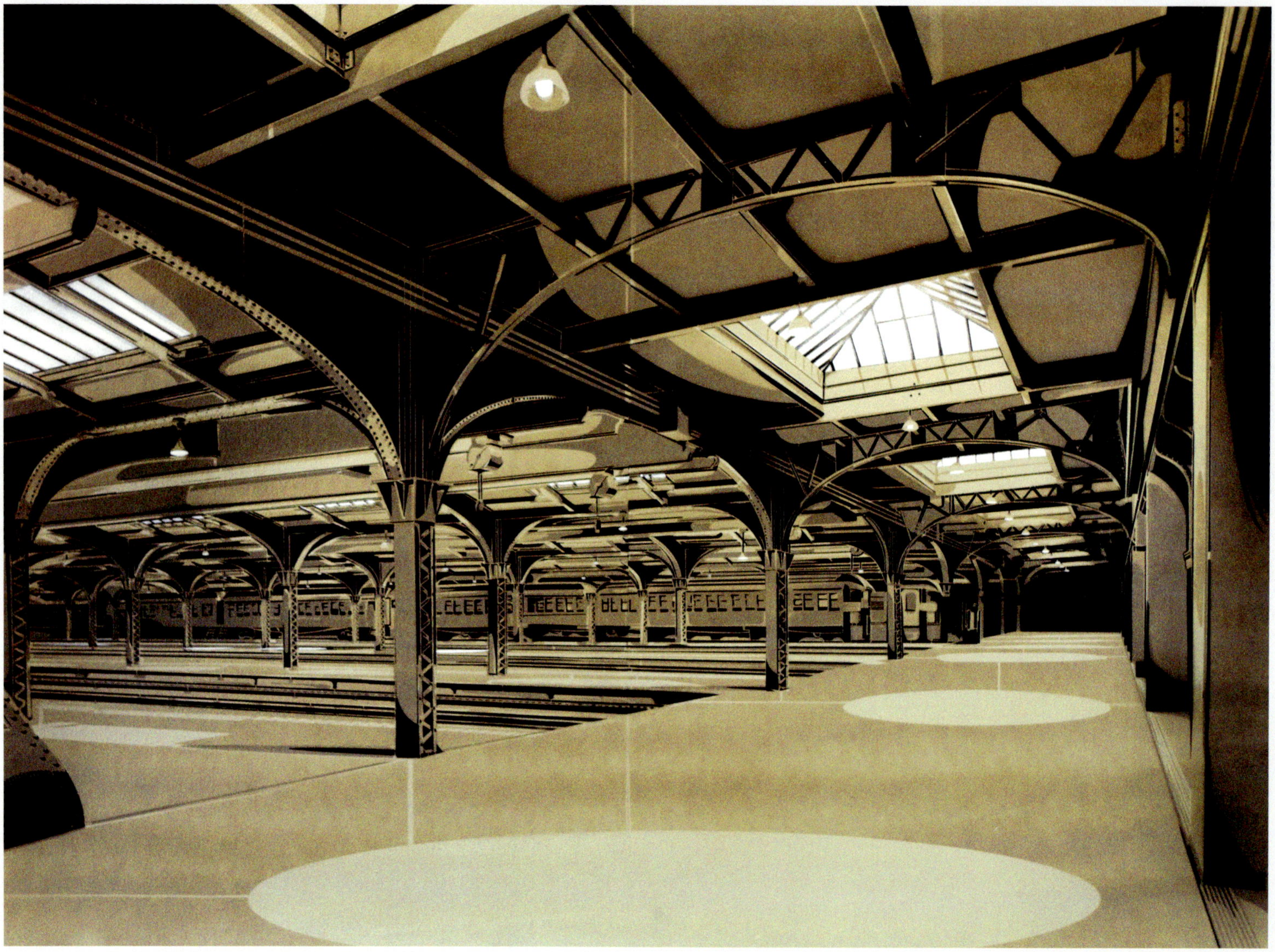

Recesses (Gold) / Stencil and aerosol on board – 123 x 91 cm – 2010

Logan Hicks

Born in Key West, United States, 1971. Lives in New York, United States.

The street is not my canvas, but rather my subject. It's the urban Möbius strip that twists the day into night under the artificial lights without so much as a pause from its inhabitants. It's a 24-hour machine that never sleeps. City streets are the blood lines that bring life to my work.

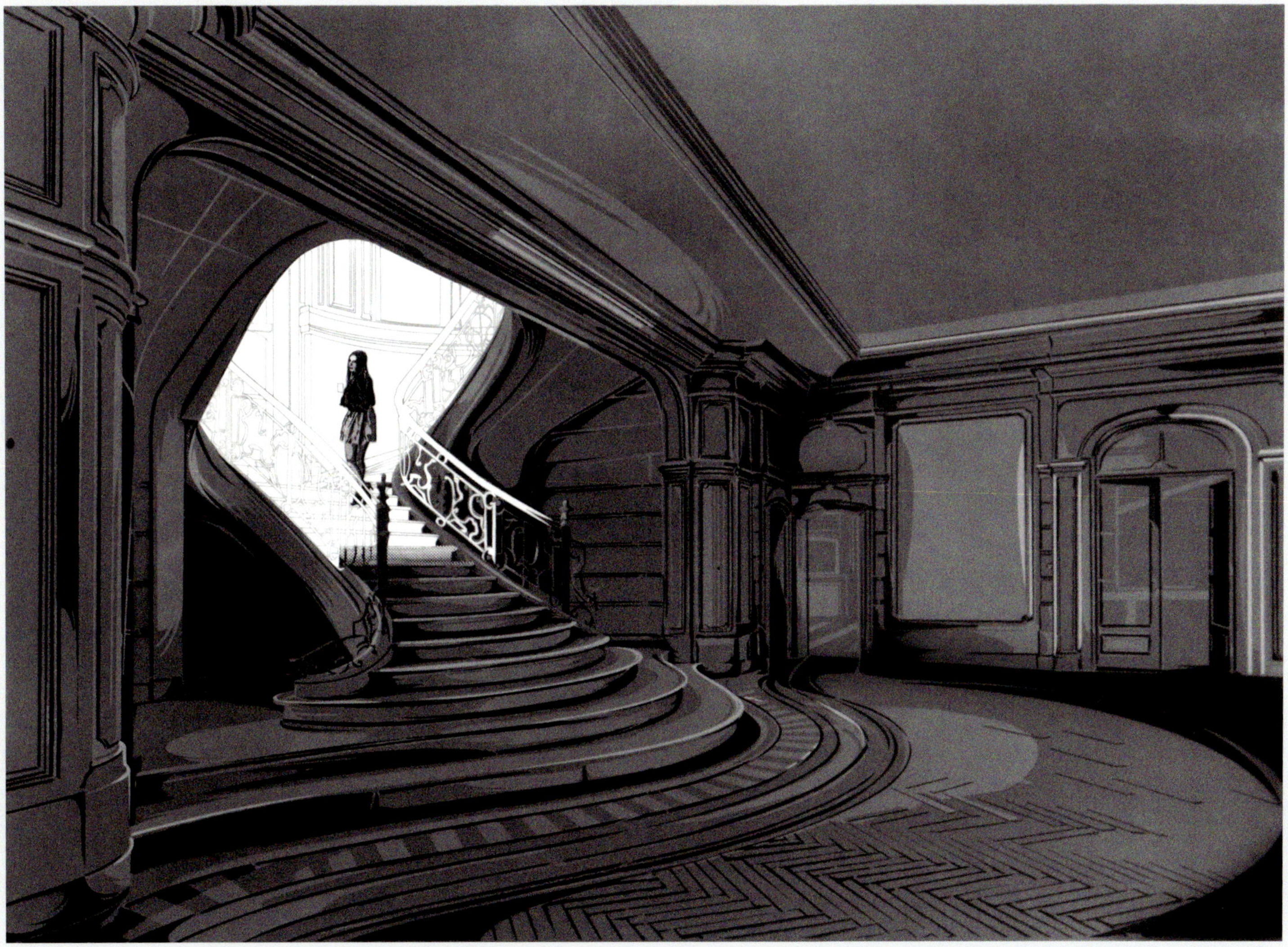

Chateau Du Loup / Stencil and aerosol on acrylic – 123 x 91 cm – 2010

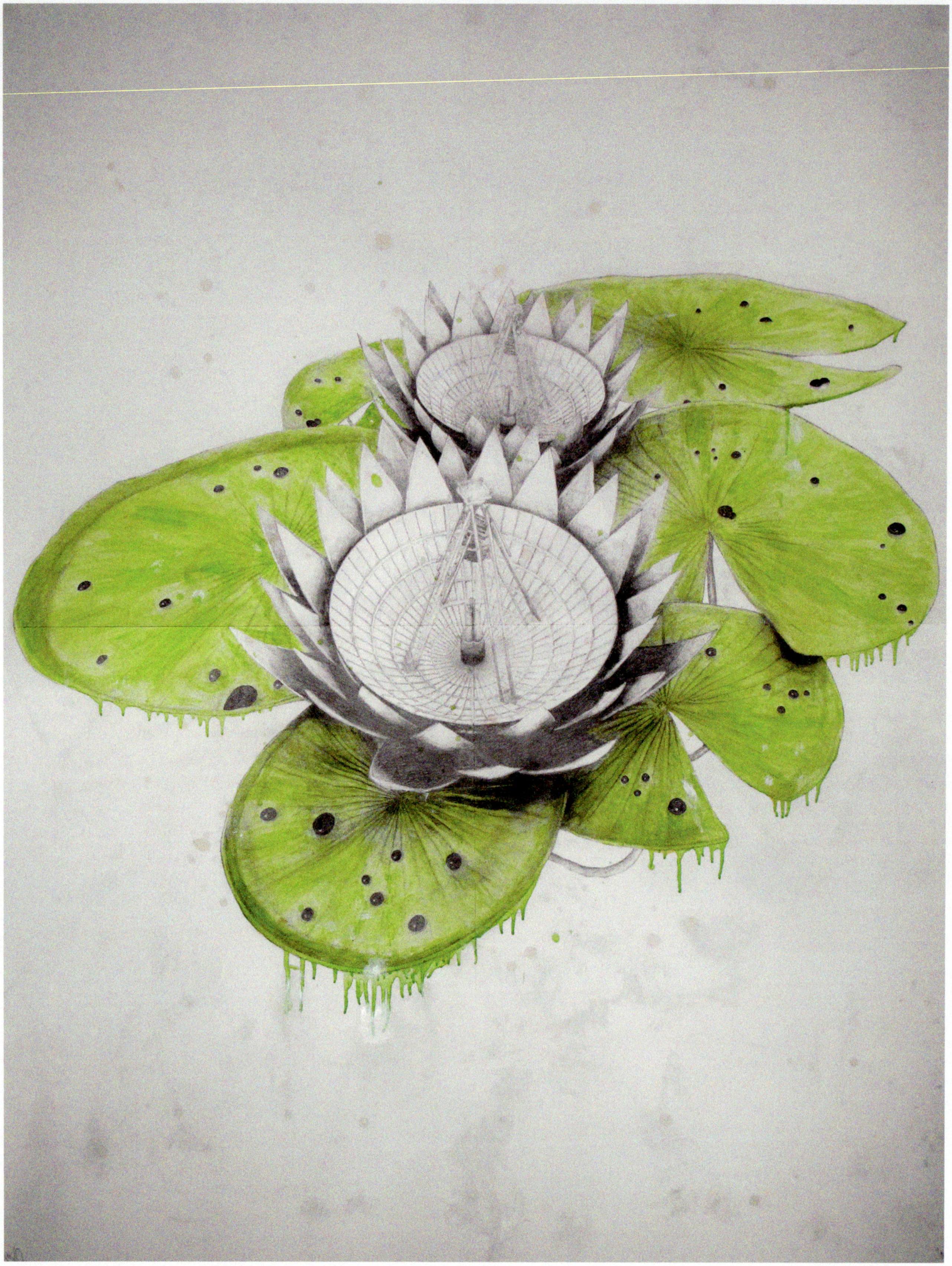

The Nympheas / Graphite and oil on paper – 100 x 130 cm – 2011

Ludo

Born in Paris, France, 1976. Lives in Paris, France.

The streets give me the liberty to spread my art without any limitations. My work started its life in this outside laboratory then evolved (or not) with different mediums inside galleries. Sometimes it's kind of hard to create inside works without the energy and textures of the street environment but it makes me develop and adapt my pieces using the time and techniques the studio allows me.

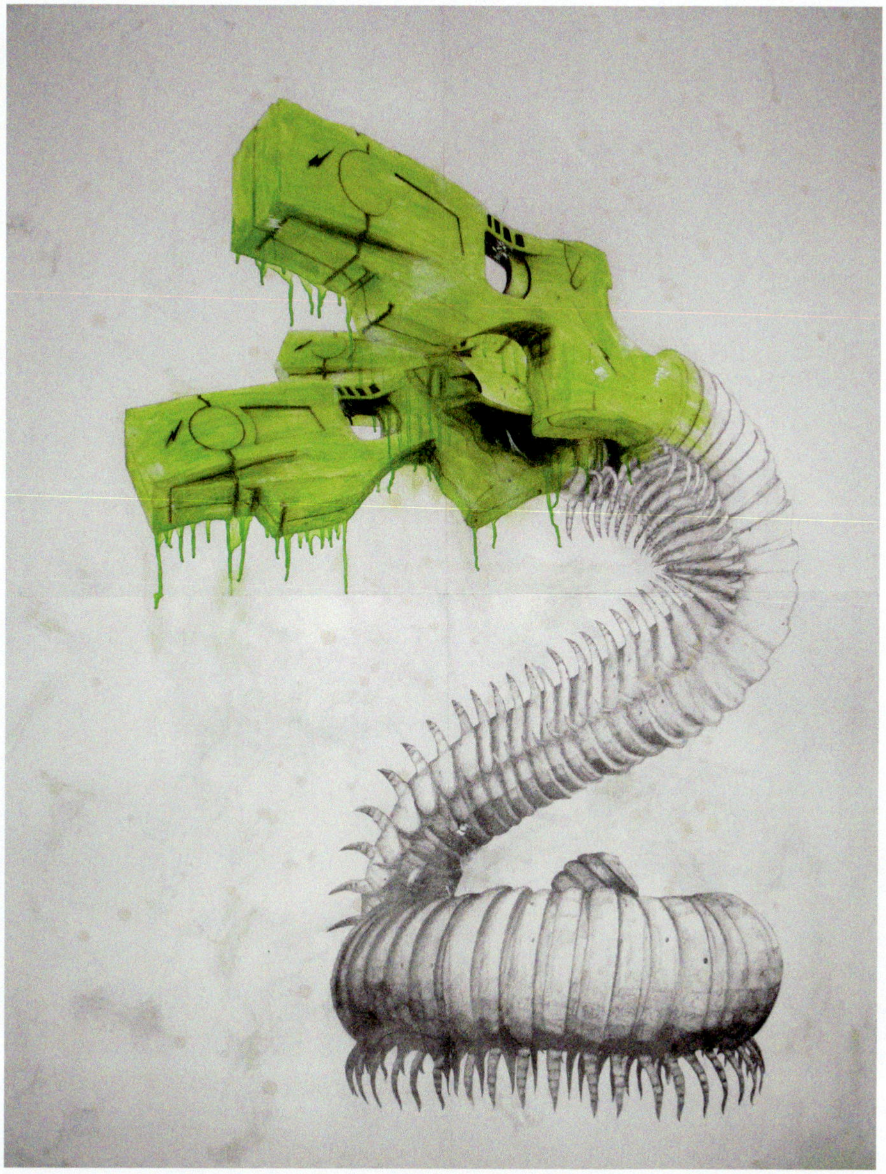

Heads Taseropode / Graphite and oil on paper – 100 x 130 cm – 2011

M-City

Born in Gdynia, Poland, 1978. Lives in Gdańsk, Poland.

Many people ask me about my inside works, if that's still street art. And I say no. For me it's something absolutely different. It's a part of painting, graphic design, sculpture, etc. I prefer to make outside works, in open spaces, dedicated to a special place. Outside works are more visible. Everyone can see and experience it. I can say something and maybe I can change a local neighborhood. I also work in galleries and I like it too, like canvases, installations but the problem is that it's just for other artists, just for curators and visitors. And for money of course.

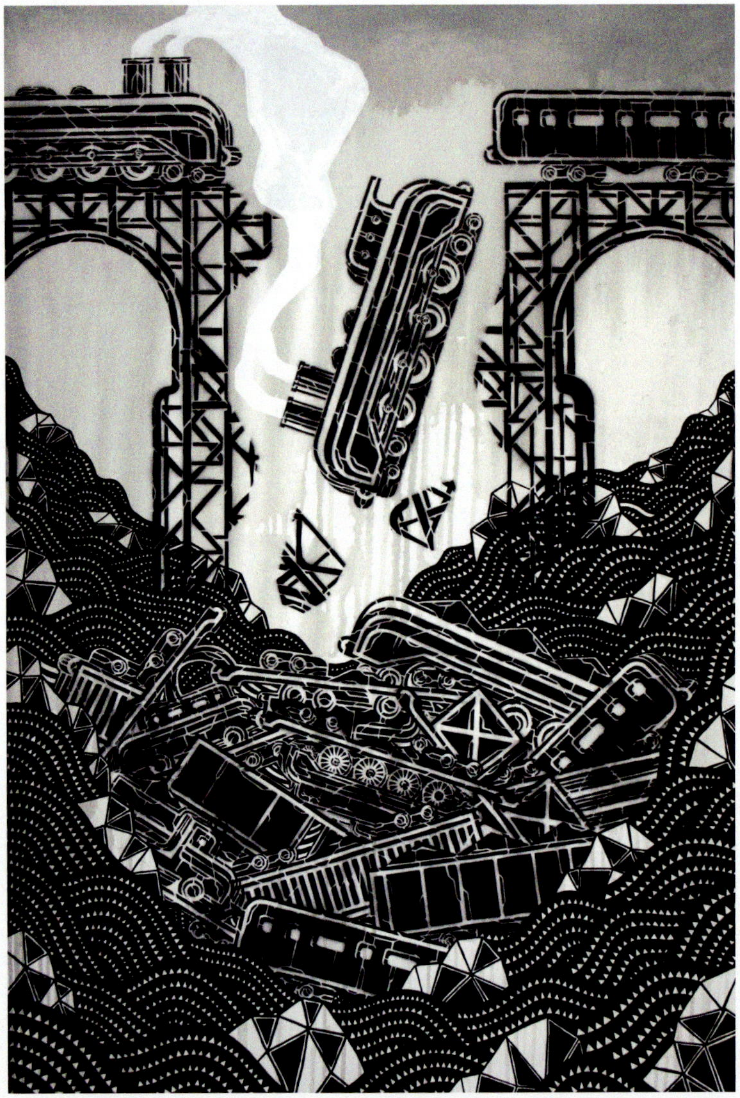

M-City 391 / Stencil, aerosol, and acrylic on canvas – 80 x 120 cm – 2011

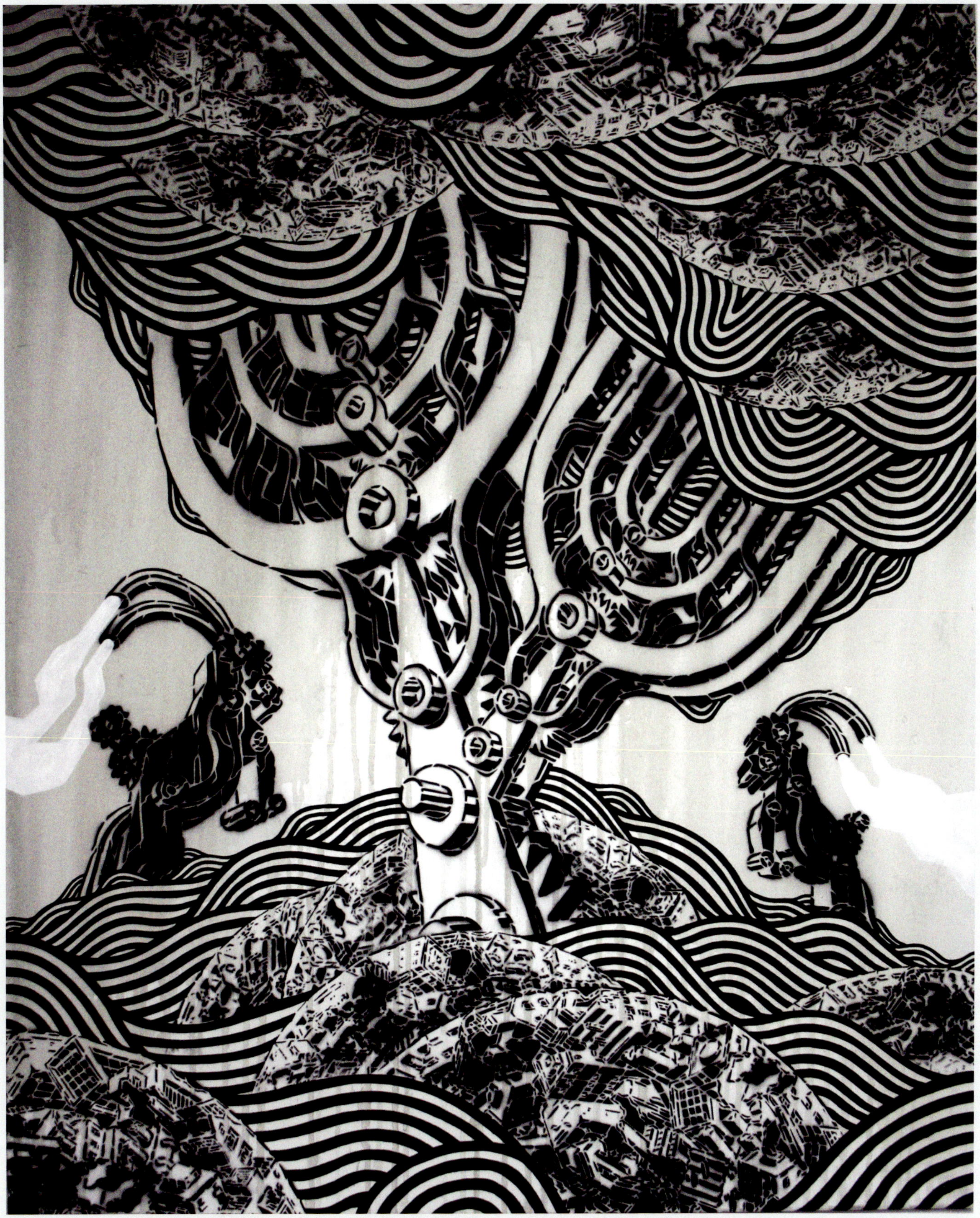

M-City 394 / Stencil, aerosol, and acrylic on canvas – 80 x 100 cm – 2011

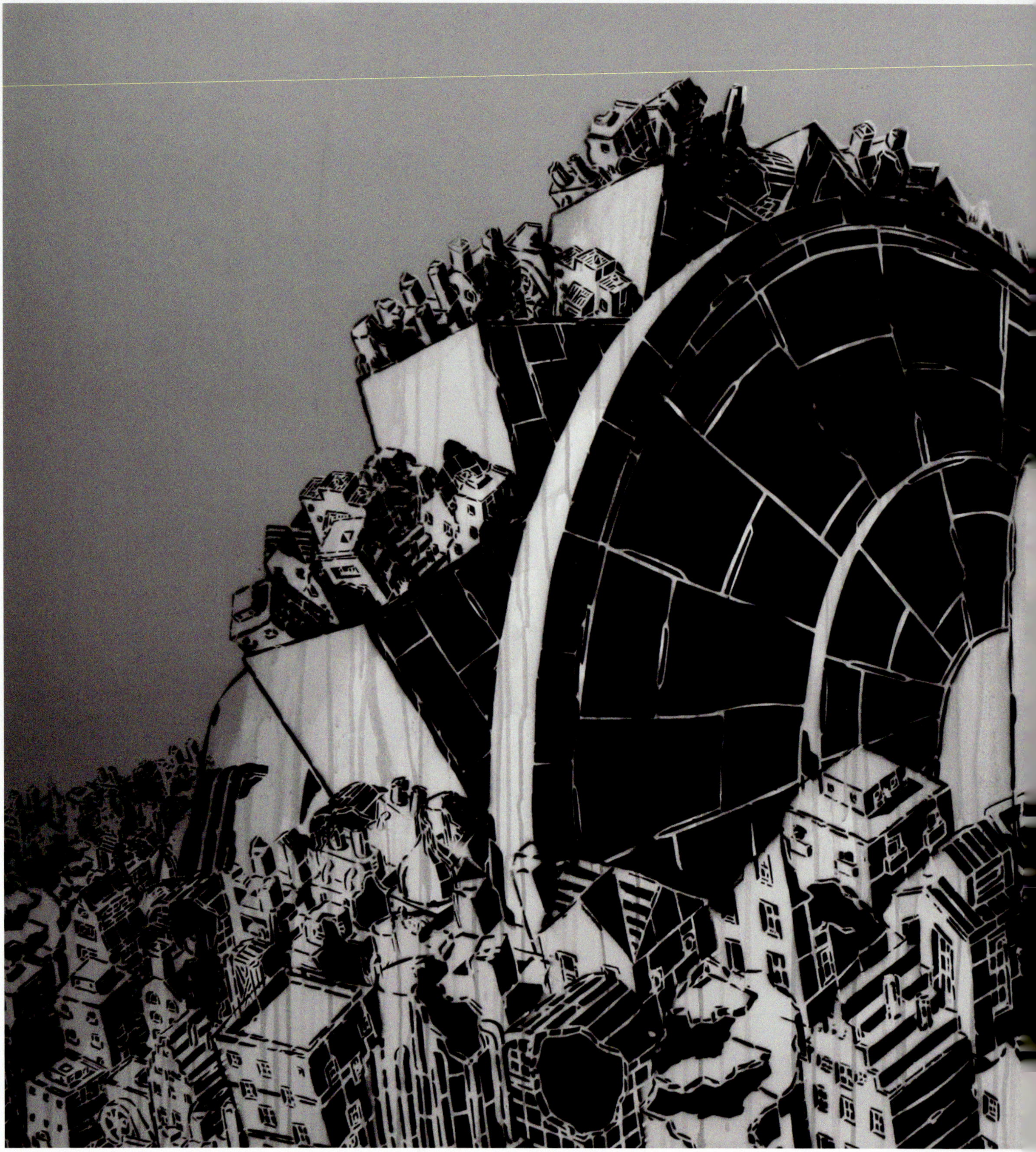

M-City 205 / Stencil, aerosol, and acrylic on canvas – 150 x 100 cm – 2009

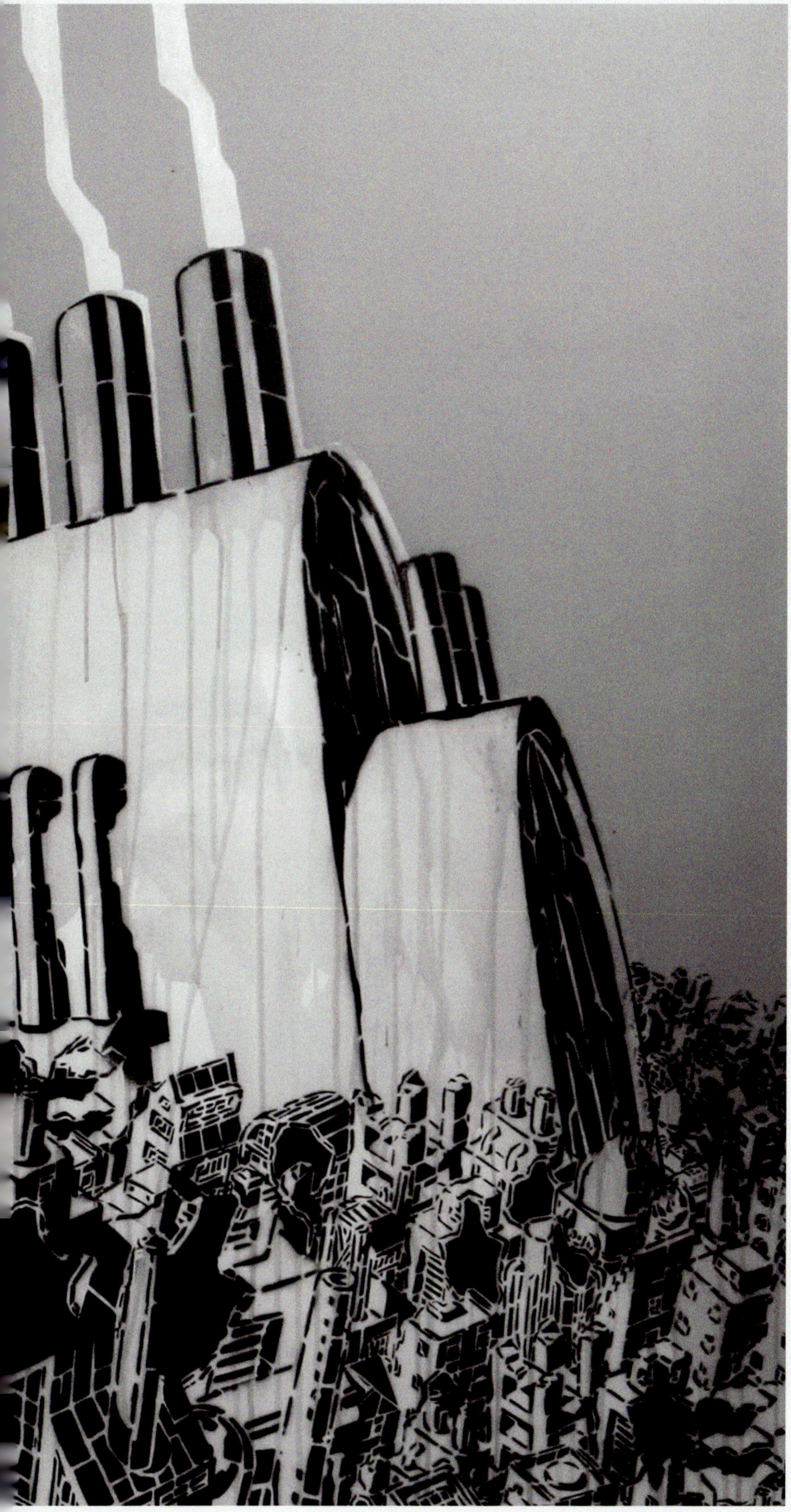

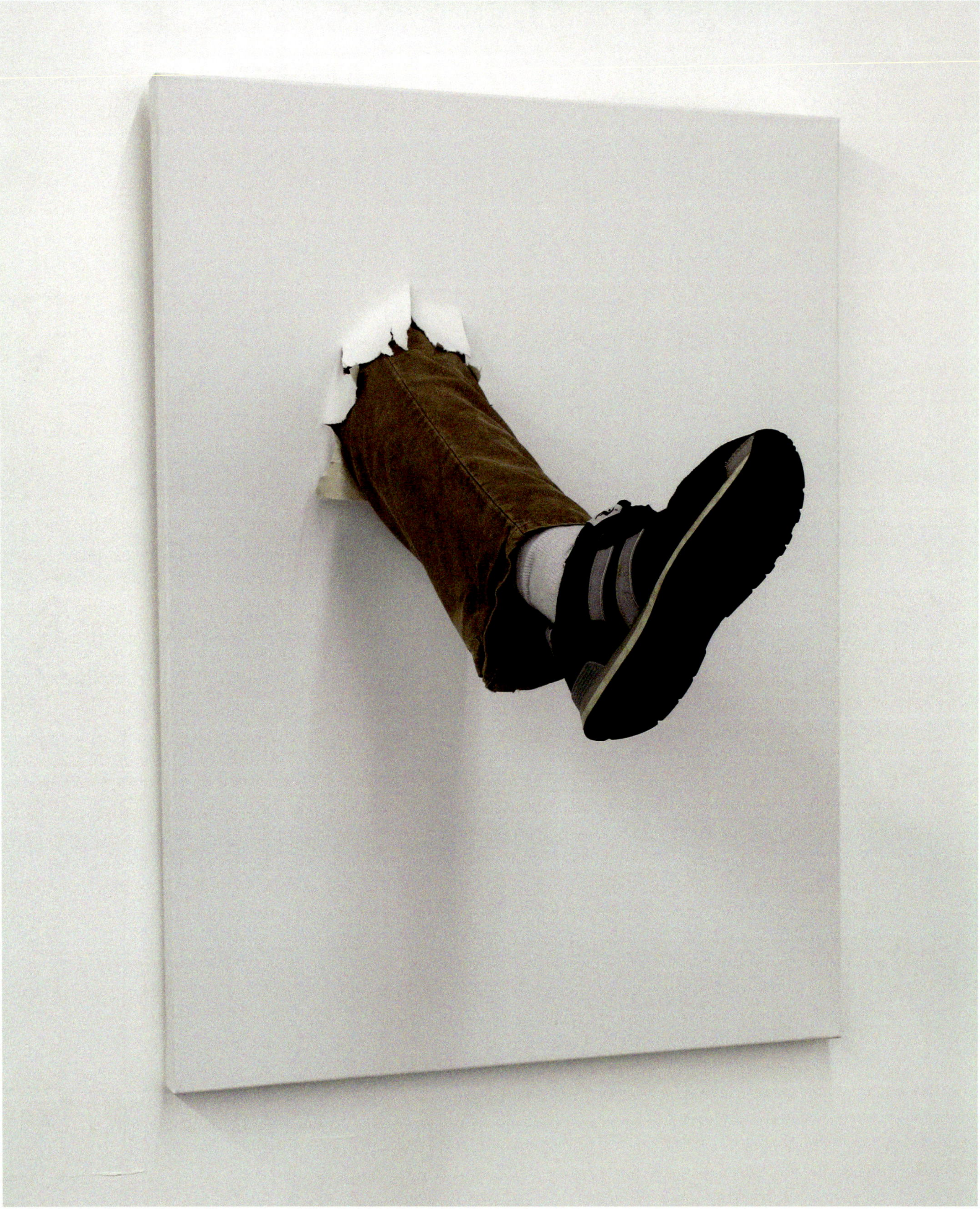

Kicked Painting Series / Mixed media – 61 x 92 cm – 2010

Mark Jenkins

Born in Fairfax, United States, 1970. Lives in Washington DC, United States.

The first place I showed my work was on the streets in Rio de Janeiro (2003). I installed a sculpture that was a cast of myself in a trash dumpster. It was picked up later that night by a garbage truck, crushed into its hull and taken off to the dump. I realized through this experience that the street was the ideal stage for my work and I've been exploring it ever since.

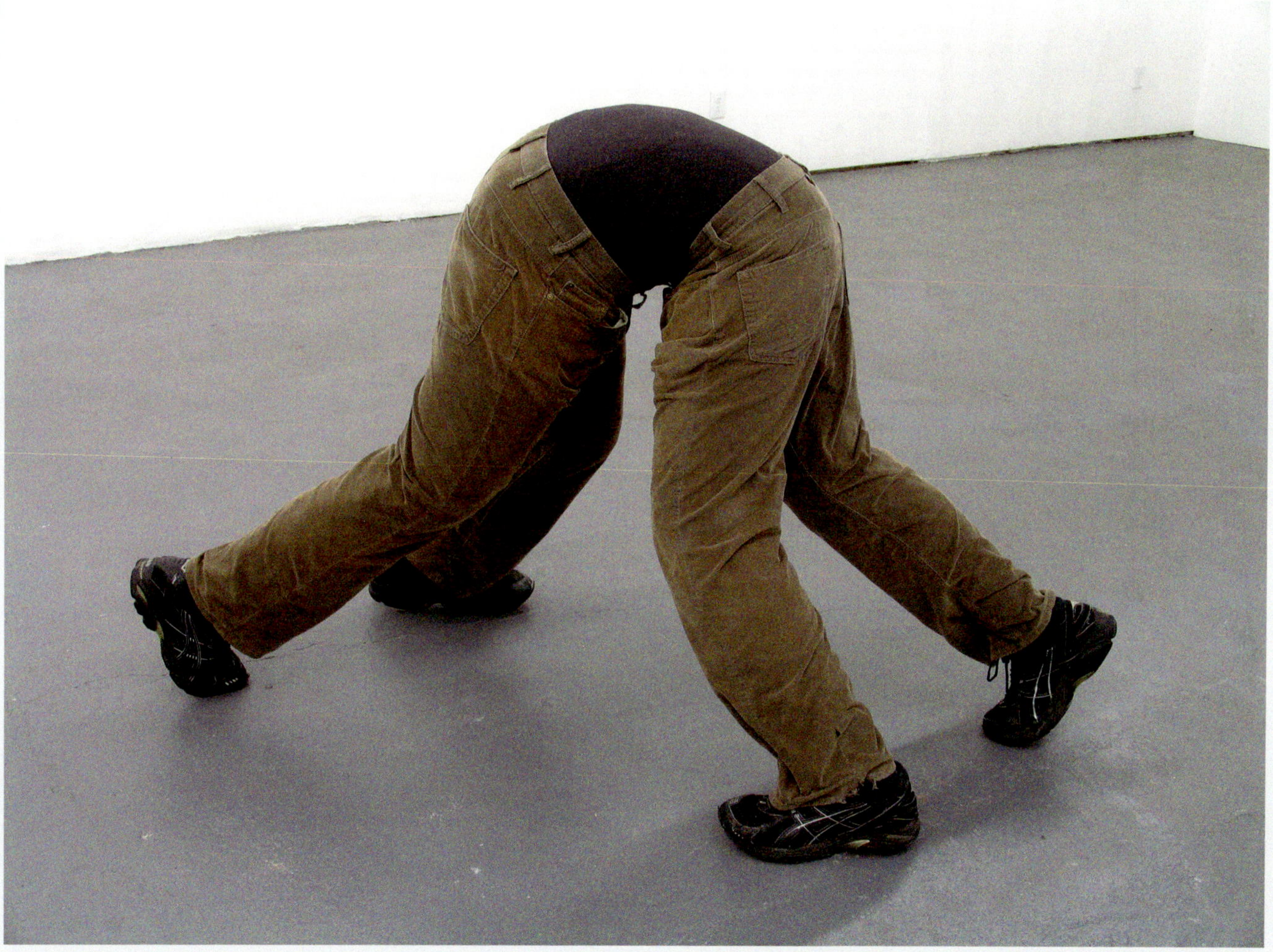

Winner Takes All | Mixed media – 170 x 74 x 124 cm – 2010

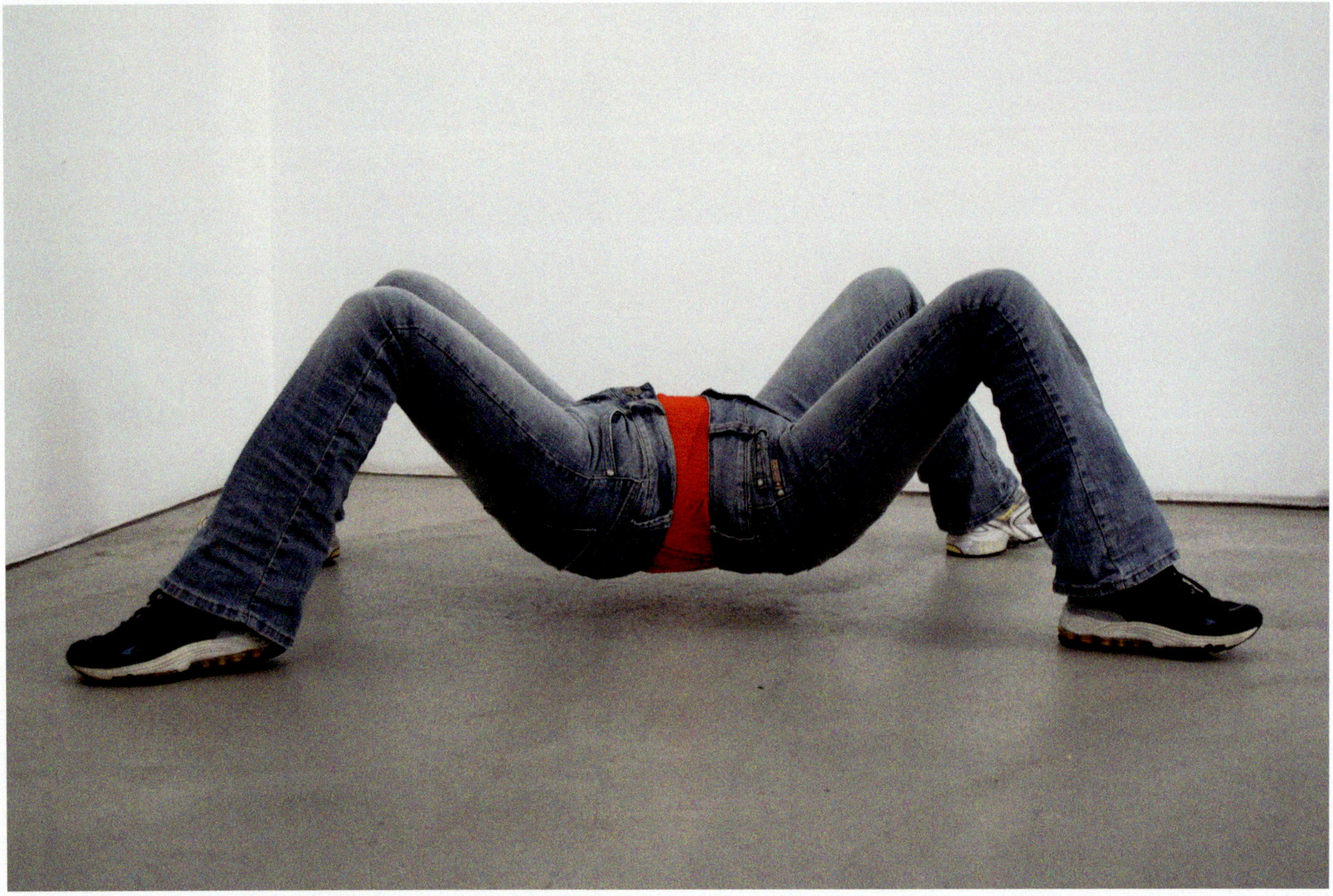

Spiderlegs / Mixed Media – 130 x 86 x 69 cm – 2010

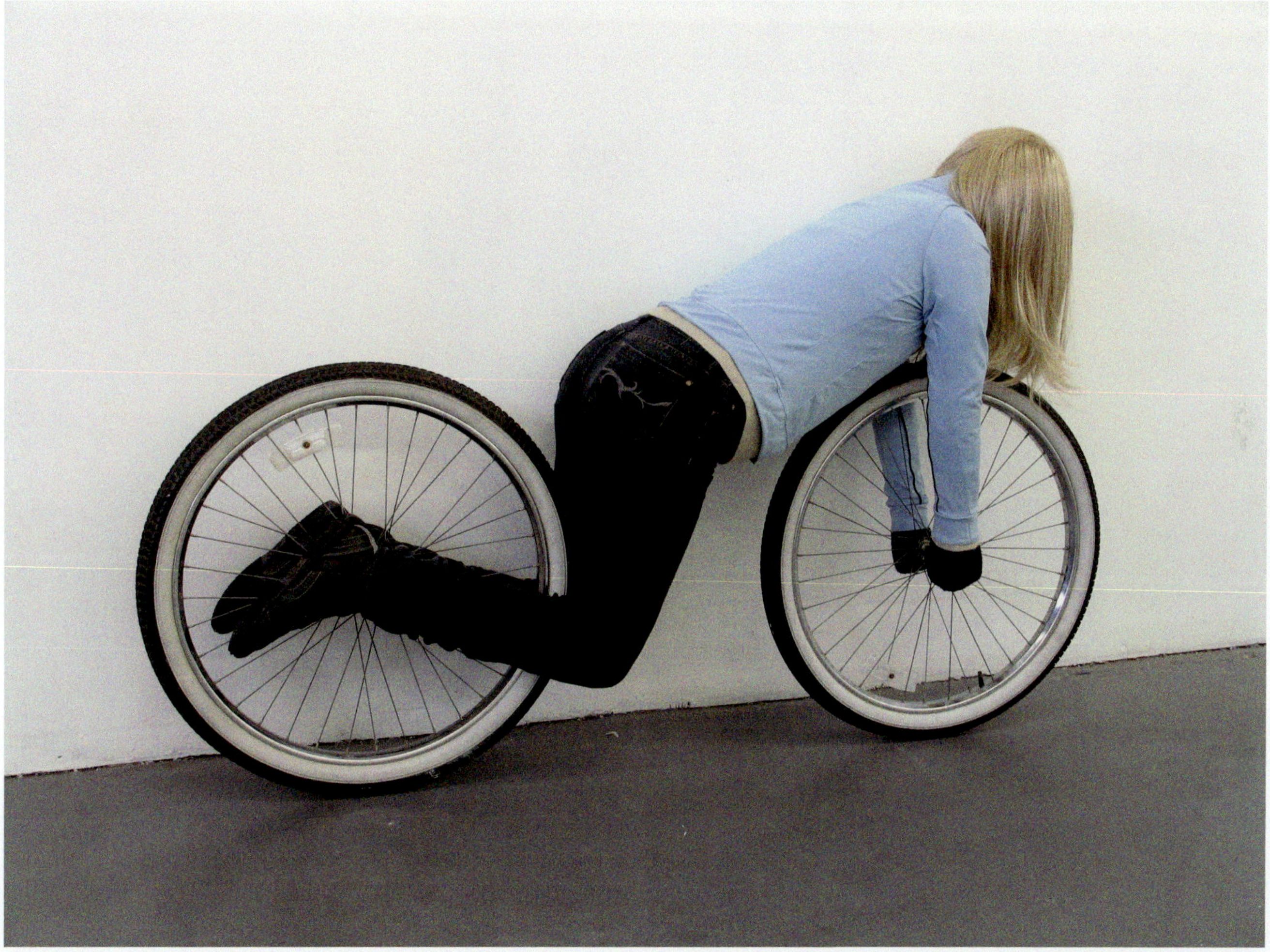

Spokes / Mixed media – 157 x 48 x 99 cm – 2010

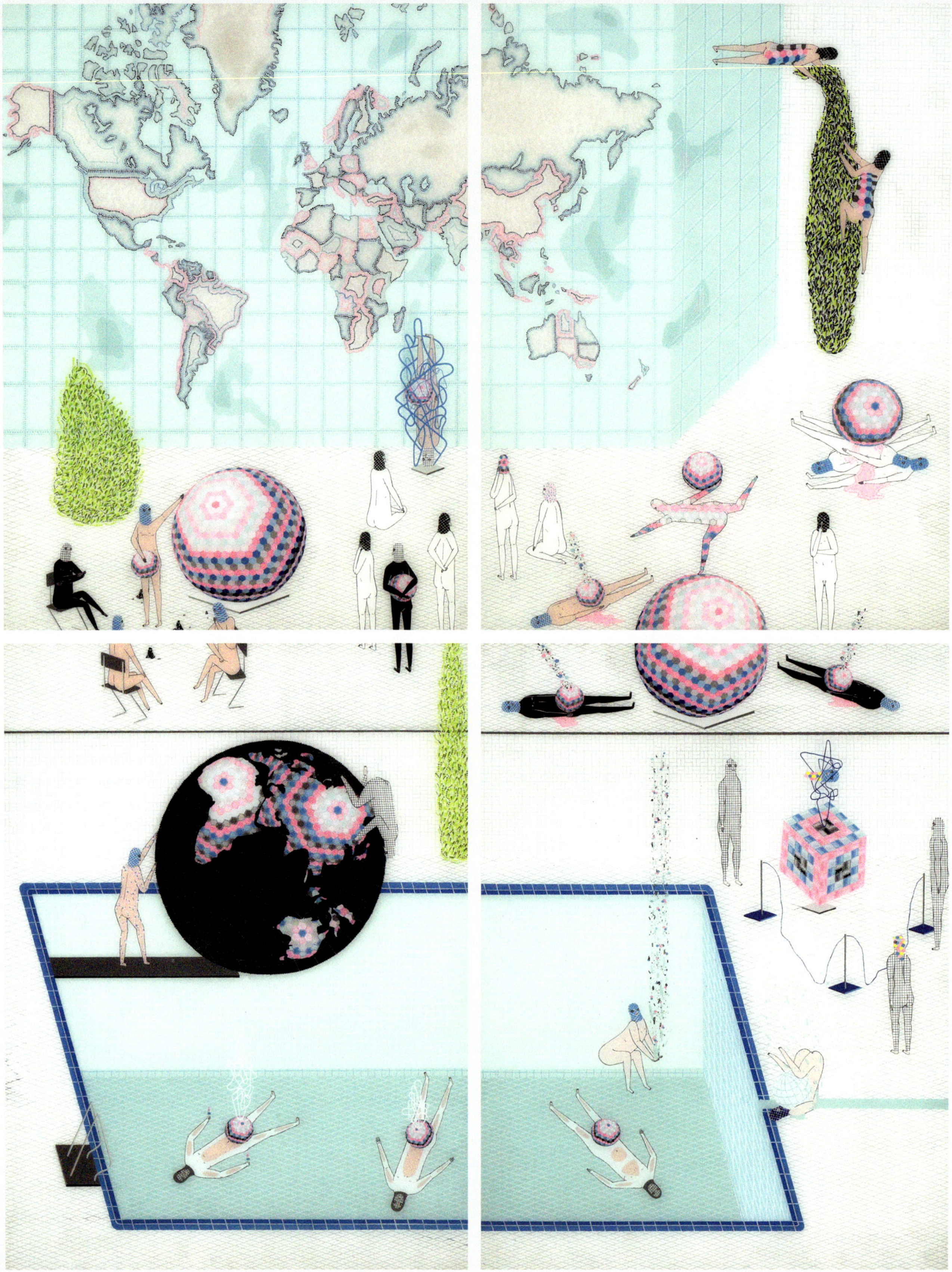

The Map Room **Quadtych** / Acrylic, ink, gouache, and resin on paper mounted on wood – 120 x 89 cm – 2011

Mark Whalen aka Kill Pixie

Born in Sydney, Australia, 1982. Lives in Los Angeles, United States.

My work is an examination of humanity; set as a forecast-projecting communication, emotion, sexuality, humor, and the greater experience of mankind. I create an ideolect where solitary individuals live in a sterile and scientific world but carry out a ritualistic investigation into metaphysic issues of the modern man. Identity, alienation, globalization, environmentalism, and creativity are turned upside down and inside out and like in the real world we the viewers are never in a state of objective knowing.

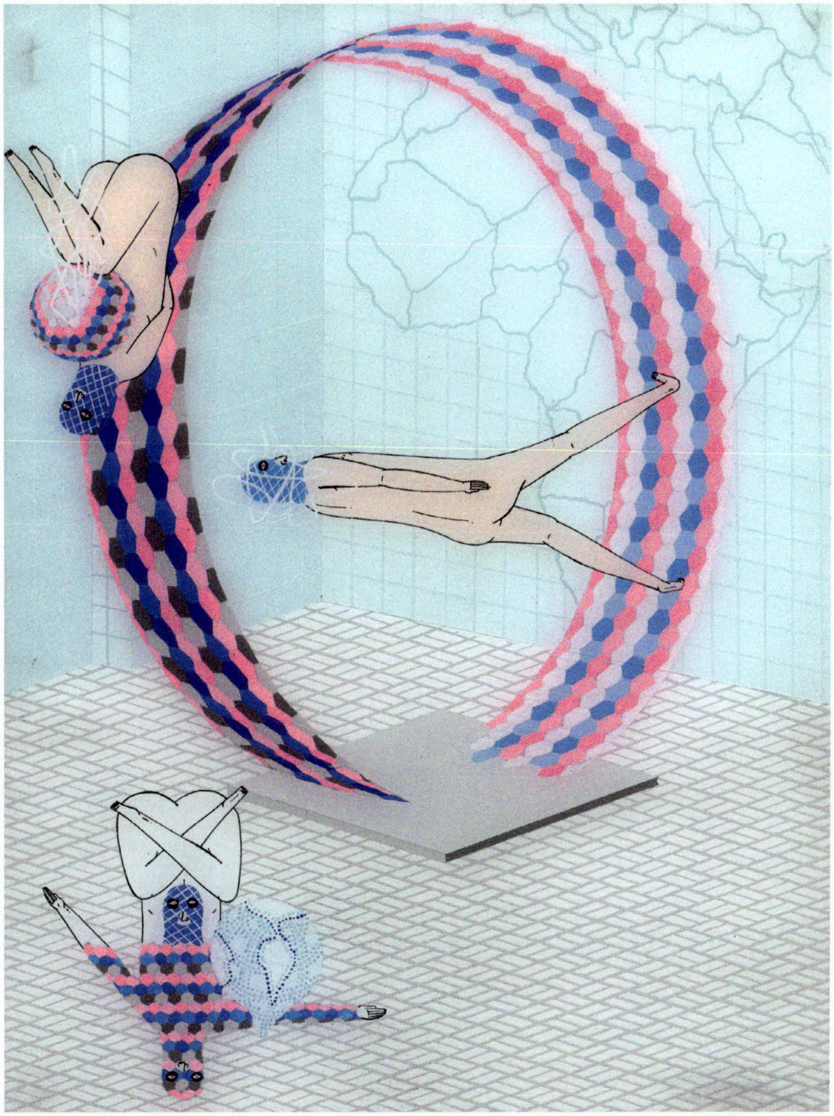

Exploration / Acrylic, ink, gouache, and resin on paper mounted on wood – 23 x 29 cm – 2011

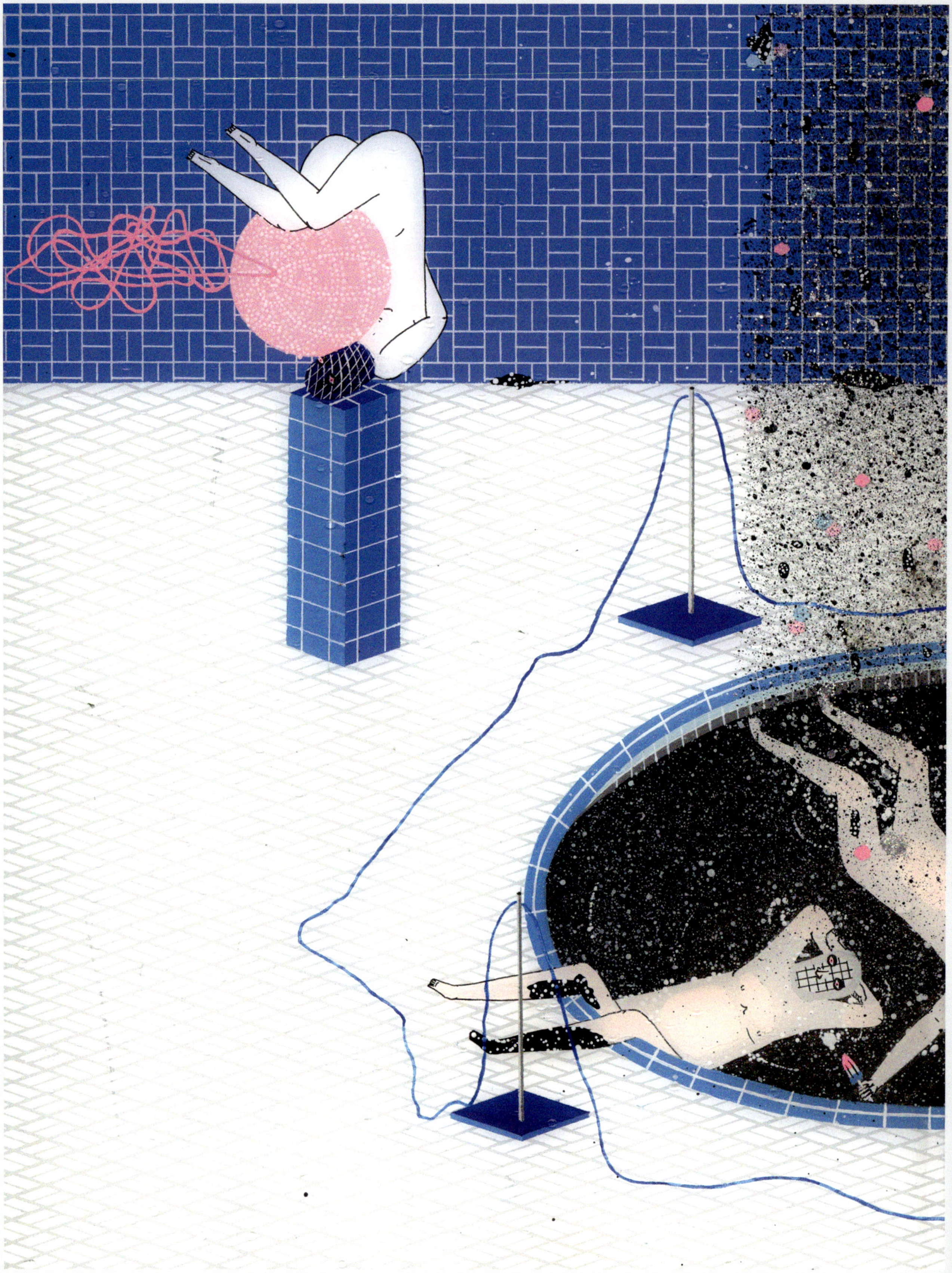

Pools **Diptych** / Acrylic, ink, gouache, and resin on paper mounted on wood – 30 x 44 cm – 2011

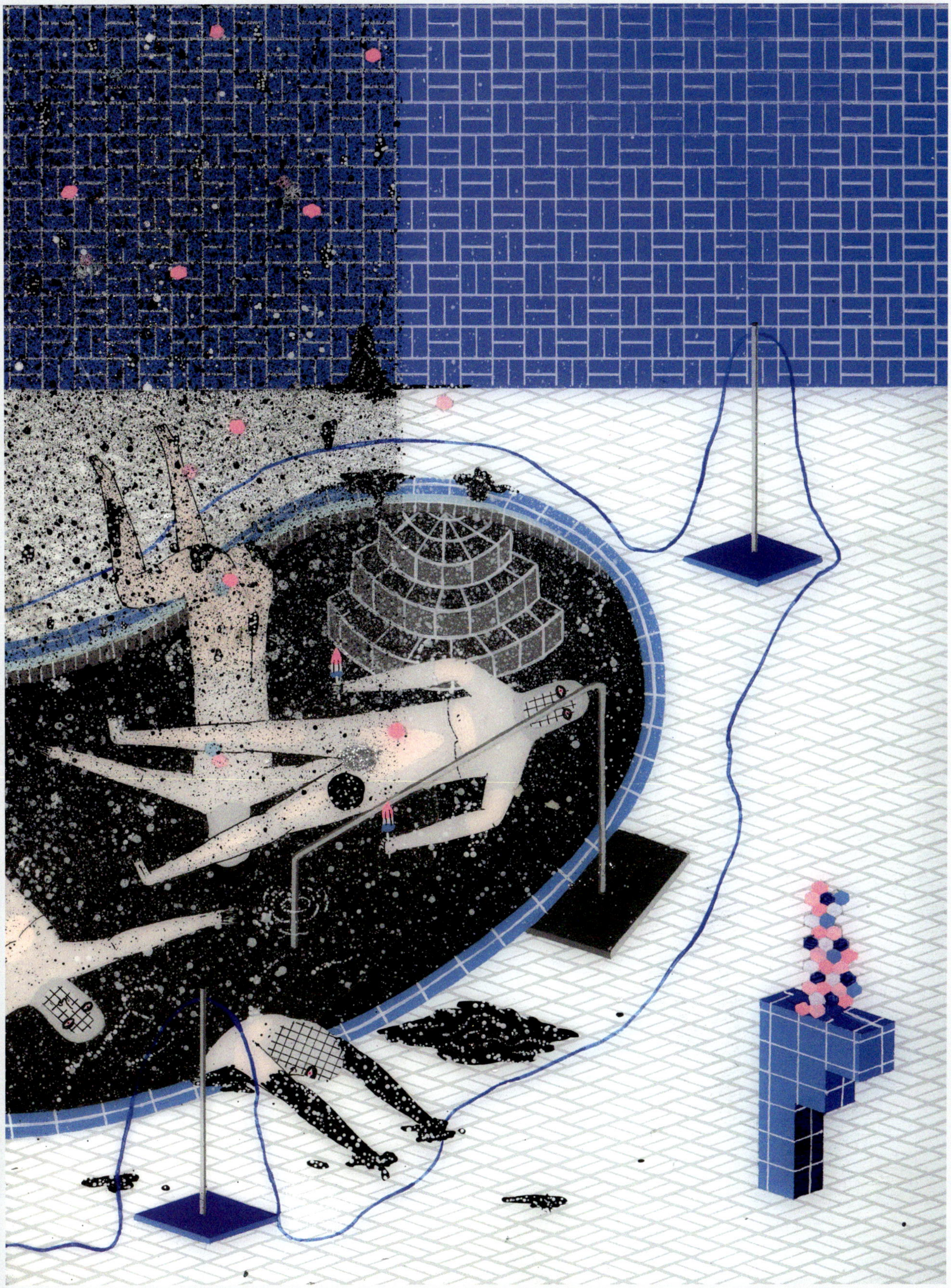

Maya Hayuk

Born in Baltimore, United States, 1969. Lives in New York, United States.

I do so many different things, that really it's not a negotiation between the street and the studio because both and all are important and symbiotic. I do prefer, over all, to paint outdoors in and on massive spaces because this work winds up belonging to everyone and everything around it in ways that a little canvas never can. The one thing that painting on objects in my studio provides that I still haven't figured out how to do on architecture in the world is the ability to defy gravity and spin surfaces around. Thanks.

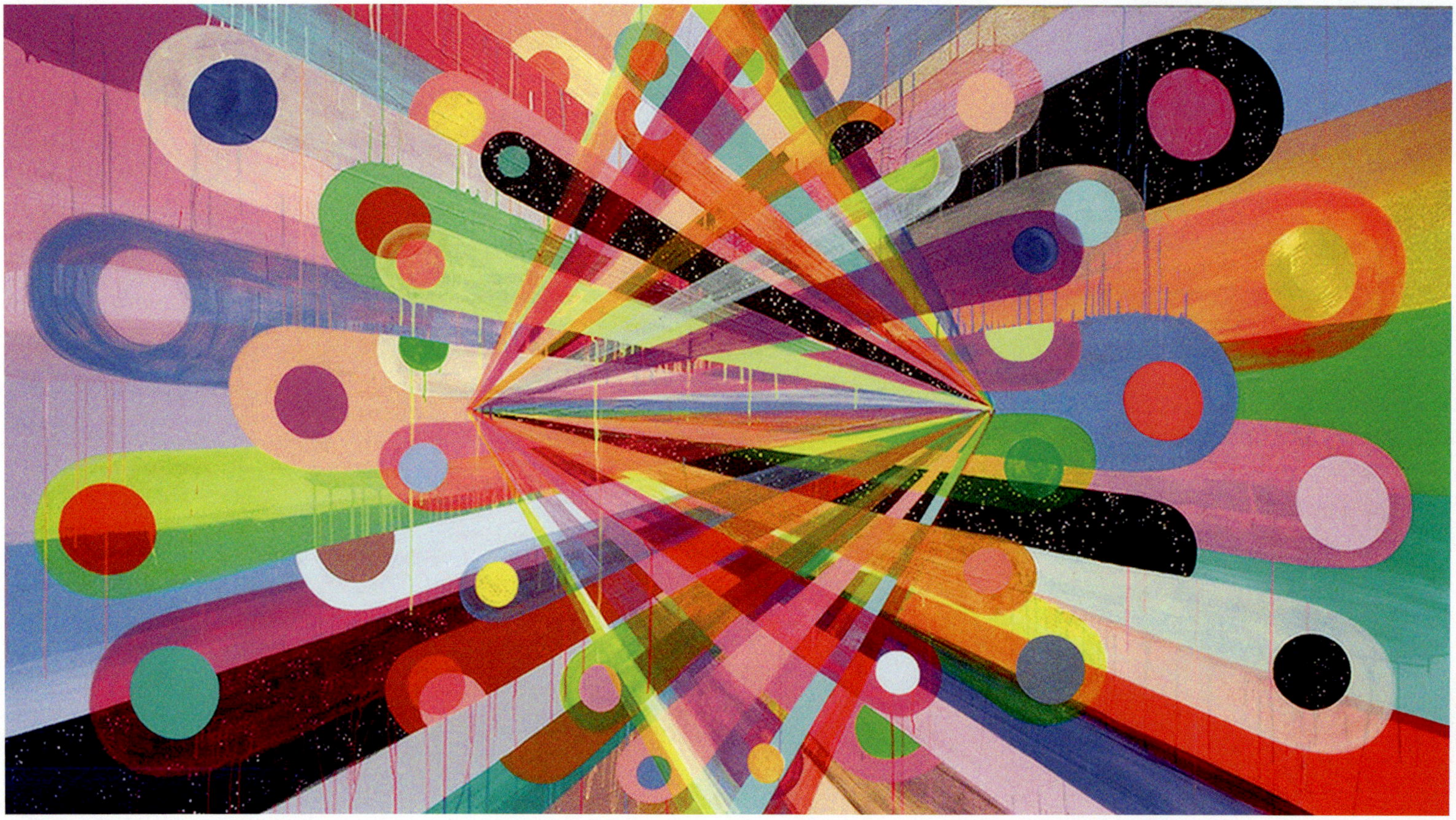

Hands Across the Universe (Portrait of Iman's Aura) / Acrylic on canvas – 213 x 152 cm – 2009

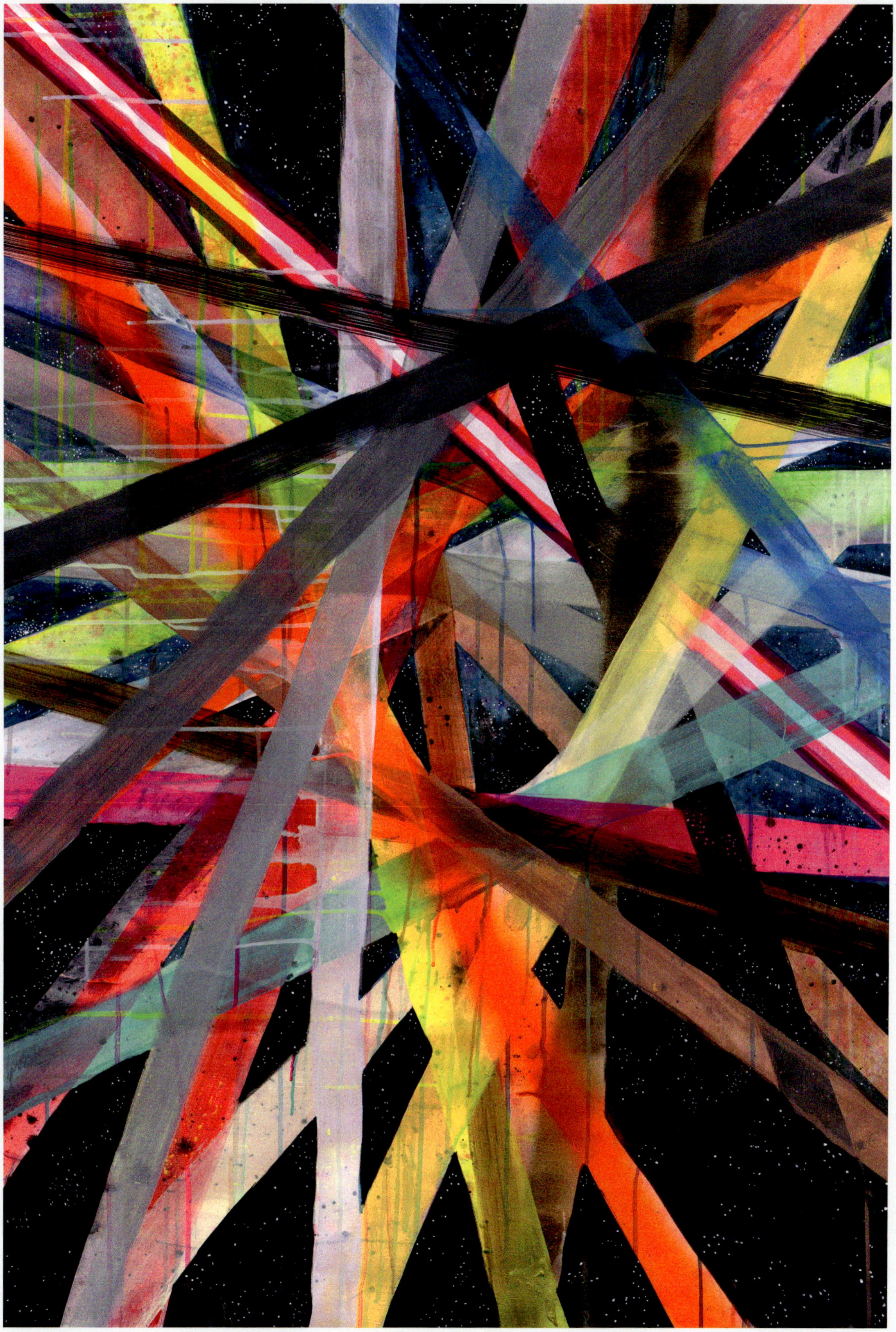

A Path for the Light / Acrylic on paper – 107 x 137 cm – 2009

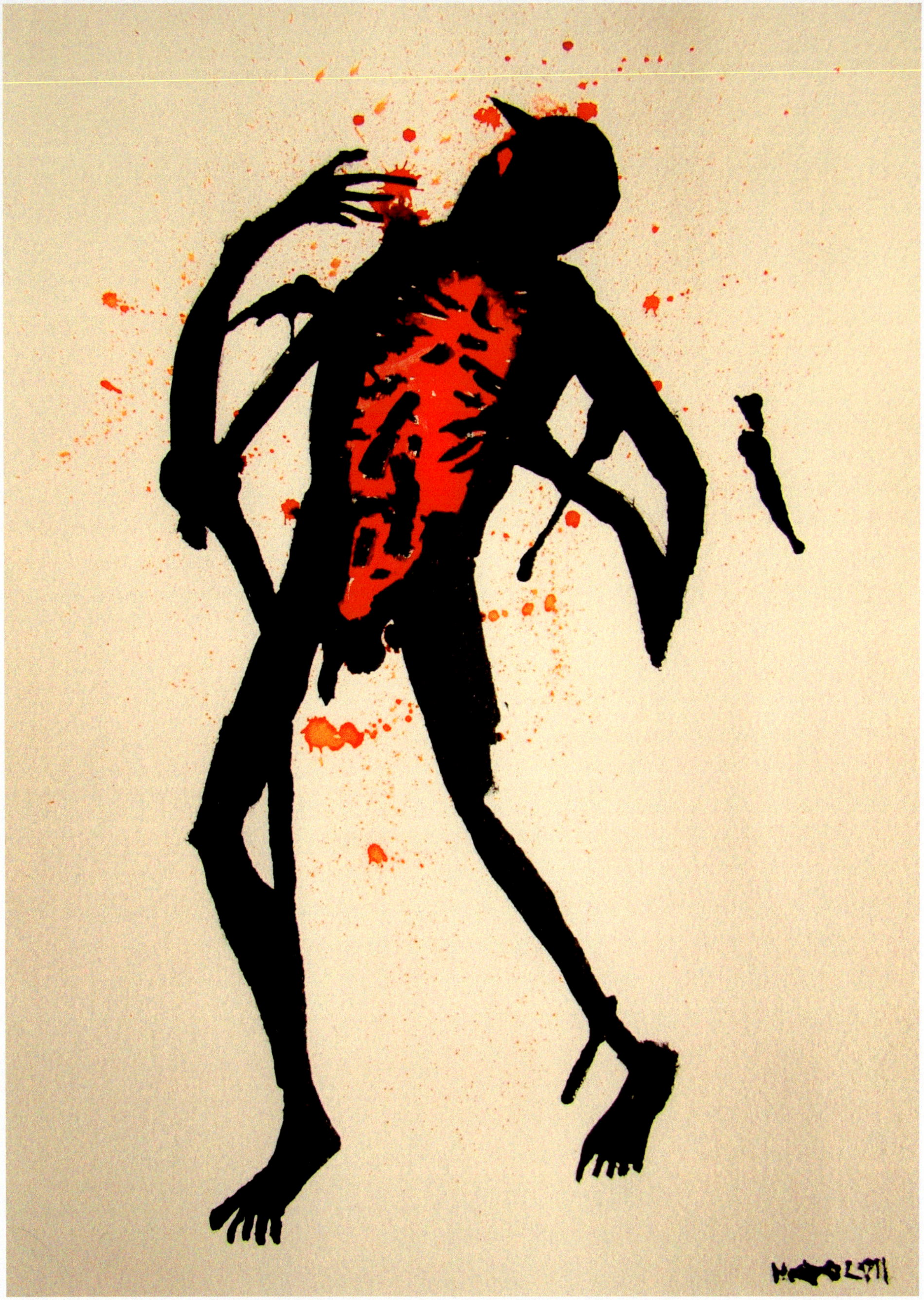

Untitled / Indian ink and ecoline on paper – 15 x 22 cm – 2010

Medo & Demência

Born in Rio Claro, Brazil, 1982. Lives in São Paulo, Brazil.

I've always used indian ink on paper, that's my main form of creation. Painting outdoors is really different because the environment acts as a big part on how the piece is going to turn out. The textures, the weather, and the noises influence a great deal on my painting. Before painting the streets I'd never thought about painting techniques, I just experiment a lot and am still trying to find a way to express my style in studio work.

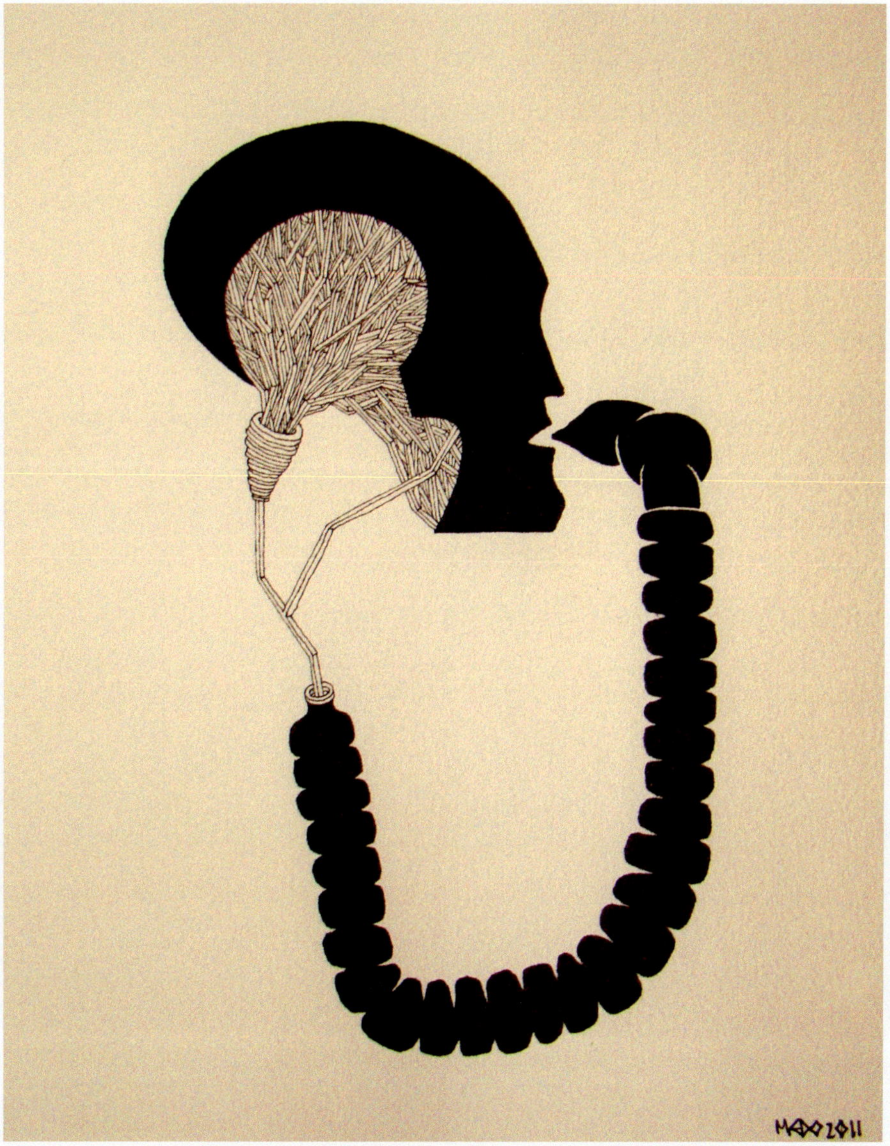

Retroalimentação / Indian ink on paper – 15 x 20 cm – 2011

Meggs

Born in Melbourne, Australia, 1978. Lives in Melbourne, Australia.

The streets initially provided me with an outlet where I first expressed my individual artwork outside of working as a graphic designer. Since then it has helped me develop the skills and confidence in my work and led to me exploring a full-time career as an artist. Through street art and graffiti I have met a network of awesome artists and lifelong friends who've taught me skills and provided me with inspiration and opportunities to produce artwork worldwide.

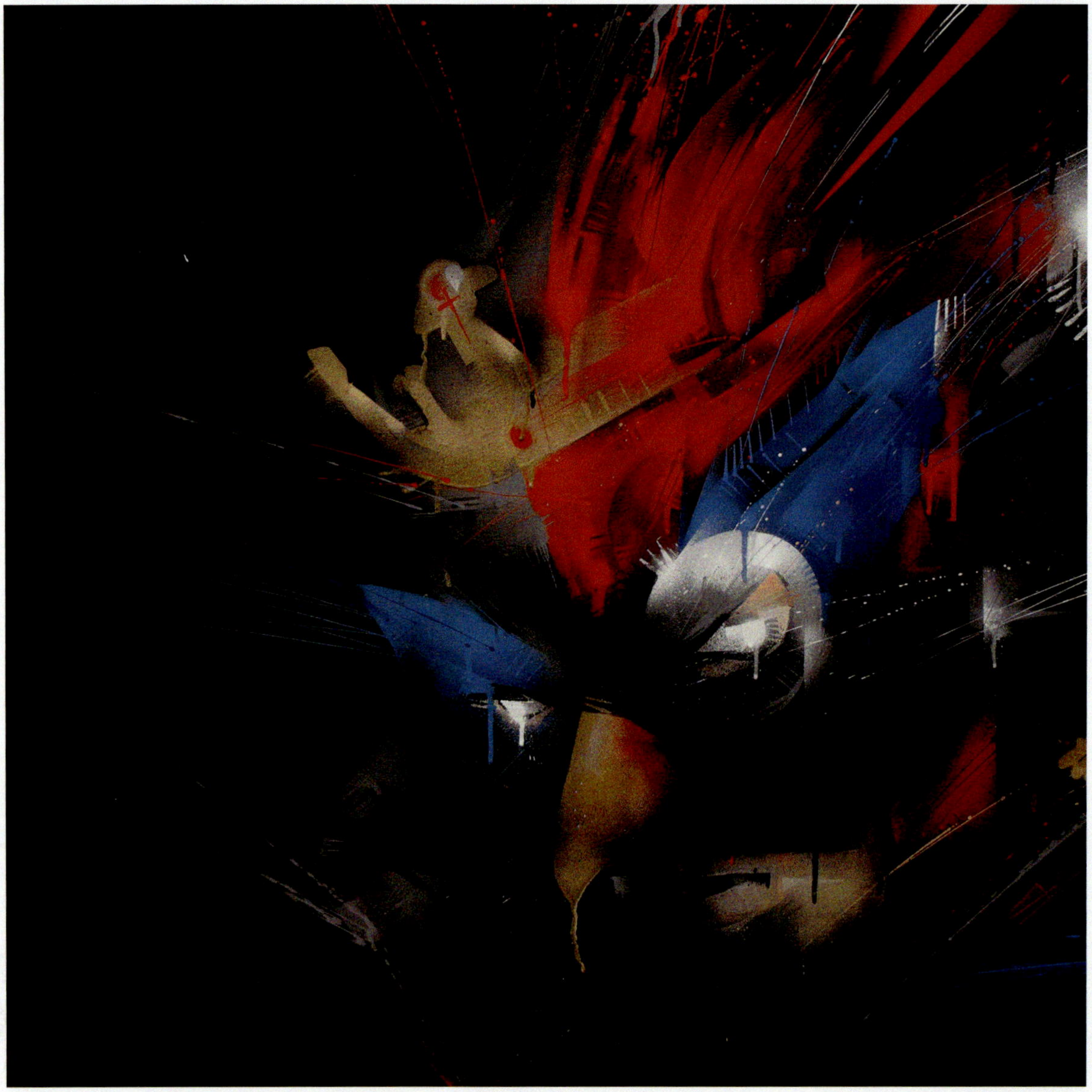

Sons of Privilege (Black) / Mixed media on canvas – 90 x 90 cm – 2010

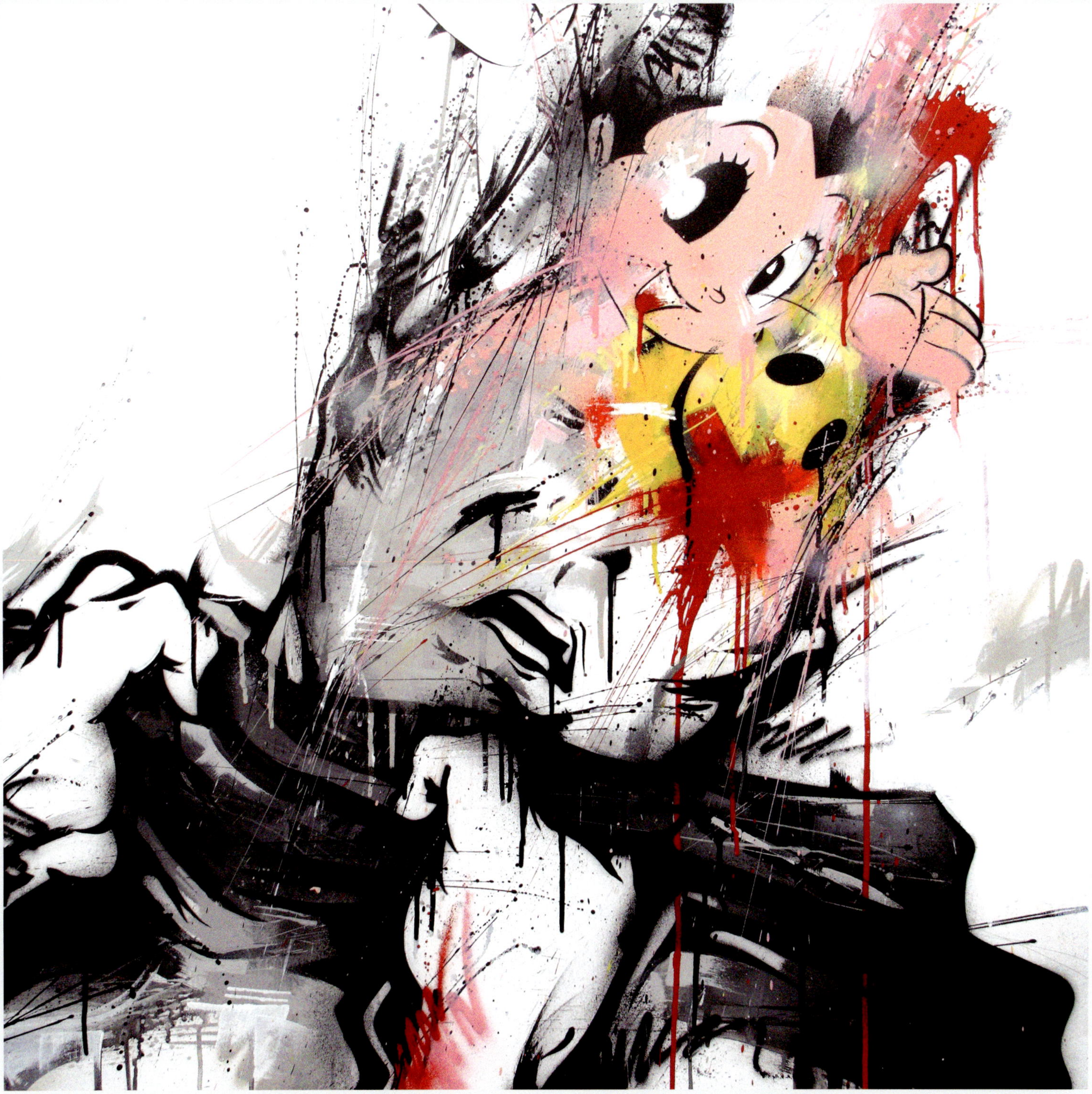

Out of Sight, Out of Mind / Mixed media on plywood – 90 x 90 cm – 2009

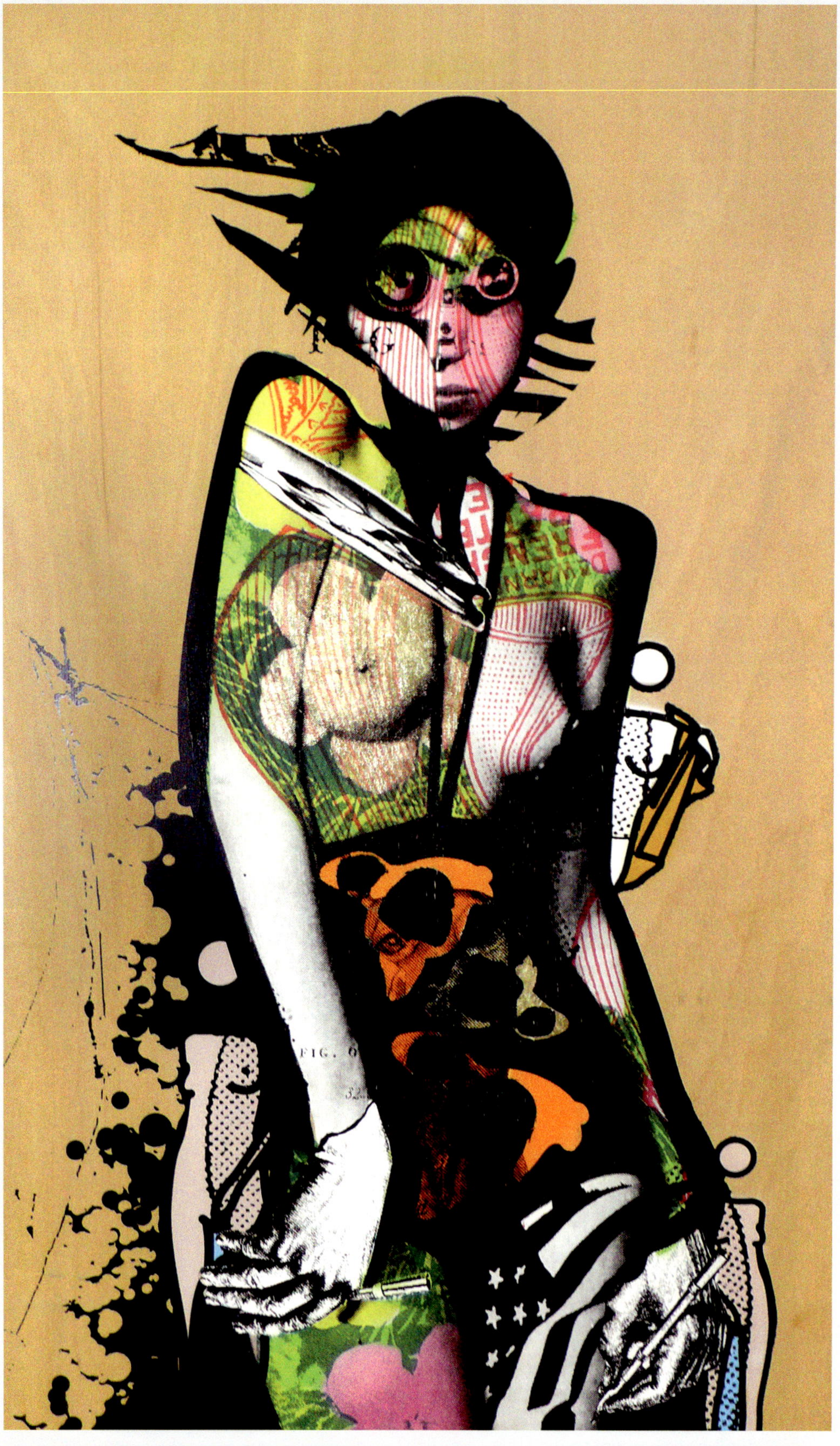

Elaine Sturtevant Did it Better than Miss / Oil and acrylic, 3 colors silkscreen, 6 colors stencil, and gold leaf on wood – 84 x 115 cm – 2008

Miss Bugs

Miss. Born in Bangor, Wales, 1979. Lives in London, England.
Bugs. Born in Bristol, England, 1979. Lives in London, England.

Our studio gallery work goes hand in hand with our street-based work. Although our street pieces play with the city landscape by camouflaging themselves; so when the viewer finds one they question their surroundings. Our studio gallery work also has to raise questions with the viewer but we have to do this by telling the story on the canvas alone!

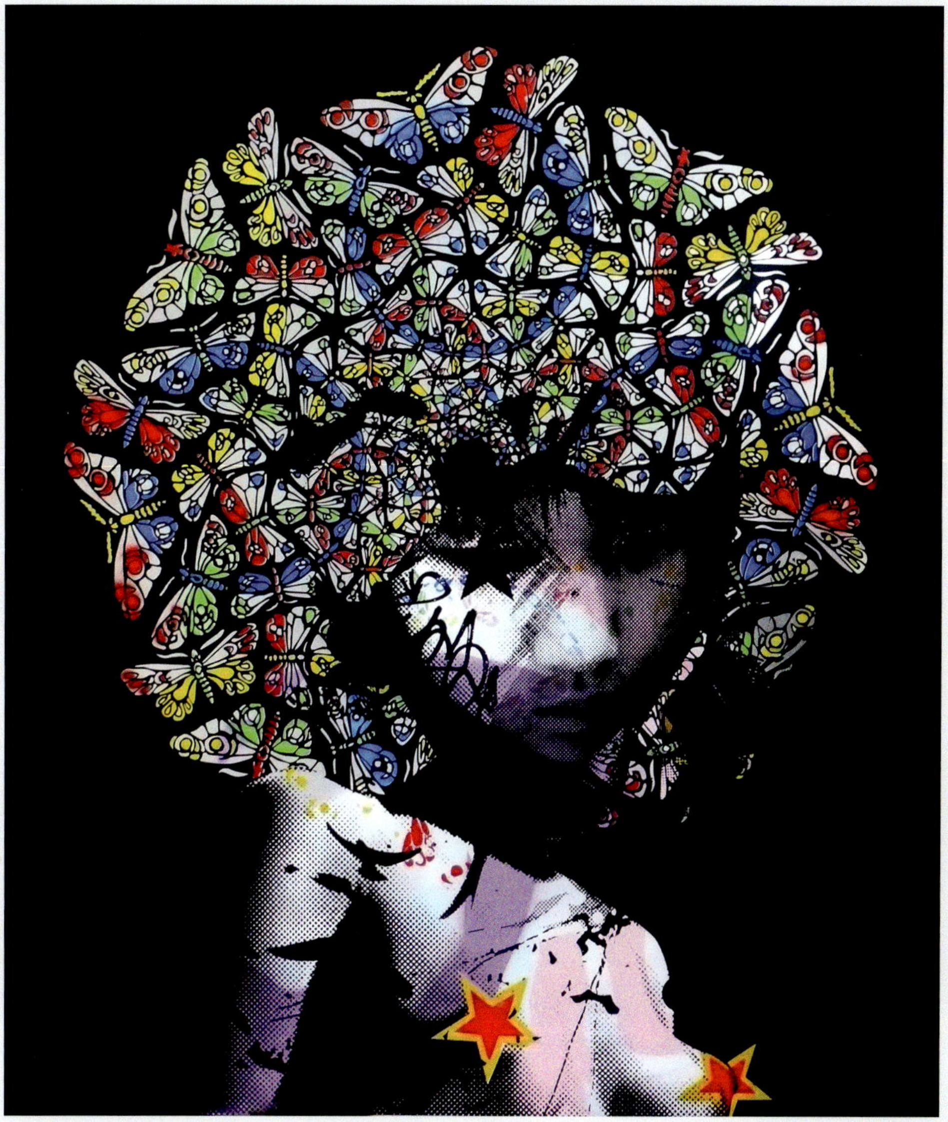

All Her Beautiful Thoughts / Oil, 1 color silkscreen, and 6 colors stencil on aluminum – 90 x 110 cm – 2009

Miss Van

Born in Toulouse, France, 1973. Lives in Barcelona, Spain.

What I keep from painting in the streets is that taste of urgency, focus the energy to paint spontaneously and intense. When I start painting a canvas, I like to finish it the same day or the next, but now I enjoy more and more taking the time to work on it, to extend the pleasure of the process, experiment, develop new techniques, improvising without fear or pressure. Working in the studio allowed me to evolve a lot technically, grow and refine, creating a space to search for new ways of painting and new materials.

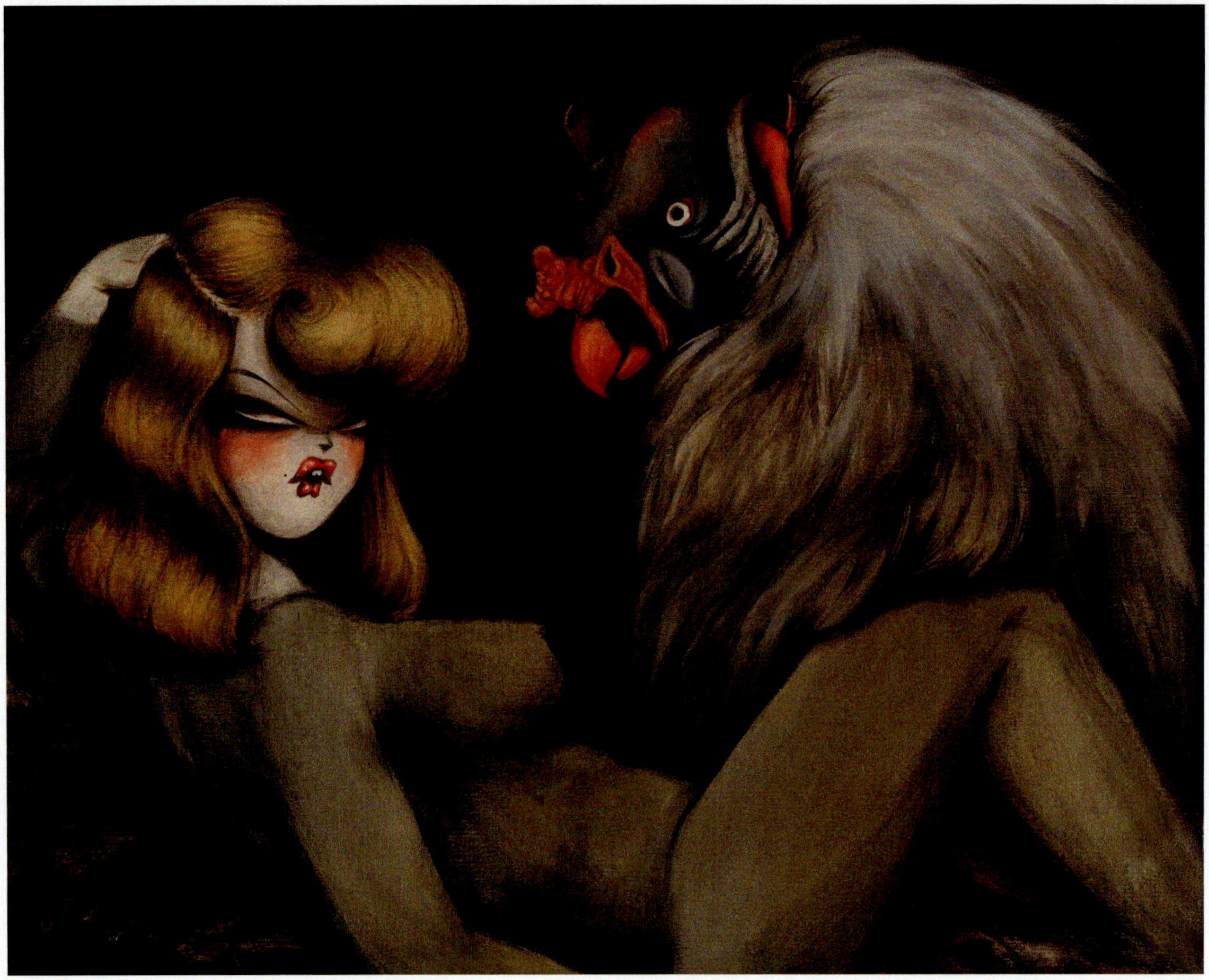

Twinkles 9 | Acrylic on canvas – 96 x 76 cm – 2010

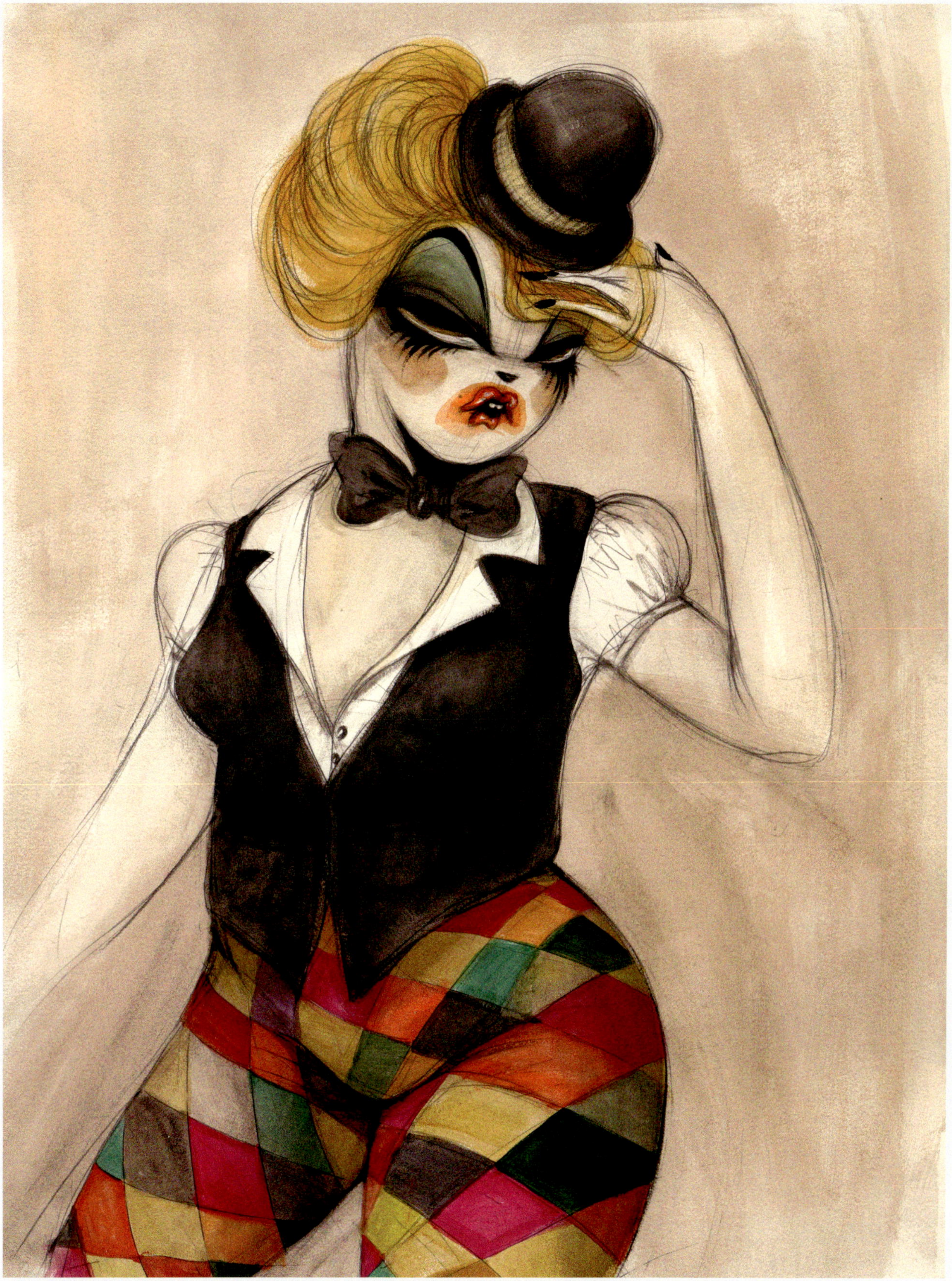

Lovestain 1 | Acrylic on paper – 65 x 85 cm – 2009

Morten Andersen aka M2theA

Born in Aalborg, Denmark, 1976. Lives in Berlin, Germany.

See colors like you hear jet planes. I sense and absorb colors and the cityscape this way, sometimes it's real loud and disturbing to me like the noise of a jet plane, frustrating cuz I wanna be at peace. Other times it's real inspiring, then I get moved by it and go do something creative. The streets provide me with that ruff and vivid energy I try to put into my paintings.

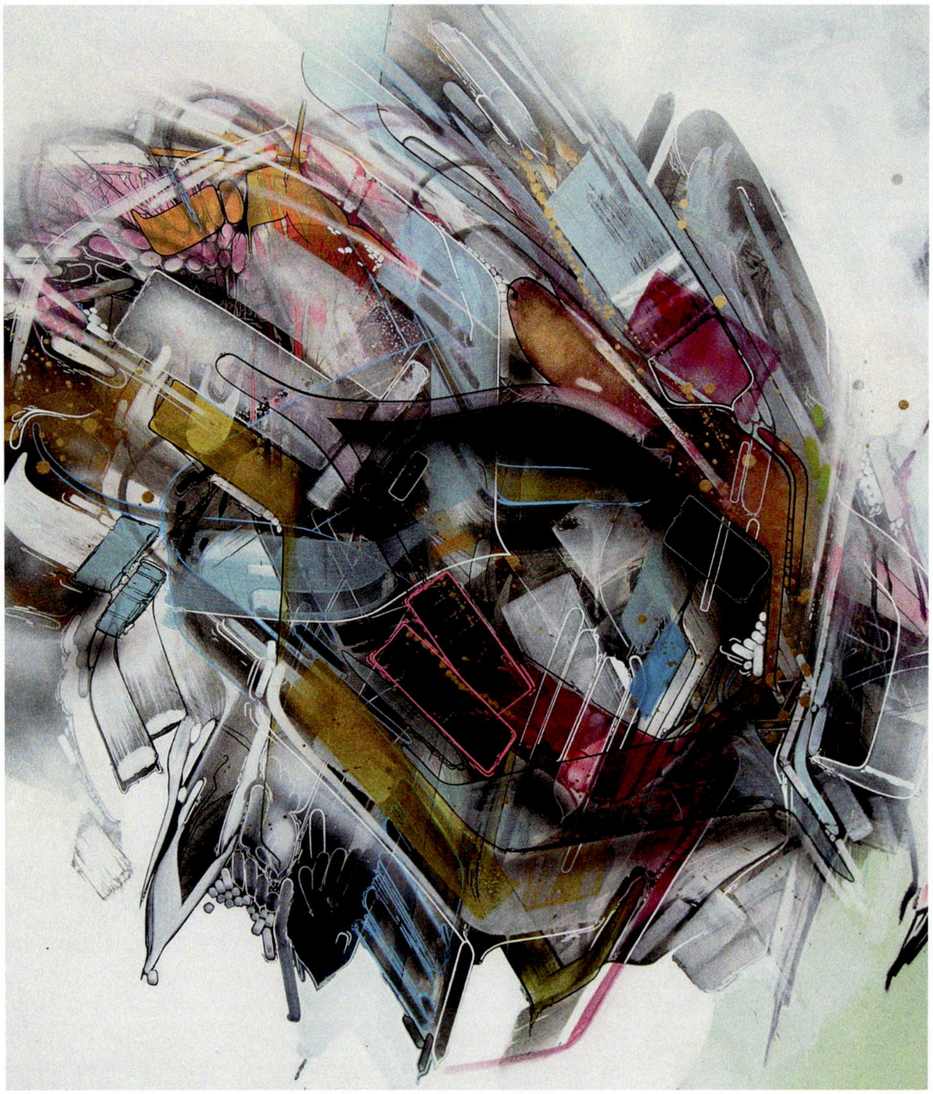

Violently Thru The Sky / Acrylic, marker, aerosol, and pen on canvas – 122 x 144 cm – 2010

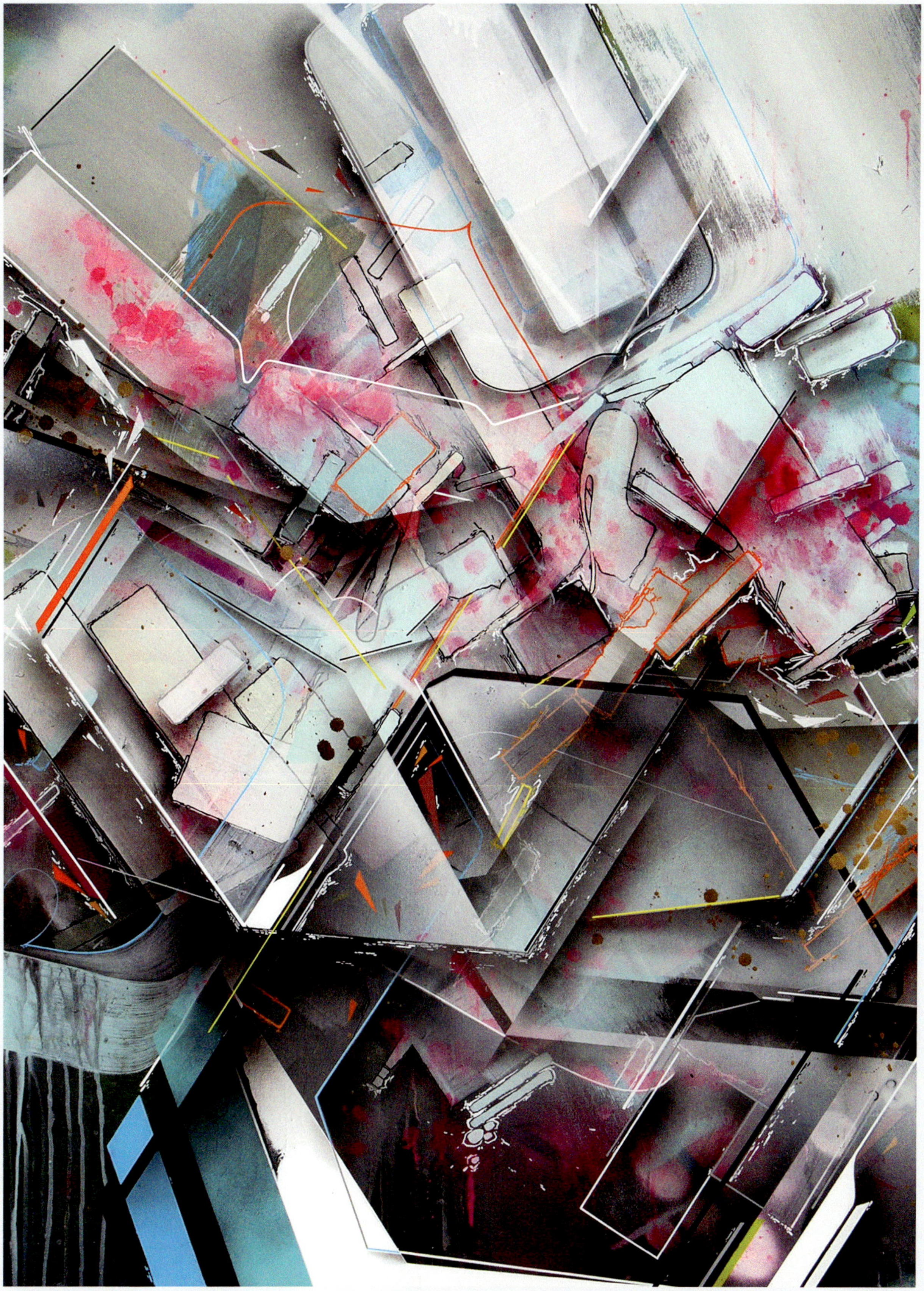

Strawberry Strata / Acrylic, marker, aerosol, and pen on canvas – 100 x 140 cm – 2011

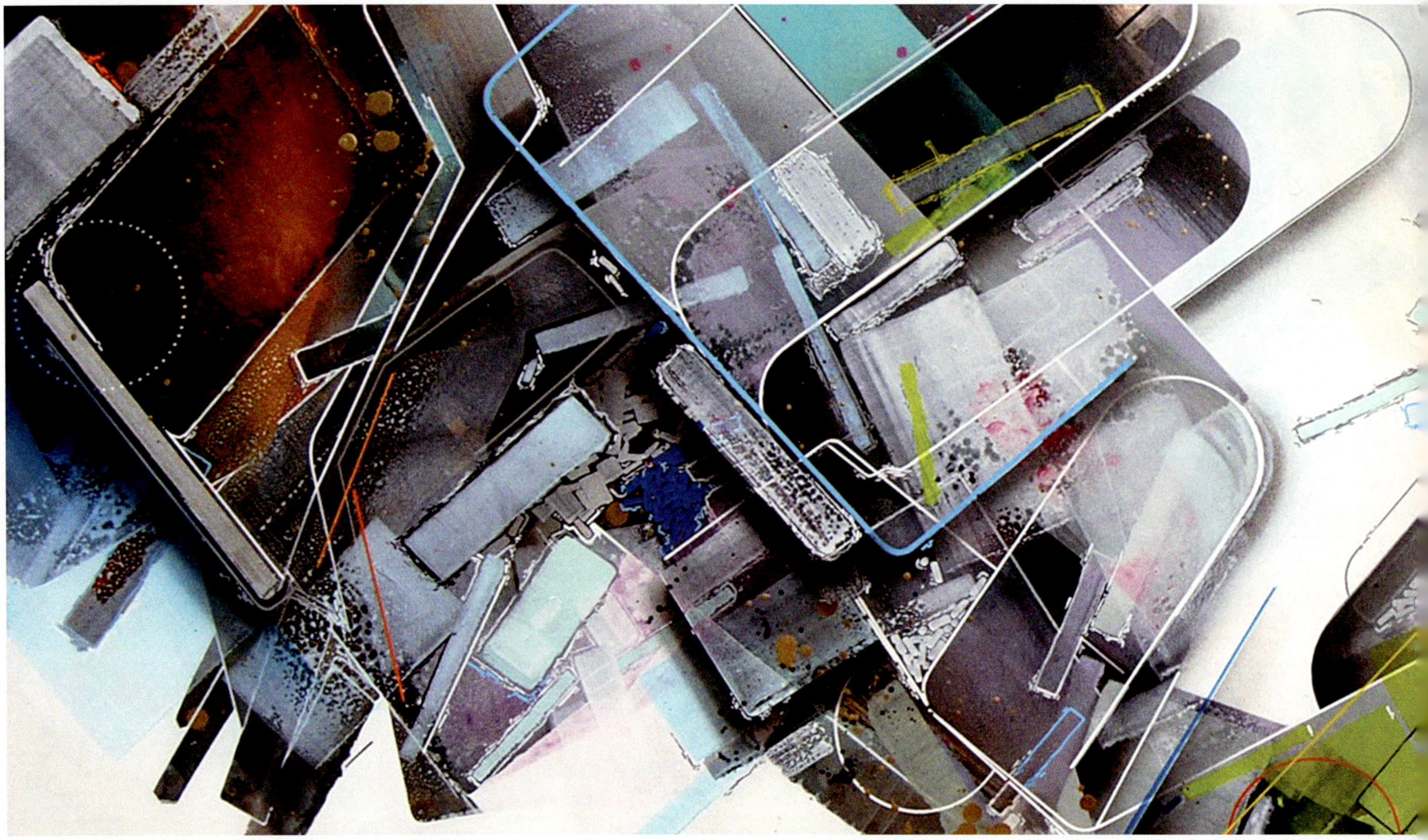

Milky Lopsided / Acrylic, marker, aerosol, and pen on canvas – 210 x 60 cm – 2011

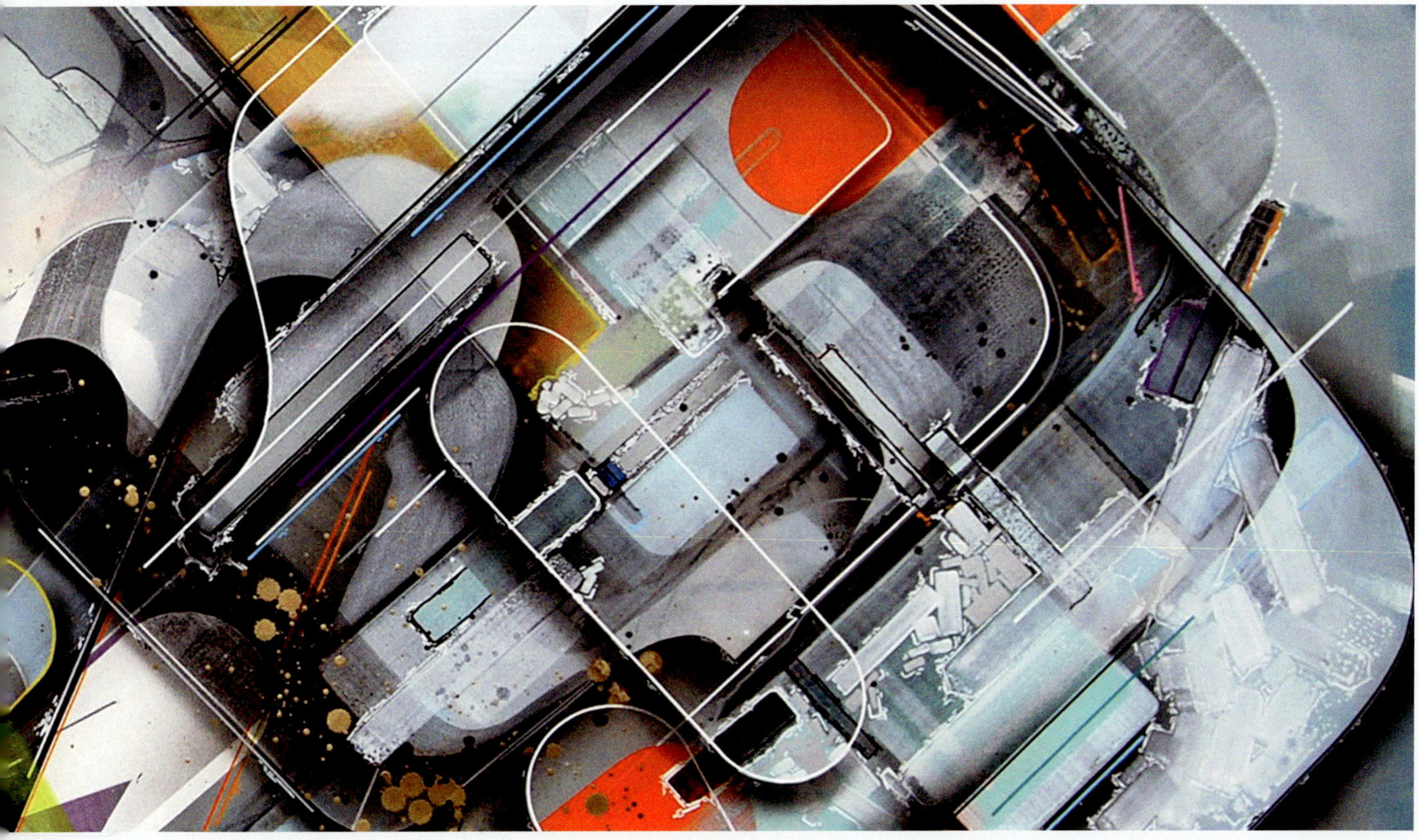

Mr. Kern

Born in Buenos Aires, Argentina, 1981. Lives in Bordeaux, France.

My childhood was very difficult, raised by wolves in a forest near Bordeaux. The practice of painting was very difficult for me: I learned to paint bite by bite. In fact the only tools which were available to me were a brush made with boar armpit hair, natural pigments as well as egg white of wild canary to mix the paint. I did what I could with what was in my reach... So for me the only thing that changes between working in the forest and the study is only the support!

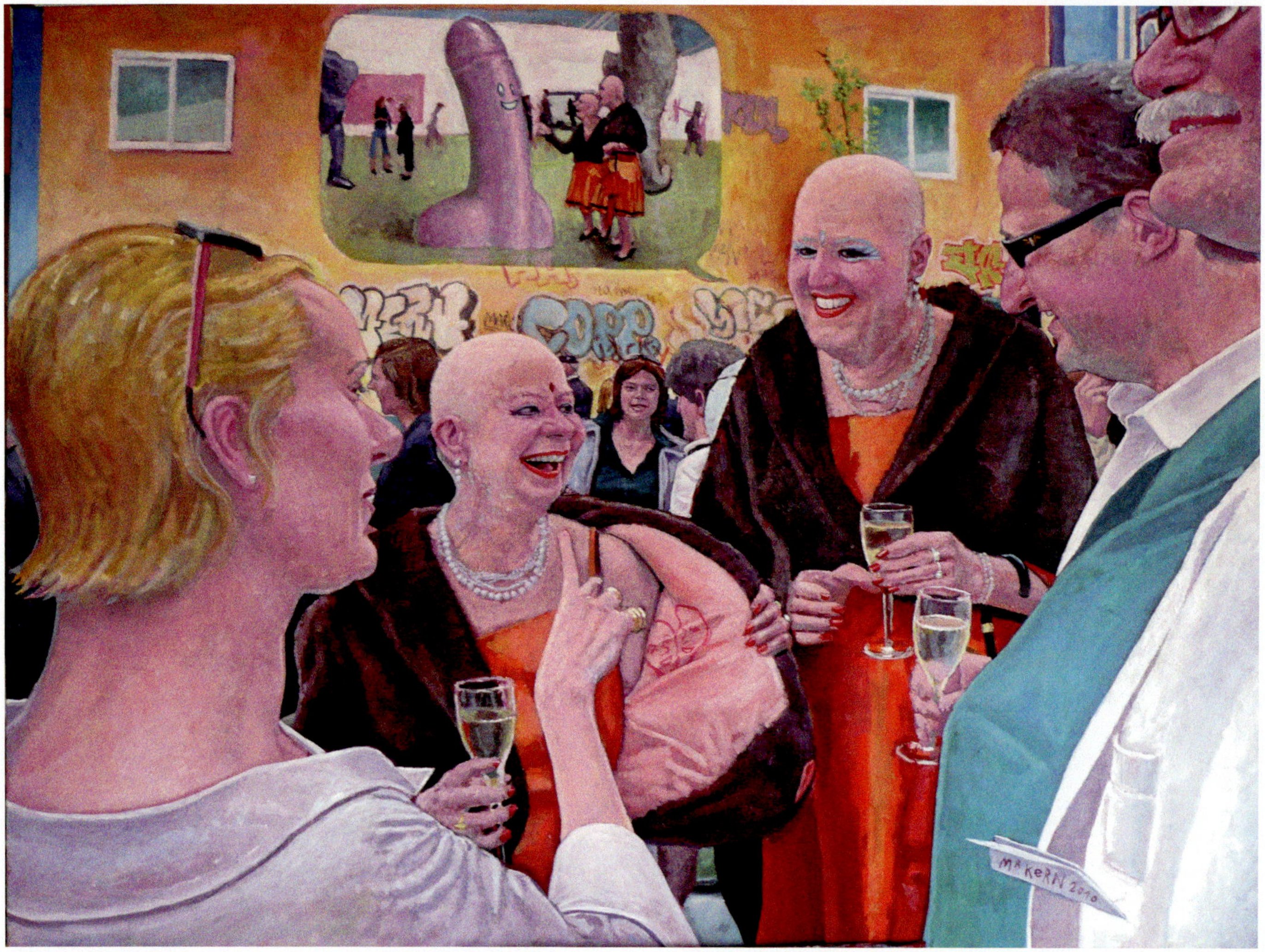

Hekel et Jekel / Acrylic on canvas – 150 x 80 cm – 2010

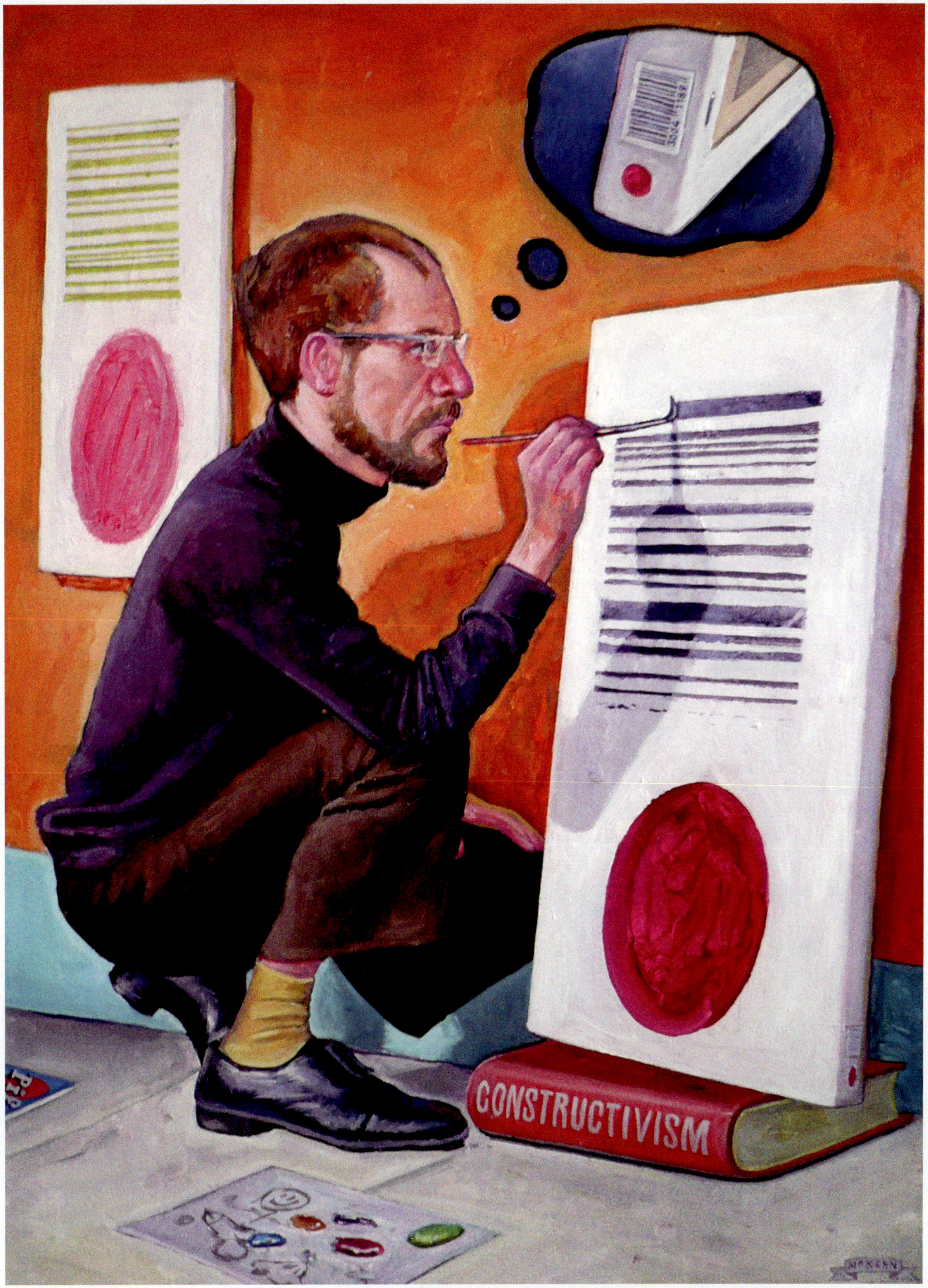

Constructiviste | Acrylic on canvas – 50 x 70 cm – 2010

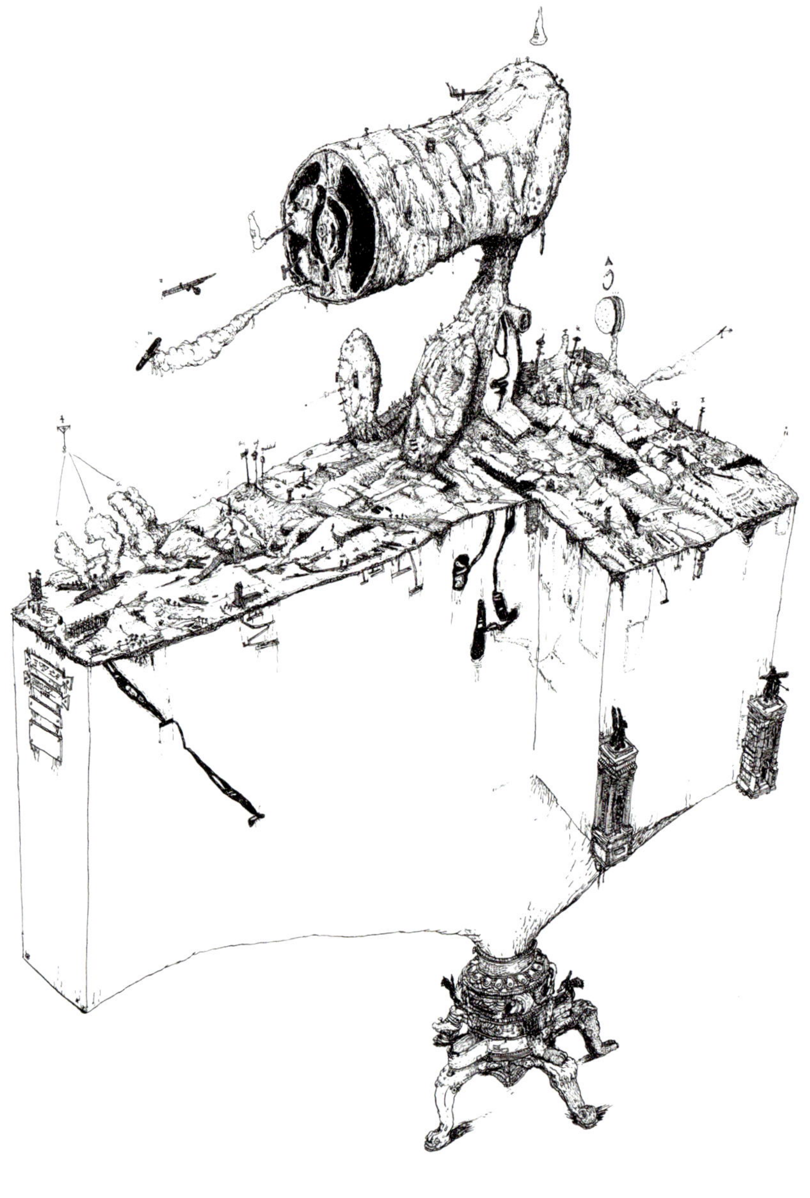

Snoop - Flackteau Nip Midway '44 / Ink on Heritage paper – 60 x 90 cm – 2010

Mudwig

Born in Stroud, England, 1980. Lives in London, England.

In a nutshell my work is predominantly about being made of meat, walking about on the land, and an inevitable disintegration and regrowth of these modes. I illustrate complex comic landscapes and abstract protrusions that are juxtaposed onto realistic imagery or photographic backdrops. The Street paintings I make are an infiltration of my odd Seussian vision onto a banally tangible environment.

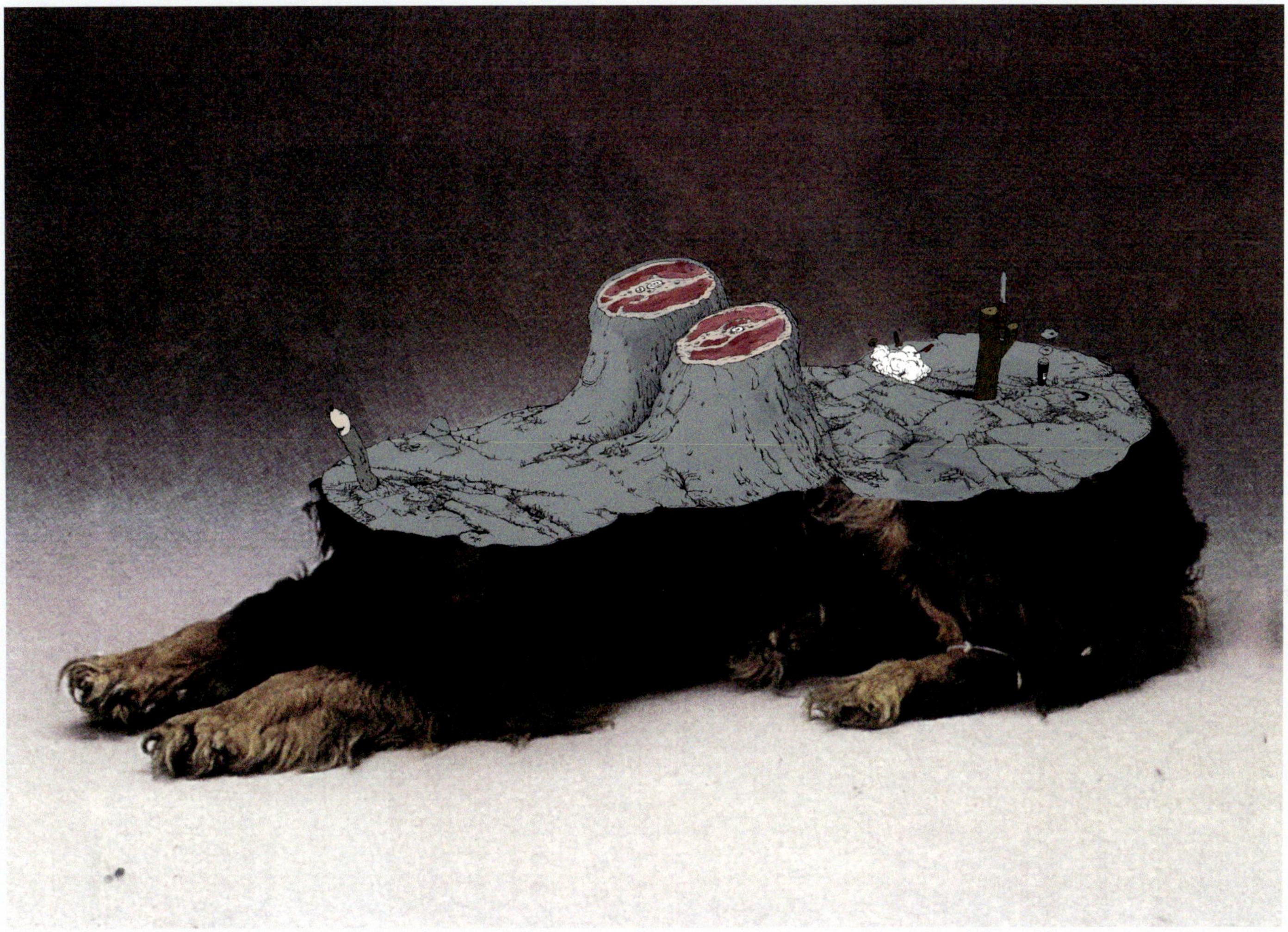

Gary Busey's Carpet Madame '91 / Acrylic and ink on poster – 90 x 60 cm – 2010

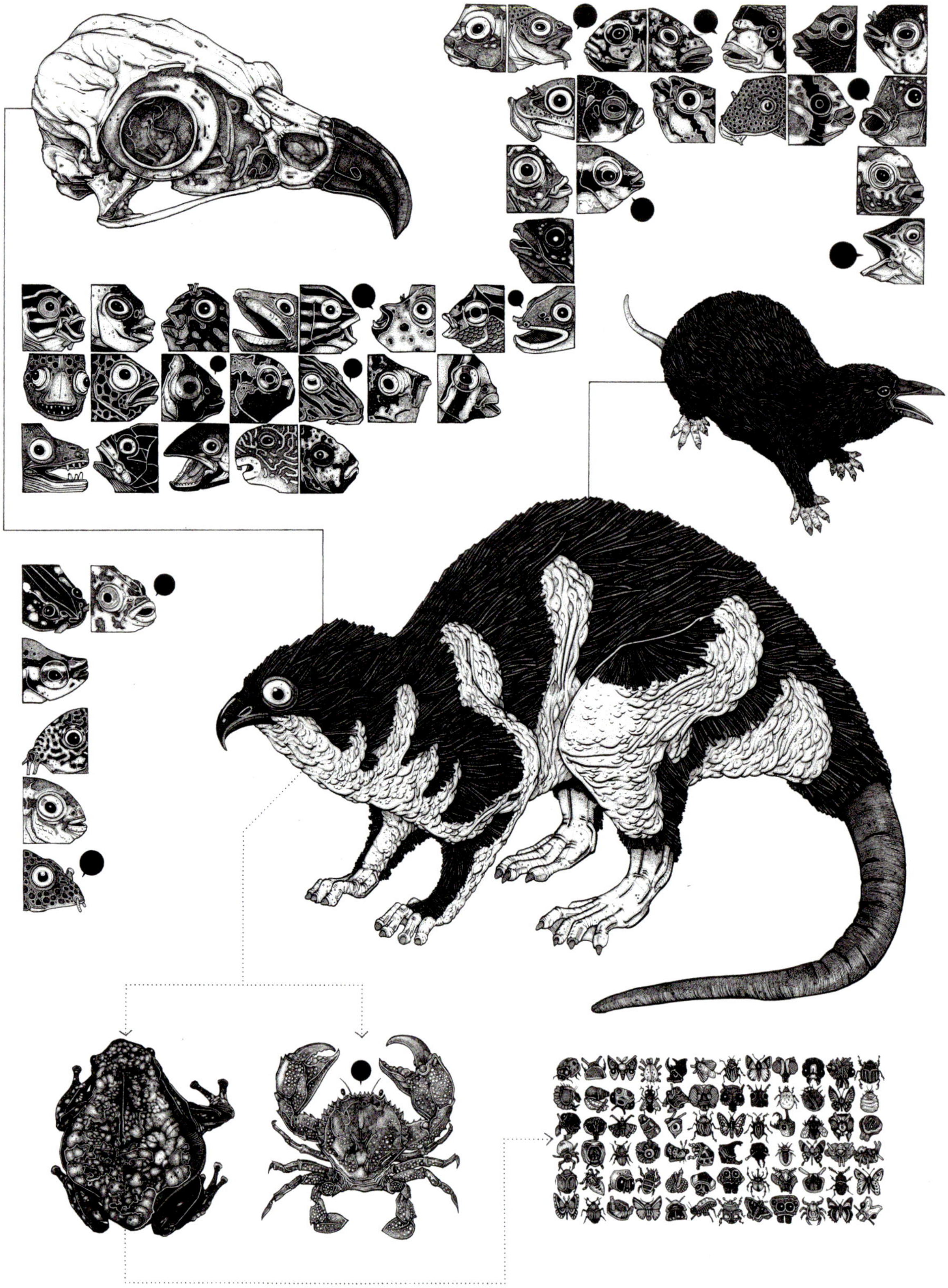

River Hunter / Pen and ink on paper – 38 x 51 cm – 2010

Nicholas Di Genova

Born in Belleville, Canada, 1981. Lives in Toronto, Canada.

When no galleries would show my work when I first started drawing seriously, the streets of Toronto became my gallery. Making work intended for a public-commuter audience was liberating, the risk of it all exhilarating. Although I rarely do work for the street these days, it is still my favorite place to discover new talent.

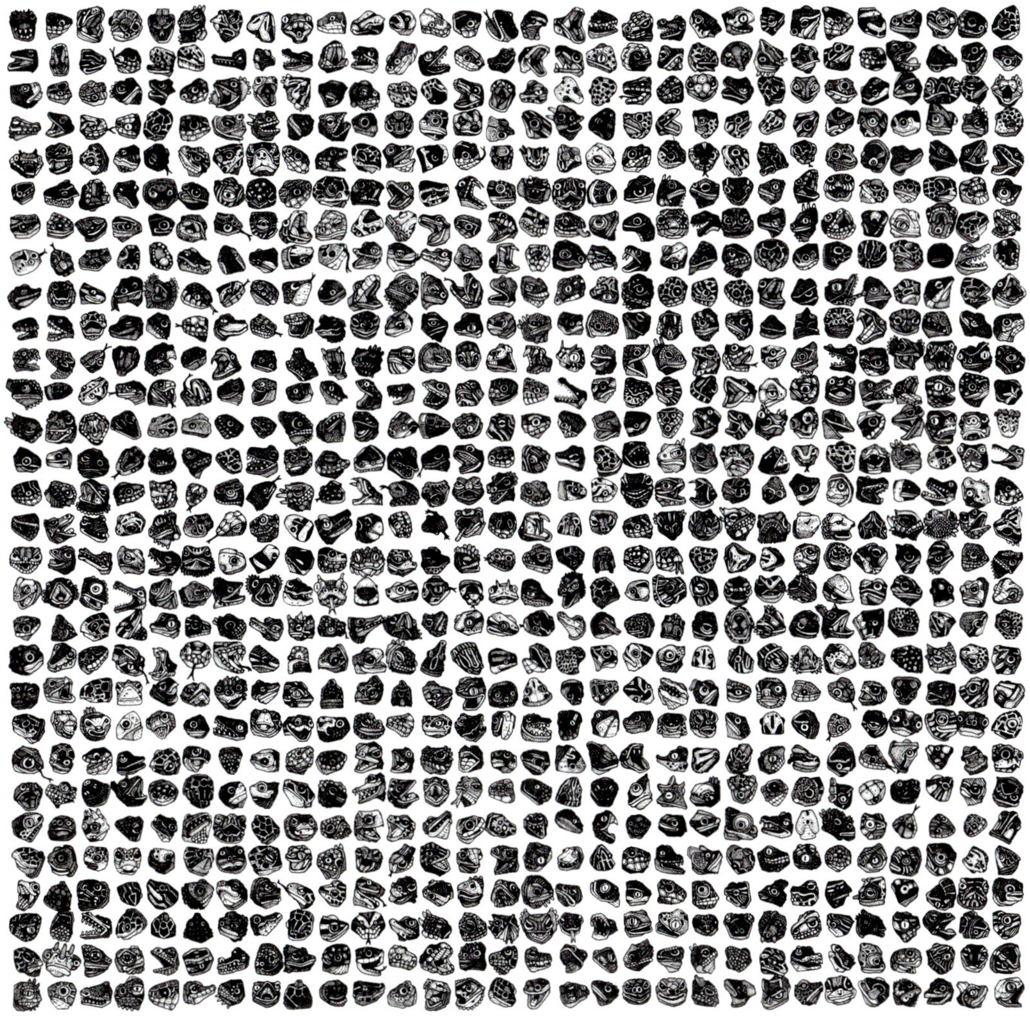

900 Reptiles / Ballpoint pen on paper – 36 x 36 cm – 2009

Okuda

Born in Santander, Spain, 1980. Lives in Madrid, Spain.

Street and my studio work are united and both paths interact. I started painting in roads and abandoned factories, and despite that now I spend days locked in my studio, I go out every week to paint the streets, which makes me feel alive.

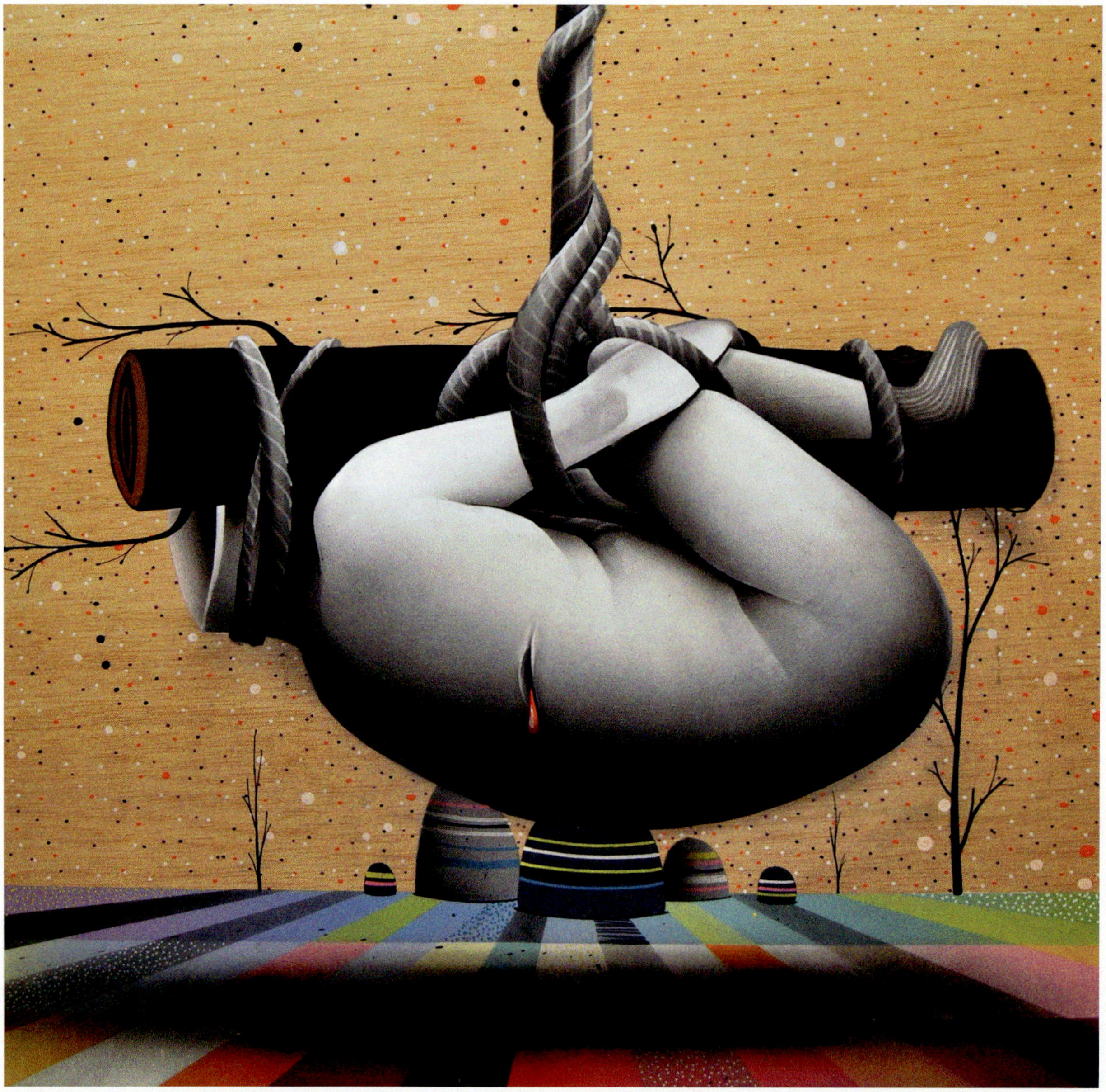

Sacrificio Natural, Victimas de sí Mismos / Mixed media on wood panel – 90 x 90 cm – 2010

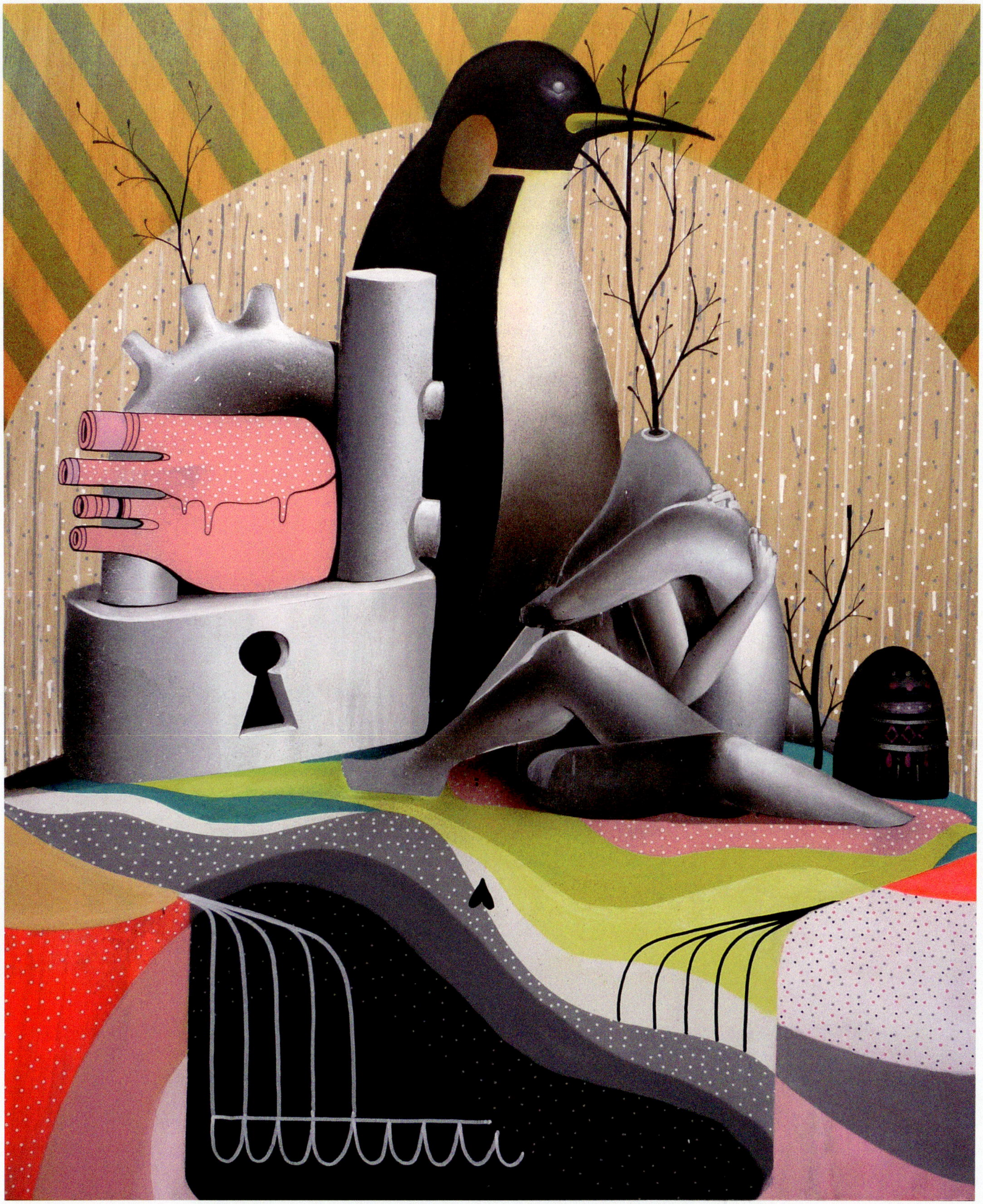

Ama Pero Odia, Falsa Realidad? / Mixed media on wood panel – 80 x 100 cm – 2010

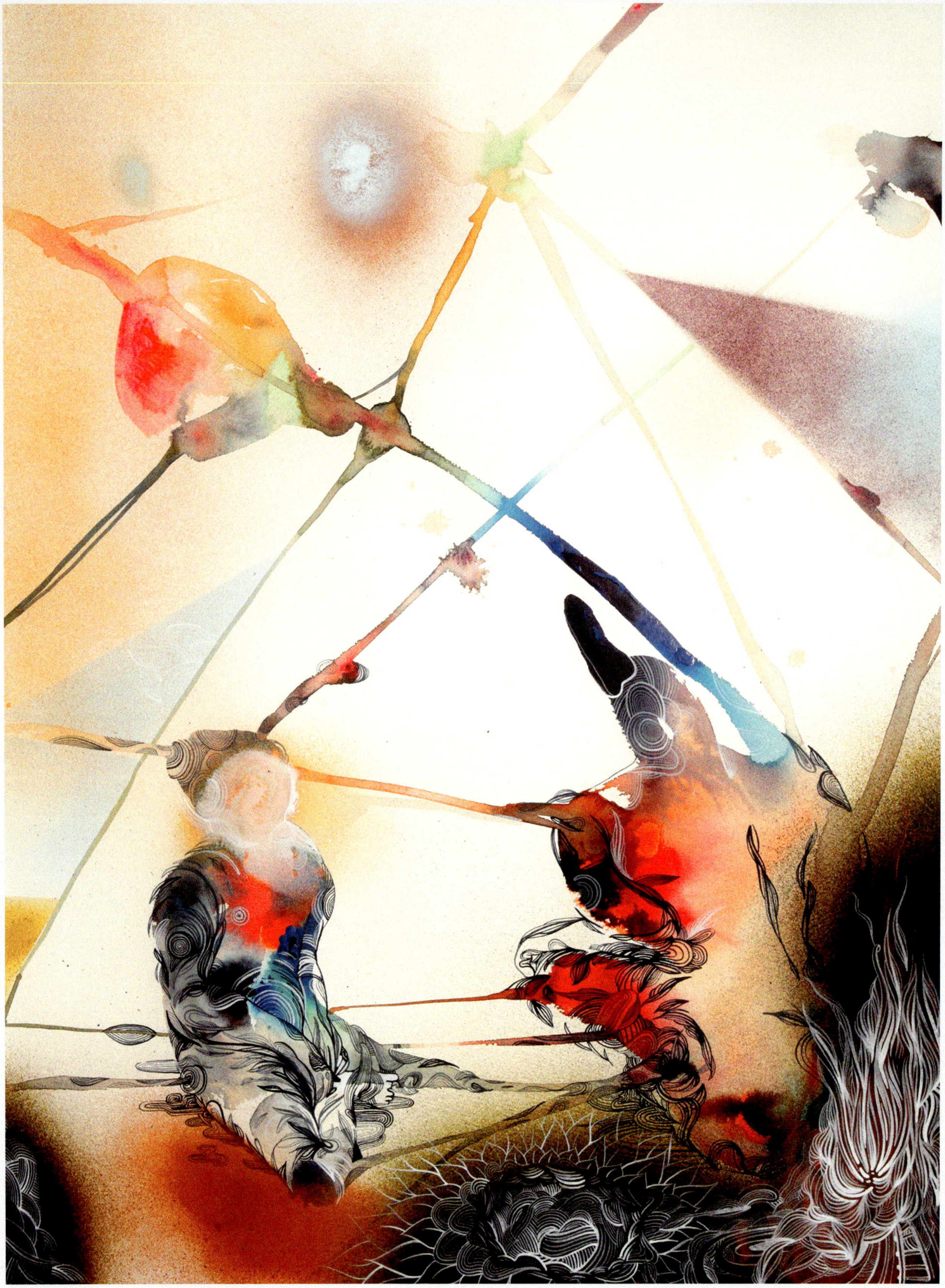

Marathon Monks Last Miles / Acrylic and ink on paper – 76 x 101 cm – 2010

Patrick Evoke

Born in Adawe, Canada, 1978. Lives in Nanjing, China.

The streets and the stuff that ends up there gets messed with endlessly. It's like the city is one giant force of creativity, one artist with multiple personalities that switches hands, her style and intentions all day and night. I love this psychotic layering. This artist and ones like her inspire me most.

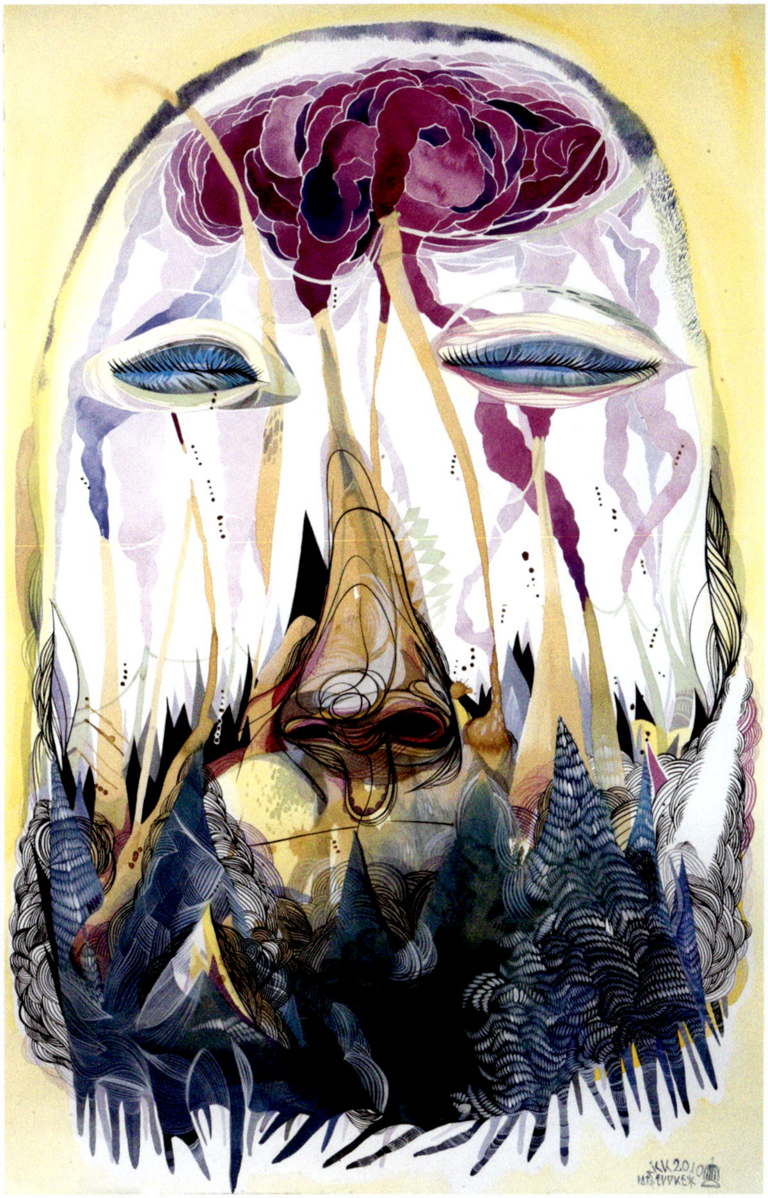

ADDwHD / Acrylic and ink on paper – 76 x 101 cm – 2010

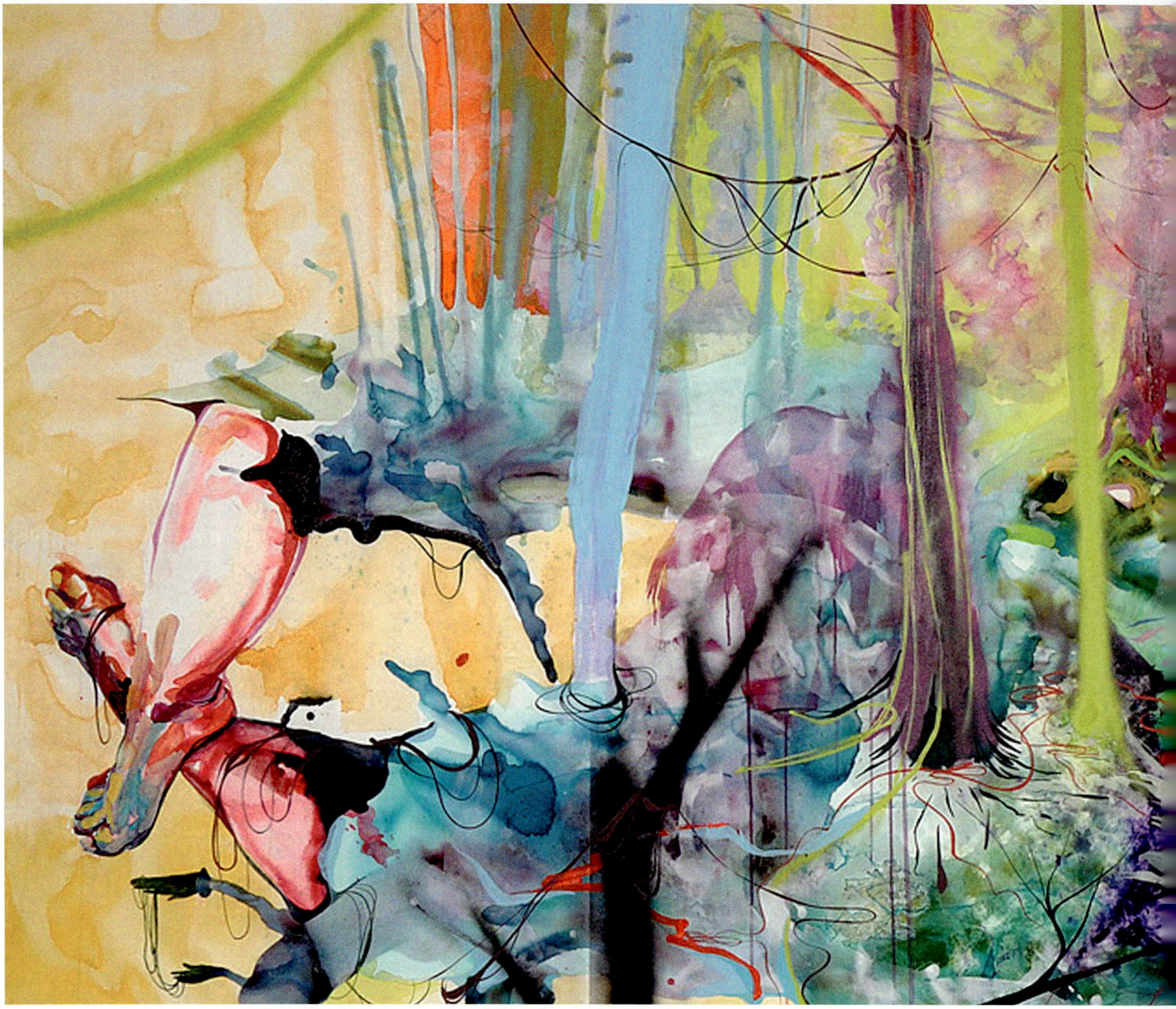

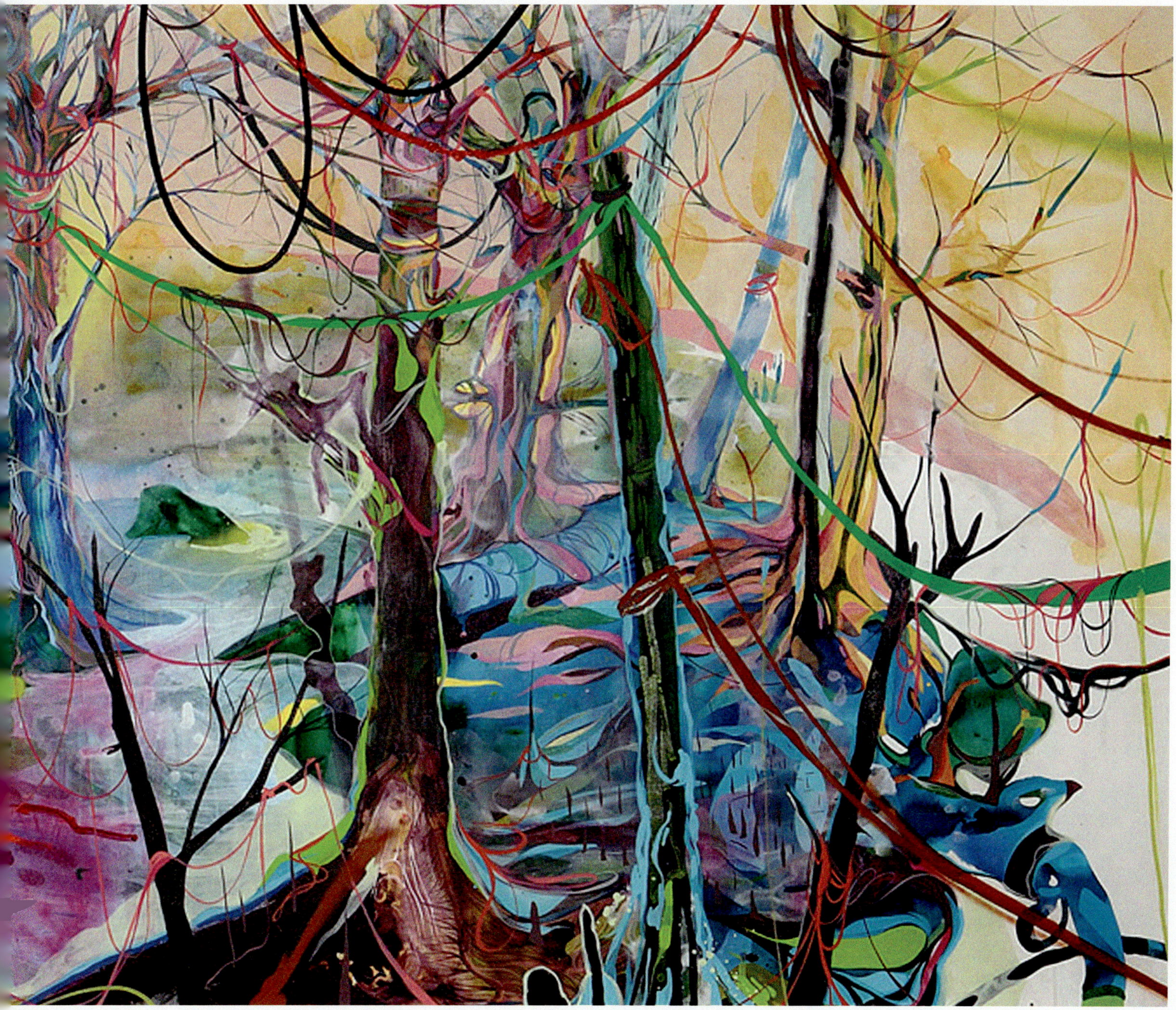

Kirk's Ferry **With Alexa Hatanaka** / Acrylic and enamel on canvas – 335 x 213 cm – 2010

Paul Insect

Born in South East, England, 1971. Lives in London, England.

Studio work can be more of a selective process, whereas work placed onto the street is much more fluid. My street work has the opportunity to speak to a different audience, and a surrounding to integrate with, whereas a white canvas, has nothing to begin with...

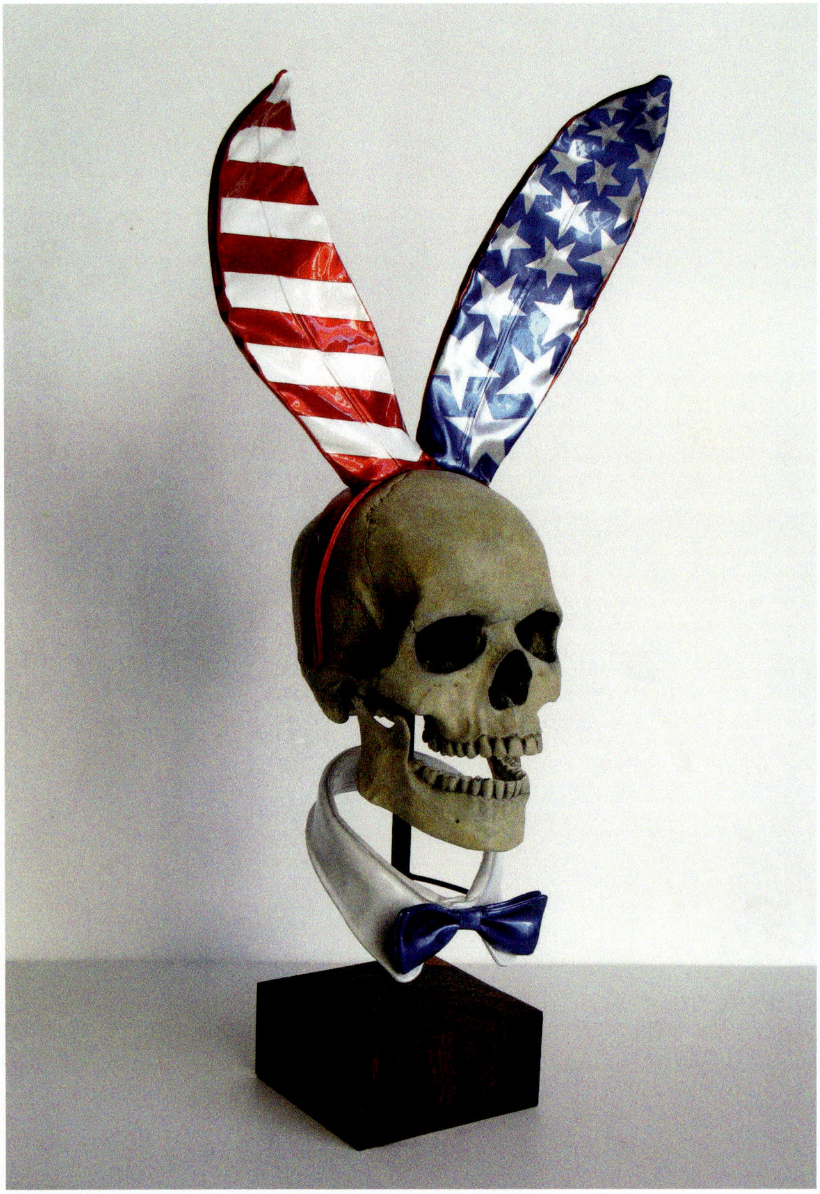

Miss July / Bronze, stainless steel, cocobola, and enamel – 27 x 57 x 20 cm – 2008

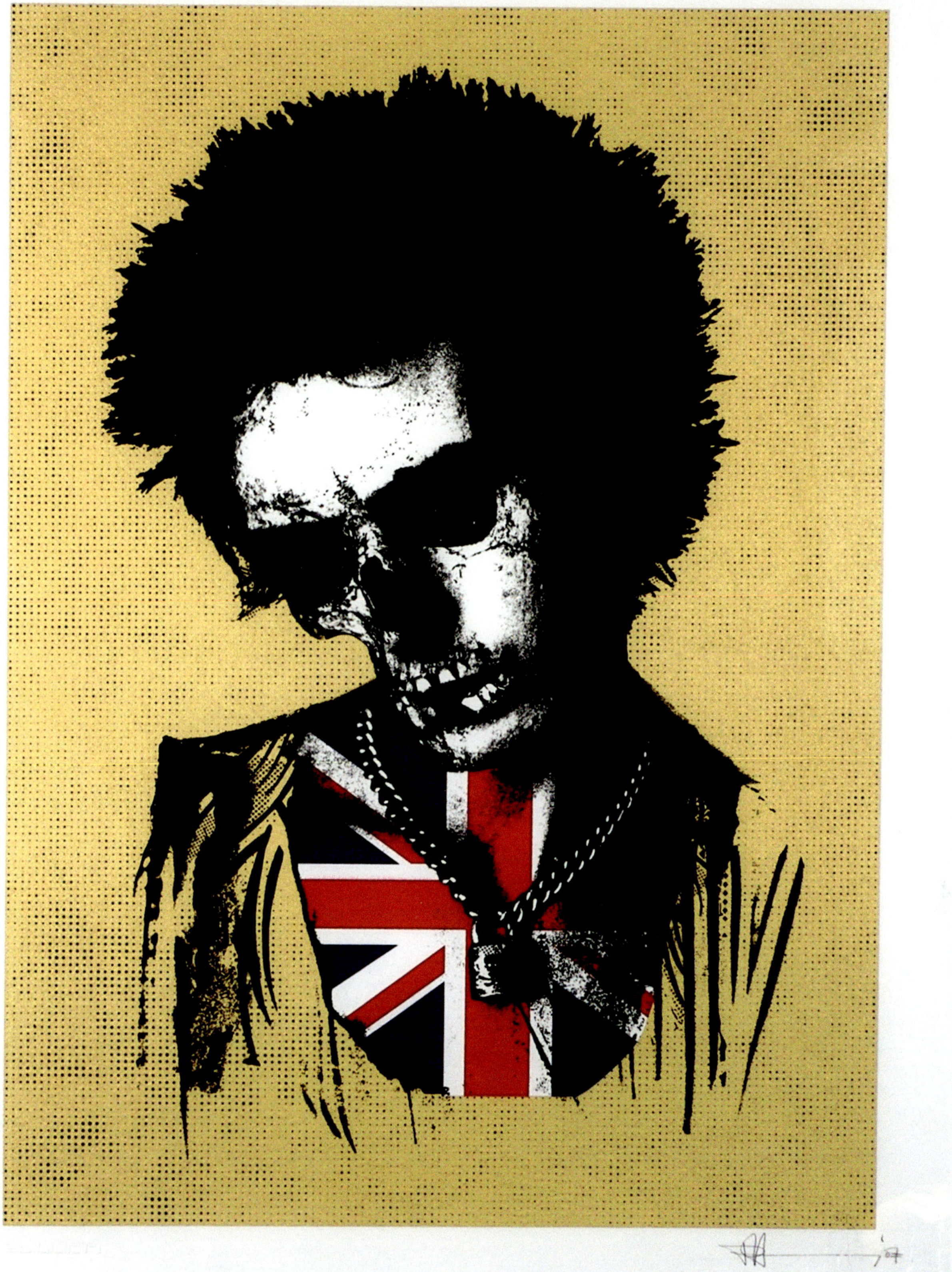

Dead Rebels, Sid | Acrylic and silkscreen – 57 x 75 cm – 2007

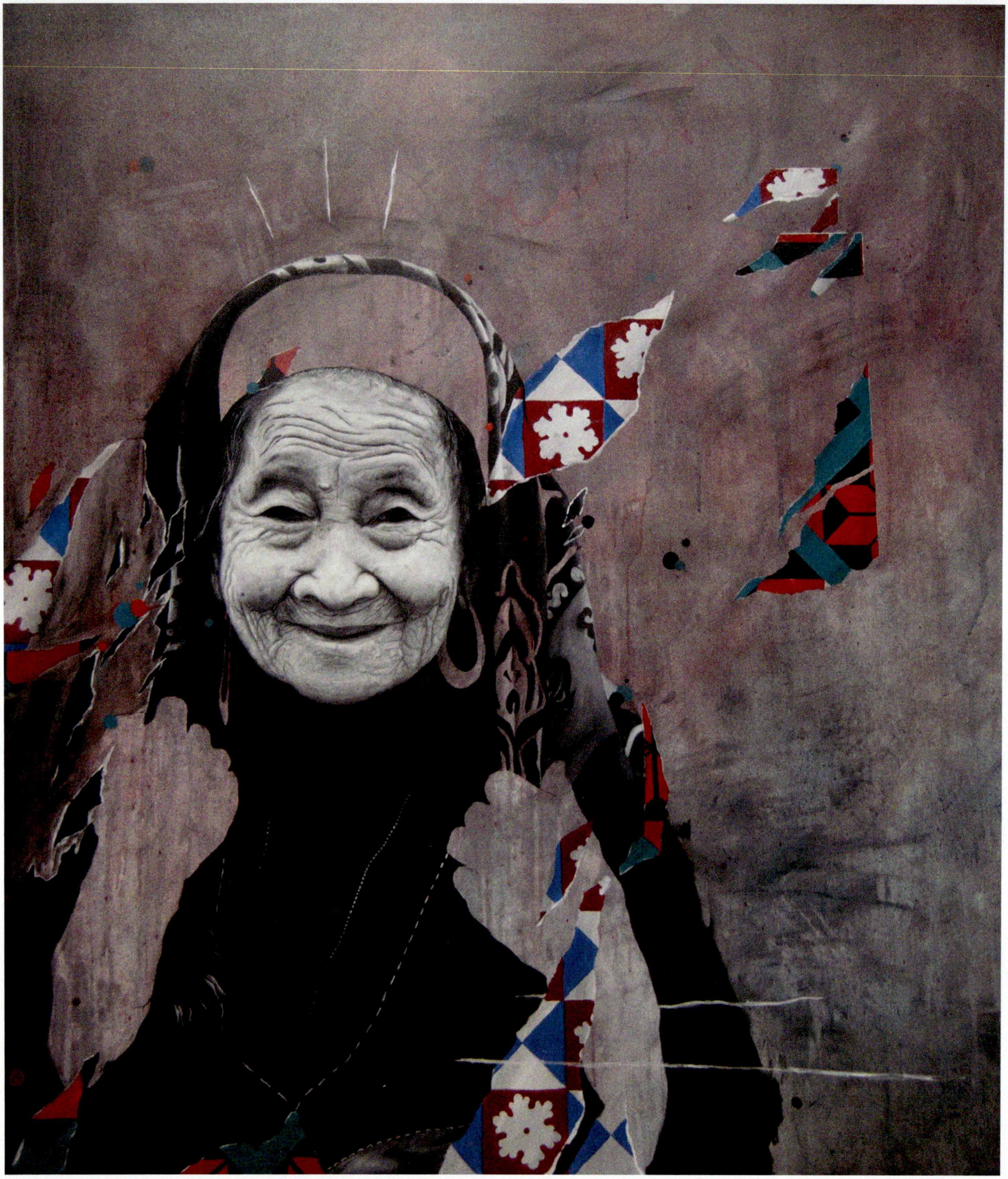

Melissa Officinalis / Oil, acrylic, and aerosol on canvas – 107 x 122 cm – 2010

Pedro Matos

Born in Santarem, Portugal, 1989. Lives in Lisbon, Portugal.

I grew up in a time and place where kids could still play safely in the streets. A few years later, Skateboarding and Graffiti took part in my life and gave me the opportunity to grow up in this interactive public space of urban life that is the street. Today, my studio practice is still very influenced by that background and the street is still where a lot of my inspiration comes from.

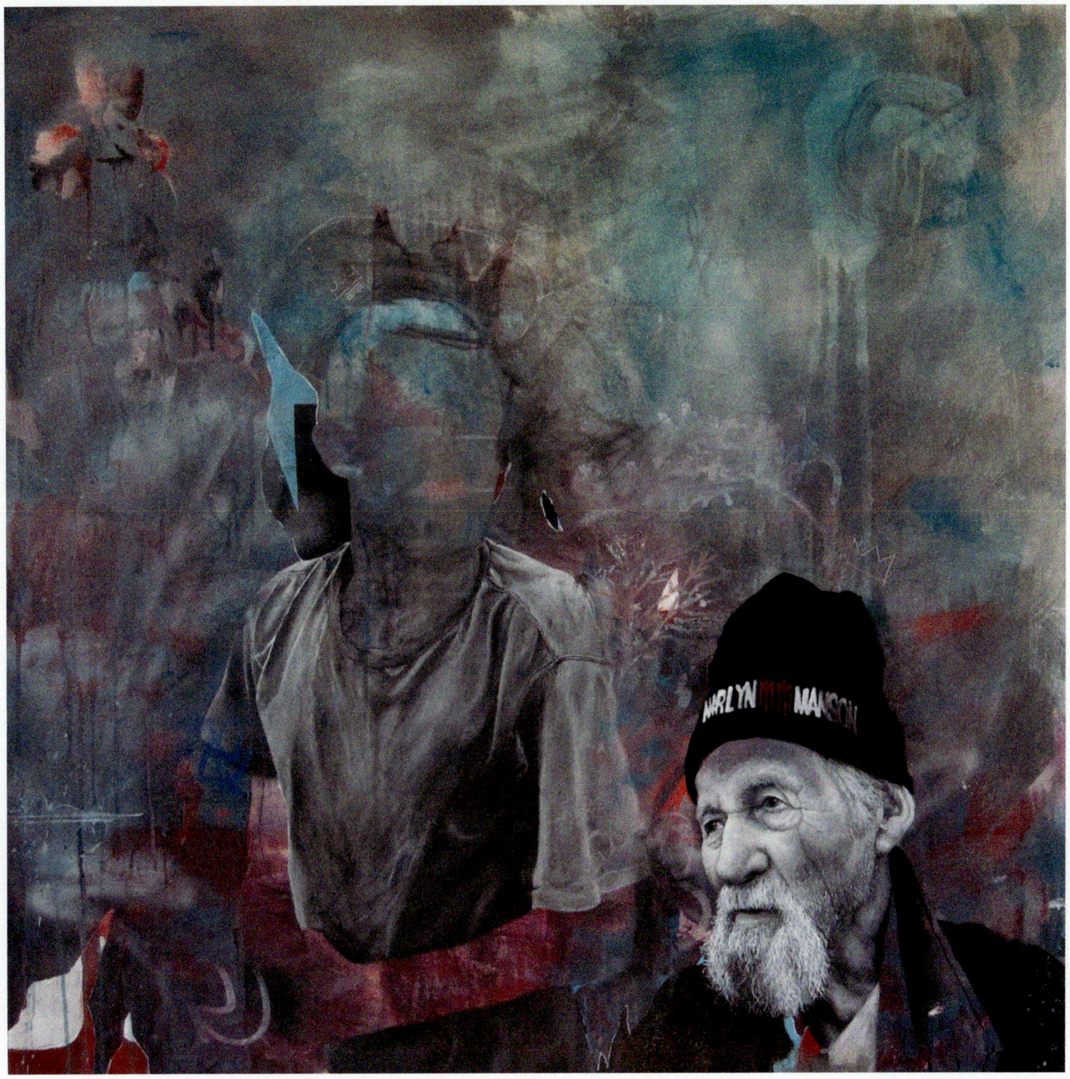

Marlyn / Oil, acrylic, and aerosol on canvas – 100 x 100 cm – 2010

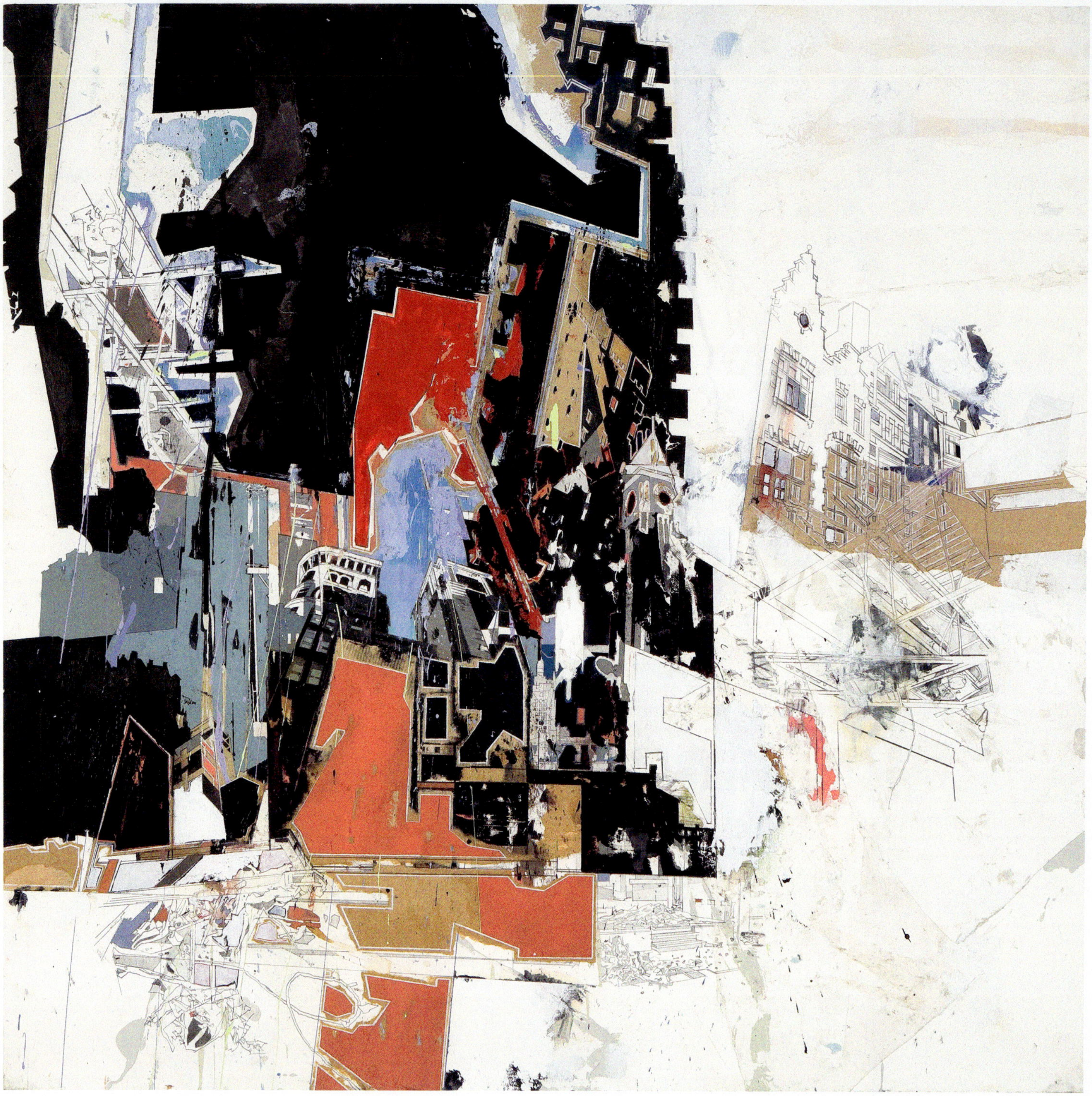

Untitled / Graphite, oil, acrylic, ink, and paper bags on paper mounted on wood – 102 x 102 cm – 2010

Peter Owen

Born in Los Angeles, United States, 1977. Lives in New York, United States.

My drawings and paintings are based on my daily experience in the city. I study the surfaces of buildings, with their layers of graffiti, advertisements, paint, and decay. The jarring colors of spray paint next to brick, iron, and cement inspire my color palette, and my compositions are full of the buildings I see every day. I attempt to describe the experience of living in a place that is continually transformed by construction and demolition, attention and neglect.

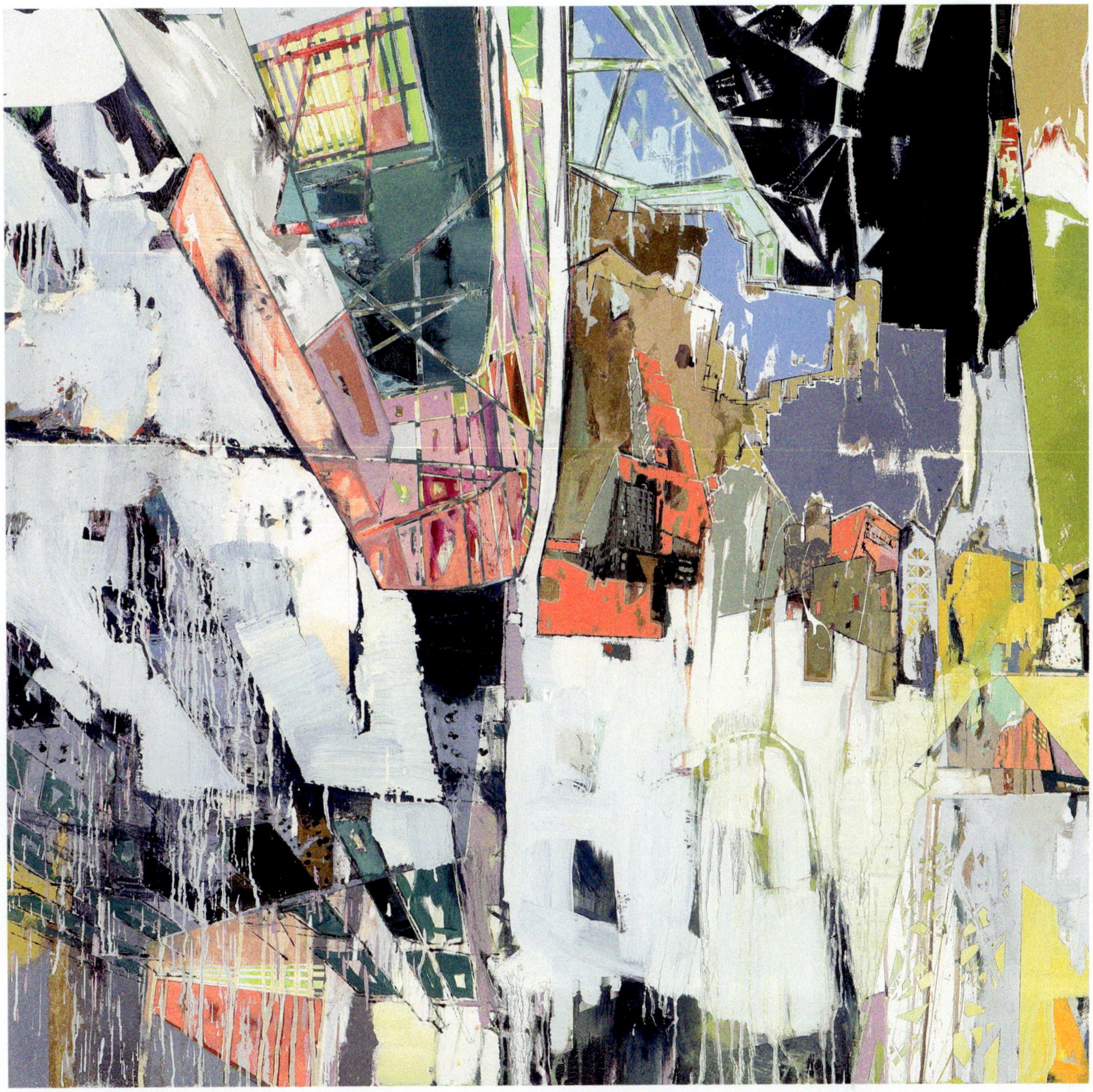

Intersection 2 / Graphite, oil, acrylic, and aerosol on wood – 152 x 152 cm – 2010

Pose

Born in Chicago, United States, 1980. Lives in Chicago, United States.

Since I came into art through graffiti and not the other way around, I try to approach studio work with the same mischievous irreverence as I would working in the street. Striving for the same sense of lawlessness and immediacy keeps my studio work authentic to my personality and my original intent of creating graffiti in the street. Inherently my work in the street influences and informs my work in the studio and vice versa.

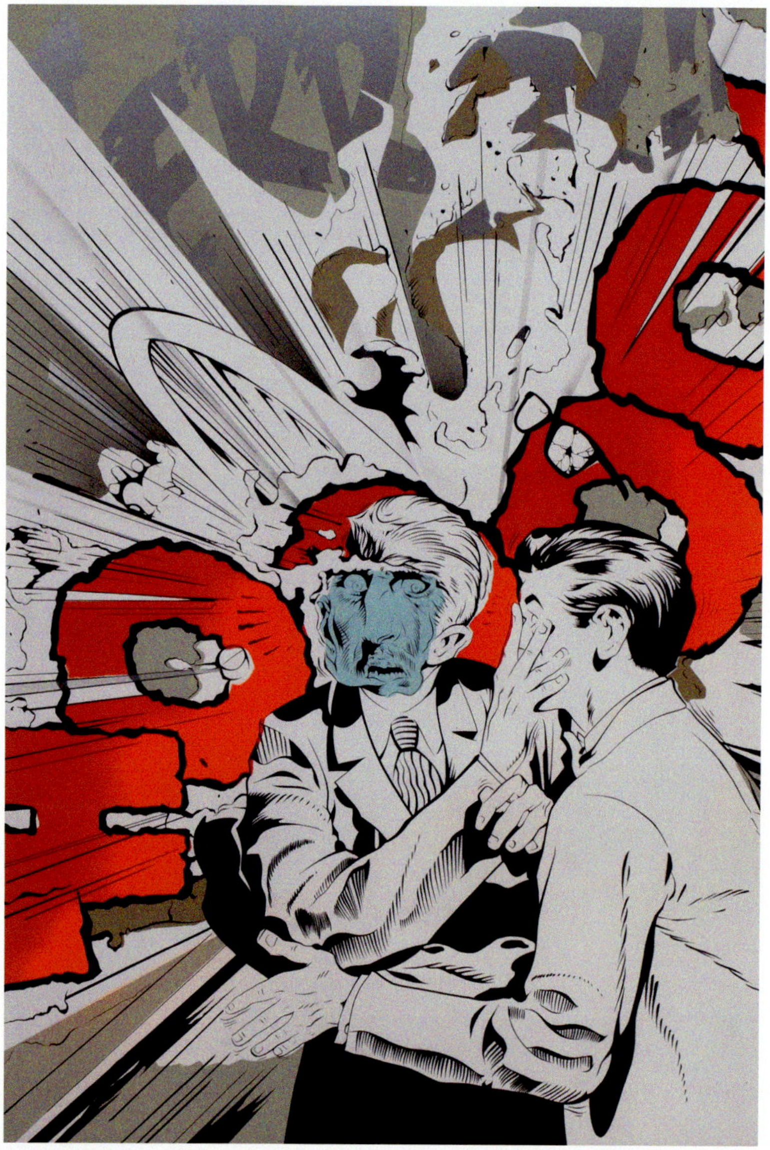

Gasface / Acrylic, gouache, and Cel-Vinyl on MDF – 121 x 182 cm – 2010

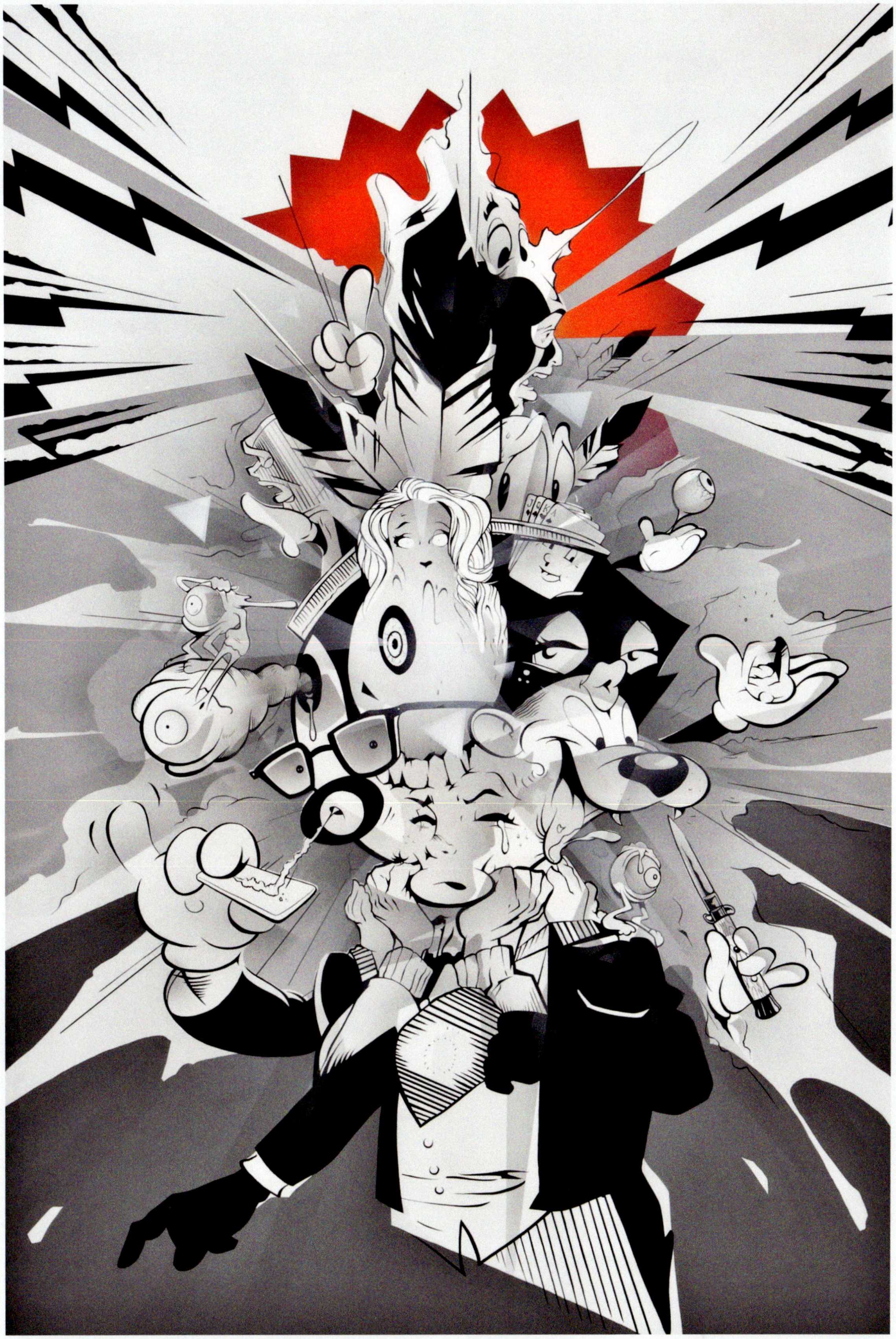

Blow Your Lid 2 / Acrylic, gouache, and Cel-Vinyl on MDF – 121 x 182 cm – 2010

Pure Evil

Born in Haverfordwest, Wales, 1968. Lives in London, England.

I enjoy walking around looking for spots to paint wherever I am. This usually culminates in a night of sporadic bunny painting wherever I might be: Moscow , Ulaanbaatar , São Paulo, London … I like the poetry of street art, how it's enhanced by the environment, just as we are shaped by our environment. Running a gallery has meant that I have had to reign in much of my vandalistic urges in my neighborhood, but if I am in a new city and there is the exciting possibility of getting caught then the adrenaline is too much and I have the urge to paint in the streets. It takes about 5–8 seconds and then im gone. Off to the next wall.

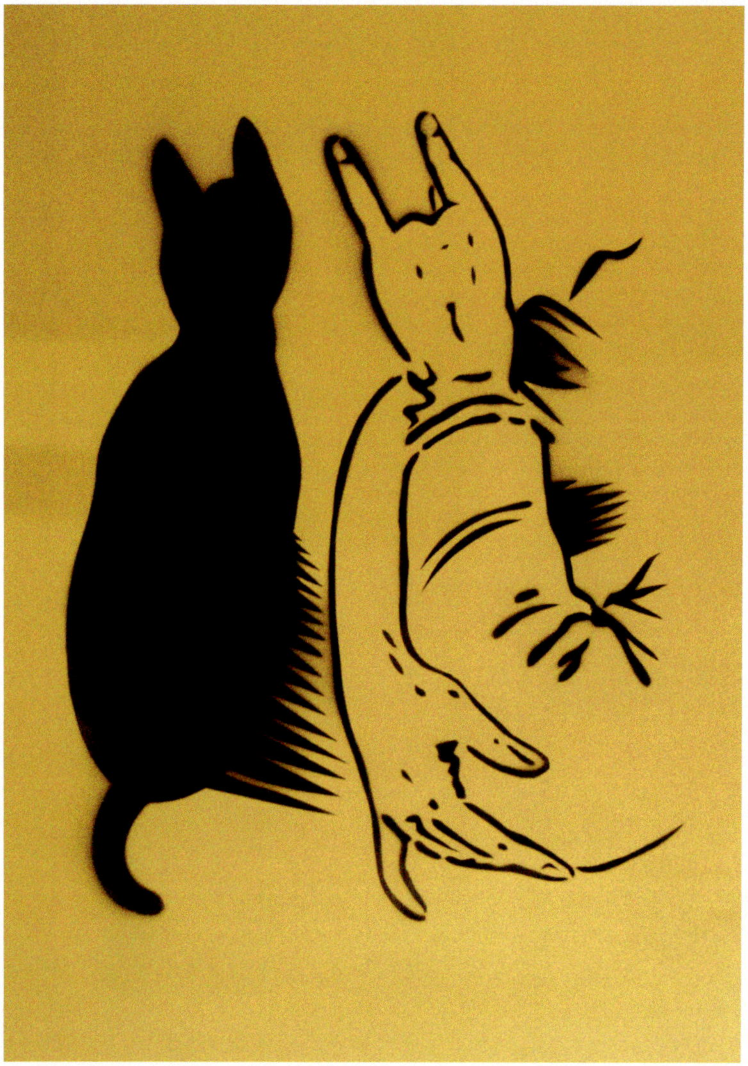

Pussyfingers / Stencil and aerosol on metallic paper – 40 x 80 cm – 2011

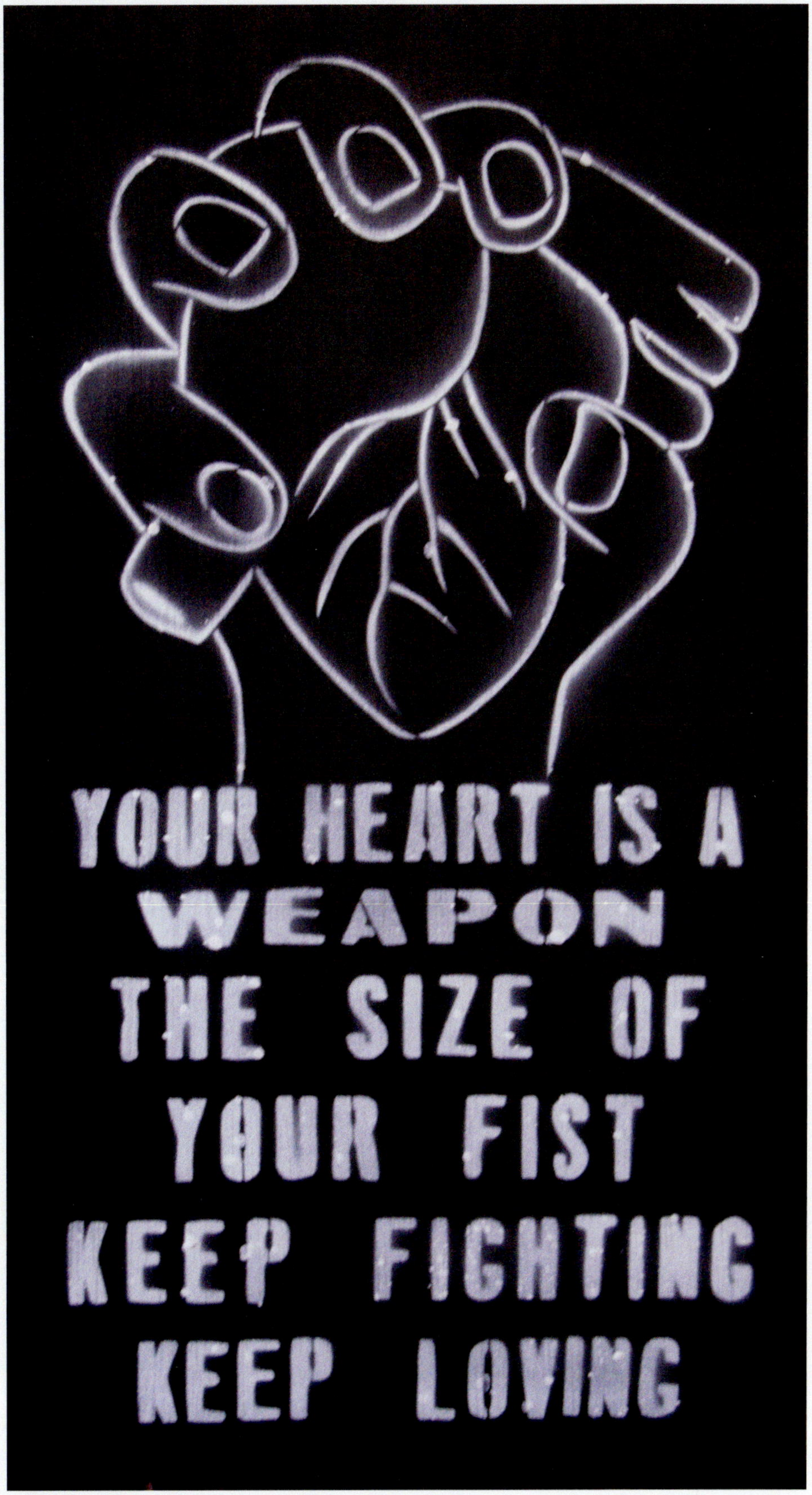

Your Heart is a Weapon / Stencil and aerosol on wood – 35 x 80 cm – 2011

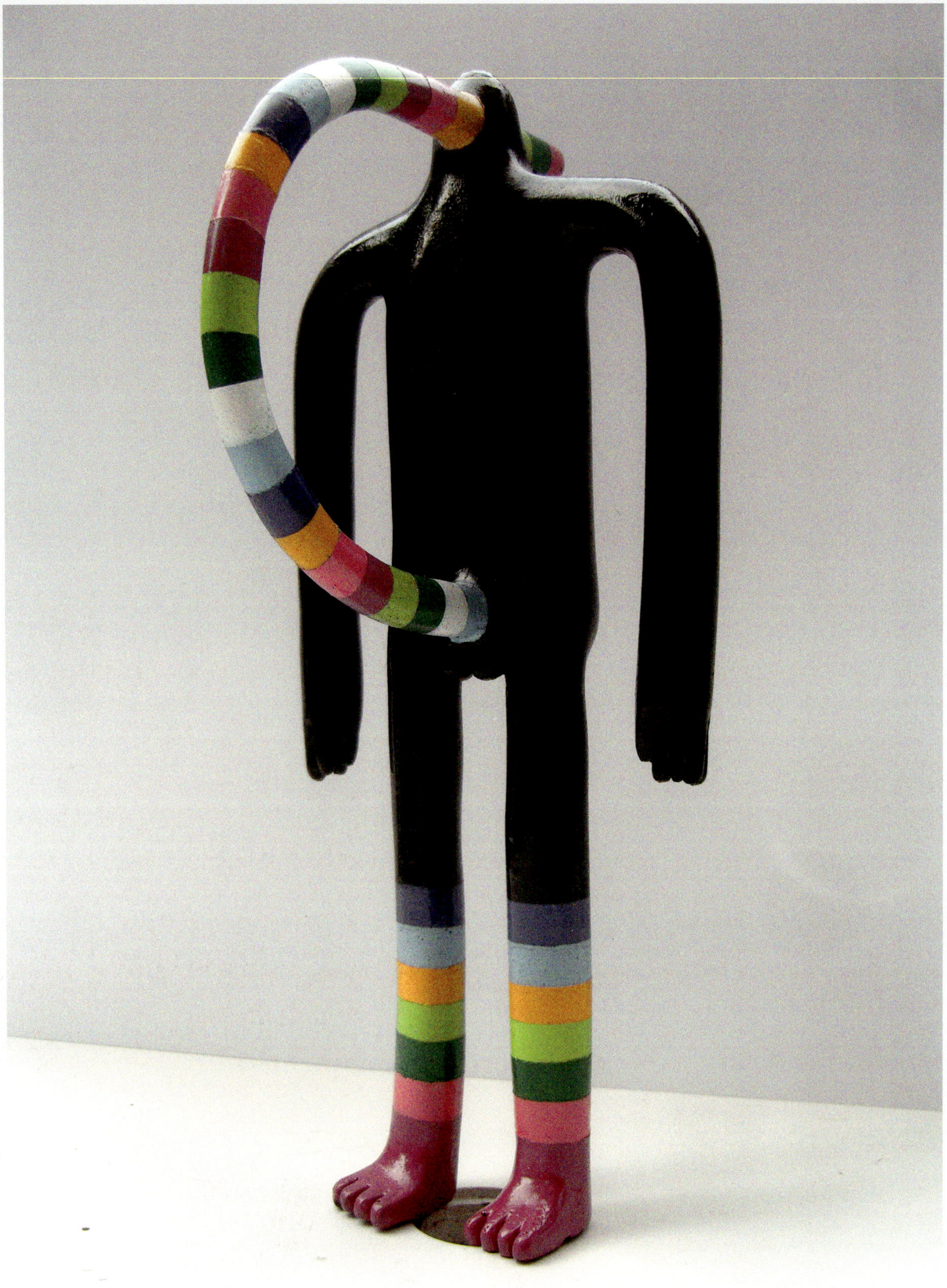

The Rainboner aka M.Irony **With Toykyo** / Resin and car varnish – 15 x 35 x 15 cm – 2007

Remed

Born in Paris, France, 1978. Lives in Madrid, Spain.

I've always enjoyed the intimity and silence of my studio. I still love and need to stare at the emptiness of a virgin canvas in order to travel into my self and beyond. In the street things are different, much easier. You need less introspection. You need to observe the life that is already on the wall, that's your starting point. I try to simplify my canvases so that the viewer can feel something deep without having me to explain anything. That's how my art has got closer to be iconic. Each visual became an icon, more than a composition of various elements or ideas. All is one, one is all.

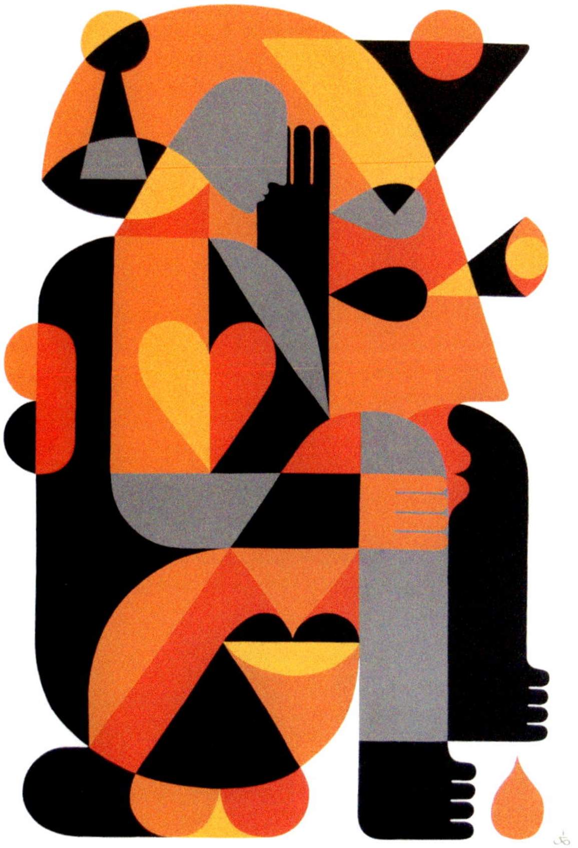

From Desire / Acrylic paint on canvas – 80 x 120 cm – 2010

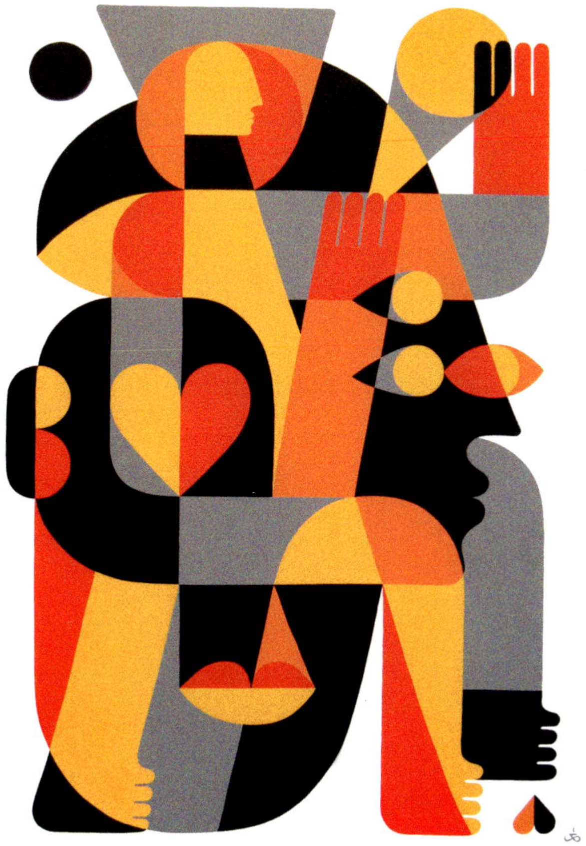

To Fulfilment / Acrylic paint on canvas – 80 x 120 cm – 2010

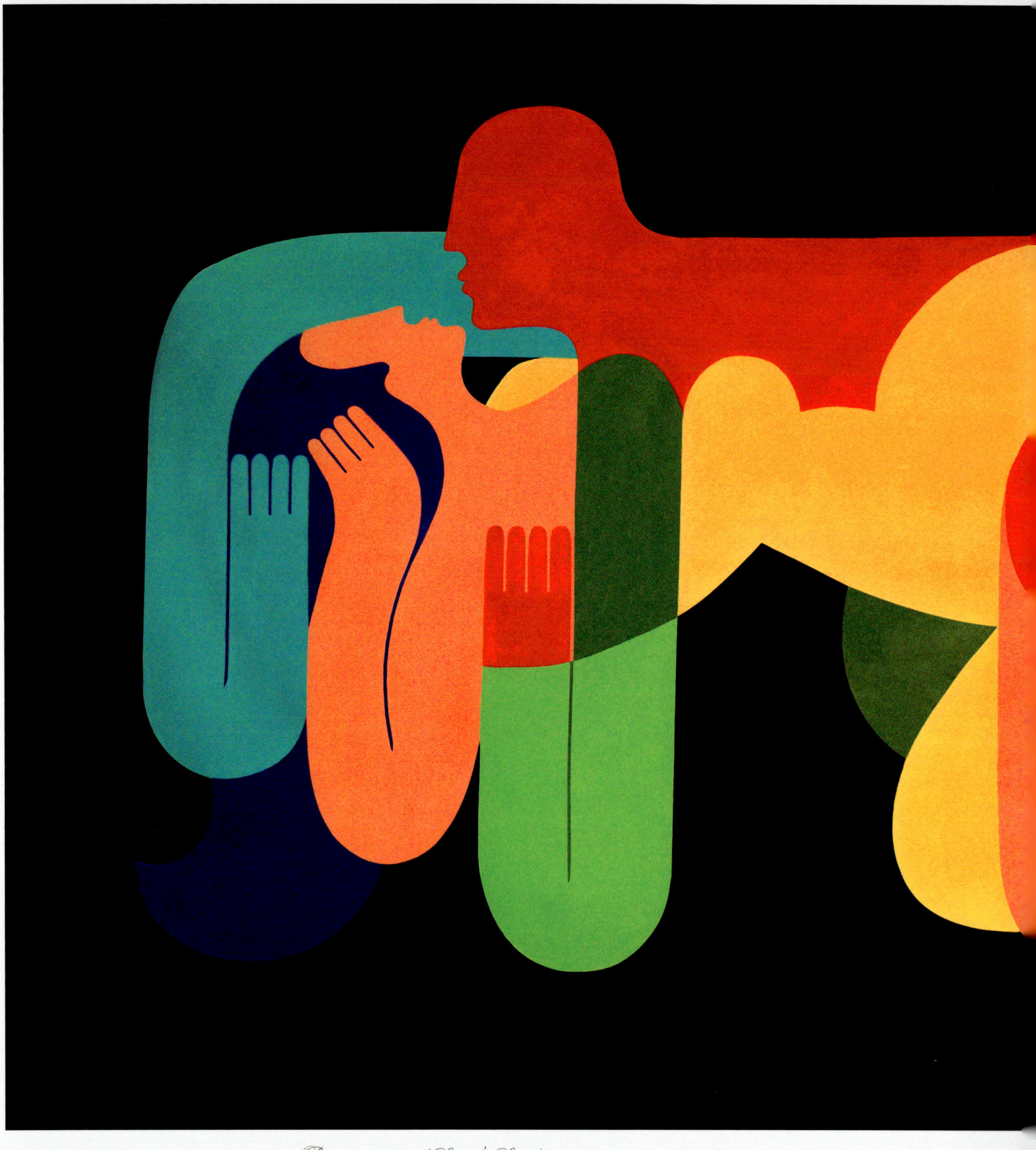

Pareja acostada (Layin' Love) | Acrylic on canvas – 190 x 115 cm – 2008

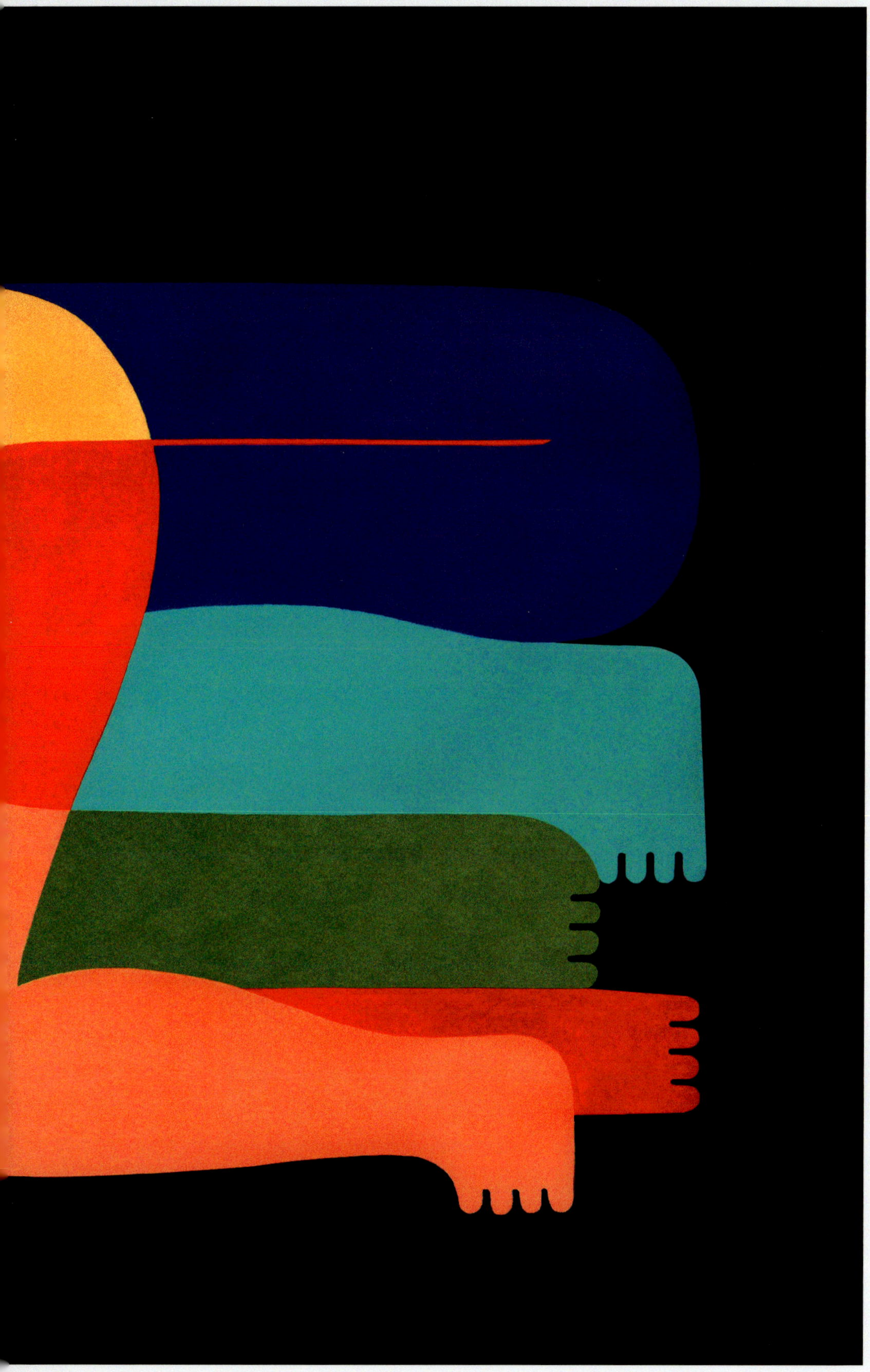

Remi-Rough

Born in London, England. 1971. Lives in London, England.

At its heart my work is about tension, balance, and structure. I identify the dynamic in certain shapes and forms and bend them to my own building texture until I feel the depth is right. The line and shape then follow... I am drawn to the rearrangement of mediums—using layers of emulsion over layers of wet spray paint—as a form of reversal and experimentation with more comfortable mediums. I hear the hum and whispers of contrasting colors and let them lead me where I need to go...

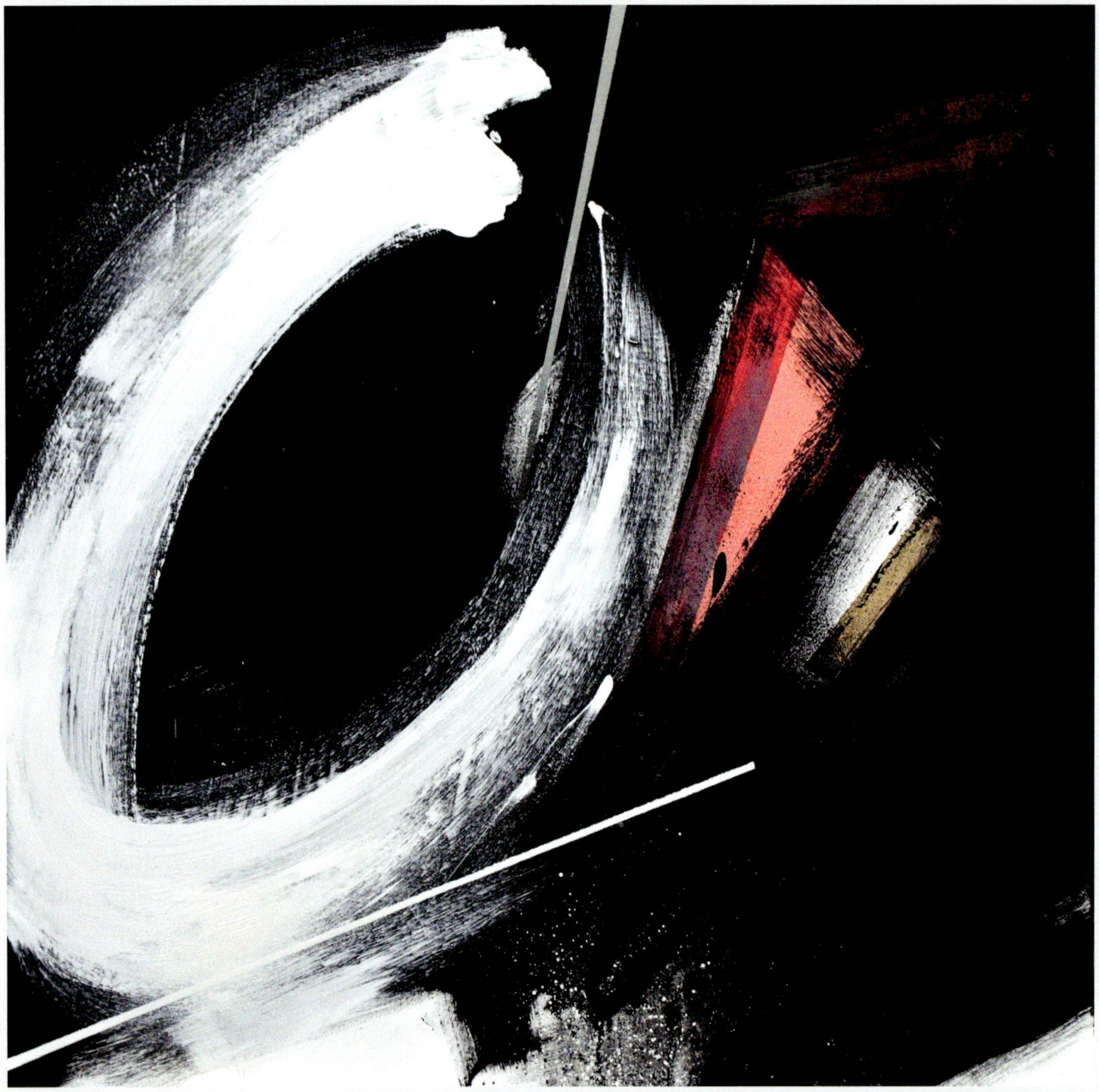

Marozia / Mixed media on canvas – 99 x 99 cm – 2011

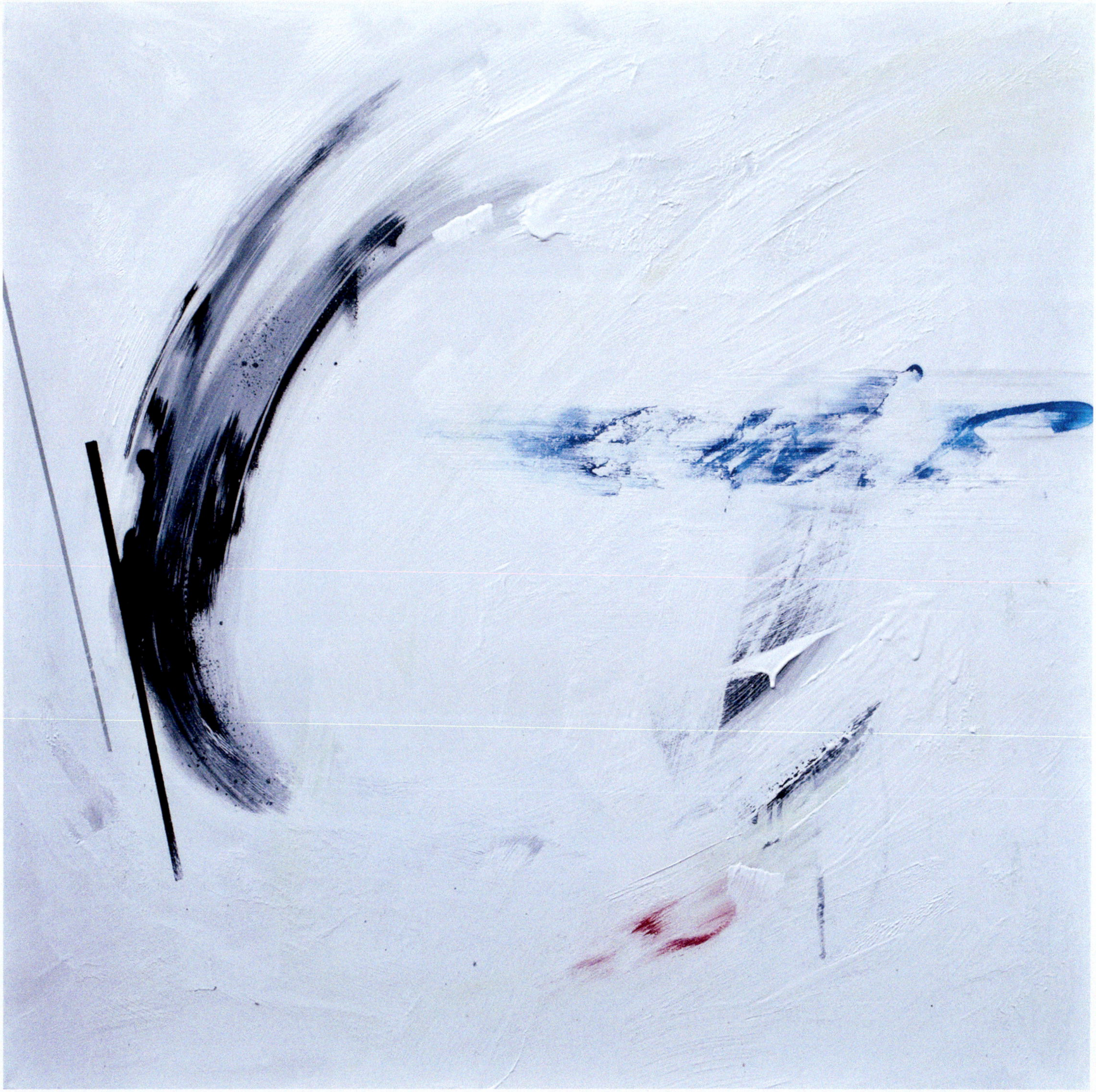

Evaristus / Mixed media on canvas – 99 x 99 cm – 2011

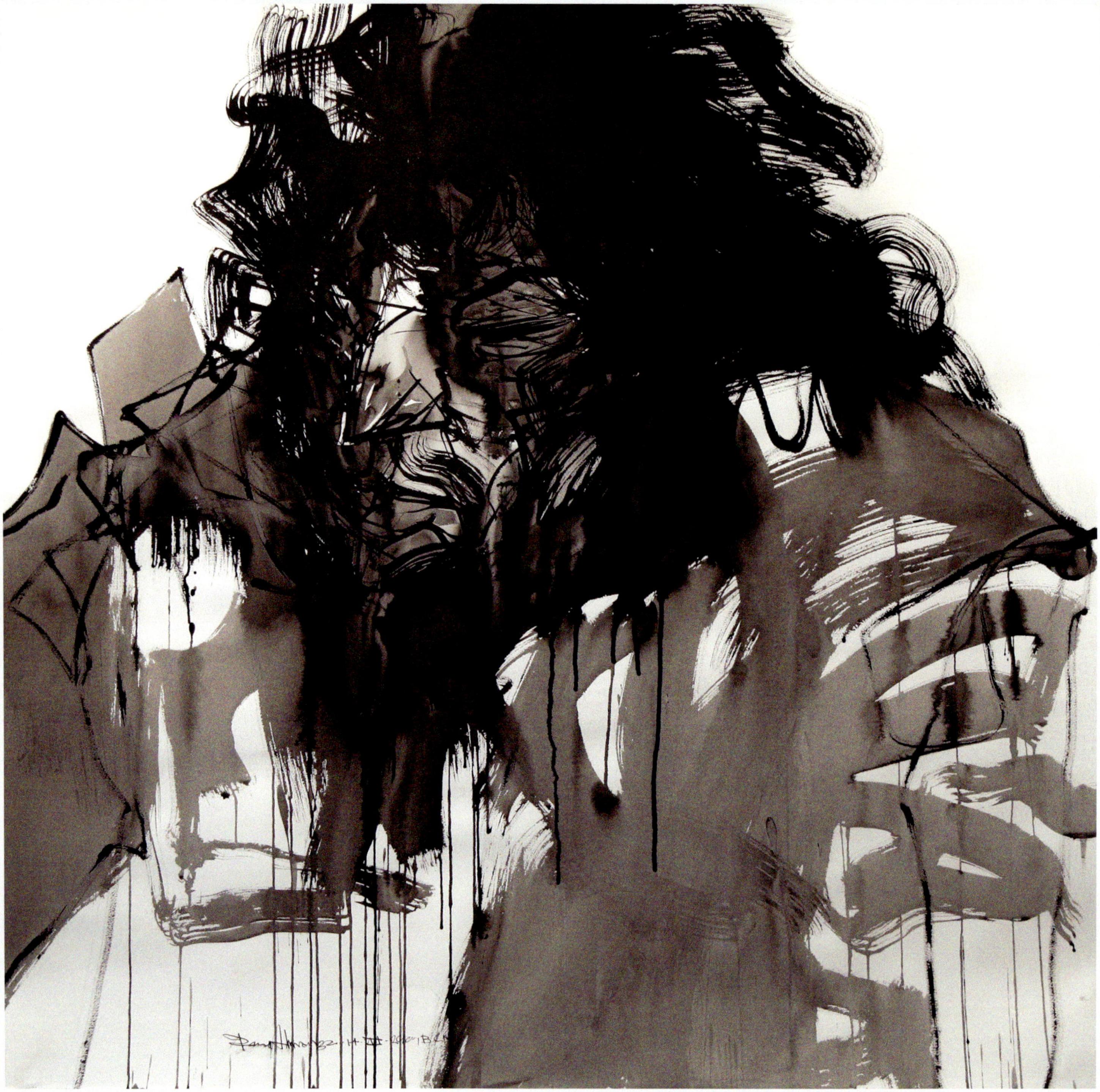

Aeonod / Indian ink on paper – 120 x 120 cm – 2010

René Almanza

Born in Monterrey, Mexico, 1979. Lives in Monterrey, Mexico.

The street, the walking and transit place of many human beings, is the ultimate environment where many views are generated, where the past, present, and future is displayed, the art takes form in the streets but returns home, to the personal space, people consume images, they digest them, they project them in their persons, then the images become part of the collective unconscious and thus they always come and go as the water cycle.

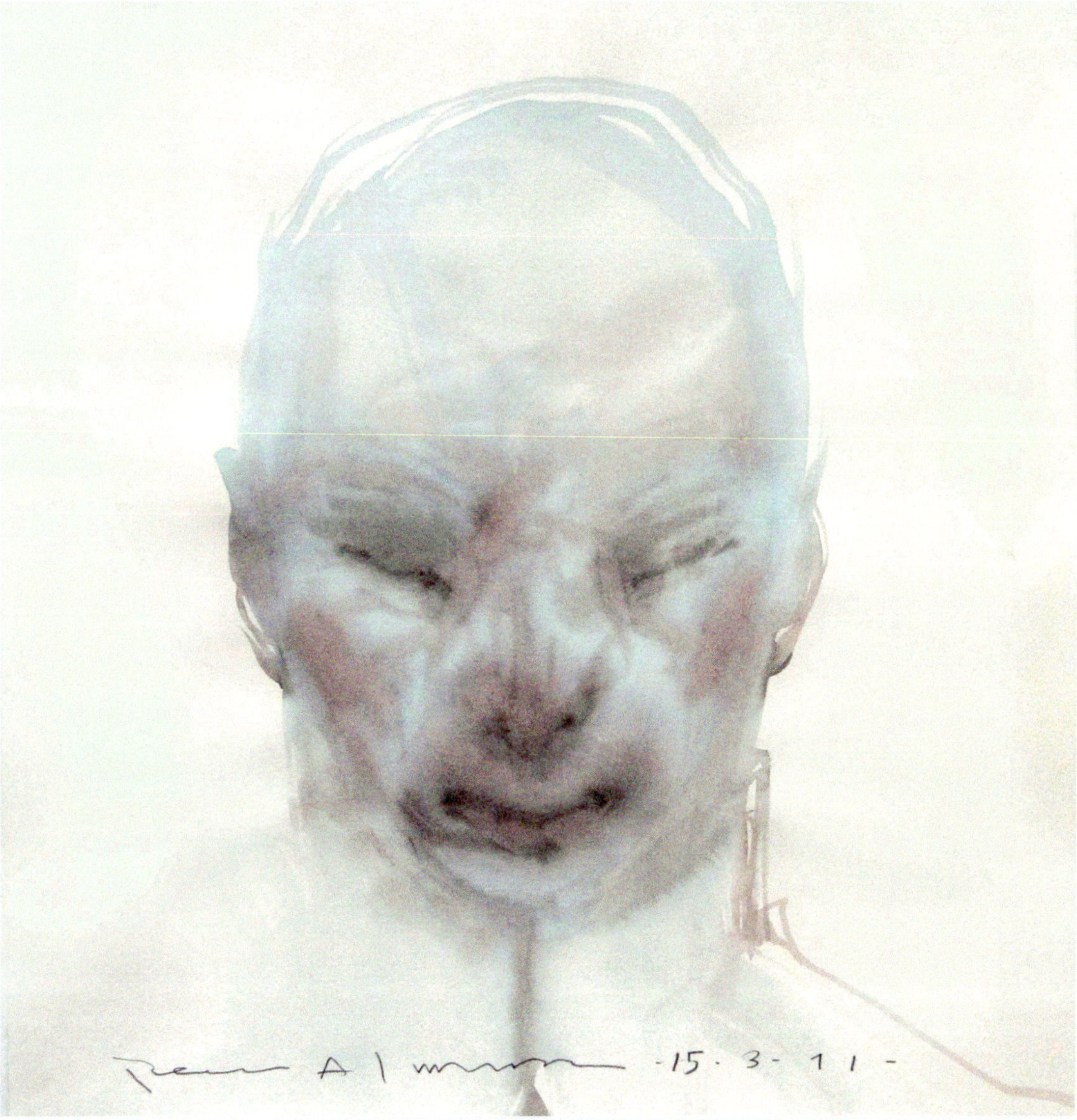

Sin título / Watercolor on paper – 48 x 50 cm – 2011

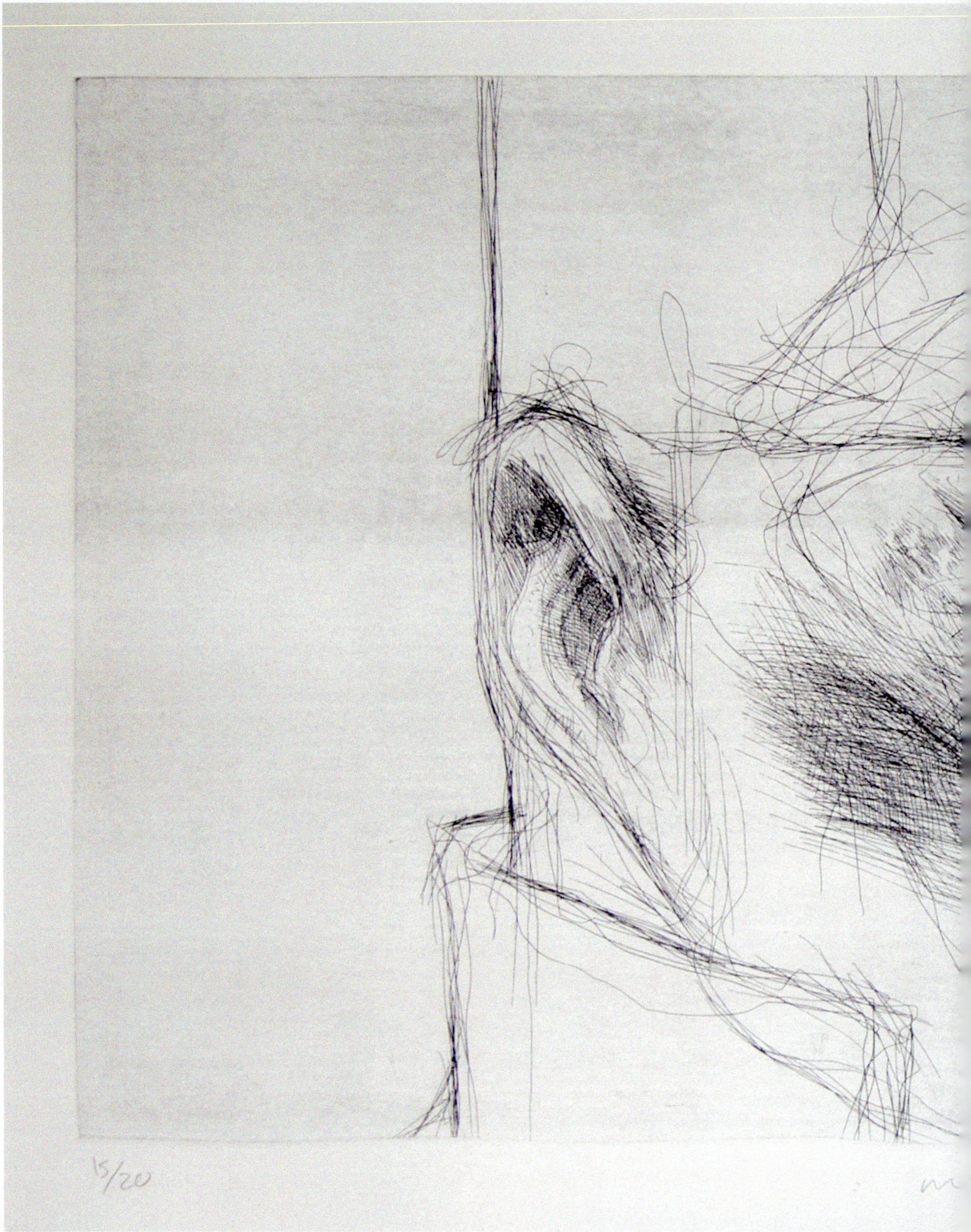
15/20

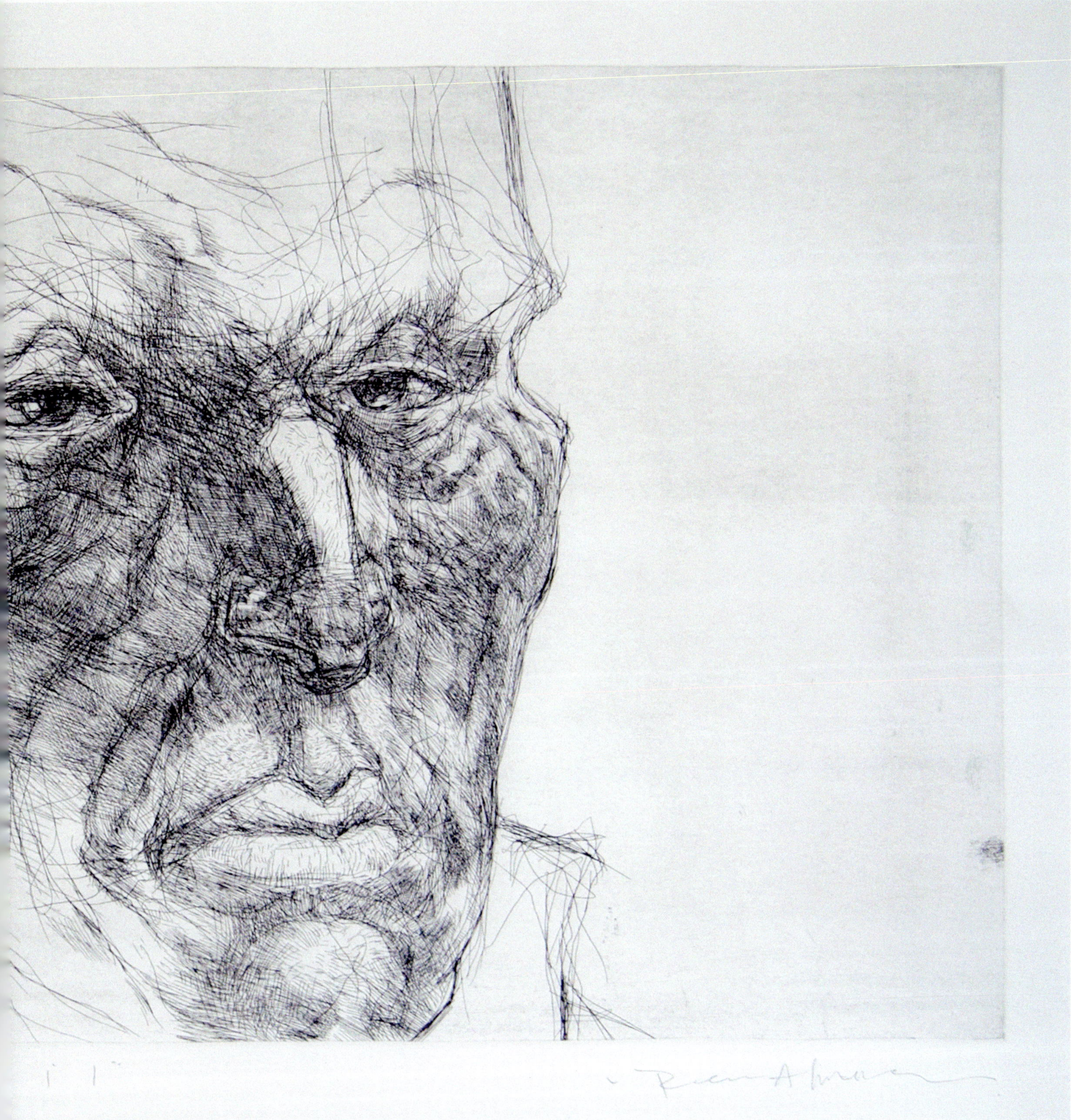

Misil II / Etching metal on paper – 110 x 70 cm – 2010

Retna

Born in Los Angeles, United States, 1979. Lives in Los Angeles, United States.

I want my text to feel universal, whether my work is in the streets or showing in a gallery, I want people from different cultures to all find some similarity in it—whether they can read it or not. My art allows me to see people all as one.

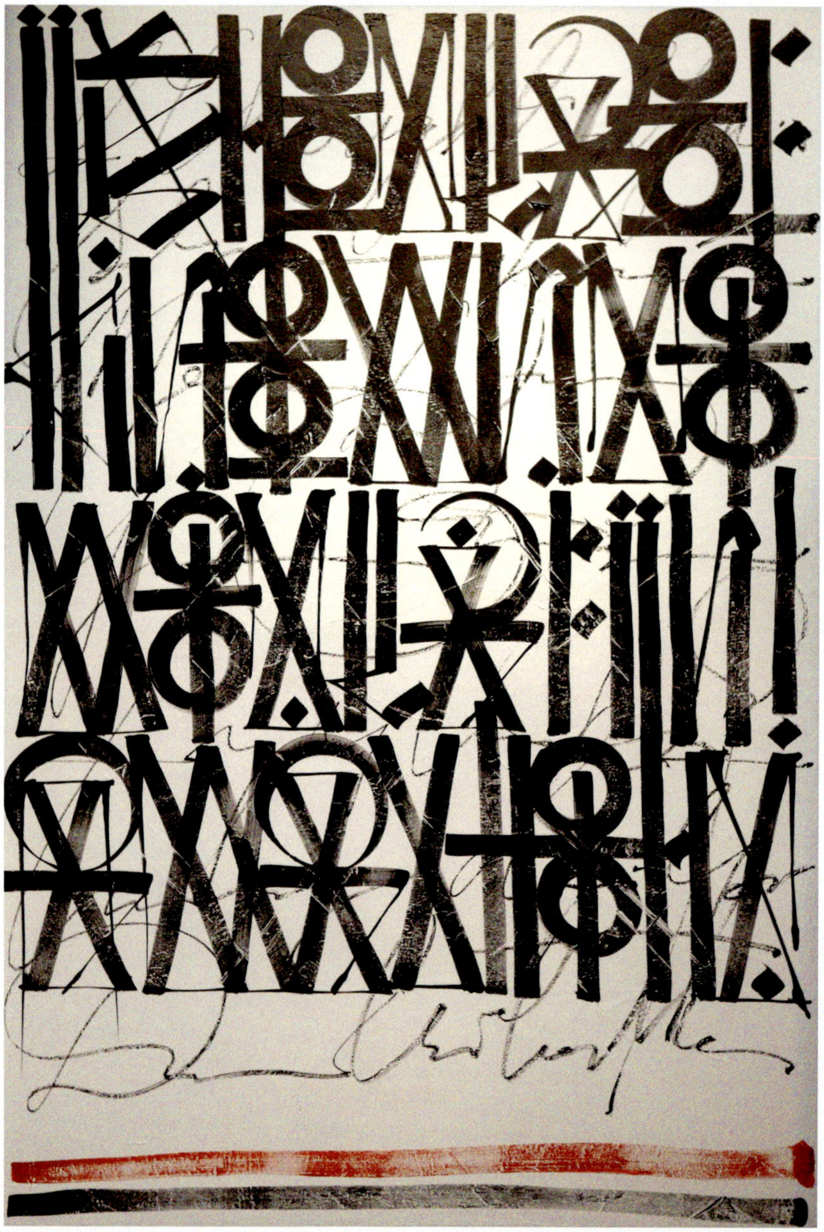

Don't Bother Me / Acrylic on canvas – 162 x 244 cm – 2011

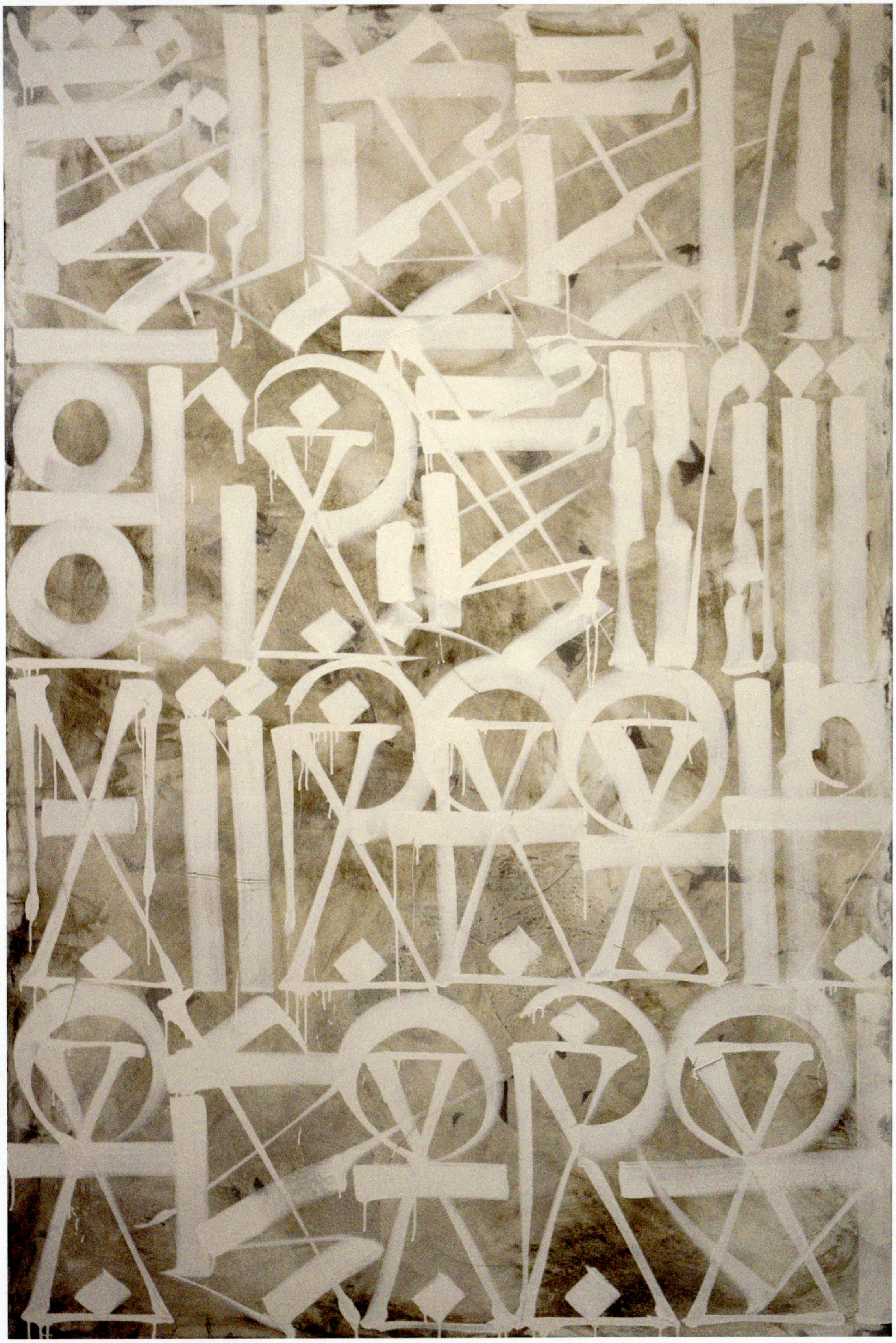

El Señor de mi Vida Pasada / Acrylic on canvas – 162 x 244 cm – 2011

Ripo

Born in New York, United States, 1983. Lives in Barcelona, Spain.

Art is a reaction to life and good art should inspire reactions to life. This holds true whether the art is in a nice white gallery setting or under a bridge next to a stinking river. Each has its own value, should be created to fit its context, and if done well will create different reactions in different people. I also believe that humor is often the best way to speak about a serious subject. Whether working indoors or outdoors I strive to create artwork based on these ideas.

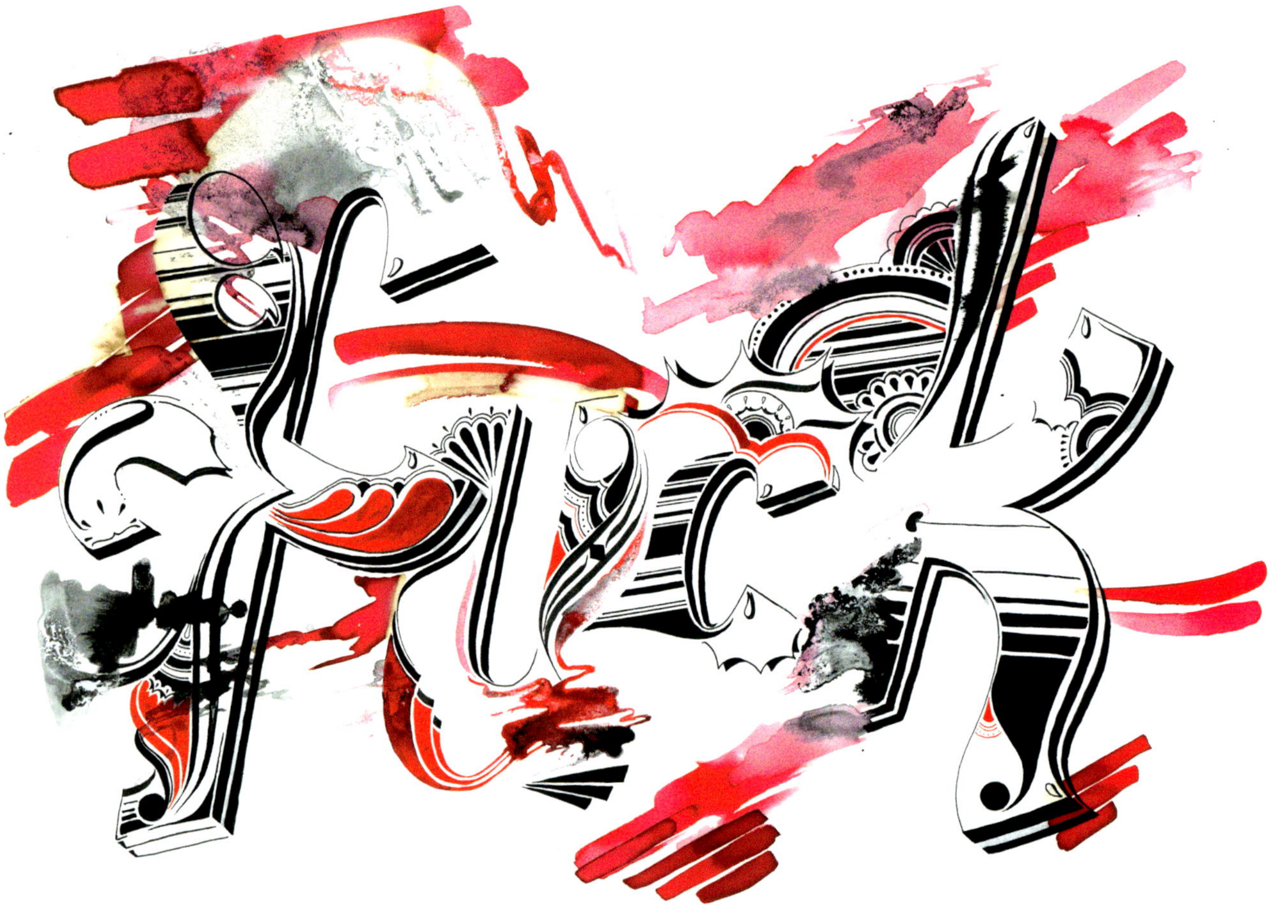

Fuck / Ink, gouache, and bleach on paper – 51 x 38 cm – 2010

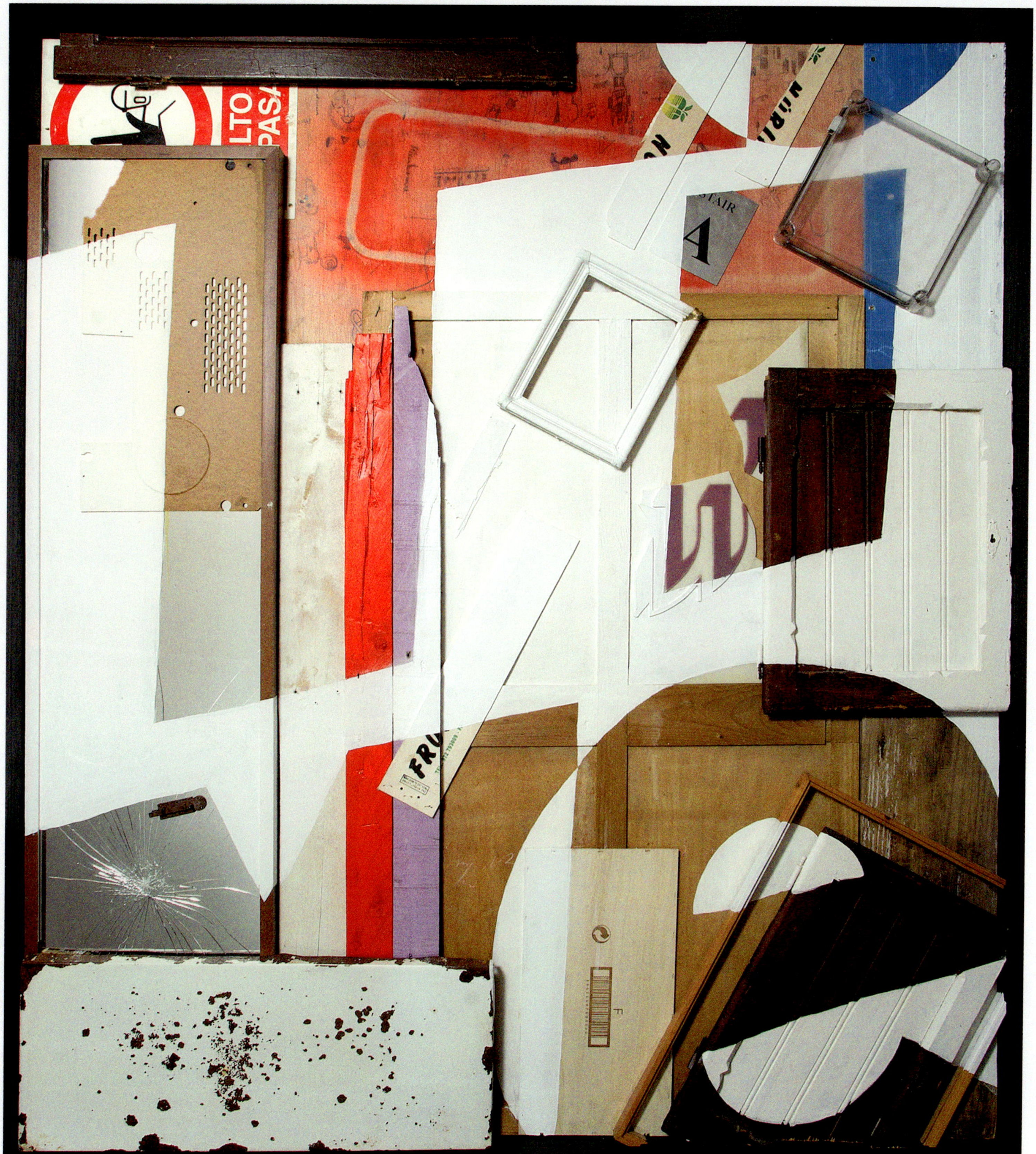

Never Enough #1 | Latex on assembled found objects – 162 x 185 x 16 cm – 2011

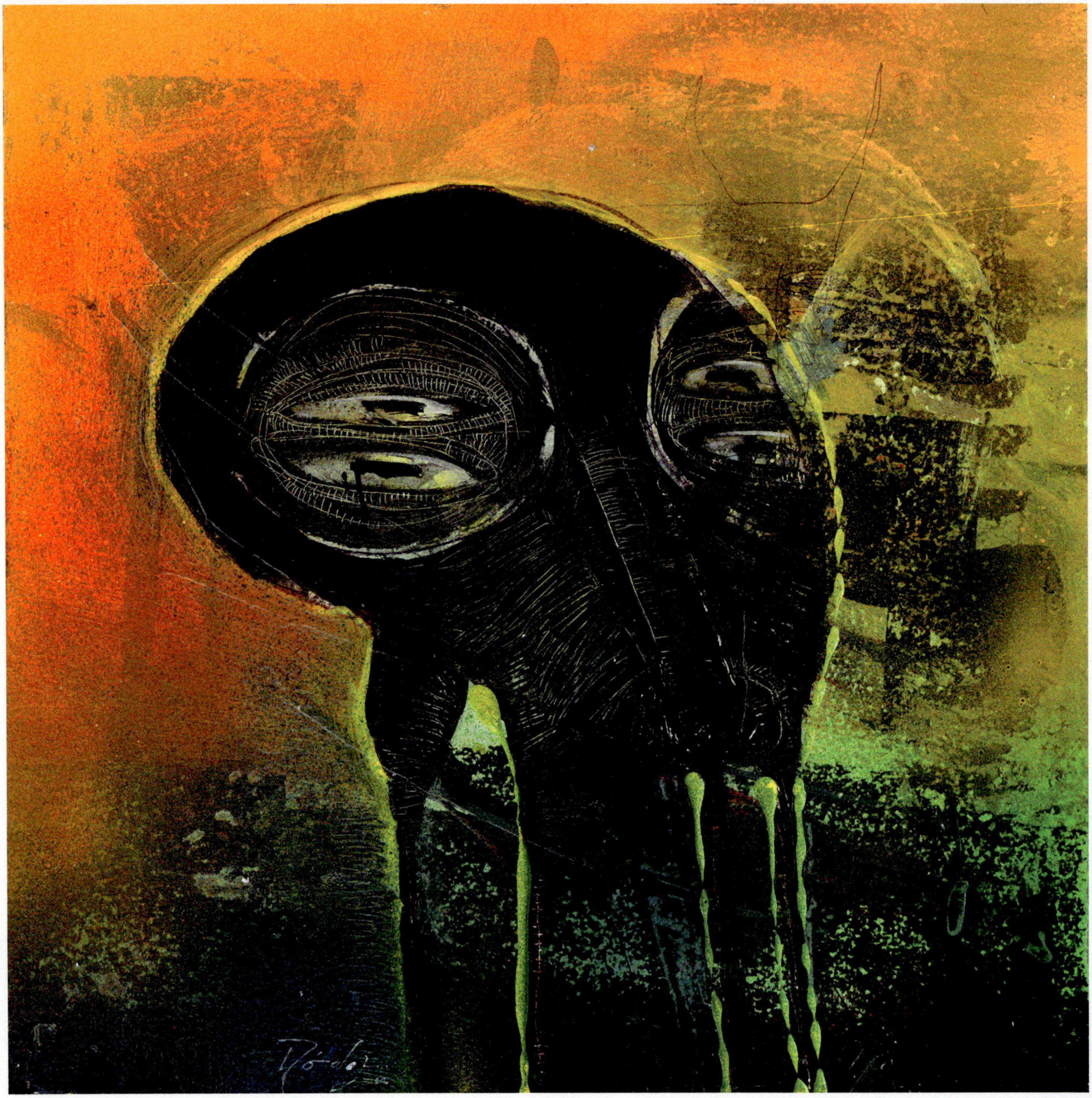

Hombre Mirando al Sur / Acrylic, latex, enamel, and aerosol on wood panel – 30 x 30 cm – 2009

Ródez

Born in Bogotá, Colombia, 1963. Lives in Buenos Aires, Argentina.

Independence generates a free spirit, then the street allows me to explore a language without relying on the critics. The street art brings me closer to new materials, mediums, and dimensions, renovating my attitude in the studio. I feel that my painting breathes joy and sincerity because it is the result of my daily experiences while walking the streets and feeling the cultural and ethnic diversity: my work is the result of a mixed culture of which I am proud.

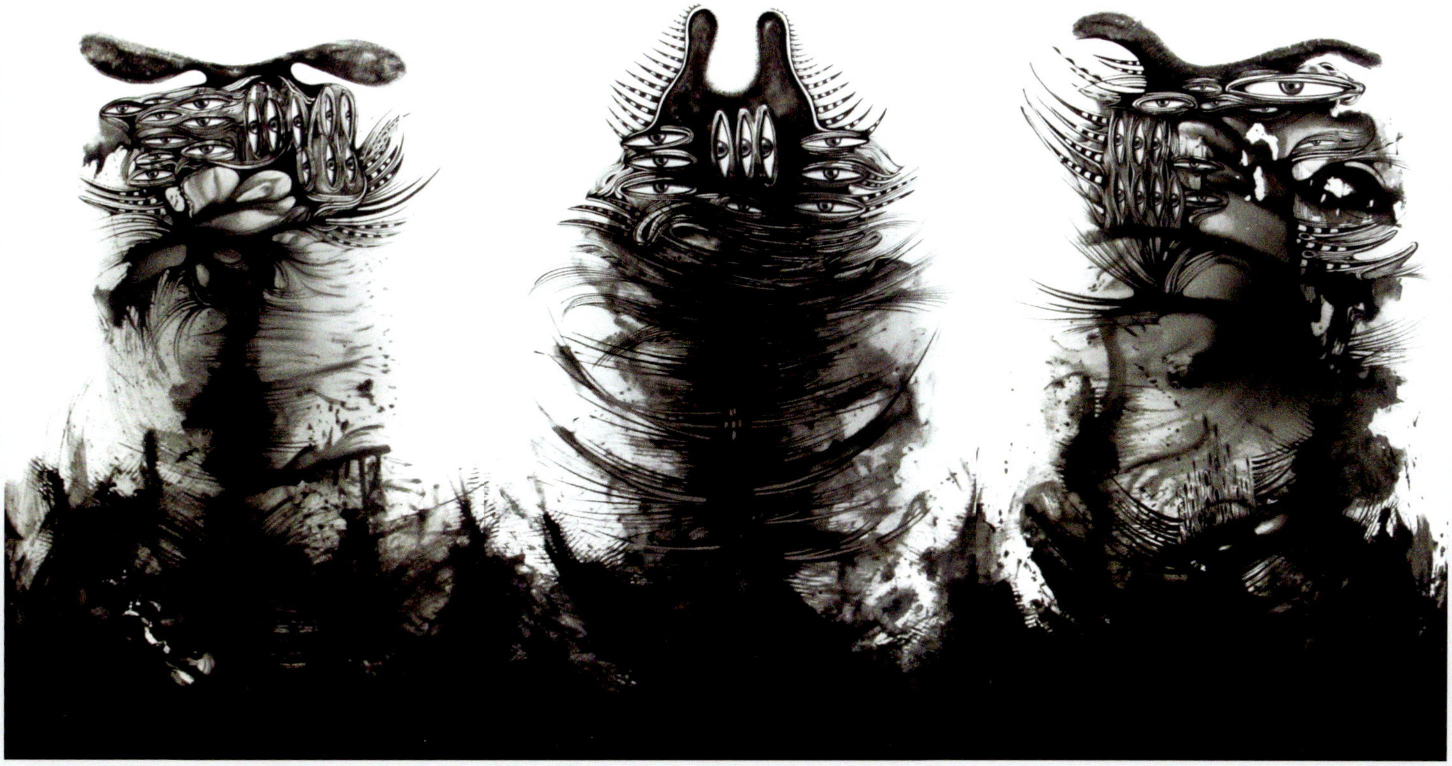

Pinta la Niña, Santamaría / Ink and acrylic on wood – 150 x 90 cm – 2010

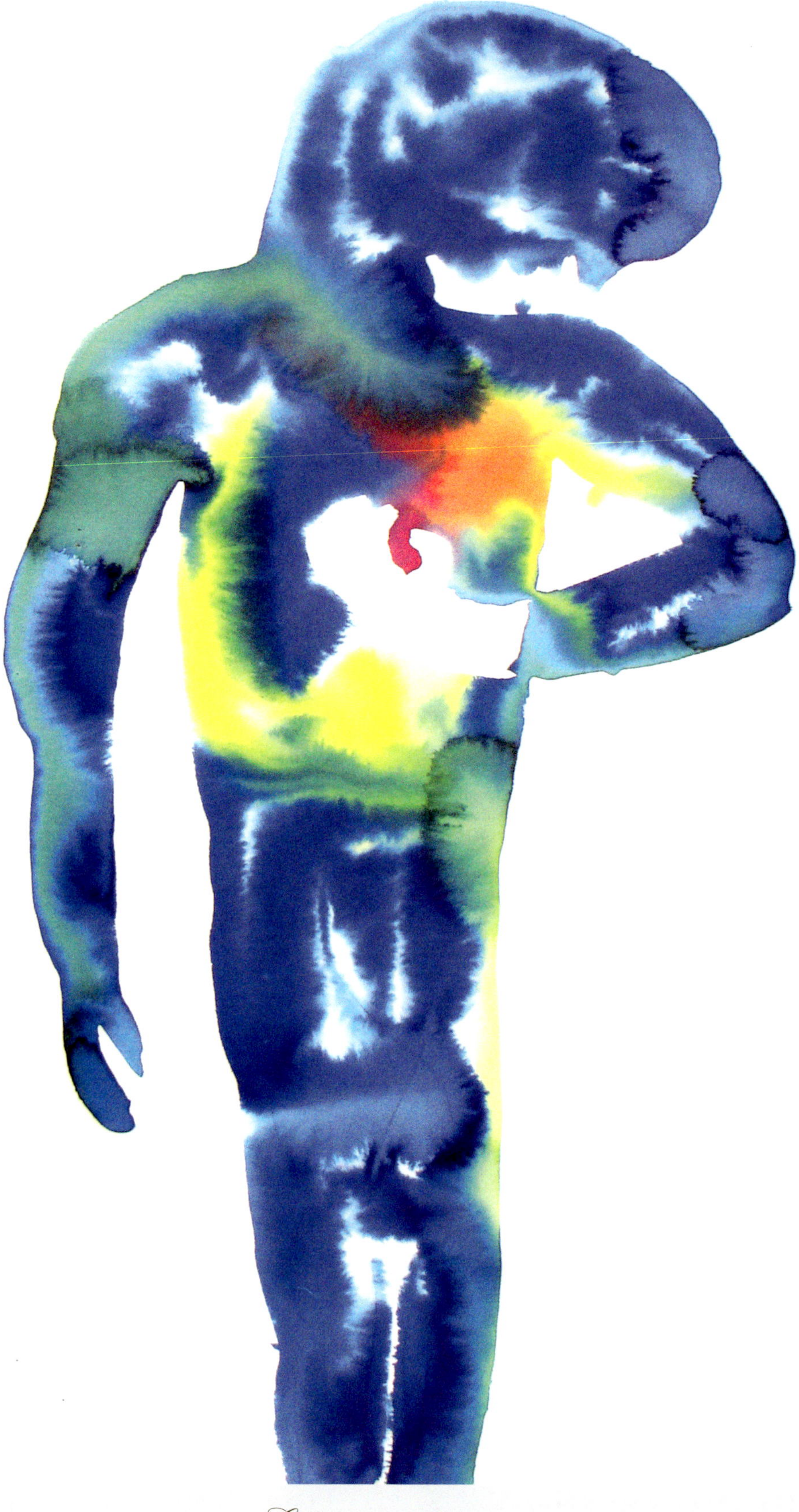

Corazón / Ink on paper – 30 x 42 cm – 2009

Sam3

Born in Elche, Spain, 1980. Lives in Murcia, Spain.

The street and the studio work are complementary. I work a lot on video animation, do experiments, documents, photographs on the outside and then it is necessary to edit this material in the laboratory. Although their destination is on the internet, today it is extremely easy to reach an audience without going through television's filters. Sometimes the reverse happens, first you have to work inside in order to take it outside, as is the case of installations. The studio is necessary even if only as a place to store the paint you use outdoors.

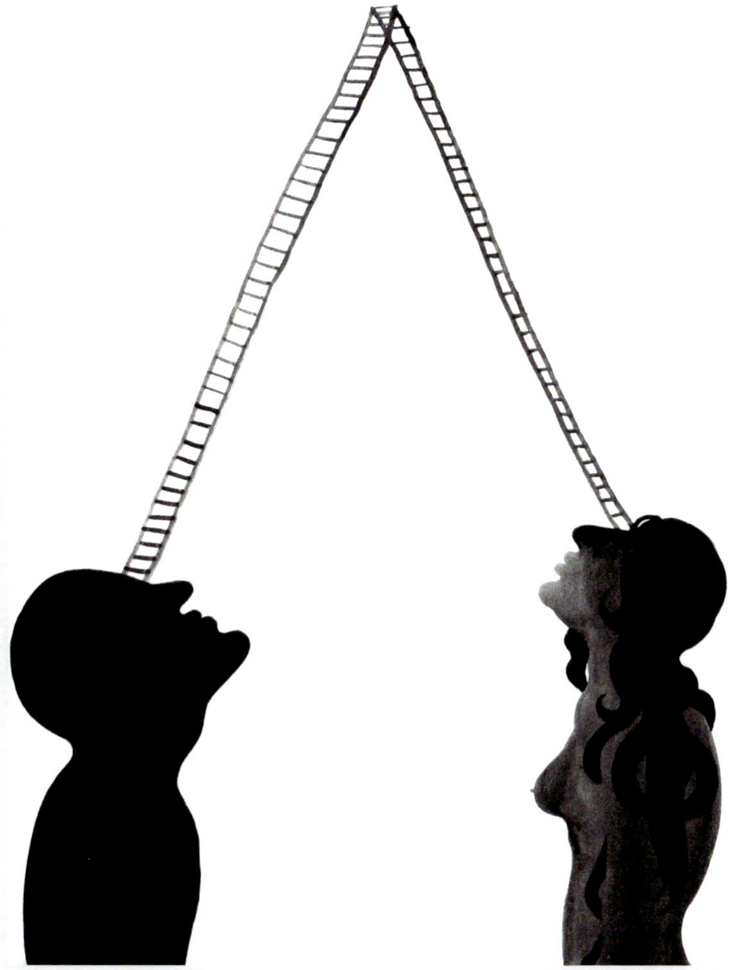

Tú y Yo / Acrylic on canvas – 61 x 91 cm – 2009

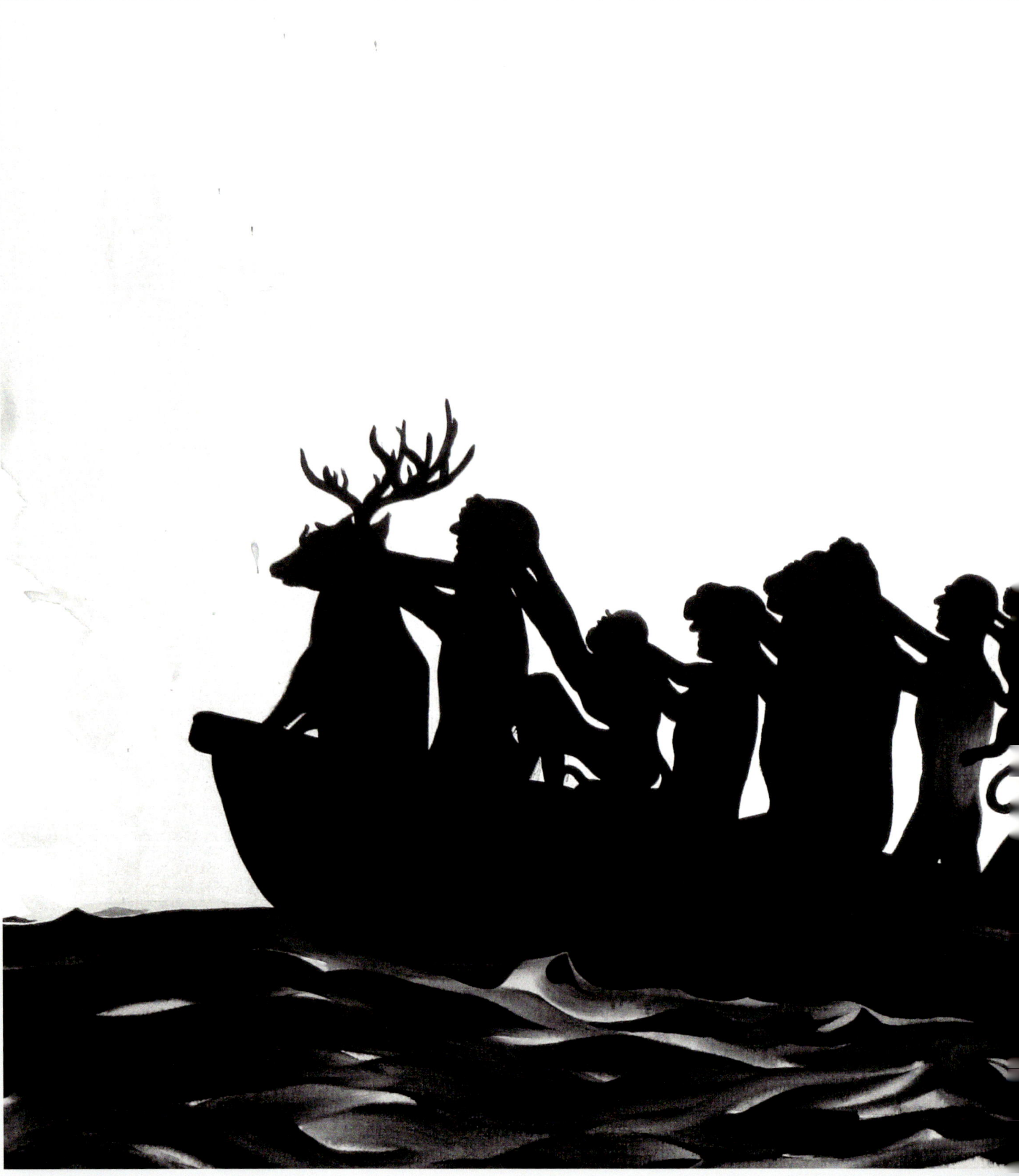

Arca de Noé | Acrylic on canvas – 91 x 61 cm – 2010

Sat One

Born in La Victoria, Venezuela, 1977. Lives in Munich, Germany.

I used to work on several projects of quite a different nature at once. Instead of perceiving them as competing parts, I learned to draw synergies out of that variety and provide every creative process its specific platform. The streets are a space to cooperate with fellow artists, where working comes along with a direct response from the public. In contrast to that, my studio is a laboratory to me—the pool of experiences from my former background builds the foundation for future experiments.

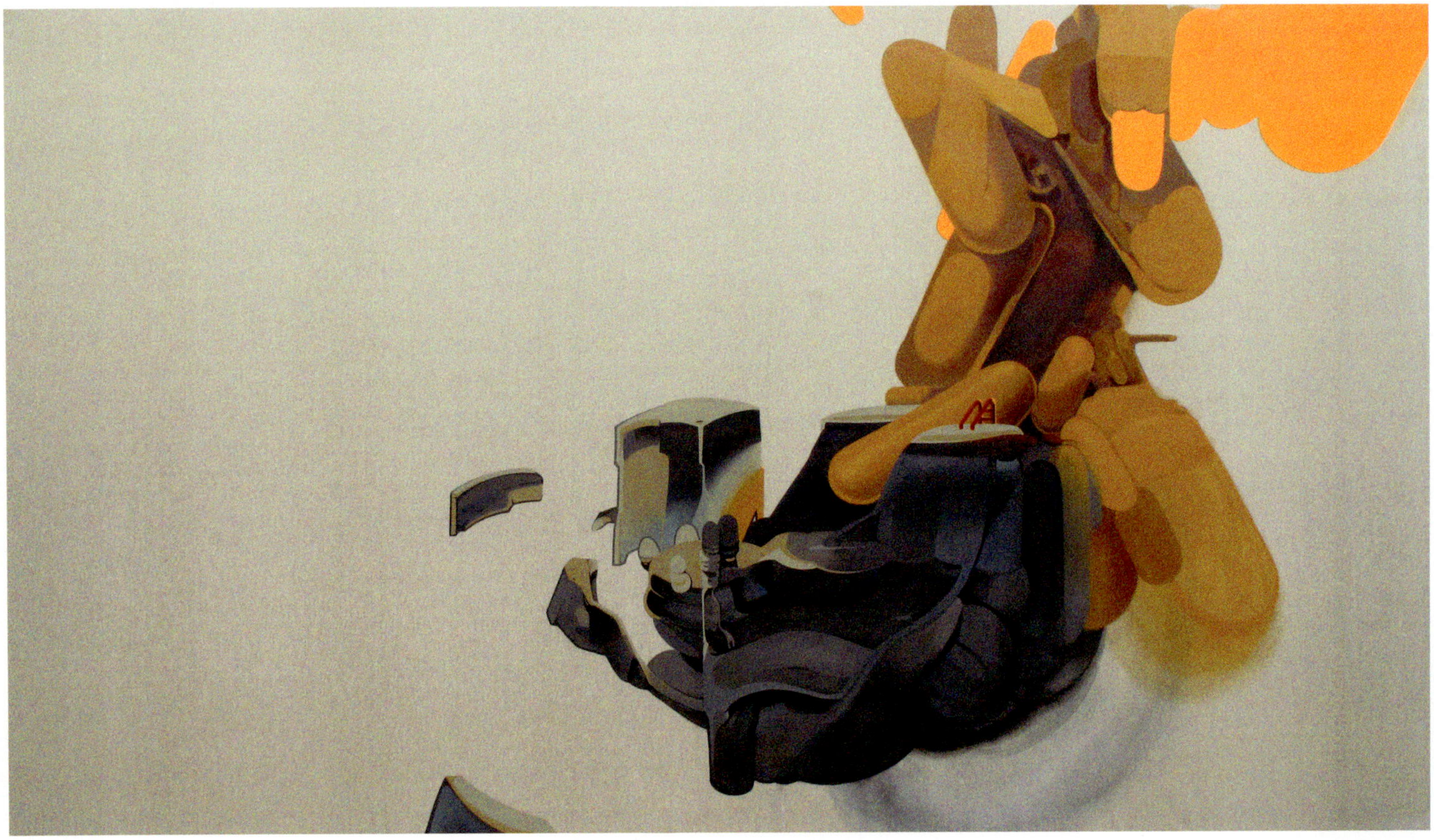

Innerspace // Acrylic on canvas – 250 x 150 cm – 2010

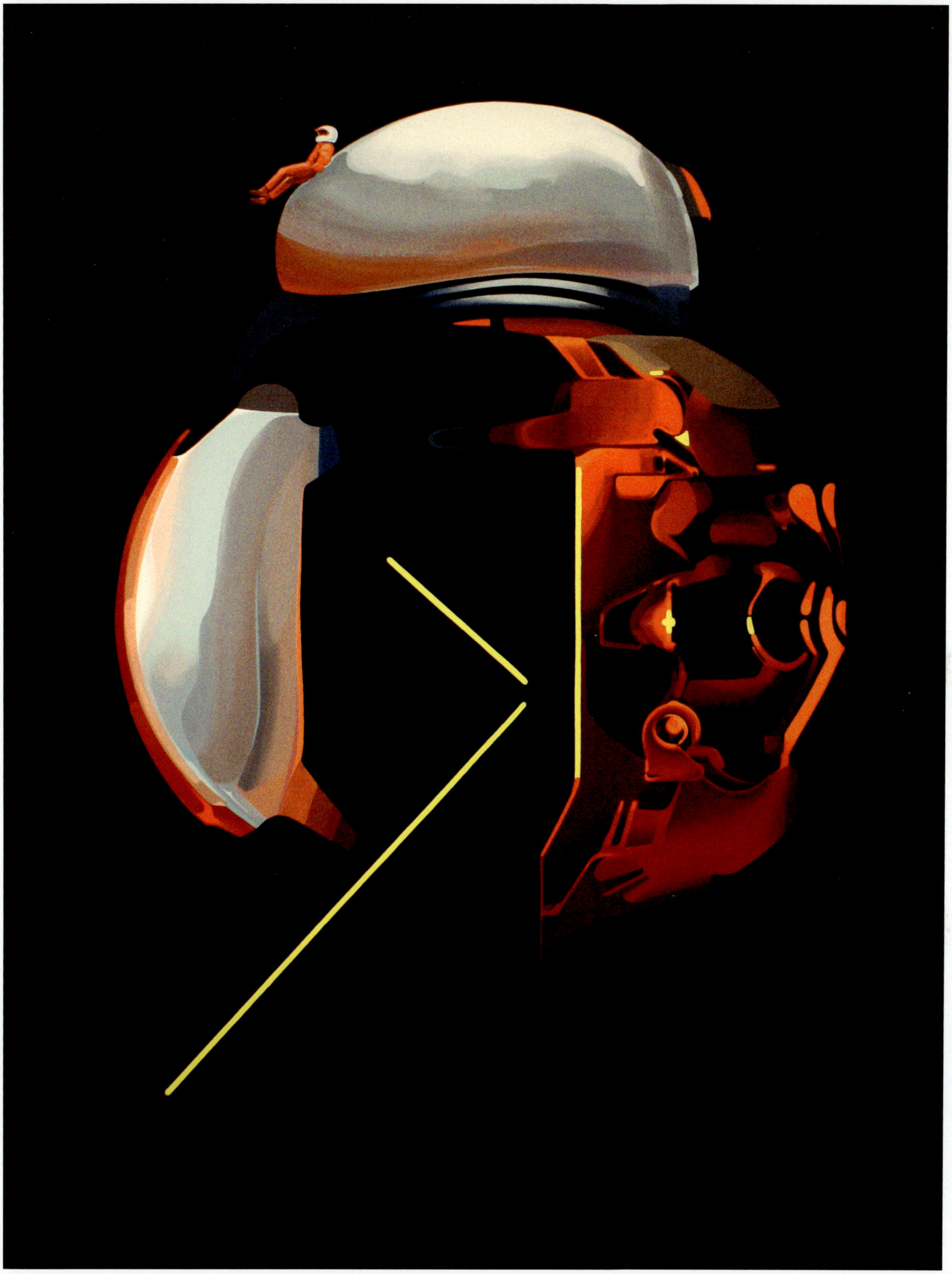

Trip Down Memory Lane / Acrylic on canvas – 130 x 175 cm – 2010

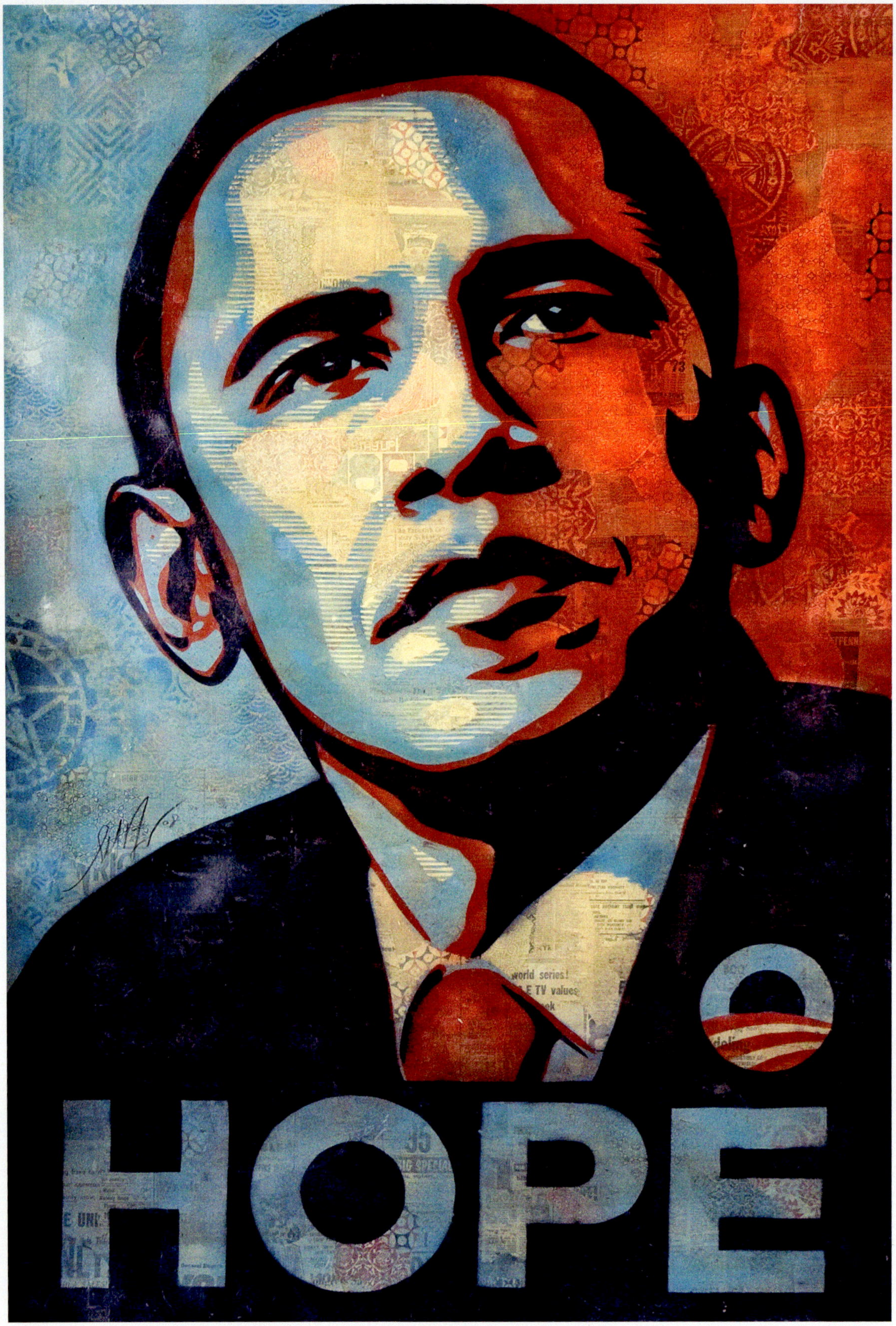

Obama Hope / Aerosol, stencil, and collage on paper – 112 x 152 cm – 2008

Shepard Fairey

Born in Charleston, United States, 1970. Lives in Los Angeles, United States.

The aesthetics of my fine art evolved from the techniques and concerns inherent to my street art. Street art is free, but must compete with well-funded advertising for attention. My illustration style strives to reduce detail in order to emphasize the iconic essence of an image. Virtually all of the sensibilities of my fine art came from doing street art.

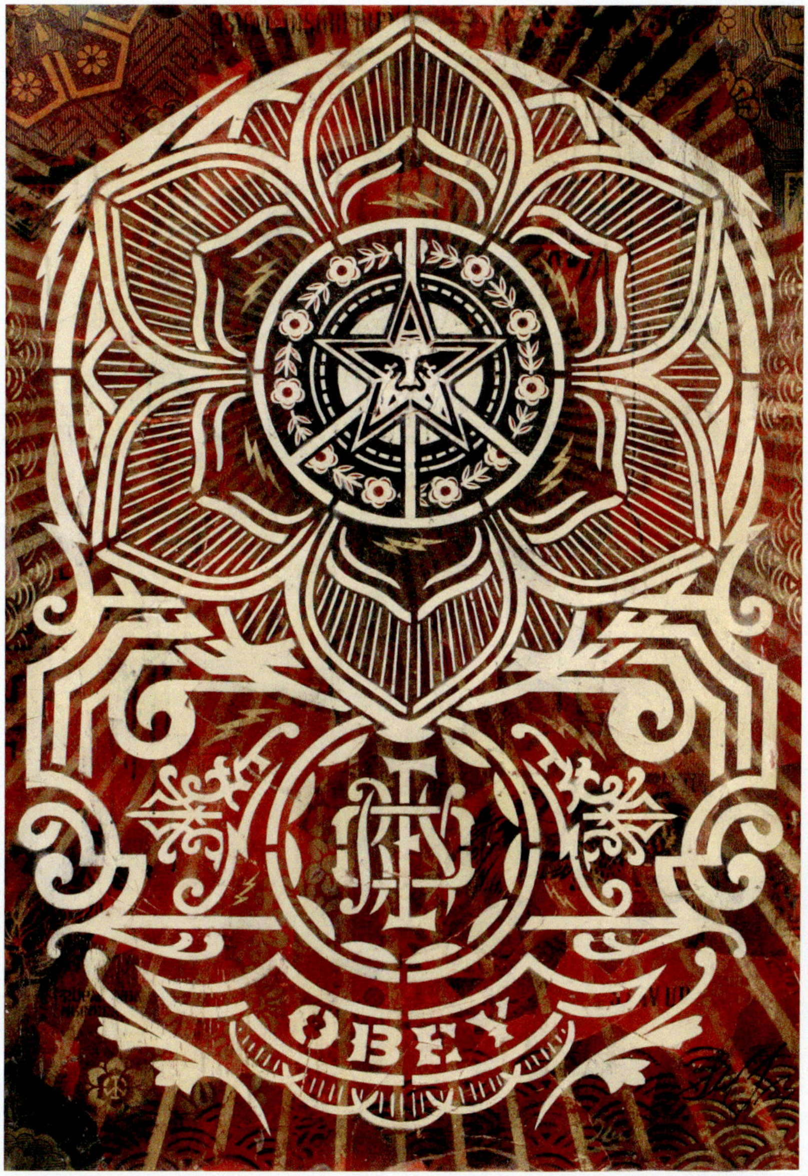

Peace Ornament / Aerosol and collage on paper – 76 x 112 cm – 2007

Sixe

Born in Barcelona, Spain 1975. Lives in Barcelona, Spain.

The studio work for me is like entering another creative dimension, a methodical and impulsive painting at the same time, united in a single space. You can work in other media and use all kinds of techniques. Being able to materialize your work to three dimensions. Both the studio and the street work gives me different things. First came the graffiti and then painting in the studio. But the two are linked and feed off one another. This way I have many more tools to express myself.

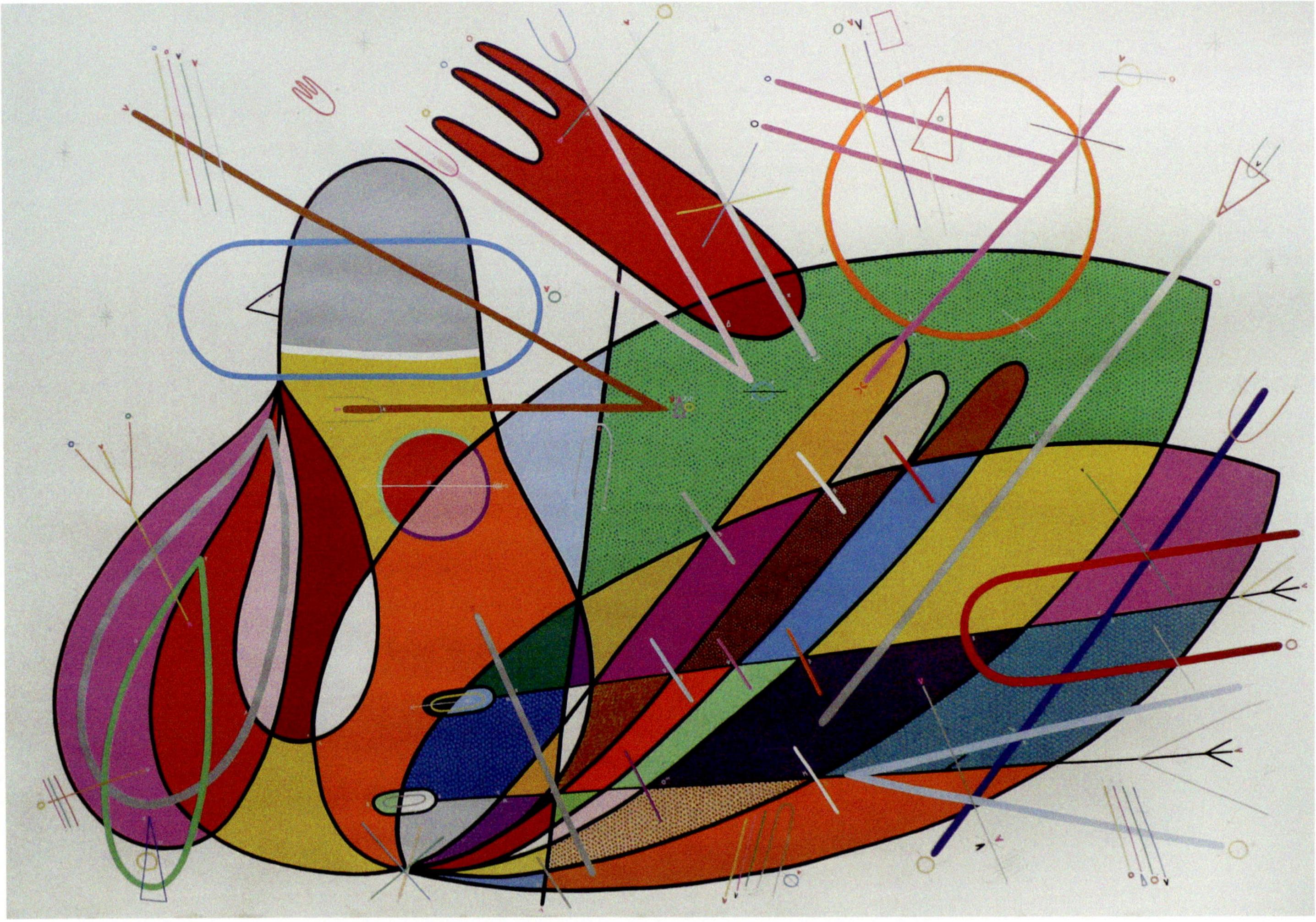

Pájaro Migas / Acrylic on paper – 195 x 150 cm – 2010

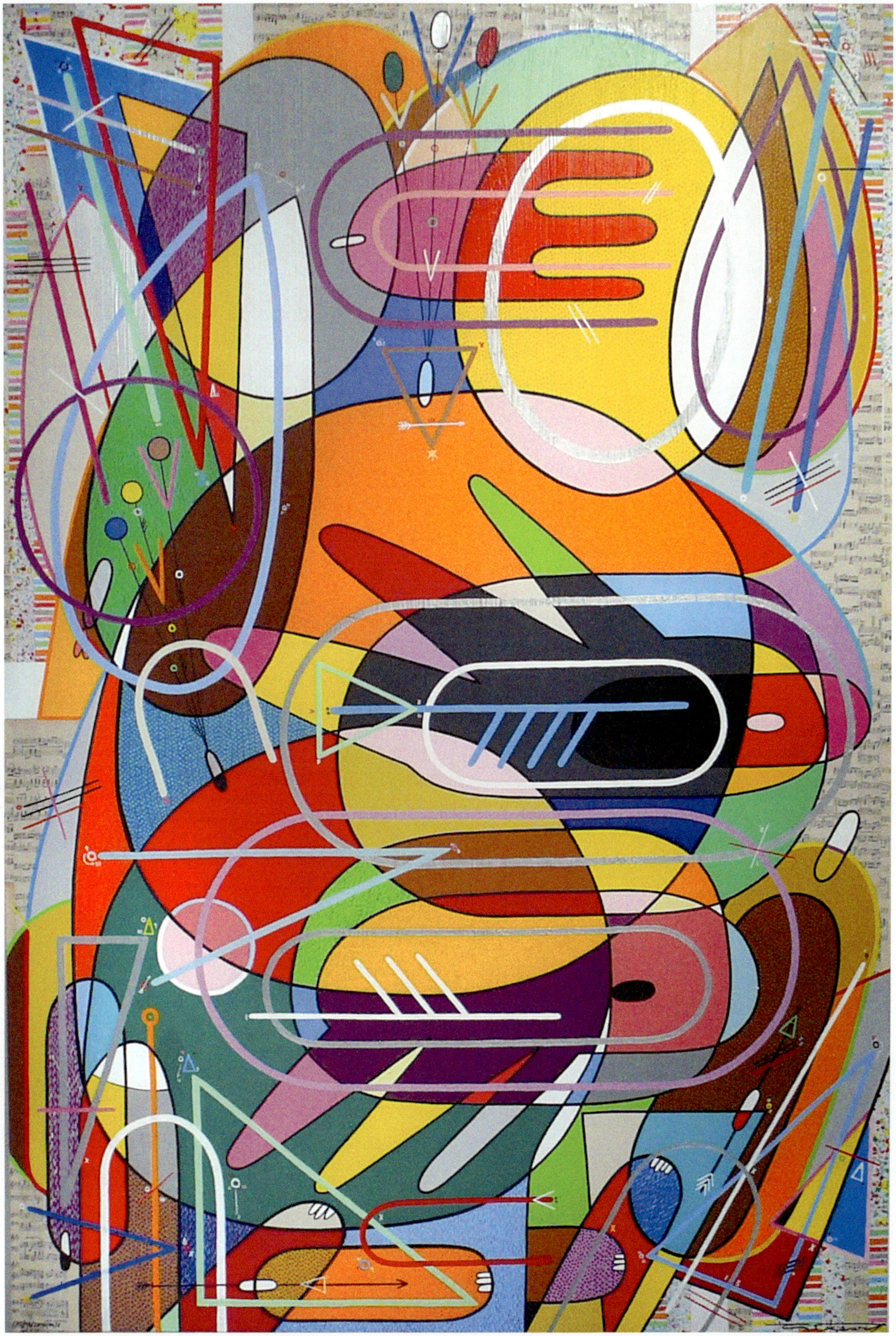

Indígenas / Acrylic on canvas – 140 x 195 cm – 2010

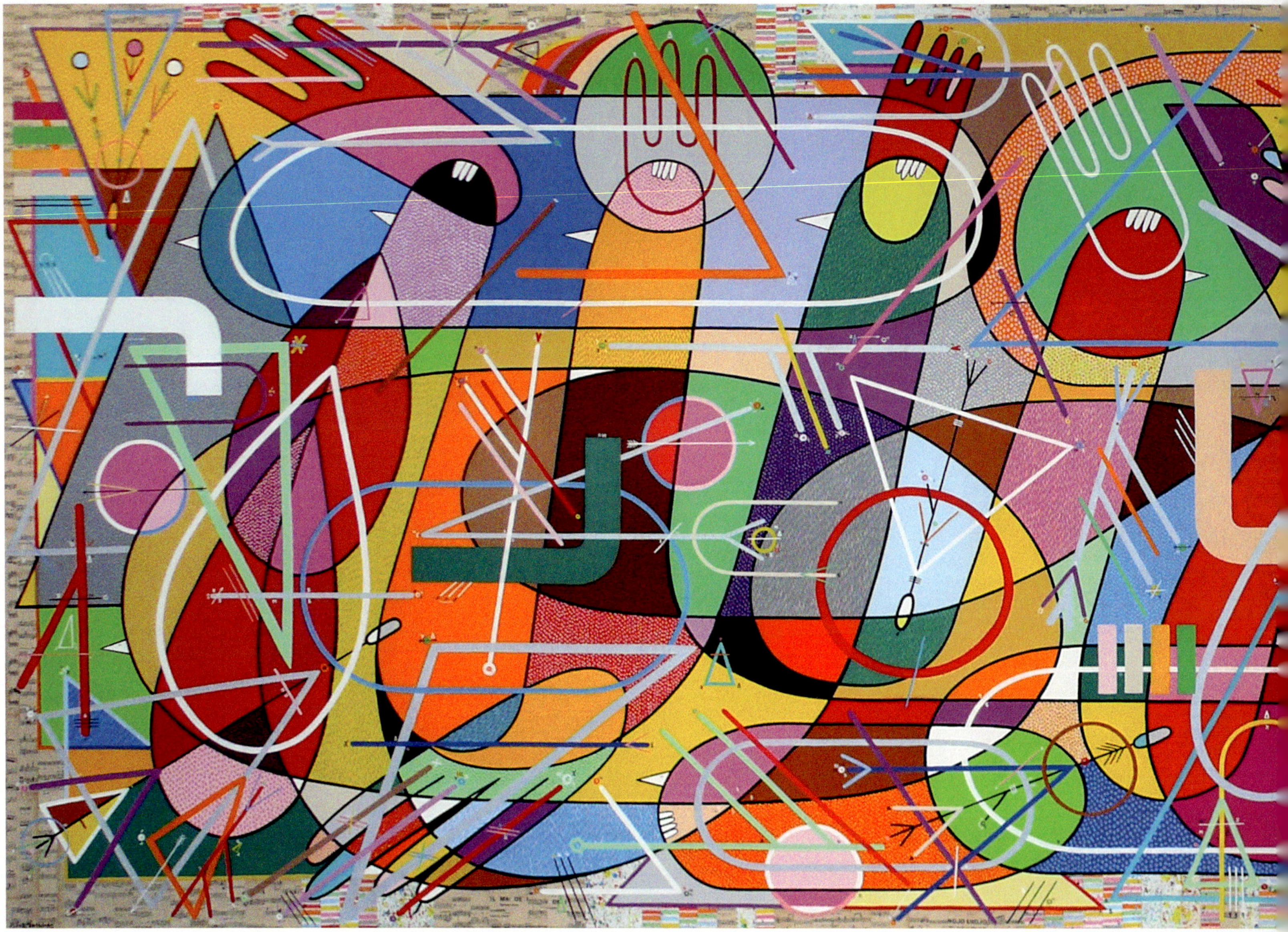

Manglar / Acrylic on canvas – 500 x 165 cm – 2010

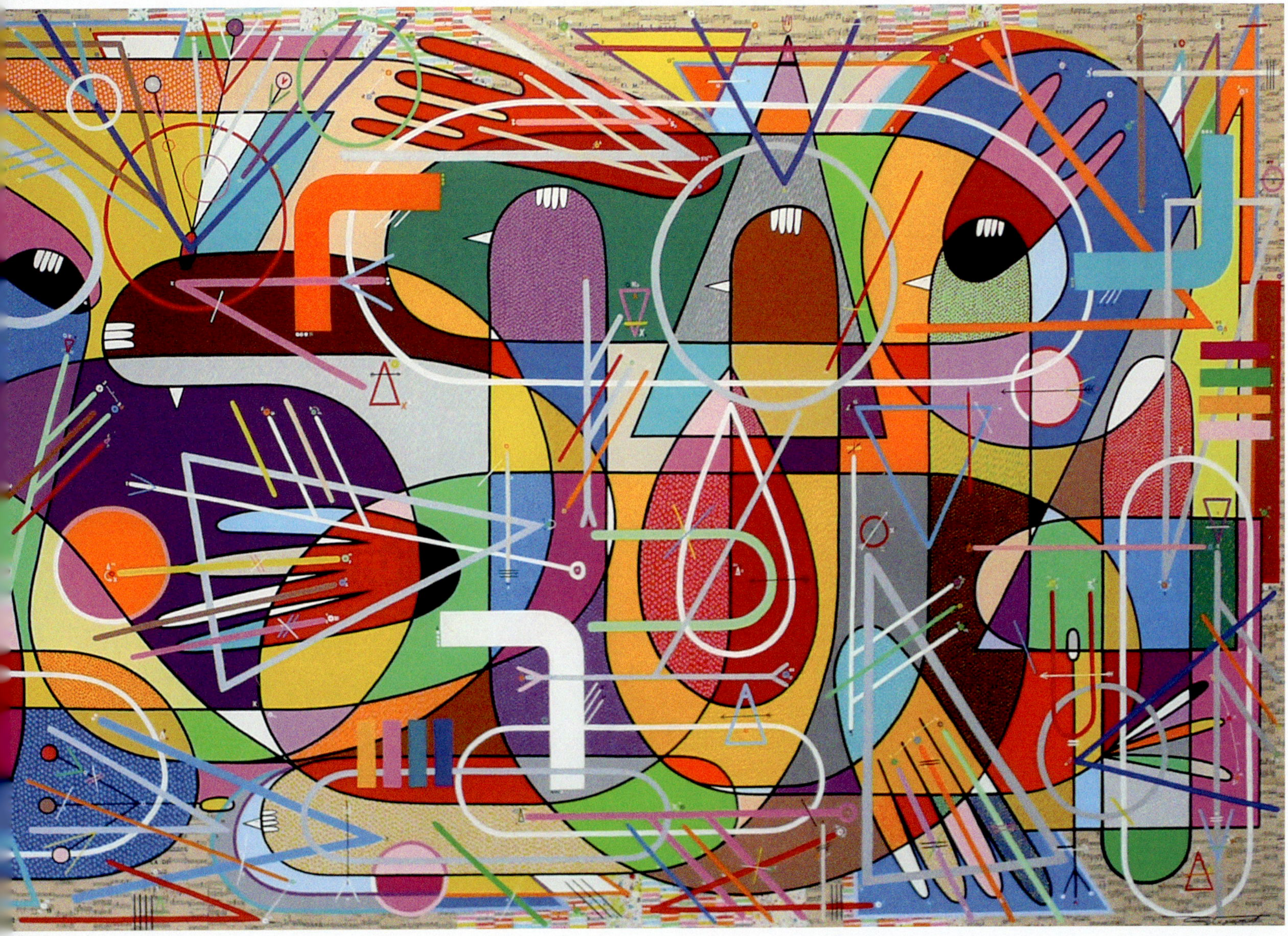

Smash 137

Born in Basel, Switzerland, 1979. Lives in Barcelona, Spain.

I call the streets my childhood home because that's where I was training and shaping up my letters for 15 years before I took them into the galleries. And don't get me wrong, I still live with my parents.

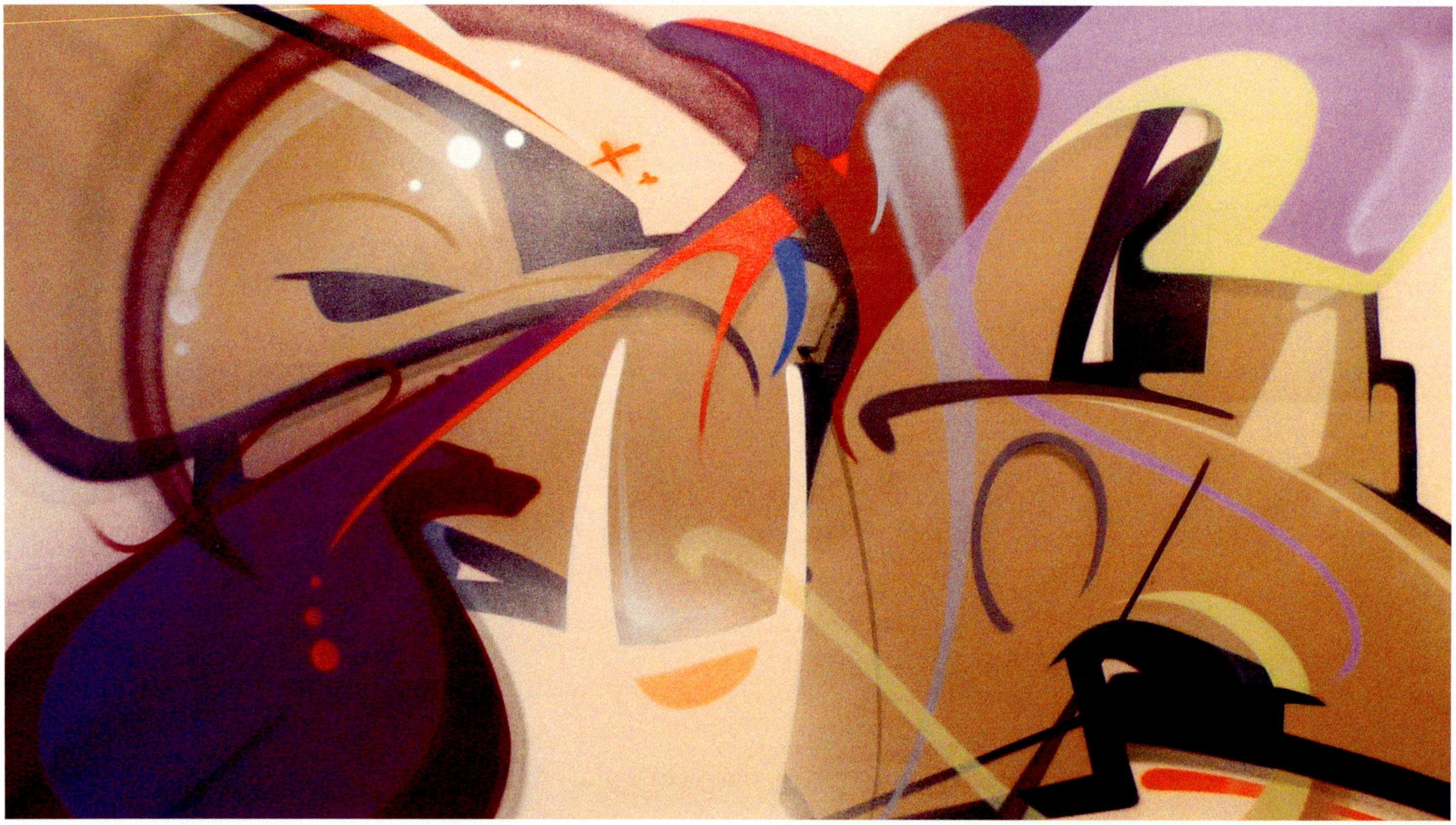

Carrer dels Escudellers / Enamel and aerosol on canvas – 210 x 118 cm – 2011

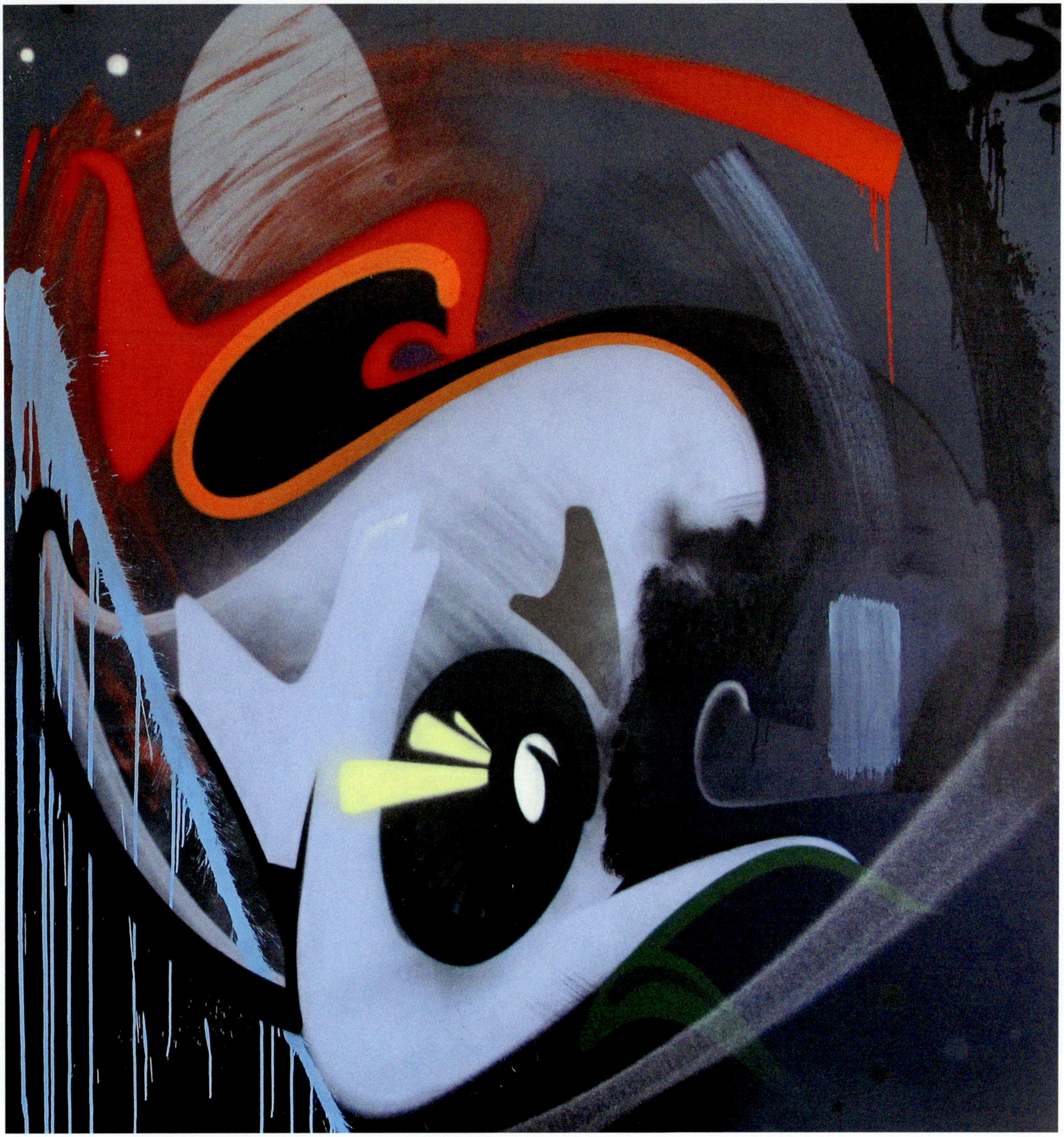

Pollo Negro / Enamel, aerosol, and ink on canvas – 170 x 180 cm – 2010

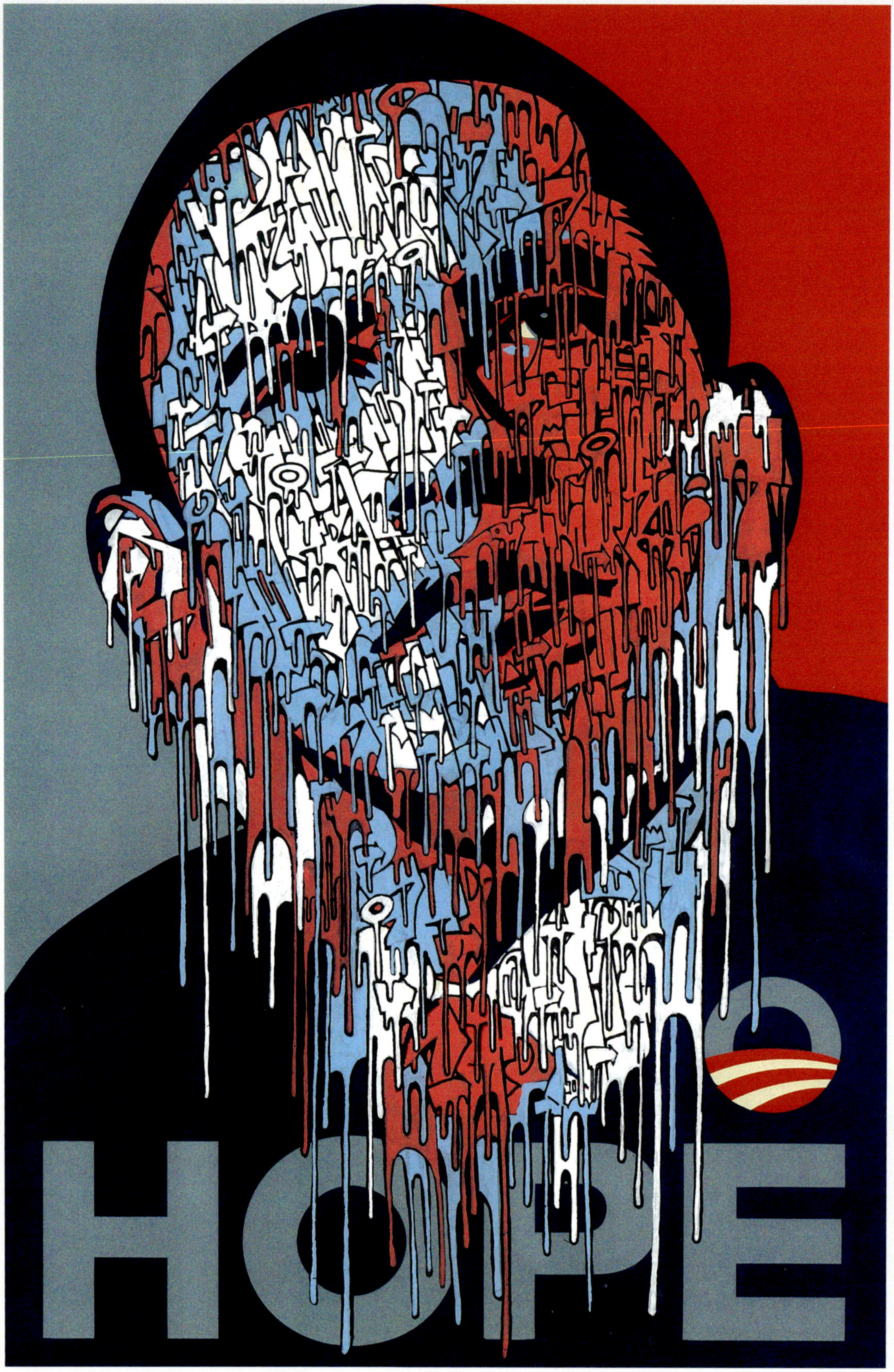

Barack / Acrylic on print – 30 x 42 cm – 2010

Sowat

Born in Marseille, France, 1978. Lives in Paris, France.

For years, I never considered painting on canvas. I was perfectly happy running around with a spray can until the Da Mental Vaporz took a studio outside of Paris. Surrounded by derelict factories and busy railroads, it instantly felt like home. The first canvas I did there was like a born again experience. For a minute I was 15 again, discovering something wild and new. I've been clinging to that feeling ever since.

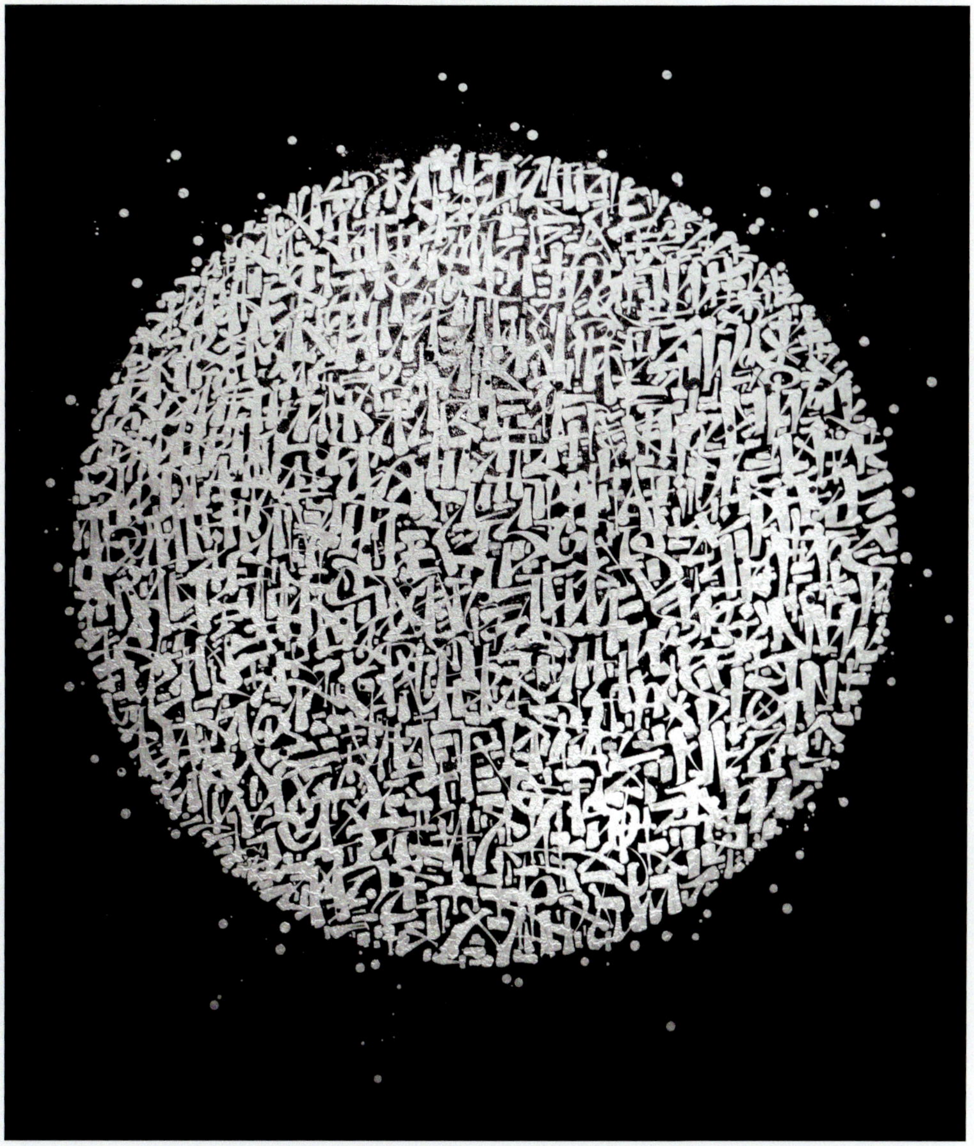

Chrome Noire / Acrylic on canvas – 120 x 140 cm – 2010

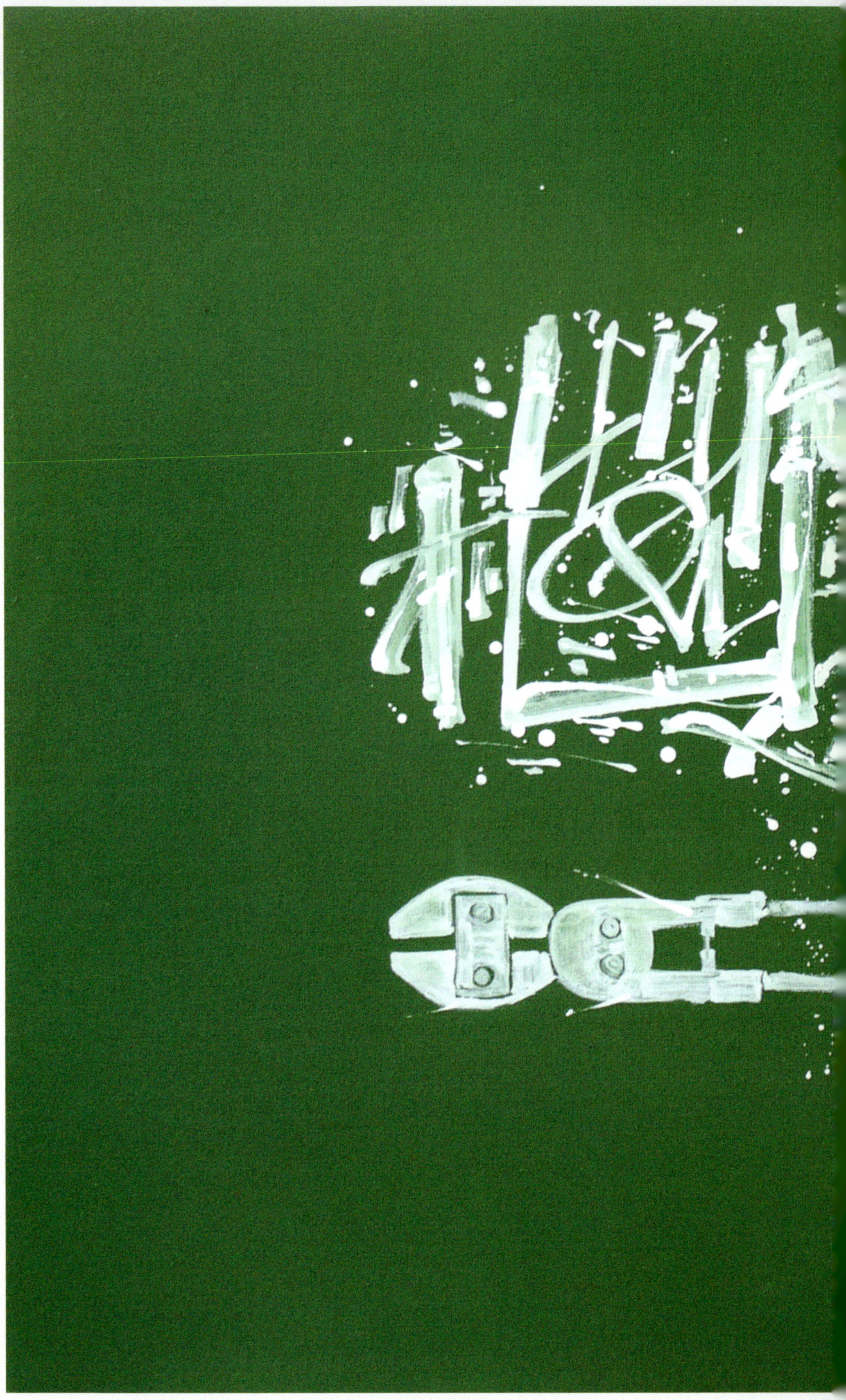

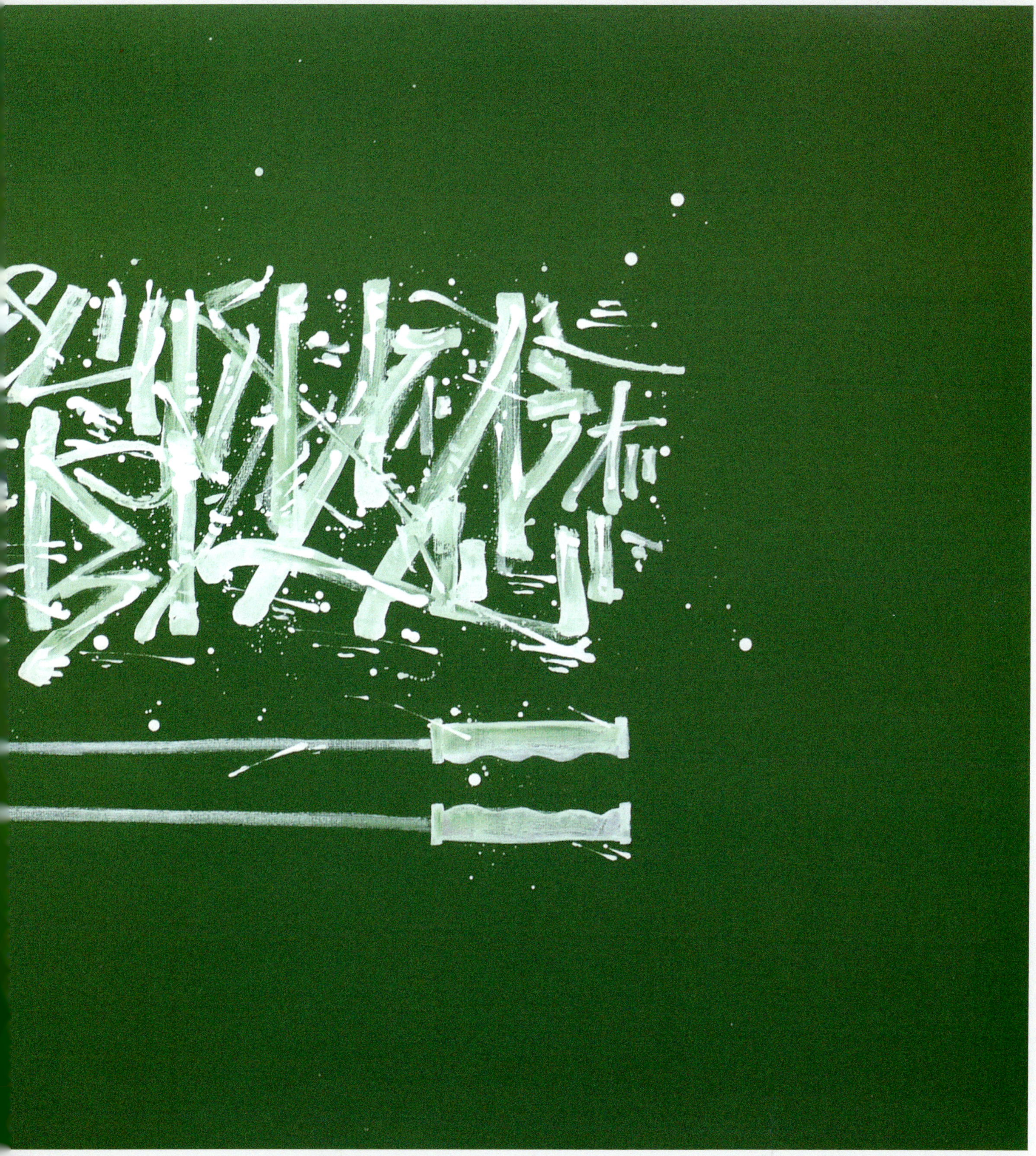

A.S. **With Bom-K** / Acrylic on canvas – 117 x 73 cm – 2009

Sten & Lex

Sten. Born in Rome, Italy, 1979. Lives in Rome, Italy.
Lex. Born in Grottaglie, Italy, 1980. Lives in Rome, Italy.

We think that there is a strong connection between our work for the galleries and museums and what we do on the street. What changes is the support: all walls on the streets are different, our woods are all similar. The wall is irregular and the images we do on the street are not squared as for the pieces off the street. Doing something on the street is much more difficult and casual and for this reason we prefer working on the street because it is irregular and impredictable. In the future we'd like to work just on the street and do no more woods for shows.

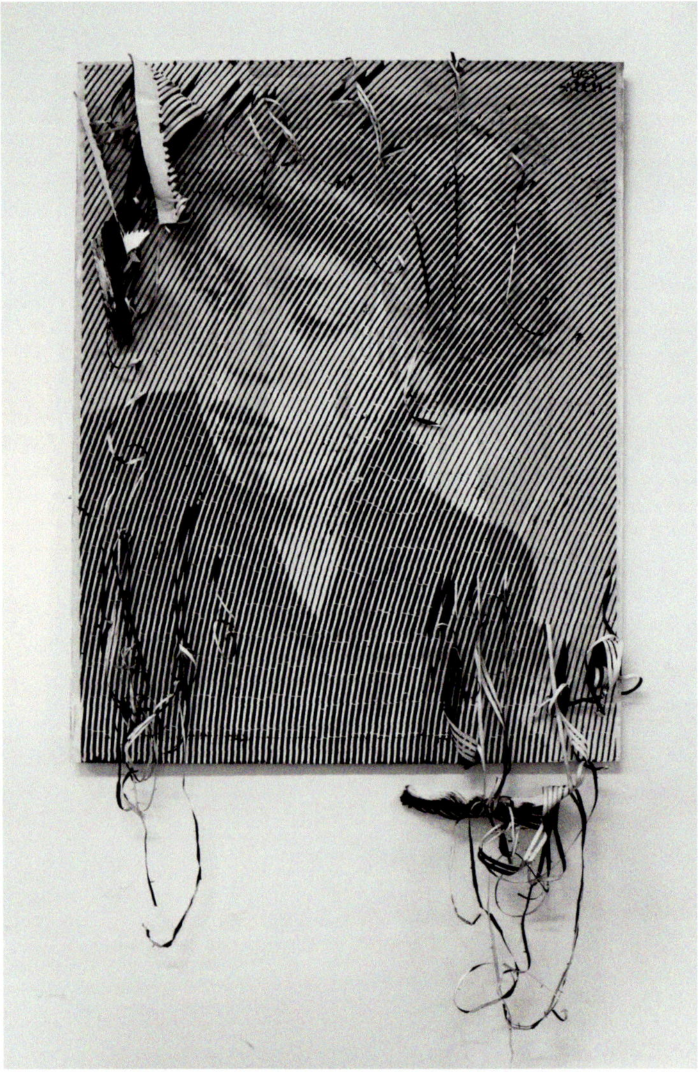

Francesca / Wheat paste matrix and acrylic on wood – 70 x 100 cm – 2010

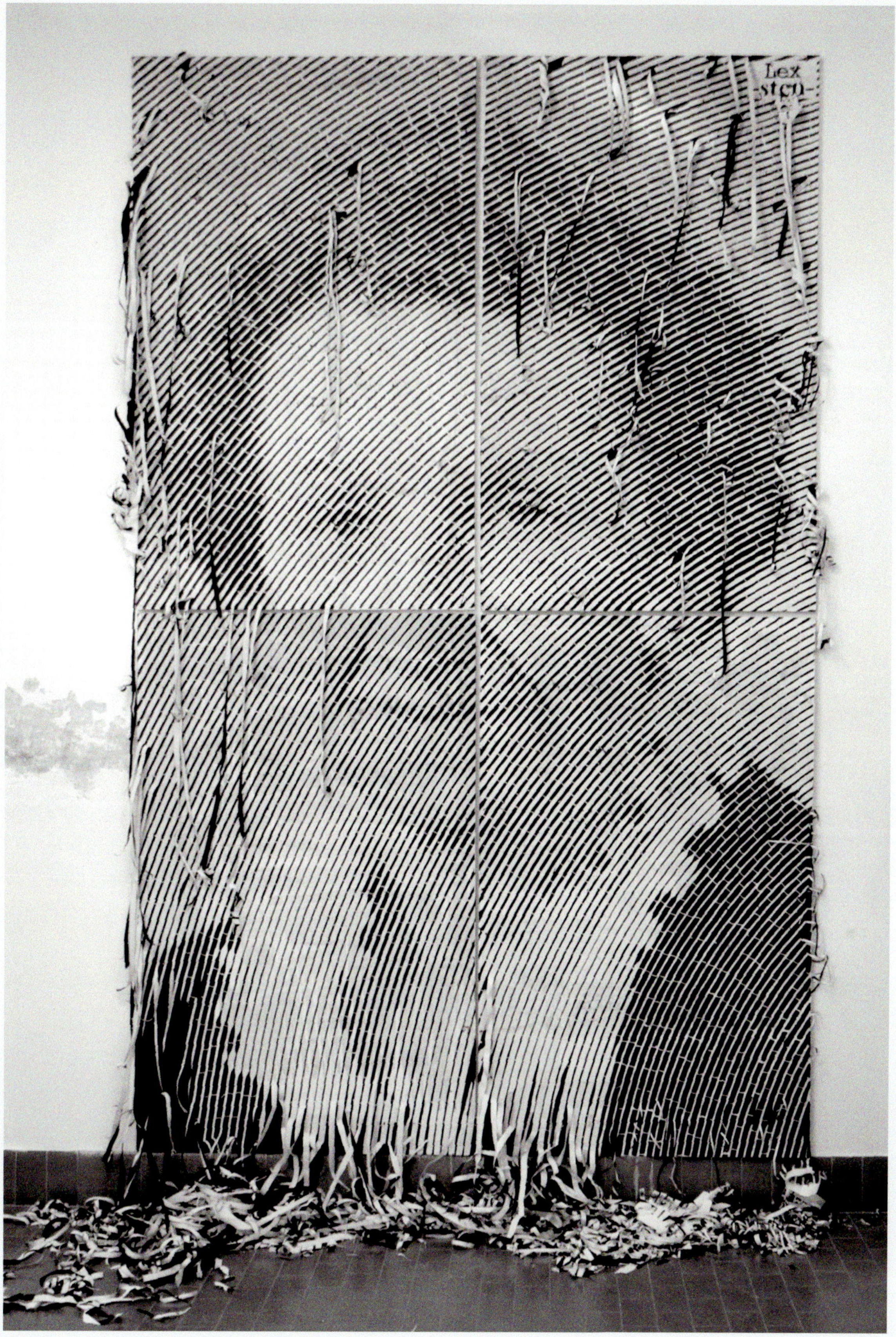

Nonna Luisa / Wheat paste matrix and acrylic on wood – 180 x 350 cm – 2010

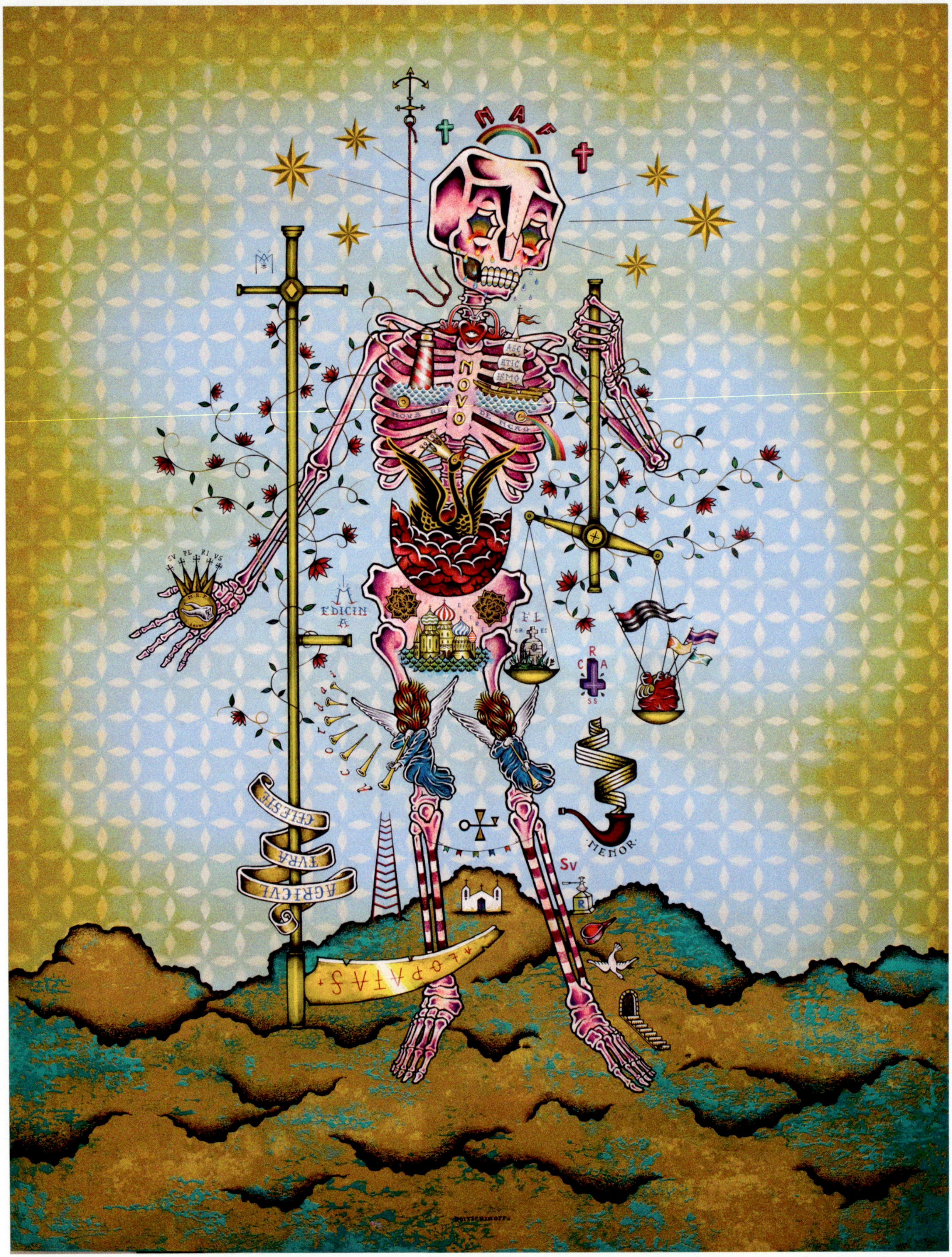

Agricultura Celeste | Acrylic on wood – 150 x 200 cm – 2010

Stephan Doitschinoff

Born in São Paulo, Brazil, 1977. Lives in São Paulo, Brazil.

Perhaps the most interesting thing about working with the public space is the interaction with people, especially those that are not part of the circuit of the arts, museums, or galleries. Once I was painting a house in a small community in Bahia. From the top of the stairs I saw this old gentleman, already at a good age, watching me paint, motionless. After a while I looked back again, waved and said "hello." He didn't respond and remained there, motionless. When I finally came down the stairs, I saw he had his eyes closed, and I said, "Hello, how are you?" As he gave no sign of life I repeated the question louder, he shook his head, rubbed his eyes as one who has just woken up and said "Oops, sorry boy, I can not take more than five minutes of standing or sitting, I just fall asleep".

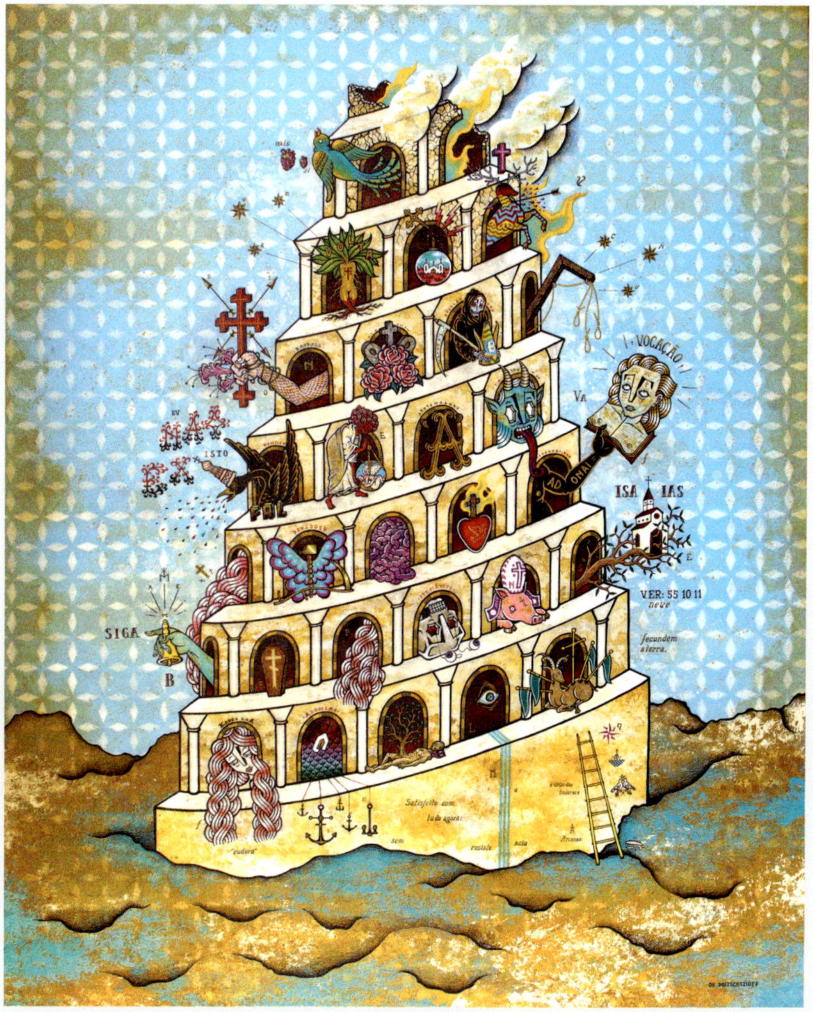

Babel | Acrylic on wood – 150 x 200 cm – 2010

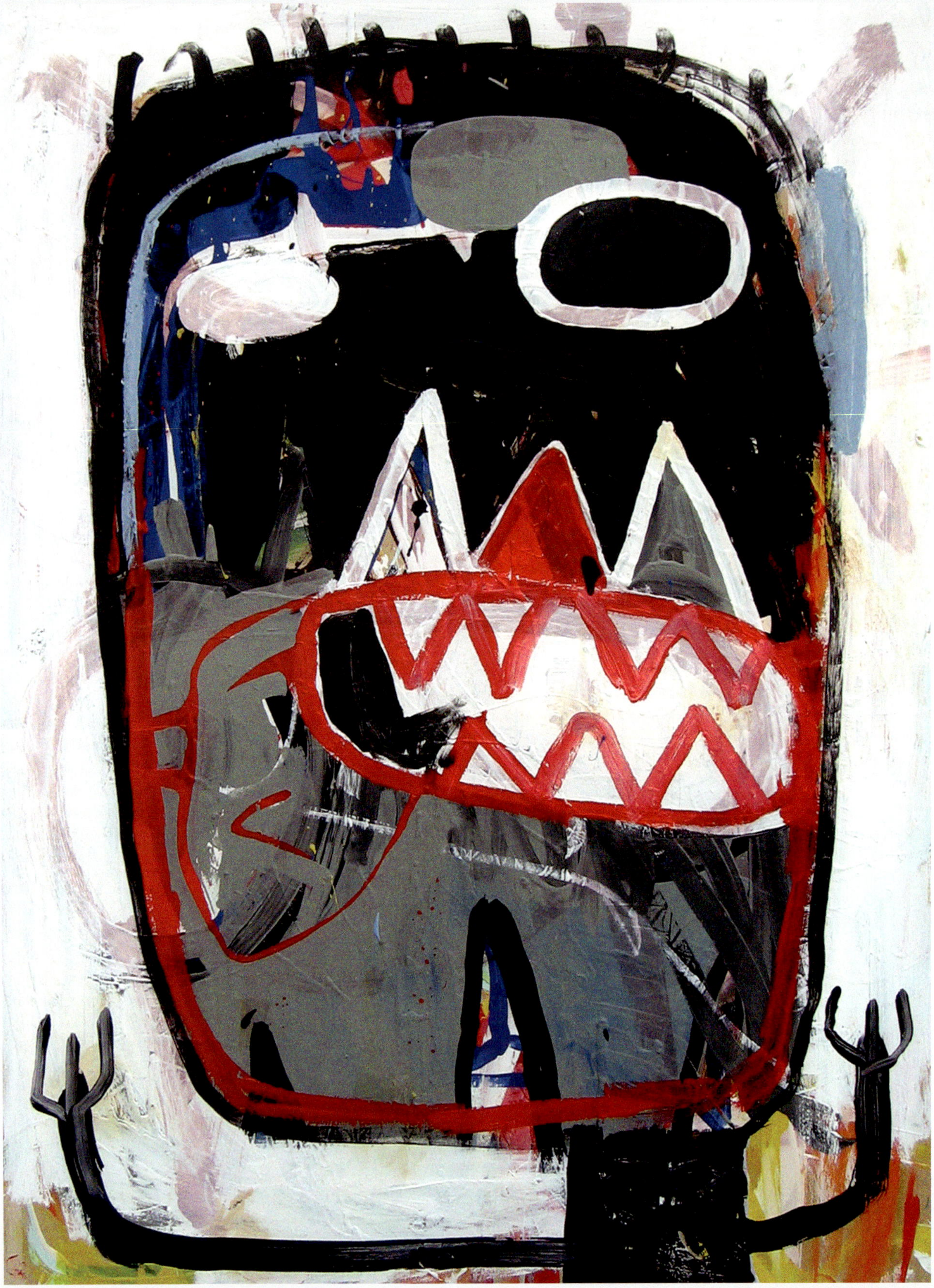

Cabezón / Acrylic on wood – 70 x 100 cm – 2009

Tee

Born in Córdoba, Argentina, 1975. Lives in Buenos Aires, Argentina.

The streets and public spaces are my sketchbook. Out is where people can react to my work, this action-reaction finishes my work. When I'm inside working on a canvas, all these images from the outside come to me and become the way I work or how I make it. When I paint in the streets the work is never finished, it's only a moment of the wall. I think the same with my draws and paintings, they are never finished, it's all a big-quick moment.

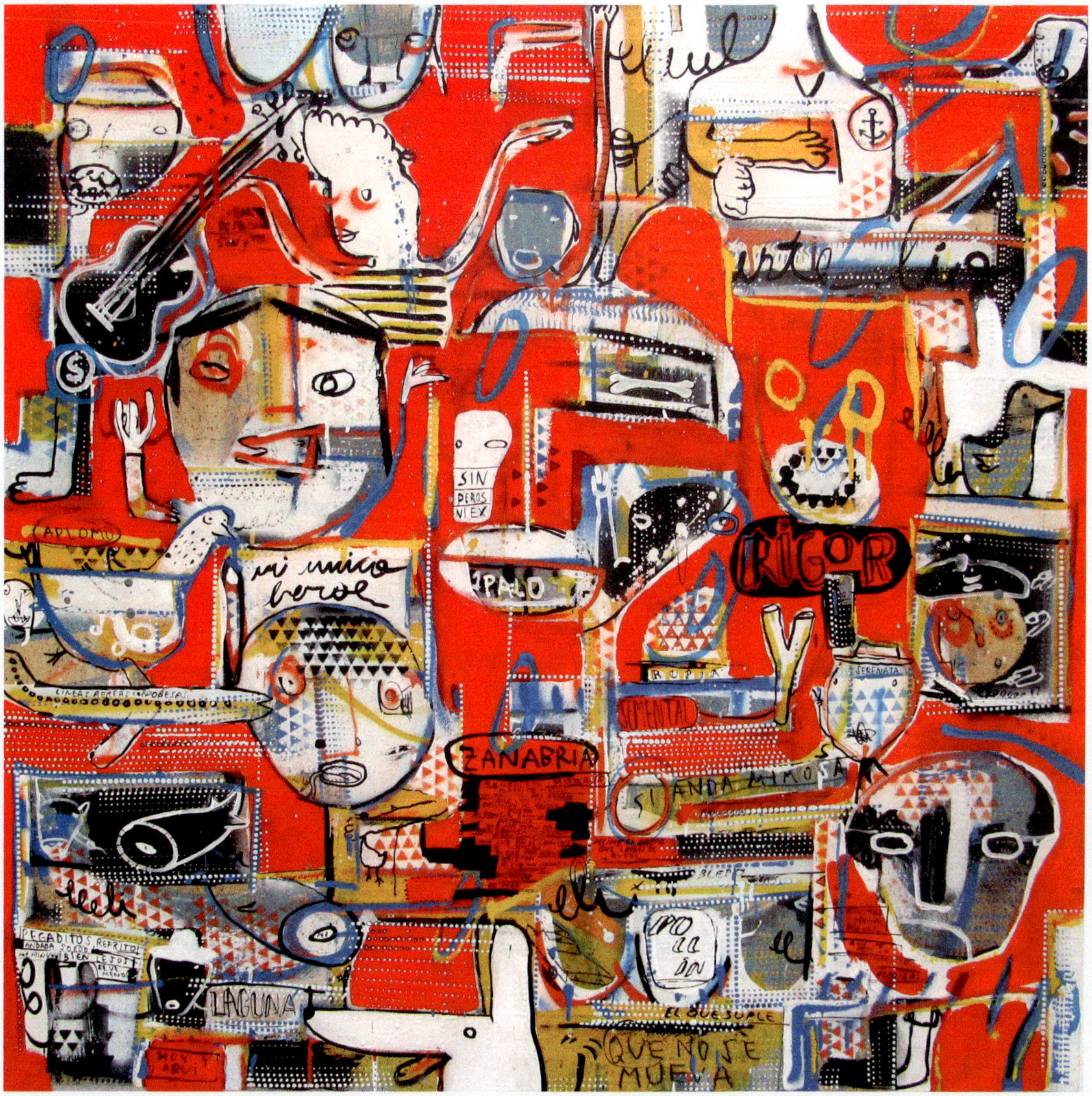

Rojo **With Tester** / Aerosol and acrylic on wood – 100 x 100 cm – 2010

Tilt

Born in Toulouse, France, 1973. Lives in Toulouse, France.

I can say I have a real love story with streets since I am 14 because of skateboarding and graffiti. There is a freedom, an authenticity, and intensity that always inspire me as an artist. I think that my actual studio work just tries to translate the energy of writing, accumulation of letters and history of the textured walls I saw during those last 20 years I've been traveling the world.

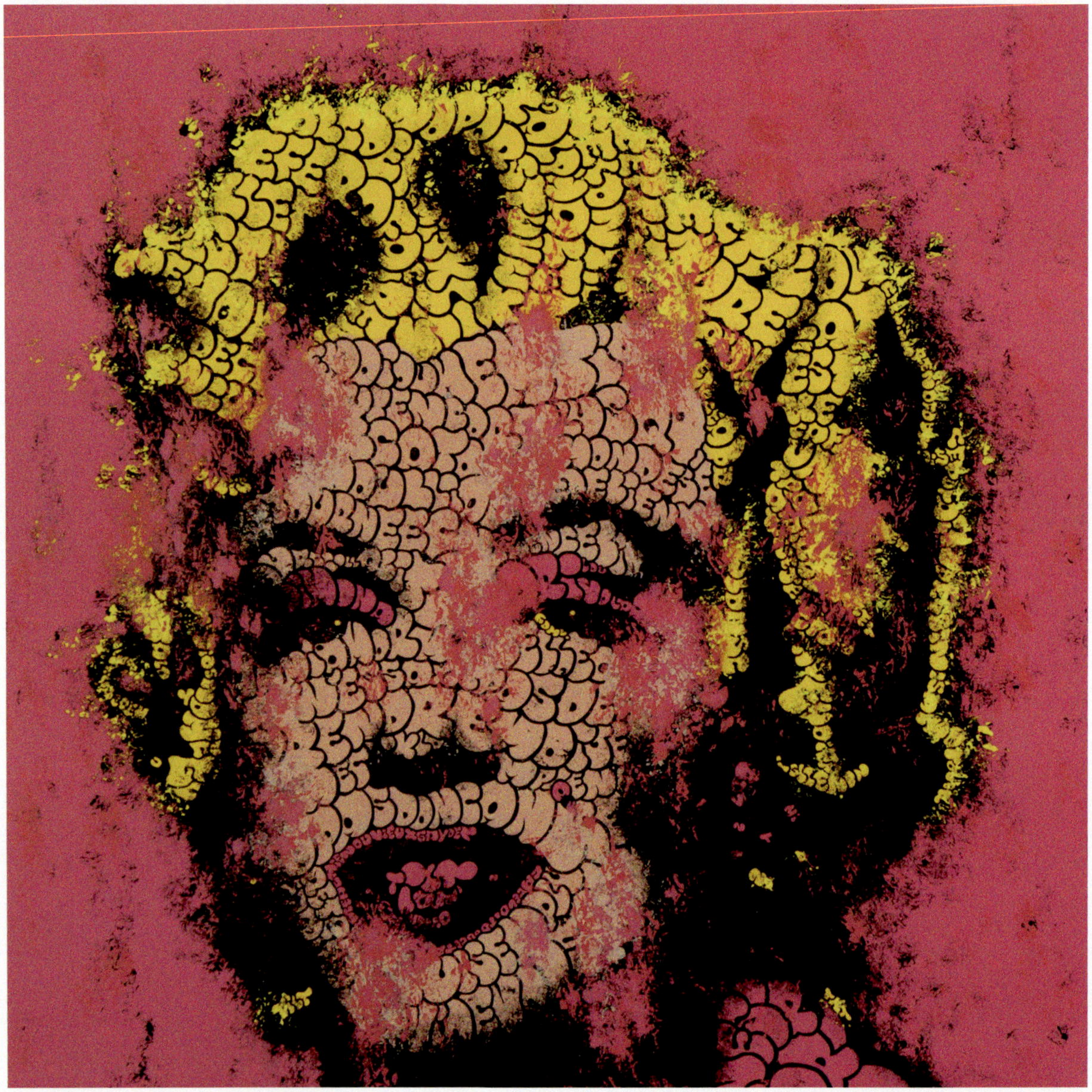

Marylin 3 / Aerosol and acrylic on canvas – 140 x 140 cm – 2010

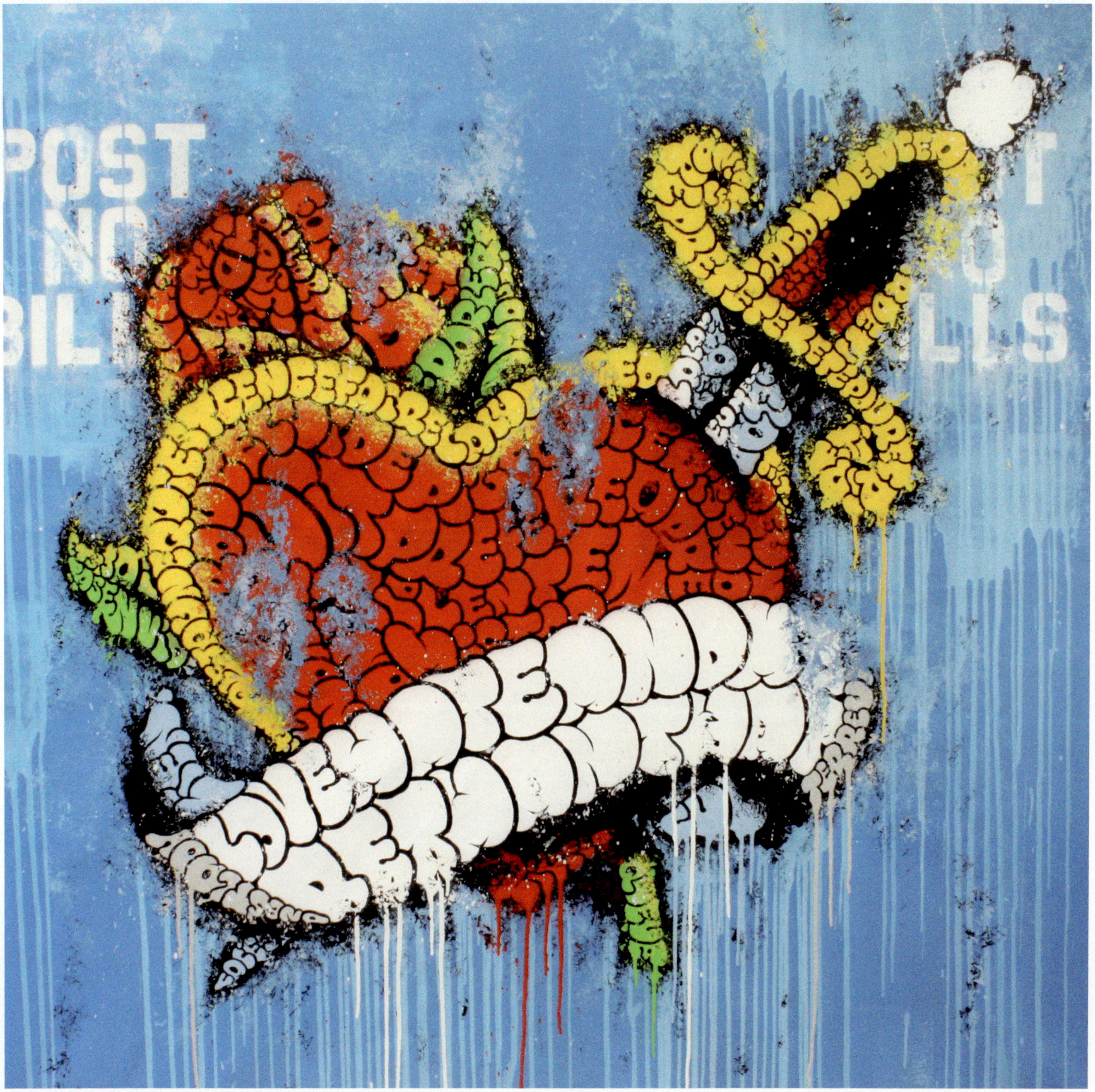

Sacre Coeur / Aerosol and acrylic on canvas – 145 x 145 cm – 2010

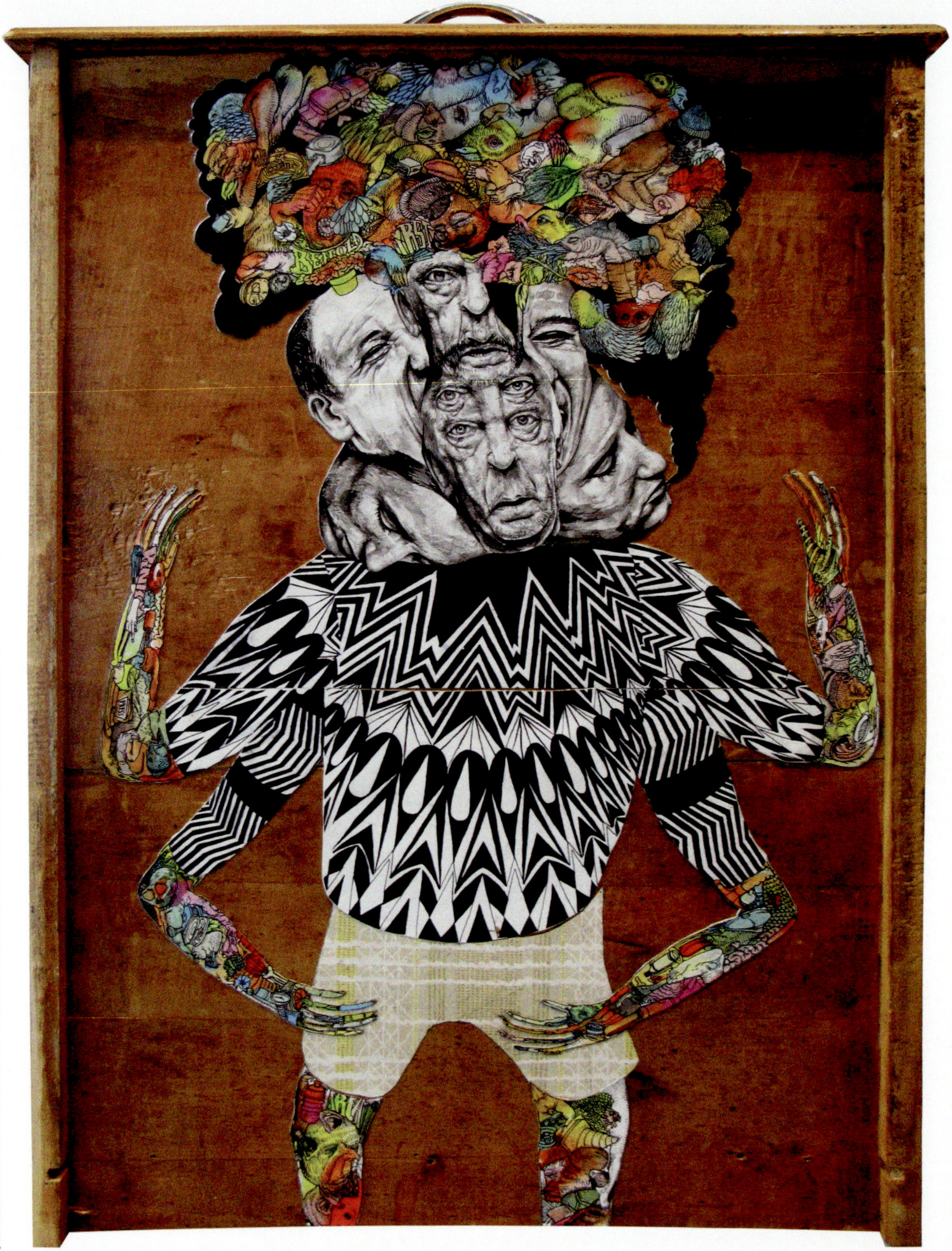

Insane / Acrylic and ink on found drawer – 45 x 91 cm – 2010

Troy Lovegates aka Other

Born in Toronto, Canada, 1972. Lives in Buenos Aires, Argentina.

When I paint indoors time is spent in my mind almost like a dream state processing what has happened lately, thinking, listening to music, relaxed. Outdoors you have to be aware of your surroundings and read everything around you, every shadow, every car, every person on the street. You don't have the time to think things through, it is more fluid and a physical adventure, maybe running, maybe an incredible new story. My paintings indoors might reflect these stories but painting inside never is as exciting.

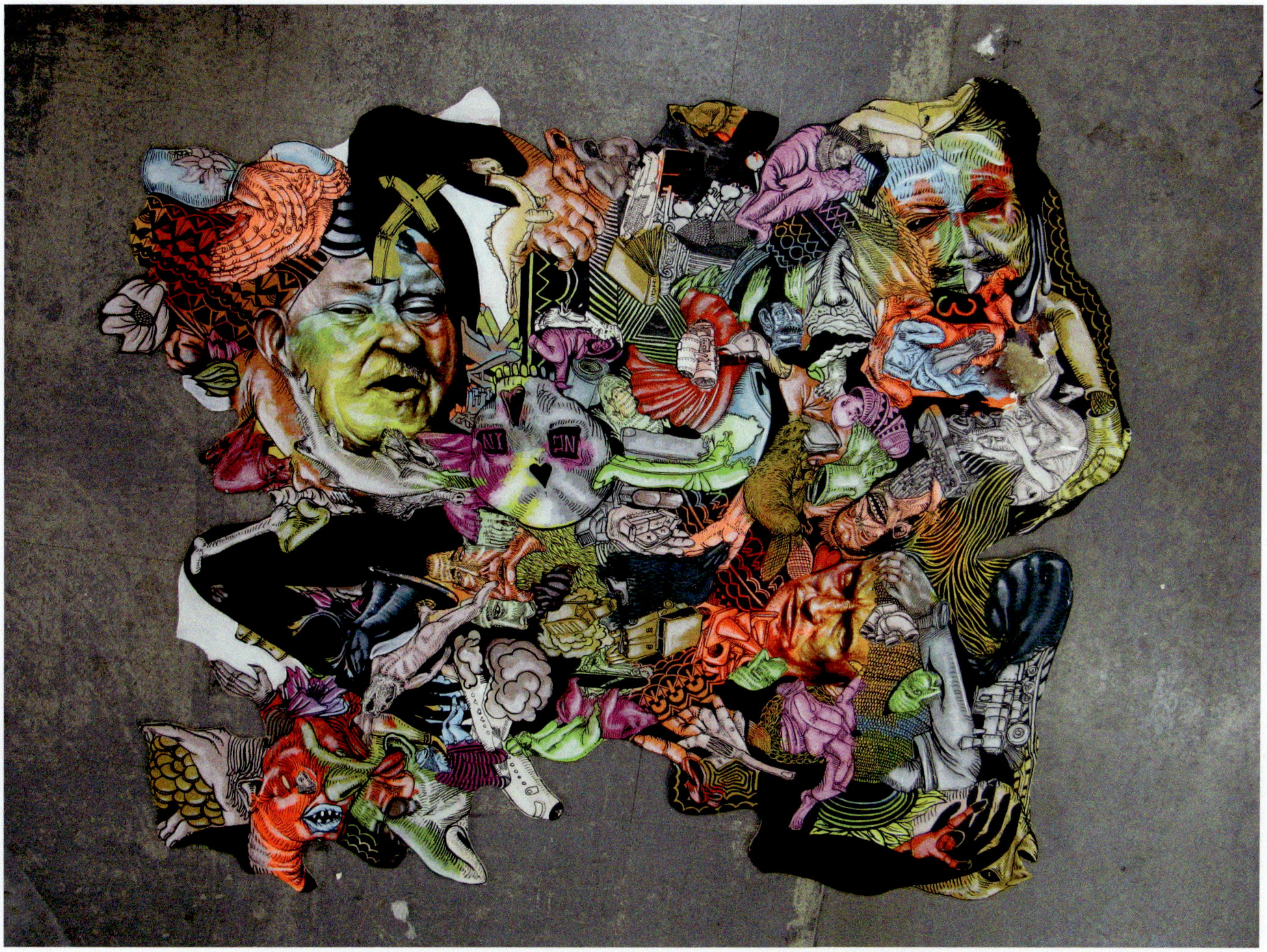

Gobblegoo / Acrylic and ink on wood – 121 x 121 cm – 2010

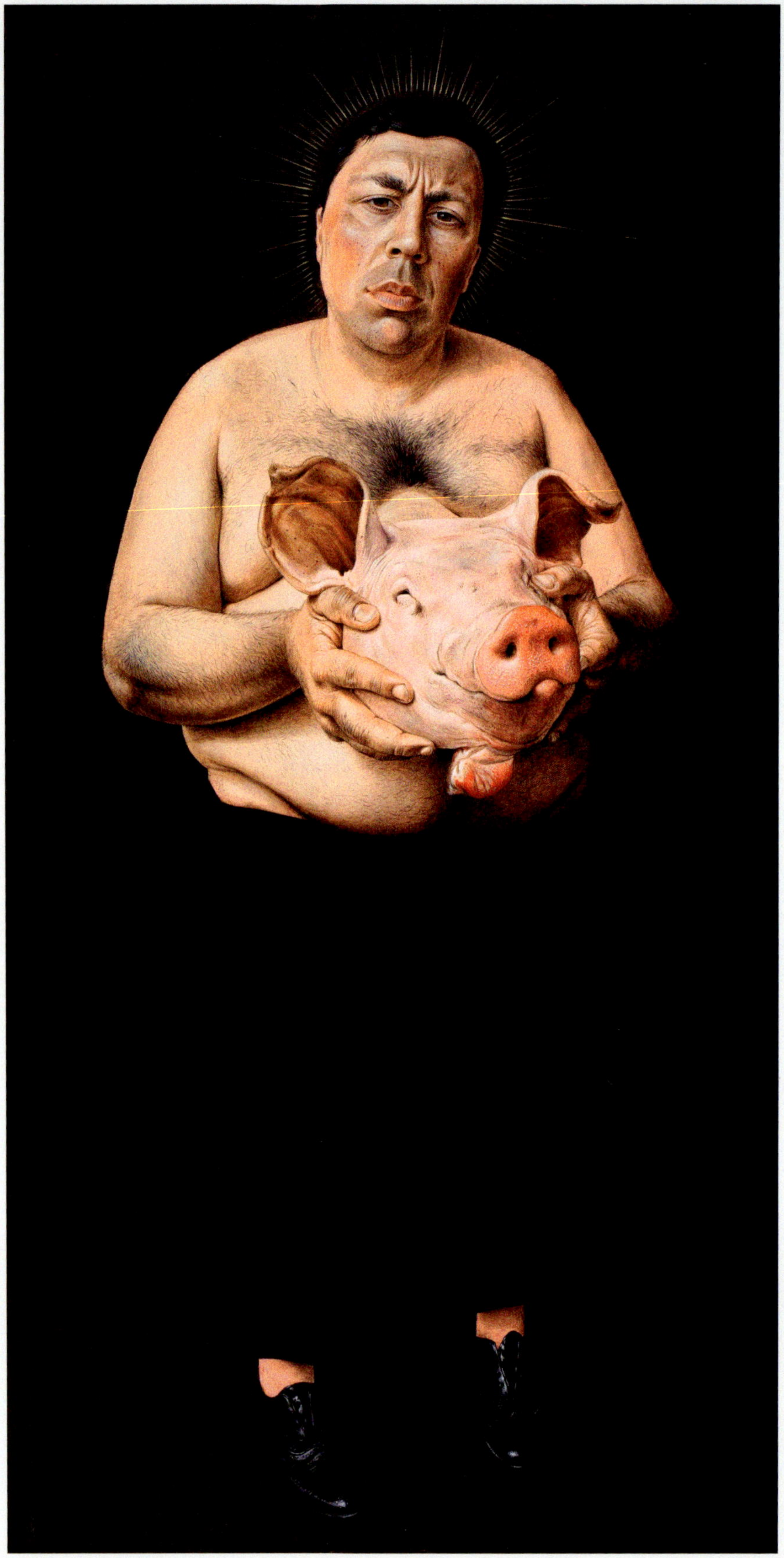

Meat / Acrylic on canvas – 61 x 122 cm – 2009

Turf One

Born in Paris, France, 1976. Lives in Montreal, Canada.

Graffiti was definitely my art school. I am self-taught and the techniques I am using today have their origins in the techniques I started developing painting walls in the early '90s… I also owe to graffiti the deep love I have for old objects and the playful relationship that I establish with them when using them to create pieces… This is a direct extension of years of exploring abandoned spaces and using them as a canvas for my work…

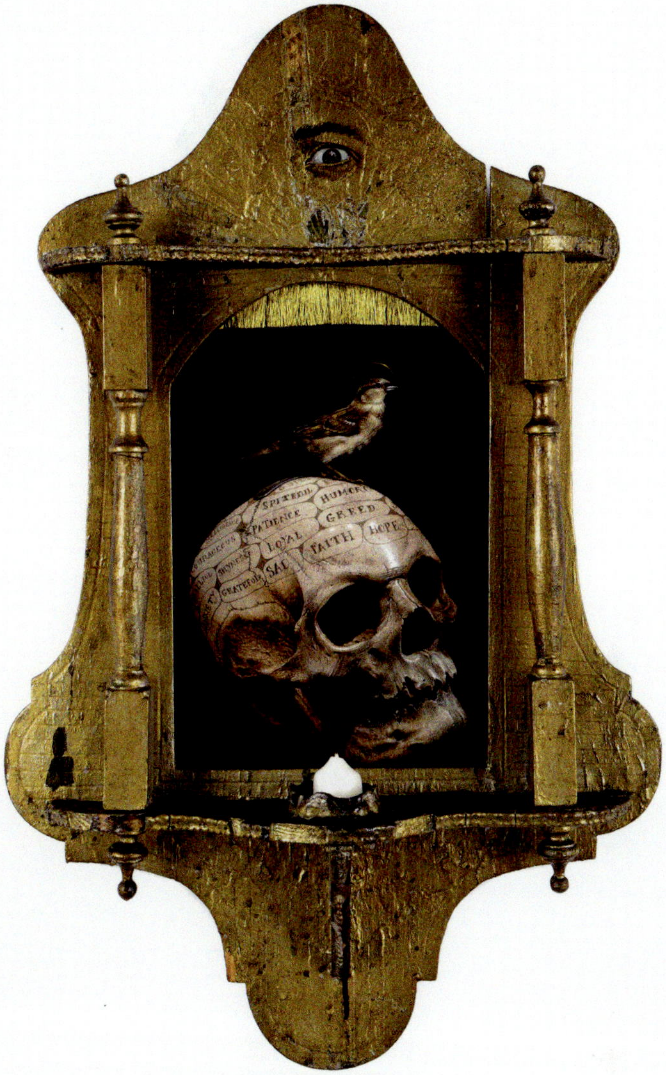

Vanita / Acrylic on wood and customized antique frame – 43 x 69 x 12 cm – 2010

Vitché

Born in São Paulo, Brazil, 1969. Lives in São Paulo, Brazil.

A dream, a scream, a way to stay alive sailing in an endless sea.

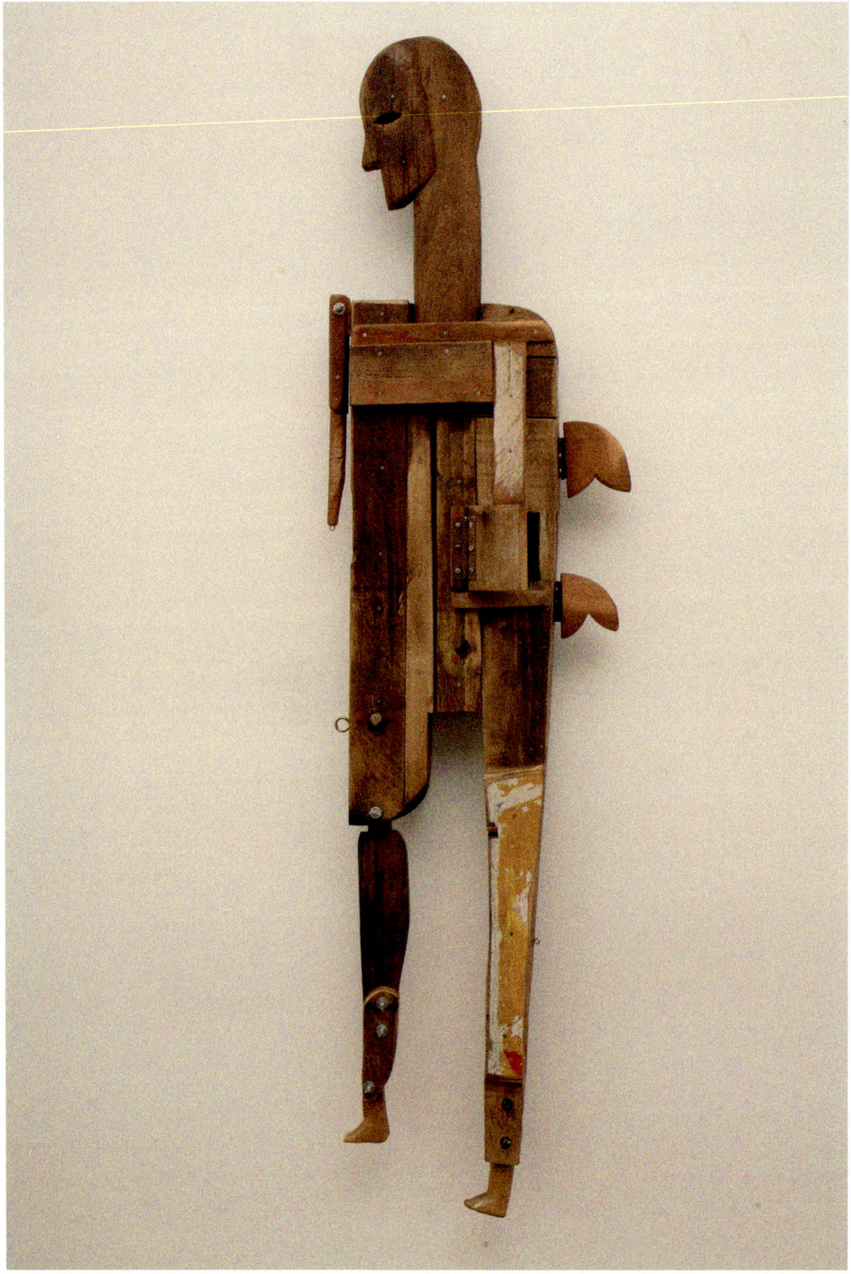

No Title / Hand-carved wood – 38 x 147 x 13 cm – 2007

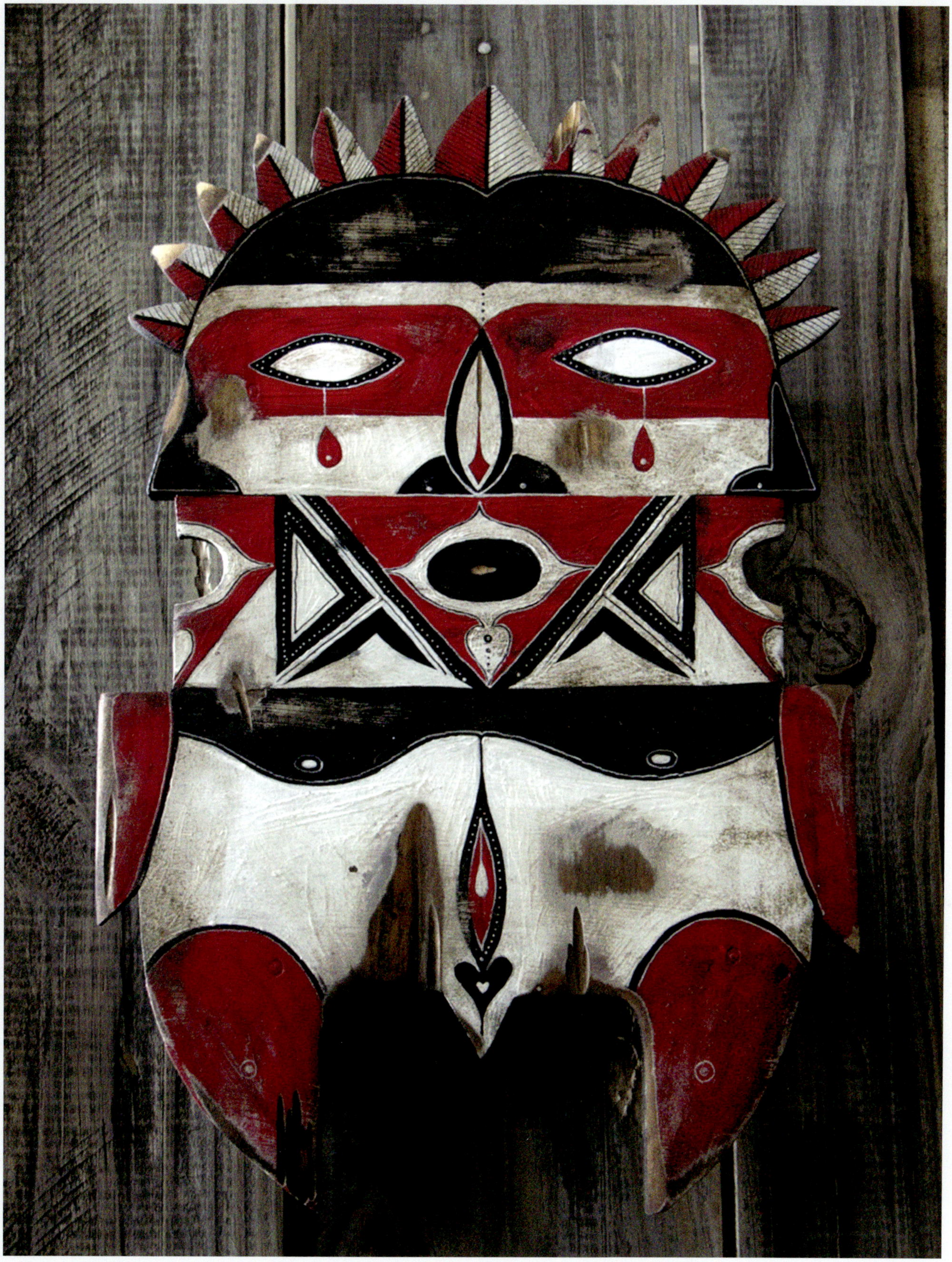

No Title / Acrylic on hand-carved wood – 25 x 30 cm – 2009

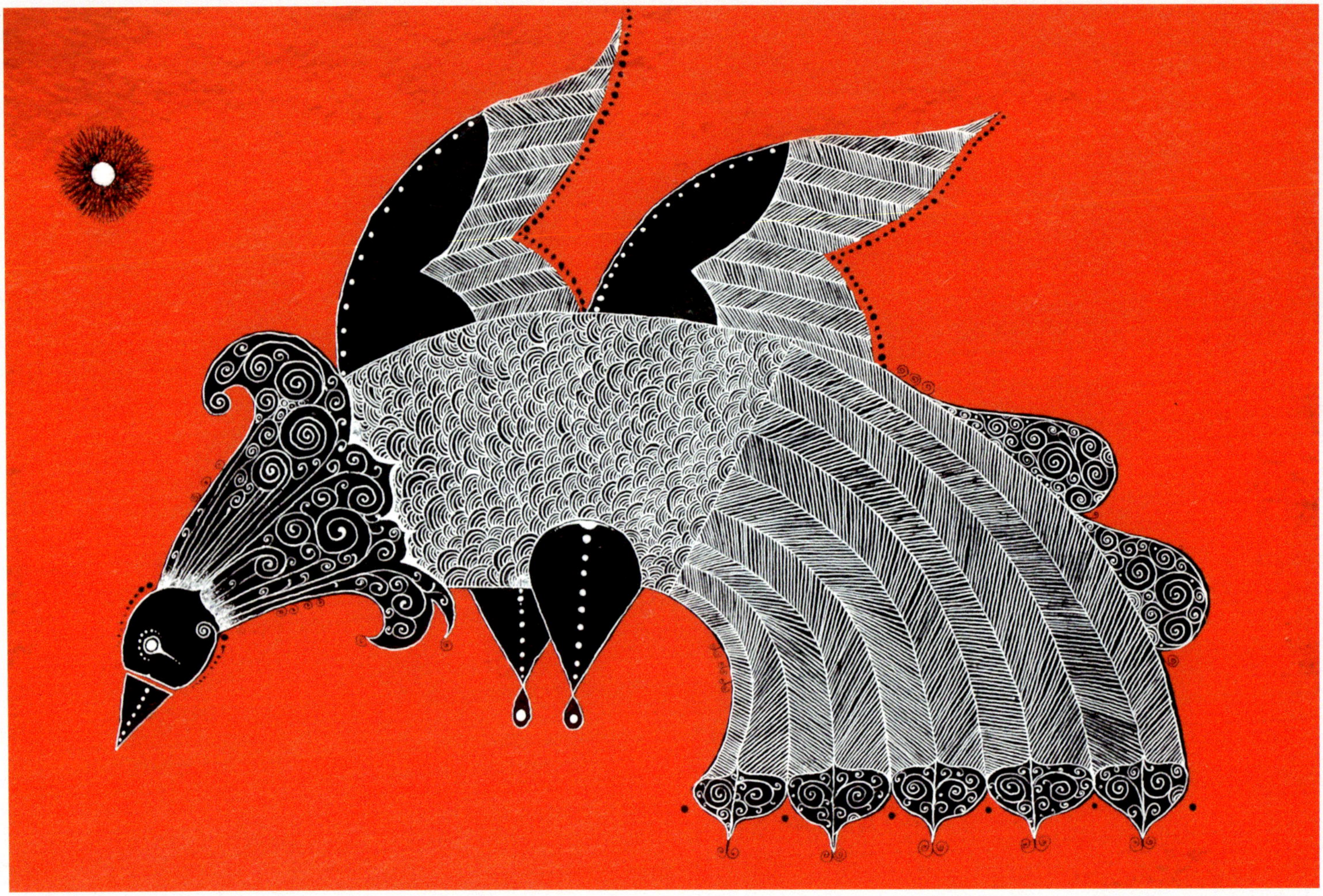

Irapuru / Mixed media on paper – 60 x 42 cm – 2010

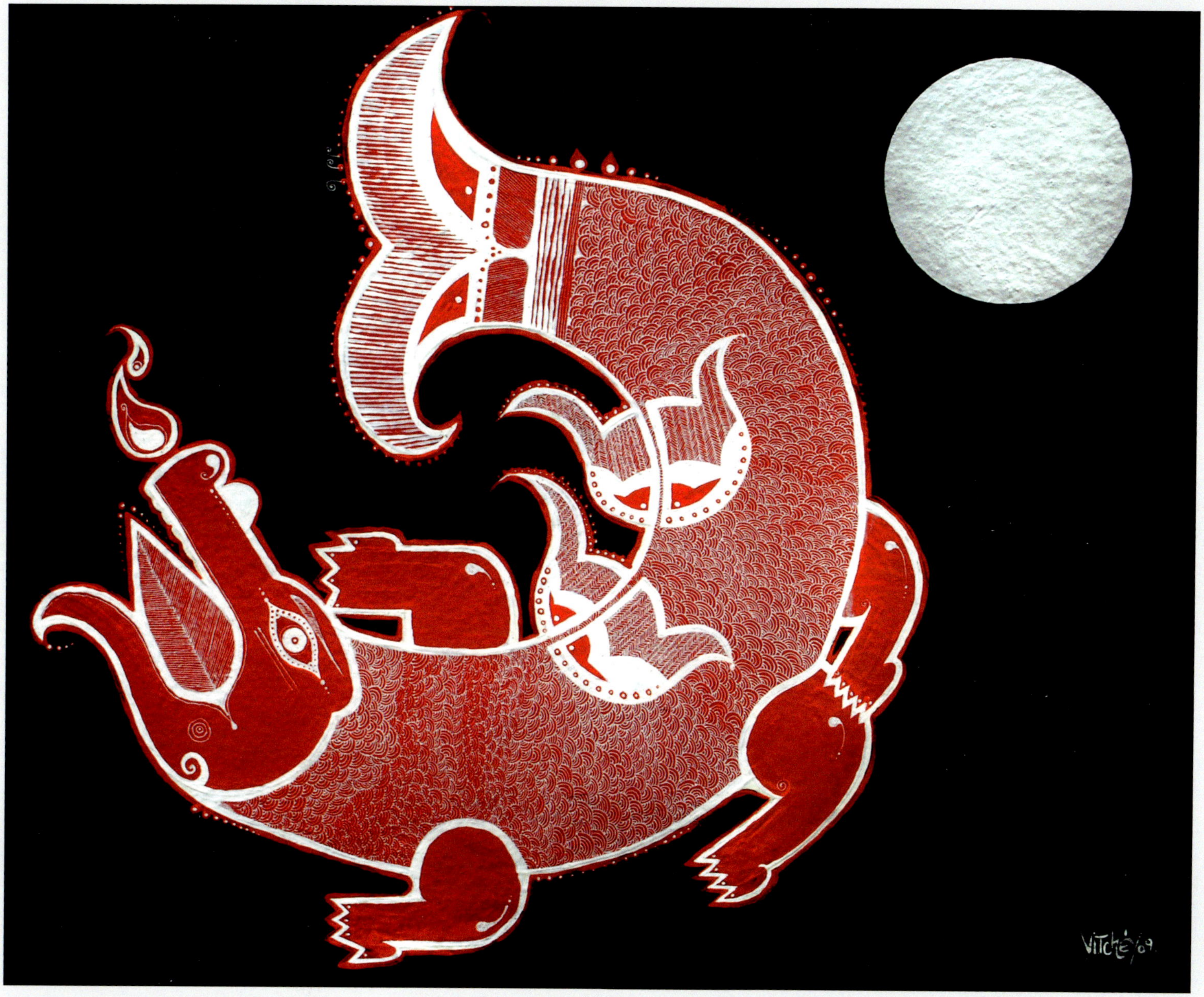

Mataku / Mixed media on paper – 62 x 51 cm – 2009

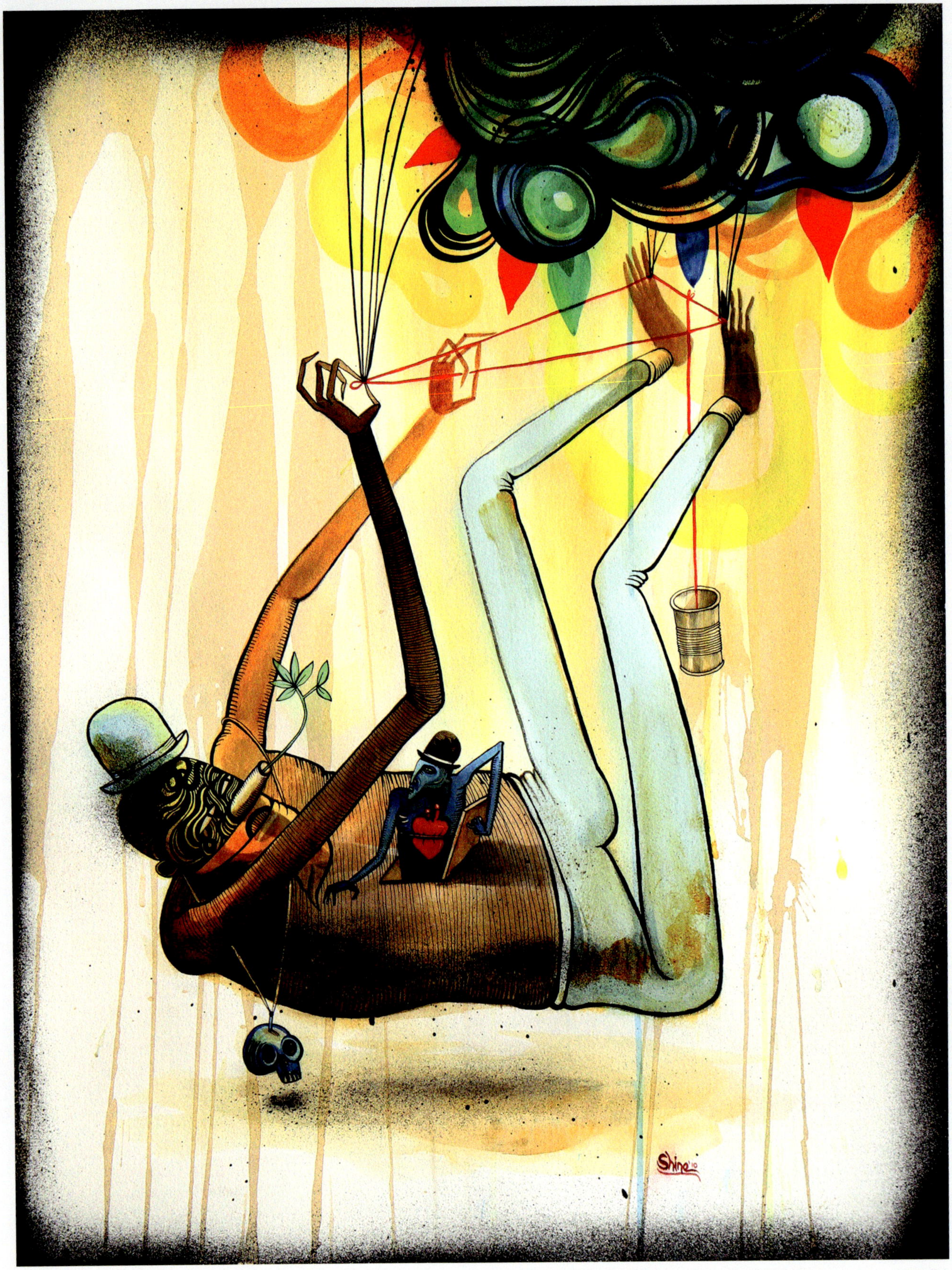

The Promise / Acrylic, aerosol, and indian ink on paper – 64 x 150 cm – 2010

Wendell McShine

Born in Trinidad and Tobago, 1972. Lives in Mexico City, Mexico.

In the streets I'm in a perpetual state of discovery. In the studio I allow things to develop naturally. I set off to exchange energy like a witch doctor and his client do. My father preached in the streets, it was crazy. Now I paint in the streets. I pay reverence to my work via animation repurposing its function. Infinite worlds rebirth themselves onto canvases and walls. It's a never ending cycle.

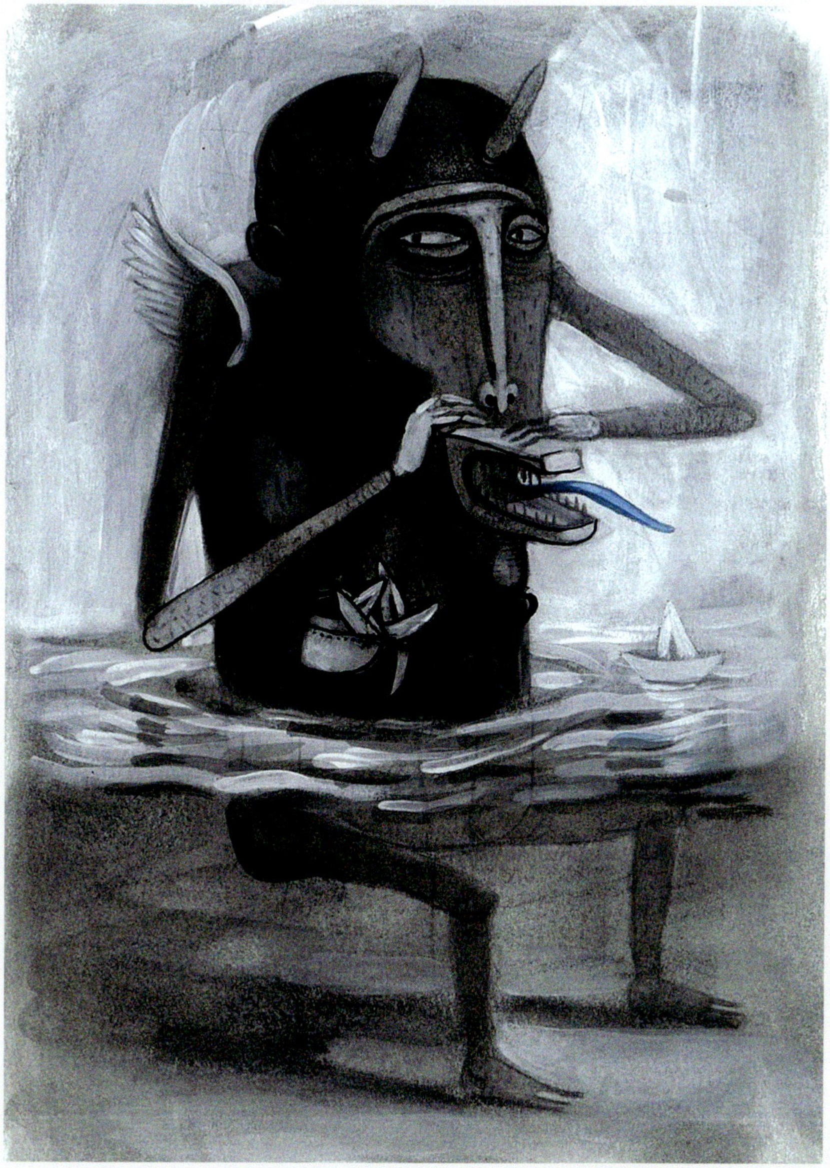

Secret of Jab Molassie / Pencil, charcoal, acrylic, and indian ink on paper – 15 x 21 cm – 2010

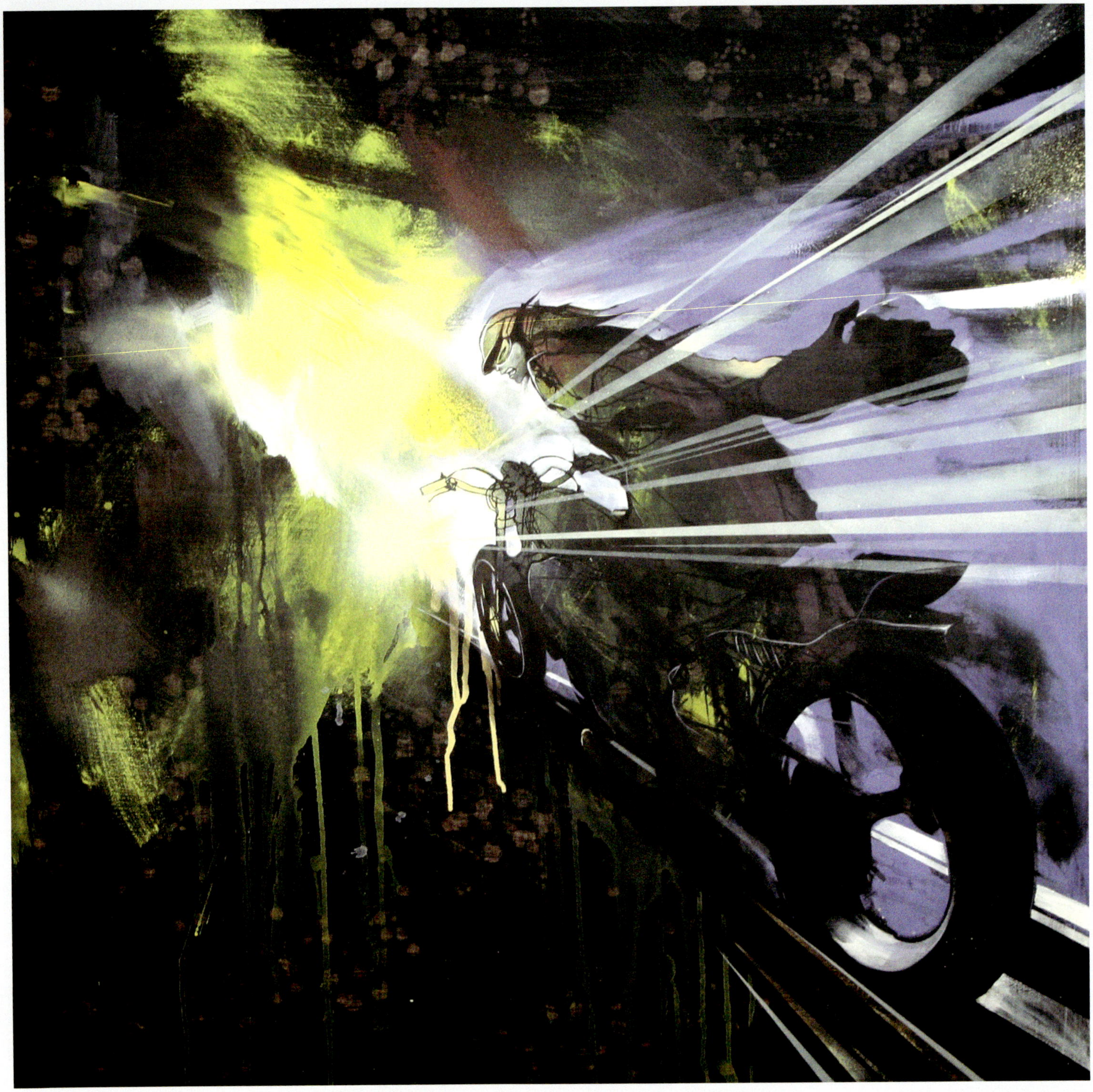

Tracker / Acrylic aerosol on printed fabric – 91 x 91 cm – 2010

Will Barras

Born in Birmingham, England, 1973. Lives in Hackney, England.

I don't work on the streets, I'm an illustrator and a painter. After beginning to work as an illustrator for a couple of years I found I was sitting in front of the computer as much, if not more than when I worked as a telephone operator, the job I had been trying to escape. So I started to think about working big. I had friends who were grafitti artists in Bristol, who taught me some basic techniques. I think my current methods of painting have been informed by my life in Bristol. I live in a city, my inspiration often comes from living, working, and traveling around the city...

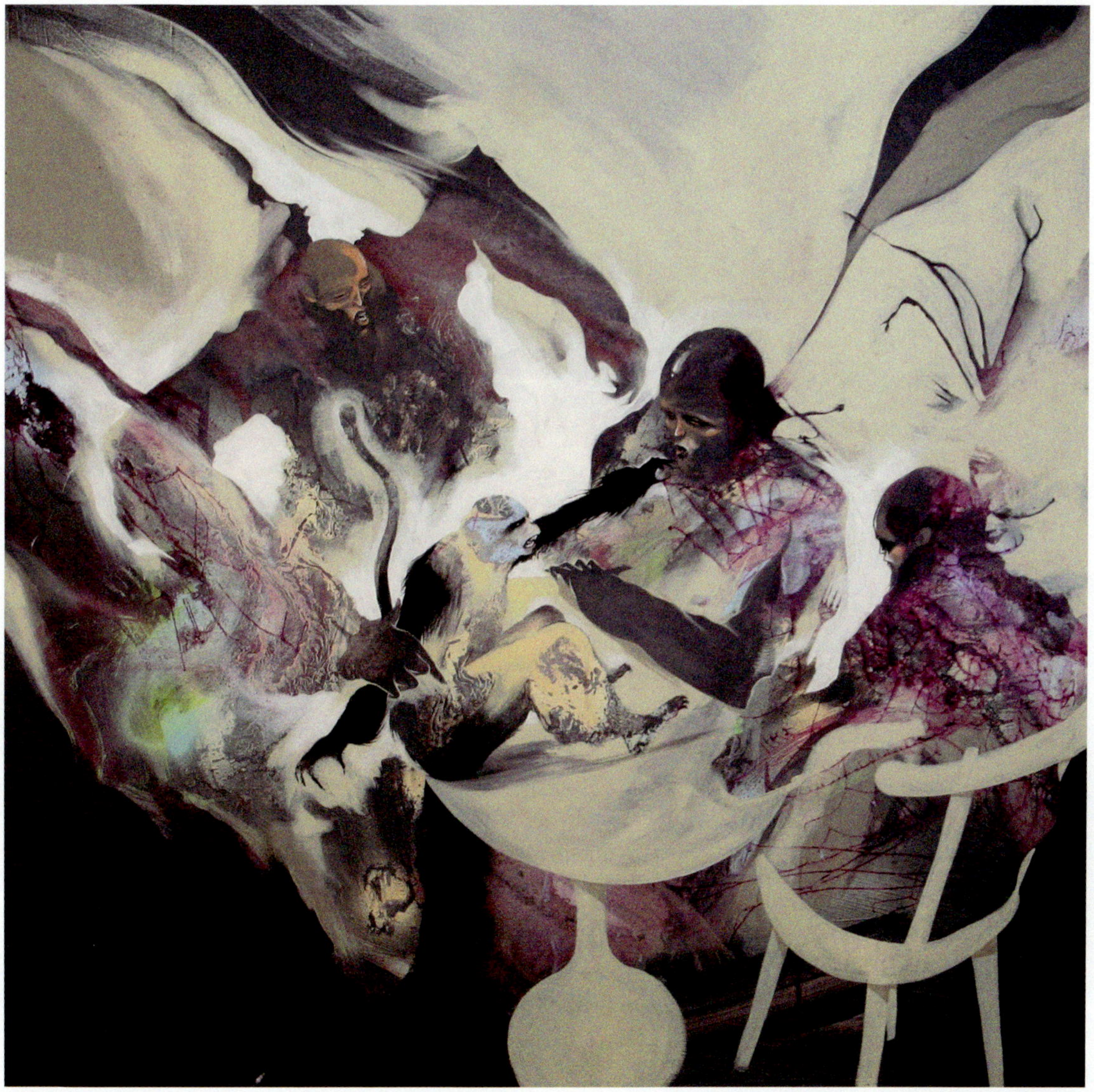

The Special | Acrylic aerosol on canvas – 91 x 91 cm – 2009

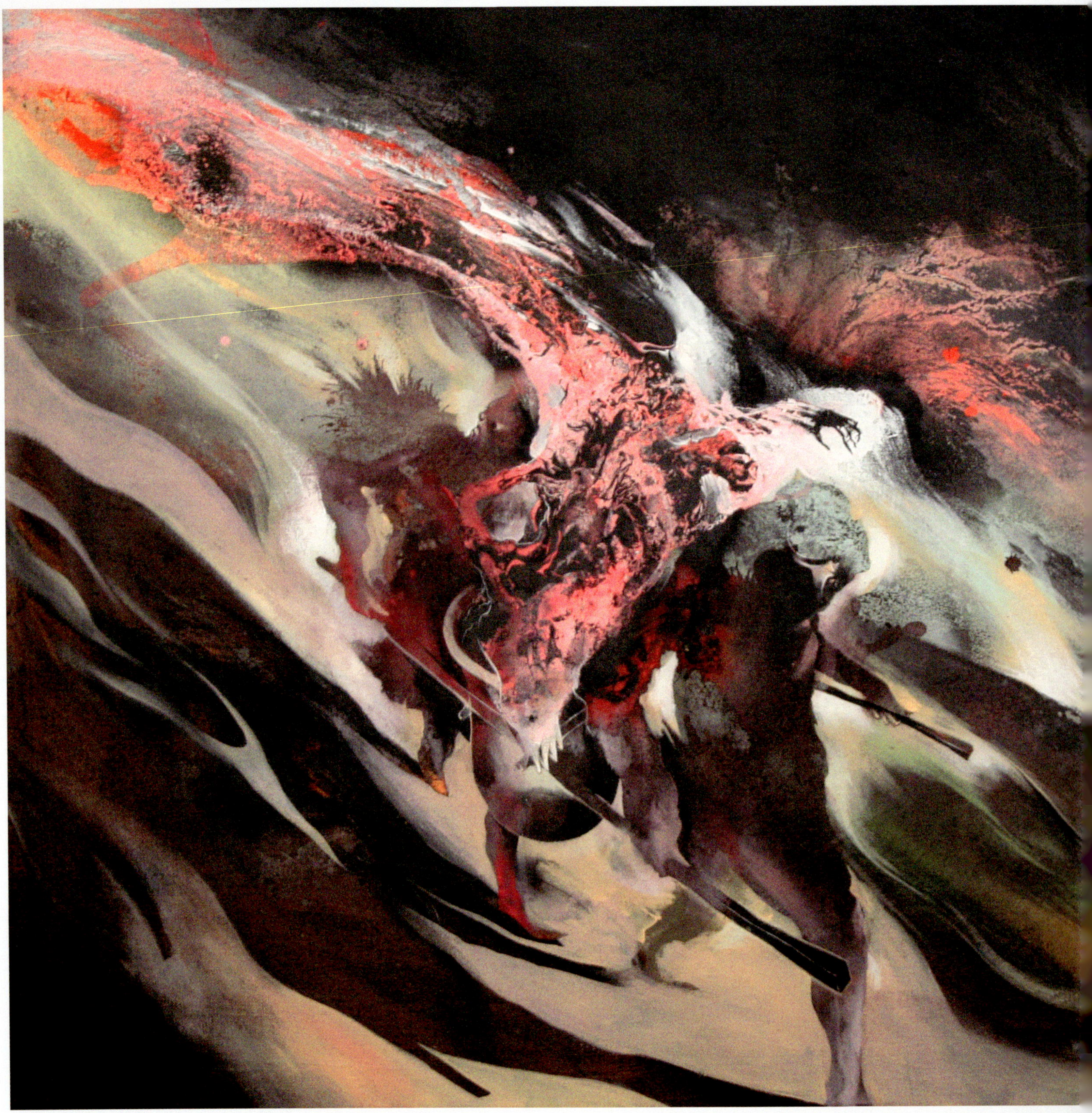

The Jago Plaetz Delivery System **Diptych** / Mixed media on linen – 184 x 92 cm – 2010

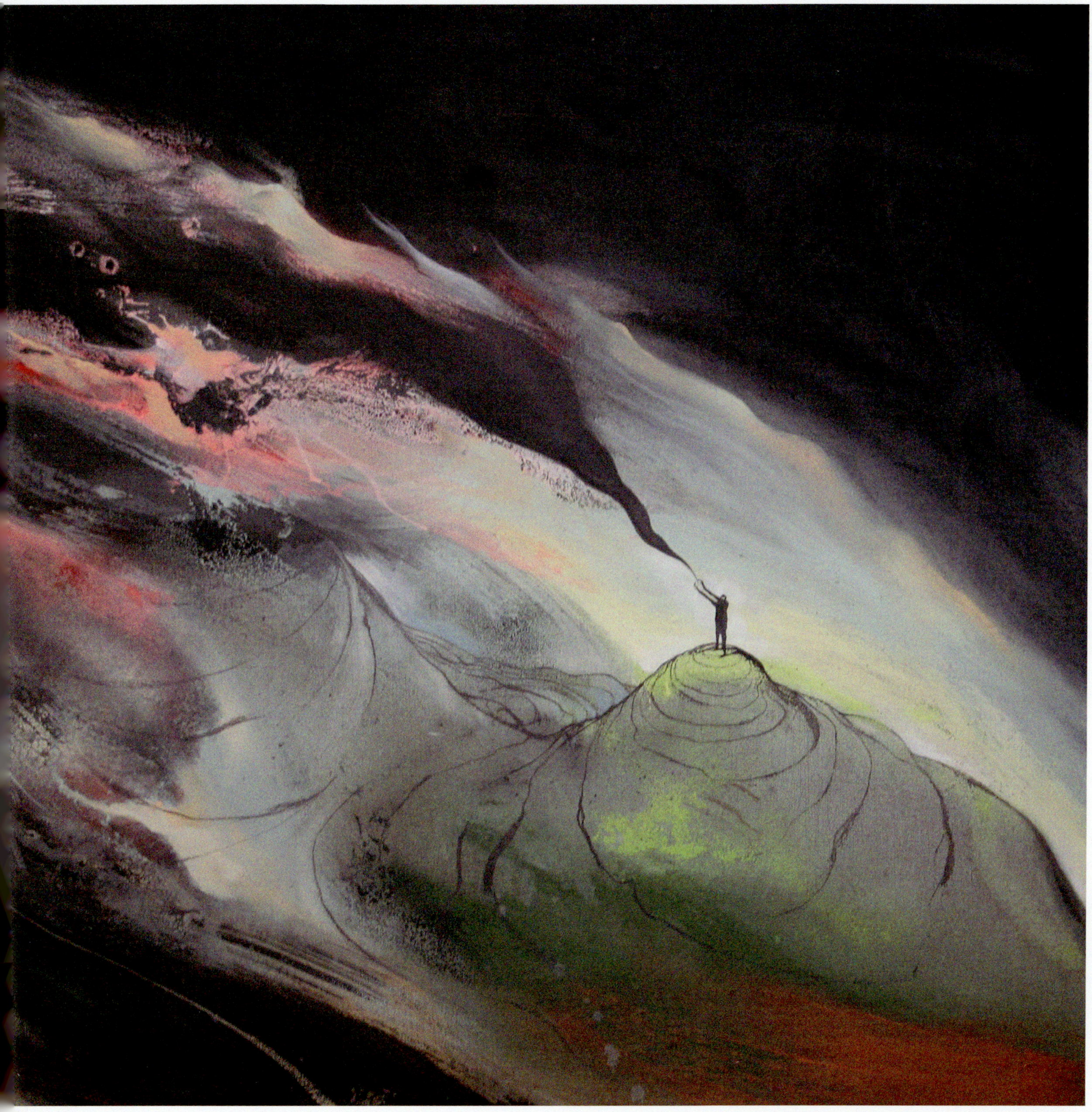

Zosen

Born in Buenos Aires, Argentina, 1978. Lives in Barcelona, Spain.

I began spraying graffiti when I was 11 in Buenos Aires. I started riding a skateboard at the same time. When I started, graffiti wasn't the big movement it is today; it was very underground and you certainly didn't make money from it. I painted in different cities of the world, from South America to North America, Europe. I really like the big walls format but also a good paint on canvas.

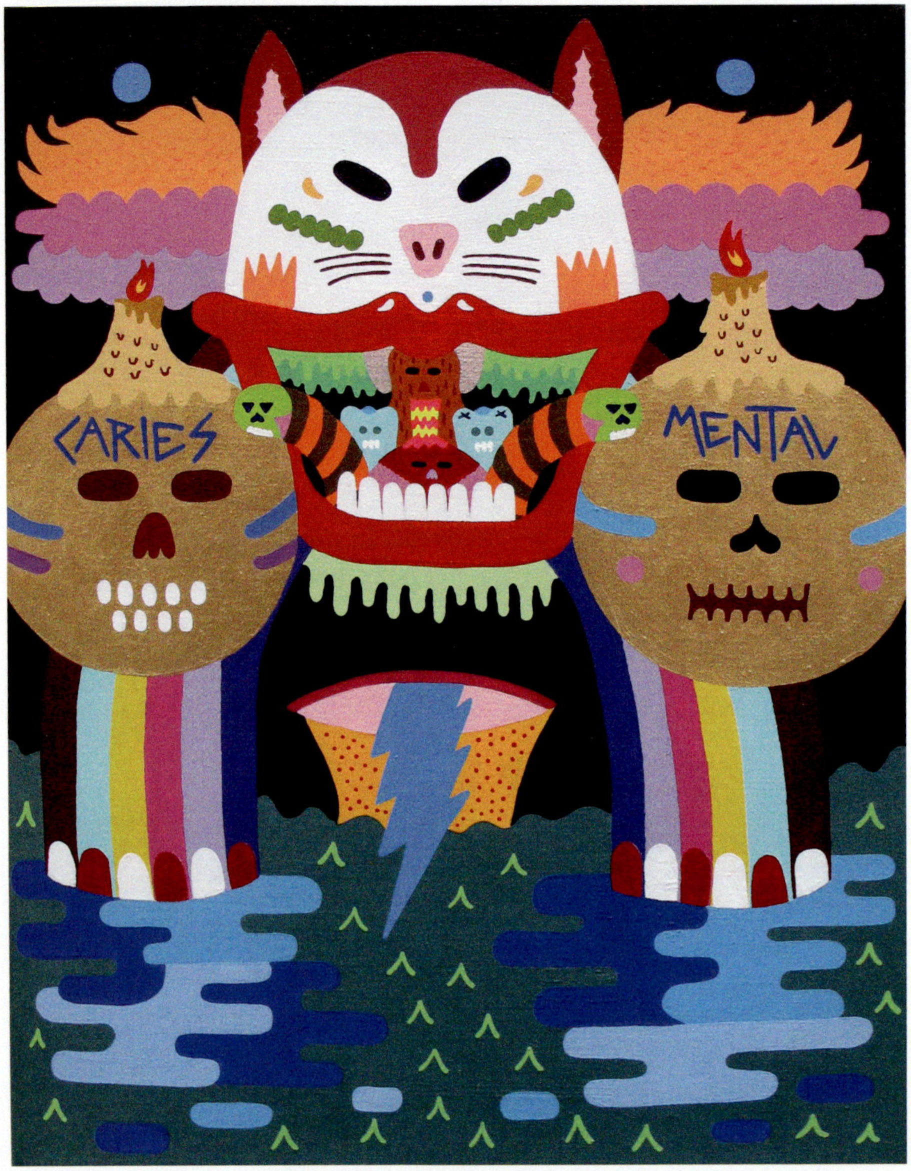

Caries Mental | Mixed media on canvas – 75 x 165 cm – 2009

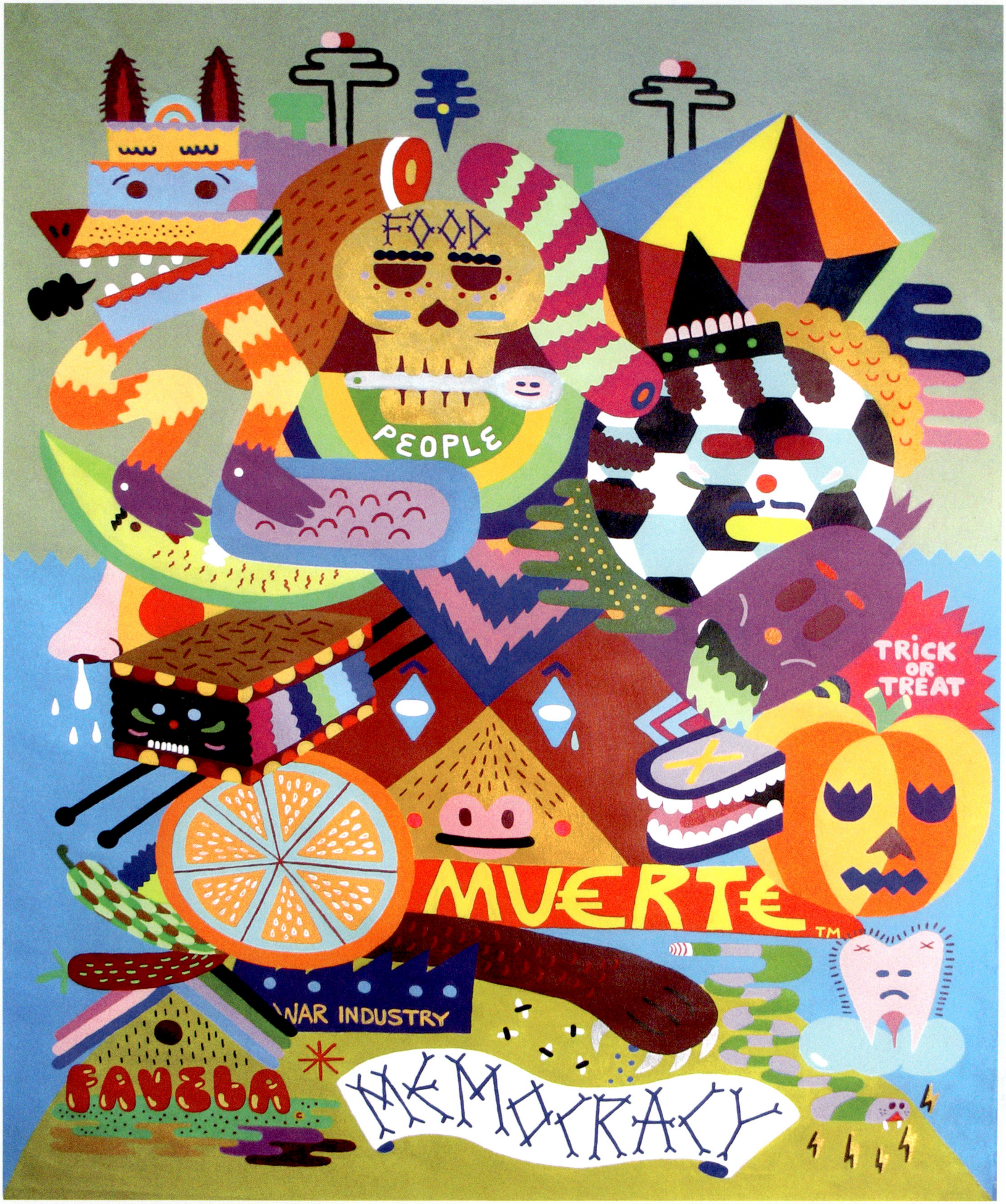

Norte - Sur / Mixed media – 120 x 150 cm – 2009

Photo Credits

All picture credits belong to the artists themselves unless indicated otherwise below.
Page numbers are indicated in bold.

Photo Cover
Evol

Alexandre Farto aka Vhils
10 – Ian Cox
17 – Matilde Meirelles

Conor Harrington
56, 57, 59 – Ian Cox

D*Face
61 – Darryl Stoodley

Doze Green
78, 79 – Adam Walclavage

Jeremy Fish
124, 125 – Randy Dodson

Jesse Hazelip
126, 127 – Randy Dodson

Johnny "KMNDZ" Rodriguez
128 – Static Medium
129 – Larry Underhill

Judith Supine
144, 145 – Brent Kerr

Okuda
192 – Nacho Abascal
193 – Oscar San Miguel

Peter Owen
202 – Etienne Frossard

Ripo
221 – Gustavo Osorio

Shepard Fairey
230, 231 – Obey Giant

Tilt
248, 249 – Vincent Sarda

Troy Lovegates aka Other
250, 251 – Derek Mehaffey

Wendell McShine
258 – Yadira Albarran Kamin
259 – Liliana Capinteyro

Acknowledgments

I dedicate this book to all the people whose artistic ethics have remained intact whether going through adversity or success.
I would like to give special thanks to Laurene, Léon, Isaac, Christine, the Dragones Voladores, Sowat, Tekila, and the Chevy.
For their trust, collaboration, and support, I would like to thank the following people:

Aaron Noble
AJ Fosik
Alexandre Farto aka Vhils
Alexandros Vasmoulakis
Alëxone Dizac
Alix Malandian
Amose
Andrew McAttee
Anthony Lister
Antony Micallef
Aranzazú Zumarán
Aryz
Axel Void
Basco-Vazko
Base 23
Ben Frost
Blek le Rat
Bom-K
Boris Hoppek
Boxi
Brandi Pickett
Brusk
C215
Cekis
Chu
Conor Harrington
D*Face
Dan Witz
Daniel Muñoz aka San
Dave Kinsey
Delta
Der
Dixon
Docteur Gecko
Dome One
Doze Green
Dran
Duncan Jago aka Mr. Jago
Eelus
Eine
Ekundayo
El Mac
Elbow Toe
Emma Valentin
Escif
Evan Roth
Evol
Faile
Faith 47
Fefe Talavera
Gaia
George Morton-Clark
Heather Jones
Herakut
Herbert Baglione
Interesni Kazki
Jane Wickstead
Jaybo
Jaz
Jeff Soto
Jenn Melvin
Jennifer Perez
Jeremy Fish
Jesse Hazelip
Jhonny "KMNDZ" Rodriguez
Joram Roukes
Jordan Seiler
Jorge Rodriguez Gerada
Josh Keyes
JR
Judith Supine
Julian Sorge
Katrin Fridriks
Kevin Cyr
Kofie
L'Atlas
Lightgraff
Liqen
Logan Hicks
Loreto Varela
Ludo
M-City
Marco Schwalbe
Mark Jenkins
Mark Whalen aka Kill Pixie
Matt Fails
Maya Hayuk
Medo & Demência
Meggs
Miss Bugs
Miss Van
Morten Andersen aka M2theA
Mr. Kern
Mudwig
Nicholas Di Genova
Okuda
Olivia Perches
Parra
Patrick Evoke
Paul Insect
Pedro Matos
Peter Owen
Pose
Pure Evil
Ralph Taylor
Remed
Remi/Rough
René Almanza
Retna
Rik Reiking
Ripo
Ródez
Saint
Sam3
Sat One
Shepard Fairey
Sixe
Smash 137
Sowat
Sten & Lex
Stephan Doitschinoff
Stephen Thompson
Susan Kendrick
Sybille Prou
Tec
Tilt
Tina Soikkeli
Tofa
Troy Lovegates aka Other
Turf One
Vega Gimeno
Vitché
Wendell McShine
Will Barras
Word to Mother
Zosen

For more information on the book and all featured artists please visit **www.wallsandframes.com**

Imprint

Walls & Frames: Fine Art from the Streets
Edited and introduced by Maximiliano Ruiz

Layout by Isaac Gimeno
Cover artworks and photography by Evol
Charlottenstr. / Stencil and aerosol on cardboard – 205 x 87 cm – 2010

Project management by Julian Sorge for Gestalten
Production management by Janine Milstrey for Gestalten
Proofreading by transparent Language Solutions
Copy editing of introduction by Christine Jayne Pettma
Printed by Main Choice

Published by Gestalten, Berlin 2011
ISBN 978-3-89955-376-5

For more information, please visit www.gestalten.com

Bibliographic information published by the Deutsche Nationalbibliothek.
The Deutsche Nationalbibliothek lists this publication in the Deutsche Nationalbibliografie; detailed bibliographic data is available online at http://dnb.d-nb.de.

None of the content in this book was published in exchange for payment by commercial parties or designers; the inclusion of all work is based solely on its artistic merit.

This book was printed according to the internationally accepted ISO 14001 standards for environmental protection, which specify requirements for an environmental management system.

This book was printed on paper certified by the FSC®.

MIX
Paper from responsible sources
FSC® C020691

Gestalten is a climate-neutral company. We collaborate with the non-profit carbon offset provider myclimate (www.myclimate.org) to neutralize the company's carbon footprint produced through our worldwide business activities by investing in projects that reduce CO_2 emissions (www.gestalten.commyclimate).

myclimate
Protect our planet